# Special Education

## SIXTH EDITION

Selected, Edited, and with Introductions by

**MaryAnn Byrnes**
*Educational Consultant*

TAKING SIDES: CLASHING VIEWS IN SPECIAL EDUCATION, SIXTH EDITION

MHID: 0-07-805048-0
ISBN: 978-0-07-805048-0

Managing Editor: *Larry Loeppke*
Senior Developmental Editor: *Jade Benedict*
Senior Content Licensing Specialist: *Shirley Lanners*
Marketing Director: *Adam Kloza*
Marketing Manager: *Nathan Edwards*
Project Manager: *Erin Melloy*
Cover Designer: *Studio Montage, St. Louis, MO*
Buyer: *Jennifer Pickel*
Media Project Manager: *Sridevi Palani*

Compositor: MPS Limited
Cover Image: Moodboard/Getty Images/RF

# Editors/Academic Advisory Board

Members of the Academic Advisory Board are instrumental in the final selection of articles for each edition of TAKING SIDES. Their review of articles for content, level, and appropriateness provides critical direction to the editors and staff. We think that you will find their careful consideration well reflected in this volume.

## TAKING SIDES: Clashing Views in SPECIAL EDUCATION

Sixth Edition

### EDITOR

**MaryAnn Byrnes**
*Educational Consultant*

# Preface

**S**pecial education is full of questions, emotions, and opinions. Public responsibility for the education of children with disabilities is a relatively new endeavor that is still exploring its identity and boundaries. Sometimes it seems that just as one set of issues is resolved (such as the creation of a range of services in public schools) a host of new challenges (such as leaving no child behind) arises. Other issues, including appropriate funding and inclusion, all but defy resolution. Through *Taking Sides: Clashing Views in Special Education*, I invite you to consider several controversial questions in this volatile and rewarding field.

*Taking Sides: Clashing Views in Special Education* has two major goals. First, to introduce key questions in special education, so readers can learn from authors who have thought extensively about educational policy and practice. Second, to encourage thinking and discussion, so readers can explore possibilities and debate the consequences of positions and actions. I hope you will find yourselves engaged and enlivened by the conversations these topics begin. Most of all, I trust your deliberations will contribute to constructive solutions to puzzles, which demand careful thinking and dedication to all our children.

Some basic principles guided the choice of selections for this book. Each selection needed to represent a widely held point of view on the question at hand. Other opinions surely exist, but the ones presented needed to be broadly held. Each had to employ solid reasoning; its position could not be easily refuted because of faulty logic. Finally, each selection needed to be interesting to read. If an article did not captivate my attention—and that of my students—I did not want it to be included.

This book includes 20 issues, addressing active debates in the field. There are three units. Unit 1, Special Education and Society, introduces questions of social policy and practice. Unit 2, Access and Accountability, highlights perspectives on educational expectations and outcomes. Unit 3, Exceptionalities, presents critical considerations about atypical learners and the treatments suggested for their benefit.

Each issue is framed as a question representing a challenge to be resolved in the policy and practice of educating children with disabilities. *Learning Outcomes* guide your reading, next an *Issue Introduction* sets the stage, extending the controversial question to its relevance in the practice of special education. Additional studies and reports on the topic are highlighted. *Is There Common Ground?* identifies areas on which both sides agree. *Challenge Questions* endeavor to stimulate your thinking as you weigh the topic at hand and its relationship to schools.

Two selections, representing contrasting points of view, are the substance of each issue. One answers the question in the affirmative (YES); the other in the negative (NO). Each selection has been published in a journal or as a report or speech. Due to page constraints, most selections have been edited. Use the heading citations to locate the entire article, along with its bibliography.

To further expand your thinking, you may want to reference the *Internet References* pages that precede each section. These contain a sampling of Internet site addresses (URLs) that represent varied points of view and offer resources as well as links to related sites and bibliographies.

The YES and NO positions on every issue express strongly held opinions. You may agree or disagree with the authors, or your own position may lie somewhere in between. Perhaps you will identify additional perspectives as you study the issues more thoroughly. You will find intentional connections between issues, demonstrating the complexity of the field. Class discussions may lead to a fresh response to the issue's question.

Doubtless, as you continue in your professional and personal lives, your thinking will change and develop. What is critical as you read this book is that you reflect on positions, possibilities, and emotions, so you can form opinions to guide your actions and decisions.

**A Word to the Instructor** An *Instructor's Manual with Test Questions* (multiple choice and essay) is available through The McGraw-Hill Contemporary Learning Series for the instructor using Taking Sides in the classroom. Also available is *Using Taking Sides in the Classroom*, a general guidebook that presents strategies and examples of using the pro–con method in classroom settings. Faculty members using this text also have access to an online version of *Using Taking Sides in the Classroom* and a correspondence service, located at www.mhcls.com/usingts/.

*Taking Sides: Clashing View in Special Education* is only one title in the Taking Sides series. The table of contents for any of the other titles can be found at the Taking Sides website at www.mhcls.com/takingsides/.

**Changes to This Edition** This sixth edition includes seven new or significantly revised Issues: *Is Disproportionally High Minority Representation in Special Education a School Problem?* (Issue 3); *Can RTI and IDEA Child Find Coexist?* (Issue 4); *Are Charter Schools a Good Choice for Students with Disabilities?* (Issue 6); *Should RTI Interventions Be Delivered by Special Educators?* (Issue 9); *Should the Government Prohibit the Use of Restraint and Seclusion in Schools?* (Issue 17); *Is ADHD a Real Disorder?* (Issue 18), and *Are Evidence-Based Practices Sufficient for Educating Students with Autism?* (Issue 19). The book *Introduction* and every *Issue Introduction* have been revised with updated research references.

**Acknowledgments** Spirited debate about *the right thing to do* has been part of my life since I became a teacher. So long as we keep children in mind, debating possibilities is exhilarating. First, and most importantly, I thank the children, educators, and parents who frame the questions and continually teach me almost anything is possible—not always easy, but possible. Next, I extend my deep appreciation to my many students, whose drive to understand *why* we do things and *how* to do their best keeps me on my toes. Additionally, I want to acknowledge the helpfulness of Jade Benedict and all the supporting staff at McGraw-Hill. And, of course, Joe.

**MaryAnn Byrnes**
*Educational Consultant*

# The Educational Experience of Disciplinary Controversy*

**A**s a long-time user of the *Taking Sides* books, I have seen first-hand their educational impact on students. A student we will call "Brittany" is a prime example. Until her role in a *Taking Sides'* panel discussion, she had not participated once in class discussions. It is probably fair to say that she was sleepwalking through the course. However, once she was assigned to a "side" of the panel discussion, she vigorously pitched in "to do battle," as she put it, with the opposing team. She described a "kind of energy" as she and the rest of her team prepared for the upcoming debate. In fact, she found herself and her teammates "talking trash" good-naturedly with the opposing team before the actual discussion, despite her usual reserve. Because she wanted to win, she "drilled down" and even did extra research.

The panel discussion itself, she reported, was exhilarating, but what I noticed afterward was probably the most intriguing. Not only did she participate in class more frequently, taking more risks in class discussions because she knew her teammates would support her, she also found herself having a position from which to see other positions in the discipline. Somehow, as she explained, her advocating a particular position on the panel, even though she knew I had arbitrarily assigned it, gave her a stake in other discussions and a perspective from which to contribute to them. Brittany's experience nicely illustrates the unique educational impact of the *Taking Sides* Series.

*Taking Sides* is designed quite intentionally to shore up some of the weaknesses of many contemporary educational settings. The unique energy that Brittany experienced is a result of *Taking Sides* specific focus on the controversial side of academic disciplines. For several good reasons instructors and textbooks have traditionally focused almost exclusively on the more factual or settled aspects of their disciplines. This focus has led, in turn, to educational strategies that can rob the subject matter of its vitality.

*Taking Sides,* on the other hand, is uniquely structured to highlight the more issue-oriented aspects of a discipline, allowing students to care about and even invest in the subject matter as did Brittany. Involvement can spur a deeper understanding of the topic and help students to appreciate how knowledge advancement is sometimes driven by passionate positions. This focus has led, in turn, to educational strategies that can rob the subject matter of its vitality.

*The full text of this essay and references are available online at: http://highered.mcgraw-hill.com/sites/0076667771/information_center_view0/

## Including the Controversial

A case could be made that a complete understanding of any discipline includes its controversies. Controversies may not be considered "knowledge" per se, depending on the discipline, but there is surely no doubt that they are part of the process of advancing knowledge. The conflicts generated among disciplinary leaders often produce problem-solving energy, if not disciplinary passions. In fact, they can drive entire disciplinary conferences and whole programs of investigation. In this sense, disciplinary controversies are not just "error" or an indication of the absence of knowledge; they can be viewed as a positive part of the discipline, a generator of disciplinary vigor if not purpose.

If this is true, then de-emphasizing the controversial elements of a discipline is de-emphasizing a vital part of the discipline itself. Students may learn accepted aspects of the discipline, but they may not learn, at least directly, the disputed aspects. This de-emphasis may not only produce an incomplete or inaccurate sense of the discipline, but it may also mislead the student to understand the field as more sterile, less emotional, and less "messy" than it truly is. The more rational, factual side is clearly important, perhaps even the more important. The question, however, is: do these more settled and perhaps rational aspects of the discipline have to monopolize courses for beginning students?

Another way to put the question might be: couldn't some portion of the course be devoted to the more controversial, thus allowing the student to engage the field in a more emotional manner? In some sense, the more settled and accepted the information is, the less students can feel they are truly participating in the disciplinary enterprise. After all, this information is already decided; there is no room for involvement in developing and "owning" the information. Students may even assume they will be punished for challenging the disciplinary status quo.

## Specific Educational Benefits

*Engaging the Discipline.* When controversy is placed in the foreground of an educational experience, it gives disciplinary novices (students) permission to participate in and perhaps even form their own positions on some of the issues in the field. After all, some issues have not been addressed; some problems have not been solved. As Brittany put it, she was ready to "do battle" with the alternative position, even though she was quite aware of the arbitrariness of her own positional assignment. She was aware that something was at stake; something was to be decided.

In other words, it is the very *lack* of resolution in a controversy that invites students to make sense of the issues themselves and perhaps even venture their own thoughts. Obviously, students should be encouraged to be humble about these positions, understanding that their perspective is fledgling, but even novice positions can facilitate greater engagement with the materials. In a sense, the controversy, and thus a vital part of the discipline, becomes their own, as the example of Brittany illustrates. She not only "owned" a disciplinary position, she used it as a conceptual bridge to engage other settled and unsettled aspects of the discipline.

*Appreciating the Messy.* Students can also experience the messiness of disciplines using *Taking Sides.* I use the term "messiness" because conventional texts are notorious for representing the field too neatly and too logically, as if there were no human involvement. If disciplines are more than their settled aspects, there are also unsettled elements, including poorly defined terms and inadequately understood concepts, which also need to be appreciated. This messiness is what led Brittany to "drill down" and do "extra research" in her preparation for her panel discussion. She knew that some of the basic terms and understandings were at play.

Good conventional texts may attempt to include these unsettled aspects, but they typically do so in a deceptively logical fashion, as though the controversy is solely rational. This presentation may not only distort these aspects of the discipline but also deliver merely a secondhand report. By contrast, *Taking Sides* books—in pitting two authors against one another—facilitate an *experience* with actual published authorities, who are struggling with the issues from completely different perspectives. In reading both articles, students cannot help but struggle *with* the authors. They do not need to be *told* that the terms of the debate are problematic; the students *experience* these terms as problematic when they attempt to understand what is at stake in the authors' positions.

*Preventing Premature Closure.* The *Taking Sides* structure also serves to prevent students from prematurely closing controversies. Premature closure can occur by underestimating the controversy's depth or deciding it without a proper appreciation for the issues involved. *Taking Sides* prevents this prematurity by helping the student to experience how two reasonable and highly educated people can so thoroughly disagree. In other words, premature closure is discouraged because real experts are countering each other, sometimes point by point.

A student would almost have to ignore one side of the controversy, one of the experts, to prematurely close the issue. Brittany, for example, reported that she became "absolutely convinced" of the validity of the first authors' position, only to have the second reading put this position into question! Obviously, if the issue could be closed or settled so easily, presumably the experts or leaders of the discipline would have done so already. Controversies are controversies because they are *deeply* problematic, so it is important for the student to appreciate this, and thus have a more profound understanding of the disciplinary meanings involved.

*Rehabilitating the Dialectic.* One of the truly unique benefits of the *Taking Sides* experience is its rehabilitation of the age-old educational tradition of the dialectic. Since at least the time of Socrates, educators have understood that a *full* understanding of any disciplinary meaning, explanation, or bit of information requires not only knowing what this meaning or information is but also knowing what it isn't. The dialectic, in this sense, is the educational relation of a concept to its alternative (see Rychlak, 2003). As dialectician Joseph Rychlak (1991) explains, all meanings "reach beyond themselves" and are thus clarified and have implications beyond their synonyms. It may be trivial to note, for example, that one cannot fully comprehend what "up" means without understanding what "down" means. However, this dialectic is not trivial when the meanings are disciplinary, such as when the political science student realizes that justice is incomprehensible without some apprehension of the meaning of injustice.

One of the more fascinating educational moments, when using *Taking Sides* books, occurs when students recognize that they cannot properly understand even one side of the controversy without taking into account another side. Brittany described learning very quickly that she clarified and even became aware of important aspects of her own position only *after* she understood the alternative to her position. This dialectical awareness is also pivotal to truly critical thinking.

*Facilitating Critical Thinking.* I say "truly" critical thinking because critical thinking has sometimes been confused with rigorous thinking (see Slife et al, 2005). Rigorous thinking is the application of rigorous reasoning or analytical thinking to a particular problem, which is surely an important skill in most any field. Still, it is not truly *critical* thinking until one has an alternative perspective from which to criticize a perspective. Recall that Brittany did not participate in class until she developed a perspective to view other perspectives. In other words, one must have a (critical) perspective "outside of" or alternative to the perspective being critiqued. Otherwise, one is "inside" the perspective being critiqued and cannot "see" it as a whole.

As many recent educational formulations of critical thinking attest, this approach means that critical thinkers should develop at least a dialectic of perspectives (one plus an alternative). That is to say, they should have an awareness of their own perspective *as facilitated by* an understanding of at least one alternative perspective. Without an alternative, students assume either they have no position or their position is the *only* one possible. A point of comparison, on the other hand, prevents the reification of one's perspective and allows students to have a perspective on their perspectives. A clear strength of the *Taking Sides'* juxtaposition of alternative perspectives is that it facilitates this kind of critical thinking.

These five benefits—engaging the discipline, appreciating the messy, preventing premature closure, rehabilitating the dialectic, and facilitating critical thinking—are probably not exclusive to controversy. However, they are, I would contend, a relatively unique *package* of educational advantages that students can gain with the inclusion of a Taking Sides approach in the classroom. Controversy, of course, is rarely helpful on its own; settled information and sound reasoning must buttress and perhaps even ground controversy. Otherwise, it is more heat than light. Even so, an *exclusive* focus on the settled and more cognitive aspects can deprive students of the vitality of a discipline and prevent the ownership of information that is so important to real learning.

**Brent D. Slife**
*Brigham Young University*

# Contents in Brief

# Contents

Gwyn W. Senokossoff, an instructor in childhood education and literacy, and Kim Stoddard, an associate professor in special education (both at the University of South Florida, St. Petersburg) describe the first author's struggles to find a diagnosis, appropriate intervention, and support for her son with childhood bipolar disorder. Scott M. Shannon, psychiatrist and former president of the American Holistic Medical Association, explains why he believes it is advantageous to look for ways to relieve stressors in a child's environment rather than seek a label, which might do more harm than good.

H. Rutherford Turnbull III, co-founder and co-director of the Beach Center on Disability at the University of Kansas, sees major changes in IDEA 2004. In line with the Bush administration's priorities, Turnbull identifies a shift toward requiring parents and students to take more responsibility for their own behavior and for relationships with schools. Tom E. C. Smith, professor at the University of Arkansas, focuses his research on disability law and inclusion. Reflecting on IDEA 2004, Smith believes that although some changes seem significant, they will make little difference in the daily practice of special education teachers.

Edward Fergus is deputy director of the Metropolitan Center for Urban Education at New York University. Previously a high school teacher, Dr. Fergus consults on issues of disproportionality. His study of over 30 districts identified common root causes of disproportionality and remedies for each one. Richard Rothstein, a research associate of the Economic Policy Institute, writes and speaks on issues of education, economics, and policy, with a focus on the achievement gap. Mr. Rothstein posits that schools alone cannot overcome the effects of poverty on a child's life and education.

Lynn S. Fuchs, a prolific scholar in the area of learning disabilities, and one of several researchers in the National Research Center for Learning Disabilities, explains how Research to Intervention (RTI) strategies can separate a struggling learner from one with specific learning disabilities (SLDs). Research results demonstrate her thinking. Jose L. Martin, partner in the law firm Richards Lindsay & Martin in Austin, Texas, represents schools in disability issues and litigation, sees promise in RTI, and also discord with IDEA that could cause tension and conflict between schools and parents. Perhaps revision of the 35-year-old IDEA is in order to recognize changes in general education.

Howard S. Adelman and Linda Taylor, co-directors of the UCLA School Mental Health Project, based in the Center for Mental Health in Schools, believe that many discipline problems could be eliminated by whole-school initiatives that create and sustain an environment that addresses positive social and emotional development as well as academics. William C. Frick and Susan C. Faircloth, assistant professors at the University of Oklahoma and the Pennsylvania State University, respectively, present dilemmas faced by principals torn between balancing the needs of one particular student who exhibits disruptive behavior with those of the rest of the student body, whose learning is affected by the single student's actions.

Mitt Romney, Republican contender for the presidency and former governor of Massachusetts, proposes to improve options for all children, especially those from low-income families and those with special needs, by using U.S. federal grant funds to increase access to more desirable, innovative charter schools. Thomas Hehir, prominent educational policymaker, agrees that charter schools can offer desirable options. Testifying in front of Congress, Hehir expresses his strong concern that the doors of charter schools are often closed to students with disabilities. He cautions that these closed doors might constitute a denial of civil rights.

Autism Speaks, an advocacy organization founded by Suzanne and Bob Wright (former executives in General Electric and NBC, respectively), together with the National Alliance for Autism Research and Cure Autism Now, presents eight arguments in support of legislation mandating health insurance coverage of autism services. Writing for the Council for Affordable Health Insurance, an organization that promotes the affordable health care access for all Americans, Victoria C. Bunce and J.P. Wieske discuss national trends in state-mandated health care benefits for children with autism, arguing that responsibility for these costs belongs elsewhere.

Mary T. Brownell, Paul T. Sindelar, and Mary Theresa Kiely, policy scholars from the University of Florida, Gainesville, and Louis C. Danielson at the American Institutes for Research link political changes with special education teacher preparation. They conclude that the future of special education rests within content-rich RTI practices. Margaret J. McLaughlin, policy architect and analyst from the University of Maryland sees a disconnect between the singular academic outcomes of NCLB/ESEA and the individualized needs of students with disabilities. Merging is not wise when some students with disabilities are treated unjustly if held to unitary academic outcomes.

Jennifer Booher-Jennings, a doctoral candidate at Columbia University when she wrote this issue, finds the accountability pressures of No Child Left Behind lead some administrators to advise teachers to focus only on those children who will improve their school's scores; other students don't count much. The U.S. Department of Education FAQ Sheet on IDEA and No Child Left Behind (NCLB) advises readers that the link between these two statutes is sound, emphasizing how they work together to ensure that every student's performance and needs receive appropriate attention.

Kevin S. McGrew, director of the Institute for Applied Psychometrics (IAP) and educational researcher, and Jeffrey Evans, consultant and educational researcher for IAP, are wary that stereotypes of individuals with cognitive disabilities are used to form limited (and limiting) expectations and self-fulfilling prophecies. James M. Kauffman, professor Emeritus of Education at the University of Virginia, Charlottesville, and special education philosopher-researcher, believes that educators and parents must acknowledge that some students with cognitive disabilities cannot reach high academic standards and are best served by programs that develop other skills.

Rosalind Vargo and Joe Vargo, parents of Ro, use their voices to tell a powerful story of their daughter's success in fully inclusive educational programs, from kindergarten through college. Amy D. Marcus, staff reporter at *The Wall Street Journal*, conveys the voices of Eli's parents and teachers as they react to his message to leave a fully inclusive program in favor of a separate special education class.

Hazel Denhart, who lectures at Portland State University, uses a disability theory perspective to analyze how students with learning disabilities perceive their experiences in higher education. Her interviewees identify social barriers that make college a less-than-welcome experience and recommend steps to reduce institutional intolerance. Melana Zyla Vickers, an editorial writer for *USA Today*, uses information from interviews with on-campus experts, professors, and students, to raise serious questions about the legitimacy of accommodations and disability services. Many of her interviewees think disabilities leading to accommodations can be purchased, to the detriment of everyone's experience.

# UNIT 3   EXCEPTIONALITIES   329

John Cloud, a staff writer for *Time Magazine* since 1997, profiles a number of extraordinarily gifted young people challenged for the first time in a specialized school that pushes them to reach their potential in a way that public schools could not. Susan Winebrenner and Dina Brulles work with educators to design and deliver cluster-based programs that address the needs of the gifted within their neighborhood school and provide options for a range of students to reach their potential.

Nathaniel Lehrman, clinical director (retired) of the Kingsboro Psychiatric Center, New York, warns that new mental health screening requirements, heralded as a way to increase the health of the nation, will intrude on basic freedoms, lead to inappropriate labels, and increase revenue for pharmaceutical companies. Mark Weist, Marcia Rubin, Elizabeth Moore, Steven Adelshiem, and Gordon Wrobel, consultants and researchers in mental health, view this screening as a way to identify those who need early intervention in order to prevent the development of debilitating mental illnesses.

The National Disability Rights Network (NDRN) has authored three major reports highlighting concerns about the use of restraint and seclusion in schools. In the face of continuing legislative gridlock, the latest report urges the U.S. federal Department of Education to issue clear guidance limiting restraint and seclusion to situations posing an imminent danger. Sasha Pudelski, government affairs manager for the American Association of School Administrators (AASA), presents her organization's position that restraint and seclusion need to be available tools in schools. Banning their use with any and all students could actually increase the potential for injury.

Evelyn B. Kelly, a science writer, journalist, and adjunct professor at the College of Education, St. Leo University, presents an encyclopedia of characteristics, causes, and interventions for the several conditions, which are all very real attention deficit hyperactivity disorders. Todd E. Elder, a faculty member in the Economics Department of Michigan State University, presents evidence from a longitudinal study indicating that the likelihood of a child's diagnosis with ADHD is more dependent on his age relative to kindergarten peers than it is to any discrete, absolute behavior characteristics.

Samuel L. Odom, Lana Collet-Klingenberg, Sally J. Rogers, and Deborah D. Hatton, researchers affiliated with the National Professional Development Center, describe a procedure for determining whether focused intervention practices have sufficient evidence to be deemed evidence-based practices (EBPs). Identifying 24 practices that meet the research criteria, the authors also provide guidance and advice about implementation. Ken Siri and Tony Lyons are fathers of children on the autism spectrum. Dr. Mark Frielich is a developmental pediatrician who practices in New York. They view children with autism as individuals whose bodies have fallen victim to a perfect storm of problems. They introduce an edited book of "cutting-edge therapies," designed to inform readers of possible treatments, many of which have not been vetted by research.

Jenna Goudreau, journalist in two prominent publications, relates the compelling stories of several parents who have had to fight with school systems and battle legal complexities to get the free appropriate public education they feel is right for their children with disabilities. Jennifer Krumins, a special education teacher and mother of a child with autism, advises parents to ease tension, stress, and pressure by finding an advocate who can serve as an "interpreter" in a complex educational system and teach them how to secure the necessary supports with a positive approach.

# Correlation Guide

The *Taking Sides* series presents current issues in a debate-style format designed to stimulate student interest and develop critical thinking skills. Each issue is thoughtfully framed with an issue summary, an issue introduction, and a postscript. The pro and con essays—selected for their liveliness and substance—represent the arguments of leading scholars and commentators in their fields.

*Taking Sides: Clashing Views in Special Education,* 6/e is an easy-to-use reader that presents issues on important topics such as *Charter Schools, NCLB,* and *Autism.* For more information on *Taking Sides* and other *McGraw-Hill Contemporary Learning Series* titles, visit www.mhhe.com/cls.

This convenient guide matches the issues in *Taking Sides: Special Education,* 6/e with the corresponding chapters in one of our best-selling McGraw-Hill Education textbooks by Taylor et al.

| Taking Sides: Special Education, 6/e | Exceptional Students: Preparing Teachers for the 21st Century by Taylor et al. |
| --- | --- |
| **Issue 1:** Are Labels Good for Kids? | **Chapter 2:** The Special Education Process: From Initial Identification to the Delivery of Services |
| **Issue 2:** Did IDEA 2004 Contain Substantial Changes? | **Chapter 4:** Students with Learning Disabilities |
| **Issue 3:** Is Disproportionally High Minority Representation in Special Education a School Problem? | **Chapter 1:** An Overview of Special Education |
| **Issue 4:** Can RTI and IDEA Child Find Coexist? | **Chapter 3:** School, Family, and Community Collaboration<br>**Chapter 4:** Students with Learning Disabilities |
| **Issue 5:** Can Whole-School Reform Reduce Discipline Problems? | **Chapter 3:** School, Family, and Community Collaboration |
| **Issue 6:** Are Charter Schools a Good Choice for Students with Disabilities? | **Chapter 2:** The Special Education Process: From Initial Identification to the Delivery of Services<br>**Chapter 3:** School, Family, and Community Collaboration |
| **Issue 7:** Should Insurance Cover Treatments/ Services for Autism? | **Chapter 11:** Students with Autism Spectrum Disorders |
| **Issue 8:** Has the Americans with Disabilities Act (ADA) Accomplished Its Goals? | **Chapter 4:** Students with Learning Disabilities |
| **Issue 9:** Should RTI Interventions Be Delivered by Special Educators? | **Chapter 2:** The Special Education Process: From Initial Identification to the Delivery of Services<br>**Chapter 3:** School, Family, and Community Collaboration |

| Taking Sides: Special Education, 6/e | Exceptional Students: Preparing Teachers for the 21st Century by Taylor et al. |
| --- | --- |
| **Issue 10:** Should Special Education and General Education Merge? | **Chapter 2:** The Special Education Process: From Initial Identification to the Delivery of Services |
| **Issue 11:** Does NCLB Leave Some Students Behind? | **Chapter 4:** Students with Learning Disabilities |
| **Issue 12:** Should Students with Cognitive Disabilities Be Expected to Demonstrate Academic Proficiency? | **Chapter 4:** Students with Learning Disabilities |
| **Issue 13:** Is Full Inclusion the Least Restrictive Environment? | **Chapter 3:** School, Family, and Community Collaboration |
| **Issue 14:** Should Colleges Be More Accommodating to Students with Disabilities? | **Chapter 3:** School, Family, and Community Collaboration |
| **Issue 15:** Do Gifted and Talented Students Need Special Schools? | **Chapter 15:** Students Who Are Gifted and Talented |
| **Issue 16:** Is Mental Health Screening an Unwarranted Intrusion? | **Chapter 13:** Students Who Are At Risk: Early Identification and Intervention |
| **Issue 17:** Should the Government Prohibit the Use of Restraint and Seclusion in Schools? | **Chapter 2:** The Special Education Process: From Initial Identification to the Delivery of Services |
| **Issue 18:** Is ADHD a Real Disorder? | **Chapter 14:** Students with Attention Deficit/Hyperactivity Disorders |
| **Issue 19:** Are Evidence-Based Practices Sufficient for Educating Students with Autism? | **Chapter 11:** Students with Autism Spectrum Disorders |
| **Issue 20:** Does Working with Parents Have to Be Contentious? | **Chapter 3:** School, Family, and Community Collaboration |

# Topic Guide

This topic guide suggests how the selections in this book relate to the subjects covered in your course. You may want to use the topics listed on these pages to search the web more easily. On the following pages a number of websites have been gathered specifically for this book. They are arranged to reflect the units of this Taking Sides reader. You can link to these sites by going to www.mhhe.com/cls.

All issues and their articles that relate to each topic are listed below the bold-faced term.

## Achievement Gap
3. Is Disproportionally High Minority Representation in Special Education a School Problem?

## Americans with Disabilities Act
8. Has the Americans with Disabilities Act (ADA) Accomplished Its Goals?

## Attention Deficit Hyperactivity Disorder
18. Is ADHD a Real Disorder?

## Autism
7. Should Insurance Cover Treatments/Services for Autism?
19. Are Evidence-Based Practices Sufficient for Educating Students with Autism?
20. Does Working with Parents Have to Be Contentious?

## Charter Schools
6. Are Charter Schools a Good Choice for Students with Disabilities?

## Cognitive Disabilities
12. Should Students with Cognitive Disabilities Be Expected to Demonstrate Academic Proficiency?
18. Is ADHD a Real Disorder?

## Disability Services
14. Should Colleges Be More Accommodating to Students with Disabilities?
18. Is ADHD a Real Disorder?

## Discipline
5. Can Whole-School Reform Reduce Discipline Problems?
17. Should the Government Prohibit the Use of Restraint and Seclusion in Schools?
20. Does Working with Parents Have To Be Contentious?

## IDEA 2004
2. Did IDEA 2004 Contain Substantial Changes?
4. Can RTI and IDEA Child Find Coexist?
11. Does NCLB Leave Some Students Behind?

## Insurance
7. Should Insurance Cover Treatments/Services for Autism?

## Labels
1. Are Labels Good for Kids?

## Minorities
3. Is Disproportionally High Minority Representation in Special Education a School Problem?

## No Child Left Behind
11. Does NCLB Leave Some Students Behind?

## Reform
5. Can Whole-School Reform Reduce Discipline Problems?

## Research to Intervention
4. Can RTI and IDEA Child Find Coexist?
10. Should Special Education and General Education Merge?

## Restraint
17. Should the Government Prohibit the Use of Restraint and Seclusion in Schools?

## Seclusion
17. Should the Government Prohibit the Use of Restraint and Seclusion in Schools?

## Stereotypes
12. Should Students with Cognitive Disabilities Be Expected to Demonstrate Academic Proficiency?

## Stressors
1. Are Labels Good for Kids?

# Introduction

I introduce . . . a bill . . . to insure equal opportunities for the handicapped by prohibiting needless discrimination in programs receiving
federal financial assistance. . . . The time has come when we can no
longer tolerate the invisibility of the handicapped in America. . . . These
people have the right to live, to work to the best of their ability—to
know the dignity to which every human being is entitled. But too
often we keep children whom we regard as 'different' or a 'disturbing
influence' out of our schools and community altogether. . . . Where is
the cost-effectiveness in consigning them to . . . 'terminal' care in an
institution?

—Senator Hubert H. Humphrey (D-Minnesota), January 20, 1972, on
introducing to Congress a bill mandating education for children with
disabilities (as quoted in *Back to School on Civil Rights,* National Council on
Disability, 2000)

Unfortunately, this bill promises more than the federal government can
deliver, and its good intentions could be thwarted by the many unwise
provisions it contains. . . . Even the strongest supporters of this measure
know as well as I that they are falsely raising the expectations of the
groups affected by claiming authorization levels which are excessive and
unrealistic. . . . [This bill also contains a] vast array of detailed complex
and costly administrative requirements which would unnecessarily assert
federal control over traditional state and local government functions.

—President Gerald Ford, November 29, 1975, upon signing federal legislation
to mandate education for children with disabilities (as quoted in *Congress and
the Nation, IV*)

Special education was born of controversy about who belongs to schools and
how far schools need to stretch to meet student needs. The debate continues.

Think hard about your school experience. When was the first time you saw
someone with a disability? What do you remember? Compare your recollections
with those of someone one generation older—and one younger. The differences
will be startling.

Did anyone remember The Room? Usually it was in the basement of the
school. Hardly anyone went into The Room. Hardly anyone came out. The kids in
The Room never seemed to be part of recess or assemblies or lunch or gym. The
teachers were also invisible. Sometimes the windows of The Room were covered
with paper. Usually the shades were drawn. Kids whispered about The Room, but
no one really knew what happened *in there*.

The students who went to school in The Room usually seemed older, bigger,
and not as smart as most of the other kids in the school. They had few books to

learn from and rarely studied any but the most basic academic subjects. No one really knew what happened to the kids in The Room once they left elementary school. There never seemed to be a Room at the high school. Difficult as it is to believe, those who made it inside The Room may have been the lucky ones.

In 1970, not all that long ago, if you were the parent of a child with a disability, your neighborhood school could say your child was not welcome—that there was no place in the school for your child. Choices were limited. You could teach your child at home (or just have him spend his days there); you could try to find a space in a school run by dedicated religious people; or you send your child to live in a faceless institution. Try looking at Burton Blatt's *Christmas in Purgatory: A Photographic Essay on Mental Retardation* (Human Policy Press, 1974) for a view of some of the worst options.

I remember The Room in the elementary schools I attended, but I never knew much about its students. I also remember the Catholic school for girls with Down syndrome, where I volunteered as a Girl Scout. The residents learned cooking and sewing while I was getting ready for high school and college. I never saw the girls outside the school and didn't know what they did when they grew into adults.

There were also the boys who sat in the back row of my classes and tried to avoid the attention of adults. The teachers hoped these boys would just be quiet and behave. The boys dropped out of school as soon as they could.

Years later, in the early 1970s, after teaching fourth grade for two years, I entered special education because I was intrigued with unlocking the puzzles that made learning so hard for some of my students. One of my early jobs was as a teacher in an updated version of The Room. It was my first experience in a small district. The day before school began, all the teachers and their students were listed in the local newspaper, along with their bus routes. I eagerly looked for my name, but instead of Mrs. Byrnes, I read "Emotionally Disturbed Classroom." For my entire time at that school, I was the *emotionally disturbed teacher.*

Times had changed somewhat since I attended elementary school. My classroom was on the main floor, next door to the third grade; we had some academic books and we had lunch and recess with everyone else. But we were still different. Each day, my students and I needed to leave our room from 11:30 to 1:30, so it could be used by the gym teacher while the gym was used as a cafeteria. Since there were only 10 of us, taking our classroom space seemed an easy solution. No one appeared to care where we went or what we did during that time. Plenty of people were surprised to see us camp out in the library, tackling *real* school work.

In contrast, think about the schools of today. Children with learning problems significant enough to be disabilities are the focus of concentrated attention. Skilled professionals and researchers strive to understand disabilities and address them with specific teaching methods and approaches. Parents and teachers actively consider ways to adapt instruction. Program options seem limitless. Many children with disabilities grow into adults who hold jobs and contribute to society instead of spending their lives in isolation at home, in institutions, or on the streets.

Despite this progress, I still know schools in which classes for students with disabilities are located in sections of the school where no one else ever goes. There are still districts where people must be reminded to include students with disabilities when counting up the number of new math books that need to be ordered. And once formal schooling ends, there are still many young adults who sit at home without jobs because there is no employment support.

Has the promise of special education been met, fallen short, or been exceeded? Has society done too much or not enough? Despite what feels like progress, arguments about special education continue. Many of them are included in this book.

As you consider the controversial issues in this volume, think about the people with disabilities *you* first remember. How did today's special education shape their lives? What about the young adults with visible disabilities working in your community? Where might they be without special education? How have the dreams of Hubert Humphrey and the cautions of Gerald Ford been realized?

## Recent History and Legal Foundations

The history of special education in American public schools is brief and defined by legislation. Private or religious schools have long offered specialized options for students who were blind, or deaf, or had mental retardation (only recently changed to intellectual disabilities). Until the last quarter of the twentieth century, public options were largely limited to residential institutions and a few *Opportunity Classes* in public schools.

After the civil rights struggles of the 1960s came the realization that another significant segment of our children—those with disabilities—were not offered a quality education. Although a few states instituted their own policies and regulations regarding education of children with disabilities, districts could still refuse to admit these students.

Successful state court cases established that children with disabilities had rights to an education. This led to the 1975 passage of U.S. federal Public Law 94-142, which offered U.S. federal funds to every public school district delivering a free and appropriate public education to all children with disabilities. Renamed the Individuals with Disabilities Education Improvement Act (IDEA) in subsequent reauthorizations, the regulations connected to these statutes form the foundation of special education. Individual states constructed legislation to clarify U.S. federal language or to extend commitments beyond the U.S. federal standard.

Elements of the No Child Left Behind Act of 2001 (NCLB) are reflected in the 2004 IDEA reauthorization. This linkage holds schools accountable for student performance; sets exacting standards for teacher qualifications; and requires that educators implement research-based instructional practices. NCLB includes accountability provisions for students with disabilities; IDEA describes intervention strategies that must take place in general education classrooms. There is much discussion about the interconnectedness of NCLB (a general education-based law) and IDEA (with its focus on special education). Both are overdue for reauthorization: some wonder if the two will eventually merge—and ponder the impact on children and teachers.

Additional legislation affects the lives of individuals with disabilities: Section 504 and the Americans with Disabilities Act (ADA). Section 504 of the Rehabilitation Act of 1973 is a civil rights statute prohibiting organizations that receive U.S. federal funds from discriminating against any individual based on a disability that substantially limits a major life activity. Reasonable accommodations must be implemented so that individuals with disabilities have equal access to the activities of such organizations. Curb cuts, lowered water fountains, and signs in Braille increased in use in response to Section 504. Since school districts receive U.S. federal funds, Section 504 forbids the exclusion of students with disabilities, although it does not address education with the detail of IDEA. You may encounter students on 504 plans. These students do not require specially designed instruction, but they might need accommodations or related services to have access to education.

Passed in 1990 and amended in 2008, the Americans with Disabilities Amendment Act (ADAA) extended the protections of Section 504 to the private sector. The

ADAA forbids businesses, governmental agencies, or public accommodations (other than churches or private clubs) from discriminating against any individual who has a disability that substantially limits a major life activity. The ADAA carries the same responsibility for accommodations as Section 504, impacting the practices of almost every employer.

Aspects of all these laws are sometimes vague and undefined. Terms are interpreted differently across the states, and businesses struggle with the range of accommodations, the meaning of "reasonable," and conflicting research results. Clarity is often achieved through the resolution of legal challenges, some of which have reached the Supreme Court. A single court decision can radically alter the obligations of an employer.

Court decisions can cause the ground to shift for schools as well. For example, as you proceed through the selections, you will encounter the debate between *least restrictive environment* and *free and appropriate public education*. Each term is critical to the development of a school's special education program, but each is also fluid in meaning. Federal law does not provide precise, operational definitions. Schools do their best to apply these terms to individual children with widely varying needs. As with businesses and the ADAA, court cases about individual children continue to define what is *restrictive* and what is *appropriate*. Medical advances refine the meaning of *education*.

## Essential Terms and Concepts

Special education has its own unique vocabulary and terms, just as any other field. Being familiar with the concepts below will increase your understanding of the issues ahead.

*Disabilities*: IDEA 2004 lists the following disabilities: autism, deaf-blindness, deafness, developmental delay, emotional disturbance, hearing impairment, intellectual disability (replacing the term mental retardation), orthopedic impairment, other health impairment, specific learning disability, speech or language impairment, traumatic brain injury, and visual impairment. Autism and traumatic brain injury were added to this list relatively recently, as a result of lobbying and research developments.

States may use unique names for disabilities, but all must be encompassed by the federal legislation. Additionally, state laws frequently augment the federal definitions of each disability with particular diagnostic criteria, satisfied through the administration of appropriate assessment tools in the "language and form most likely to yield accurate information about what the child knows and can do academically and functionally" (IDEA 2004).

Note that the list of disabilities does not include children who need instructional assistance solely because of language differences, cultural differences, or lack of instruction. In order for a child to be considered eligible for special education, the school's educational team must determine that a disability exists.

*Federal definition of a child eligible for special education:* According to IDEA, this is a child with a disability who is not making effective progress in school because of that disability and who requires specially designed instruction and/or related services in order to make progress in school. Federal legislation applies to individuals from birth to the receipt of a high school diploma or age 22. In most states, public schools are charged with educational responsibility beginning on a child's third birthday.

*Individualized Education Program (IEP)*: IDEA requires each child's educational team, including parents, to meet at least annually to formulate this agreement, which describes the education of a child with a disability. The IEP outlines the impact of the student's disability, current educational status, necessary accommodations, the nature and amount of services to be provided to the child, and target goals for each year. All educators are bound to abide by the terms of an approved IEP. Services cannot be delivered—nor can they be ended—without signed parental approval. Parents who disagree with evaluations or services have the right to seek redress through administrative hearing and/or legal suit.

*Related services*: These supportive, noneducational services enable a child with a disability to access the general curriculum. Related services include, but are not limited to the following: transportation, various therapies, assistive technology, mobility instruction, social work, and medical services for diagnostic or evaluation purposes.

*Free and appropriate public education (FAPE)*: This cornerstone of IDEA guarantees that special education and related services are provided at no cost to parents. The word "appropriate," never clearly defined, has been the source of much controversy and litigation. The impact of the word "free" has strained many school budgets.

*Continuum of services*: Special education services take many forms and are delivered in varied settings. Inside classrooms, these can range from consulting with a teacher on the format of a test, to team teaching between a special educator and an English teacher, to 1:1 services from a paraprofessional. Outside the general education class, specially designed instruction might be delivered to small groups of children with disabilities. A few children are taught in separate classes or schools (day, residential, or hospital) that enroll only children with disabilities. The entire spectrum of options, known as the continuum of services, must be considered when designing individualized special education programs.

*Least restrictive environment (LRE)*: Another key element of IDEA, this phrase refers to each school's responsibility to ensure that "to the maximum extent appropriate, children with disabilities . . . are educated with children who are nondisabled; and that . . . removal from the regular educational environment occurs only if the nature or severity of the disability is such that education in regular classes with the use of supplementary aids and services cannot be achieved satisfactorily." Here, too, differing interpretations of undefined terms can lead to disagreement and litigation.

*Inclusion*: This word may be one of the first that comes to mind when special education is mentioned. Surprisingly, the term inclusion does not appear in any federal legislation. Its meaning differs across states, districts, and even within schools, often changing from year to year. Defining and applying this term has resulted in inspiration as well as confusion, frustration as well as opportunity, creativity as well as litigation. The common element in all definitions involves increasing the participation of children with disabilities in general education classes.

# Differing Orientations

Underlying the controversies in *Taking Sides: Clashing Views in Special Education* are four distinct perspectives, each of which affects the way people envision a solid special education program. Although disagreements cannot always be reduced to one of these, it is likely that people who support differing sides of an issue question will also be on opposite sides of the following dynamics.

## Medical or Educational Model?

The medical model of special education views disabilities as conditions that can be improved, remedied, remediated, and perhaps prevented. Medical model adherents seek a specific treatment or therapy to address the physical, psychological, or cognitive issues, which result in school problems. Specialized diets or procedures for gastrointestinal problems are examples of medical interventions.

Those who follow an educational model aim to address the impact of a disability on school performance directly. Proponents focus on improving educational success through teaching skills or particular strategies that compensate for areas of difficulty. Peer tutoring and co-teaching are both educational interventions.

## Special Need or Disability?

Children can have a special need, but not a disability. Laws about special education specifically exclude children whose learning difficulties are due to language differences, cultural differences, poverty, or lack of instruction. Neither do they include students who are gifted and talented. Almost everyone can remember struggling with learning at one point in life. Children in each of these groups may not have their needs met without extra attention from someone.

Special education is about the education of children who have a disability rather than those who struggle. This delineation causes controversy. If we know children whose lives place them at risk for failure, should we wait till that failure occurs before we give help or should we expand special education to include them? If we expand special education by including these children, are we helping them or burdening them with a stigmatizing label? Is special education the only way to address learning differences?

## General Education or Special Education Responsibilities?

In the early 1970s, millions of children with disability were excluded from school. U.S. federal laws mandated their education, which initially occurred mostly in secluded locations by specialized teachers. Seeing these students progress, teachers and parents began to seek out special education services. In many districts, special education ceased being a stigma and became a desired resource, particularly when budget stress increased class sizes and reduced overall supports.

As the number of children receiving services increased, resistance rose to the expansion and costs of special education and to its separation from the overall school curriculum. This backlash resulted in tighter definitions, restricting services to those who are truly disabled and increasing expectations that classroom teachers assume responsibility for a wider range of children.

NCLB took these deliberations one step further, introducing the idea that students should not be considered for special education if it can be determined that they have not experienced research-based classroom instruction. Interventions by the general education teacher are required as part of the evaluation process. IDEA 2004 encourages teachers to adopt Response to Intervention strategies before seeking special education. Will schools initiate and sustain general education supports for all children, lessening the pressure for special education?

## Academics or Functional Skills?

The accountability provisions of NCLB redefined the connection between general education personnel and special education personnel. Because schools must be answerable for the academic achievement of students in special education, *where* students learn has become less important than the knowledge they acquire.

Learning priorities must be considered. The majority of students with disabilities can make good academic progress, with appropriate support. Sometimes teams determine that functional skills to support success in daily living are a higher priority. In the past, students with both emphases could receive a high school diploma. With the advent of high stakes testing, this is often no longer possible. Will heightened standards result in better outcomes for students with disabilities? Will students be equally prepared for adulthood?

# Understanding Controversy

Precisely because the issues surrounding special education are so powerful, and the stakes for children are so high, it is vital that we engage actively in their resolution. To achieve this end, it is essential to recognize differences and collaborate to reach common ground.

## Disagreements about Applying the Law

Parents and teachers must come to agreement about the best way to meet the needs of a child with a disability. Honorable people may be equally committed to the goal of a free and appropriate public education in the least restrictive environment, but differ on the definition and application of these terms. Although few argue about the meaning of *free*, some parents and teachers prefer focused instruction in small groups of children with similar learning needs, whereas other parents and educators feel the letter and spirit of the law can only be met when all children (regardless of individual need) are taught solely within the general education classroom.

Two children may be very similar, but have dramatically different special education programs because the preferences and reasoning of their educational teams differ. Since each child is unique, and can experience only one option at a time, it is impossible to guarantee which choice will lead to the best outcome. In fact, the *best* option may change as the child grows and develops.

Sometimes the differing views of parents and teachers lead to heated arguments. Everyone wants to help; often the disagreement is about which path to take. Because we see children as individuals—as our future—these controversies often reach to our core.

The keys to coming to consensus involve listening, learning, and being open to new information and fresh perspectives. Equally important is evaluating each source of information, and each course of action, in a measured, careful way, even if it differs substantially from what you feel is right. Often, putting yourself in the other person's place helps. What would I do if this were my child? What would I do if I were the teacher?

It helps to focus on the child in the middle of this discussion. As with most issues regarding children, the best solution is achieved when the adults involved put aside beliefs, attitudes, emotions, and pride and strive to understand what the other person wants and why they want it. This can be very difficult to do.

## Disagreements about Interpreting Facts and Figures

Although some of the questions in this *Taking Sides* address decision making about individual children, others require the interpretation of objective facts. Analyzing these controversies requires a different approach.

For example, educators and legislators often argue about the significant increase in costs and the number of students receiving special education. Although this is a debate that deserves examination, it is also one that highlights the importance of evaluating information carefully. Meaning often depends on the context used for interpretation.

Consider the following statement: "Federal law first insisted in 1975 that public schools educate disabled students. Since then, the portion of students receiving special education services has increased 64%. Today, 13.5% of all public school students have been diagnosed with a disability. Special education, it turns out, is no longer particularly special at all" (Winters & Greene, www.forbes.com, 2009).

How could the number of children in special education more than double? There must be a way to slow this trend. At this rate there won't be any money to buy books. Perhaps the law is poorly written. Perhaps districts are not evaluated closely enough. Perhaps parents are too unreasonable or administrators too ready to provide any service requested. Which is it?

Additional information might affect the interpretation. In 1973, the Senate Labor and Public Welfare Committee documented "more than seven million deaf, blind, retarded, speech-impaired, emotionally disturbed or otherwise handicapped children in the United States . . . only 40 per cent were receiving an adequate education, and many were not in school at all" (*Congress and the Nation, IV*, 1973). The enrollment statistics cited by Winters and Greene begin with 1976, the first year after U.S. federal law called for a free and appropriate public education for all children with disabilities.

Millions of children with disabilities were not *in* school in 1976, so their addition to the rolls made a big impact. Many children were in institutions, which declined in size and scope as school doors opened. Many underserved children became identified as having a disability and entered the special education count. How should these children be counted? Does this information change your conclusion?

Background information about statistics or seemingly objective facts can affect your understanding of their meaning and, with it, your position on the issue. Bringing to light the assumptions made by others may do the same.

Some believe special education enrollments have risen due to *invisible disabilities* invented by those looking for a cause, an excuse for poor performance, or any way to get extra help for their children. Some believe teachers seek special education to mask their own inability to teach students whose language and/or culture does not match their own. Still others contend science is becoming more adept at understanding learning and behavior; in doing so, researchers discover evidence explaining why some students struggle and productive strategies to facilitate learning.

Some maintain that society has become looser and more permissive. Drugs and alcohol are more available. Children are not supervised the way they used to be and are influenced heavily by exposure to media representations of violent behavior. Others point to statistics on poverty, one-parent homes, three-job parents, and the disintegration of family and community supports to explain increasing numbers of students who push the limits of courtesy, tolerance, and the law.

Some are proud that medicine is making remarkable strides, sustaining one-pound babies and victims of tragic accidents or chronic illnesses, who survive, returning to school ready to learn. Others are concerned that these miracles of life require extensive support and extraordinary methods beyond the scope of schools. Many contend that vaccines invented to sustain health actually lead to disabilities.

Each perspective puts a different spin on the analysis of enrollment figures in special education. The interpretation you choose to accept depends on the argument you find most compelling. Careful deliberation of all information helps you formulate your own opinion and understand the opinions of others.

## Being Aware of Bias

Each of us brings to every discussion our own background and inclinations. We cannot help but apply these to the issues in this book. In fact, those individual experiences may very well lead to creative options that change the course of a debate. As you begin to tackle your first issue, I offer the following reflections, gathered from students, parents, and colleagues.

*Acknowledge and be mindful of your own experiences.* If you, or a family member, encountered special education (or the lack of it), you may have formed strong opinions about its worth. If you have not had direct experience, your community's media coverage of special education may have shaped your thoughts. Recognize the impact of your experience and consider its influence as you debate the issues.

*Be cautious of solutions that claim to apply equally to every situation.* Two children with autism can be as different from each other as two *typical* seventh-grade children. Urban and suburban elementary schools pose very different sets of possibilities and limitations. Appropriate strategies in kindergarten usually transfer poorly to 10th grade.

*Think of possibilities rather than limitations.* It is easy to say, "That can't be done," and be constrained by what you have already observed. Creative solutions emerge from asking, "How could we do this?"

*Consider the impact of roles, motivations, and perspectives.* Teachers come to their work because they want to help children grow and learn. Special education professionals believe in the ability to help children with disabilities become productive learners and adults. Parents seek educators who are dedicated to helping children reach their potential. District administrators serve two masters. First, they believe in the power of education and want to clear financial and legal hurdles so that teachers can focus on children as much as possible. Second, they understand that they are entrusted with the finite resources of a community and must be answerable for their decisions in a way that will sustain the confidence of the citizens. Finally, legislators are committed to ensuring equal treatment and benefit to constituents whose lives span a wide range of circumstances.

*All of these roles* demand responsibility and accountability. The tasks of each role shape opinions and decisions. The outlook of people holding each role can lead to distinctly different perspectives, powerful arguments, and creative solutions. Consider the background of each of the authors you read as you evaluate their viewpoint. What in their backgrounds led them to their respective conclusions?

## Final Words

As you read the selections in this book and discuss them with your colleagues, your challenge is to sort through competing arguments and information to form your own opinions about the education of children with disabilities. Perhaps you will have opportunities to apply your point of view to an issue within your community or school. Perhaps you will discover practices in those schools that will change your opinion on an issue.

Controversies in special education will likely endure. The topics will change, but there will always be arguments about the right thing to do for children who seem to need so much.

Your own contributions will reflect the way you use experience and new knowledge. You might be tempted to search for global answers. You might find yourself frustrated by limited options. You might devise a unique solution that works perfectly for your district and your school.

As a special education administrator, especially in the spring, I often woke up in the middle of the night with a seemingly irresolvable problem running and running and running through my brain. Usually it involved balancing competing views of how to help a child. None of the options seemed totally satisfactory. A wise friend suggested I let go of the feeling that I needed to solve the problem alone and, instead, ask others to discuss together the pros and cons of each avenue. This suggestion has always served me well as I struggle over issues of doing the right thing for children; I have been comforted by knowing my colleagues were awake, too. I hope the issues in this *Taking Sides* keep you thinking at night and that my friend's suggestion helps you reach your own conclusions about educating children with disabilities.

# Internet References . . .

## The School Mental Health Project

Based at the University of California Los Angeles, The School Mental Health Project (SMHP) was created in 1986 to pursue theory, research, practice, and training addressing mental health and psychosocial concerns through school-based interventions. SMHP works closely with districts, agencies, and organizations across the country to develop and disseminate effective resources and practices. The website contains an array of resources about controversial topics, positive programs, and research-based recommendations.

**http://smhp.psych.ucla.edu**

## Individuals with Disabilities Education Improvement Act of 2004

The final Individuals with Disabilities Education Act (IDEA) regulations are more than 1,700 pages long. Should you want to consult them as a primary source, they can be found at this site:

**www2.ed.gov/policy/speced/guid/idea/idea2004.html**

## RTI Network

"The RTI Action Network is dedicated to the effective implementation of Response to Intervention (RTI) in school districts nationwide. Our goal is to guide educators and families in the large-scale implementation of RTI so that each child has access to quality instruction and that struggling students—including those with learning disabilities—are identified early and receive the necessary supports to be successful."

**www.rtinetwork.org**

## The Equity Alliance at ASU

"The Equity Alliance at ASU works with principals, teachers, parents, community members, students, school boards, and other school leaders to create the conditions necessary for culturally responsive schools. Committed to inclusive education, the Equity Alliance values diversity, pushes the boundaries of traditional thinking, and leads by example."

**www.equityallianceatasu.org**

## National Charter School Resource Center

The National Charter School Resource Center was authorized in the 1990s to issue competitive grants to expand the number of high-quality charter schools providing financial assistance for planning, program design, and initial implementation of public charter schools; evaluation of the effects of charter schools; and the dissemination of information about charter schools and successful practices in charter schools. This website includes links to primers on implementing special education in charter schools.

**www.charterschoolcenter.org/**

# Special Education and Society

*It seems simple enough. All students—including those with a disability—have a right to education. Unfortunately, society needed to be compelled by force of law to provide that education. The boundaries of required services are interpreted as frequently by the words of litigation as by the decisions of educators. Opportunities for some are interpreted as limitations for others. Recent education reform laws stress the benefits of schoolwide models, rather than reliance on special education as the only source of student support. At the same time, the line separating medical and educational needs becomes increasingly blurry. The costs of society's commitment to include everyone become increasingly contentious with strained finances. The spirit and the letter of the laws need to be interpreted as each educational dimension changes.*

- Are Labels Good for Kids?

- Did IDEA 2004 Contain Substantial Changes?

- Is Disproportionally High Minority Representation in Special Education a School Problem?

- Can RTI and IDEA Child-Find Coexist?

- Can Whole School Reform Reduce Discipline Problems?

- Are Charter Schools a Good Choice for Students with Disabilities?

- Should Insurance Cover Treatments/Services for Autism?

# ISSUE 1

## Are Labels Good for Kids?

**YES: Gwyn W. Senokossoff and Kim Stoddard**, from "Swimming in Deep Water: Childhood Bipolar Disorder," *Preventing School Failure* (vol. 53, no. 4, 2009)

**NO: Scott M. Shannon**, from *Please Don't Label My Child: Break the Doctor-Diagnosis-Drug Cycle and Discover Safe, Effective Choices for Your Child's Emotional Health* (Chapter 1: The High Cost of Labeling) (Rodale, 2007)

---

### Learning Outcomes

**At the conclusion of this issue, readers will be able to:**

- Compare and contrast the positions of the YES and NO selections addressing whether labels are beneficial or harmful to children.
- Describe the strengths and the weaknesses of each side's arguments.
- Identify the range of options parents pursue when seeking help for their children.
- Discuss the implications of each position for school teams considering a student who struggles.

---

### ISSUE SUMMARY

**YES:** Gwyn W. Senokossoff, an instructor in childhood education and literacy, and Kim Stoddard, an associate professor in special education (both at the University of South Florida, St. Petersburg) describe the first author's struggles to find a diagnosis, appropriate intervention, and support for her son with childhood bipolar disorder.

**NO:** Scott M. Shannon, psychiatrist and former president of the American Holistic Medical Association, explains why he believes it is advantageous to look for ways to relieve stressors in a child's environment rather than seek a label, which might do more harm than good.

$\mathbf{Y}$our child has changed. Her activity level is way up; she sleeps fitfully, and very little. Without sufficient sleep, her schoolwork declines and her temper flares at home and on the playground. You cannot sleep when she is restless and neither can your spouse or other children, so you all have less patience. Her school calls frequently, interrupting your focus at work. Nothing you or your partner does makes a difference—not rewards, not reasoning, not punishment. Everyone has suggestions for you; none seems to work. Can't you feel the tension?

This issue examines a situation you are likely to encounter as an educator: a child is in distress. Numerous possibilities could account for the behavior changes in the child described above. Her activity level could signify ADHD (attention hyperactivity disorder), infected tonsils that disrupt her breathing (and thus her sleep), sensitivity to the crying of a new baby, worries about school performance, or one of the disorders discussed in the YES and NO selections. Her parents want to find relief for the child, the rest of the family, and the school. You are all part of a team.

In the YES selection, Senokossoff and Stoddard describe how hopeless the first author felt when her youngest son, Matthew, began to exhibit unusual and extreme behaviors. As his mother, Gwyn Senokossoff could not understand what was causing Matthew's behavior. Worse, she did not know how to help him or his teachers. While reading a book on childhood bipolar disorder, Matthew's mother recognized her son. Finding this label helped Senokossoff understand Matthew, explain him to others, and identify appropriate medications and interventions.

In the NO selection, Scott M. Shannon acknowledges the pressures parents feel when they see their child suffering. Through his own practice as a psychiatrist working with children and adolescents, and his own experience as a parent, Shannon understands that it is natural for parents to want to relieve their child's distress. He expresses concern, however, that finding a label for the child's difficulties all too often leads to medications—sometimes several. Although these drugs might relieve the symptom, he cautions that they may have unintended consequences, including masking the real reason for the child's distress.

Krasny (*Reuters.com*, 2010) reported results of a recent study revealing that the number of preschool children diagnosed with bipolar disorder has doubled over the last decade. The number of children whose difficulties have been diagnosed as serious mental disorders has more than tripled in the last 15 years (Carey, *New York Times*, 2006). This may be a consequence of the 1994 revision of the *DSM-IV*, which greatly increased the number of disorders described. Perhaps this increase correlates with the rising number of pharmaceutical interventions available. Carey also wonders whether people are becoming more open about discussing their problems, seeing diagnostic labels (often more than one) as a way to get services.

Thomas Knestrict (*EP Magazine*, 2009) studied families who identified their children as having severe disabilities. He relied on parent perception and did not require confirmation of severity by doctors or schools. His parent-participants told him that one way they became more resilient was to move beyond a label, considering the child's changes and growth without constant reference to what others define as *normal.*

People also have different views of how difficult it is to obtain a label for a child's behavior and/or learning problems. Matthew's mother notes that some professionals focus on the family and environment and are unwilling to consider medical possibilities. Senokossoff saw a number of reluctant doctors before finding one who was "willing and able" to provide the diagnosis needed for specific medication. That doctor, and others, identified overlapping conditions and additional medications, all of which helped Matthew "focus" and "calm down."

In contrast, Shannon cited numerous examples of physicians and other professionals who are quick to provide a label, and reluctant to look beyond a symptom to consider the whole individual and his/her environment. Shannon's patient Melanie, along with her parents, discovered that her symptoms were substantially lessened by increased family time, not a label.

Labels can serve a purpose. Describing a set of behaviors with a term helps people discuss conditions and behaviors. Medically, we can differentiate between flu symptoms and those of a cold. In his compelling narrative (*Unstrange Minds,* 2007), Roy Richard Gringer conveys his pleasure that a label exists to talk about autism and his daughter's experiences. According to Grinker (2007), the label opens doors to research, services, and supports. In his opinion, a particular set of behavior exists: they do not disappear if there is no label. Without the label, there might not be understanding and targeted services. Matthew was angry when he was punished for behavior people did not understand was beyond his control.

Labels can have negative consequences. Shannon mentions Johnny, who thought his ADHD label meant his "brain was broken;" which affected his confidence in attempting school tasks. Tom Hehir (*Educational Leadership,* 2007) has no problem with labels, but does oppose ableism, an attitude that views people through stereotyped lenses of what someone with a disability supposedly cannot accomplish.

The bumper sticker "Jars Should Be Labeled, Not People" is distributed by PeopleFirst (www.peoplefirst.org.uk), a British organization that promotes the practice of seeing people as individuals rather than as disabilities: a child who has autism rather than an autistic boy. Seeing the person first focuses on the individual, not the label.

Labels change over time, reflecting new knowledge and perceptions. In 2006, the 130-year-old American Association on Mental Retardation renamed itself the American Association on Intellectual and Developmental Disabilities. Responding to its community, the new name communicates a progressive approach and moves beyond a diagnostic term that is all-too-often used as an insult. IDEA, the federal special education law, now uses the term *intellectual disability* instead of mental retardation. States sometimes have unique labels for various disabilities. These may or may not match the terms used in the DSM or IDEA.

Over 25 years ago, Stainback and Stainback (1984) recommended that the medical model of naming behavior and learning patterns be discarded because "deviant labels" are hurtful and create bureaucracies and artificial barriers. They preferred a world in which every child is provided with a unique education. Schools would be flexible, delivering help to every child who needs it.

In these days of shrinking budgets and ever-increasing pressures on schools, it is important to consider whether costly individualized services would exist if there were no labels and focused special education laws. In this time of managed care and pharmaceutical solutions, it is equally important to consider how physicians will be able to gather the information required to make the best treatment decision.

Gwyn Senokossoff sought assistance through a medical model that identifies overlapping disorders and uses medication as a key to treatment. She remembers Matthew as an active, headstrong baby and wonders if the trauma of their move might have triggered latent medically based symptoms. Scott Shannon likely would have preferred to explore the family's move rather than prescribe medication as a first intervention.

Gwyn W. Senokossoff and
Kim Stoddard

# Swimming in Deep Water: Childhood Bipolar Disorder

Several years ago on Oprah Winfrey's booklist, there was a book called *The Deep End of the Ocean*. This book was later made into a movie starring Michelle Pfeiffer. In the book, a woman loses her 3-year-old son in a hotel in Chicago, and he is missing for over 10 years before he is reunited with his family. Throughout this mother's journey, she must find the courage to go on with her life and raise her other two children. At times, she feels like she is swimming in the deep end of the ocean.

That is exactly how I (G. W. Senokossoff) felt 2 years ago when my youngest son, Matthew, began to struggle and exhibit extreme—and sometimes unusual—behaviors in school and home. I have always loved children and waited a long time to have my own. Being an educator, I am supposed to be good with kids, yet I did not know how to fix Matthew's problems. I hope that sharing our story will help other children, parents, and teachers who are dealing with similar situations to get the support that they desperately need.

Also, 2 years ago, my sons and I moved into our new home, at which time they enrolled in new schools. Matthew was starting first grade and his teacher was my friend and former colleague. As the year progressed, I began to receive notes about Matthew's work and behavior. His teacher indicated that he was often off-task, did not complete his work, and wandered around the classroom disturbing the other children. When the teacher asked him to return to his seat or when his classmates complained, he would roar like his favorite dinosaur. At other times, Matthew would sit at his desk and destroy school supplies or draw on himself. When the teacher confronted him, according to Matthew, it was always someone else's fault. He often said that his classmates were bothering or teasing him. Also, Matthew is very sensitive to and stimulated by noise. When his teacher raised her voice or the classroom became noisy, he would become agitated.

At the first parent–teacher conference, Matthew was given an academic instructional plan because he was not performing on grade level. He refused to complete the writing assessment. My son, who learned to read during the first few months of kindergarten and absorbed facts and could repeat them at will, was struggling in the first grade.

At the same time, we were dealing with unusual behaviors at home. Matthew was getting up at all hours of the night. Sometimes, he would wake me

From *Preventing School Failure,* vol. 53, no. 4, Winter 2009, pp. 89–93 (Notes omitted). Copyright © 2009 by Routledge/Taylor & Francis Group. Reprinted by permission via Rightslink.

up; at other times, I would hear him and check on him. A few times, he climbed out of his bedroom window to wander around or look for things such as bats. Also, Matthew was fascinated by fire. One morning, my other son and I awoke to the fire alarm. Matthew had taken out the grill lighter from the top shelf of a closet where I had hidden it, and he had set his behavior chart on fire.

In addition to his sleeplessness, Matthew became angry when he made a poor choice and was given consequences or when he felt misunderstood. His temper tantrums grew; he became increasingly aggressive and went into rages that often lasted hours.

In September, a psychiatrist diagnosed Matthew with Attention Deficit with Hyperactivity Disorder (ADHD) and prescribed a stimulant and eventually an antidepressant to combat his anger; however, the tantrums continued. Also, Matthew had trouble making and keeping friends in our neighborhood and at school. Several times, I had to apologize to other parents for his behavior. Although Matthew's tantrums started at home with his family, he soon began to act out in public and at school. During this time, I could not figure out what was wrong. My child was out of control and I did not know how to help him. Then, during one session with our therapist, she asked me if I had read the book *The Bipolar Child*. I had not, so I bought the book and, after reading the first few chapters, knew that my son had childhood bipolar disorder (CBD).

As the year progressed, Matthew continued to have trouble at school, especially during less structured times, such as physical education and lunch. Although he was reading on a fourth-grade level and able to complete all of his assessments successfully, he was still off-task for a large part of the day. Then, in April, we found a pediatric psychiatrist who specialized in ADHD and bipolar disorder. During our first meeting, he gave us the diagnosis that we needed to get the proper medication for Matthew. Since then, Matthew qualified for the gifted program, which he attends once a week. He is currently in a third-grade inclusion classroom. With his current medication, Matthew's behavior has stabilized and I continue to work with a therapist on various behavior intervention strategies.

## Bipolar Disorder

The challenges that Matthew and his family face because of his bipolar disorder affect more than 750,000 children a year. Unfortunately, many children go undiagnosed or misdiagnosed as ADHD, conduct disordered, oppositionally defiant, and depressed. As many as 80% of children with bipolar condition are undiagnosed for up to 10 years before receiving appropriate services to treat it. The discipline strategies that most schools use—repeated detentions with a final result of suspension—are ineffective for most children, especially for those with bipolar condition. Many school personnel lack an understanding of the condition, whereas the child and family continue to feel the stigma and guilt associated with the child's behavior problems.

Researchers first identified bipolar disorder in the early 1800s. Although bipolar disorder is the most prevalent psychotic disorder in adults, most professionals consider the onset of the condition to rarely occur before puberty. The research for CBD is in its infancy. The first diagnostic criteria for CBD occurred in the early 1960s with the use of adult criteria. As professionals began to apply the same diagnostic criteria and treatment for children, they realized adult onset and CBD manifest themselves in different ways. In addition, researchers found that treatment that is considered effective for adults can actually exacerbate the condition in children, which has prompted more specific investigation into childhood and adolescent bipolar disorder as separate conditions from adult onset.

## CBD

CBD occurs before adolescence and, in many cases, results in more severe behavior problems. Although CBD is considered a low-incidence disability, it occurs more often than the combined incidence of common childhood illnesses such as juvenile diabetes, cancer, AIDS, and epilepsy. Furthermore, the disorder is more difficult to diagnose in children because of the infancy of the field and overlap of other mitigating conditions such as ADHD.

Those who manifest early-age onset often have mood changes that shift from manic to depressive (referred to as *rapid cycling*), which often result in irritable behavior and frustrating tantrums. Also, delusions and hallucinations occur more frequently in childhood onset than in adult or adolescent onset. Misdiagnosis of CBD often occurs because the overt behaviors of the student are so disruptive that educators view it as a behavioral rather than medical issue. In addition, 70–90% of children with CBD also have ADHD, whereas 19% of children with ADHD are also identified as having CBD. Both conditions may result in hyperactivity, irritability, and distractibility. However, the child with CBD may also exhibit behaviors such as grandiosity, flight of ideas, racing thoughts, and a decreased need for sleep. The stimulant medication prescribed for children with ADHD often exacerbates the bipolar condition, which results in an acceleration of the cycling behavior. Unfortunately, professionals often look at the children's environment and blame poor parenting skills and a lack of discipline in the home. Among parents of adopted children, behavioral problems sometimes are attributed to attachment disorder and researchers have suggested psychotherapy for treatment. Unfortunately, the probability of recovery from CBD also diminishes when there is too much time between the first symptoms and the actual treatment.

The likelihood that a child will recover from CBD increases when educators and other professionals are knowledgeable of the condition and various variables that may affect a student with a predisposition for the disorder. Children with bipolar disorder may appear outgoing, personable, highly energetic, and goal directed in the manic phase. Often, parents and teachers value and reinforce these characteristics during the early school years. The difference between appropriate and manic behaviors is the intensity and frequency of the behaviors. Children in the manic phase may not be able to stop their behavior. They must constantly be doing something and believe that they can do just about anything well. They also require little sleep. Children with ADHD seem to be in constant motion, involved in undirected behavior, and sleep through the night. Children with CBD need only 3–4 hr of sleep and when awake routinely perform multiple tasks that are all goal directed. When the depressive episode appears, an astute teacher may notice the change and begin to investigate why such a drastic change has occurred in the student. The depressive episode may include the following: lack of enjoyment in life, change in appetite, fatigue, feelings of worthlessness or guilt, poor concentration, and thoughts of death and suicide. Over 50% of individuals are diagnosed with bipolar disorder during a depressive episode. Because most children exhibit rapid cycling, it may be difficult for teachers, parents, or other professionals to see a discrete completion of one phase and the beginning of the next. Most adults with bipolar disorder have episodes that last 1–3 months, followed by normal day-to-day functioning behavior between phases.

The quick interepisode recovery for children with bipolar disorder often results in disruptive behavior because of their irritability and frustration with the rapid changes in their mind and body. Children themselves refer to it as the inability to shut off their brain. It is a roller-coaster ride in which they have no control, so they act out because of frustration and anxiety over the situation. In most classrooms in which a child is disruptive, the teacher imposes consequences for inappropriate behavior. Therefore, a child who has CBD does not seem to have control over his or her behavior, so the consequences add further frustration and may escalate the acting out behavior to a more significant degree.

Because of the frenzied and erratic behavior of children with CBD, many are socially rejected by their peers. Reports on children with bipolar disorder indicate that more than 50% of them have no friends, are made fun of by others, and have poor relationships with their siblings. Furthermore, they may face academic challenges because of the increased risk for learning disabilities and a higher likelihood of deficits in cognitive functioning, math, and verbal memory. When children with CBD experience stress, their episodic behavior increases. Across the elementary grades, the stress that accompanies the increased academic demands seems to play a role in the increase in episodic behaviors or the triggering of bipolar behaviors.

## Adolescent Onset Bipolar Disorder

Although concerns for adolescent bipolar disorder are similar to adults, there are differences in the manifestation of the disorder. Adolescents with bipolar disorder have similar manic characteristics as children; however, the manifestation of the behavior may be slightly altered. Adolescents with bipolar disorder often feel a sense of grandeur and importance in life, believe that rules are for others and do not apply to them, and manifest cockiness in the classroom. They may continually question a teacher's skills in the classroom and even extend this point by failing a class to prove that the teacher was incompetent. Adolescents show longer episodic behavior but still may cycle as in childhood onset. The challenges that adolescents with bipolar disorder face are similar to the challenges that all adolescents face, but with an increase in the intensity and severity of the problems. In addition, adolescents with bipolar disorder face a greater risk for drugs and alcohol abuse, as well as a higher rate of suicide. Also, 30% of adolescents with bipolar disorder attempt suicide by the age of 18, and many of them turn to drugs and alcohol to cope. Drug and alcohol addiction occurs in approximately 39% of adolescents with bipolar disorder. The hypersexuality of adolescents with bipolar disorder can have serious consequences that include increased risk of communicable diseases and pregnancy. Accordingly, it is important to develop a treatment plan that enables adolescents to maintain a degree of stability in overall emotional development.

## Treatment and Services

In the beginning, the treatment for children and adolescents with bipolar disorder followed the same treatment plan as adult onset. However, as researchers studied the effects of pharmacological intervention, concerns arose over the effectiveness of the drugs, especially the exacerbation of manic behavior. Most experts believe the best long-term intervention includes a multimodal treatment plan involving psychosocial therapy, educational training, and maintenance medication. Most professionals support the practice of stabilizing the mood swings before treating other mitigating disorders such as ADHD, OCD, or depression. In addition, most professionals contend that each new disability should be treated in a sequential manner to determine interactive factors of multiple medications.

The key to long-term effective treatment of CBD is monitoring the effects of each medication and the mix of multiple drug interactions; this monitoring must occur at home and in school. Teachers must report changes in students' mood and overt behaviors. It is useful if teachers keep anecdotal charts to record the date, time of behavior, and duration of behaviors. In addition, the inclusion of a mood chart helps students and teachers identify the mood of students at particular times of the day. Also, a mood chart may help professionals to identify any correlations between behaviors and moods that occur throughout the school day.

Researchers have not established any clear guidelines on the maximum length of pharmacological treatment for children and adolescents. For adults, the recommendation is to begin to taper drug use after 18 months when possible. In some cases, drug intervention is needed for a much longer period of time.

The unintended side effects of medication often hinder successful treatment of children and adolescents. For example, weight gain is a concern for all individuals, and some female adolescents refuse the medication despite the effectiveness of mood stabilization drugs. In addition, with medication, there can be increased difficulty with cognitive functioning, including problems with word retrieval and memory. Thus, it is important to monitor the effectiveness of the drug on the child's mood and how the drug affects the child. A proper diet and exercise may help to reduce the negative side effects of the medication. Also, researchers have found that exercise assists with mood elevation in individuals who have been diagnosed with bipolar conditions.

## Teachers' Role

Teachers play a critical role in understanding students with bipolar disorder and assisting them in being successful in school. School personnel should have some knowledge on the characteristics that a child with bipolar behavior may convey, such as inappropriate emotional response (e.g., laughing hysterically, crying for no reason), inappropriate or precocious sexual behavior, rapidly changing moods in a short period of time, defiance of authority, daredevil behavior, excessive involvement in multiple projects, delusions and hallucinations, sleeping too little, extreme sadness or loneliness, and racing thoughts and speech patterns.

The distinguishing difference between bipolar disorder and situational behavior problems that are due to extenuating circumstances is the intensity and duration of the behavior. It would be normal for an individual to be extremely sad because of the loss of a loved one. However, it would be abnormal for an individual to be extremely sad because of being asked to sit at his or her desk to begin class.

After a student is diagnosed with bipolar disorder, an individual education plan (IEP) should be written under the *other health impaired* category. The IEP should cover accommodations for the student and a means to assess progress throughout the year. The following accommodations provide a student with the support to be successful in the classroom: (a) consistent scheduling of courses, (b) area for debriefing when emotions overwhelm the student, (c) notice of changes in the schedule beforehand, (d) a staff member in the school to talk with when emotions are overwhelming, and (e) flexibility in the length and difficulty of assignments when needed because of cycling of behavior.

A student with bipolar disorder is no different from a student with diabetes, asthma, or epilepsy. The overt behavior of a student with a bipolar disorder is often beyond his or her control even with medication. Assuring the student that he or she is a welcome part of the school community—as well as establishing an understanding of the needs of the child—will provide a stabilizer for the student and assist him or her in succeeding in the classroom.

## At-Home Support for a Child with Bipolar Disorder

There are several useful strategies that parents of children with bipolar disorder may use at home. Flexibility, patience, conflict-resolution skills, and consistency are essential. Flexibility, or the ability to adjust the schedule to the child's needs, is important. For instance, if the parents are entertaining guests at home or going out to attend an event and the child becomes agitated or irritable, it is advantageous to have a quiet place at home where he or she can go to calm down. However, the parents may need to leave the event early to care for their child. The ability to exercise patience is essential, as is ignoring minor negative behaviors and focusing on more positive responses.

Also, strong conflict-resolution skills are important. Being able to deflate a growing tantrum is crucial. Often, parents deal with many stresses concurrently and lose patience with misbehavior; however, negative, loud behavior only stimulates and escalates the child's behavior. Although people don't want to excuse poor behavior, they have to de-escalate the situation first. After the child is calm again, they should discuss the consequences of his or her actions.

The final, most important strategy is consistency, which children with bipolar disorder need in addition to structure. Routines are critical. Parents should have a morning routine that the child follows and set a timer. Also, parents should have a homework and bedtime routine. In the 2 years that the doctors were diagnosing and stabilizing Matthew, he was frequently late to school and our mornings were often a battle. Matthew is very rigid, or black-and-white, in his thinking, and he has difficulty making quick transitions. Setting up routines has helped him to know exactly what to expect.

In addition to routines, I helped Matthew set goals, and he earned rewards for meeting his goals. Many times, his rewards centered around time spent doing a favorite task. Also, Matthew has strategies that he used when he began to feel frustrated or stressed. These strategies include taking deep breaths, unclenching his fists, and moving to a quiet area to regain control. These strategies have significantly helped Matthew learn to cope.

Family dynamics are also affected. Matthew has a teenage brother who has learned how to remain calm and be helpful to him. It has been difficult for his brother, though, because of the focus and constant care that is required for Matthew. I have tried to support our older son in other ways.

# Conclusion

The first doctor that we worked with hesitated to diagnose Matthew. Many psychiatrists are reluctant to diagnose children. After many struggles, I found a pediatric psychiatrist who was willing and able to help Matthew. We were also working with a highly skilled therapist. Matthew's rages have greatly diminished and he is learning to control his behavior and accept responsibility for his actions.

Current research suggests that many children are born with bipolar disorder and may not be diagnosed until adolescence. Also, children with bipolar disorder may not exhibit severe behaviors until they experience a traumatic event that triggers the symptoms. With Matthew, it may have been our move. When I look back at Matthew's behavior over the years, it is clear that he was always an active and headstrong child. As a baby, he often did not sleep through the night, and, as a toddler, he had tantrums. However, many toddlers go through similar stages, and Matthew did not display severe behavior problems until we moved to a new home.

Because CBD is not a well-known problem, there is limited support for children with a bipolar disorder and each family's story may differ. Parents should seek medical treatment and academic support for their children. Many professionals are not well informed on how to deal with these children. Yet, the incidence of pediatric bipolar disorder has been increasing steadily since World War II, and schools will need to learn to support these children and their families.

Remember the voice of one child with bipolar disorder:

> Hi, I'm Matthew. I'm going to tell you what it feels like to have Bipolar disorder. I've been made fun of by other children. If you have this problem don't attempt to fix it yourself. Instead go find an adult and tell them what happened. When I'm angry I feel like I want to hurt the person who made fun of me but I don't. School was the hardest. Almost everyone in my class was making fun of me. At P. E. my classmate was making fun of me. Then he ran off laughing. It was hard to listen to my teacher. I was off task and thinking about other things then I wouldn't hear the teacher. Well . . . I'm on Summer Break and I'm out of school so I don't need that much medicine oh! Did I mention that I took medicine? Nope guess not. The medicine helps me focus, calm down a little and go to sleep. Well that's it for me. [*sic*].

# Please Don't Label My Child: Break the Doctor-Diagnosis-Drug Cycle and Discover Safe, Effective Choices for Your Child's Emotional Health

## Lost to a Label

Labeling is what happens when our children show signs of distress and trouble and we, the well-meaning adults in their lives, intervene. On the face of it, we do the right thing when we are able to identify the symptoms of "dis-ease" in our children and turn to experts for help. But something curious happens when we defer—with the best of intentions—to doctors, psychologists, health care providers, educators, and other "experts" in order to help our children. Too often, the *relief of symptoms* becomes the sole goal of treatment, and our children wind up labeled and medicated but feeling no better.

I don't mean to be the voice of doom and gloom about this, and of course, it can be useful—even crucial—to first aggressively treat the symptoms a child exhibits. What does alarm me, however, is how many of our children are being treated *only* on a symptomatic level and thus become lost to their labels. When this happens, the true source of the upset often remains unidentified and unaddressed. . . . [O]ne of the most frightening aspects of overlabeling [is that] more and more kids are on two or more psychiatric drugs at a time. This is true despite there being little or no research on what the effects of combining such drugs has on children.

. . . How did we get into this situation of overlabeling our kids? I believe it's a problem of well-intentioned parenting colliding head-on with a rigid and label-oriented medical culture. Parents have kids who are suffering, and they want to find relief for them. They turn to a medical system that rewards quick diagnosis over thoughtful and reflective care and prizes the myth of "silver bullet" treatment over accurate understanding. . . . Labels, to many parents, appear at first glance to be a kind of lifeboat. Who wouldn't be relieved and hopeful when whatever ails their child is quickly and succinctly identified? But the long-term cost of labeling outweighs any short-term relief of symptoms.

Instead of stopping to contemplate what brain stressors might be undermining a child's ability to enjoy emotional and mental well-being, we parents have a tendency to panic at the signs of upset in our children, to become fearful in the face of serious symptoms. When this happens, our good parental intentions go bad.

How do I know this? First, I am a parent who has had to resist the urge to label my own kids whenever the going gets tough for them—or for me. Second, I am a child psychiatrist whose practice is bursting at the seams with children who have been aggressively (and often erroneously) diagnosed with and treated for major psychiatric problems but who are not getting better. Third, I speak to professional groups around the country, and I hear firsthand how frustrated and concerned my colleagues are with the current situation. Labeling our children often cripples them instead of liberating them. The very labels that we turn to in order to help our children can actually do more harm than good.

## Psychiatric Labels: Hard Science?

. . . [P]sychiatry [is] . . . not a hard science. There is no blood test or brain scan we can use to diagnose a condition like ADHD. Psychiatric diagnosis is based on the personal observation and judgment of the practitioner, which are colored by temperament, interest, skill, level of knowledge, degree of training, and innumerable other factors. . . .

Psychiatry does very little research into the reliability of our diagnostic system in actual clinical practice. One reason may be that the results are so embarrassing and destructive to psychiatry that no one wants to consider them. [Consider] one such example, reported in May 2006 in *Clinical Psychiatry News*. In this study 376 patients at a large psychiatric hospital in Tucson, Arizona, were readmitted within 30 days of their initial discharge, and very few received the same diagnosis. Fewer than half of the patients with bipolar disorder were given the same diagnosis. Ninety percent of patients with schizoaffective disorder got a new and different diagnosis. In this study 255 people had two admissions; only 50 of these (less than 20 percent) were given the same diagnosis. If they had three admissions, only 7 of 82 patients (9 percent) received the same label. When they were readmitted four times, only 2 of 27 (7 percent) got the same tag. The poor souls who were sick enough to be admitted more than four times batted zero for 12. The researcher who did this study gave this advice: "Take the prior diagnosis with a grain of salt because other diagnosticians may not be as careful as you." I don't think I could have said it better. Can you imagine what the diagnostic reliability would have been if these patients had been children? Everyone in the field of psychiatry knows that kids are much harder to diagnose, simply because they are "moving targets" as they constantly grow, change, and mature.

We psychiatrists have some understanding of how the human brain functions, but we have very little understanding of what causes the brain to malfunction in ways that cause emotional or mental disorders. In order to organize and "codify" the way we think about mental disruptions, psychiatry has evolved around an ever-expanding encyclopedia of terminology that gives a diagnostic name to a symptom or cluster of symptoms. These psychiatric terms are the labels I've been referring to, and they can be found in the *DSM-IV* (*Diagnostic and Statistical Manual of Mental Disorders*), . . . the official handbook created by and for psychiatrists that names and defines mental disorders.

[When] [t]he *DSM* . . . was first published in 1952, [it] contained 106 mental disorders.When it was updated in 1968, there were 182. . . . [In] the most current edition . . . edited in 1994, there are more than 300 mental disorders identified . . . : Could the numbers of serious mental and emotional disorders really have *tripled* in 42 years? The answer is no. I believe the proliferation of mental and emotional disorders . . . reflects our tendency toward "diagnosis creep," toward our willingness to find illness where there may be simply difference.

The labels we most frequently give to kids include the acronyms for and names of some complex and serious mental, emotional, and social disorders. These disorders, though once thought to be very rare in children, are being diagnosed (and misdiagnosed) at alarming rates. (In the 1970s, ADHD was considered quite rare, and only about 150,000 American children were thought to have it. Today, nearly four million American kids are labeled with ADHD, and most of them are also being given very powerful drugs to "control" it.) . . .

## The Advantages of Labels

Diagnostic labels were designed to facilitate healing. There is no doubt about this. Using such labels is not only crucial to guiding appropriate treatment, it also provides a source of much-needed relief for the parents of any child who is suffering. Once a diagnosis is made, parents experience an immediate sense of reassurance that the problems that plague their child are understood and will be addressed. With a diagnostic label in hand, parents can often break out of the isolation that comes with having a seriously troubled child. They can then find support among parents with kids who have been similarly diagnosed. They can also do research and learn more about the diagnosis, which, one hopes, will help them learn more about their child.

As a physician, finding a suitable diagnosis gives me a departure point, an entrée into treating a child, and this is a crucial first step in any good treatment. I turn to diagnostic labels daily in my own practice and use them to get a handle on the symptoms that may be debilitating a child under my care. I use these labels cautiously, however, as I'm aware of the tendency (even in myself) to become persuaded that the diagnosis—or the label—is the end point of treatment.

## The Disadvantages of Labeling

Of course, there are negative consequences of diagnostic labeling, even when the diagnosis is correct.

For one, a physician who has chosen a diagnosis may stop looking for other causes of a child's symptoms. For example, when a child is labeled

ADHD, the adults around him may then miss the fact that his symptoms indicate a stress reaction to some traumatic experience or signal the stress brought on by an undetected learning disability. The kind of myopic thinking that an overreliance on labels promotes can have terrible consequences, including prolonged and unnecessary suffering for our kids. . . . Once a diagnostic label is applied, it is often understood so rigidly that many potentially helpful treatment options are ignored (or disallowed by insurers), much to the detriment of the child in question.

Of course, the greatest cost of labeling is the effect on our children. Children who are labeled in some way (however well-intentioned and therapeutically appropriate that label may be) feel separated from their peers, which takes a terrible toll on their self-esteem. Children have difficulty distinguishing a label from who they are; they also believe that because they have earned a label, they are somehow "less than," "broken," or "sick."

This tendency toward labeling is dangerous because it fractures and fragments the way we look at things, particularly how we view our kids. Instead of seeing robust, complicated, three-dimensional people, we start to see our kids as being one-dimensional. When we begin to identify and know our kids only by the symptoms they exhibit, we have, however inadvertently, abandoned them.

Even when a good diagnosis is made and a child is relieved of terrible symptoms, the stigma surrounding the initial diagnostic label may prompt the child to view himself as being somehow defective or "bad." He may come to see himself as nothing more than a problem to be solved rather than as the lovable and breathtakingly complex human being he is. Putting a label on him distorts his—and our—perception of who he is.

There is also social stigma that comes with diagnostic labeling. I find the ADHD label to be particularly noxious for kids. Take Johnny, a pleasant and playful 9-year-old. . . . His parents, who were very concerned about him, wanted to know if he indeed had ADHD, as diagnosed by his pediatrician. I actually did confirm the diagnosis and agreed with the use of stimulants to treat Johnny's symptoms. The drugs worked wonders in terms of allowing him to focus and concentrate, but it wasn't until I spent some time with Johnny in therapy and worked with him on the self-esteem issues brought on by the diagnosis that his performance in school began to improve. After a term of school under my care, Johnny brought home passing grades for the first time—even in math, his most difficult subject. I asked him what he thought had changed. "I used to think my brain was broken—isn't that what ADHD means?" he said. "Now I know it isn't, and so I can enjoy my schoolwork, even math."

Although labeling Johnny brought him symptomatic relief, he needed to refuse to identify himself with that label in order to thrive. . . .

## Multiple Labels

One of the true travesties of the epidemic of labeling is co-morbidity, which, in plain English, means the application of more than one diagnosis. On average, every child who is seen by a child psychiatrist comes away with not one but three different diagnoses. This means that children who are identified as being ADHD are also tagged as being depressed. Or a child who has OCD may also be diagnosed as having mild bipolar disorder. Although one may find reassurance in this, thinking that our children are being looked at comprehensively, what co-morbidity indicates to me, more than anything else, is how profoundly complex our children are and how poorly our diagnostic system serves them. . . .

## Incorrect Labels

Sometimes, kids are diagnosed with the wrong condition entirely. When this happens, you have a serious problem on your hands. Not only will the child not get the treatment she needs, she will continue to suffer—and so will her parents. The off-target treatment she does receive may not help at all, and it may even aggravate her symptoms. This happens very frequently with ADHD; I see kids all the time who are dealing with the effects of terrible, unacknowledged brain stressors. Instead of identifying the problem, someone slaps an ADHD tag onto these kids, and they continue to suffer, legitimately. If a child is anxious— and stress causes great anxiety in all of us—being given stimulants may make him more so. If he has endured an unspoken trauma, he will continue to suffer unless that trauma is acknowledged and addressed by the caregivers around him. All doctors—myself included—make this mistake at times. . . . Here's an example of how damaging an inaccurate diagnosis can be.

## Nick

When Nick was 6, he lived with his mother, who struggled to manage a busy job . . . while raising three children on her own. Nick's father, a bright but underachieving computer programmer who liked to drink, had finally left his wife—and their kids—in the rural small town he had taken them to. . . . Not long after the divorce, Nick's first-grade teacher called his mother to complain that the boy would not sit still and pay attention and that he was seriously disrupting the class.

Nick's mother took him to see their family doctor, who immediately became annoyed with Nick because he refused to sit still and insisted on rummaging through the doctor's supplies. The doctor promptly diagnosed ADHD and prescribed Ritalin. The medication seemed to help Nick to sit still and focus—for a few days. Then things got worse. His mother . . . became too depressed to be emotionally available to her children. Nick began to further act out at home and at school. The doctor upped the Ritalin dose, and after Nick failed to improve over the next few weeks, he raised it again. Nick began to hit kids at school and his siblings at home. When his teachers or his mother asked him to do something, he did the opposite, or he threw things and screamed. He became a tempest of a boy. In response, his doctor added the antipsychotic drug Risperdal . . . to control the aggressive behavior.

On high doses of Ritalin and Risperdal, Nick was somewhat more manageable, although he became lethargic and began to gain weight. Because of his severe behavior and aggression, the school moved him into a classroom with other "high-needs" kids, most of whom had learning difficulties and poor social skills.

In the meantime, Nick's mother sought help for herself [and]. . . decided to move back home. . . .

When I met him, Nick was 9 years old and obese (although his mother told me he had been thin most of his life). His clothes and hair were disheveled. He didn't seem to care how he looked; he didn't seem to care much about anything. To my astonishment, he related to me on the intellectual level of a teen. . . . He compensated for an overall lack of social skills with a sharp and sarcastic sense of humor. . . . He was observant, intelligent, and a bit eccentric but clearly his own person. . . .

As we talked and I had the chance to watch Nick, I saw that he had some mildly compulsive traits. Specifically, he liked to order and count some of his possessions. I decided to taper his medications and do some testing. His IQ was over 140 for analytic skills, which is higher than all but about 1 percent of the population. Although he lagged in some academic areas, his greatest shortfall was in his social skills. The bottom line was that Nick didn't have ADHD at all. He was bored by school and had been extremely stressed by his family's turmoil. . . .

Off medication, Nick was a handful: He was energetic, talkative, sarcastic, curious, testy, and stubborn. However, his mother, who now had more psychological ballast and generally felt better . . . realized that his "hyperactivity" surfaced mainly when he was bored or upset. At my urging, she agreed to put Nick into an educational program specifically designed for kids with two areas of uniqueness. . . . His teachers encouraged his curiosity and intellect while providing special instruction in developing stronger social skills. They were also tolerant of his need for stimulation and movement.

Nick is now 11. He has lost some weight and makes more effort with his appearance and personal hygiene. The only medication he takes is a very low dose of a drug called Luvox . . . to help him with his compulsions. Relaxation training and calming herbs have helped him feel on more of an even keel. He enjoys his family and his home life and is loved by his mother, brother, and sister.

Nick is the perfect example of a child who became lost in a label. In his case, his hyperactive and frustrated behavior blinded the adults around him to his high intelligence and his thirst for knowledge. . . .

## Minimizing the Harmful Effects of Labeling: A Holistic Approach

. . . [I]t's our responsibility to minimize the harm these labels do. . . . We must be willing to look at any and all aspects of a child's life that seem to be off-kilter and not just focus on the symptoms that are most apparent to adults. . . . I sometimes find that I can do the most good if I don't apply any diagnostic label at all. That's what I did when Melanie's parents came to see me.

### Melanie

I spent two sessions trying to understand 9-year-old Melanie, but I made little headway until I had the chance to spend some time with her parents. Both are engineers who work long hours, but they're devoted to their only child. The family came to me because Melanie was struggling with anxiety, sad moods, and a volatile temper. . . . She had already been . . . given two very different diagnostic labels (depression, from the family doctor, and intermittent explosive disorder, from a psychologist). Melanie's parents were hoping I could resolve this diagnostic confusion for them.

After seeing the girl three times, I told her parents that she was somewhat fragile emotionally, which meant she needed a lot of support and attention from them. Then I outlined a very rich and holistic treatment plan for her. They seemed pleased by how comprehensive all this was, but I sensed some hesitation. . . . Finally, Melanie's mother spoke up: "But what is her diagnosis, Doctor?"

I believed that Melanie was feeling great stress due to the lack of a steady, consistent emotional connection with her busy and distracted though well-meaning parents. Of course, I couldn't say this out loud, so instead I told them that I would need their help in making a diagnosis. "Melanie . . . is suffering from either a mood disorder, an anxiety disorder, oppositional defiant disorder, intermittent explosive disorder, or parent-child conflict." I asked both parents to watch her very closely and at the end of each day, to sit down with her and together decide which category she fell into on that day. . . . I sent them out the door with the symptom checklist for each of the five disorders and a firm commitment to work hard on this assignment until we met the following week.

After five more sessions, this strategy bore amazing fruit. Melanie's parents were spending so much time with her—really connecting with her—that they declared that she really didn't fit into any of the five categories. They had given Melanie such high-quality attention and time over the 6 weeks that she had become much more relaxed and happy. She had also shed much of her anger. A bonus of this "treatment plan" was that her parents were working less and spending more time focused on their child and their home life. Both parents remarked about how . . . much happier they had all become.

. . . I could have taken the easy route with Melanie and diagnosed her as having a mood disorder. I would have then prescribed antidepressant medication, which would have cleared up her symptoms. But the label—and the treatment—wouldn't have touched the true stress at the heart of Melanie's problem: her lack of connection with her overworked and emotionally unavailable parents. . . . [R]esisting the urge to label her allowed her parents to look at her in new ways. They began to address the stress that was at the root of her problem. By doing this—without the aid of drugs or labels—they began a healing process that will strengthen Melanie's mental and emotional health for the long haul.

## How We Can Avoid Labels and Drugs and Heal Our Kids

Everyday, I see kids who are labeled, and everyday, their parents ask me questions like these: "Does Johnny have ADHD?" "I was told Mary has bipolar disorder—will this ruin her life?" "My insurance company will pay for treatment only if Billy's diagnosis fits into one of these five categories. Do any of them fit him?" "My son wants to enlist in the Marines, but they say that since he was diagnosed with bipolar disorder, he can't. Why is this?"

These are important questions, but to my mind, the parents are not asking quite the right ones. Instead, they should be wondering: "Why is my child being labeled with such a serious disorder?" "Why has my child gone from being many things (a son, a student, a friend, an athlete) to being only this?" And finally, "What is keeping my child from enjoying the kind of mental and emotional health that she should have?"

. . . Our kids, given the chance, can tell us (even in nonverbal ways) what's bothering them. It's our job to listen to them attentively and openly, to resist labeling them, and to work to remove the stressors from their lives that are blocking their mental and emotional health.

# EXPLORING THE ISSUE

## Are Labels Good for Kids?

## Challenge Questions

- Compare and contrast the positions of the YES and NO selections regarding whether labels are good for kids.
- Which selection makes the best case for its argument? Why?
- What do you think would have happened if Gwen Senokossoff had seen Scott Shannon about Matthew? Construct their dialog.
- Consider the children discussed in the YES and NO selections. In each case, if you were the parent, would you seek a label? What would influence your decision?
- Consider each of the children again, but from the perspective of a teacher who has been asked for advice by a parent. Would you advise that the parent seek a label? What would influence your recommendations?

## Is There Common Ground?

All three authors consider the complexity of multiple diagnoses and conflicting (often medical) interventions. All three reveal that, once pressing behaviors were addressed, the children described were seen as academically capable, perhaps even gifted. They agree that it is important to help every child reach his/her own potential, growing into a strong, resilient adult.

Kennedy, Banks, and Grandin (*Bright, not broken,* 2011) discuss twice exceptional (2e) children. Parents and teachers see these children as gifted, but attention/behavior difficulties mask that strength. These authors worried that they, themselves, focused more on the label attached to the attention/behavior and lost sight of the giftedness. They believe a whole child approach, with emphasis on the child's gifts, will result in a more balanced, happy child.

## Additional Resources

Carey, B. (2006, November 11). What's wrong with a child? Psychiatrists often disagree. *New York Times.* Retrieved November 11, 2006 from www.nytimes.com

Grinker, R. R. (2007). *Unstrange minds.* Cambridge, MA: Basic Books.

Hehir, T. (2007). Confronting ableism. *Educational Leadership, 64*(5), 9–14.

Kennedy, D. M. & Banks, R. S., with Grandin, T. (2011). *Bright not broken: Gifted kids, ADHD and autism.* San Francisco, CA: Jossey-Bass.

Knestrict, T. (2009). Welcome to Holland: Helping families develop resiliency. *EP Magazine, 39*(1), 36–39.

Krasny, R. (2010, January 15). *Bipolar diagnosis jumps in young children: Study.* Retrieved January 15, 2010 from www.reuters.com.

Shannon, S. M. (2007). *Please don't label my child: Break the doctor-diagnosis-drug cycle and discover safe, effective choices for your child's emotional health.* New York: Rodale.

Stainback, W. & Stainback, S. (1984). A rationale for the merger of special and regular education. *Exceptional Children, 51*(2), 102–111.

# ISSUE 2

## Did IDEA 2004 Contain Substantial Changes?

**YES: H. Rutherford Turnbull, III,** from "Individuals with Disabilities Education Act Reauthorization: Accountability and Personal Responsibility," *Remedial and Special Education* (vol. 26, no. 6, pp. 320–326, 2005)

**NO: Tom E. C. Smith,** from "IDEA 2004: Another Round in the Reauthorization Process," *Remedial and Special Education* (vol. 26, no. 6, pp. 314–319, 2005)

---

### Learning Outcomes

**At the conclusion of this issue, readers will be able to:**

- Compare and contrast the positions of the YES and No selections and references addressing whether IDEA 2004 contributed to substantial changes in special education practices.
- Describe the strengths and the weaknesses of each side's arguments.
- Identify specific changes in special education practice as a result of IDEA 2004.
- Explore how local schools have addressed changes made in IDEA 2004.

---

**ISSUE SUMMARY**

**YES:** H. Rutherford Turnbull III, co-founder and co-director of the Beach Center on Disability at the University of Kansas, sees major changes in IDEA 2004. In line with the Bush administration's priorities, Turnbull identifies a shift toward requiring parents and students to take more responsibility for their own behavior and for relationships with schools.

**NO:** Tom E. C. Smith, professor at the University of Arkansas, focuses his research on disability law and inclusion. Reflecting on IDEA 2004, Smith believes that although some changes seem significant, they will make little difference in the daily practice of special education teachers.

$T$he Education of All Handicapped Children Act was passed in 1975. It opened school doors for millions of excluded children with disabilities from ages 3 to 22 (or high school graduation). States were offered some federal funding for providing a Free and Appropriate Public Education (FAPE) to these students. Linked to funds came many detailed regulations. The 1997 reauthorization as the Individuals with Disabilities Education Act (IDEA 97) opened classroom doors, mandating access to the general education curriculum and participation in large-scale assessments.

The fifth reauthorization of IDEA began in 2001. Despite good intentions, the new Individuals with Disabilities Education Improvement Act (still called IDEA) was not signed by then President Bush until 2004. The process to formalize regulations was also expected to move quickly, but these were not posted in *The Federal Register* until mid-August, 2006, becoming official 60 days later.

Next, state governments aligned their unique state laws with new federal regulations. The former can exceed, but not fall below, federal standards. Not until state regulations are formulated do educators and parents learn what they must do to comply with any reauthorization.

Current IDEA information is available through the respective state department of education and/or the U.S. federal website: http://idea.ed.gov. Reauthorization of IDEA is again due, but no specific timelines have been established.

The last reauthorization occurred in a highly charged atmosphere. No Child Left Behind (NCLB) was impacting schools, holding them accountable for the progress of all children (including those with disabilities). The Fordham Foundation had just released a comprehensive analysis of the accomplishments and shortcomings of IDEA (*Rethinking Special Education for a New Century,* 2001) as had the President's Commission on Excellence in Special Education (2002). Both called for increased accountability, reduced paperwork, and stronger controls in what each perceived as rampant litigation.

Reauthorization of IDEA 2004 addressed many of the criticisms. Substantial changes were made in the following areas:

- Increased alignment with NCLB, including the definition of highly qualified teachers and the requirement to use services and techniques "based on peer-reviewed research (PRR) to the extent practicable"
- Use of Response to Intervention (RTI), as a general education methodology and as an alternative means of identifying students with specific learning disabilities
- Paperwork reduction through elimination of short-term objectives (except for students with significant cognitive needs) and pilots of a multiyear Individualized Education Program (IEP)
- Flexibility in IEP practices, including "excusal" of some participants
- Increased requirements for specificity from parents seeking due process remedies
- More administrative latitude in disciplinary proceedings, including manifestation determination

This issue revisits IDEA 2004 to reflect on the impact of its changes, several of which are treated more expansively in other issues. The YES and NO

**25**

selections differ dramatically in their interpretation of the significance of the reauthorization. Analyze the accuracy of the authors' predictions in light of those who have studied IDEA 2004's impact and formulated topics for the next reauthorization.

In the YES selection, H. Rutherford Turnbull, III contends IDEA 2004 was substantially altered in ways that would engineer society and change behavior. He finds that the new provisions substantially increased the responsibilities of parents and students.

In the NO selection, Tom E. C. Smith predicts that although a number of the new elements of IDEA 2004 appeared promising, they would have little real impact on the daily practices of schools. He sees that the core element of IDEA—providing a Free and Appropriate Public Education—remained unchanged.

Scholars and practitioners have addressed the reauthorization elements of RTI, the use of research-based/peer-reviewed practices, paperwork reduction, and IEP practices. Their findings and experiences form the basis of recommendations for the impending reauthorization. Consider how they compare with the predictions of this issue's authors.

RTI, in varying forms, is now firmly in process, according to a majority of superintendents responding to an *Education Week* survey (Samuels, *RTI: An approach on the march,* 2011, www.edweek.org). Adoption has generated sufficient controversy to be the focus of Issue 6: Are Charter Schools a Good Choice for Students with Disabilities? and Issue 9: Should RTI Interventions Be Delivered By Special Educators?

IDEA 2004 directs teachers to use educational strategies documented to be successful through PRR, to the extent practicable. Related to the term *scientifically based research* in NCLB, PRR techniques must have been deemed effective through research rigorously reviewed by other scholars (peers) and published in peer-reviewed journals.

Fulfilling the PRR directive is complicated. The unique nature of disabilities makes it difficult to locate a group of similar-enough children of the same age who would be available for study. Rigorous evaluation of educational methods requires a control group (which does not receive the treatment under study); few educators or parents feel comfortable assigning children to uncertain situations. A technique may appear promising, but not for the same disability and age as the student at hand. There may be conflicting evidence about a technique's efficacy. This topic is considered in Issue 19: Are Evidence-Based Practices Sufficient for Educating Students with Autism?

In the midst of this complexity are children who need to be taught and teams (including parents) who cannot wait for research to evaluate each method and each disability. Online resources such as the National Dissemination Center for Children with Disabilities (http://nichcy.org/research) contain extensive information on educating children with disabilities in a research-focused environment. An extensive discussion of the challenges posed by this element, including information on litigated-decisions, has been presented by Etscheidt and Curran (2010) in *Exceptionality,* itself a peer-reviewed journal.

Several contributors to *Rethinking* described special education as consumed with documenting compliance through reams of paper. IDEA 2004 appeared to take paperwork reduction seriously. Meetings could be streamlined; short-term objectives were eliminated for most students; and pilot projects for multiyear IEPs were funded.

Reports of success are mixed, for both IEP procedures and data collection. Some states decided to retain the use of short-term objectives for all students; no changes were effected. Other states adopted the practice. In a document outlining issues for the IDEA's next reauthorization the National School Board Association (*NSBA Issue Brief, IDEA: Early preparation for reauthorization*, 2010, www.nsba.org) praised the removal of "unnecessary bureaucracy, paperwork, legal process, and expense."

Determining the impact of "excusal," a practice in which a member of the IEP team can be excused from attendance under certain circumstances is difficult. One can never know how that person's absence affects the IEP that is constructed (Etscheidt, *Preventing School Failure,* 2007).

Turnbull referenced increased parental responsibility in due process actions. NSBA felt these became less cumbersome and less contentious with the tightened standards of IDEA 2004. Referencing an effort in his state to pilot streamlined IEP procedures, attorney Robert Crabtree (*Federation for Children with Special Needs Newsline,* 2011) saw "nothing at all of benefit" in forfeiting critical rights, and recommended that parents take time to carefully consider their choice. The NSBA report anticipates some groups will strive to regain some of the protections lessened in IDEA 2004. This topic is developed further in Issue 20: Does Working with Parents Have to Be Contentious?

IDEA 2004 increased administrative latitude in disciplinary practices for students with disabilities and encouraged positive behavioral intervention. For detail on this topic, read Issue 5: Can Whole School Reform Reduce Discipline Problems?

The heralded multiyear paperwork reduction pilots hit a snag, demanding manpower exceeding the capacity of any state (Samuels, *Education Week,* 2006). "Massive" amounts of data were required to document progress on issues such as parent involvement and disproportional representation (Samuels, *Education Week,* 2005). The IDEA Data Accountability Center (www.ideadata.org) offers a window into the multitude of information the U.S. Department of Education endeavors to collect, analyze, and disseminate.

Just as *Rethinking* affected the IDEA 2004 reauthorization, a current Fordham report is poised to affect the next. *Shifting Trends in Special Education* (Scull & Winkler, 2011, www.edexcellence.net) describes special education as "a field in flux" that "needs a make-over for the twenty-first century." For the first time since its inception, the overall number of students covered by IDEA has declined, although there is little consistency across states. Scull and Winkler wonder if the decline reflects the success of early interventions, such as Response to Intervention or the undesirable use of an NCLB loophole allowing schools with low numbers of students with disabilities to skirt accountability.

The key to understanding and making change, according to Scull and Winkler, is improved data collection and analysis. Currently, states create their own definitions and procedures. Meaningful comparative analyses can occur only when states are unified in using terms and definitions.

System changes take time to implement. The challenges of RTI and PRR alone require considerable energy and resources; and the results of these initiatives take even longer to be experienced. It is essential to acknowledge progress along the way.

The upcoming reauthorization seems far removed from educators—in fact, that's what Smith said. As the next IDEA reauthorization becomes a reality, Dale (*TEACHING Exceptional Children,* 2011) suggests ways teachers can influence the process, including written commentary. Teachers possess a credible and practical insight that made a difference to Dale when he worked at the Pennsylvania Education Department. Should you doubt that input makes a difference, consider that the U.S. Department of Education reviewed over 5,500 public comments before finalizing regulations for IDEA 2004. Your experience might raise an important idea.

# YES

H. Rutherford Turnbull III

# Individuals with Disabilities Education Act Reauthorization: Accountability and Personal Responsibility

It is important at the outset to recognize that law is a form of behavior modification. It regulates the behaviors between the government and the governed, and it shapes the behavior of both. In this respect, the law plays its traditional role of social engineering—shaping the ways that society operates.

Seen in this light, the reauthorized Individuals with Disabilities Education Act (IDEA; 2004) engineers society and shapes behavior in three basic ways. First, it authorizes the expenditure of federal funds and shapes how those funds and the complementary state and local educational agencies' funds are spent, and it aligns those funds and their expenditure patterns with the earlier IDEA (1997) and with the No Child Left Behind Act of 2001 (NCLB). It continues to be—but becomes more like—a *school reform* law. Second, IDEA grants rights to students and their parents: It continues to be a *civil rights* law. Third, IDEA particularizes the relationships that students and their parents have with local and state educational agencies. It partakes of social reform on a large scale—more like a *"welfare state"* reform law than a civil rights or school reform law.

Taking these three approaches to social engineering as a whole, and based on a close analysis of IDEA's text, it becomes clear that IDEA is more consistent than ever with other federal policies that impose accountability standards and procedures on the beneficiaries of federal largesse. The accountability that IDEA (1997) and NCLB imposed on the schools is now imposed on the students and their parents as well. To support this argument, it is appropriate to begin with analyzing IDEA as an education law, then showing how IDEA retains its basic nature as a civil rights statute, and finally discussing its new accountability and responsibilities provisions, their origins, their relationships to other disability laws, and their implications as welfare law reform.

From *Remedial and Special Education,* vol. 26, no. 6, November/December 2005, pp. 320–326. Copyright © 2005 by Hammill Institute on Disabilities and Sage in association with American Rehabilitation Counseling Association (ARCA). Reprinted by permission via Rightslink.

# IDEA as Education Law

When Congress reauthorized IDEA in 2004, it aligned IDEA with the Elementary and Secondary Education Act (ESEA; 1965), as amended by the . . . NCLB. To understand how this is so, it is helpful to describe the six principles that underlie NCLB (Erwin & Soodak, 2005) and show how IDEA connects to them.

The most obvious and, therefore, the first to be mentioned principle of NCLB is *accountability* for the outcomes (results) of education. NCLB's provisions for the mandatory assessment of student proficiency during the elementary school years are its principal means for ensuring accountability. In 1997, IDEA provided that students with disabilities will have a right to participate in state and district assessments. In 2004, IDEA provides that students will participate, with accommodations and sometimes by alternate assessments, in the NCLB assessments. . . . The significant change is not that the students will engage in the state and district assessments, but that IDEA now references and therefore aligns with NCLB.

To support its accountability principle, NCLB adopts a second principle, the *highly qualified teacher* principle. Without a qualified teacher corps, improved student outcomes will be elusive, and accountability for those outcomes difficult to achieve. Accordingly, IDEA (2004) requires special education staff to be highly qualified. . . . The second principle is a means to achieve the first.

NCLB's third principle is also a means to achieve its ends: The highly qualified teachers will use *scientifically based instruction* (SBI; sometimes called *evidence-based instruction*). IDEA reiterates the SBI requirement through several different provisions:

1. It disqualifies a student from IDEA benefits if the student's educational needs or deficiencies result from "a lack of appropriate instruction in reading, including the essential components of reading instruction," as defined in . . . the Elementary and Secondary Education Act of 1965, as amended by NCLB. . . .
2. It restricts a student from being classified as having a specific learning disability by authorizing an LEA to "use a process that determines if the child responds to scientific, research-based intervention as part of the evaluation procedures." . . .
3. It requires a student's special education, related services, and supplementary aids and services (as set out in the student's . . . IEP) to be "based on peer-reviewed research to the extent practicable." . . .
4. It authorizes the SEA and LEAs to support preservice and professional development (inservice) activities that train educators to use "scientifically based instructional practices." . . .
5. It authorizes "whole-school approaches, scientifically based early reading programs, positive behavioral interventions and supports, and early intervening services" that can prevent students from being classified into special education. . . .
6. It defines "highly qualified" teachers in terms that originate in NCLB. . . .

7. It authorizes the SEA and LEAs to expend Part B money for "early intervening services" that are coordinated with their NCLB activities. . . .
8. It sponsors research, training, demonstration, and other programs that align with NCLB. . . .

NCLB's fourth principle is *local flexibility,* the theory being that too many restrictions are imposed on SEAs and LEAs by too many federal laws and that if the SEAs and LEAs have more flexibility to use their federal funds as suitable to meet their particular needs, they will achieve more acceptable outcomes. Thus, fiscal and programmatic flexibility advances agency accountability, and site-based management is sanctioned. Similarly, IDEA recognizes that SEAs and LEAs have the primary responsibility for educating students with disabilities and that there is a limited role for the federal government (Sec. 601)(c)(6). It is appropriate, then, for IDEA to seek to reduce federal paperwork requirements . . . and to grant SEAs and LEAs more discretion in how they use Part B funds. . . .

NCLB's fifth principle relates to *safe schools,* the theory being that agency accountability and student proficiency are unlikely to be realized when the teaching and learning environment is unsafe. To advance the safe school and acceptable outcome approach, IDEA retains the 1997 provision that allows an LEA to put a student into an interim alternative educational setting for a maximum of 45 days if the student carries weapons or drugs to school or injures others, but it now allows the LEA to take into account any "unique circumstances" relative to that student and his or her conduct. This vague provision is consistent with the flexibility principle, but it targets the discipline issue, not the expenditure issue: The LEA needs to be able to exercise its discretion to carry out the safety principle and thereby advance the accountability principle.

Moreover, IDEA (2004) also makes it more difficult for a student to prove that his or her behavior and disability are causally connected. . . . Under the 1997 law, the student's IEP team had discretion (the statute used the word "may") to conclude that the student's behavior was not a manifestation of his or her disability if (a) the student's IEP and placement were "appropriate," and special education services, supplementary aids and services, and behavior intervention strategies "were provided consistent with" the student's IEP; (b) the student's disability did not "impair" the student's ability to understand "the impact and consequences" of his or her behavior; and (c) the student's disability did not "impair" his or her ability "to control the behavior" for which the school would be disciplining the student.

Under the 2004 reauthorization, however, the discretionary "may" has been deleted. In its place, IDEA (2004) provides that the student's "conduct shall be determined to be a manifestation" of his or her disability under certain conditions. Furthermore, those conditions are more stringent. Instead of the original three conditions, there are now only two, and each is itself more exacting. One is that the student's conduct "was caused by, or had a direct and substantial relationship to" the student's disability. Note the change; "caused" and "direct and substantial relationship" are more immediately connected to the conduct than the two 1997 standards of "did not know" and "could not control." The other condition is that the student's conduct was "the direct result" of the LEA's "failure to implement" the student's IEP. Note again the change: Gone is the 1997 language about services not being provided "consistent with" the student's IEP and placement. "Causation" and "direct relationships" are now clearly more connected to conduct than "consistency" or fidelity of implementation.

NCLB's sixth principle is *parent participation and choice*. This has always been one of IDEA's six principles: the right to be involved in a nondiscriminatory evaluation, to be on the IEP team, to have access to and control over the release of records, and to be eligible for membership on various SEA or LEA advisory boards.

The new IDEA (2004) retains these provisions but clarifies that parents have responsibilities as well. Section 612(a)(10) limits tuition reimbursement and conditions it on the parents' giving an LEA notice and opportunity to cure alleged violations of the student's right to FAPE. Section 614(a)(1)(D) imposes duties on parents with respect to the initial evaluation, and Section 614(c)(3) does the same with respect to reevaluations. Sections 615(b)(5) and (e) make mediation available and create premediation meetings. Section 615(b)(6) creates a 2-year statute of limitations and thus requires parents to complain in a timely way. Section 615(a)(7) obligates parents to notify the LEA concerning "the nature of the problem of the child" and the "proposed resolution" of the problem of the child (not "of the school") and thus imposes on them the duty to specify what is wrong with their child and what the LEA should do for their child. Section 615(c)(E) restricts the parents' (and LEA's) right to amend their due process hearing complaint: The parents have to get their complaint right the first time around, or else the school cannot respond, because it would always be subject to being caught off guard by another and different complaint. Section 615(d)(1)(A) provides that parents may receive the procedural safeguards notice only once a year (with some exceptions), rather than on demand as often as they want it. Section 615(f)(1) requires parents and the LEA to hold a prehearing "resolution session" and to provide sufficient final notice so that the parents' complaint might be resolved before the hearing. Section 615(f)(2) requires the parents to disclose all evaluations and recommendations that they intend to use in the hearing. Section 615(f)(3)(C) creates a 2-year statute of limitations, counting from the time when a parent knew or reasonably should have known that a local educational agency violated IDEA, thus putting the parents to the task of regularly monitoring their child's education. Section 615(i)(3) regulates that award of parents' attorneys' fees and allows a court to charge the LEA's fees to the parents' attorneys if the parents' complaint is frivolous or if the parents do not proceed in good faith during the pendency of any hearing, trial, or appeal.

In summary, the reauthorized IDEA (2004) imposes many new duties on students and their parents, giving them the message that they are personally responsible for their conduct—a point that the following discussion expands.

# IDEA as Civil Rights Law

IDEA is still a civil rights law. Section 612(c) parrots the Americans with Disabilities Act (1990; the disability community's civil rights law) by proclaiming that the nation's disability policy consists of ensuring equal opportunity, full participation, independent living, and economic self-sufficiency. The very term *equal opportunity* derives from the equal protection clause of the 14th Amendment (prohibiting a state from denying anyone in its jurisdiction the "equal protection" of the law), and the 14th Amendment itself was the basis on which students with disabilities first gained access to the schools as a matter of constitutional right. More than this, however, IDEA retains the original six principles that endow it as a civil rights law.

Section 612 codifies the *zero rejection* principle by continuing to require that the state plan to provide for the education of *all* students with disabilities and by retaining the "no cessation" provision. Moreover, the Section 615 discipline provisions ensure that students with disabilities will have procedural and substantive protection against discipline that might terminate their right to an education or alter the nature of FAPE for them.

Sections 614(a)–(c) continue the *nondiscriminatory evaluation* principle by retaining the safeguards for nondiscriminatory evaluation. The requirement that the evaluation now must attend to the student's academic, developmental, and functional characteristics simply makes the evaluation more specific. Moreover, the evaluation team still needs to determine the "relative contribution" of "cognitive, behavioral, physical, and developmental factors" to a student's educational needs. Thus, three characteristics, or domains, become the focus of an evaluation under the IEP: academic (consistent with NCLB), developmental, and functional (consistent with the "alternate assessment" provisions of IDEA). The four contributing factors—cognitive (a surrogate for academic), behavioral, physical, and developmental—must be evaluated and taken into account, separately and collectively.

Section 614(d) retains the *appropriate education* principle by setting out the required content of a student's IEP—the theory being that if the content standard is met, the student's education will "benefit" the student and thus meet the *Rowley* definition of "appropriate."

Section 615(f), however, minimizes the "process" component of the *Rowley* definition by providing that a procedural violation constitutes the denial of a free, appropriate public education only if it impedes the student's right to such an education, significantly impedes the parents' opportunity to participate in decision making, or causes a deprivation of educational benefits. This provision seems to codify case law: no significant procedural harm, no substantive foul.

Several sections of the 2004 IDEA restate the *least restrictive environment* principle. Section 612(a)(5) and Sections 614(b)(2)(A) and (c)(1)(B)(iv) continue to ensure that the student may participate and have the opportunity to make progress in the general curriculum. They also retain the requirement that the student's IEP must advance the student's participation in the general curriculum, extracurricular, and other school activities, consistent with the principle of the least restrictive environment.

Likewise, two sections of IDEA (2004) retain the *procedural due process* principle. Section 614 retains the procedural safeguards related to evaluation, program, and placement, and Section 615 retains the procedural due process protections related to grievances, although, as noted earlier, it adds new provisions regarding dispute resolution and mediation and makes it more difficult for a student to resist unilateral placement (see the "unique circumstances" provision) and to prove manifestation of a disability.

Finally, Sections 614 and 615 retain the *parent participation* principle by conferring opportunities on the parents to participate in decisions affecting their child's education.

By retaining its original six principles, IDEA remains a foundation for the 18 core concepts and the related nine overarching principles of disability policy. For example, the zero rejection principle reflects the core concept of *antidiscrimination*. The nondiscriminatory evaluation principle reflects the core concept of *classification*. The appropriate education principle reflects the core concept of *individualized appropriate services*. The least restrictive environment principle reflects the core concept of *integration*. The procedural due process principle reflects the core concept of *accountability*. The parent participation principle reflects the core concept of *empowerment and participatory decision making*.

These core concepts reflect constitutional principles (*life, liberty,* and *equality*) and ethical principles (*dignity, family as foundation,* and *community*). Thus, for example, the NCLB principles of accountability, highly qualified teachers, and scientifically based instruction reflect the core concepts of accountability, professional and system capacity development, and individualized appropriate services, respectively. The principle of local flexibility reflects the core concept of accountability. The principle of safety reflects the core concept of protection from harm. The principle of parental participation and choice reflects the core concept of empowerment and participatory decision making.

The fact that NCLB reflects some of the same core concepts of disability policy as IDEA is significant: It shows how very universalistic and less exceptionalistic IDEA has become. It is "mainstream" disability policy, of course, but it also has become part of the mainstream of education policy.

## Two Preludes to IDEA as Accountability Policy

Two reports predicted that the reauthorized IDEA would focus far more on student and parental accountability than it had in the past. The first was *Rethinking Special Education for a New Century.* The second was the report of the President's Commission on Excellence in Special Education (2002). Both reports made similar critiques of special education, and both sought similar improvements to IDEA. Both focused on outcome rather than process, on a model of prevention rather than failure, and on children with disabilities as "general education children first" (President's Commission, 2002). Both reports paid attention to IDEA as an education law but less attention to IDEA as a civil rights law. Most significantly, both reports argued that IDEA leads students with disabilities to have unacceptable outcomes, low expectations, and a diminished sense of personal responsibility.

The point about personal responsibility was made most directly in *Rethinking*, in the chapter by Horn and Tynan, who argued that one of IDEA's "unintended negative consequences" included the "application of an accommodation philosophy to populations better served with prevention or intervention strategies." The "accommodation model," when applied to some "low- and under-achieving students," replaces a goal of "independence" with one of "lifetime dependence on special accommodations, often at tax-payers' expense." The accommodations, and especially the discipline provisions, have been "teaching students in special education that they are entitled to operate under a different set of rules than everyone else." These accommodations constitute "encouragement for special education students to see their disability as rationale for a life-time entitlement to special accommodations." The consequence of these accommodations is that the "end game" of independence has been forgotten: "special education in far too many instances serves to separate, not integrate, through the use of special rules and procedures not available to non-disabled students." Special education "seems focused on encouraging a lifetime entitlement to special accommodations." The "true victims" are the students themselves; they learn that there are "two standards" and they are "encouraged to rely upon special accommodations rather than being challenged to achieve at high levels."

Horn and Tynan's critique has a basic message: IDEA creates dependency. That message is consonant with the messages given by welfare law reform during the last decade, as the following discussion makes clear.

# IDEA as Welfare Law

By analyzing the messages that Congress and the Supreme Court have been giving in welfare and disability policy during the past decade, and by bearing in mind Horn and Tynan's critique, it becomes obvious that IDEA extends the basic message of personal responsibility that was the core of welfare reform. This message also relates as much to personal responsibility as it does to social obligations and the social contract.

## Congress, the Supreme Court, and the Principle of Personal Responsibility

Congress reformed welfare programs in 1996 by enacting the Personal Responsibility and Work Opportunity Reconciliation Act (PRWORA). This law targeted a subpopulation that allegedly had "learned" to be dependent—namely, families who had been supported by aid-to-dependent-families programs. PRWORA authorized time-limited and conditional cash grants, requiring the head of family to enroll in some educational program or work and entitling the family to receive the grants for only 2 years.

In a nutshell, PRWORA declared an end to learned dependency and imposed responsibilities on heads of families; it taught welfare beneficiaries that they should not continue to expect different treatment from other citizens. It signaled that people should expect less from their government and more from themselves. It proclaimed the renaissance of self-reliance and a work-ethic policy that asserts that everyone has a responsibility to contribute to society.

Similarly, IDEA reflects the theory that special education "teaches" students with disabilities to expect "different" treatment in society. This is a fundamental premise of the Finn et al. report and the Horn and Tynan chapter: The discipline provisions "teach" students with disabilities that they are different, can behave in different (and less acceptable, less conforming) ways and still expect to be treated differently ("no cessation" under Section 612, and special procedural safeguards, including manifestation determinations, under Section 615). The reauthorized IDEA sent a different message, as the many provisions cited earlier demonstrate.

In PRWORA and IDEA, Congress did more than restate the "responsibility" principle. Fundamentally, it restated the quid pro quo of the social contract: Society will do something for you if you cannot do it for yourself, but you first must be responsible for yourself. Self-reliance precedes social support. Personal responsibility precedes social dependency.

The Supreme Court also has advanced the principle of personal responsibility, principally (in its disability-law cases) in *Sutton v. United Air Lines* (1999). In this case, the court held that in determining whether the ADA protects a person, it is permissible to take into account whether the person can or does mitigate his or her disability. If a person's impairment is or can be mitigated, that person does not have a disability. *Sutton*'s message and subtext is clear: If you can mitigate your disability, you should, and if you do not, ADA will not cover you.

Following *Sutton,* the Supreme Court made a deliberate effort to reduce the number of people that the ADA covers. The best example is its decision in *Williams v. Toyota*. There, the court declared that the "major life activities" that a person's impairment must significantly limit are performing household chores, bathing, and brushing one's teeth; those activities do not include being able, with accommodations, to perform a particular job. By reducing the number of people who are entitled to accommodations because they have disabilities, the court adopted the premise of *Rethinking* and the President's Commission (2002), namely, that too many people have been included as "disabled" and that it is better social policy to restrict admission to disability entitlements than to allow people to enter the disability category easily. . . .

The Supreme Court's message, then, is congruent with Finn et al., the report of the President's Commission (2002), and the reauthorized IDEA (2004): Disability policy and law should benefit fewer, not more people, and it should teach those who do qualify and those who seek to qualify as having a disability that they have obligations as well as rights and entitlements.

## IDEA and the Principle of Personal Responsibility

The reauthorized IDEA (2004) restates the principle of personal responsibility in at least two ways. In this respect, IDEA is consistent with the message that Congress sent in PRWORA and the Supreme Court sent in the ADA employment cases.

First, as noted earlier, IDEA grants a variety of rights to students' parents to participate in decisions about their child's education, but it also imposes duties on them as they do participate. Moreover, IDEA also makes the personal responsibility theme explicit, . . . with respect to the students themselves. Here, Congress declares that students' education can be made more effective when educators have "high expectations" of them and enable them to "meet their developmental goals," to meet the "challenging expectations that have been set for all children," and to "be prepared to lead productive . . . adult lives." . . . Under an analysis of IDEA as welfare law, the provisions about meeting "developmental goals" arguably refer to students' behavior, not just to their academic achievement. Likewise, under the same analysis, the provisions about "lead[ing] productive . . . adult lives" arguably refer to being economically self-sufficient, working and contributing to the nation's economy, or making other socially valued contributions.

Second, as also explained earlier, IDEA allows LEAs to take into account "any unique circumstances on a case-by-case basis" when determining whether to order a change in a student's placement because of conduct that violates school rules. . . . This provision is a Damoclean sword: The "unique circumstances" are a thin hair that can protect the student or, if it is cut, cause the sword of discipline to strike the student. In either event, it permits LEAs to take into account whether the student chose to act responsibly or was incapable of making that choice.

The reauthorized IDEA (2004) also makes it more difficult for students to defend themselves against a disciplinary sanction by alleging "manifestation." As pointed out above, the reauthorized law requires students to prove that their conduct was "caused by" or had a "direct and substantial relationship" to their disability. It also removes the lax standard that the student's services were not delivered "consistent" with the IEP and replaces it with the standard that the LEA must fail to implement the student's IEP and thereby directly cause the student's conduct.

## Rights and Responsibilities Within IDEA: Teaching New Lessons

The changes in IDEA's parent participation and student discipline provisions impose a duty of responsibility on parents and students alike. These beneficiaries must either follow new, highly specific procedures and standards or justify why they do not.

The new IDEA, then, teaches parents and students that they have responsibility for their own actions. It intends to shape their behavior by causing them to unlearn their alleged sense of entitlement to act in certain ways. It seeks to reduce their dependency on the schools and to increase their dependency on themselves. It calls on them to be more self-reliant and self-governing. It bears repeating: Section 601(c)(5)(A) proclaims that students' education can be made more "effective" if there are "high expectations" for them (including both behavioral expectations and academic expectations) and ways of "strengthening the role and responsibility of parents." . . .

## IDEA, Title I of ESEA, and the New Morbidity

It is not just in its parent and student rights provisions that IDEA reveals that it is a welfare law. There is also a clear line between (a) IDEA and its concern with student outcomes, especially outcomes for ethnically and linguistically diverse students . . . (b) NCLB and the special provisions for Title I schools (i.e., for "poor students" in school); and (c) the "new morbidity." The term *new morbidity* refers to evidence that disability has a positive correlation with poverty and other demographic factors, such as family structure, ethnicity/ culture, language, and geography.

IDEA and NCLB focus especially on students whom the new morbidity affects—under IDEA, students from minority populations (Sec. 601(c)(10)–(13)), and under NCLB, the Title I eligible ("poor") students. PRWORA and welfare reform focused on these students' families. Together, IDEA and NCLB continue the PRWORA welfare reform policies passed nearly a decade ago and the *Sutton* line of cases.

# Conclusion

It seems unseemly to argue that the reauthorized IDEA is, at its core, part of the reforms that PRWORA and *Sutton* launched more than half a decade before Congress turned its attention to IDEA. Somehow, the notion that students' and parents' rights were sacrosanct had become the conventional wisdom. Yet the transitory nature of "conventional wisdom" is apparent in the very terms that define the concept itself: *Conventional* refers to the conventions, the mores, of a certain time, place, and culture. As our country's history shows, conventions and mores change; the underlying principles (the so-called six principles of IDEA and the so-called core concepts of disability policy) may not have changed, but the ways in which they are expressed in practice and codified in law do.

So it seems to be with the reauthorized IDEA. The conventional notion that rights are paramount now seems to be descendant, not ascendant. At the same time, the notion that rights entail responsibilities is ascendant; this notion does not supersede the importance of rights, but it does assert that, in our society, rights and responsibilities go hand in hand. This is a message of paramount importance to the special education and disability communities. Whether these communities will hear that message—which is sure to be repeated in debates about Social Security, Medicaid, and ADA—and how they will respond to it if they hear it are the stuff of the future.

Tom E. C. Smith  **NO**

# IDEA 2004: Another Round in the Reauthorization Process

The Individuals with Disabilities Education Act (IDEA; 1997) has once again been reauthorized. Although the reauthorization was thought to be on a fast track when it was initially begun in 2001, the law was finally passed in November 2004 and signed by President Bush in December 2004. The Individuals with Disabilities Education Improvement Act (2004), still to be referred to as IDEA, contains some significant changes; however, after careful review, the changes may not be as significant as first thought.

Certainly, the lives of children with disabilities in this country have been forever altered as a result of federal legislation. Beginning with the passage of Public Law 94-142, the Education for All Handicapped Children Act, in 1975, federal policies and federal dollars have been an integral component of special education. Overall, there is no doubt that the lives of children with disabilities have improved significantly. Let us review some of the major changes that have resulted from this law; some of the changes made in previous reauthorizations; and finally, some of the major changes associated with IDEA 2004.

## Public Law 94-142

When Public Law 94-142 (the Education for All Handicapped Children Act) was passed in 1975, the state of special education was vastly different from what it is today. Prior to its passage, Congress found that up to 1 million of the estimated 8 million children with disabilities in the United States were excluded from public school services, and another 3 million were being served inappropriately. The original four purposes of P.L. 94-142 included

- to assure that all children with disabilities have available to them . . . a free appropriate public education which emphasizes special education and related services designed to meet their unique needs
- to assure that the rights of children with disabilities and their parents . . . are protected
- to assist States and localities to provide for the education of all children with disabilities
- to assess and assure the effectiveness of efforts to educate all children with disabilities

From *Remedial and Special Education,* vol. 26, no. 6, November/December 2005, pp. 314–319.

Public Law 94-142 resulted in many changes in the way children with disabilities were identified and provided with services. Prior to its passage, special education was a mere footnote in U.S. educational statistics. There were fewer than 3.5 million children with disabilities served in public schools, mostly in isolated, self-contained settings; and teacher preparation for special education was a minor activity. Some of the major requirements of P.L. 94-142 included the following:

- Child Find. Schools were required to locate children with disabilities and initiate the referral process to determine their eligibility for services under this act.
- Individualized Education Program (IEP). Every child served in special education must have an IEP. Although not intending to do so, the IEP requirement resulted in massive amounts of paperwork for special education teachers.
- Least Restrictive Environment (LRE). To the maximum extent appropriate, children with disabilities should be educated with their non-disabled peers. This resulted in "mainstreaming" and the practice of including many students with disabilities in general education settings.
- Nondiscriminatory Assessment. All children must be given a comprehensive assessment prior to determining their eligibility for special education, and this assessment must be administered in such a way as not to discriminate against individuals from different cultural/language groups.
- Related Services. Services that are necessary for a child to benefit from special education, such as physical therapy or transportation, must also be provided.
- Due Process Rights. Children with disabilities, and their parents, must be afforded certain due process rights, including the right of notice and consent prior to actions affecting their child and the right to a due process hearing to resolve complaints and disagreements between parents and the school.
- Funding. Congress said that the federal government would eventually fund up to 40% of the excess costs of educating students with disabilities. Although Congress still has not come close to the 40% level, hundreds of millions of dollars have supported programs under this legislation.
- Free, appropriate public education (FAPE). Schools were required to provide a free, appropriate public education to all students with disabilities. This includes determining the eligibility of children and developing and implementing an IEP for each child. All of the services to children under this act must be provided without cost to the parents.

Although there were many other provisions in the original P.L. 94-142, these were the ones having the greatest impact.

Since P.L. 94-142 was passed, there have been several reauthorizations that have made changes in the law. Although some of these changes have been significant, they have not altered the basic requirements of the original legislation. All children with disabilities must be referred, evaluated, and determined to be eligible or not; all eligible students must have IEPs; and all must be provided with a free, appropriate public education, meaning they must be

*Table 1*

### Key Components of Reauthorizations of P.L. 94-142/IDEA

| Reauthorization | Key components |
|---|---|
| 1983 (P.L. 98-199) | 1. Provided incentives for states to serve preschool children with disabilities. |
| | 2. Required states to collect information and address issues related to students transitioning from school to post-school. |
| (P.L. 101-457) | 1. Mandated services for children 3-5 lowering all of the requirements of P.L. 94-142 to include 3-5 year old children. |
| | 2. Provided for attorney's fees in due process or court cases where parents prevailed. |
| (P.L. 101-476) | 1. Added autism and traumatic brain injury to the list of disabilities covered under IDEA. |
| | 2. Changed the name of the act from the Education for All Handicapped Children Act to the Individuals with Disabilities Education Act. |
| | 3. Required schools to initiate transition services no later than age 16. |
| 1997 (P.L. 105-17) | 1. Required schools to initiate transition planning no later than age 14. |
| | 2. Required schools to include behavior intervention plans for students with behavior problems. |

served in the least restrictive environment. Some of the major changes associated with successive reauthorizations up to 1997 are included in Table 1.

# IDEA 2004

The reauthorization of IDEA in 2004 included a name change: The word "improvement" was inserted, making the official title of the legislation the "Individuals with Disabilities Education Improvement Act." However, the law is still referred to as IDEA. Several significant changes were included in the reauthorization. The following section will describe these changes and discuss the actual implications of the changes.

## Highly Qualified Teachers

IDEA 2004 includes a requirement that special education teachers meet the "highly qualified" mandate introduced in the No Child Left Behind Act (NCLB; 2001) legislation. This is the first reauthorization of IDEA that includes any specific requirements related to teacher qualifications. Until this act, determining the qualifications of teachers had always been left to the states. IDEA 2004 now requires teachers to be "highly qualified." Highly qualified means that

1. All special education teachers must be highly qualified under the NCLB definition; also, special education teachers must have a state special education certification; not hold an emergency, temporary, or provisional certification; and have at least a bachelor's degree.

2. Special education teachers who teach content courses and are the teachers of record for those courses must meet the NCLB *highly qualified* requirements. This means that they must be licensed in the subjects taught, similar to general classroom teachers under NCLB.

The ramifications of this addition to the legislation are just now being understood. The Council for Exceptional Children (CEC) has referred to this component of the law as "an extraordinary federal intrusion into what has been the domain of States and the profession." CEC has added that these requirements are bureaucratic, impractical, unsound, and intrusive. Many special education teachers have been involved in providing instruction and support to students in subject areas, especially in middle and high schools. Getting these teachers licensed in these content areas will undoubtedly cause many problems. Teachers are allowed to become licensed through state high objective state standard of evaluation (HOUSSE) options, which is a way states can license teachers under NCLB; however, for the immediate future, these requirements will create problems for many teachers, local districts, and states.

## Funding

Finally, more than 30 years since the passage of P.L. 94-142, Congress appears to be ready to meet its promise of full funding for IDEA. P.L. 94-142 said that Congress would fund special education programs under the law at a rate up to 40% of excess costs for educating children with disabilities. Congress has never come close to the 40% level. In fact, federal funding for IDEA has never reached the 20% level. IDEA 2004 lays out a path for full funding. The law authorizes Congress to fund IDEA for $12.36 billion for fiscal year 2005 and an additional $2.3 billion each year through 2011, when full funding will be achieved.

## Individualized Education Programs

The level of paperwork associated with special education has increased significantly since the passage of P.L. 94-142. In some cases, special education professionals seem to spend as much time on paperwork as on programs for their students. Excessive paperwork has actually been cited by some teachers as their primary reason for leaving the teaching profession. The 2004 reauthorization has made some changes directly targeting a reduction in paperwork. One of the changes incorporated in IDEA 2004 is deleting the requirement that IEPs include short-term objectives, except for students who are assessed using alternative assessment procedures that are aligned with alternate achievement standards. Eliminating short-term objectives hopefully will not have a negative impact on appropriate programming but will result in a reduction of paperwork.

Another change in IEPs relates to transition requirements. Whereas IDEA 1997 required schools to include transition planning in IEPs when the child reached 14 years of age, IDEA 2004 only requires schools to include a statement of transition goals based on age-appropriate transition assessments beginning with the first IEP that will be in effect when the child reaches 16 years of age.

IDEA 2004 also provides some flexibility in attendance at IEP meetings by permitting team members not to attend if their area of expertise is not needed, as agreed by other team members, and not to attend if they provide written information related to the IEP meeting prior to the meeting, again with team approval. IEPs can also be modified during the year without the entire team being present if the school and parents agree to a written amendment after the original IEP is developed. These provisions should help limit the number of times that complete teams have to get together to develop and modify IEPs. It also keeps some school personnel from having to attend meetings when their expertise is really not needed.

Finally, relative to the IEP, IDEA 2004 has established a 15-state pilot program for multiyear IEPs. States can apply for participation in the pilot program. Under the pilot program, states can develop IEPs for up to 3 years on a trial basis. Whereas students' progress toward achieving their 3-year goals would have to be measured annually, IEPs would not have to be rewritten on an annual basis. This pilot program, advocated by many professionals and some professional organizations, will determine if students can receive FAPE using multiyear IEPs, just as they receive FAPE using annual IEPs. If the results of the pilot program are positive, it is likely that all states will be able to move to multiyear IEPs.

## Due Process Requirements

The original P.L. 94-142 included specific due process requirements, including the right to notice and consent and the right to a due process hearing. Parents must give consent prior to the initial evaluation and placement of their child in special education, and they must be notified prior to other actions dealing with their child. IDEA 2004 continues to require that schools obtain consent prior to initial evaluation and placement. If parents refuse their consent for initial evaluation, schools may pursue this denial through due process. However, parental refusal of consent to special education placement may not be pursued by the school through due process. In this situation, the child is not considered a child with a disability under IDEA, and the school district is not responsible for ensuring FAPE for the child.

IDEA 2004 also includes some significant changes related to due process hearings. Parents have been able to recoup attorney fees in situations where they prevailed in due process hearings and court cases, but the schools have not been able to recoup attorney fees in situations where they prevailed. IDEA 2004 enables schools to recoup costs in certain situations from the parents and parents' attorneys.

Specifically, IDEA 2004 says that the court may award fees to the prevailing state education agency (SEA) or local education agency (LEA) against parents' attorneys who (a) file a complaint or other cause of action that is frivolous, unreasonable, or without foundation or (b) continue to litigate after litigation clearly has become frivolous, unreasonable, or without foundation. The prevailing SEA or LEA may also be awarded fees by the courts against the parents' attorney or against the parents if the complaint or subsequent cause of action was presented for any improper purpose (e.g., to harass, cause delay, or increase the cost of litigation).

It is hoped that these provisions will reduce the number of complaints, due process hearing requests, and court actions, unless the situation truly merits those actions. Schools have complained in the past that some parents are filing complaints to retaliate against a school or school personnel and that often parents or their attorneys continue the litigation process to enhance the level of attorney fees. The fact that parents and their attorneys can be held accountable for these fees in situations where the courts think their actions are unwarranted may reduce the level of complaints.

## Expulsion and Suspension

Disciplinary procedures for students with disabilities have been a highly debated topic for many years. In fact, disagreements on disciplining students with disabilities have been a major stumbling block in successfully reauthorizing IDEA on several previous occasions. Advocates for children with disabilities have resolutely supported students and opposed disciplinary procedures for this group of children that did not take the effect of the child's disability into consideration. This has resulted, correctly, in schools having to consider the impact of the disability on the behavior. If a suspension was for fewer than 10 days, and the student did not already have a series of suspensions that might add up to 10 days, then the school could suspend the student, similar to suspending any other student. However, if the suspension or expulsion added up to more than 10 days, the schools had to conduct a manifestation determination to determine the relationship, if any, between the disability and the inappropriate behavior. If a relationship was found to exist, then the school could not remove the student. If no relationship was found, the child could be removed from the school but the school had to continue to provide FAPE.

IDEA 2004 makes some changes to the disciplinary procedures for children with disabilities. Similar to IDEA 1997, prior to any suspension or expulsion for more than 10 days, a manifestation determination must be made. If no relationship is found, then the school may suspend or expel the student, similar to a student without disabilities. In this case, however, the school must continue to provide FAPE to the student. If there is a relationship between the disability and the behavior, then the school may not expel or suspend the student. A relationship is found if the behavior was caused by or had a *direct and substantial* relationship to the child's disability, or if the school had failed to implement the child's IEP. IDEA 2004 adds the *direct and substantial* language, possibly making it more difficult to determine that the behavior is related to the disability. If the manifestation determination concludes that there is a relationship between the disability and the behavior, then a functional behavior assessment is conducted and a behavior intervention plan is developed. The child is returned to the original placement unless both parties agree to a change of placement. The parents or the school may appeal a decision. In this case, the student will remain in the alternative placement until appeals are exhausted. An expedited hearing process is held.

In certain instances (e.g., the child has a weapon, is using or in possession of drugs, or inflicts serious bodily injury on someone), the child may be removed for up to 45 school days without regard to whether the behavior is a manifestation of the disability. This action can be taken without a hearing officer's involvement. IDEA 1997 said that a child could be removed for 45 days; by changing this to 45 *school* days, IDEA 2004 in effect allows a substantial increase in the period of time the child can be removed. Again, parents may appeal this decision and have an expedited hearing. While under appeal, the student remains in the placement that resulted from the inappropriate behavior, not the student's placement before the behavior occurred.

## Eligibility for Students Classified as Having LD

Overidentification of students as having learning disabilities (LD) has been a concern for many years. Indeed, with more than 50% of all students with disabilities in this classification, many professionals have long been concerned about the use of a discrepancy formula to determine eligibility. Some have agreed that the use of this formula, which requires a severe discrepancy between IQ and achievement scores, has led to overidentification. Although IDEA has never required a discrepancy formula, many states and local education agencies have adopted this model of LD.

IDEA 2004 makes a point that a discrepancy between achievement and aptitude is not required to classify a student as having LD. It further states that schools may use a child's response to intervention as part of their eligibility process. Therefore, a school may choose to implement intervention programs, such as reading programs, and, if a child responds positively to the program, determine that a child is not eligible under IDEA. IDEA 2004 gives schools this flexibility. This language was added to IDEA 2004 in an attempt to limit the number of students identified as eligible for special education services who may simply be experiencing difficulties resulting from inappropriate instruction. If interventions are successful, there is no reason to identify the child as having LD and being eligible for special education.

## Other Changes

In addition to the aforementioned changes in IDEA 2004, there are many other changes that schools will be implementing. These include

- changing definitions of *assistive technology device*
- optional establishment of a risk pool with up to 10% of IDEA funds reserved for state-level activities for high-cost activities and supports
- allowing up to 15% of a school's IDEA funds for prereferral interventions
- flexibility in using Part C funds
- including homeless children in child-find activities
- allowing reevaluations of students not more than once each year and not more than every 3 years, unless school and parents agree it is not necessary
- conducting evaluations in the language or form most likely to yield accurate results, not necessarily in the child's native language

# Conclusions

IDEA 2004 includes some significant changes to IDEA 1997; however, in many instances, practices will remain relatively similar. The basic requirement of IDEA—to provide a free, appropriate public education to children with disabilities—has not changed. There are numerous changes, but some of the notable ones include (a) adding NCLB language related to highly qualified special education teachers; (b) increasing funding to the authorized 40% level over a period of years through 2011; (c) changing eligibility for classification as having LD; (d) adding flexibility to attendance at IEP meetings; (e) creating a pilot demonstration for multiyear IEPs; (f) deleting the requirement for short-term objectives on the IEP; and (g) modifying suspension and expulsion requirements.

These notable changes may or may not have a significant impact on schools. Obviously, one change that could negatively affect schools is the requirement that special education teachers meet the NCLB *highly qualified* standard. With special education teachers already in short supply, adding this bureaucratic requirement could only exacerbate the situation, without improving educational opportunities for children with disabilities. Only time will determine the impact of this requirement, as school personnel and professional organizations lobby for a change. Increasing funding for special education could have a dramatic impact on services. However, the first budget proposal from the White House after the passage of IDEA 2004 added only $500 million to the IDEA budget, as opposed to the more than $2 billion called for in the legislation. Therefore, although it initially looked like a movement toward full funding would be made, reality has already set in that the likelihood of such an increase is low.

Changes made in the IEP requirements appear to be major. However, it is unlikely that, previously, all individuals participated in IEP development and changes at every meeting. In practice, IEPs were often developed by one individual or a small number of individuals and were likely changed without a formal IEP meeting. The changes in IDEA 2004 only legitimize those actions. Not having to include objectives might reduce some of the paperwork associated with IEPs; however, there still must be ongoing efforts to ensure that adequate progress is being made toward the student's annual goals. Finally, the multiyear IEP seems to be an idea that could significantly reduce paperwork. However, this is only a pilot program for up to 15 states, and even in schools that participate in the program, school personnel must determine if progress is being made toward the multiyear goals on at least an annual basis.

So, finally, IDEA has been reauthorized once again. Although the 3 years of debate focused on many of the same issues that have been dealt with in each reauthorization—discipline, due process rights, attorney fees, overidentification—the result is similar in many ways to the "old" law. As always, the changes do not satisfy everyone and, in fact, may not satisfy anyone. Hopefully, however, with each reauthorization of IDEA, realizing the original intent of P.L. 94-142 becomes more likely: meeting the needs of each child with a disability in the most appropriate way.

# EXPLORING THE ISSUE

## Did IDEA 2004 Contain Substantial Changes?

## Challenge Questions

- Compare and contrast the positions of the YES and NO selections and references regarding whether IDEA 2004 contributed to substantial changes in special education practice.
- Which selection makes the best case for its argument? Why?
- Which author made the most accurate prediction about the impact IDEA 2004 would make?
- Which of the IDEA 2004 changes did your state implement? How were these decisions made? What has been the impact of the changes on teachers?

## Is There Common Ground?

Turnbull and Smith agree on the fundamental principles and elements of IDEA. They agree that the driving force behind IDEA is ensuring that students with disabilities have a FAPE. They also agree that some of the changes to IEP practices could make a significant difference for students, educators, and parents.

## Additional Resources

Crabtree, R.K. (2011) Should You Ever Waive Rights? Newsline, *32*(2) http://fcsn.org/newsline/v32n2/waive_rights.php

Crabtree, R. K. (2011). Should you ever waive rights? *Federation for Children with Special Needs Newline, 32*(4).

Dale, R. E. (2011). How to influence the IDEA regulations. *TEACHING Exceptional Children, 43*(5), 62–68.

Etscheidt, S. & Curran, C. M. (2010). Peer-reviewed research and Individualized Education Programs (IEPs): An examination of intent and impact. *Exceptionality, 18,* 138–150.

Etscheidt, S. (2007). The excusal provision of the IDEA 2004: Streamlining procedural compliance or prejudicing rights of students with disabilities? *Preventing School Failure, 51*(4), 13–18.

National School Boards Association. (2010). *Issue brief: Individuals with Disabilities Education Act (IDEA): Early preparation for reauthorization.* Retrieved on July 1, 2010 from www.nsba.org

Samuels, C. A. (2011, March). RTI: An approach on the march. Special Report: *Monitoring progress: Response to Intervention's Promise and Pitfalls, Education Week,* S2–S5.

Samuels, C. A. (May 2, 2006). Paperwork-Reduction Pilots Off to Slow Start. Education Week. *25*(34).

Samuels, C. A. (November 8, 2005). States Face a December Deadline to Submit Special Education Data. Education Week. *25*(11).

Scull, J. & Winkler, A. M. (2011, May). *Shifting trends in special education.* Retrieved on June 24, 2012 from www.edexcellence.net

Smith, T. E. C. (2005). IDEA 2004: Another round in the reauthorization process. *Remedial and Special Education, 26*(6), 314–319.

Samuels, C. A. (2006). *Advocacy for parents key to IDEA case. Education Week,* April 11.

Samuels, C. A. (2005). *Revised IDEA shifts control of special education research. Education Week,* January, 25.

Turnbull, H. R., III. (2005). Individuals with Disabilities Education Act reauthorization: Accountability and personal responsibility. *Remedial and Special Education, 26*(6), 320–326.

# ISSUE 3

## Is Disproportionally High Minority Representation in Special Education a School Problem?

YES: **Edward Fergus**, from "Distinguishing Difference from Disability: The Common Causes of Racial/Ethnic Disproportionality in Special Education," www.niusi/leadscape.org, March 23, 2012

NO: **Richard Rothstein**, from "Whose Problem Is Poverty?" *Educational Leadership* (vol. 65, no. 7, pp. 8–13, 2008)

---

### Learning Outcomes

**At the conclusion of this issue, readers will be able to:**

- Compare and contrast the positions of the YES and NO selections addressing the impact schools can make on reducing disproportional representation of minorities in special education.
- Describe the strengths and the weaknesses of each side's arguments.
- Identify steps to take in determining the degree of disproportionality that exists in their own community.
- Compare the selections' recommendations with practices in his/her school.

---

### ISSUE SUMMARY

**YES:** Edward Fergus is deputy director of the Metropolitan Center for Urban Education at New York University. Previously a high school teacher, Dr. Fergus consults on issues of disproportionality. His study of over 30 districts identified common root causes of disproportionality and remedies for each one.

**NO:** Richard Rothstein, a research associate of the Economic Policy Institute, writes and speaks on issues of education, economics, and policy, with a focus on the achievement gap. Mr. Rothstein posits that schools alone cannot overcome the effects of poverty on a child's life and education.

**D**isproportionality occurs whenever a group's representation in a category differs significantly from its proportion of the total population. In underrepresentation, the target group appears in lower proportions than it exists in the population. In overrepresentation, the target group is present in larger proportions.

Laws and programs for students with disabilities were built on the accomplishments of the civil rights movement. However, since 1968 (Dunn, *Exceptional Children*), there has been concern that African American children are disproportionately represented in special education, and resegregated into substantially separate classes.

U.S. federal regulations address disproportionality in special education, considering both overrepresentation and underrepresentation. IDEA97 mandated that states collect and report special education enrollment information by race and ethnicity. IDEA 2004 requires that states and districts establish policies and procedures to "prevent the inappropriate overidentification or disproportionate representation by race and ethnicity of children as children with disabilities"; examine data to determine if significant disproportionality exists; use federal funds to provide "early intervening services" to reduce significant overrepresentation; and document their efforts (and results) at reducing disproportionality (*Dialog guides for IDEA 2004 regulations*, www.ideapartnership.org) States reported confusion when formulating their own definitions of "significant disproportionality" and "inappropriate identification" (Burdette, 2007, www.nasdse.org).

Several methods are used to calculate special education enrollment statistics; each reveals a different perspective (Skiba, Simmons, Ritter, Gibb, Rausch, Cuadrado, & Chung, *Exceptional Children*, 2008). The Composition Index compares a target group's representation in the entire population with its percentage in an area of special education (e.g., African American students are 17 percent of the total school population, but 33 percent of students are identified as "mentally retarded"). The Risk Index and Relative Risk Ratio compare a group's representation in special education to that of other groups (2.64 percent of African American students identified as "mentally retarded" compared with 1.18 percent of White students).

Index results are far from consistent. Ratios vary widely across districts and states (Guiberson, *Preventing School Failure*, 2009). Representation varies by race and by disability category. Despite a multitude of statistics, the causes of disproportionality, and effective remedies, are elusive.

Accurate study of disproportionality is affected by the complexity of both racial designation and language status. The 2010 Census contained 15 racial categories as well as the opportunity to select more than one. As more people have a multiracial heritage (think of Tiger Woods), analyzing by racial category will be increasingly challenging. People selecting the same race may have linguistic/cultural differences that impact their school experiences differentially. Ford, Moore, Whiting, and Grantham (*Roeper Review*, 2008) observe that much research is "colorblind," providing little information on the participants, and obscuring information about specific racial/linguistic groups. They recommend researchers specify the racial identity of participants and broaden inquiry to embrace successful individuals of all races.

Eligibility qualifications for special education differ across states. Some states use no discrete disability categories; others use unique terms for particular disabilities. Some states have strict criteria for classification into a disability; others are vague.

Despite disparate reporting options and definitional complications, there is widespread agreement that children of color, especially African American boys, are disproportionately overrepresented in special education. This seems especially so in the socially defined disabilities of intellectual disabilities (formerly referred to as mental retardation), emotional disturbance, and specific learning disabilities.

This issue explores the complex subject of disproportional minority representation in special education. Two contrasting remedies are presented; many others exist. The references in this section are recommended to obtain a more textured understanding of disproportionality.

Two influential reports were issued in 2002: *Minority Students in Special and Gifted Education* (Donovan and Cross) from the National Research Council (NRC) and *Racial Inequality in Special Education* (Losen and Orfield) from the Civil Rights Project at Harvard (CRP). Because of their depth, continuing relevance, and contrasting recommendations, these continue to be the foundation for discussions of disproportionality.

Directed by the NRC and Congress to update a 1982 study of overrepresentation, the committee led by Donovan and Cross also considered minority underrepresentation in gifted and talented programs. After reviewing existent research, Donovan and Cross highlighted contributing environmental variables. They cited risks inherent in poverty, including environmental hazards, and concluded that children who have encountered these conditions come to school at greater risk. There are actual differences in school readiness. Through systems of tiered intervention, schools can address student performance, but environmental issues must become matters of "political priority."

Guided by compelling voices of community leaders concerned about children wrongly placed in special education, CRP commissioned leading scholars to analyze conditions and contributing factors, and to generate solutions. Losen and Orfield concluded that minority children in special education have not received a substantial benefit. The authors believed that poverty and the environment could not explain disproportionate representation of African American children. The collective findings led to recommendations that racial disproportionality should become a top school priority, facilitated (if necessary) through federal and state oversight.

Both studies addressed racial bias. The NRC study noted that the effects of prejudice are often subtle and intangible. Losen and Orfield observed that it is difficult to determine whether disproportionality results from intentional, biased behaviors, but described what happens in schools as a "subset" of the racial impacts in society.

In the YES selection, Edward Fergus, who consults widely with districts cited by the U.S. federal government for their disproportionality, discusses the results of a multiyear data-driven study of 30 school districts. Common root causes, with the most significant impact on the rate of disproportionality, were found in three specific areas: gaps in curriculum and instruction implementation; limited beliefs of student ability; and inconsistent pre-referral practices. Fergus recommends specific remedies for each of the three areas, along with strategies and resources educators can employ to address disproportionality in their own schools. These strategies are geared to helping educators avoid confusing difference with disability.

In the NO selection, Richard Rothstein, who writes extensively on issues of public policy and education reform, presents a contrasting view of the achievement gap and its solution. Rothstein asserts that it is time to acknowledge the pervasive impact poverty has on student learning. Poor children—most of whom are African American—experience fewer medical services, more residential mobility, and increased family stress related to poverty. Teachers cannot overcome these challenges alone. Civic and business leaders must act to limit socioeconomic inequities rather than blaming educators. Neither group can succeed without the other.

Barton and Coley (*Parsing the achievement gap II,* 2009) cite research support for the relationship between life experiences and school achievement; closing the persistent gap is too large a task for teachers alone. However, the authors indicate some people fear that looking at external factors will provide schools with excuses not to do their best. Conversely, blaming schools distracts attention from the responsibility to create public policies to prevent learning gaps.

Poverty's impact on learning generates energetic debate. Based on personal family experiences at a number of economic levels, Ruby Payne (*Educational Leadership,* 2008) discusses the culture of intergenerational poverty. Throughout her writings and extensive school consultation, she maintains that the impact of poverty can be somewhat alleviated by direct teaching of the differences between home and school language and expectations. Lisa Delpit, a well-known scholar on the school experiences of African American children, believes poverty is a "convenient" explanation for school performance (*Multiplication is for white people: Raising expectations for other people's children,* 2012). Delpit accepts some of Payne's recommendations, but finds Payne's analysis incomplete.

Researchers criticize deficit models that use a disability label to situate school difficulties as problems within a child. Teams exploring a child's school difficulties should consider the entire context for those struggles: student characteristics, family dynamics, life experiences, school conditions, and, not least, limits reflecting teacher tolerance (Hart, Cramer, Harry, Klingner, and Sturges, *Remedial and Special Education,* 2010). Others extend the deficit model to criticize teachers. Hoover (*TEACHING Exceptional Children,* 2012) encourages teachers to consider the cultural and linguistic diversity of their students, and reducing referrals to special education by recognizing that differences are not the same as disabilities.

Cultural differences are the focus of another line of reasoning. Gorski (*Educational Leadership,* 2008) urges educators to stop trying to "fix" children and turn their efforts to increasing the responsiveness of schools. Other researchers emphasize the need for teachers to consider how cultural norms might differ between themselves and their students (Cartledge, Singh, and Gibson, *Preventing School Failure,* 2008).

Reflecting the belief that a responsive school environment is essential, Reschly (National Comprehensive Center for Teacher Quality, 2009) counters myths about disproportionality and offers a solution. First myth: people differ; there will always be differential representation across disability categories; precisely even proportions will never occur. Additionally, students referred for special education are truly struggling with learning. IDEA asks for remediation of *significant* disproportionality. Reschly asserts that the remedy for disproportionality lies in the use of solid instructional practices and regular progress assessments in general education classrooms.

Although doctors identify the most visible disabilities, approximately 90 percent of referrals to special education are made by general education teachers: 73 percent to 90 percent of those referred are found eligible (Harry and Klingner, *Why are so many minority students in special education?* 2006). Examining research published between 1968 and 2006, Waitoller, Artiles, and Cheney (*The Journal of Special Education,* 2010) were surprised at how seldom the topic of disproportionality occurred in journals focused on general education.

Experts at the National Center for Culturally Responsive Educational Systems (NCCRESt), now located at The Equity Alliance at ASU (www .equityallianceatasu.org), rejected the binary notion that learning problems resided either in the child or in the special education system. Their endeavors affected a historic conceptual shift by advancing the premise that disproportionality needs to be addressed by both general education and special education professionals (Artiles, Kozleski, and Gonzalez, 2010, Final report, www .nccrest.org). Only a systems approach, including all educators, will resolve a situation as complex as disproportionality.

Adelman and Taylor (*Schools and the challenge of LD and ADHD misdiagnoses,* 2011, www.smhp.psych.ucla.edu) advocate a transactional perspective that considers the interaction of child and environment. Type I problems are caused by difficulties in the environment. Type II problems are caused equally by factors in the environment and in the person. Type III problems are due to factors in the individual. Careful evaluation of all components ensures that intervention (if any is required) focuses on the elements most likely to improve the situation.

# YES

Edward Fergus

# Distinguishing Difference from Disability: The Common Causes of Racial/Ethnic Disproportionality in Special Education

## Distinguishing Difference from Disability

Since Lloyd Dunn's report on the overrepresentation of Black and Latino students in special education countless federal, state and district reports, as well as research studies exist that document the various facets of educational practice impacting these rates. Most recently the over-representation picture is troubling: in 2008, the school enrollment of Blacks (15.5%) differed greatly from their representation in special education (20.4%) and among students with an Emotional Disturbance classification (29.1%); while enrollment of Whites (55.5%) was mirrored in special education (55.9%) and among students with an ED classification (56.3%). This disproportionate representation is at the heart of the issue. According to a report released in 2006 by the U.S. Department of Education, one important consequence of over-representation has to do with the educational access and participation that students who are placed in special education experience once they become part of the special education population. Fortunately, we know a great deal regarding the effect of disproportionality on the educational and social mobility of racial/ethnic minority groups. For example, students are less likely to receive access to rigorous and full curriculum; limited academic and post-secondary opportunities; limited interaction with "abled" or academically mainstreamed peers and increased sense of social stigmatization; and a permanence in their placement.

Given some of the negative consequences of special education placement, there is urgency in understanding the practices that lead to identification and placement and why it happens disproportionately to Black, Latino and Native American student populations. In the absence of a research base for why Black, Latino and Native American representation in special education is not proportionate to their representation in general education, then educators must consider whether our local, state, and national educational policies and practices place racial/ ethnic minority and low-income student groups at risk. In this article, I highlight some of the common policies, practices and beliefs that place racial/ethnic minorities and low-income students at risk.

# Addressing Disproportionality: State Performance Plan Indicators 9 and 10

Each year state education departments inform school districts whether they have met the measure of racial/ethnic disproportionality in special education. The formula and the threshold of what is disproportionate vary across the country. In supporting states to create equitable school systems for all students, the Equity Alliance at ASU recognizes that the disproportionate representation of culturally and linguistically diverse students in special education programs is both a result and an indicator of inequitable practices in schools. This Equity In Action is intended to provide educators and researchers with the most comprehensive, praxis-oriented information on identifying and reducing disproportionality in schools.

Since 2004, the Metropolitan Center for Urban Education has housed the New York State Center on Disproportionality (also known as the Technical Assistance Center on Disproportionality [TACD]—www.steinhardt.nyu.edu/metrocenter/tacd). TACD's work has involved assisting school districts cited for disproportionality to:

1. Understand the citation
2. Identify the root causes of this outcome
3. Develop a strategic plan for addressing the root causes
4. Implement the plan and develop capacity to continuously monitor rates of disproportionality

Over the course of developing and piloting a data-driven process (2004–2010) for identifying root causes, we've gained insight into not only the root causes but also the driving forces (internal and external to district) of these root causes. Our data driven root cause process focused on examining various areas of the schooling process in order to understand the interaction of school practice (inputs) and student outcomes. This process involved examining the following three areas:

- Quality of curricular and instructional supports (e.g., type of core program, stage of core program implementation, capacity of instructional staff, and learning outcomes of students).
- Intervention services for struggling students (e.g., type of available interventions, frequency of intervention usage, stage of implementation, length of intervention implementation, and number of students participating in intervention programs by race/ ethnicity, gender and grade level).
- Predominant cultural beliefs (perceptions of race and class, perceptions of different learning styles versus a disability, perceptions of how race and class interact in school practice, and cultural responsiveness of current policies and practices).

The examination of this data for the last 6 years across 30 districts has resulted in our identification of common root causes of disproportionality. These causes are not the only ones but tend to be present in every district and maintain the most significant effect on the rate of disproportionality in school districts.

# Unpacking the Common Causes of Disproportionality

## Topic 1: Gaps in Curriculum and Instructional Implementation Disproportionately Affect Struggling Learners

Endemic in most school districts is the question of instructional wellness which includes responsiveness—does and can our instruction maximize the learning capacity of all students? In our data-driven root cause process, multiple causes emerged as contributing to disproportionality rates. The wellness of instruction and curriculum as it is represented in instructional support teams/teacher assistance teams, intervention services, assessment, and gifted and talented programs continuously emerged as maintaining gaps in practices that disproportionately affected struggling learners.

1. Minimally articulated core curriculum and consistent support of teaching ability. Due to various factors, many school districts did not have in place a current curriculum and/or agreement on instructional approaches that considered the range of learners. As a result, students who persistently could not attain proficiency on the state exam were promptly considered for special education services. Additionally, some districts were continuously changing or adding curriculum, assessment and instructional strategies from year to year. Although every school district contends with such changes, we found that in our districts such structural changes affected struggling learners the most. For example, practitioners tended to comment that they lacked the ability to adequately service students at the lowest quartile of performance. Therefore instructional staff were experiencing a steep learning curve regarding a new curriculum and/or assessment, meanwhile feeling inadequate to address skill deficiencies with students even based on the prior curriculum or assessment.

   The policy change in IDEA 2004 regarding response to intervention (RtI) has greatly pushed the conversation among practitioners to recognize the impact of an inadequate curriculum, particularly in reading, on struggling learners. Many of our school districts are acknowledging the absence of a reading series and program as preventing them from truly understanding and locating the reading capacity of students in grades K-5.

   *Remedy:* Identification and sustained implementation of appropriate reading and math core program that is sequenced K-12. Additionally, sequenced and sustained support for non-tenured and tenured teaching staff to build ability to effectively implement curriculum and/or assessment, as well as instructional capacity.

2. Too many interventions for struggling learners. In our examination of curriculum and the related interventions, we found that many school districts maintained an exhaustive list of interventions for students demonstrating academic difficulty. The overabundance of interventions for

struggling learners indicated that staff were not proficient in differentiating the core curriculum to address the needs of a range of learners. Unfortunately, without a well articulated core curriculum and instructional program that services all students, this gap disproportionately affected not only struggling learners but also new students to the districts (including newly arrived English Language Learners).

*Remedy:* Identification and implementation of targeted, evidence-based, intervention programs for students demonstrating academic difficulty while core curriculum program is re-developed.

3. Inconsistent knowledge of the purpose and implementation of assessments. Various school districts were utilizing assessment tools that were developed to screen students at risk for reading difficulty as measures of diagnosing reading skill deficiency. This appeared to be a result of inconsistent knowledge surrounding these assessments, that is, what information it captured, how to translate the assessment information into targeted interventions, etc. In another district, the Kindergarten screening being used maintained a specific threshold of which students were potentially at risk and the common practice with this assessment was to go 25% above that threshold and identify all those students as "not ready" for their school environment. This inconsistent knowledge base regarding assessments allowed for the implementation of interventions and strategies that were not tailored to meet the specific needs of struggling learners. Therefore, instructional support teams and/or child study teams would receive information about a child's reading difficulty sometimes after months or a year of inadequate interventions.

   *Remedy:* Continuous professional development on purpose, application and interpretation of curriculum, assessment and instructional strategies.

4. Poorly structured intervention services for struggling learners. In New York State and New Jersey, academic intervention services are legislated to exist for struggling learners, particularly in Title 1 school districts. However, our root cause process revealed the implementation of these programs was inconsistent and as a result, the intervention process became the gateway for special education referrals. For example, students referred and classified tended to reach below basic proficiency over multiple school years. Meanwhile the academic intervention staff did not receive training on how to move students from far below basic proficiency up toward proficiency; staff tended to receive training focused on moving students that would assist a school in reaching Adequate Yearly Progress (AYP), which are generally those students *just below proficiency*. The long-term effect is twofold:

   1. Students who are far below proficiency are not given the adequate and sustained opportunity to accelerate their learning.
   2. Students who are barely into proficiency tend to "slide" in and out of proficiency thus, they are constantly receiving instruction and

interventions that is only enough to get them to proficiency but not enough to master academic skills.

*Remedy:* Re-development of a tiered system of academic supports for struggling learners, identification of research-based interventions for targeted groups of students, and targeted professional development for academic intervention staff (i.e., non-tenured and tenured, including content specialists).

## Topic 2: Inconsistent Pre-Referral Process

1. Inconsistency in referral process, including referral forms. School districts are generally good at ensuring they abide by special education regulations, including referral timeframes, involvement of practitioners, etc. However we found that school districts maintained inconsistent pre-referral information, as well as different forms for each school building in a district. Again, much of these system inconsistencies were not intentional but rather reflective of the bifurcation existing in the district between special education and general education. In many instances special education directors would describe how they could only suggest to building administrators about adopting one common referral form or insisting on general education teachers to complete the specifics of the pre-referral strategies.

   *Remedy:* Development of a common process and form for pre-referral; outline an annual evaluation process for examining the efficiency and effectiveness of this process. Provide training on appropriate interventions and fidelity of implementation for general education teachers.

2. Limited information regarding intervention strategies. One of our steps in the root cause process is to conduct a records review of a representative sample of files; this ranged from 40 to 100 files, depending on the number of students receiving special education services. On most forms we found a text box in which general education teachers would describe the strategies they'd already tried. In most instances general education teachers annotated how moving a student's seat, matching them with a buddy, or providing the content or skill again but at a slower pace did not work, even though they considered it a practical strategy. The plethora of strategies lacked any sense of feasibility as competent strategies and also lacked any sense of summative evaluation as to their impact. Teachers tended not to note any type of pre/post evaluative summary—instead the standard answer was "I tried and it didn't work." Even with the addition of response to intervention (RtI) in IDEA 2004, which forced school districts to revamp their pre-referral/problem-solving team forms so that they request information about interventions provided by general education teachers, there still existed a gap in knowledge among practitioners regarding what is and is not an intervention in Tier 1.

   *Remedy:* Provide training on evidence-based interventions and fidelity of implementation for general education teachers and instructional support teams/teacher assistance teams.

## Topic 3: Limited Beliefs About Ability

1. Special education is viewed as fixing struggling students. In most school districts, the general and special education staff rarely interact with each other. Through our root cause process, we worked with a cross district team that included general and special education teachers, administrators, content specialists, etc., and more often than not there were disconnects in the conversation due to a limited understanding among practitioners regarding what constitutes a disability. General education teachers tended to express the belief that special education maintains the "magic fairy dust" that will "fix" the learning capacity and outcomes of students. Some of this belief may be due to the reality that prior to the addition of response to intervention in IDEA 2004, special education processes were perceived as organized to provide services to students who fell outside of the normal curve of academic performance. Though RtI is part of the water stream of conversation in most school districts, for some practitioners in our districts RtI is viewed as the new process for "getting a student classified" versus a process for ensuring quality instruction and interventions.

   ***Remedy:*** General and special education participate in professional development regarding curriculum, assessment and instructional strategies together, including special education regulations; analysis of data regarding interventions for struggling students must involve general and special education teachers.

2. Poor and racial/ethnic minority students are viewed as not "ready" for school. We commonly heard school district staff struggling with the idea that somehow being poor/low-income and being from a racial/ethnic minority group compromises how "ready" these students are for their school environment. More specifically, school and district staff at times perceived the cultural practices of the home environment as making low-income and racial/ethnic minority children unable to learn or contradicting school practices. In one district, many of the participants rallied around the concept of "urban behavior" as a driving force of why the Black students were in special education. In another district, an ESL teacher hypothesized that English Language Learners were over-represented in special education with speech/language impairment because in "Latin culture they listen to music loud." Yet another district hypothesized the Latino and ELL students were such a distraction in the classroom that they could be better served with "other disability groups." Such perspectives are not solely found in school districts cited for racial/ethnic disproportionality; in fact, such perspectives can be found in many urban, suburban and rural districts as well. Part of the difficulty with such a belief is that it is a distraction from engaging how teaching matters in learning outcomes. That is, we found practitioners were willing to cite the family and community (e.g., poverty, limited reading materials at home) as the reason why poor/low-income and racial/ethnic minority students were struggling academically, meanwhile attributing the academic performance of proficient students to their teaching practice. So there needs to be a paradigm alignment regarding the connection between

teaching and learning, as well as an understanding of how to harness the types of knowledge students demonstrate.

Additionally, these predominant beliefs regarding poor/low-income and racial/ethnic minority students as "different" also resulted in students feeling a sense of stereotype threat and vulnerability because [of] their low-income or racial/ethnic minority status as a "risk" factor. In several districts, for example, we conducted focus groups with students to ascertain what it took to get good grades; low-income and racial/ethnic minority students often reported feeling that they were seen and treated as "different." In one particular district, the boys in two of the elementary schools talked about "only girls" as getting good grades.

*Remedy:* Continuous professional development around creating culturally responsive school environments with particular sessions on stereotype threat, vulnerability, racial/ethnic identity development within the five developmental domains, examination of whiteness, and cultural developmental expressions as additive not subtractive.

# Conclusion

In order to embark on a process of remedying a district or school of disproportionate representation, one must begin with a substantive inquiry into why and how these patterns exist. The following are suggested steps:

1. **Develop a district/school-wide team:** This team must be comprised of administrators, general and special teachers, intervention and reading specialists, parents, curriculum and assessment coordinators, etc. The purpose of the team will be to jointly collect, examine, interpret, and outline the core root causes.
2. **Conduct an analysis of disproportionality rates:** At the onset a thorough analysis of disproportionality rates must be conducted. We suggest utilizing TACD's Disproportionality Data Analysis Workbook, which contains the necessary calculations.
3. **Conduct a survey of culturally responsive practices:** At the heart of disproportionality is the recognition that racial/ethnic minority groups are over represented in special education, and as such there needs to be a consideration as to whether school practices are responsive to culturally and linguistically diverse populations. We suggest utilizing a tool such as the School Self-Assessment Guide for Culturally Responsive Practice.

In summary, the disproportionate representation of racial/ethnic minority and low-income students in special education occurs because of complex intersections. Therefore, educators, schools, and school systems have a responsibility to engage a deliberate inquiry process that critiques existing practices and policies against a [criterion] of responsiveness to the populations of students served.

**Richard Rothstein**

**NO**

# Whose Problem Is Poverty?

**I**n my work, I've repeatedly stressed this logical claim: If you send two groups of students to equally high-quality schools, the group with greater socioeconomic disadvantage will necessarily have lower *average* achievement than the more fortunate group.

Why is this so? Because low-income children often have no health insurance and therefore no routine preventive medical and dental care, leading to more school absences as a result of illness. Children in low-income families are more prone to asthma, resulting in more sleeplessness, irritability, and lack of exercise. They experience lower birth weight as well as more lead poisoning and iron-deficiency anemia, each of which leads to diminished cognitive ability and more behavior problems. Their families frequently fall behind in rent and move, so children switch schools more often, losing continuity of instruction.

Poor children are, in general, not read to aloud as often or exposed to complex language and large vocabularies. Their parents have low-wage jobs and are more frequently laid off, causing family stress and more arbitrary discipline. The neighborhoods through which these children walk to school and in which they play have more crime and drugs and fewer adult role models with professional careers. Such children are more often in single-parent families and so get less adult attention. They have fewer cross-country trips, visits to museums and zoos, music or dance lessons, and organized sports leagues to develop their ambition, cultural awareness, and self-confidence.

Each of these disadvantages makes only a small contribution to the achievement gap, but cumulatively, they explain a lot.

I've also noted that no matter how serious their problems, all disadvantaged students can expect to have higher achievement in better schools than in worse ones. And even in the same schools, natural human variability ensures a distribution of achievement in every group. Some high-achieving disadvantaged students always outperform typical middle class students, and some low-achieving middle class students fall behind typical disadvantaged students. The achievement gap is a difference in the *average* achievement of students from disadvantaged and middle class families.

I've drawn a policy conclusion from these observations: Closing or substantially narrowing achievement gaps requires combining school improvement with reforms that narrow the vast socioeconomic inequalities in the United States.

Rothstein, Richard. From *Educational Leadership*, April 8, 2008, pp. 8–13. Copyright © 2008 by Richard Rothstein. Reprinted by permission of the author. Richard Rothstein (riroth@epi.org) is a Research Associate at the Economic Policy Institute. He is the author of *Class and Schools* (Teachers College Press 2004) and *Grading Education. Getting Accountability Right* (Teachers College Press 2008).

Without such a combination, demands (like those of No Child Left Behind) that schools fully close achievement gaps not only will remain unfulfilled, but also will cause us to foolishly and unfairly condemn our schools and teachers.

## Distorting Disadvantage

Most educators understand how socioeconomic disadvantage lowers average achievement. However, some have resisted this logic, throwing up a variety of defenses. Some find in my explanations the implication that disadvantaged children have a genetic disability, that poor and minority children can't learn. They say that a perspective that highlights the socioeconomic causes of low achievement "blames the victim" and legitimizes racism. Some find my analysis dangerous because it "makes excuses" for poor instruction or because demands for social and economic reform "let schools off the hook" for raising student achievement. And others say it's too difficult to address nonschool problems like inadequate incomes, health, or housing, so we should only work on school reform. The way some of these critics see it, those of us who call attention to such nonschool issues must want to wait until utopian economic change (or "socialism") becomes a reality before we begin to improve schools.

Some critics cite schools that enroll disadvantaged students but still get high standardized test scores as proof that greater socioeconomic equality is not essential for closing achievement gaps—because good schools have shown they can do it on their own. And some critics are so single-mindedly committed to a schools-only approach that they can't believe anyone could seriously advocate pursuing *both* school and socioeconomic improvement simultaneously.

## Seeing Through "No Excuses"

The commonplace "no excuses" ideology implies that educators—were they to realize that their efforts alone were insufficient to raise student achievement—would be too simple-minded then to bring themselves to exert their full effort. The ideology presumes that policymakers with an Olympian perspective can trick teachers into performing at a higher level by making them believe that unrealistically high degrees of success are within reach.

There's a lack of moral, political, and intellectual integrity in this suppression of awareness of how social and economic disadvantage lowers achievement. Our first obligation should be to analyze social problems accurately; only then can we design effective solutions. Presenting a deliberately flawed version of reality, fearing that the truth will lead to excuses, is not only corrupt but also self-defeating.

Mythology cannot, in the long run, inspire better instruction. Teachers see for themselves how poor health or family economic stress impedes students' learning. Teachers may nowadays be intimidated from acknowledging these realities aloud and may, in groupthink obedience, repeat the mantra that "all children can learn." But nobody is fooled. Teachers still know that although all children can learn, some learn less well because of poorer health or less-secure homes. Suppressing such truths leads only to teacher cynicism and disillusion. Talented teachers abandon the profession, willing to shoulder responsibility for their own instructional competence but not for failures beyond their control.

Mythology also prevents educators from properly diagnosing educational failure where it exists. If we expect all disadvantaged students to succeed at levels typical of affluent students, then even the best inner-city teachers seem like failures. If we pretend that achievement gaps are entirely within teachers' control, with claims to the contrary only "excuses," how can we distinguish better from worse classroom practice?

## Who's Getting Off the Hook?

Promoters of the myth that schools alone can overcome social and economic causes of low achievement assert that claims to the contrary let schools "off the hook." But their myth itself lets political and corporate officials off a hook. We absolve these leaders from responsibility for narrowing the pervasive inequalities of American society by asserting that good schools alone can overcome these inequalities. Forget about health care gaps, racial segregation, inadequate housing, or income insecurity. If, after successful school reform, all adolescents regardless of background could leave high school fully prepared to earn middle class incomes, there would, indeed, be little reason for concern about contemporary inequality. Opportunities of children from all races and ethnic groups, and of rich and poor, would equalize in the next generation solely as a result of improved schooling. This absurd conclusion follows from the "no excuses" approach.

Some critics urge that educators should not acknowledge socioeconomic disadvantage because their unique responsibility is to improve classroom practices, which they *can* control. According to such reasoning, we should leave to health, housing, and labor experts the challenge of worrying about inequalities in their respective fields. Yet we are all citizens in this democracy, and educators have a special and unique insight into the damage that deprivation does to children's learning potential.

If educators who face this unfortunate state of affairs daily don't speak up about it, who will? Educators and their professional organizations should insist to every politician who will listen (and to those who will not) that social and economic reforms are needed to create an environment in which the most effective teaching can take place.

And yes, we should also call on housing, health, and antipoverty advocates to take a broader view that integrates school improvement into their advocacy of greater economic and social equality. Instead, however, critical voices for reform have been silenced, told they should stick to their knitting, fearing an accusation that denouncing inequality is tantamount to "making excuses."

## What We Can Do

It's a canard that educators advocating socioeconomic reforms wish to postpone school improvement until we have created an impractical economic utopia. Another canard is the idea that it's impractical to narrow socioeconomic inequalities, so school reform is the only reasonable lever. Modest social and economic reforms, well within our political reach, could have a palpable effect on student achievement. For example, we could

- Ensure good pediatric and dental care for all students, in school-based clinics.
- Expand existing low-income housing subsidy programs to reduce families' involuntary mobility.
- Provide higher-quality early childhood care so that low-income children are not parked before televisions while their parents are working.
- Increase the earned income tax credit, the minimum wage, and collective bargaining rights so that families of low-wage workers are less stressed.
- Promote mixed-income housing development in suburbs and in gentrifying cities to give more low-income students the benefits of integrated educations in neighborhood schools.
- Fund after-school programs so that inner-city children spend fewer non-school hours in dangerous environments and, instead, develop their cultural, artistic, organizational, and athletic potential.

None of this is utopian. All is worth doing in itself, with the added benefit of sending children to school more ready to learn. Educators who are unafraid to advocate such policies will finally call the hand of those politicians and business leaders who claim that universal health care is too expensive but simultaneously demand school reform so they can posture as defenders of minority children.

In some schools, disadvantaged students are effectively tracked by race, denied the most qualified teachers and the best curriculum. Failure is both expected and accepted. Unfortunately, some educators do use socioeconomic disadvantage as an excuse for failing to teach well under adverse conditions. But we exaggerate the frequency of this excuse. Some teachers excuse poor practice, but others work terribly hard to develop disadvantaged students' talents. Where incompetence does exist, we should insist that school administrators root it out.

But consider this: The National Assessment of Educational Progress (NAEP), administered to a national student sample by the federal government, is generally considered the most reliable measure of U.S. students' achievement. Since 1990, the achievement gap between minority and white students has barely changed, feeding accusations that educators simply ignore the needs of minority youth. Yet average math scores of black 4th graders in 2007 were higher than those of white 4th graders in 1990. If white achievement had been stagnant, the gap would have fully closed. There were also big math gains for black 8th graders. The gap stagnated only because white students also gained.

In reading, scores have remained flat. Perhaps this is because math achievement is a more direct result of school instruction, whereas reading ability also reflects students' home literacy environment. Nonetheless, the dramatic gains in math do not suggest that most teachers of disadvantaged students are sitting around making excuses for failing to teach. Quite the contrary.

# Reticent About Race

It is puzzling that some find racism implied in explanations of why disadvantaged students typically achieve at lower levels. But to understand that children who've been up at night, wheezing from untreated asthma, will be less attentive in school is not to blame those children for their lower scores. It is to explain that we can enhance those students' capacity to learn with policies that reduce the epidemic incidence of asthma in low-income communities—by enforcing prohibitions on the use of high-sulfur heating oil, for example, or requiring urban buses to substitute natural gas for diesel fuel—or provide pediatric care, including treatment for asthma symptoms. Denying the impact of poor health on learning leads to blaming teachers for circumstances completely beyond their control.

The fact that such conditions affect blacks more than whites reflects racism in the United States. Calling attention to such conditions is not racist. But ignoring them, insisting that they have no effect if teaching is competent, may be.

Some critics lump my analyses of social and economic obstacles with others' claims that "black culture" explains low achievement. Like other overly simplistic explanations of academic failure, cultural explanations can easily be exaggerated. There is, indeed, an apparent black–white test-score gap, even when allegedly poor black and white students are compared with one another or even when middle class black and white students are compared with one another. But these deceptively large gaps mostly stem from too-broad definitions of "poor" and "middle class." Typically, low-income white students are compared with blacks who are much poorer, and middle class black students are compared with whites who are much more affluent. If we restricted comparisons to socioeconomically similar students, the residual test-score gap would mostly disappear.

But probably not all of it. Responsible reformers are seeking to help low-income black parents improve child-rearing practices. Others attempt to reduce the influence of gang role models on black adolescents or to raise the status of academic success in black communities. Generally, these reformers are black; white experts avoid such discussions, fearing accusations of racism.

This is too bad. If we're afraid to discuss openly the small contribution that cultural factors make to achievement gaps, we suggest, falsely, that we're hiding something much bigger.

# Dancing Around the Issue

I am often asked to respond to claims that some schools with disadvantaged students have higher achievement, allegedly proving that schools alone *can* close achievement gaps. Certainly, some schools are superior and should be imitated. But no schools serving disadvantaged students have demonstrated consistent and sustained improvement that closes—not just narrows—achievement gaps. Claims to the contrary are often fraudulent, sometimes based on low-income schools whose parents are unusually well educated; whose admissions policies accept only the most talented disadvantaged students; or whose students, although eligible for subsidized lunches, come from stable working-class and not poor communities.

Some claims are based on schools that concentrate on passing standardized basic skills tests to the exclusion of teaching critical thinking, reasoning, the arts, social studies, or science, or of teaching the "whole child," as middle class schools are more wont to do. Increasingly, such claims are based on high proportions of students scoring above state proficiency standards, defined at a low level. Certainly, if we define proficiency down, we can more easily reduce achievement gaps without addressing social or economic inequality, But responsible analysts have always defined closing the achievement gap as achieving similar score distributions and average scale scores among subgroups. Even No Child Left Behind proclaims a goal of proficiency at "challenging" levels for each subgroup. Only achieving such goals will lead to more equal opportunity for all students in the United States.

## Beyond Either/Or

Nobody should be forced to choose between advocating for better schools or speaking out for greater social and economic equality. Both are essential. Each depends on the other. Educators cannot be effective if they make excuses for poor student performance. But they will have little chance for success unless they also join with advocates of social and economic reform to improve the conditions from which children come to school.

# EXPLORING THE ISSUE

## Is Disproportionally High Minority Representation in Special Education a School Problem?

## Challenge Questions

- Compare and contrast the positions of the YES and NO selections regarding whether restraint and seclusion should be available tools to educators.
- Which selection makes the best case for its argument? Why?
- If poverty and environmental problems were alleviated, what differences would we see?
- Will the uniform expectations of a common core curriculum ensure general education attention to the needs of all children or motivate educators to seek assistance through special education?
- Will improved general education practices relieve disproportionality?
- Consider how to evaluate and address the existence of disproportionality in an all-minority school.
- Does disproportionality exist in your district? If so, what steps are in place to reduce it? Do conversations involve both general and special education practices? What part do community members play?

## Is There Common Ground?

Fergus and Rothstein agree that minorities are disproportionally represented in special education. Low-income minorities are especially vulnerable, for myriad reasons. The authors also agree that disproportionality is complex and that the remedy is broader than special education alone. Both are adamant that it is essential to reduce the causes of disproportionality. American children's future is at stake.

## Additional Resources

Adelman, H. S. & Taylor, L. (2011). *Schools and the challenge of LD and ADHD misdiagnoses*. Retrieved July 6, 2011 from http://smhp.psych.ucla.edu/pdfdocs/ldmisdiagnoses.pdf

Artiles, A., Kozleski, E., & Gonzalez, J. (2010). *Final report: How the Disproportionality Center Changed the nature of the conversation about disproportionality in special education*. Retrieved March 24, 2012 from www.nccrest.org

Barton, P. E. & Coley, R. J. (2009). *Parsing the achievement gap II.* Princeton, NJ: Educational Testing Service. Retrieved June 1, 2009 from www.ets.org/research/pic

Burdette, P. (2007). *State definitions of significant disproportionality.* National Association of State Directors of Special Education. Retrieved August 10, 2007 from www.nasdse.org

Cartledge, W., Singh, A., & Gibson, L. (2008). Practical behavior-management techniques to close the accessibility gap for students who are culturally and linguistically diverse. *Preventing School Failure, 52*(3), 29–38.

Delpit, L. (2012). *Multiplication is for white people: Raising expectations for other people's children.* New York: The New Press.

Dialog guides for IDEA 2004 regulations. (2004). Retrieved May 26, 2008 from www.ideapartnership.org

Ford, D. Y., Moore, J. L. III, Whiting, G. W., & Grantham, T. C. (2008). Conducting cross-cultural research: Controversy, cautions, concerns, and considerations. *Roeper Review, 30,* 82–92.

Gorski, P. (2008). The myth of the "culture of poverty." *Educational Leadership, 65*(7), 32–36.

Guiberson, M. (2009). Hispanic representation in special education: Patterns and implications. *Preventing School Failure, 53*(3), 167–176.

Harry, B. & Klingner, J. (2006). *Why are so many minority students in special education? Understanding race and disability in schools.* New York: Teachers College Columbia University.

Hart, J. E., Cramer, E. D., Harry, B., Klingner, J. K., & Sturges, K. M. (2010). The continuum of "Troubling" to "Troubled" behavior: Exploratory case studies of African American students in programs for emotional disturbance. *Remedial and Special Education, 31*(3), 148–162.

Hoover, J. J. (2012). Reducing unnecessary referrals: Guidelines for teachers of diverse learners. *TEACHING Exceptional Children, 44*(4), 39–47.

National Research Council. (2002). *Minority students in special and gifted education.* In Committee on Minority Representation in Special Education. M. S. Donovan and C. T. Cross (Eds.), Washington, DC: National Academy Press, 1–14.

Payne, R. (2008). Nine powerful practices. *Educational Leadership, 65*(7), 48–52.

Reschly, D. J. (2009). *Overview Document: Prevention of disproportionate special education overrepresentation using Response to Intervention.* National Comprehensive Center for Teacher Quality. Retrieved May 1, 2010, from www.ncctq.org

Skiba, R. J., Simmons, A. B., Ritter, S., Gibb, A. C., Rausch, M. K., Cuadrado, J. & Chung, C. (2008). Achieving equity in special education: History, status, and current challenges. *Exceptional Children 74*(3), 264–288.

Waitoller, F. R., Artiles, A. J., & Cheney, D. A. (2010). The miner's canary: A review of overrepresentation research and explanations. *The Journal of Special Education, 44*(1), 29–49.

# ISSUE 4

## Can RTI and IDEA Child Find Coexist?

YES: **Lynn S. Fuchs**, from "NRCLD Update on Responsiveness to Intervention: Research to Practice" (National Research Center on Learning Disabilities, 2007), www.nrcld.org, February 25, 2008

NO: **Jose L. Martin**, from "Legal Implications of Response to Intervention and Special Education Identification" (n.d.), www.rtinetwork .org, April 25, 2012

---

### Learning Outcomes

**At the conclusion of this issue, readers will be able to:**

- Compare and contrast the positions of the YES and NO selections addressing whether RTI and IDEA's Child Find requirements can coexist.
- Describe the strengths and the weaknesses of each side's arguments.
- Discuss whether the flexibility of RTI outweighs the due process protections of IDEA.
- Compare concepts in the YES and NO selections to procedures in local schools.

---

### ISSUE SUMMARY

**YES:** Lynn S. Fuchs, a prolific scholar in the area of learning disabilities, and one of several researchers in the National Research Center for Learning Disabilities, explains how Research to Intervention (RTI) strategies can separate a struggling learner from one with specific learning disabilities (SLDs). Research results demonstrate her thinking.

**NO:** Jose L. Martin, partner in the law firm Richards Lindsay & Martin in Austin, Texas, represents schools in disability issues and litigation, sees promise in RTI, and also discord with IDEA that could cause tension and conflict between schools and parents. Perhaps revision of the 35-year-old IDEA is in order to recognize changes in general education.

$S$LD is the disability designation for the majority of students covered by IDEA. It is the only disability specifically defined in IDEA, and the only one for which assessment methodology is addressed.

Students with SLD encounter significant learning difficulties not attributable to other disabilities, such as intellectual disabilities or a sensory impairment. They have not experienced environmental, cultural, or economic disadvantage. They have received quality instruction. In other words, all the conditions for learning are present, but learning is not occurring at a developmentally typical rate.

Prevalence rates for SLD vary from approximately 15 percent of all special education students in Kentucky to 60 percent in Iowa (Cortiella, *The state of learning disabilities*, 2011). This variation likely reflects inconsistent approaches to identification, using SLD as "the sociological sponge that wipes up the spills of general education" (Gresham, LD Summit, 2001).

Historically, identification of SLD relied on finding a significant discrepancy between a student's ability (usually measured by an IQ test) and academic achievement. Many complained that this process required students to "wait to fail" since the discrepancy often does not become significant during the earliest school years.

Courts found a lack of evidence in favor of the discrepancy model as well as documented standardized test bias against minority children and English language learners (Zirkel, CEC, 2006). These challenges, along with concern for the sheer numbers of students in this category, motivated Congress to address SLD identification directly.

IDEA 2004 signaled a dramatic shift in the way schools could identify students as having SLD. Districts are now directed that they must not require that teams rely solely on finding an IQ/achievement gap. Instead, teams "may use a process which determines if a student responds to scientific, research-based intervention." Schools are permitted to use the approaches in combination.

To ensure that the quality of classroom instruction was strong, and could not be the reason for a child's learning problems, Congress wrote Response to Intervention (RTI) into IDEA 2004. Instruction and assessment through RTI involves gathering student progress information on a consistent basis, beginning with universal screening. All students are to experience research-based classroom instruction (Tier 1). Students whose regular in-class assessments show an unsatisfactory rate of growth receive more intense general education services and progress-monitoring (Tier 2). Those not responsive to this level of assistance move on to Tier 3 or higher. If a comprehensive evaluation rules out the exclusionary factors listed above, the student could be considered for special education, perhaps under the SLD designation. Some districts consider Tier 3 the same as special education.

IDEA contains several provisions designed to protect the rights and education of individual students with disabilities. Through the Child Find provision, districts must actively seek any child who may have a disability and offer to conduct an evaluation to determine special education eligibility. Extensive regulations govern the evaluation process as well as the formation and implementation of the IEP by a team, including parents. Due process rights provide an avenue for parents who want to challenge school proposals or practices.

This issue focuses on the question of whether RTI and the current IDEA Child Find practices can coexist. New RTI practices in general education offer options for a range of services to children, but districts seeking to use RTI options may violate Child Find regulations. Parents accepting this new design may be forfeiting some hard-won legal rights.

In the YES selection, Lynn Fuchs, whose research identifies both benefits and risks in using RTI, believes the number of students found to have SLD will be reduced by effective general education intervention. Checking student progress on a regular basis and providing data-based intervention as soon as a need appears will help many children learn successfully. Acknowledging that evaluation under RTI may take longer than the traditional one-step assessment, Fuchs envisions a more open process, in which students move fluidly between special education and general instruction. In another issue (issue 9: Should RTI Interventions Be Delivered by Special Educators?), Fuchs expands this idea to propose that special education and Tier 3 become the same. Identifying some potential due process risks that need to be refined, she believes RTI and IDEA together form a strong safety net for all children.

In the NO selection, school-focused attorney Jose L. Martin sees much promise in the general education changes, but has grounds to think they conflict with IDEA as currently written. RTI has brought many benefits, including the possibility for early responsiveness to student needs. Unfortunately, the tiered instructional system may interfere with IDEA Child Find provisions and put students, families, and educators at risk. Martin describes a number of potential dispute scenarios in which a district's drive to implement RTI tiers conflicts with a parent's legal request for a special education evaluation. Martin speculates that this tension can only be resolved through IDEA's next reauthorization (now more than 5 years overdue).

Compton (*Journal of Learning Disabilities*, 2006) talks about "the nudges" necessary to help children learn. Everyone needs little nudges from time to time. A need for stronger and longer nudges might signify a disability. RTI is designed as a system of progressively more intense nudges, within the general education environment, enabling students to receive supplementary instruction without a disability label that some find stigmatizing (Brown-Chidsey, *Educational Leadership*, 2007). Litty and Hatch approve of interventions and monitoring, but are concerned about how long interventions take (*Early Childhood Education Journal*, 2006). Children with disabilities need the big nudge of special education, not delaying tactics that waste valuable time.

RTI was formulated, in part, to avoid the situation in which children needed to wait to fail before they could be considered for special education. Ironically, although individualized services are available earlier, some believe the length of time spent in RTI tiers may result in a parallel wait to fail situation.

Voices of parents and advocates are heard as part of a lengthy *Education Week RTI Report* (Kelleher, 2011). Some parents maintained that their children remained in Tier 2 for multiple years without showing progress; others that they had to "push pretty hard" for a special education evaluation rather than remain in RTI. Three sets of parents, from different states, declined an interview for fear of retaliation against their children. Other parents raved about the progress their children made under RTI; some had enough trust to leave behind due process protections of IDEA.

Fluid movement between services is one of the hallmark differences between RTI and IDEA. As a student demonstrates difficulty, she can move to a more intense tier. As her performance improves, she can move to a less intense tier and perhaps to no additional assistance at all. Under the current IDEA, movement between levels and types of service must be formalized in an IEP; no change can be made without written parental agreement.

Ideally, RTI acts as a prevention tool, focusing teacher attention on students who are progressing slowly. Interventions address difficulties before they become severe enough to warrant disability status. Students and teachers no longer need wait for the discrepancy to reach significance. With these improvements in general education, services might be provided faster and some students might not develop a discrepancy at all (Cortiella, www.ncld.org, 2012; Wanzek and Vaughn, *Remedial and Special Education*, 2011).

Emerging proficiency in English can contribute to low standardized test scores, which might be misinterpreted as a disability (Hoover, *TEACHING Exceptional Children*, 2012). Careful attention to student progress might also reduce inappropriate SLD determinations in English language learners.

The ongoing and active assessment of student progress also encourages schools to look beyond the scores of a single child. Finding a pattern of struggle across a grade level—or within a classroom—can lead to a consideration of whole-school curriculum or program changes (Ervin, www.rtinetwork.org, n.d.).

As a closing note, although the number of students identified as SLD rose consistently through the 1990s, that number declined by 14 percent during the first decade of this century (Cortiella, *The state of learning disabilities*, 2011). Several explanations are possible, including diagnosis-shift due to the meteoric rise of individuals on the autism spectrum. However, this is also the time period in which RTI began to be practiced: the reduction could be the result of improvements in general education—or of students whose parents were dissuaded from asking for IDEA's protections.

# YES

Lynn S. Fuchs

# NRCLD Update on Responsiveness to Intervention: Research to Practice

## What RTI Is

Students with SLD make up the majority of school-age individuals with disabilities. The number of students with SLD increased (from 1.2 million in 1979–1980 to 2.9 million in 2003–2004). Many policymakers and school administrators are concerned about the numbers of students with SLD. The concern is that some of these students may be capable of learning without special education if they are provided effective general education.

The usual method for identifying SLD relies on the difference between IQ and achievement. Research now shows that this method has many problems. For example, children who read poorly have similar characteristics, regardless of whether they have a discrepancy between IQ and achievement. Also, the size of discrepancy does not indicate the severity of the SLD. Moreover, data obtained through an assessment of the IQ-achievement discrepancy do not inform instruction in important ways.

RTI is a promising model for a new way to identify SLD as a student's failure to respond to teaching methods that research has shown to work well for most students.

*Here is one example of an RTI process.*

**Step 1:** All students in a school are given short tests. The aim is to identify those students whose scores are low and so seem to be at risk of developing a learning disability.

**Step 2:** The progress of these at-risk students is checked for five to eight weeks. A short test is given each week. Students whose progress is low in response to *general education instruction (Tier 1)* are identified.

**Step 3:** These students receive *small-group instruction (Tier 2 and Beyond intervention)* for nine to 20 weeks. This instruction usually consists of three to four sessions per week. Each instructional session lasts 30 to 40 minutes. Each week,

Fuchs, Lynn S. From *National Resource Center on Learning Disabilities*, Winter 2007. Published in 2007 by U.S. Office of Special Education Programs/Department of Education. www.nrcld.org

a short test measures the student's progress. They also are tested at the end of instruction. *Students who respond well to the intervention return to Tier 1 (general education) instruction.* Responding well means the student has improved each week during instruction and has a satisfactory achievement score at the end of the intervention. Student progress continues to be checked to catch any student who is not able to keep up a good rate of learning while back in general instruction.

**Step 4:** *Students whose response to small-group instruction is poor are given a comprehensive evaluation.* A poor response is a low rate of improvement each week and a low achievement score at the end of the intervention.

**Step 5:** To answer questions that arose during Tier 2 and Beyond, a *comprehensive evaluation* is conducted using valid and reliable data collection measures that are targeted specifically to student needs. The aim is to determine whether it is correct to identify the student as having a learning disability. A student may be identified as having some other disability—for example, mental retardation, speech/language delay, or emotional or behavioral disorder.

**Step 6:** *Special education is delivered with a more intensive instructional program.* Progress continues to be checked each week. If at any time data indicate that the student is not progressing adequately with the instructional program, the special educator changes the program. *Once a student has a strong rate of learning and reaches a satisfactory performance level, the student exits special education and returns to Tier 1 general education instruction.* The student's progress in Tier 1 instruction continues to be checked so that corrective action may be taken as needed.

The reasoning behind this RTI method of identifying learning disabilities is this: When a student does not respond to generally effective interventions both at Tier 1 and at Tier 2 and Beyond, the quality of instruction is not a likely reason for poor academic progress and, instead, may provide evidence of a disability.

## Benefits

An RTI model may offer several benefits. First, an RTI model for identifying students with SLD has the benefit of *early identification and intervention.* Students at risk for SLD can be screened as early as January of kindergarten or September of first grade. This decreases the likelihood that students will slip through the system without detection of their learning problems.

A second potential benefit of an RTI model of SLD identification is *systematic screening, which reduces screening bias.* Systematic screening, which involves testing all students, decreases reliance on teacher-based referral. This reduces possible teacher bias and reduces the variability in SLD identification practices. Referral and identification for SLD vary in part because teachers differ in their views about how students perform and why they may be learning poorly. This variability in teachers' views and attributes results in missed opportunities to serve students with SLD.

A final potential benefit of RTI is *linking identification assessment with instructional planning.* Presently, the assessment process for documenting a discrepancy between IQ and achievement takes a lot of resources. At the same time, the resulting test scores have little connection with planning effective instruction. Many special and general education teachers find results from traditional tests are not much help in designing instruction. Using RTI to identify students as having SLD keeps the assessment focus on the student's learning. The RTI model switches the emphasis from assessment for identification to instructionally relevant assessment. It involves monitoring student progress and systematic testing of changes in instruction.

## Risks

Despite the promise of an RTI model for identifying learning disabilities, key conceptual issues need to be sharpened. RTI methods need to be further specified and studied.

One potential pitfall of RTI is *whether strong intervention models and measures are available to produce strong learning outcomes.* For schools and teachers to be able to use RTI, instructional procedures that are shown to be effective across teachers and schools must be available. In addition, measures are required to follow learning over time. These tools are available for some, but not all, academic areas. They are better developed at some grade levels. For example, a fair amount of work has been accomplished in beginning reading to provide the groundwork for both RTI intervention and measurement procedures. By contrast, in math, spelling, and writing, measurement procedures for tracking growth are well established, but more research is needed on validated intervention methods for testing responsiveness to instruction. More information is available at the early grades than for older students.

A second potential pitfall concerns *having enough trained professionals available.* To use an RTI model in the thousands of school districts in this country, large numbers of trained professionals are required. They will need the knowledge and skills to put in place defined tutoring methods or to solve problems through research. They also will need the knowledge and skills to monitor student learning, to interpret the assessment results, and to make decisions about eligibility. Moreover, using RTI requires a new way of thinking about assessment and instruction for many professionals, including school psychologists, special and general educators, and principals. To date, RTI models have been implemented only on a small scale by highly trained personnel in research settings. Using RTI on a large scale, in many school systems and many states, has not yet been tested. It will require developing and carrying out an ambitious training agenda for school professionals.

Finally, *RTI practitioners will need to determine when to begin due process and parental involvement.* Does due process begin with problem-solving adaptations to general education or with the intensive short-term preventive instruction?

Is it delayed until the student is found to be unresponsive to instruction and a special education classification is imminent? On the one hand, due process early in the identification process may be essential to protect against students getting caught in a cycle in which they linger between general education and some layer of services short of special education, without parents being aware or having input. On the other hand, initiating due process early in identification will be costly and will add considerable time and personnel requirements to identification. Clearly, discussions are needed about due process in such a changed identification system.

# How NRCLD's Research Is Helping Schools Implement RTI

*Two large studies* have been conducted, one in *reading* and the other in *math,* in which students were followed over time.

## Reading

NRCLD worked in 42 classrooms across 10 schools. Some schools had large numbers of high-poverty families, and other schools had large numbers of middle-class families. Students from these classrooms were selected for taking part based on low scores on brief reading measures given at the beginning of first grade. These 252 students were randomly assigned to receive the instruction or not at the beginning of January, depending on how they actually improved during the fall.

### Instruction Group
Students who had been randomly assigned to receive small-group instruction (and who did not improve much in reading during the fall) continued to receive reading instruction in the general education classroom. They also took part in Tier 2 small-group instruction for nine weeks. Small-group instruction consisted of three, 45-minute sessions per week.

### Control Group
By contrast, students who had been randomly assigned to the control group (and who did not improve much in reading during the fall) continued to receive all of their reading instruction in the general education classroom. They did not receive small-group instruction.

### Findings
At the end of first grade, students who had received small-group instruction read substantially better than students who did not receive small-group instruction. Many fewer students qualified as SLD given the various methods we used to define SLD. The alternative ways of defining SLD at the end of first grade, some based on traditional methods of discrepancy between IQ and

achievement and others based on RTI approaches, designated different students as having a learning disability.

## Math

We conducted a study similar to the reading study but not identical. We worked in 41 classrooms across 10 schools. Some schools had large numbers of high-poverty families, and other schools had large numbers of middle-class families. Based on their math scores near the beginning of first grade, students from these classrooms were designated as not at risk for SLD in math (127 children) or as at risk for SLD in math (569 children). The at-risk children were randomly assigned to receive small-group instruction or not beginning in November.

### Instruction Group

Students who had been randomly assigned to receive small-group instruction continued to receive math instruction in the general education classroom. They also took part in Tier 2 small-group instruction for 20 weeks. This instruction consisted of three, 30-minute sessions per week.

### Control Group

By contrast, students who had been randomly assigned to the control group continued to receive all of their math instruction in the general education classroom. They did not receive small-group instruction.

### Findings

At the end of first grade, students who had received small-group instruction computed and understood math concepts substantially better than students who did not receive small-group instruction. Many fewer students qualified as SLD given the various methods we used to define SLD. The alternative ways of defining SLD at the end of first grade, some based on traditional methods of discrepancy between IQ and achievement and others based on RTI approaches, designated different students as having a learning disorder.

## Conclusions

From these studies, we draw several conclusions that should influence how schools conduct RTI.

1. One-time testing at the beginning of the year does not provide an adequate basis for identifying children who need Tier 2 and Beyond small-group instruction intervention. Instead, one-time testing can be used to identify a pool of students whose progress then needs to be monitored, using brief weekly tests, for five to eight weeks. Then, a

slope of improvement (that is weekly rate of gain) can be calculated to determine which children have progressed nicely in response to the Tier 1 general education program and which children require Tier 2 and Beyond intervention.

2. Tier 2 and Beyond small-group instruction can be effective in promoting better achievement. It also can be effective for sorting out children who will learn well with well-designed instruction versus children who require more intensive special education. With Tier 2 and Beyond small-group instruction, fewer children finish first grade with the kinds of academic deficits that make them appropriate for disability certification.

3. This RTI process can provide a sound basis for identifying students to receive a comprehensive special education evaluation.

4. Tier 2 and Beyond instructors need to be well trained and supervised for Tier 2 and Beyond benefits to accrue. With training and supervision, formal teaching certification is not necessary. Continuing problem solving to address the learning needs and behavioral challenges of individual students needs to be provided by a licensed teacher who has a strong teaching background.

5. Different methods for quantifying "response" to Tier 2 and Beyond small-group instruction will result in different numbers of students being identified for comprehensive special education evaluation. Some methods work better than others at identifying students with severe academic deficits. One method that appears to work well is to define adequate response as students demonstrating (a) a strong rate of improvement during small-group instruction as well as (b) adequate final performance at the end of small-group instruction.

6. Some students who demonstrate adequate response to small-group instruction will fall behind again when they return to Tier 1 general education without the continuing support of small-group instruction. For this reason, it is important that schools continue to monitor the progress of these students with brief weekly assessments so that corrective actions may be taken when needed, including returning to Tier 2 and Beyond small-group instruction.

# Frequently Asked Questions About RTI

## Will This Process Delay Identification?

The RTI process takes longer than a traditional one-step comprehensive evaluation. However, beginning at Tier 2, students are receiving services designed to remediate their learning problems—a prevention strategy. The aim is that the prevention built into RTI will reduce the number of students incorrectly identified as having a disability because they have not received strong instruction. It may help many students get on an upward track toward successful academic outcomes. Also, RTI facilitates prevention and identification early in the primary grades. In contrast, the traditional method of identifying a discrepancy between IQ and achievement often occurs later in schooling, since it may be many grades before a sizeable discrepancy accrues.

## Does Each Child Have to Go Through RTI or Can a Child Have a Traditional Assessment?

Schools honor parent requests for a traditional one-step comprehensive evaluation, in lieu of the RTI process. Legislation suggests that the evaluation of a child suspected of having a disability must include a variety of assessment tools and must not rely on any single measure.

## What Does "Research-Based Intervention" Mean?

A research-based intervention constitutes a set of practices. Each of those practices is tested and evaluated in controlled studies. Each practice must be shown to be effective. In a controlled study, students are matched (found to be similar) according to the criteria important to the study. Students are randomly assigned to a treatment or no treatment group. The outcomes for students in both groups are compared.

## Who Initiates an RTI Process?

Typically, children are identified to take part in Tier 2 and Beyond interventions based on their universal screening scores, when students are tested once, at the beginning of the school year. Many times, such universal screening is supplemented with short-term progress monitoring (for example, over five weeks) to determine the student's response to general education.

## What Will Be Required for Professional Development?

An RTI process of SLD identification will require professional development to prepare school staffs to do the following activities:

- Collect and interpret screening scores using existing data or individually administered brief assessments on all students
- Ensure the quality of general education by selecting strong curricula and by conducting observations to document that those strong curricula have been used well. This requires examining class-wide patterns of response to determine when teachers require assistance to improve the quality of their instructional programs and then providing that assistance
- Collect continuing progress-monitoring data and interpret the data
- Design Tier 2 and Beyond programs that incorporate validated intervention protocols
- Implement those Tier 2 and Beyond programs with fidelity.

### *Who Is Responsible for the Various Activities Required to Implement RTI as a Method of SLD Identification?*

Faculty in a school building must work collaboratively to implement RTI as a method of SLD identification. In some schools, the work is distributed as follows:

| Task | Responsibility |
| --- | --- |
| Collecting screening data using existing data or individually administered brief assessments on all students | Teachers & trained aides |
| Interpreting screening data | Special educators & school psychologists |
| Ensuring the quality of general education | Curriculum specialists at the school or district level, school psychologists, teachers, & parents |
| Collecting continuing progress-monitoring data | Teachers & trained aides |
| Interpreting progress-monitoring data | Special educators & school psychologists |
| Designing Tier 2 and Beyond programs that incorporate validated intervention protocols | Special educators & school psychologists |
| Implementing Tier 2 and Beyond programs with fidelity | Trained aides under the supervision of special educators & school psychologists |
| Conducting the Step 4 evaluation | Special educators & school psychologists |

## How Long Will the Comprehensive Evaluation Be and What Professional Is Likely to Give the Step 4 Assessment?

The comprehensive evaluation should be specifically targeted to answer questions that arise during Tier 2 and Beyond instruction. It should be done in collaboration with the perspective of the student's general education teacher. Typically, answering these relevant questions involves only a small number of relatively brief tests. For example, if mental retardation is suspected as the disability category, school psychologists might administer the Vineland Adaptive Behavior Scale along with a two-sub-test Wechsler Abbreviated Scale of Intelligence instead of giving a full-blown intelligence test to rule out mental retardation.

## What Proportion of Students Is Likely to Be Identified as at Risk (for Tier 1 Monitoring) and for the Tier 2 and Beyond Diagnostic Trial?

The proportion of students identified for different steps in the RTI process depends largely on the quality of general education. When general education instruction is of questionable quality, research suggests that 20 percent to 25 percent of a school population is likely to be identified as at risk and demonstrate unresponsiveness to Tier 1. Of course, providing the Tier 2 and Beyond diagnostic instructional trial to 25 percent of a school population challenges a school's resources. In contrast, research also suggests that with high-quality general education, only 9 percent to 10 percent of students will be identified as at risk and respond inadequately to Tier 1, with approximately half those students responding to high-quality Tier 2 and Beyond instruction. Clearly, a need exists to ensure high-quality general education. In a similar way, integrity of the RTI process requires a strong Tier 2 and Beyond diagnostic instructional trial.

Jose L. Martin

 **NO**

# Legal Implications of Response to Intervention and Special Education Identification

The Response-to-Intervention (RTI) movement is enabling public education in the United States to evolve from a reactive model in which students had to seriously deteriorate before being moved on to special education programs, to one that emphasizes early and high-quality research-based interventions in regular programs that generate useful data with which to make key decisions for each struggling student. This evolution, however, has taken place against a backdrop of legal requirements for special education referrals and evaluations that remain almost unchanged from those of more than 30 years ago. The meeting of RTI innovations and the traditional child-find requirement of the Individuals with Disabilities Education Improvement Act of 2004 has many scratching their heads over exactly how the rules fit into the modern intervention era.

## Child-Find Under IDEA 2004

Child-find is the term used to describe the legal duty imposed by IDEA 2004 on public school districts to "find" children who may have a disability and be in need of special education services. Under the law, schools have an affirmative duty to identify, locate, and evaluate students who they suspect may have a disability, in order to evaluate them for potential eligibility for special education services. It is not enough for schools to wait until parents ask about or request a special education evaluation based on suspicion that their child may have a disability and struggling in school as a result. Schools must . . . ascertain when there are reasonable grounds to suspect disability and the potential need for special education services.

. . . [T]he school's obligation to evaluate a student is triggered when a school district has reason to suspect both that (1) the student has a disability, and (2) a resulting need for special education services. Once that "trigger" is pulled, schools must evaluate the child within a reasonable time to meet IDEA 2004's requirements and avoid exposure to child-find legal challenges and compensatory services claims. . . .

# The Push for Early Interventions and RTI

In 2004, the Congress acted on concerns about the increasing number of students in special education, and the related suspicion that many students currently classified as having a specific learning disability (SLD) might have avoided the need for special education if instructional support and interventions had been provided to them at an early stage in their education. Thus, the backdrop was set in place for a move to reform to the manner in which schools should identify students with SLD—the largest population served by special education. This reform, moreover, was to take advantage of existing and emerging research on SLD, as well as modern ideas on how to meaningfully address the needs of struggling students within regular education.

By the time IDEA was reauthorized in 2004, a variety of experts from different disciplines noted that the special education system in the United States represented a "wait-to-jail" model, rather than a system that focused first on quality interventions within the regular education environment, followed by case-by-case educational decision making based on struggling students' response to high-quality research-based interventions. This sea change in educational thinking and modernization in SLD evaluations . . . has come to be encapsulated in the phrase Response to Intervention, or RTI. . . .

This evolution, however, is not taking place without incident. The RTI movement, has generated a new tension between the desire to apply early high-quality interventions to struggling students and the legal duty to comply with IDEA'S traditional child-find requirements. And, while schools are establishing RTI programs as educational initiatives, the child-find mandate of IDEA represents a legal requirement, violation of which can mean real liability for schools.

# New Questions Mean New Disputes

There is no lack of consensus on the outline of IDEA'S child-find requirements, or about the positive benefits of expanded opportunities for interventions for struggling students within regular education programs. The child-find obligation imposed under IDEA, however, is currently applied in a context where public schools are simultaneously focusing on providing quality regular education interventions for struggling students prior to referring them for an IDEA evaluation. In many situations, campuses, referral teams, and classroom teachers are being asked to provide documentation that they have implemented serious interventions to address a student's difficulties in the classroom before a referral is allowed to proceed to evaluation. The advent of RTI methodology, together with an expanding range of interventions available outside of special education, has thus created a tension with the schools' duty to comply with child-find, particularly in cases where parents approach schools with concerns about their children's performance or outright request testing.

While schools are expending resources and energies on making effective use of interventions outside of special education for struggling students, however, the child-find requirement remains ever-present and mostly unchanged.

Another fact is that a number of students who meet criteria for regular educa-tion interventions may in fact be struggling in the classroom due to the effects of learning disabilities.

Given the existing dynamic, new and difficult questions have arisen about how the child-find requirement of IDEA works in the context of expanded reg-ular education interventions and RTI methodology. These questions include the following:

- At what point should schools suspect that students who are struggling with the curriculum while receiving regular education interventions might actually have a specific learning disability?
- How long should a student receive regular interventions before a school initiates an IDEA evaluation?
- Is the child-find obligation triggered if a child moves through tiers of interventions with some improvement, but nevertheless continues to show deficits in achievement?
- How should schools handle parents' requests for evaluations when interventions have only just been initiated and/or appear to show promise?
- How can schools avoid failure-to-identify IDEA hearing claims while attempting to make best use of regular education interventions prior to a referral?

It is in answering these questions that we are likely to see the complex legal disputes in this area of education. Questions may be raised about the timeliness of implementation of high-quality interventions, the rate of the student's progress in the interventions, the timeline for interventions, and situations where parents are encouraged to allow interventions to proceed only to lead to limited response and an ultimately delayed placement in spe-cial education. Some parents may feel that participating in the RTI process ultimately led to a delay in having special education services provided to their children and may attempt to seek legal redress in the form of compensatory services. . . .

# The Federal Regulation on Referral

The federal regulation addressing referrals to special education—in the all-important context of potential learning disabilities—envisions that interven-tions will be considered for a struggling child, but at the same time it respects the parents' ultimate right to request an evaluation at any time. The regula-tion in question states that schools must promptly seek parental consent to evaluate a child for special education, under regular timeframes, if the child has not made adequate progress after an appropriate period of time when pro-vided with appropriate instruction, and whenever the child is referred for an evaluation.

Another regulation addressing initial evaluations in all situations also serves to emphasize that "either a parent or a public agency may initiate a request for an initial evaluation to determine if the child is a child with a disability." The United States Department of Education (ED) commentary accompanying the regulation indicates that the same timelines and procedures applicable to all initial evaluations would apply to evaluations involving students with potential LDs. The only exception to the regular timelines to complete evaluations is in situations where the school staff and parents mutually agree in writing to extend the timeline, ostensibly to allow additional time for interventions to proceed. The USED commentary also reminds us that interventions can be provided during the weeks while the evaluation is conducted, a point made in response to concerns that parents, by requesting evaluation, could "short-circuit" or opt out of the intervention process. . . . In sum, however, the referral scheme under IDEA'S federal regulations respects the parent's right to request an evaluation with no specialized exception for circumstances where the school is attempting high-quality research-based interventions.

. . . Although schools can, technically, refuse to refer the student, they must then provide parents with written notice of refusal and notice of IDEA procedural safeguards (since parents must be informed that they can challenge the school's refusal to evaluate the student). This course of action also creates the possibility that the school will face a failure-to-identify legal action challenging the refusal to evaluate. If the parents can prove that there are reasonable grounds to suspect disability and the need for special education services (admittedly not a high threshold), then the school will lose the case, will be ordered to evaluate the student, and will likely be liable for the parents' attorneys' fees. . . .

## Common RTI/Child-Find Misconceptions

The advent of RTI, together with the modernization of the SLD evaluation process, has given rise to some common notions and confusion spots that can lead schools awry in complying with child-find while also implementing RTI programs. Some of these misconceptions include the following:

- RTI interventions are a mandatory prerequisite to LD evaluation
- Intervention programs must be implemented for the entire period of instruction
- In tiered intervention models, all tiers must be completed prior to referral
- Data from RTI intervention programs is a mandatory part of an LD evaluation

The most entrenched misconception involves the need for RTI data as part of SLD evaluations. Although individual states may, if they wish, make the use of RTI data mandatory, the federal statute or regulations do not. . . .

In addition, the component of the SLD evaluation under which the team must rule out that the performance difficulties are not caused by lack of appropriate instruction does not require high-quality research-based instruction or interventions—plain, appropriate, regular instruction in regular classes with periodic progress assessments (e.g., classroom quizzes and tests) can meet this requirement. . . . [A]lthough provision of high-quality research-based interventions would certainly meet—and, indeed, would exceed—the requirement for "appropriate" instruction, it is not required.

Consequently, ED stated in a 2011 letter that "it has come to the attention of the Office of Special Education Programs (OSEP) that, in some instances, local educational agencies (LEAs) may be using Response to Intervention strategies to delay or deny a timely initial evaluation for children suspected of having a disability." The memo states that while ED supports RTI initiatives and programs, "the use of RTI strategies cannot be used to delay or deny the provision of a full and individual evaluation, . . . to a child suspected of having a disability. . . ." The memo also reiterates . . . that IDEA and its regulations currently "allow" the use of RTI data as part of the criteria for determining if a child has a specific LD, as opposed to mandating such an evaluation procedure. The memo therefore concludes that "it would be inconsistent with the evaluation provisions [of the IDEA regulations] for an LEA to reject a referral and delay provision of an initial evaluation on the basis that the child has not participated in an RTI framework." . . .

## Parental Requests for IDEA Evaluation

Certainly, a school addressing the difficulties of a student who is struggling academically is free to consider, explore, and apply its range of intervention options prior to deciding on a referral for special education evaluation. The circumstances change, however, when the parent approaches the school asking for special education testing. Because the parent not only has a right to request evaluation, but can initiate legal action against a school that fails to act on their request, a parent referral places the school in a unique situation. As recent case law indicates, these scenarios can easily lead to disputes. The cases that illustrate the present tension between RTI and child-find seem to break down into distinct types.

In one variety of case, the parent approaches the school with concerns about the child's performance, some suspicions of disability, and questions about initiating an evaluation. The school responds by providing interventions, but takes no action on the requested evaluation, and provides neither prior written notice under IDEA explaining its refusal to evaluate, nor notice of IDEA procedural safeguards. The parents, getting no straight answers on their request for evaluation, subsequently initiate legal action claiming a child-find violation. This type of case is characterized by school staff laboring under misconceptions about RTI programs and child-find, confusion in communications with parents, and by a lack of collaborative decision making.

In another type of case, the parent requests an evaluation of their struggling child but, after conferring with the school, agrees to the interventions proposed by the school instead. Likewise, in these scenarios, the school provides neither prior written notice, nor notice of IDEA rights. Later, however, the parent files a legal action alleging a child-find violation. These scenarios are marked by school staff lobbying parents to accept provision of interventions in lieu of a referral and a lack of compliance with procedural requirements (usually because the school does not see itself as having refused an evaluation outright). But, the courts tend to take the position that if a parent asks for an evaluation but does not get it, the school has de facto refused the evaluation request, even if it never actually said the word "no." Schools tend to lose this type of case.

In yet another form of RTI/child-find dispute, the school provides interventions over a period of time with the parents' agreement, although it subsequently conducts an evaluation once the student's response to interventions appears to slow. The parents, feeling that the school has tarried too long in deciding to evaluate, request a due process hearing to seek compensatory services. The results in these cases tend to hinge on whether the students were positively responding to initial interventions, and whether the school acted in a timely fashion to evaluate the child when intervention response began to lag. At times, the cases also turn on whether state law required the school to provide a certain amount of intervention prior to referral. If the student was progressing with interventions, if the school acted quickly to evaluate the student once progress slowed, or if a state law requires interventions prior to referral, the school tends to prevail in the dispute.

Lastly, in another type of scenario, the parents and the school collaboratively agree on proceeding with interventions rather than pursue an evaluation. The decision making is by consensus, collaborative, and with parents receiving full information of all options, including their right to request an evaluation. For various reasons, litigation nevertheless erupts, but schools tend to fare well in these scenarios.

. . . Ultimately, the key question is how schools can both make effective use of available high-quality research-based interventions while at the same time avoiding potentially complicated child-find legal claims. . . . The tension between the two priorities, therefore, is one that must be addressed with a carefully balanced approach.

## Active Steps for Schools to Avoid RTI-Based Child-Find Disputes

From an IDEA liability standpoint, the main challenge for schools attempting to implement interventions for struggling students prior to referral for a special education evaluation is avoiding disputes with parents. . . . [T]he key to this balancing effort lies in actively involving parents as partners in the decisions regarding interventions and the timing of a special education evaluation. This effort could include the following operational steps:

1. Providing parents with detailed information on the range of regular education interventions available (pamphlets, research support, rates of success, etc. . . .)
2. Meeting with parents to discuss intervention options, agreed timelines, and available courses of action
3. Making clear to parents their right to request an IDEA evaluation and providing written notice of IDEA procedural safeguards

4. Reaching a consensus on a course of action in a collaborative manner
5. If the consensus decision is to pursue regular education interventions, sharing progress data frequently with parents
6. Initiating follow-up communication regarding progress or lack thereof
7. Convening follow-up meetings to review progress and renew consensus on current course of action
8. Documenting the steps above.

Parents who are partners in the intervention decision-making process will be less likely to raise legal challenges, and evidence of consensual action will be important should the matter lead to litigation. The issue is of importance, because there will be situations where even after application of high-quality interventions, the student does not make sufficient progress, an IDEA evaluation takes place, and the student is placed in special education. Thus, parents should be informed that there are no guarantees that regular education interventions will work.

Schools that invest resources and time on RTI-oriented intervention programs should also use RTI's data-based approach to study the effectiveness of the program on school-wide and district-wide bases. The important question to answer with the data is the degree to which the interventions are proving effective in reducing the need for special education referrals by improving student performance on the whole. In other words, what schools need to know is whether their RTI program is yielding positive results in the form of student improvement, to the point that the need for IDEA referrals is reduced. If the data show that a substantial number of students who, in the past, would have been evaluated do in fact improve significantly with interventions and thus do not need referral, then the program is being successful. If, on the other hand, most of the students who would have been referred in the past simply get referred at a later time—after a potentially lengthy intervention period—then the program might appear to simply be slowing down or delaying the eventual referral and evaluation process. Certainly, the RTI movement did not intend to replace the discrepancy-based wait-to-fail SLD model with yet another version of a wait-to-fail model that requires failure in potentially lengthy RTI' programs prior to referral to IDEA.

# Referral Decisions versus Eligibility Decisions

With all of the discussion about preventing unnecessary referrals to special education, we should not forget that IDEA eligibility requires two separate findings: (1) meeting of state and federal criteria for at least one IDEA disability eligibility category, and (2) a resulting need for special education (i.e., specially designed instruction). A complexity is presented, however, when a school is capable of successfully providing high-quality and beneficial individualized instruction to a student with disabilities as part of its regular education program.

This scenario raises a concrete legislative question: Does the 35-year-old definition of "specially designed instruction" require modernization as a broader and deeper range of instructional intervention options becomes available within regular education? This question will likely be fodder for upcoming legislative discussion when IDEA is again reauthorized in a timeframe fully within the RTI era. As a broader range of struggling students' needs can be met outside of the special education system, IDEA might evolve to reflect this reality by updating its definition of special education services. Perhaps this debate will also lead to reform in child-find and referral rules, in recognition of schools' local intellectual and resources investments in high-quality intervention programs. For now, however, it is clear we are in a time where reform is taking place and effecting change on a system-wide basis, which inevitably leads to some degree of tension and confusion. The benefits of moving forward, however, are simply too significant to turn away.

# EXPLORING THE ISSUE

## Can RTI and IDEA Child Find Coexist?

## Challenge Questions

- Compare and contrast the positions of the YES and NO selections regarding whether RTI and the current IDEA can coexist.
- Which selection makes the best case for its argument? Why?
- What, if any, changes do you think should be made in the legal foundations for RTI and IDEA with respect to identifying children who might have a disability? Support your decision with information from this issue.
- What plans does your local school have to ensure that parents are partners in making the decision between RTI interventions and a referral for special education evaluation?
- What should parents consider when deciding to choose the promises of fluid services in RTI in favor of IDEA's protections?

## Is There Common Ground?

Lynne Fuchs and Jose L. Martin have several points of agreement. They agree that RTI has promise to teach children effectively, before their needs escalate. They believe RTI has resulted in a vast positive change to general education, and value the collaborative spirit behind both RTI and IDEA. This collaboration will be essential to resolving disputes between RTI and IDEA, for the benefit of the same children. Finally, both authors emphasize the critical responsibility to honor a parent's request for a special education evaluation, no matter how strong the RTI program.

## Additional Resources

Brown-Chidsey, R. (2007). No more "waiting to fail." *Educational Leadership, 65*(2), 40–45.

Compton, D. L. (2006). How should "unresponsiveness" to secondary intervention be operationalized? It's all about the nudge. *Journal of Learning Disabilities, 39*(2), 170–173.

Cortiella, C. (2011). *The state of learning disabilities: Facts, trends and indicators.* New York: National Center for Learning Disabilities.

Cortiella, C. (2012, January 18). *RTI and the special education evaluation and eligibility process.* Retrieved January 20, 2012 from www.ncld.org

Ervin, R. A. (n.d.). *Considering Tier 3 within a Response-to-Intervention model.* Retrieved May 4, 2012 from www.rtinetwork.org

Gresham, F. (2001). *Responsiveness to intervention: An alternative approach to the identification of learning disabilities.* Retrieved March 22, 2008 from www. nrcld.org/resources/ldsummit/index.html

Hoover, J. J. (2012). Reducing unnecessary referrals: Guidelines for teachers of diverse learners. *TEACHING Exceptional Children, 44*(4), 39–47.

Kelleher. (2011, March). Parents skeptical of RTI's benefits. Special Report: *Monitoring progress: Response to Intervention's Promise and Pitfalls,* XXX: *Education Week,* S14–S15.

Litty, C. G. & Hatch, A. J. (2006). Hurry up and wait: Rethinking special education identification in kindergarten. *Early Childhood Education Journal, 33*(4), 203–208.

Wanzek, J. & Vaughn, S. (2011). Is a three-tier reading intervention model associated with reduced placement in special education? *Remedial and Special Education, 32*(2), 167–175.

Zirkel, P. A. (2006). *The legal meaning of specific learning disability for special education eligibility.* Alexandria, VA: Council for Exceptional Children.

# ISSUE 5

## Can Whole-School Reform Reduce Discipline Problems?

**YES: Howard S. Adelman and Linda Taylor,** from "Rethinking How Schools Address Student Misbehavior and Disengagement," *Addressing Barriers to Learning* (vol. 13, no. 2, 2008), http://smhp.psych.ucla.edu

**NO: William C. Frick and Susan C. Faircloth,** from "Acting in the Collective and Individual 'Best Interest of Students': When Ethical Imperatives Clash with Administrative Demands," *Journal of Special Education Leadership* (vol. 20, no. 1, pp. 21–32, 2007)

---

### Learning Outcomes

**At the conclusion of this issue, readers will be able to:**

- Compare and contrast the positions of the YES and NO selections addressing whether whole-school reform can reduce discipline problems.
- Describe the strengths and the weaknesses of each side's arguments.
- Identify varied approaches to supporting and reacting to student misbehavior.
- Outline the requirements of manifestation determination.

---

#### ISSUE SUMMARY

**YES:** Howard S. Adelman and Linda Taylor, co-directors of the UCLA School Mental Health Project, based in the Center for Mental Health in Schools, believe that many discipline problems could be eliminated by whole-school initiatives that create and sustain an environment that addresses positive social and emotional development as well as academics.

**NO:** William C. Frick and Susan C. Faircloth, assistant professors at the University of Oklahoma and the Pennsylvania State University, respectively, present dilemmas faced by principals torn between balancing the needs of one particular student who exhibits disruptive behavior with those of the rest of the student body, whose learning is affected by the single student's actions.

IDEA ensures free and appropriate public education for students with disabilities. Students with emotional/behavioral disabilities are among those accorded this right. These students typically experience difficulty complying with general school rules and social conventions. Some may internalize conflict; withdrawing, and perhaps hurting themselves. Others react aggressively, externalizing their conflict. Although both types of behavior must be addressed; externalizing behavior is usually the most problematic for teachers. Students with other disabilities can also demonstrate behaviors that are challenging for teachers; imagine a child with attention deficit hyperactivity disorder (ADHD) in a setting that requires tightly controlled behavior.

Educators encounter a dilemma when students with a disability violate school norms. The behavior (e.g., starting a fight) breaks the rules, but the student starting the fight has a disability that affects the ability to restrain impulses. Repeated suspensions for the same behavior could effectively expel the student, depriving him of legally protected education and services, constituting a change of placement. Ignoring the action sends a troubling message to peers, and fails to increase socially appropriate behavior.

In its early authorizations, IDEA emphasized academic access; there was no mention of "the troublesome topic of discipline" (Osborne & Russo, *ELA Notes,* 2007). IDEA 97 remedied that oversight by stipulating that students should not be removed from school for behavior that was a manifestation of their disability or the result of an inappropriate IEP. Behavior unrelated to the disability could receive the standard consequence. Unfortunately, IDEA 97 contained no precise definition of the term *manifestation* (Osborne & Russo). Often the appropriateness of the IEP became the primary focus of discussion, removing or delaying disciplinary consequences.

IDEA 2004 tightened legal requirements regarding manifestation determination, making it easier to discipline students with disabilities (Zirkel, *Journal of Special Education Leadership,* 2006). The emphasis shifted from whether the IEP was appropriate to whether it had been implemented. A tougher standard now exists for finding specific behavior directly related to the disability. Schools have broader latitude to send students with disabilities to short-term alternate facilities for longer periods of time. Parents now bear the burden of proof if they disagree with the school's determination regarding manifestation.

In contrast with these heightened standards, schools are also encouraged to adopt systems of positive behavioral interventions and support (PBIS). Like right to intervention (RTI), PBIS encompasses a range of interventions designed to model and support positive behavior rather than focus on punishing negative behavior. Trussell (*Intervention in Schools and Clinic,* 2008) comments that PBIS schools create environments that support both social and learning outcomes, preventing the emergence of problem behaviors.

This issue's controversy deals with the challenge of addressing student misbehavior. A whole-school approach, with differentiated levels of support, provides one option. Attending differentially to the needs of individuals is another. As you read the YES and NO selections, think about how your school approaches behavior and discipline.

In the YES selection, Howard S. Adelman and Linda Taylor maintain that disciplined students might become disengaged, unmotivated to continue learning. Acknowledging the pressures on teachers, Adelman and Taylor advocate school improvement efforts that incorporate positive behavioral supports to minimize the occurrence of undesirable behavior, and re-engage troubling students, whether or not they have a disability.

In the NO selection, William C. Frick and Susan C. Faircloth analyze the words of high school principals trying to balance the needs of the whole student body with those of individual students with disabilities. These leaders are comfortable providing instructional accommodations and adaptations to meet student needs, but unsettled by the ethical dilemmas they face when trying to be fair to everyone in disciplinary matters. Unbending discipline standards and structures—even those meant to be well-intentioned through IDEA—may not satisfy the individual needs of a particular student.

Two key resources support educators interested in pursuing a PBIS model. The federally funded technical assistance website (www.pbis.org) contains extensive resources and links to state PBIS contacts. A comprehensive guide to mental health and school improvement, developed by Adelman and Taylor (http://smhp.psych.ucla.edu/mhbook/mhbookintro.htm, 2008), emphasizes the importance of including counselors, psychologists, and school social workers in school reform to create an array of proactive practices that do not depend on a disability label for access.

Another perspective holds that some students just do not thrive in traditional schools, exceeding the tolerance level of teachers and administrators (Quinn, Poirier, Fuller, Gable, & Tonelson, *Preventing School Failure,* 2006). These students often flourish in alternative learning environments, which provide a unique blend of structure, support, and flexibility.

Alternative schools have seen a dramatic increase recently, perhaps due to mismatches between today's expectations and student performance. Students with disabilities account for 12–19 percent of alternative school enrollment (Bullock, *Preventing School Failure,* 2006). There is no single definition of an alternative school, but Tissington (*Preventing School Failure,* 2006) identified three varieties. Type I schools focus on educational specialties, such as magnet schools; Type II schools address disciplinary issues and are sometimes seen as the last chance before expulsion; Type III alternatives are therapeutic, delivering specialized treatment for students with disabilities.

The specialized focus of alternative schools helps students become re-engaged with academics while simultaneously working with their families to improve social and emotional skills (Hughes & Adera, *Preventing School Failure,* 2006). Although alternatives strike a balance between safe schools and keeping troubling children in school, Van Acker (*Preventing School Failure,* 2007) cautions that grouping children with behavioral issues in one place eliminates role models and could exacerbate negative behavior.

Ross Greene (*Educational Leadership*, 2010) believes that challenging behavior could be a sign of lagging skills. Students would rather not misbehave, but when the demands of a situation outstrip their current skills, some act out. Instead of responding with uniform consequences or interventions, Greene recommends engaging the student in collaborative problem solving during which both adult and student voice concerns and brainstorm a path forward. Rather than "what" the student did, Greene's method focuses more on "why and when" the behavior occurred. If the solution does not address the problem, the problem grows.

Troubling, aggressive, unacceptable behavior might begin with bullying—playground pushing, shoving, and rude language. This behavior is stressful for teachers and more difficult to tackle than instructional challenges. Unfortunately, without intervention, bullies can become increasingly aggressive and antisocial (Crothers & Kolbert, *Intervention in School and Clinic*, 2008).

Intervention is now legally mandated in most states. Anti-bullying legislation is on the books in 48 states; the first law passed in 1999, partially in response to the Columbine shootings (Sacco, Silbaugh, Corredor, Casey & Doherty, *Overview of state anti-bullying legislation and other related laws*, 2012, http://cyber.law.harvard.edu). These laws varied widely in definitions, expectations, and required training for school personnel.

In *Bullying and students with disabilities* (2011, www.ncd.gov), Young, Ne'eman, and Gelser report that very little research and policy address this particular topic. Existing studies showed that students with visible and invisible disabilities were "uniquely vulnerable and disproportionately impacted by the bullying phenomena." The briefing paper suggests that bullying could jeopardize the civil rights of students with disabilities, limiting their access to education because of social isolation and ridicule. Simultaneously, the authors note that when students with disabilities are suspected of exhibiting bullying behavior, IDEA's rules regarding manifestation determination override any state-specified consequences.

Educators weigh strategies to address an individual's behavior as well as comprehensive approaches to building a schoolwide set of expectations, consequences, and supports. Legal requirements affect decisions. This area is challenging, but must be actively discussed by every faculty.

# YES

Howard S. Adelman
and Linda Taylor

# Rethinking How Schools Address Student Misbehavior and Disengagement

T he essence of good classroom teaching is the ability to create an environment that first can mobilize the learner to pursue the curriculum and then can maintain that mobilization, while effectively facilitating learning. The process, of course, is meant not only to teach academics but [also] to turn out good citizens. While many terms are used, this societal aim requires that a fundamental focus of school improvement be on facilitating positive social and emotional development/learning.

Behavior problems clearly get in the way of all this. Misbehavior disrupts. In some forms, such as bullying and intimidating others, it is hurtful. And, observing such behavior may disinhibit others. Because of this, discipline and classroom management are daily topics at every school.

Concern about responding to behavior problems and promoting social and emotional learning are related and are embedded into the six arenas we frame to encompass the content of student/learning supports. How these concerns are addressed is critical to the type of school and classroom climate that emerges and to student engagement and re-engagement in classroom learning. As such, they need to be fully integrated into school improvement efforts.

## Disengaged Students, Misbehavior, and Social Control

After an extensive review of the literature, Fredricks, Blumenfeld, and Paris conclude: *Engagement is associated with positive academic outcomes, including achievement and persistence in school; and it is higher in classrooms with supportive teachers and peers, challenging and authentic tasks, opportunities for choice, and sufficient structure.* Conversely, for many students, disengagement is associated with behavior and learning problems and eventual dropout. The degree of concern about student engagement varies depending on school population.

In general, teachers focus on content to be taught and knowledge and skills to be acquired—with a mild amount of attention given to the process

From *Addressing Barriers to Learning,* vol. 13, no. 2, Spring 2008, pp. 1–2, 4–6. Copyright © 2008 by UCLA Center for Mental Health in Schools. Reprinted by permission. http://smhp .psych.ucla.edu of engaging students. All this works fine in schools where most students come each day ready and able to deal with what the teacher is ready and able to teach. Indeed, teachers are fortunate when they have a classroom where the majority of students show up and are receptive to the planned lessons. In schools that are the greatest focus of public criticism, this certainly is not the case.

What most of us realize, at least at some level, is that teachers in such settings are confronted with an entirely different teaching situation. Among the various supports they absolutely must have are ways to re-engage students who have become disengaged and often resistant to broadband (nonpersonalized) teaching approaches. To the dismay of most teachers, however, strategies for re-engaging students in *learning* rarely are a prominent part of pre- or in-service preparation and seldom are the focus of interventions pursued by professionals whose role is to support teachers and students. As a result, they learn more about *socialization* and *social control* as classroom management strategies than about how to engage and re-engage students in classroom learning, which is the key to enhancing and sustaining good behavior.

## Reacting to Misbehavior

When a student misbehaves, a natural reaction is to want that youngster to experience and other students to see the consequences of misbehaving. One hope is that public awareness of consequences will deter subsequent problems. As a result, a considerable amount of time at schools is devoted to discipline and classroom management.

An often stated assumption is that stopping a student's misbehavior will make her or him amenable to teaching. In a few cases, this may be so. However, the assumption ignores all the research that has led to understanding *psychological reactance* and the need for individuals to maintain and restore a sense of self-determination. Moreover, it belies two painful realities: the number of students who continue to manifest poor academic achievement and the staggering dropout rate in too many schools.

Unfortunately, in their efforts to deal with deviant and devious behavior and to create safe environments, too many schools overrely on negative consequences and plan only for social control. Such practices model behavior that can foster rather than counter the development of negative values and often produce other forms of undesired behavior. Moreover, the tactics often make schools look and feel more like prisons than community treasures.

In schools, short of suspending a student, punishment essentially takes the form of a decision to do something that the student does not want done. In addition, a demand for future compliance usually is made, along with threats of harsher punishment if compliance is not forthcoming. The discipline may be administered in ways that suggest the student is seen as an undesirable person. As students get older, suspension increasingly comes into play. Indeed, suspension remains one of the most common disciplinary responses for the transgressions of secondary students.

As with many emergency procedures, the benefits of using punishment may be offset by many negative consequences. These include increased negative attitudes toward school and school personnel. These attitudes often lead to more behavior problems, anti-social acts, and various mental health problems. Because disciplinary procedures also are associated with dropping out of school, it is not surprising that some concerned professionals refer to extreme disciplinary practices as "pushout" strategies.

In general, specific discipline practices should be developed with the aim of leaving no child behind. That is, *stopping misbehavior must be accomplished in ways that maximize the likelihood that the teacher can engage/re-engage the student in instruction and positive learning.*

The growing emphasis on positive approaches to reducing misbehavior and enhancing support for positive behavior in and out-of-the-classroom is a step in the right direction. So is the emphasis in school guidelines stressing that discipline should be reasonable, fair, and non-denigrating (e.g., should be experienced by recipients as legitimate reactions that neither denigrate one's sense of worth nor reduce one's sense of autonomy).

Moreover, in recognizing that the application of consequences is an insufficient step in preventing future misbehavior, there is growing awareness that school improvements that engage and re-engage students reduce behavior (and learning) problems significantly. That is why school improvement efforts need to delineate

- efforts to prevent and anticipate misbehavior
- actions to be taken during misbehavior that do minimal harm to engagement in classroom learning
- steps to be taken afterwards that include a focus on enhancing engagement. . . .

# Focusing on Underlying Motivation to Address Concerns About Engagement

Moving beyond socialization, social control, and behavior modification and with an emphasis on engagement, there is a need to address the roots of misbehavior, especially underlying motivational bases. Consider students who spend most of the day trying to avoid all or part of the instructional program. An *intrinsic* motivational interpretation of the avoidance behavior of many of these youngsters is that it reflects their perception that school is not a place where they experience a sense of competence, autonomy, and/or relatedness to others. Over time, these perceptions develop into strong motivational dispositions and related patterns of misbehavior.

## Misbehavior Can Reflect Proactive (Approach) or Reactive (Avoidance) Motivation

Noncooperative, disruptive, and aggressive behavior patterns that are *proactive* tend to be rewarding and satisfying to an individual because the behavior itself is exciting or because the behavior leads to desired outcomes (e.g., peer recognition [and] feelings of competence or autonomy). Intentional negative behavior stemming from such approach motivation can be viewed as pursuit of deviance.

Misbehavior in the classroom may also be *reactive,* stemming from avoidance motivation. This behavior can be viewed as protective reactions. Students with learning problems can be seen as motivated to avoid and to protest against being forced into situations in which they cannot cope effectively. For such students, many teaching situations are perceived in this way. Under such circumstances, individuals can be expected to react by trying to protect themselves from the unpleasant thoughts and feelings that the situations stimulate (e.g., feelings of incompetence, loss of autonomy, [and] negative relationships). In effect, the misbehavior reflects efforts to cope and defend against aversive experiences. The actions may be direct or indirect and include defiance, physical and psychological withdrawal, and diversionary tactics.

## Interventions for Reactive and Proactive Behavior Problems Begin with Major Program Changes

From a motivational perspective, the aims are to (a) prevent and overcome negative attitudes toward school and learning, (b) enhance motivational readiness for learning and overcoming problems, (c) maintain intrinsic motivation throughout learning and problem solving, and (d) nurture the type of continuing motivation that results in students engaging in activities away from school that foster maintenance, generalization, and expansion of learning and problem solving. Failure to attend to motivational concerns in a comprehensive, normative way results in approaching passive and often hostile students with practices that instigate and exacerbate problems.

After making broad programmatic changes to the degree feasible, intervention with a misbehaving student involves remedial steps directed at underlying factors. For instance, with intrinsic motivation in mind, the following assessment questions arise:

- Is the misbehavior unintentional or intentional?
- If it is intentional, is it reactive or proactive?
- If the misbehavior is reactive, is it a reaction to threats to self-determination, competence, or relatedness?
- If it is proactive, are there other interests that might successfully compete with satisfaction derived from deviant behavior?

In general, intrinsic motivation theory suggests that corrective interventions for those misbehaving reactively requires steps designed to reduce reactance and enhance positive motivation for participation. For youngsters highly motivated to pursue deviance (e.g., those who proactively engage in criminal acts), even more is needed. Intervention might focus on helping these youngsters identify and follow through on a range of valued, socially appropriate alternatives to deviant activity. Such alternatives must be capable of producing greater feelings of self-determination, competence, and relatedness than usually result from the youngster's deviant actions. To these ends, motivational analyses of the problem can point to corrective steps for implementation by teachers, clinicians, parents, or students themselves.

# Promoting Social and Emotional Learning

One facet of addressing misbehavior proactively is the focus on promoting healthy social and emotional development. This emphasis meshes well with a school's goals related to enhancing students' personal and social well being. And, it is essential to creating an atmosphere of "caring," "cooperative learning," and a "sense of community" (including greater home involvement).

In some form or another, every school has goals that emphasize a desire to enhance students' personal and social functioning. Such goals reflect an understanding that social and emotional growth plays an important role in

- enhancing the daily smooth functioning of schools and the emergence of a safe, caring, and supportive school climate
- facilitating students' holistic development
- enabling student motivation and capability for academic learning
- optimizing life beyond schooling.

An agenda for promoting social and emotional learning encourages family-centered orientation. It stresses practices that increase positive engagement in learning at school and that enhance personal responsibility (social and moral), integrity, self-regulation (self-discipline), a work ethic, diverse talents, and positive feelings about self and others.

It should be stressed at this point that, for most individuals, learning social skills and emotional regulation are part of normal development and socialization. Thus, social and emotional learning is not primarily a formal training process. This can be true even for some individuals who are seen as having behavior and emotional problems. (While poor social skills are identified as a symptom and contributing factor in a wide range of educational, psychosocial, and mental health problems, it is important to remember that symptoms are correlates.)

## What Is Social and Emotional Learning?

As formulated by the Collaborative for Academic, Social, and Emotional Learning (CASEL), social and emotional learning (SEL) "is a process for helping children and even adults develop the fundamental skills for life effectiveness. SEL teaches the skills we all need to handle ourselves, our relationships, and our work, effectively and ethically. These skills include recognizing and managing our emotions, developing caring and concern for others, establishing positive relationships, making responsible decisions, and handling challenging situations constructively and ethically. They are the skills that allow children to calm themselves when angry, make friends, resolve conflicts respectfully, and make ethical and safe choices."

CASEL also views SEL as "providing a framework for school improvement. Teaching SEL skills helps create and maintain safe, caring learning environments. The most beneficial programs provide sequential and developmentally appropriate instruction in SEL skills. They are implemented in a coordinated manner, school-wide, from preschool through high school.

Lessons are reinforced in the classroom, during out-of-school activities, and at home. Educators receive ongoing professional development in SEL. And families and schools work together to promote children's social, emotional, and academic success."

Because of the scope of SEL programming, the work is conceived as multi-year. The process stresses adult modeling and coaching and student practice to solidify learning related to social and emotional awareness of self and others, self-management, responsible decision making, and relationship skills.

## Natural Opportunities to Promote Social and Emotional Learning

Sometimes the agenda for promoting social and emotional learning takes the form of a special curriculum (e.g., social skills training, character education, [and] assets development) or is incorporated into the regular curricula. However, classroom and school-wide practices can and need to do much more to (a) capitalize on *natural* opportunities at schools to promote social and emotional development and (b) minimize transactions that interfere with positive growth in these areas. Natural opportunities are one of the most authentic examples of "teachable moments."

An appreciation of what needs more attention can be garnered readily by looking at the school day and school year through the lens of goals for personal and social functioning. Is instruction carried out in ways that strengthen or hinder development of interpersonal skills and connections and student understanding of self and others? Is cooperative learning and sharing promoted? Is counterproductive competition minimized? Are interpersonal conflicts mainly suppressed or are they used as learning opportunities? Are roles provided for all students to be positive helpers throughout the school and community?

The Center's website offers specific examples of natural opportunities and how to respond to them in ways that promote personal and social growth. . . .

## The Promise of Promoting Social and Emotional Learning

Programs to improve social skills and interpersonal problem solving are described as having promise both for prevention and correction. However, reviewers tend to be cautiously optimistic because so many studies have found the range of skills acquired are quite limited and so is the generalizability and maintenance of outcomes. This is the case for training of specific skills (e.g., what to say and do in a specific situation), general strategies (e.g., how to generate a wider range of interpersonal problem-solving options), as well as efforts to develop cognitive-affective orientations, such as empathy training. Reviews of social skills training over several decades conclude that individual studies show effectiveness, but outcome studies often have shown lack of generalizability and social validity. However, the focus has been mainly on social skills training for students with emotional and behavior disorders.

Recent analyses by researchers involved with the Collaborative for Academic, Social, and Emotional Learning (CASEL) suggest that "students who receive SEL programming academically outperform their peers, compared to those who do not receive SEL. Those students also get better grades and graduate at higher rates. Effective SEL programming drives academic learning, and it also drives social outcomes such as positive peer relationships, caring and empathy, and social engagement. Social and emotional instruction also leads to reductions in problem behavior such as drug use, violence, and delinquency."

# Promotion of Mental Health

Promotion of mental health encompasses efforts to enhance knowledge, skills, and attitudes in order to foster social and emotional development, a healthy lifestyle, and personal well-being. Promoting healthy development, well-being, and a value-based life are important ends unto themselves and overlap primary, secondary, and tertiary interventions to prevent mental health and psychosocial problems.

Interventions to promote mental health encompass not only strengthening individuals but also enhancing nurturing and supportive conditions at school, at home, and in the neighborhood. All this includes a particular emphasis on increasing opportunities for personal development and empowerment by promoting conditions that foster and strengthen positive attitudes and behaviors (e.g., enhancing motivation and capability to pursue positive goals, resist negative influences, and overcome barriers). It also includes efforts to maintain and enhance physical health and safety and *inoculate* against problems (e.g., providing positive and negative information, skill instruction, and fostering attitudes that build resistance and resilience).

While schools alone are not responsible for this, they do play a significant role, albeit sometimes not a positive one, in social and emotional development. School improvement plans need to encompass ways the school will (1) *directly facilitate* social and emotional (as well as physical) development and (2) *minimize threats* to positive development (see references at end of this article). In doing so, appreciation of differences in levels of development and developmental demands at different ages is fundamental, and personalized implementation to account for individual differences is essential.

From a mental health perspective, helpful guidelines are found in research clarifying normal trends for school-age youngsters' efforts to feel *competent, self-determining,* and *connected with significant others.* And, measurement of such feelings can provide indicators of the impact of a school on mental health. Positive findings can be expected to correlate with school engagement and academic progress. Negative findings can be expected to correlate with student anxiety, fear, anger, alienation, a sense of losing control, a sense of hopelessness and powerlessness. In turn, these negative thoughts, feelings, and attitudes can lead to externalizing (aggressive, "acting out") or internalizing (withdrawal, self-punishing, delusional) behaviors.

Clearly, promoting mental health has payoffs both academically and for reducing problems at schools. Therefore, it seems evident that an enhanced commitment to mental health promotion must be a key facet of the renewed emphasis on the whole child by education leaders.

## Concluding Comments

Responding to behavior problems and promoting social and emotional development and learning can and should be done in the context of a comprehensive system designed to address barriers to learning and (re)engage students in classroom learning. In this respect, the developmental trend in thinking about how to respond to misbehavior must be toward practices that embrace an expanded view of engagement and human motivation and that includes a focus on social and emotional learning.

Relatedly, motivational research and theory are guiding the development of interventions designed to enhance student's motivation and counter disengagement. And, there is growing appreciation of the power of intrinsic motivation.

*Now, it is time for school improvement decision makers and planners to fully address these matters.*

William C. Frick and
Susan C. Faircloth

 **NO**

# Acting in the Collective and Individual "Best Interest of Students": When Ethical Imperatives Clash with Administrative Demands

The focus of this investigation was on how secondary principles interpret the experience of leadership decision making as a moral activity in relation to a specific ethical lens, the Ethic of the Profession, and its associated Model for Promoting Students' Best Interests. This ethical framework elevates the profession of educational leadership by positing a central moral ideal in the form of an injunction of special duty: "serve the best interests of the student" whereby "promoting the success of all students" by focusing on the individual needs of children. The Ethic of the Profession is an eclectic framework incorporating established ethical paradigms of justice, care, critique, and community not as totally distinct, incommensurable moral reasoning, but as complementary—a "tapestry of ethical perspectives that encourage . . . rich human response to . . . many uncertain ethical situations." The Ethic of the Profession indicates that a disparity exists between diverse ethical perspectives related to the education of students, professional codes meant to inform decision making and conduct, and the personal moral values of administrators that influence their judgment and behavior. When reflective school leaders attempt to integrate established ethical paradigms and professional and personal codes of ethics, the result is often moral dissonance, or a "clashing of codes." In responding to this inevitable discord, the Ethic of the Profession is grounded in a reasoned consideration of the educational shibboleth "serve the best interests of the students."

The student's best interests are the focal point of the Ethic of the Profession. A model for determining the best interests of the student consists of a robust focus on the essential nature of individual rights, the duty of responsibility to others for a common interest, and respect as mutual acknowledgment of others as having worth, value, and dignity unto themselves.

An important consideration for this investigation was the distinction practicing secondary school administrators make between the best interests of the student (one) and the best interests of the students (all or most). In reviewing the literature on the best interests of students, Walker indicates

William C. Frick and Susan C. Faircloth. From *Journal of Special Education Leadership*, 20(1), March 2007, pp. 21–22, 23, 24, 25–29 (excerpts). Copyright © 2007 by Council of Administrators of Special Education (CASE). Reprinted by permission.

that "the interests of children supersede the interests of all other interests." Walker argues, however, that it may be very difficult to know with precision and appositeness what the best interests of students might be. The Ethic of the Profession and its Model for Promoting Students' Best Interests clearly and intentionally refer to the best interests of the student (one) as opposed to the best interests of students (group, many, or all). This ethical frame does not recognize a difference between the two perspectives and purports that

> if the individual student is treated with fairness, justice, and caring, then a strong message is sent to all students that they will be treated with similar justice and caring and that they should treat others similarly. Thus, rights carry with them responsibilities, so much so that the rights of one individual should not bring harm to the group.

The (individual) student's best interests are at the center of the Ethic of the Profession and, according to this decision-making framework, individuals (particularly students) possess inherent worth and dignity unto themselves and they need not strive to maintain their value. With this said, educational leaders must first decide if the individual is acting responsibly in asserting his or her rights. If not, there are opportunities to teach responsibility, which is challenging and requires vigilance, but the potential is great for students to share responsibility for their own development.

## Purpose of the Study

. . . [The] primary intent in this study was to pilot the use of this frame in the field of education leadership to test the explanations and definitions of what professional moral practice entails, defined by the Ethic of the Profession and its Model for Promoting Student's Best Interests, compared to the explanations and definitions practitioners use. The focus was on practicing administrators' understanding of the expression "the best interests of the student" and additional aspects of moral practice and reasoning removed from classroom or seminar settings.

## Method

As part of the overall study from which this specific research is derived, verification was sought as to whether or not educational leaders could relate experiences of discord between organizational policies and professional expectations meant to inform judgment, decision making, and conduct and their own personal moral values (whether held privately or expressed publicly). In addition, this research investigation sought to know and understand how the expression "the best interests of the student" was defined and used in decision making. . . .

### Participants

. . . A range of people occupying the position of secondary school principal were sought as participants for this research. Secondary principals were selected because of their work in managing the size, scale, and level of problems associated with a complex and often bureaucratic service organization. This range of participants constituted a broad variety of individual and contextual factors and backgrounds. . . . Three female and eight male principals participated in this study. One male and one female were black and the other nine were white. Participants ranged in age from 35 to 55 years old and had worked in their administrative role from 2 to 19 years. The size of student enrollment in participants' respective schools ranged from 80 to 2200, with two principals serving in rural schools, three serving in suburban schools, three serving in suburban/ metro schools, and three in urban schools. . . .

## Findings

As a result of the focus and stamina required to lead an entire school organization, each participant in this study indicated in some fashion a sharp distinction and clear difference between the best interests of individual students and the best interests of students as a group. The distinction administrators made was markedly different from the conceptual framework guiding this study. They viewed the work of deciding and acting in the best interests of the student body as being qualitatively different from working with individual students. Participants indicated that balancing the two priorities was difficult, but essential, within the confines of a bureaucratic institution.

In their daily work, most principals thought about the best interests of students in general, as a corporate body, and when specific student-related issues came to their attention they would alter their perspective on students' best interests and focus on unique, individual student needs. This pattern of thought was prevalent and consistent across participants in terms of their interpretation of the expression "the best interest of the student." . . .

A young, male high school principal put it this way: "You look at each situation, and I think [about] a decision: How many kids can I impact versus how many may I not impact, across the board?" A similar attitude was expressed by a veteran high school administrator who said:

> I think there are times when you have to do things in the collective best interests. There is no question you have to do things sometimes that a student may have to have an issue sacrificed for the benefit of the entire student body, or for the safety of the student body, or for a variety of reasons. And because we do work within a system, we're not working in a private setting where we can handle each student individually: we're working in a system where we have to handle the entire global group. So yeah, people are sometimes, I hate to say people are sacrificed, but their issue may be sacrificed for the benefit of all. That's a bureaucratic issue.

Another principal communicated the view of focusing primarily on individual student needs and best interests as specified in the Model for Promoting Students' Best Interests when he explained, "Given certain circumstances, you can send a message to the entire student body based on what happens to an individual." Although he believed focusing on a case by case treatment of individual students can have some effect on the best interests of the entire student body, this level of individual interaction was not sufficient for ensuring a complete consideration of the best interests of all students under his supervision.

Although the principals' first order of business was considering, deciding, and acting in the best interests of students as a group, they were cognizant of the potential danger of the distinction, especially when, according to one participant, "you just give people what they need" at an individual rather than a group level. The perspectives participants held about balancing what was in the best interests of one student as opposed to an entire group were diverse. Most believed that public schooling was becoming increasingly individualized and student centered, with planning and interventions designed to address the needs and talents of every student, whereas other principals expressed their frustration with public education and organizational life where "political correctness" and a "one size fits all approach" dictated how to respond when addressing students' needs or seeking to serve their best interests.

The majority of the principals focused on special education policy to illustrate the qualitative difference, in their view, between the best interests of the student (one) and the best interests of the students (all or most). It was difficult for principals to address the best interests of the student (one), although they would have liked to, because of policies and protections for groups of students. One aspect (instructional) of the policies and protections resonated with their moral notions of equity, fairness, and social justice whereas the other aspect (discipline) was morally troubling and restrictive and did not address the best interest of the individual student.

The two contrasting views, one of student-centered discretion and the other a one size fits all way of doing business, were fueled by the same source—special education mandates and the provisions of the Individuals with Disabilities Education Improvement Act (IDEIA) and the No Child Left Behind Act (NCLB). Most principals fully supported IDEIA and the current direction of public education. For example, a female high school principal indicated that "what's best for all is not necessarily what's best for the individual. Education these days is working toward the needs of each child, [such as] differentiation of instruction and curriculum in the classroom. This is a good thing." This view was also held by a young, male, rural high school principal who imagined that public education will eventually remake itself into an endeavor centered on serving individual student needs, promoting each student's success, and attending to "best interests" at an individual/personal level. He said:

> I think we're always going to make [decisions for] the best interests
> of the whole. That's been the direction of education, but then we are
> prescribing more of what is in the individual best interests of certain
> students, and it's likely to continue on that track. I think we're going to
> be doing more of that now. . . . Every day we think about our services
> for special education; what we're doing in special education. I think
> we've got to service kids. I think we're obligated to do that, [but] I think
> we're overprotective of special education. I think it's a copout when we
> put the responsibility to work with low achieving or special needs kids

on special education teachers. I think it's everybody's responsibility to work with those special needs kids. . . . I think there'll be a point where, I mean people keep laughing about this, and they've been laughing about this 10, 15, 20 years ago when they said, "Every kid is going to have an IEP. I think we're headed that way, I really do. We're headed in a direction where we're really individualizing a lot of decision making and the way things are being done."

Other principals took a completely different perspective on the "direction education was headed." One middle school principal believed that the balance between the individual and the group was skewed more toward the group, particularly in instructional matters. He was deeply disturbed by this type of attitude and indicated that uniform treatment of all students did not achieve the goals and purposes of public education. He said:

> I think we have a philosophy in education today that we believe that one size fits all. . . . There needs to be more recognition of the uniqueness of mankind and individual needs in that one size doesn't fit all—people haven't sensed that uniqueness or that specialness in a sea of numbers. And I think that sometimes we lose masses because that's not occurring.

Expressing this position in a more critical tone, a veteran high school principal did not mince words about his viewpoints when it came to the restrictions placed on him by special education policy when desiring to make decisions in, what he believed to be, the best interests of students. He spoke primarily about student discipline and how the balance between individual and group is skewed because of the standards of uniform treatment he must comply with based on federal, state, and district policy. His frustration was about treating every student in a protected class the same way, or within the parameters of restrictive policy mandates, without being granted the administrative discretion and decision making necessary to respond to students in their best interests. . . . He indicated:

> Public education dictates to you what you can and can't say, or do, or feel, or be; because you are all things to all people—that's the nature of public education. And a result of that, being all things to all people . . . my own personal positions are inconsequential for the most part, unless it's a major philosophical issue. There are many things that are [a major philosophical issue], but because we live in a politically correct world, we cannot deal with things that are actual . . . and so as a result of that, we cannot act on what we know to be true, we have to act on what the public perceives to be acceptable, so that is a dilemma sometimes.

The same principal illustrated the tension he feels when complying with special class protections and his desire to respond morally, decide and act ethically, and deal with students as individuals. The extended quote that follows illustrates the importance, for this principal, of engaging and responding to students on a personal and individual level rather than being forced to decide and act in the best interests of students as a group. According to this participant, there is a moral danger in dictated and uniform prescriptions for attending to and managing students as a group that essentially ignore or do away with administrative discretion.

> I have special education questions every single day. What's best for the child? Well in this building we have 470 special education students. So there's a large group, and I think the moral questions come every day: What's right for those particular students? I think, in weighing that out [it] combines with What's right then for regular education students? You look at them as separate tracks. Clearly the moral dilemma is there: 'How can I treat two people who do the same thing totally differently and still acquire some integrity of fairness?' The answer is you can't. So you do the best you can. Knowing the fact that if I have a special education student sitting here, he has a knife on him; he's OK to have that knife on him because he is a special education student. And I have a regular education student with the same knife on him, and I have to expel him for a year and this [special education] kid doesn't get anything because it's OK—that's a moral dilemma for me. It's a moral dilemma for me when I have a special education student extort money from a student in the hallway, and I have a regular education student extort money in the hallway, and I have to suspend one or expel one and not the other. It's a moral dilemma when . . . I have a special education student punch a teacher in a fight and a regular education student punch a teacher in a fight [and] one's expelled for assaulting staff, the other one gets nothing because the parent won't agree to a suspension. That's a moral dilemma for me—that's a problem for me, because that's wrong. No matter how you cut that up in my mind that's wrong. I know there's somebody . . . somewhere that could cut that up in their own mind and make that right. I can't do that, and I've not been able to do that over 32 years' time. Pretty sure it won't change in the next five or ten.

More than half of the principals in this study focused on special education policy to illustrate the qualitative difference, in their view, between the best interest of the student (one) and the best interests of the students (all or most). Results of this study, specific to handling special education student issues, indicate that it is difficult to address the best interests of the student (one), although the participants would have liked to, because of educational policies and protection for groups of students. Although the instructional aspects of the policies and protections resonated with participants' moral notions of equity, fairness, and social justice, the disciplinary aspects of the same policies and protections were morally troubling and restrictive and did not address the best interest of the individual student.

## Discussion

The turbulent intersection of education policy, professional ethics, and personal morality became evident as participants talked about working with students on an individual basis. . . . Serving the best interests of the student meant being fair and acting fairly, and in the eyes of participants who talked about fairness as a principle or virtue, the rule or quality was immensely important. However, fairness required responding with personal investment to each student based on their unique needs, not being inextricably tied to formulaic procedures or regulations that did not allow for reasonable distinctions between equality and equity. As one respondent indicated, "You just give people [students] what they need" at an individual level. It seems that participants would not want to be questioned about why they were not doling out the same treatment or responding and acting in the same, uniform manner toward every student.

. . . The principals in this study described the difficulties they experienced, both externally by way of publicly defending their decisions and actions to others and internally as a moral struggle between their own sense of fairness as equity and the uniform procedures and policies that were to be applied equally to all students.

Principals expressed, in a variety of ways, the importance of treating students equitably. . . . Another principal put the matter this way:

> I think we struggle with what is fair and consistent. We have to treat everybody as an individual, but we have to be consistent with our discipline. I know sometimes we have to weigh it. How is it going to be looked at by the rest of the kids or the faculty if one thing happens to this kid who did the same behavior as another kid? See, they don't get the background information. . . . You definitely have to keep your faculty happy; you have to be supportive and let them know you're backing them up, but they don't know that we can't treat everybody the same sometimes for the same behavior because there's circumstances out there. I wish some people would just understand that and even parents too.

# Implications

## Implications for Practice

This study raises important questions regarding . . . preparing building-level administrators, to respond to the dilemmas that arise when the best interests of the individual student clash with the best interests of students as a whole. The potential for such dilemma is clearly illustrated by the increasing demand on school leaders to meet the individual needs of children with special educational needs as mandated by the IDEIA and the often competing demands of NCLBA, which may be described as being directed toward the more collective interests of students as a group rather than individual students.

## Implications for Policy

To assist school leaders in navigating these potential ethical and administrative dilemmas, policy makers must give increased attention to the ways in which the implementation of current and future policies affects school leaders' abilities to respond to individual student needs as well as fosters and sustains inclusive learning environments for all students. An example of such action includes recent federal policy discussions pertaining to the use of the Response to Intervention (RTI) model, which may have the potential to assist educators in more effectively addressing student academic and learning needs as well as disciplinary and behavioral issues. Using the RTI model may assist building-level principals and their staff in mitigating what principals, such as those in this study, identify and experience as qualitative differences between responding to the best interests of the student (one) and responding to the best interests of the students (all or most). As noted earlier in the findings, in addition to the instructional aspects of special education policies and protections, it may be easier for some school leaders to equate the provision of instructional accommodations and adaptations with the moral notions of equity, fairness, and social justice, whereas the disciplinary aspects may be viewed as morally troubling, restrictive, and at odds with the practice of meeting the best interest of the individual student. Again, this illustrates the potential for both administrative and ethical dilemmas for school leaders. . . .

## Conclusion

As discussed, principals in this investigation expressed satisfaction in their press for equitable responses to student learning needs, particularly for those students identified as requiring special instructional services. In contrast, participants reported a significant unsettledness with special class protections that dismiss, and thereby limit, the principal's ability to take fair and just disciplinary actions. These findings suggest that secondary principals, who play a significant role in special education leadership in their respective building assignments, experience a moral tension between serving the best instructional interests of each identified student under their supervision and care and the disciplinary policies and procedural regulations that limit, according to participants' perspectives, moral discretion, ethical judgment, and reasonable retributive justice pertaining to student disciplinary matters. Although special education disciplinary policies and procedural regulations were created and enforced to preserve students' rights to a free and appropriate education as a protected class, some principals ironically view these policies and regulations as morally and ethically inadequate in addressing individual student needs.

Given the complexity of today's educational system, it is imperative that school leaders be skilled in balancing the competing demands that emerge from the challenge to meet the best interests of the students as well as the best interests of all students. According to Donaldson, leadership that builds commitment to mutual moral purposes positions school leaders to respond justly and equitably to "increasingly diverse student needs and increasingly demanding societal needs . . . as agents of a 'free, appropriate education' for every American child" (pp. 49–50). Building such a commitment in the face of "pluralistic pressures" from a wide range of constituencies is one matter (Gardner, 1990), but attending to the best interests of the student in face-to-face encounters must be the first order of the day for school administrators. Before building broad and lasting collective commitment to moral purposes, principals need to find ethical satisfaction in the decisions they make, about individual students.

# EXPLORING THE ISSUE

## Can Whole-School Reform Reduce Discipline Problems?

## Challenge Questions

- Compare and contrast the positions of the YES and NO selections regarding whether whole-school reform can reduce discipline problems.
- Which selection makes the best case for its argument? Why?
- How do your local schools address behavior, bullying, and discipline? How do they measure up to recommended practices?
- What are the practices your school follows regarding manifestation determination? How do they compare with the information in this section?

## Is There Common Ground?

This issue's authors share the belief that safe schools are essential to learning and that teaching is to be valued over punishment. They also agree that it is challenging, but essential, to strike a balance between what is good for the student body and what is good for a single student.

## Additional Resources

Adelman, H. S. & Taylor, L. (2008b). *Mental health in school and school improvement: Current status, concerns and new directions.* Center for Mental Health in Schools. Retrieved February 6, 2008 from http://smhp.psych.ucla.edu/mhbook/mhbookintro.htm

Bullock, L. M. (2006). Introduction to the special issue: Alternative schooling—A viable approach to educating our children and youth. *Preventing School Failure, 51*(1), 3–4.

Crothers, L. M. & Kolbert, J. B. (2008). Tackling a problematic behavior management issue: Teachers' intervention in childhood bullying problems. *Intervention in School and Clinic, 43*(3), 132–139.

Greene, R. (2010). Calling all frequent flyers. *Educational Leadership, 68*(2), 28–34.

Hughes, A. F. & Adera, B. (2006). Education and day treatment opportunities in schools: Strategies that work. *Preventing School Failure, 51*(1), 26–30.

Osborne, A. G., Jr. & Russo, C. J. (2007). Making the manifestation determination under IDEA 2004. *ELA Notes,* Second Quarter, 4–7.

Quinn, M. M., Poirier, J. M., Fuller, S. E., Gable, R. A., & Tonelson, S. W. (2006). An examination of school climate in effective alternative programs. *Preventing School Failure, 51*(1), 11–17.

Sacco, D. T., Silbaugh, K., Corredor, F., Casey, J., & Doherty, D. (2012, February 23). *An overview of state anti-bullying legislation and other related laws.* The Kinder & Braver World Project. Retrieved June 2, 2012 from http://cyber.law.harvard .edu/sites/cyber.law.harvard.edu/files/State_Anti_bullying_Legislation_Overview_0 .pdf

Tissington, L. D. (2006). History: Our hope for the future. *Preventing School Failure, 51*(1), 19–25.

Trussell, R. P. (2008). Classroom universals to prevent problem behaviors. *Intervention in School and Clinic, 43*(3), 179–185.

Van Acker, R. (2007). Antisocial, aggressive, and violent behavior in children and adolescents within alternative education settings: Prevention and intervention. *Preventing School Failure, 51*(2), 5–12.

Young, J., Ne'eman, A., & Gelser, S. (2011). *Bullying and students with disabilities: A briefing paper from the National Council on Disabilities.* Retrieved June 2, 2012 from www.ncd.gov

Zirkel, P. A. (2006). Manifestation determinations under the Individuals with Disabilities Education Act: What the new causality criteria mean. *Journal of Special Education Leadership, 192*, 3–12.

# ISSUE 6

# Are Charter Schools a Good Choice for Students with Disabilities?

YES: **Mitt Romney**, from *A Chance for Every Child: Mitt Romney's Plan for Restoring the Promise of American Education* (2012), www.mittromney.com, May 24, 2012

NO: **Thomas Hehir**, from "Hearing on The All Students Achieving through Reform Act of 2009, H.R. 4330," Hearing Before the Committee on Education and Labor, House of Representatives, 111th Cong. (2010) (Statement of Mr. Thomas Hehir), http://edlabor.house .gov/documents/111/pdf/statements/20100224GMHearingStatement.pdf

---

### Learning Outcomes

**At the conclusion of this issue, readers will be able to:**

- Compare and contrast the positions of the YES and NO selections addressing whether charter schools are a good choice for students with disabilities.
- Describe the strengths and the weaknesses of each side's arguments.
- Consider the options parents should weigh when considering charter school enrollment for their child with a disability.
- Identify challenges that face charter schools endeavoring to enroll students with disabilities.

---

### ISSUE SUMMARY

**YES:** Mitt Romney, Republican contender for the presidency and former governor of Massachusetts, proposes to improve options for all children, especially those from low-income families and those with special needs, by using U.S. federal grant funds to increase access to more desirable, innovative charter schools.

**NO:** Thomas Hehir, prominent educational policymaker, agrees that charter schools can offer desirable options. Testifying in front of Congress, Hehir expresses his strong concern that the doors of

**113**

charter schools are often closed to students with disabilities. He cautions that these closed doors might constitute a denial of civil rights.

School choice, a major component of education reform, offers parents alternatives to their neighborhood school. States determine the breadth of choice available. Intra-district options range from open-enrollment programs to magnet schools emphasizing thematic education. Depending on state law, charter schools may be considered part of a school district or a distinct district unto themselves.

Today's 5,000 charter schools owe their existence to a Minnesota law passed in 1991. Post-Katrina, the majority of New Orleans children attend charter schools, many of which are operated by the Orleans Parish School Board, which also oversees traditional schools (Weber, http//works.bepress.com, 2009). Some companies, referred to as education management organizations (EMO), coordinate a network of schools. Green Dot (www.greendot.org) focuses its efforts on Los Angeles. KIPP Schools (Knowledge is Power Program: www.kipp.org) are found across the country.

Charter schools are funded by direct transfers from the public schools' annual budget. When a child moves from a public school to a charter school, a sum of money, intended to cover per pupil operating costs, is transferred from the public school to the charter school.

States determine the regulations governing charter schools, each of which must be approved by an authorizer to gain existence. Proposers present a charter containing a mission statement, performance goals, and accountability procedures. States may designate local school districts to review, approve, and monitor charter schools or delegate this responsibility to private agencies. The National Association of Charter School Authorizers (www.qualitycharters.org) supports and represents member agencies.

Charter and private schools are exempt from many of the rules that structure (some say bind) public schools. Charters have the latitude to create unique and innovative curricula. They do not need to hire licensed teachers. Union contracts are rare, although some are beginning to appear. This range of flexibility is intended to stimulate more attractive alternatives for all children, compared to those found in bureaucracy-laden neighborhood public schools.

Although free from many regulations, privately funded and charter schools must abide by U.S. federal laws ensuring equal access to educational opportunities for students with disabilities. Although these regulations prohibit discrimination through the Americans with Disabilities Act (ADA), many of IDEA's specific protections are not always made available.

Charter schools typically enroll a lower percentage of children with disabilities than public schools (CREDO, 2010). The students with disabilities who are enrolled usually have mild disabilities, although some charter schools focus entirely on students with severe disabilities. This issue focuses on whether charters are a good choice for students with disabilities.

In the YES selection, Mitt Romney, Republican contender for the presidency of the United States, describes an educational system strengthened by robust, well-funded charter schools. In Romney's vision, children from low-income environments and those with disabilities find hope in the creative innovation possible in charter schools. Their access would be enhanced by overhauling two key U.S. federal laws (ESEA and IDEA) to provide individual sums of money so that parents could choose the best school.

In the NO selection, Tom Hehir, an educational leader in many arenas, proclaims his support for charter schools. At a congressional hearing on legislation to create competitive grants to replicate successful charter schools, Hehir testified that the charter school experiment would be in jeopardy if schools don't serve the full range of students. He worried about possible civil rights violations that might arise from continued under-enrollment of children with disabilities. In his testimony, Tom Hehir also calls for accountability. Acknowledging that charters may serve students with disabilities in inclusive settings, he voices concern that their numbers are small, and include few children with severe disabilities. To ensure that students with disabilities have equal opportunity, and that charter schools are fairly evaluated, Hehir urged Congress to require equal access as a condition of receiving U.S. federal funds.

Speaking at the same congressional hearing, Greg Richmond, president and CEO of the National Association of Charter School Authorizers, expressed pleasure at the Obama administration's support for charters, but concern about little administrative financial support for oversight activities. He believes strongly that charters offer fine educational opportunities, but cautions that some may need the structured monitoring of an authorizer to ensure that all children have access to those opportunities.

Education Secretary Arne Duncan likes charter schools because they "think differently" (Duncan 2009). Signaling the Obama administration's belief that charters make a significant contribution to student learning, criteria for receiving Race to the Top funds included a requirement that states encourage and support charters, along with other innovative school programs. Additionally, applicants must have provided assurance that low-performing schools might be turned over to a charter-management organization.

Robin Lake and Bethany Gross author *Hopes, fears, and reality*, an annual report examining current controversies and evidence regarding charter schools (2012, www.crpe.org). In a chapter focusing on students with "special needs," Lake and Gross comment, like Romney, that many of these students "have never been adequately served in public education." Simultaneously, they find common ground with Hehir, observing that on average, charter schools enroll a smaller percentage of students with disabilities than do their local public schools. This average masks a considerable range, with some schools focusing on students with a particular disability and other charters reporting no students with disabilities. Lake and Gross note that there is no definitive reason for this variation; a number of possibilities exist. Some students could be counseled away from admission by schools who feel their mission is not a good fit for the student; other students might leave their formal special education designation behind as they find a match with a charter's unique program.

Issued biennially, the Center for Education Reform (CER) disseminates results of annual surveys of charter schools. The most recent report (*Annual survey of America's charter schools*, 2010, www.edreform.com) highlights the creative programs its respondents provide. Small group instruction, extended school time, and independent teachers help charters "excel" at creating programs and curricula that better support what CER describes as "children who are being failed by a one-size-fits all education system."

Secretary Duncan shares observations with the authors of both selections. Mitt Romney notes variability in the outcomes of charter schools, but is impressed by the "dramatically positive" results with disadvantaged students. While lauding charter schools, Secretary Duncan also expressed concern that charter accomplishments are inconsistent. Studies by CREDO (http://credo.stanford.odu/home, 2010), a Stanford-based research organization focusing on education reform, presented data calling into question the achievements claimed by charter schools. On average, students in public and charter schools performed equally well. Referring to such findings as "a wake up call," Duncan encouraged charter schools to seek the accountability outlined in their charters.

Duncan also emphasizes the cautions voiced by Tom Hehir: the promise of charter schools must include the same student body that exists in public schools. In a report titled *Charter schools and students with disabilities: Preliminary analysis of the legal issues and areas of concern* (2012, www.cleweb.org), the Council of Parent Attorneys and Advocates urges policymakers to hold charter schools to their pledge—for all students.

The Council for Exceptional Children (CEC) (www.cec.sped.org), the largest international professional organization advocating for children with disabilities, emphasizes that charters need to abide by the ADA and Section 504 so that children with disabilities have equitable access. CEC offers an additional perspective. Some children with disabilities and their parents may decide to forfeit their special education status when enrolling in a charter, believing the instructional environment worth the trade-off. When these students move on to higher education or employment, they may encounter barriers if they seek legally allowed accommodations. Since they were not considered to have a disability during school years, establishing that status might be challenging. Perhaps it won't be needed. Perhaps this is the outcome of choice.

# YES

**Mitt Romney**

## A Chance for Every Child: Mitt Romney's Plan for Restoring the Promise of American Education

### . . . Part I: The Imperative of Education Reform

Education has always been central to the American Dream. Families immigrated to the United States to secure a better education and a better life for their children. Parents saved from even the most modest paychecks to help their children pay for college. Students graduated from both high school and college confident that with their hard work would come valuable skills, with those skills a good-paying job, and with that job the promise of prosperity and an even better future for the next generation. Education guaranteed freedom—both the economic freedom of self-sufficiency and the individual liberties that only a democracy of well-informed citizens can protect.

The connection between education and prosperity could not be clearer. We know, for instance, that receiving a high school diploma is one of the most potent antidotes to poverty. Only 2 percent of those who graduate from high school, get a full-time job, and wait until age 21 and get married before having children end up in poverty. By comparison, that figure is 76 percent for those who fail to do all three. We know that improvements in education lead to improvements in productivity, which are in turn the key to increases in wages and our standard of living. We even know that education improves health and happiness, reduces unemployment, and strengthens the fabric of our society. With access to quality education comes broader opportunity and greater equality.

Sadly, today that American Dream too often represents only a dream. In many corners of the nation, children have no access to an effective school that can give them the opportunity they deserve. Across the nation, our school system is a world leader in spending yet lags on virtually every measure of results. Higher education is becoming at once more important and more unaffordable than ever, stretching family finances and producing new graduates who have too much debt and not enough of the skills they need to succeed in the modern economy.

Each in its own way, these challenges compound the immediate fiscal and economic crises facing the nation. In the long term, they pose serious threats to the equality of opportunity in our society, and to our competitiveness in the 21st century global economy. To restore America's promise, and get Americans working again, we must achieve meaningful reform in our education system.

## The Imperative of K-12 Education Reform: Countless Reforms But Few Results

The challenges we face are not new. Since *A Nation at Risk* was published almost thirty years ago, our country has understood the urgent need for reform. Yet today, fewer than 75 percent of freshmen graduate within four years of entering high school, and far too many who do graduate require remediation when they enroll in college. In a recent survey of more than 10,000 of its graduates, the Harvard Business School identified America's K-12 education system as one of our nation's greatest competitive weaknesses—only the dysfunction of our political system itself scored worse. On the latest international PISA test, American high school students ranked 14th out of 34 developed countries in reading, 17th in science, and 25th in math. China's Shanghai province led the world in all three subjects, outperforming the United States by multiple grade levels in each. These results are unacceptable in their own right, and a sobering warning of a potential decline threatening our nation's future.

Our K-12 system also poses one of the foremost civil rights challenges of our time: the achievement gap facing many minority groups. The average African American or Hispanic student performs at the same level in 12th grade that the average white student achieves in 8th grade. More than one in three African American and Hispanic students fails to graduate from high school within four years of entering. This unconscionable reality flows as a direct consequence from the poor quality of the schools that serve disproportionately minority communities in low-income areas. For example, African American and Hispanic children make up only 38 percent of the nation's students overall, but 69 percent of the students in schools identified by states as the lowest performing. The tragic result is that instead of providing an escape from the cycle of poverty, our education system is reinforcing it.

Politicians have attempted to solve these problems with more spending. But while America's spending per student is among the highest in the world, our results lag far behind. We spend nearly two-and-a-half times as much per pupil today, in real terms, as in 1970, but high school achievement and graduation rates have stagnated. Higher spending rarely correlates with better results. Even the liberal Center for American Progress acknowledged in a recent study that "the literature strongly calls into question the notion that simply investing more money in schools will result in better outcomes," and reported from its own research that most states showed "no clear relationship between spending and achievement" even after adjusting for other factors like the cost of living.

Tinkering around the edges and using money to fix the problem has proven fruitless. The recent infusion of stimulus funds has only served to delay the difficult budgetary decisions facing states, which now stand at the edge of a fiscal cliff. Providing more funding for the status quo will not deliver the results that our students deserve, our country needs, and our taxpayers expect. More than ever before, fiscal responsibility and resourcefulness are required to refocus investments and deliver results.

Unfortunately, rather than embracing reform and innovation, America remains gridlocked in an antiquated system controlled to a disturbing degree by the unions representing teachers. The teachers unions spend millions of dollars to influence the debate in favor of the entrenched interests of adults, not the students our system should serve. The efforts of teachers will be central to any successful reform, but their unions have a very different agenda: opposing innovation that might disrupt the status quo while insulating even the least effective teachers from accountability. Sadly, these priorities do not correlate with better outcomes for our children. To the contrary, teachers unions are consistently on the front lines fighting against initiatives to attract and retain the best teachers, measure performance, provide accountability, or offer choices to parents.

In defense of the failed system, unions spend hundreds of millions of dollars to curry the favor of political leaders. This money is taken from teachers as a condition of their employment, with many teachers forced to pay almost $1,000 in union dues each year. During the last presidential election the National Education Association (NEA) spent more on federal, state, and local elections than any other organization in the country, with more than 90 percent of those funds going to support Democrats. It is no wonder that America's K-12 system is stagnant, when the very individuals charged with ensuring children's success are forced to fund efforts to stifle reform, while parents and children have no one to speak on their behalf. Real change will come only when the special interests take a back seat to the interests of students.

Across the nation, glimmers of success offer reason for hope. Charter school networks such as the KIPP Academies, Uncommon Schools, and Aspire Public Schools are producing remarkable results with students in some of our nation's most disadvantaged communities. Florida Virtual School and other digital education providers are using technology in new ways to personalize instruction to meet students' needs. In Massachusetts, whose schools have led the nation since Romney's time as governor, students' math achievement is comparable to that of the top-performing national school systems worldwide. In our nation's capital, the D.C. Opportunity Scholarship Program has achieved high school graduation rates above 90 percent in inner-city communities where barely half of public school students are earning their diplomas. These successes point the way toward genuine reform. They also underscore the broader struggles and show how far we have to go. . . .

# Part II: Mitt Romney's Plan for Reform

As president, Mitt Romney will pursue genuine education reform that puts parents and students' interests ahead of special interests. These reforms will ensure that students have the skills they need to succeed after graduation. To meet this goal, states must give parents the information and choices they need to enroll their children in good schools. Those schools must be held to high standards and be able to hire and retain the best teachers. Students must have diverse and affordable options for higher education that will give them the skills they need to compete in the global economy, and when they graduate they must be able to find jobs that provide a rewarding return on their educational investment.

## Mitt Romney's Plan for K-12 Education: Supporting Teachers, Increasing Choice, and Emphasizing Results

Ensuring that all children in the United States have access to a K-12 education that equips them to pursue their dreams is both a fundamental American value and essential for lasting economic prosperity. Sadly, we have long fallen short in this vital task, especially when it comes to the education of our most disadvantaged students. The cause is not a lack of public investment: as a nation we spend over $11,000 annually on each student enrolled in K-12 education, more than almost any other country. Nor can we assign blame to those leading our classrooms. American schools are filled with talented and passionate educators who know that the system desperately needs reform and want to be a part of a brighter future for our children. What we need is leadership from state and federal policymakers to free public education from a paralysis that keeps our schools and students from reaching their full potential.

To that end, we must dramatically expand parental choice over the education their children receive and unleash the power of innovation and technology to drive improvement. We must call on states to set high academic standards, hold schools and teachers responsible for results, and ensure that families and taxpayers have accurate information about school performance and spending. And we must reward effective teachers for their excellence in the classroom so that others like them will be attracted into the profession. In short, a Romney Administration's agenda for K-12 education will be organized around the following principles:

**Promoting Choice and Innovation.** Empowering parents with far greater choice over the school their child attends is a vital component of any national agenda for education reform. To start, low-income and special-needs children must be given the freedom to choose the right school and bring funding with them. These students must have access to attractive options, which will require support for the expansion of successful charter schools and for greater technology use by schools. And parents must have reliable, transparent, user-friendly information on how their own children and their schools are performing. Just as innovation and technology moved the nation into the Information Age, so too can they catapult our schools into the 21st century.

**Ensuring High Standards and Responsibility for Results.** States must have in place standards to ensure that every high school graduate is prepared for college or work and, through annual testing, hold both students and educators accountable for meeting them. The results of this testing, for both their own children and their schools, must be readily available to parents in an easy to understand format. And both parents and taxpayers should have detailed and timely information on school and district spending to ensure accountability for the use of public funds.

**Recruiting and Rewarding Great Teachers.** A world-class education system requires world-class teachers in every classroom. Research confirms that students assigned to more effective teachers not only learn more, but they also are also less likely to have a child as a teenager and more likely to attend college. Policies for recruitment, evaluation, and compensation should treat teachers like the professionals they are, not like interchangeable widgets. We must eliminate barriers to becoming a teacher that are based on credentials unrelated to classroom effectiveness. We must reward those teachers who contribute the most to student learning and provide them with advancement opportunities. And we must insist on contract provisions that allow for the removal of those educators who are unable to do the job effectively.

# The Federal Role

Achieving this vision will require a partnership between the states and the federal government. As Tennessee Senator and former U.S. Secretary of Education Lamar Alexander wisely notes, "there is a difference between a national concern, which education is, and a federal government solution driven by Washington." Overly prescriptive federal policy mandates have a chilling effect on state and local efforts to improve schools by diverting resources toward compliance with the letter of the law, not its underlying intent. Federal fiscal requirements too often stifle local innovation and prevent spending on effective programs for fear of triggering federal audits.

As a former governor, Mitt Romney knows that states and localities are best-positioned to reform their education systems and must take the lead in implementing these core principles free of federal micromanagement. Under Romney's leadership as governor, Massachusetts expanded parental choice, maintained high standards, and sought to hold schools and teachers responsible for their performance. During his tenure, Massachusetts became the first state to lead the nation in both reading and math in both fourth and eighth grade and fared well against the top nations in math and science. Other states, such as Florida under Governor Jeb Bush, have made dramatic progress in closing race- and income-based achievement gaps by embracing these same principle. . . . Indiana Governor Mitch Daniels and Louisiana Governor Bobby Jindal have advanced similarly ambitious reforms expanding choice and accountability.

Yet Romney also knows that the federal government cannot ignore the troubled state of American K-12 education. The federal government is uniquely positioned to provide financial support for the education of our neediest students and to require states and districts to tell the truth about how their schools and students are performing. Washington also has a critical role to play in enhancing competition among education providers by eliminating local education monopolies and supporting choice for parents and students. A Romney Administration will align federal funding and policies with the principles of expanded choice and innovation, high standards and accountability, and emphasis on recruiting and rewarding excellent teachers.

## Promoting Choice and Innovation

Through Title I of the Elementary and Secondary Education Act (ESEA) and the Individuals with Disabilities Education Act (IDEA), the federal government provides more than $25 billion of financial support annually for the education of high-need students. These two programs account for roughly two-thirds of baseline federal spending on K-12 education, but have largely failed to achieve their desired results—namely, improved student achievement. We need a new approach, one that expands parental choice by attaching federal funding to the students it is intended to support rather than dispersing it to districts through complex, politically-motivated formulas.

A Romney Administration will work with Congress to overhaul Title I and IDEA so that low-income and special-needs students can choose which school to attend and bring their funding with them. The choices offered to students under this policy will include any district or public charter school in the state, as well as private schools if permitted by state law. Eligible students remaining in public schools will also have the option to use federal funds to purchase supplemental tutoring or digital courses from state-approved private providers rather than receiving Title I services from their district. To ensure accountability, students using federal funds to attend private schools will be required to participate in the state's testing system.

Choice is only valuable if good choices are available. To expand the supply of high-performing schools in and around districts serving low-income and special-needs students, states accepting Title I and IDEA funds will be required to take a series of steps to encourage the development of quality options: First, adopt open-enrollment policies that permit eligible students to attend public schools outside of their school district that have the capacity to serve them. Second, provide access to and appropriate funding levels for digital courses and schools, which are increasingly able to offer materials tailored to the capabilities and progress of each student when used with the careful guidance of effective teachers. And third, ensure that charter school programs can expand to meet demand, receive funding under the same formula that applies to all other publicly-supported schools, and access capital funds.

Charter schools are public schools of choice that are run independently and freed from many of the rules and regulations governing traditional school districts. Thanks to a strong and growing bipartisan base of support, the charter movement is over 5,600 schools strong and serves more than two million students in 41 states and Washington, D.C. While the performance of individual charter schools in improving student achievement varies, the most successful among them are having dramatically positive effects while working with some of the nation's most disadvantaged students. A growing number of charter and education management organizations are taking these effective models to scale. Under a Romney Administration, more funds will be allocated to grow the number of high-quality charter schools and create the conditions under which they can flourish.

The successful D.C. Opportunity Scholarship Program has put into practice many of these principles in our nation's capital. Enacted by Congress with the support of local elected officials, the program offers 1,600 students scholarships to attend private schools of their choice. The U.S. Department of Education's official evaluation of the program confirms that it dramatically increased graduation rates for scholarship recipients. The program also saves taxpayers money because scholarship amounts are substantially less than per-pupil spending in D.C. Public Schools. . . . A Romney Administration will expand the D.C. Opportunity Scholarship Program, offering more students a chance to attend a better school and providing a model of parental choice for the nation.

This unprecedented series of steps will use the power of parental choice to hold our education system responsible for results and set in motion the innovation we so desperately need. Our state and local leaders dedicated to reform will finally be equipped to implement real change, and our best educators will finally have the outlets they need to translate their commitment and creativity into opportunities for children. When this expanded choice is coupled with greater transparency, and an overriding emphasis on placing a quality teacher in every classroom, America will finally be able to ensure a chance for every child.

# Hearing on The All Students Achieving through Reform Act of 2009, H.R. 4330

## Introduction

My name is Thomas Hehir. I am a Professor of Practice at the Harvard Graduate School of Education where I teach courses on educating students with disabilities and federal education policy. I also work as a consultant in the area of special education primarily with large city school districts. My clients have included New York City, Los Angeles, San Diego, and Baltimore among others. I have spent my entire career in the field of special education as a classroom teacher, local administrator in both Boston and Chicago, and as a university professor. I also served as Director of the Office of Special Education Programs for the U.S. Department of Education during the first six years of the Clinton Administration.

In relationship to today's hearings I do not purport to be an expert on all aspects of charter schools. My expertise is primarily in special education. My knowledge of charter schools is based on work I have done in San Diego and Los Angeles assisting these districts to improve their programs for students with disabilities. I have also supervised two doctoral students who have conducted research on the participation of students with disabilities in charters in Massachusetts and New Orleans, and reviewed the literature in this area in preparation for teaching my courses. Further I have consulted with faculty colleagues who have done research on charters, and consulted with many of my former students who run charters. I have done research in three charter-like "pilot schools" in Boston that have enrolled a diverse population of students with disabilities that are outperforming their urban counterparts. I have also had the opportunity to speak with numerous parents of children with disabilities who have enrolled their children in charters or have considered the option.

I would like to state from the onset that I am a proponent of charter schools. I believe that parents, particularly those who reside in urban and low-income areas, should have choice within the public system. The need for choice is even greater for families of students with disabilities given the huge variability between schools in implementing the *Individuals with Disabilities Education Act* (IDEA).

Statement from Hearing on the All Students Achieving through Reform Act of 2009, Hearing before the Committee on Education and Labor. From U.S. House of Representatives, H.R. 4330, February 24, 2010.

# The Opportunity Charters Present for Special Populations

Charters provide choice to all parents. For parents of students with disabilities, choice is highly valued due to the high degree of variability that exists across public schools in educating their children. Though we have made great strides in improving educational offerings for students with disabilities, noncompliance with IDEA continues in many schools. Affluent parents sometimes move to get their children into schools that welcome their children and provide them with a high-quality education. I have done work with a high school in the Boston suburbs that does a great job including students with disabilities. I have met a number of parents who moved to this community simply to allow their children to attend this school. Poor and middle-class parents do not have that option. Charters can and in some cases do provide this option.

Some charter schools have even been created by activists who are seeking a more inclusive and effective option for children with disabilities. The Mary Lyons School, Boston Arts Academy pilot schools, Democracy Prep Charter in Harlem, and Chime Charter in Los Angeles are examples of schools that from their onset have sought to be inclusive of a diverse population of students with disabilities.

There is also evidence that charters may serve students with disabilities in more inclusive settings than traditional public schools. Chris Wilkens, a doctoral student at Harvard, found that urban charters in Massachusetts were more likely to serve similar students with disabilities in inclusive settings than traditional urban public schools. His research also found that overplacement of African American students in special education was far less of a problem in charters than traditional urban public schools.

Many charters focus intently on individualization that is a central tenet of IDEA. Others such as the KIPP schools focus on explicit direct instruction needed by many students with disabilities and other students who may struggle in school. These approaches may account for some of the lower levels of special education identification in charter schools. To the extent that these practices prevent inappropriate referrals to special education, they should be encouraged.

A similar dynamic exists for English language learners and other special populations. Like students with disabilities, English language learners participate in charters in much smaller numbers than they exist in the population at large. However, some advocates for English language learners have seized upon the opportunity provided by charters to promote better education for these children. For instance, the National Council of La Raza has supported the establishment of over 50 charters in their efforts to expand educational opportunity for this population.

# The Problem of Charters and Special Populations

Research on the participation of special populations and charters demonstrates that in most places these students are underrepresented. For instance in the area of disability, charters generally serve fewer children with disabilities than traditional public schools. When one looks at students with more significant or complicated disabilities in general, charters serve far fewer students and in many instances none at all. Research conducted in a number of major cities bears this out. In San Diego, close to 10% of all students now attend charter schools. Though the enrollment of students with disabilities in traditional public schools overall approaches 12%, the average enrollment of students with disabilities in non-conversion (from scratch) charter schools during the 2005–2006 school year was 5.8% (Hehir & Mosqueda, 2008). With respect to students requiring extensive special education services, the imbalance is even more dismal. For example, during the 2005-06 school years, there were only three children with mental retardation in all San Diego non-conversion charter schools *combined*; traditional schools across the district, meanwhile, educated almost one thousand students with mental retardation. That same year, non-conversion charter schools in San Diego educated just two students with autism.

The picture is quite similar in Los Angeles. The enrollment of students in charter schools throughout the city is large (approximately 8%). The enrollment of students with disabilities across the district averages over 11%, while the enrollment of students with disabilities in independent charter schools averages fewer than 7% (Independent Monitors Office, 2009). As in San Diego, the distribution of disability types within independent Los Angeles charter schools is skewed; for students with disabilities requiring extensive special education services, the likelihood they will be enrolled in independent charter schools is one-fourth that of traditional public schools.

Similar data emerges for charters serving urban areas in Massachusetts. For the 2006–07 school years, the percentage of enrolled students with disabilities in traditional urban schools was 19.9%, while the percentage of enrolled students with disabilities enrolled in urban charter schools was significantly lower, 10.8%. As is the case in Los Angeles and San Diego, significantly fewer students were enrolled in all urban charter schools who had more substantial needs such as mental retardation, emotional disturbance, and autism. Several cities' charter schools enrolled none of these students.

The underenrollment of English language learners in charters mirrors that of students with disabilities in many places. In Boston where approximately 20% of students are English language learners, only one charter school enrolled more than 4%. In NYC a similar pattern emerges where the district enrollment is 15% English language learners and the charters serve approximately 4%.

As for disadvantaged students, there is some evidence that charters in some places may enroll a more advantaged population. However, the vast majority of charters are enrolling large numbers of disadvantaged students.

# Why Is Underrepresentation a Problem?

The underrepresentation of special populations in charter schools is a problem on a number of levels:

   a. First low participation rates raise potential civil rights concerns. Students with disabilities, English language learners and homeless students have rights as American citizens both granted to them by the Constitution and within various federal education laws. Anecdotal information suggests that some parents are discouraged from applying to charter schools and that some charter schools "send back" students with complicated needs to traditional public schools. America has opened doors to previously excluded groups through the Civil Rights Act, the IDEA and The Elementary and Secondary Education Act. The federal government needs to assure that discrimination is not occurring within the charter sector.

b. The "experiment" that charters represent is compromised when charters do not serve the same populations as traditional public schools. One of the primary justifications for allowing charters to exist is to demonstrate better approaches for educating students for whom the current education system has failed. If they fail to serve representative populations, their claims to being exemplary are significantly compromised.

c. The failure of charters to enroll representative populations of students from special populations can disadvantage traditional public schools financially. As the San Diego school system demonstrates, the financial responsibility for educating students with disabilities rests with the traditional public schools. Yet, the charters receive roughly the same amount of money per-capita. It should be noted the per-capita cost in most school districts includes the cost of educating special populations and that this cost is higher per pupil. For instance, the cost of providing language supports to English language learners or transportation to homeless students increases the financial burden on school districts. In the case of students with disabilities, this cost can be much higher. The population least represented in charters, students with low incidence and more complex disabilities, are the most expensive for schools to educate.

d. There is financial incentive for charters not to educate students for whom additional costly services may be necessary. Under the current system, many charters receive the same amount of money per student whether they educate students with more complex needs or not. Many charters, like many traditional public schools, encumber most of their money on the first day of school by hiring staff. When an unforeseen need arises during the year, they may not have the resources to address that need. In traditional public schools the central office may step in with needed support or the anticipated needs of students from special populations are budgeted upfront. Some charters have established similar mechanisms but many have not. Therefore, when a child with additional needs becomes apparent the charter may not have the resources to meet this need. I am aware of charters that have not even budgeted for a single special education teacher upfront.

# Policy Considerations

In my opinion, it is time for policy makers to directly address the issue of imbalanced enrollment of students from special populations in charter schools. Though some may have argued in the past that charter schools needed time to get established, and to have flexibility to experiment, they are now a well-established segment of our education system. The charter choice should be available to all students and parents. Toward that end I believe the federal government has a role in assuring equity and promoting more effective public school choice for parents of children from special populations. The following recommendations are offered:

> **(1) The federal government should require states to proactively address issues of access involving special populations as a condition for receiving federal funds.**

The US Department of Education historically has played a crucial role in promoting equity in education in the areas of racial desegregation, gender equity and disability access among others. The lack of access for special populations to some charters raises serious equity and civil rights concerns. At a minimum, states should be required to submit their authorizing regulations to their Departments of Education for approval. States should further be required to investigate charters that enroll significantly fewer students from special populations than their surrounding area contains. It is important to emphasize here that states should be allowed flexibility as there should not be an expectation that charters always mirror the population of the surrounding area. Some charters may have lower special education counts simply because they have been successful in eliminating inappropriate referrals to special education. Others may have been established to serve English language learners. These innovations should not be discouraged. The point here is that the state needs to reasonably assure the federal government that special populations' access to charters is not impeded.

States should also be required to assist charter operators in meeting their obligations to provide access to special populations. The vast majority of charter operators I have met want to address the needs of all students. Again, this may take many forms and states should be allowed a good deal of flexibility in meeting this requirement.

> **(2) The federal government should establish a federal technical assistance center focusing on the needs of students from special populations in charter schools.**

This center would primarily serve the states in meeting their obligations detailed above. Such a center could provide states with model authorizing documents as well as information about successful practices in charters serving special populations. This model has worked very effectively in IDEA and the Elementary and Secondary Education Act as a vehicle to promote better practices in the schools.

> **(3) Fund research on serving special populations in charter schools.**

Though I am sure Congress has gotten advice from many quarters on how to address these issues, there is no consensus on the range or extent of the problems concerning special populations and charter schools. I believe this issue is important enough to warrant a National Research Council study. Such a study would provide an objective picture of the current state of charters and special populations and identify promising practices. Congress should also fund a research program to investigate ways in which charters can better serve special populations.

## Final Reflections

This past year I assisted my cousin in choosing an elementary school in Boston for her four-year-old twin boys. Having worked in the Boston system from 1977 to 1987, I was pleasantly surprised at how much the system had improved. My cousin is currently considering two public charters and two traditional public schools for the boys. All four are strong choices. This contrasts to the system I left where parents were often given few or no choices and were forced to send their children to underperforming schools. I believe Boston is a far better system for a number of reasons but one is parental choice. Boston outperforms most major cities on the National Assessment of Educational Progress as does the state of Massachusetts. Parental choice is deeply embedded in the state as well. The challenge facing Massachusetts as well as Congress is how we make this choice real for all parents.

Finally, in doing research for this testimony I relied on an old and tested method; Facebook. I posted a request for assistance to my former students many of whom work in charters. They responded well to their old professor. One related that she was working as a psychologist in a major city with troubled youth many of whom are in the foster care system. Many of her students have opted for charters in lieu of large impersonal high schools that had utterly failed them. She found that charters had been particularly effective in serving GLBT youth who felt unsafe in traditional high schools. Another student related how her sister had placed her son in a local charter school and how happy she was that she was not forced to send him to an underperforming elementary school. However, she has another child with disabilities for whom this choice was not an option. For her disabled daughter, she had no choice and was forced to place her in the same underperforming school she avoided for her son. She has been forced to file for a due process hearing in order to get an acceptable choice for her. This will be a huge financial burden on the family. Public school choice is an incomplete option for this family.

It's time for the adults who run charters and for those who authorize them to act. The charter "experiment" has gone on long enough. Access to all must become a priority. When PL 94-142 was passed in 1975 opening up the doors of schools to thousands of previously excluded students with disabilities Congressman Miller stated, "I believe the burden of proof . . . ought to rest with the administrator or teacher who seeks for one reason or another to remove a child from a normal classroom. . . ." We need to provide that same logic to charter schools and special populations. The burden of proof should fall on government officials, charter school operators and charter advocates who need to take proactive responsibility to deal with the very real issues of access for special populations.

I hope Congress leads the way.

Thank you.

# EXPLORING THE ISSUE

## Are Charter Schools a Good Choice for Students with Disabilities?

## Challenge Questions

- Compare and contrast the positions of the YES and NO selections regarding whether charter schools are a good choice for students with disabilities.
- Which selection makes the best case for its argument? Why?
- What is the status of special education enrollment in the charter schools in your town/city?
- How can charters claim success without enrolling the full range of students?
- Discuss what would be gained/lost by overhauling IDEA and ESEA to provide funds parents can use in the way they see best.

## Is There Common Ground?

Both Mitt Romney and Tom Hehir view education as a critical contributor to success in adult life. They share a belief in the possibilities of charter schools and support the idea of choice for parents seeking the best education for their children.

## Additional Resources

Center for Education Reform. (2010). *Annual survey: America's charter schools.* Retrieved September 16, 2010 from www.edreform.com

Center for Research on Educational Outcomes. (2009). *Multiple choice: Charter school performance in 16 states.* Retrieved from www.credo.stanford.edu

Center for Research on Educational Outcomes. (2010). *Charter school performance in New York City.* Retrieved from www.credo.stanford.edu

Council for Exceptional Children. *Charter Schools and Special Education,* Retrieved March 12, 2010 from www.cec.sped.org

Duncan, A. (2009, June 22). *Turning around the bottom 5 percent: Address by the Secretary of Education at the National Alliance for Public Charter Schools Conference.* Retrieved March 8, 2010 from www.ed.gov/news/speeches/2009/06/0622209.html

Lake, R. J. & Gross, B. (2012). Making choice work for students with special needs. In Robin Lake and Bethany Gross (Eds). *Hopes, fears, & reality: A balanced look at American charter schools in 2011*. Center on Reinventing Public Education (Chapter 4). Retrieved May 20, 2012 from www.crpe.org

Romney, M. (2012). *A chance for every child: Mitt Romney's plan for restoring the promise of American education*. Retrieved May 24, 2012 from www.mittromney.com

# ISSUE 7

## Should Insurance Cover Treatments/Services for Autism?

YES: **Autism Speaks,** from *Arguments in Support of Private Insurance Coverage for Autism-Related Services* (February 2009), www.autismspeaks.org

NO: **Victoria C. Bunce & J.P. Wieske,** from *Health Insurance Mandates in the States 2009* (The Council for Affordable Health Insurance, 2009), www.cahi.org, February 10, 2009

---

### Learning Outcomes

**At the conclusion of this issue, readers will be able to:**

- Compare and contrast the positions of the YES and NO selections addressing whether insurance companies should cover treatments/services for children with autism.
- Identify the strengths and the weaknesses of each side's arguments.
- Explain how autism services are funded.
- Discuss the difficult decisions parents of young children with autism must make.

---

### ISSUE SUMMARY

**YES:** Autism Speaks, an advocacy organization founded by Suzanne and Bob Wright (former executives in General Electric and NBC, respectively), together with the National Alliance for Autism Research and Cure Autism Now, presents eight arguments in support of legislation mandating health insurance coverage of autism services.

**NO:** Writing for the Council for Affordable Health Insurance, an organization that promotes the affordable health care access for all Americans, Victoria C. Bunce and J.P. Wieske discuss national trends in state-mandated health care benefits for children with autism, arguing that responsibility for these costs belongs elsewhere.

$\mathbf{H}$ow many parents can afford $30,000 to educate their child? What about $60,000 or $72,000? Each of these is an estimate of the *annual* cost for services to a child with autism. The numbers vary as do children with autism spectrum disorders (ASDs). The more severe the autism, the more extensive the need for intensive services and the higher the cost.

One child in eighty-eight is diagnosed with autism, according to the Centers for Disease Control (CDC). Most children are diagnosed before the age of 3. CDC reported a 78 percent increase in diagnoses between 2002 and 2008 (*Morbidity and Mortality Weekly Report,* March 2012). A number of possible explanations exist: broader interpretation of the category of autism; improved diagnostic tools; increased public awareness; and a shift to autism from other disability categories.

Children with ASDs present with significant difficulties in communication, language, and social interaction. They may also have seizures, gastrointestinal difficulties, and other physical disorders.

There is broad agreement that early intervention is essential (Abt Associates, 2008). No single treatment has been found universally effective, although Applied Behavior Analysis (ABA) has the most research support, especially for children at the more severe end of the autism spectrum. ABA services are typically provided in a 1:1 setting, for at least 20 hours per week.

Parents are bombarded with alternative treatment options, some of which claim to cure autism. These options, ranging from chelation to sensory integration therapy to strict diets and supplements, are also costly and not often covered by insurance.

Taking a broad view, Ganz (*Archives of Pediatric and Adolescent Medicine,* 2007) projected the lifetime societal costs of *each* person with autism at $3.2 million. Components of this staggering amount include therapies and services, lost parental work productivity, respite care, additional medical complications, and lifetime care and support. Legal fees and the cost of diet foods would raise the total.

Faced with managing treatment expenses long before their child is eligible for services under IDEA, some parents mortgage their homes; tap into retirement savings; and/or declare bankruptcy (Foden, www.iancommunity.org, 2008). Others tackle complex bureaucracies and waiting lists to secure Medicaid eligibility waivers for their child (Reinke, *EP,* 2009).

Parents also turn to their health insurance. Many find their policies deny coverage of autism-related services because certain treatments are considered "experimental and unproven," and therefore not likely to be helpful (Abramson, NPR.org, 2007). Some insurance companies have blanket exclusions for any child with autism: no coverage for anything related to autism, ever (Abt Associates, 2008). Once diagnosed, the child is viewed as having a preexisting condition and may never be insurable.

Consider the ongoing national debates about health care in general and the Patient Protection and Affordable Care Act, one of the signature accomplishments of the Obama administration. Although the Act precludes dismissing autism as a preexisting condition, not all insurance companies or policies are required to abide by this standard. The Mental Health Parity Act requires mental health services (including behavioral therapies) at the same level as physical health, but these services are provided on an episodic, rather than long-term basis. Many private insurance companies engage in deliberations about coverage for preexisting conditions, including services for those with autism.

Movements have arisen to force health insurance companies to change their practices with regard to children with autism. Individual families, and organizations focused on autism, have lobbied legislators in several states to mandate coverage, especially for ABA. Autismcrisis.org describes itself as a grassroots organization focusing energy on identifying potential conflicts of interest between individual legislators and the health care industry.

The Abt Associates (2008) report cited in this section analyzed evidence submitted to the Pennsylvania legislature as it considered passing an autism mandate. Abt determined that the evidence presented supported the need and effectiveness of the bill. Consequently, Pennsylvania's legislation instituted an annual expenditure cap on payments (adjustable for inflation), and no lifetime cap. Funding for medicines, tests, and therapeutic services was included.

No one questions the necessity of early intervention services, although there is considerable disagreement about which services make a difference, and how much change can be expected. The YES and NO selections illustrate the heated debate about funding treatments.

The YES selection was prepared by Autism Speaks (www.autismspeaks.org), an organization dedicated to improving awareness, advocacy, and life conditions for people with autism and their families. Autism Speaks sees services as a health care responsibility. Children with autism have concurrent medical problems, but are sometimes denied coverage by health insurance companies who would cover the same service for children without the diagnosis of autism. The selection's eight arguments supporting mandated coverage by private health insurance companies have been used across the country as individual states debate mandates.

The NO selection comprises two short reports written by Victoria C. Bunce and J.P. Wieske from the Council for Affordable Health Insurance (CAHI), which advocates for affordable health care for all. One introduces a survey of mandates currently in place across the country, highlighting the growing popularity of autism mandates. The next expands on autism mandates. CAHI argues that health insurance should be reserved for covering short-term needs, not the long-term care required by children with autism.

The CAHI selection projects the financial impact of burgeoning mandates. The authors assert that health insurance companies are increasingly being required to cover services beyond their mission of short-term health care. Each new mandate leads to increased health care premiums and decreased services for everyone. Legislators are using mandates to avoid providing programmatic options. Schools are skirting their IDEA responsibilities.

In the midst of Virginia's contemplation of an autism mandate, Rituparna Basu (the-undercurrent.com, 2009) acknowledged the financial stress incurred by parents, but believes the outcomes would either reduce services (in order to contain added costs) or increase premiums for everyone (making coverage unaffordable for some). Basu asks, "If it is unfair to parents of autistic children to have to pay their children's medical bills, how much more unfair is it for other parents to have to pay the same bills?" Basu views mandated coverage as "enforced charity."

The late Dr. Stephen Parker (http://blogs.webmd.com, 2008) addresses the "border war" "between two titans—the health insurance industry and the educational system." Conveying each titan's arguments through imaginary dialog, Parker thinks it shameful that we are fighting about care for some of our neediest. He decides that "autism is primarily an educational, not a medical, challenge." Unfortunately, he also concludes that schools are "woefully underfunded," and that "she-bear advocates" will be needed to secure services from schools strapped for cash.

In the center are parents trying to do what is best for their small child. Family financial challenges are far greater than for parents of typical children (Parish, Roe, Grinstein-Weiss, Richman, & Andrews, M. E. *Exceptional Children,* 2008). Work demands must be balanced with the unpredictable needs of their children (Jackson, *The Boston Globe,* 2008). The National Council on Disability (www.ncd.gov, 2009) found limited or nonexistent health insurance for individuals with disabilities throughout their lives.

# YES

# Arguments in Support of Private Insurance Coverage of Autism-Related Services

## Executive Summary

**A**utism is a complex neurobiological disorder and is the fastest growing serious developmental disability in the U.S. The Centers for Disease Control estimates that 1 in 110 children has autism. These children require extensive services from medical professionals. Early intervention is critical to gain maximum benefit from existing therapies. Most private health insurance plans do not provide coverage for Applied Behavior Analysis (ABA) and other autism-related services.

This document contains eight arguments in favor of requiring private health insurance policies to cover the diagnosis and treatment of autism spectrum disorders for individuals under the age of 21. These arguments are based on epidemiological, social, and economic studies of the children and families affected by autism and prove the significant long-term financial and public health benefits of this requirement.

We first point out that children with autism have substantial medical needs and have a difficult time accessing necessary treatments through Medicaid and private health insurance. Most insurance policies contain specific exclusions for autism. This is a hardship for many families, who are often forced to cope with delayed, inadequate, and fragmented care through the Medicaid system. Often, families must pay for costly treatments out-of-pocket or forego them.

We then review some of the many studies and reports that document the effectiveness of intensive behavioral therapies in the treatment of autism. An autism insurance mandate should specifically target coverage of Applied Behavior Analysis (ABA) and other structured behavioral therapies, which are the most effective forms of treatment and have the best outcomes, both in human costs and in long-term economic benefits.

We then comment on the experiences of several states with insurance reform. Their experiences show that the policy holder costs resulting from the passage of legislation requiring comprehensive autism services have been relatively small.

Finally, we point out that the mandate offers hope that children with autism will need less intensive care in the future. They will, in short, have a better chance at a normal life. . . .

# What Is Autism?

Autism is a complex neurobiological disorder that typically lasts throughout a person's lifetime. It is part of a group of disorders known as autism spectrum disorders (ASD). Today, 1 in 110 individuals is diagnosed with ASD, making it more common than pediatric cancer, diabetes, and AIDS combined. It occurs in all racial, ethnic, and social groups and is four times more likely to strike boys than girls. Autism impairs a person's ability to communicate and relate to others. It is also associated with rigid routines and repetitive behaviors, such as obsessively arranging objects or following very specific routines. Symptoms can range from very mild to quite severe.

*Argument 1:* **Mandated private health insurance coverage will provide services that are desperately needed by children with autism, who have greater health care needs than children without autism.**

Children with autism have a tremendous need for services from trained medical professionals. These children are at risk for a range of other medical conditions, including behavioral or conduct problems, attention-deficit disorder or attention-deficit/hyperactivity disorder, stuttering, stammering, and other speech problems, depression and anxiety problems, bone, joint, or muscle problems, ear infections, hearing and vision problems, allergies (especially food allergies), and frequent and severe headaches. These problems greatly affect their overall health and their need for and use of health care services.

A . . . study by James G. Guerney and others highlights the broad medical needs of children with autism. Using data from the National Survey of Children's Health, Guerney showed that relative to children without autism, children with autism require more services for physical, occupational, and speech therapy. Children with autism are also much more likely to have poor health, to require medically necessary care for behavioral problems, and to be using medications. [P]arents of children with autism were more likely to report the presence of a variety of concurrent medical conditions and the need for more visits to a range of medical service providers than parents of children without autism.

This reform of private health insurance coverage will address the broad medical needs of children with autism. It will ensure that these children will receive the full range of therapies necessary to ameliorate their condition.

*Argument 2:* **Treatments for autism are difficult to access, often inadequate, and frequently delayed. Denied coverage by private group health insurance companies, parents are often forced either to pay out-of-pocket or forego the treatments their children need.**

Children with autism face barriers in accessing early intensive behavioral treatments and other therapies. According to the Institute of Medicine, the term "access" is defined as "the timely use of personal health services to achieve the best possible health outcomes." For a child with autism, lack of access to services can be the cause of inconsistent and uncoordinated care. Children with autism often experience barriers to access with even greater frequency than children with other special health care needs. In fact, one study found that "over one-third of the children with autism were reported to have experienced an access problem with respect to specialty care from a medical doctor in the preceding 12 months." A study of the Tennessee Medicaid system, TennCare, found that for children with autism, "the rate of service use was only one tenth what should be expected based on prevalence rates." . . .

Within the Medicaid system, the amount of public money spent for services for developmental disabilities including autism is now eight times the rate of spending just a few decades ago. Medicaid accounts for 75% of all funding for services for the developmentally disabled, making it the largest single public payer of behavioral health services. Children with disabilities comprise a significant portion (15%) of all Medicaid recipients, and an even more significant portion (31%) of disabled children use the Medicaid system as their primary insurer.

Medicaid suffers from very low reimbursement rates that make it difficult for many locations to retain service providers. Moreover, services that can be accessed through the Medicaid system are often inadequate at meeting the specific needs of a child with autism. The system operates as a short-term service provider, tending to push children through treatment as quickly as possible. The success of the Applied Behavior Analysis, however, depends in part, on the amount of time the child with autism spends with the provider of the therapy.

The failings of Medicaid point to the importance of the private health care system in providing services to children with autism. But nationwide there are very few private insurance companies or other employee benefit plans that cover Applied Behavior Analysis and other behavioral therapies. Most insurance companies designate autism as a diagnostic exclusion, "meaning that any services rendered explicitly for the treatment of autism are not covered by the plan, even if those services would be covered if used to treat a different condition." . . .

Families that refuse to allow their children to suffer through the inadequate Medicaid system and are denied coverage by their private health insurance carriers often end up paying for therapies out of their own pockets. For these families, the financial burden is immense. Without the negotiating powers of an insurance company behind them, out-of-pocket prices are extremely high. Parents can often spend upwards of $50,000 per year on autism-related therapies, often being forced to wager their own futures and the futures of their non-autistic children to pay for necessary autism-related therapies. Children whose parents cannot afford to pay for behavioral and other therapies and who cannot access adequate therapies through the Medicaid system simply go without these interventions.

*Argument 3:* **Mandated private insurance coverage will bring effective autism services within the reach of the children who need them. The efficacy of Applied Behavior Analysis (ABA), the centerpiece of this legislative mandate's benefits, has been established repeatedly.**

Private health insurance coverage of autism services will allow children with autism to access Applied Behavior Analysis (ABA), a proven treatment for their condition. Several studies have shown that as many as 47 percent of the children that undergo early intensive behavioral therapies achieve higher education placement and increased IQ levels. A significant portion of children who receive ABA are placed into mainstream educational settings. Children who begin their treatment with minimal IQ levels end treatment with substantially higher levels of intellectual functioning. These results have been shown to last well beyond the end of treatment. As such, the effectiveness of ABA therapy has allowed many children to forego costly intensive special education in the future. . . .

*Argument 4:* **Government and scientific organizations have endorsed Applied Behavior Analysis (ABA) and other structured behavioral therapies.**

ABA is the treatment of choice for autism. Its efficacy has been recognized in a number of prominent reports, including the following:

- **The 2001 U.S. Surgeon General's Report on Mental Health,** which states, "Among the many methods available for treatment and education of people with autism, applied behavior analysis (ABA) has become widely accepted as an effective treatment. Thirty years of research demonstrated the efficacy of applied behavioral methods in reducing inappropriate behavior and in increasing communication, learning, and appropriate social behavior."
- **The New York State Department of Health** assessed interventions for children ages 0-3 with autism, and recommended that "behavioral interventions for reducing maladaptive behaviors be used for young children with autism when such behaviors interfere with the child's learning or socialization or present a hazard to the child or others."
- **The Maine Administrators of Services for Children with Disabilities** notes in their report that "There is a wealth of validated and peer-reviewed studies supporting the efficacy of ABA methods to improve and sustain socially significant behaviors in every domain, in individuals with autism. Importantly, results reported include 'meaningful' outcomes such as increased social skills, communication skills, academic performance, and overall cognitive functioning. These reflect clinically significant quality of life improvements. While studies varied as to the magnitude of gains, all have demonstrated long-term retention of gains made."
- **The National Institute of Mental Health** reports, "The basic research done by Ivar Lovaas and his colleagues at the University of California, Los Angeles, calling for an intensive, one-on-one child–teacher interaction for 40 hours a week, laid a foundation for other educators and researchers in the search for further effective early interventions to help those with ASD attain their potential. The goal of behavioral management is to reinforce desirable behaviors and reduce undesirable ones."
- **The National Institute of Child Health and Human Development** lists Applied Behavior Analysis among the recommended treatment methods for Autism Spectrum Disorders.

- **The National Research Council's** 2001 report on Educating Children with Autism acknowledged, "There is now a large body of empirical support for more contemporary behavioral approaches using naturalistic teaching methods that demonstrate efficacy for teaching not only speech and language, but also communication."
- **The Association for Science in Autism Treatment** recommends ABA-based therapies, stating, "ABA is an effective intervention for many individuals with autism spectrum disorders."

*Argument 5:* **To combat the difficulty many families face in accessing Applied Behavior Analysis (ABA) and other structured behavioral treatments through public insurance, . . . states have passed autism insurance mandates that specifically require private insurance companies to provide coverage of these therapies, thus creating a public–private partnership for the provision of care.**

While there are several states that have passed autism-specific private insurance mandates, very few states specifically mandate coverage for ABA and other structured behavioral therapy programs. Without coverage of these crucial, medically necessary, evidence-based therapies, the effectiveness of most mandates is severely diminished. . . .

*Argument 6:* **The costs of the proposed benefit are small and will have very little impact on the cost of health insurance premiums for the individual consumer.**

. . . The Council for Affordable Health Insurance, a research and advocacy association of insurance carriers, released its annual report on state health insurance mandates, *Health Insurance Mandates in the States 2007*. The report defined a mandate as "a requirement that an insurance company or health plan cover (or offer coverage for) common—but sometimes not so common—health care providers, benefits and patient populations." Using this definition, the report identified legislative mandates for autism benefits in ten states: Colorado, Delaware, Georgia, Iowa, Indiana . . . , Kentucky, Maryland, New Jersey, New York, and Tennessee. The report assessed the incremental cost of state-mandated benefits for autism in these ten states *as less than one percent.*

The Council's modest estimate of incremental premium costs is consistent with state government estimates across the country. Prior to enactment of Indiana's sweeping legislation, the Indiana Legislative Services Agency estimated additional premium costs as ranging from $.44 per contract per month to $1.67 per contract per month. In vetoing Ryan's Law in South Carolina, Governor Mark Sanford estimated that the bill, with its $50,000 maximum yearly benefit for behavioral therapy, would add $48 annually to insurance policies. And in Wisconsin, where . . . Assembly Bill 417 would provide the same broad coverage Indiana's statute mandates, the Department of Administration estimates policy increments of between $3.45 and $4.10 per month—about the same as Governor Sanford's estimate for Ryan's Law.

The cost estimates for Indiana, South Carolina, and Wisconsin—all states whose legislation allows a maximum benefit that can be considered high—suggest that an average autism insurance coverage mandate will cost approximately $50 annually per policy holder. For only a modest effect on premium cost, this insurance reform holds the promise of significantly improving the lives of thousands of children.

*Argument 7:* **By improving outcomes for children with autism, mandated private insurance coverage will decrease the lifetime costs of treating and providing services and will actually result in an overall cost savings in the long run.**

A . . . study by John W. Jacobson and others titled, *Cost-Benefit Estimates for Early Intensive Behavioral Intervention for Young Children with Autism—General Model and Single State Case,* examined the cost/benefit relationship of early intensive behavioral intervention treatment at varying levels of treatment success. The study used estimates of costs for early intensive behavioral interventions (EIBI) from childhood (age three) through adulthood (age 55) based on prices in the Commonwealth of Pennsylvania and compared these costs with the expected amount of income the child would earn later in life to arrive at an estimated cost savings.

With a success rate of 47 percent for early intensive behavioral intervention therapy (as determined by Lovaas), Jacobson's study found that cost savings per child served are estimated to be from $2,439,710 to $2,816,535 to age 55.

The study also accounts for the initial investment in early intervention by concluding that, with an initial annual cost of $32,820, the total cost-benefit savings of EIBI services per child with autism or PDD for ages 3–55 years average from $1,686,061 to $2,816,535 with inflation.

According to a 2005 Government Accounting Office (GAO) report, "the average per pupil expenditure for educating a child with autism was more than $18,000 in the 1999–2000 school year. This amount was almost three times the average per pupil expenditure of educating a child who does not receive any special education services." With this insurance reform in place, more children would be able to access the early intervention services they need. That investment will, in the long run pay benefits, both economic and social, to the greater population.

*Argument 8:* **Without passage of legislation requiring private health insurance coverage for autism, the costs associated with autism will continue not only to affect families, but will have far-reaching social effects as well.**

The cost of autism is borne by everyone. Michael L. Ganz's study of the societal costs of autism, *The Lifetime Distribution of the Incremental Societal Costs of Autism,* examined how the large financial burdens of autism affect not only families with an autistic child but society in general.

Ganz broke down the costs associated with autism into two distinct categories, direct costs and indirect costs. Direct costs include direct medical costs, such as physician, outpatient, clinic services, dental care, prescription medications, complementary and alternative therapies, behavioral therapies, hospital and emergency services, allied health, equipment and supplies, home health, and medically related travel, as well as direct nonmedical costs, such as child care, adult care, respite and family care, home and care modification, special education, and supported employment. Indirect costs include productivity losses for people with autism (calculated by combining standard average work-life expectancies for all men and women with average income and benefits and estimated age- and sex-specific labor force participation rates).

According to Ganz's study, direct medical costs reach their maximum during the first five years of life, averaging around $35,000. As the child ages, direct medical costs begin to decline substantially and continue to decline through the end of life to around $1,000. Ganz goes on to report, "The large direct medical costs early in life are driven primarily by behavioral therapies that cost around $32,000 during the first 5-year age group and decline from about $4,000 in the 8- to 12-year age group to around $1,250 for the 18- to 22-year age group."

In terms of direct medical costs "the typical American spends about $317,000 over his or her lifetime in direct medical costs, incurring 60% of those costs after the age of 65 years. In contrast, people with autism incur about $306,000 in incremental direct medical costs, which suggests that people with autism spend twice as much as the typical American over their lifetimes and spend 60% of those incremental direct medical costs after age 21 years."

The study also found the indirect costs of autism to be significant as well. While in the first 22 years of life, indirect costs are mostly associated with lost productivity for the parents of a child with autism, the costs from age 23 on are associated with lost productivity of the actual individual with autism. . . . The impact of this lost productivity can have enormous ramifications for the tax base of an entire society and the future of the older generation as their children with autism transition into adult care.

Ganz posited that direct medical costs "combined with very limited to non-existent income for their adult children with autism combined with potentially lower levels of savings because of decreased income and benefits while employed, may create a large financial burden affecting not only those families but potentially society in general."

Without the help of private insurance coverage, families affected by autism may never be able to pull their heads above water and provide their children with the medically necessary, evidence-based treatments that they need. It is to the advantage of these families, to the 1 in 150 children affected by autism, and to all of society that private health insurance coverage is provided for these services.

## Conclusion

A legislative mandate for coverage of autism asks private insurance companies to make a limited, but significant, contribution to help pay for medically necessary, evidence-based treatments that have been established to be of the greatest impact in fighting this terrible disorder.

Unbelievably, it is not uncommon for insurance carriers to have line-item exclusions for treatment of individuals diagnosed with autism. Across the nation, children with autism are routinely denied insurance benefits for treatment of their disorder. We believe that private insurance companies must contribute their fair share and partner in the financial burdens with these families.

With every new child diagnosed with autism costing an estimated $3 million over his or her lifetime, the current practices are both unfair and not cost effective in the long run for states and their citizens. Autism Speaks is confident that many more state governments will recognize the significant long-term cost benefits found in these legislative measures, will do what is right for their constituents, and will pass legislation requiring private health insurance coverage of autism services.

Victoria C. Bunce
and J. P. Wieske

 **NO**

# Health Insurance Mandates in the States 2009

**A** health insurance "mandate" is a requirement that an insurance company or health plan cover (or offer coverage for) common—but sometimes not so common—health care providers, benefits and patient populations. They include:

- Providers such as chiropractors and podiatrists, but also social workers and massage therapists;
- Benefits such as mammograms, well-child care and even drug and alcohol abuse treatment, but also acupuncture and hair prostheses (wigs); and
- Populations such as adopted and non-custodial children.

For almost every health care product or service, there is someone who wants insurance to cover it so that those who sell the products and services get more business and those who use the products and services don't have to pay out of pocket for them.

**The Impact of Mandates.**  While mandates make health insurance more comprehensive, they also make it more expensive because mandates require insurers to pay for care consumers previously funded out of their own pockets. We estimate that mandated benefits currently increase the cost of basic health coverage from a little less than 20% to perhaps 50%, depending on the number of mandates, the benefit design and the cost of the initial premium. Mandating benefits is like saying to someone in the market for a new car, if you can't afford a Cadillac loaded with options, you have to walk. Having that Cadillac would be nice, as would having a health insurance policy that covers everything one might want. But drivers with less money can find many other affordable car options; whereas when the price of health insurance soars, few other options exist.

**Why Is the Number of Mandates Growing?**  Elected representatives find it difficult to oppose any legislation that promises enhanced care to potentially motivated voters. The sponsors of mandates know this fact of political life. As a result, government interference in and control of the health care system is steadily increasing. So too is the cost of health insurance.

By the late 1960s, state legislatures had passed only a handful of mandated benefits; today, the Council for Affordable Health Insurance (CAHI) has identified **2,133** mandated benefits and providers. And more are on their way.

How do state legislators justify their actions? One way is to deny a mandate is a mandate. For example, legislators may claim that requiring health insurance to cover a type of provider—such as a chiropractor, podiatrist, midwife or naturopath—is not a mandate because they aren't requiring insurance to pay for a particular therapy. But that's a distinction without a difference; if insurance is required to cover the provider, it must pay for the service provided. . .

**How Is the Research Compiled?**   Since 1992, the Council for Affordable Health Insurance staff has tracked the introduction and passage of health insurance mandates in every state, but not until 2004 did we make this information available to the public. To corroborate our own findings, we survey every department of insurance and talk with other industry experts.

The question is sometimes raised why our mandate count may differ from other groups that identify state mandates. We do not currently differentiate between the individual and small group markets, especially since many states are blurring that traditional distinction by, for example, allowing "groups of one" (i.e., one person is considered a group) to be classified as a small group under federal law. Also, we do not differentiate between a benefit that is mandated and one that must only be offered. Our actuaries advise us that the cost to provide that policy is the same: If the mandate is offered, it is essentially a mandated benefit because only those interested in the mandate will take advantage of it. In addition, states sometimes exempt either the individual or small group markets from specific mandates, or may only apply that mandate to insurance companies that are domiciled in the state (e.g., a Blue Cross policy). Finally, states may pass a mandate in one legislative session only to come back in a later session and either expand or reduce the original bill's scope. That propensity to revise mandate legislation in subsequent years is one of the reasons why we don't include information on when the mandate originally passed.

**Mandates and Standard Coverage.**   Just because we list something as a mandate doesn't necessarily mean it should be excluded from a standard health insurance policy. Many mandates listed here should be and often are included in comprehensive coverage. The purpose . . . is to tabulate the number of benefits mandated by the states and assess their impact on the cost of insurance—not to make judgments about which mandates should or should not be included in a health insurance policy.

**Assessing the Cost of Mandates. . . .**   CAHI's independent Actuarial Working Group on State Mandated Benefits analyzed company data and their experience and provided cost-range estimates—less than 1%, 1–3%, 3–5% and

5–10%—if the mandate were added to a policy that did not include the coverage. These estimates are based on real health insurance policies and are not based on theory or modeling. However, mandate legislation differs from bill to bill and from state to state. For example, one state may require insurance to cover a limited number of chiropractor visits per year, while another state may require chiropractors to be covered equally with medical doctors. The second will have a greater impact on the cost of a health insurance policy than the first. It would be impossible to make a detailed assessment of the cost of each state's mandates without evaluating each piece of legislation. Thus, the estimated cost level . . . is considered typical but may not apply to all variations of that mandate. Further, the additional cost of a mandate depends on the benefits of the policy to which it is attached. Example: A prescription drug mandate costs nothing if a policy already covers drugs, but can be very costly if added to a policy that doesn't cover drugs.

**A Caution about Comparisons and Cost Estimates.**   Because mandates can drive up the cost of health insurance, it would be easy to assume that the states with the most mandates would also have the highest premiums. While that may be true in some states, it is not necessarily so. Some mandates have a much greater impact on the cost of health insurance than others. For example, mental health parity mandates, which require insurers to cover mental health care at the same levels as physical health care, have a much greater impact on the cost of premiums than would mandates for inexpensive procedures which few people need. In addition, mental health mandates often include mini-mandates within them, like coverage for autism diagnosis and treatment.

It may be tempting to think that since a particular mandate doesn't add much to the cost of a health insurance policy, there is no reason for legislators to oppose it. The result of this reasoning is that many states have 40, 50 or more mandates. Although most mandates only increase the cost of a policy by less than 1%, 40 such mandates will price many people out of the market. It is the accumulated impact of dozens of mandates, not just one that makes health insurance unaffordable.

**New Mandates to Watch: Federal Mandates.**   Historically, Congress deferred health insurance regulation to the states. But with the passage of the Health Insurance Portability and Accountability Act of 1996 (HIPAA), that has begun to change. Congress is increasingly willing and even eager to micromanage health insurance benefits.

[F]ederal health insurance mandates . . . lay out certain requirements that specific state mandates must adopt, because they affect states' health insurance coverage benefits laws. While federal law does not mandate employers of any size offer health insurance coverage, it does require employers who choose to offer insurance that their plans meet certain federal requirements with regard to, for example, mental health, mastectomy and maternity benefits. And states, which still have the primary responsibility for regulating insurers, can require health insurance policies offered by businesses to include certain benefits that must meet the minimum federal requirements. . . .

There are two new federal mandates from 2008: The Mental Health Parity and Addiction Equity Act, which expands the previous federal mental health parity laws to include substance abuse benefits, and Michelle's Law, which requires the continuation of health insurance coverage for full-time college students who take a medical leave of absence (otherwise, they would have become ineligible for dependent-student status under a parent's health insurance plan).

**Emerging Mandates.**    Several mandates are growing in popularity, and we expect to see even more legislative activity in the near future. For example: autism and treatment for its various complications is becoming one of the most discussed mandates.

Autism is a brain disorder that affects three areas of development: communication, social interaction, and creative or imaginative play. In the past, autism has fallen under the broader category of mental health, but one of the latest state legislative trends is to pass a standalone autism mandate separate from mental health benefit mandates. To be clear, health insurance does and should cover physical medical conditions faced by those with autism. In addition, it will usually cover many mental health conditions. However, autism advocates are pushing to have health insurance required to cover areas that would be more accurately described as education. We do not question the benefits of the various educational therapies for autism, and we certainly sympathize with the financial plight of some families faced with significant new care-related expenses, but we do question whether some of the therapies are within the scope of traditional health insurance.

It is also important to point out that federal law plays a role in autism coverage. Under the 2004 Individuals with Disabilities Education Act, or IDEA (PL 108-446), early intervention and special education programs must provide related services and treatments to children with autism. So there could be some overlap with state health insurance mandates. If legislators want to help these families, they could go beyond the IDEA scope and create programs that do just that and fund them from general revenues rather than try to force those costs onto health insurance, which will just increase others' premiums. (For a more in-depth look at the autism issue, see CAHI's "The Growing Trend Toward Mandating Autism Coverage")

In addition, we have reported in the past that several states are trying to extend dependent coverage to people who are clearly past childhood—up to age 30 and even older. The problem is that children between the ages of 2 and 18 are the healthiest segment of the population. Since the vast majority of them don't use many health services, their premiums are very low, which helps young families because they tend to be early in their working careers and so have relatively low incomes. And even though health care costs for young adults are higher, insurers will usually continue to cover them into college and graduate school, if they remain dependents. The important point is that restricting children's coverage to children keeps the premiums low, helping young families. If insurers must start including those who are well into adulthood, premiums for "dependents coverage" will rise, making it unaffordable for many young families.

The question that every legislator needs to ask is: When does one person's or group's need to have some new or traditionally uncovered procedure or therapy paid for by health insurance outweigh the majority's need to keep premiums affordable?

Fortunately, there is evidence that some legislators are getting CAHI's message. At least 30 states now require that a mandate's cost must be assessed before it is implemented. And at least 10 states provide for mandate-lite policies, which allow some individuals to purchase a policy with fewer mandates more tailored to their needs and financial situation.

**The Rest of the Story.**    The mandates enumerated here don't tell the whole story. States have other ways of adversely affecting the cost of health insurance. For example, several states have adopted legislation that requires health insurers selling in the individual market to accept anyone who applies, regardless of their health status, known as "guaranteed issue." Or they limit insurers' ability to price a policy to accurately reflect the risk an applicant brings to the pool, known as "community rating" or "modified community rating."

Both guaranteed issue and community rating can have a devastating impact on the price of health insurance, especially as younger and healthier people cancel their coverage, leaving the pool smaller and sicker. Thus, in the aggregate, mandates drive up the cost of health insurance. But determining the impact in a particular state requires careful analysis of each piece of mandate legislation, as well as other regulations that have been promulgated. . .

## The Growing Trend Toward Mandating Autism Coverage

Autism and treatment for its various complications is becoming one of the most discussed and demanded state benefit mandates. But there is a growing debate over whether, and to what extent, autism is a health-related condition as opposed to a behavioral condition or educational challenge. While health insurance does and should cover health-related aspects of autism, policymakers who want to ensure that families facing the real financial and other challenges posed by autism should develop safety net programs that meet their needs, rather than trying to impose autism-related costs on health insurance.

**Mental Health or Habilitative Services?**    Currently, health insurance does and should cover physical medical conditions faced by those with autism. In addition, it will often cover many mental health-related conditions. However, autism advocates want to require health insurance to cover therapies more accurately described as educational.

One problem is how to categorize autism treatment: Does it fall under mental health or habilitative services? If autism is a mental health condition, it is more likely to be covered by health insurance. If under habilitative services, then it should be considered long-term care.

A mental health benefit mandate provides for the payment of mental health evaluation and treatment, but sometimes at a higher out-of-pocket cost for the patient, or limitations are imposed on the coverage. Historically, mental health services have higher patient cost-sharing and shorter visit limits than services for physical illness or injury. Mental health parity laws try to minimize or eliminate this difference by requiring the same limitations and cost-sharing for mental health as for traditional medical care.

Habilitative services treatments, by contrast, include occupational, physical and speech therapies for children with a congenital or genetic birth defect, including autism. The goal of such services is to enhance the child's ability to function.

**Coverage for Autism.**   Under a federal law passed in 2004, the Individuals with Disabilities Education Act, or IDEA, public early intervention and special education programs must provide related services and treatments to children with autism. However, only roughly 3 percent of autistic children's needs are met under IDEA, and President Obama has expressed support for even more comprehensive federal coverage.

State legislatures traditionally have grouped autism in the broader category of mental health, but one of the latest state legislative trends is to pass an autism mandate separately from mental health benefit mandates.

Autism support groups want mandate legislation that provides for evaluation and treatment of autism, as well as specific services such as school mainstreaming.

**Which States Cover Autism?**   The question of whether autism is a mental health condition covered under health insurance varies from state to state. One of the problems is that scientists and doctors are not certain what causes autism, and so historically treatment differs from one person to the next. Plus autism-coverage advocates often vary in how they interpret existing laws.

- For example, Autism Speaks reports eight states with health insurance autism benefits.
- However, several autism blogs report a higher figure and point to a Connecticut Office of Legislative Research (OLR) report dated December 2006 that says 17 states have some level of coverage for autism, including 10 that require coverage for autism through their laws mandating mental illness coverage. Six of those states have specific autism laws.
- In July 2008, the Connecticut OLR came out with an additional report that broke down the autism mandate differently. Researchers reported that 22 states besides Connecticut mandate some amount of coverage for the treatment of autism—which is consistent with CAHI's own tracking of the autism mandate. Of these, eight require coverage for behavioral treatment services for autism (Arizona, Florida, Indiana, Kentucky, Louisiana, Pennsylvania, South Carolina and Texas) and five plus Connecticut require other coverage related to autism (Colorado, Georgia, Maryland, New York and Tennessee). Nine states and Connecticut include autism in their mental health mandate laws (California, Illinois, Iowa, Kansas, Maine, Montana, New Hampshire, New Jersey and Virginia).

The Autism Society of America is more consistent with the Connecticut OLR report and several autism blogs. The Society's scope is broader than Autism Speaks, and it includes all types of coverage that addresses autism benefits, not just behavioral support.

CAHI has tracked 39 states that have mental health benefit mandates on their books (of which 30 specifically include autism), 47 that have state mental health parity laws and at least three have habilitative services for children.

There was additional autism-mandate activity during the 2008 legislative session. For example, Arizona, Connecticut, Florida, Illinois, Louisiana, Pennsylvania and South Carolina now have state mandate laws. And Hawaii adopted a resolution that requests a study of the social and financial impact of adding an autism mandate to health insurance coverage.

Even so, states are increasingly looking to insurers to cover more—or all—of the costs of caring for autistic children. Not because health insurers have any particular expertise in, or even responsibility for, autism. Legislators want insurers to cover more of the costs simply so the state doesn't have to.

**The Push for Expanded Autism Coverage.** Autism is a serious problem in the country, and we still don't understand the causes or the cure. The Centers for Disease Control reported in 2007 that one in 150 children has this disorder. And there is a growing recognition that autism should be identified early and treated—hence the American Academy of Pediatrics' recent recommendation that all U.S. children be formally screened for autism twice by the age of two.

We do know these children need significant amounts of care. That's why Wisconsin's approach, which set up the Children's Long-Term Care Community-Based Waiver (or CTLS) to provide a range of services to qualifying individuals, makes the most sense. It provides more integrated care than could possibly be provided by health insurance.

In addition, autism support groups and their families are looking for more financial relief from and coverage for Applied Behavior Analysis and other therapies which, according to proponents, contain some of the most effective forms of treatment, best outcomes and long-term economic benefits. Proponents believe that health insurance companies should assume the financial burden—typically in the range of $50,000 per year per child—for autistic children that families and school districts have borne.

Insurance carriers argue that most medically related treatments are already covered for autism. In addition, they note that autism is an individually based disorder, and so there is often no clear standard of care to determine the appropriate therapy. Further, some see behavioral therapy not as a medical benefit but an educational one. For example, "play therapies" can require up to 10 separate interactions per day, ensuring the child remains focused on the world around him. The therapy may be provided by unlicensed care providers (and/or parents) who can be trained to use the methods very effectively. Some of the other therapies address developmental delays, which are not typically covered under health insurance.

While various educational therapies for autism may be beneficial, and while we recognize that many families struggle under the related financial burdens associated with autism, we question whether some of these therapies are within the scope of traditional health insurance.

**The Cost of Autism Coverage.** CAHI's actuarial working team estimates that an autism mandate increases the cost of health insurance by about 1 percent. But they caution us that figure may be rising for two reasons. The incidence of autism appears to be growing, and there is a trend to cover more services, which will drive up the cost of each covered individual. If these trends continue, as we expect, the cost of mandating coverage will move into the 1 to 3 percent range.

**Conclusion.**   Private health insurance, with companies and individuals frequently changing plans or health care networks, doesn't provide the consistent care autistic children need. If legislators want to help these families, they should create programs specifically targeted to meet their needs and properly fund them from general revenues—better than Congress did under the IDEA program—rather than try to force the costs onto health insurance, which will just increase everyone's premiums.

# EXPLORING THE ISSUE

## Should Insurance Cover Treatments/Services for Autism?

## Challenge Questions

- Compare and contrast the positions of the YES and NO selections regarding whether health insurance should cover the costs of autism treatments.
- Which selection makes the best case for its argument? Why?
- Does your state mandate private insurance companies to cover treatments/services for individuals with autism? What is your insurance company's policy about covering these services?
- Should health insurance continue to cover treatment after children enter school, or should treatment become part of educational expenses?

## Is There Common Ground?

There is no question that children with autism need services, nor that these services are expensive. Almost everyone would agree that few families can afford $50,000 per year to educate one child and that there is a serious impact of this same annual amount on a school district, especially a small one. For $50,000, a teacher and paraprofessional could be hired for a class of 25 children. In tight fiscal times, this choice causes pain and anger. Simultaneously, health insurance companies struggle with competing demands for increased services and affordable costs. It is ironic that the diagnosis of autism makes children eligible for some intensive services, but shuts them out of others.

## Additional Resources

Abramson, L. (2007, September 26). *Family wins suit for autistic son's health care*. Retrieved November 28, 2008 from www.npr.org/templates/story/story.php?storyId=14577821

Autism Speaks. (2008). *Arguments in support of private insurance coverage for autism-related services*. Retrieved March 18, 2009 from http://dhhs.nv.gov/autism/TaskForce/2008/ATF_Report_08/Appendix%20E.pdf

Abt Associates. (2008). *Autism spectrum disorders mandated benefits review panel report: Evidence submitted concerning Pennsylvania HB 1150*. Durham, NC: Abt Associates.

Basu, R. (2009, March 1). *Who should pay for autism treatment?* Retrieved February 11, 2010 from http://the-undercurrent.com/blog/who-should-pay-for-autism-treatment/

Bunce, V. C. & Wieske, J. P. (2009a). *Health Insurance Mandates in the States 2009*. The Council for Affordable Health Insurance. Retrieved February 10, 2009 from www.cahi.org

Bunce, V. C. & Wieske, J. P. (2009b, March). The growing trend toward mandating autism coverage. *The Council for Affordable Health Insurance's Issues & Answers* (152). Retrieved March 27, 2009 from www.cahi.org

Foden, T. J. (2008, June 18). *Autism and health care: Sticker shock*. Retrieved January 25, 2010 from www.iancommunity.org/cs/therapies_treatments/insurance_overview

Ganz, M. L. (2007). The lifetime distribution of the incremental societal costs of autism. *Archives of Pediatric and Adolescent Medicine, 161*(343), 349. Retrieved February 10, 2010 from www.archpediatrics.com

National Council on Disability. (2009). *The current state of health care for people with disabilities*. Retrieved October 4, 2010 from www.ncd.gov/newsroom/publications/2009/publications

Parish, S. L., Roe, R. A., Grinstein-Weiss, M., Richman, E. L., & Andrews, M. E. (2008). Material hardship in U.S. families raising children with disabilities. *Exceptional Children, 75*(1), 71–92.

Parker, S. (2008, September 29). *Autistic kids: Who should pay?* Retrieved February 11, 2010 from http://blogs.webmd.com/healthy-children/2008/09/autistic-kids-who-should-pay.html

U.S. Department of Health and Human Services, Centers for Disease Control and Prevention. (2012, March). Prevalence of autism spectrum disorders—Autism and Developmental Disabilities Monitoring Network, 14 sites, United States, 2008. *Morbidity and Mortality Weekly Report, 81*, 3. Retrieved April 9, 2012 from www.cdc.gov/mmwr/

Reinke, T. (2009). Filling in the gaps: Medicaid waivers add to the continuum of resources for people with autism. *EP Magazine, 39*(4), 68–69.

# Internet References . . .

## Office of Civil Rights Website

The Office of Civil Rights site contains abundant information. A search for "Protecting Students with Disabilities" leads to the extensive FAQ regarding the relationship between Section 504 and the education of children with disabilities.

**www2.ed.gov/about/offices/list/ocr**

## Americans with Disabilities Act (ADA)

This site contains information on the breadth of topics covered by the ADA, including education, but ranging to business, transportation, and health care. Links take readers to an array of U.S. federal departments tasked with ADA responsibilities. ADA e-mail updates are available.

**www.ada.gov**

## Reauthorization of the Elementary and Secondary Education Act (ESEA)

This government-sponsored website contains current information on the reauthorization of the Elementary and Secondary Education Act, known as No Child Left Behind in its 2001 version. It includes updates on current legislative activities as well as administration actions.

**www.ed.gov/blog/topic/esea-reauthorization/**

## What Works Clearinghouse

The What Works Clearinghouse was established in 2002 by the U.S. Department of Education's Institute of Educational Sciences to provide educators, policymakers, researchers, and the public with "a central and trusted source of scientific evidence of what works in education."

**http://ies.ed.gov/ncee/wwc/**

## Intervention Central

This site contains strategies, tools, and publication resources to assist in classroom intervention and assessment.

**www.interventioncentral.org**

# Access and Accountability

*T*hirty years ago, special education was concerned with getting students with disabilities into schools. Next, the conversation turned to opening classroom doors, so students with disabilities had access to typical peers and were included in school experiences. Current deliberations revolve around access to the general curriculum—the real work of schools. With access has come accountability. Now that the doors are open, Americans all must be accountable for the learning that goes on inside. As this new step in inclusionary practice takes shape, legislators and educators debate whether the next development is a truly seamless system of education, no longer needing the designations, protections, and paperwork of special education.

- Has the Americans with Disabilities Act (ADA) Accomplished Its Goals?
- Should RTI Interventions Be Delivered by Special Educators?
- Should Special Education and General Education Merge?
- Does NCLB Leave Some Students Behind?
- Should Students with Cognitive Disabilities Be Expected to Demonstrate Academic Proficiency?
- Is Full Inclusion the Least Restrictive Environment?
- Should Colleges Be More Accommodating to Students with Disabilities?

# ISSUE 8

## Has the Americans with Disabilities Act (ADA) Accomplished Its Goals?

YES: **John Hockenberry**, from "Yes, You Can," *Parade Magazine* (pp. 4–5, 2005, July 24), http://archive.parade.com/2005/0724/0724_ disabilities.html, July 24, 2005

NO: **Lynda A. Price, Paul J. Gerber, & Robert Mulligan**, from "Adults with Learning Disabilities and the Underutilization of the Americans with Disabilities Act," *Remedial and Special Education* (vol. 28, no. 6, pp. 340–344, 2007)

---

### Learning Outcomes

**At the conclusion of this issue, readers will be able to:**

- Compare and contrast the positions of the YES and NO selections addressing whether the ADA has achieved its goals.
- Describe the strengths and the weaknesses of each side's arguments.
- Explain how recent amendments of the ADA are likely to change school practice.
- Determine which elements of the ADAA will be most challenging to implement.

---

ISSUE SUMMARY

YES: John Hockenberry, an award-winning television commentator, radio host, and foreign correspondent, who happens to use a wheelchair, celebrates the increased access brought about by implementation of the Americans with Disabilities Act (ADA).

NO: Lynda A. Price, Paul J. Gerber (university faculty members and researchers), and Robert Mulligan (a district special education administrator) contend that the opportunities for ADA-mandated access are underused by individuals with learning disabilities.

$\mathbf{A}$s described in this section, three fundamental U.S. federal laws affect the lives of individuals with disabilities: Section 504 of the Rehabilitation Act of 1973 (Section 504), the Americans with Disabilities Act (ADA), and the Individuals with Disabilities Education Act (IDEA). This issue focuses on the first two.

Section 504 and the ADA aim to prevent discrimination against people with disabilities. They impact the lives of children with disabilities who do not require the protections of IDEA, as well as those who are not in school. The laws also apply to accessibility in employment, businesses, public facilities, restaurants, and theaters.

Section 504 is a civil rights statute prohibiting organizations receiving U.S. federal funds from discriminating against anyone based on a disability that substantially limits a major life activity. Reasonable accommodations must be implemented, so individuals with disabilities have equal access to the activities of the organization. Since all school districts receive U.S. federal funds, Section 504 covers two groups: students and employees.

Students served under IDEA are automatically covered by Section 504. Students with disabilities who do not require the specially designed instruction of IDEA often have 504 Plans, although these are not required by statute. A 504 plan specifies accommodations and related services necessary to ensure equal access to the educational experience.

The ADA, passed in 1990 by the first President Bush, extended the civil rights responsibilities of Section 504 to businesses (other than churches or private clubs) that do not receive U.S. federal funds. The ADA carries the same responsibility for reasonable accommodations as Section 504, impacting the practices of almost every employer.

The ADA was reauthorized in 2008 and is now referred to as the Americans with Disabilities Amendment Act (ADAA). Congress explicitly emphasized its original intent for broad coverage, countering Supreme Court decisions that had narrowed the scope of ADA's applicability. Through a conforming amendment to Section 504, the coverage of both laws became essentially the same; they are now frequently addressed together, as they will be here.

This issue is somewhat unusual for Taking Sides. As customary, the YES and NO selections present contrasting views—this time of the success of the ADA. Both selections were written before the act was amended. Congress clearly felt the answer to the issue's question was no; changes were necessary to reach the intended goal. The content in this section addresses the new aspects of ADAA. Consider the selections in light of perceived previous accomplishments and how the ADAA will impact society.

In the YES selection, John Hockenberry, a prominent journalist and foreign correspondent, shares his personal experiences with the ADA. At the age of 19, he became a paraplegic in a car accident. He now uses a wheelchair in his daily travel and in his overseas assignments. Hockenberry reminds readers of the increased access that we now take as commonplace. Commenting on how curb cuts and other accommodations make his own travels possible, Hockenberry reminds us that some ADA-generated changes, such as curb cuts, also assist people who do not have disabilities. Twenty years ago, the idea that a man in a wheelchair could use the subway (much less report from a far-away country) was an unlikely dream. For Hockenberry, the pre-amendment ADA did achieve its goals.

In the NO selection, Lynda A. Price and Paul J. Gerber, university professors whose research focuses on the employment of adults with learning disabilities, are joined by Robert Mulligan who directs district special education services. These three authors present evidence that adults with specific learning disabilities do not tap into ADA-mandated benefits once they leave public schools. Although these young adults heard about accomplishments of individuals with disabilities as they attended school, fully covered by IDEA, they are reticent to speak up after graduation. These findings are cause for concern, since half the students served by special education are categorized with this disability. As you read, consider whether the recent amendments would change the observations and opinions of these authors.

Questions about the differences in the ADAA/504 are answered officially in two FAQs from the U.S. Department of Education Office for Civil Rights (*Protecting students with disabilities*, 2012, www2.ed.gov/about/offices/lists/ocr). Key points follow:

1. A broader definition of disability is established. Individuals may fall under the protection of this law if they are regarded as having a disability. Eligibility may apply if an impairment is episodic or in remission. Students who previously may not have been determined to have a disability under these laws may now qualify.
2. The disability must "substantially limit (any) major life activity."
3. Determination of disability existence must be made without consideration of mitigating measures.

The significant changes were made in the second and third points. The list of major life activities has been expanded to include learning, reading, concentrating, and thinking. Although these might ordinarily be considered by schools, educators must now consider the full range of life activities. An allergy may not substantially affect a child's learning, but its existence could establish a disability and trigger ADAA coverage.

The third point concerns the use of mitigating measures. These often ameliorate the effects of a disability so as to make it all-but-unnoticeable. Consider medication a person takes for a seizure disorder. Without it, this individual's ability to attend and concentrate would be significantly impacted. With medication, the person can focus and complete grade-level work: the medication has mitigated the impact of the disability. Over time, the courts decided that the impact of the mitigating measure could be considered when making eligibility decisions; this individual might not have been eligible if medication totally controlled the condition. ADAA clarifies that narrowed perspective; individuals cannot be denied protection because they use mitigating measures (Kaloi & Stanbury, 2009, www.LD.org). This person could now be determined to have a disability, even though the seizure disorder would be all-but-unnoticeable with the medication.

The existence/effect of a mitigating measure can, however, be considered in determining if there is a need for services or accommodations. For example, the student's seizure disorder is completely controlled by medication taken at home. With medication, the student succeeds in school. In this case, the team could find that a disability exists, but that no services or accommodations are needed.

Given ADAA's changes, Weatherly (*inCase*, 2012, January–March) advises schools to adopt a two-stage process when considering 504 eligibility. First, make a disability determination in accordance with the new standards. Next, decide whether any services or accommodations are necessary, and whether these should be documented within a 504 plan. The reverse course of action would apply to students who no longer require IDEA services; if their disability still exists, the team should consider 504 eligibility.

Returning to the focus of this issue, recall that the driving force behind these laws was the desire to eliminate discrimination against individuals on the basis of a disability. Equal access provides opportunities for individuals to develop and demonstrate their abilities. John Hockenberry experiences a successful journalism career, not life in a limited environment. Not everyone has had the same experience.

On the 21st anniversary of the ADA, Nirvi Shah (*Education Week*, July 2011, www.edweek.org) was startled by information from the 2010 Census. Even with the protection and services of IDEA, 28 percent of individuals with disabilities have not earned their high school diploma, compared to 12 percent of the adult population. Of people age 16 and over, 21 percent of those with disabilities live in poverty, compared to 11 percent of those without a disability. For those who do work, the annual salary for individuals with disabilities is approximately $10,000 less than the salary for individuals without disabilities. Contemplate whether these outcomes are related to the practices Section 504/ADAA address.

Students with disabilities are increasingly enrolling in postsecondary education programs. Describing the situation for individuals with learning disabilities (who comprise approximately half of all students in special education), Candace Cortiella (*The state of learning disabilities*, National Center for Learning Disabilities, 2011) reported that high school graduation rates are increasing, but individuals with learning disabilities pursue postsecondary education, and obtain a college degree, at a far lower rate than their peers.

Most colleges and universities have centers to assist students in obtaining accommodations and communicating with faculty members. As with employment, individuals must self-disclose their disability and request support. Despite support centers, college can be more isolating than high schools. College faculty are unfamiliar with disabilities or the policies related to student rights and accommodations (Hong, Ivy, Gonzalez, & Ehrensberger, *TEACHING Exceptional Children*, 2007). Frustrated students give up and drop out.

IDEA 2004 increased emphasis on transition planning. Beginning with the IEP in place when the student turns 16, educational teams must consider postsecondary goals related to training, education, employment, and independent living. An action plan must be created for securing postsecondary services to reach these goals. This emphasis may increase attention to the development of self-advocacy skills necessary for successful postsecondary experiences.

Focusing on awareness and self-advocacy skills, Connor (*TEACHING Exceptional Children*, 2012) notes that the largest challenge for students may be to assume control and responsibility for leading their own learning. Among several suggested skills, Connor recommends that students become comfortable and knowledgeable about their disability status and needs as well as the rights and protections of Section 504/ADAA. Appreciating the responsibility for, and benefits of, self-disclosure will enable students to make informed decisions.

Perry Zirkel, a legal scholar who focuses in the area of special education, offers advice about ADAA implementation. Providing a sample Section 504/ADA Student Eligibility Form, Zirkel counsels educators to be lenient when determining a disability, and prepared to give the benefit of the doubt (Zirkel, *TEACHING Exceptional Children*, 2009). Because of the ADAA changes, the number of individuals found eligible for 504/ADAA is expected to rise (Zirkel, *Principal*, 2012). Zirkel advises special educators to be ready to help their general education colleagues adjust to this change.

Elements of the ADAA have shifted. Time, experience, and Court decisions will determine how the changes affect the goal of ensuring that people with disabilities have fair and equal access.

# YES

John Hockenberry

## Yes, You Can

Careful! You might miss the light show. If you surrender to any nervousness or caution and avoid looking at me when I roll by in my wheelchair, you'll miss the fireworks in my front wheels: tiny, colored electric lights that blaze out red, blue and green when they turn. That's right. I have electric scooter wheels on my wheelchair, and the greatest thing about them is how they grab the nervous eyes of some folks and pull them in. "Awesome!" people will say to me as I race across the Brooklyn Bridge. "Hey, that's cool!" I'll hear at an airport as I race to catch a plane. *"Really cool."*

It was two 6-year-old girls who convinced me that high-profile, sparkly wheels were a big improvement over my quiet, in-the-shadows approach to being disabled in public. Those two girls are my oldest twin daughters, Zoe and Olivia. They are almost 7 now, and all of their lives they have ridden on their daddy's lap. Doctors may call me a paraplegic. Strangers might say I am "wheelchair bound." But to my daughters, I have always been a daddy who comes with his own playground apparatus. In their short lives, oblivious of the fears and anxieties of adults, they have known a wheelchair only to represent a warm, safe place.

## Going Public

These days, Zoe and Olivia are nearly too big to ride comfortably on my lap anymore, and I will miss them terribly when they stop climbing up altogether. (At least I still have 4-year-old Zach and Regan, our second set of twins!) But I look into the faces of my children and see a sunrise of hope that people with disabilities are experiencing 15 years after the passage of the Americans with Disabilities Act (ADA).

Almost two decades into this landmark civil rights law, people determined to share their distinct talents have begun to take their places in the American mainstream. The signs of their presence go far beyond handicapped parking spaces and wheelchair ramps. Thanks to their persistence, today you are as likely to see a person with a disability on the ski slopes as you are in your workplace. And the momentum is picking up. All across the U.S., people with and without disabilities are bringing about lasting changes in their communities: There are city and state building codes, such as Michigan's, that go beyond federal law by mandating that doors, passageways and bathrooms be unobstructed. There is the unique federal and civic partnership that designed and built wheelchair access into Boston's venerated Fenway Park, which for decades was off-limits to the disabled. And there is the Center for Creative Play, a universally accessible indoor playspace in Pittsburgh, Pa., for children of all abilities, which projects such a powerful "Welcome, all!" message that families drive hours just to play there. Taken one at a time, these are small changes you might miss unless you modify old assumptions and look at the world with new eyes.

## Strength in Numbers

Even the battles today are different. Fifteen years ago, there might have been a debate over whether someone like Tony Sylvester, a young man born with spina bifida, could even go to a public school. Recently, Tony, 19 and a graduate of Wauwatosa West High School in suburban Milwaukee, Wis., waged a tough campaign for his varsity letter. Tony's a forward for the highly ranked Wheelin' Wizards—a wheelchair basketball team that competes with other disabled athletes, independent of their high schools. To appeal the school superintendent's decision to deny the letter, Tony and his mother, Tish, got advice from a powerful ally—IndependenceFirst, a Milwaukee-based organization that helped them pack a school-board meeting with disabled athletes, coaches, parents and the media. As a result, Tony was awarded his letter—a big W, which he wears proudly.

No doubt, there is strength in numbers—and the numbers are growing. IndependenceFirst, the group that helped Tony and Tish, is just one of about 500 Independent Living Centers across the U.S. that have grown up with the ADA. Typically nonresidential, private and nonprofit (though many are state-supported), these community-based centers provide services and act as advocates for people with disabilities. . . . There also are 10 federally funded ADA & information technology centers in the U.S. to help businesses, architects and schools comply with the law by providing information, training and technical assistance. . . .

Clearly, there are fewer excuses today for being inaccessible and indifferent to the disabled. But, in the end, a truly inclusive world will depend on the efforts and courage of those who are not disabled—in a word, society at large. After all, the Civil Rights Act of 1964—which had the backing of the courts, the police and the National Guard—still has not wiped out racism.

## It's Up to You, Too

Meanwhile, local victories like Tony Sylvester's boost morale for the bigger struggles that lie ahead. For instance, employment for people with disabilities has not improved significantly since the passage of the ADA. Disabled unemployment has stood near 70% for the past two decades. The ADA itself has suffered setbacks in court decisions and by its own limitations. Businesses can be exempted from the ADA by claiming that compliance is an "undue burden."

And houses of worship do not have to comply at all, even though thousands have because it is the right thing to do. Enforcement of the ADA is left to the courts, where the vast majority of lawsuits are thrown out before they ever reach trial.

Perhaps the most significant accomplishment of the Americans With Disabilities Act is that it has widened the expectation that there ought to be some way in for people with disabilities. One telling example is an incident that occurred a few years ago when I was riding on the New York City subway. The train was declared "out of service" and pulled into a station without an elevator—one of many. The conductor ordered all passengers off the train. With the exception of me and a few women with strollers, everyone got off and trudged up the steps to the sidewalk.

When the conductor offered me no help, my only option was to hop out of my wheelchair and lug myself up the filthy subway stairs on my keister. But then one of the stroller women laid into the conductor: "What's your plan for this man? Is he just supposed to stay down here forever? Is that your plan?" She was riled up on my behalf. "We're not stupid people," she continued. "There's a law that says you have to have a plan. Everybody knows that."

## We All Benefit

The conductor went from ignoring a solitary man in a wheelchair to being intimidated by a volunteer SWAT team of Brooklyn moms. He told all of us to stay on the train, then drove us to the next elevator station. The stroller mom looked at me and said with a smile, "You're the guy on TV, right? I love your work." I thanked her and left the train in awe of the anonymous outraged lady who had saved the powerless TV star. Her outrage represented something deeper: an expectation that has grown up with the ADA that disabled people have certain rights that cannot be denied. That's what saved me: her expectation—*our shared expectation*—that there is a place for all in America.

It's not like only the disabled benefit from this. Those ladies with their strollers have me to thank for the sidewalk ramps they love. And do you think that young office workers in the gym realize that it is the deaf they have to thank for the captions on the TV screens that allow them to follow their stocks while they huff and puff? Having a place for all is both the American dream and the engine of our success. We've been working on this freedom thing for the past 229 years. As my daughters might say: It's high time for some awesome, sparkly wheels.

## What You Should Know

On July 26, 1990, the Americans With Disabilities Act was signed into law, eliminating discrimination in employment, transportation and public accommodations for the nation's 50 million disabled adults and children. Still, to this day, many with physical and mental disabilities do not get their due. To learn more or for technical-assistance materials, . . . call the ADA Information

Line at 1-800-514-0301. (During business hours, specialists help you apply the law to your own situation.) For TTY, call 1-800-514-0383.

- Employers interested in hiring the disabled can consult the Employer Assistance and Recruiting Network (EARN), a free service of the Department of Labor. . . .

Lynda A. Price, Paul J. Gerber,
and Robert Mulligan

 **NO**

# Adults with Learning Disabilities and the Underutilization of the Americans with Disabilities Act

**A**t its signing in 1990, then U.S. President George H. W. Bush commented that the Americans with Disabilities Act (ADA) had moved people with disabilities from an era of paternalism to one of empowerment. In essence, the ADA was constructed to markedly change the way that people with disabilities would participate in society. In the ensuing years, the ADA has had a positive effect on people with disabilities, but, when examined more closely, there are questions about whether the ADA has met its potential with all populations of people with disabilities, one of them being learning disabilities (LD).

The part of the ADA that has the most impact on people with learning disabilities is Title 1, which governs practices in the area of competitive employment. Provisions of law are carefully articulated, with precise concepts such as *disability*, *qualified*, *essential functions*, and *reasonable accommodation*. In order for a person with LD to effectively use the ADA, these concepts must be understood. Likewise, some other things need to be mastered pertaining to the learning disability itself. Knowledge of one's challenges, the process of self-disclosure, and monitoring performance under the auspices of the ADA via self-advocacy procedures are most important.

A review of the extant research literature on LD and the ADA is one avenue of discovery. Another is a review of commonly used ADA materials to

1. teach and prepare students with LD during their last years of high school,
2. train professionals about LD and the ADA, and
3. inform consumers (adults with LD and parents) about their rights and prerogatives under the ADA.

. . . This article seeks to uncover the state of the art regarding people with LD and the ADA, especially in terms of preparing for transition.

Price et. al., Linda A. From *Remedial and Special Education*, vol. 28, no. 6, November/December 2007, pp. 340–344 (excerpts). Copyright © 2007 by Hammill Institute on Disabilities and Sage in association with American Rehabilitation Counseling Association (ARCA). Reprinted by permission via Rightslink.

# Review of ADA Research

## Business and Industry and the ADA

At the beginning of the ADA era, Gerber probed the knowledge and under-standing of the ADA from executive officers, human resource directors, and personnel managers of nine Virginia companies, some Fortune 500 compa-nies, national companies, and regional companies. It was apparent that the focus of business and industry was on compliance with the ADA, primarily for people with physical and sensory disabilities. At that time, LD were thought of as an enigma or not considered at all. There was even confusion about the true meaning of learning disabilities, which were sometimes equated with mental retardation. Gerber's conclusion indicated a shift in the role and responsibility for people with LD beyond their K–12 school experience:

> It must be remembered that business and industry are not expert when it comes to issues of disability, including learning disabilities. Therefore, the successes of people with learning disabilities will not be contingent upon law and the efforts of business alone. It will be linked to the capabilities and performance of individuals with learning disabilities themselves.

The onus of responsibility had clearly shifted as the expectations of the beyond-school culture set in. People with LD had to be able to effectively advocate for themselves. As adults, they had to be knowledgeable about their "LD profile," know how to self-disclose, and know how to use the provisions of the ADA to their benefit.

In a follow-up study to Gerber's work, Price and Gerber gauged the impact of the ADA (Price). Nine employers . . . were studied to see how people with LD were faring with the ADA in 1998. . . . As in the 1992 study, managers, supervisors, and human resource administrators were interviewed. The results of the study were essentially the same. Moreover, it was very clear that employ-ers were most willing to "work with" employees with LD under the provisions of the ADA. Also, they saw the effectiveness of the ADA being predicated on a partnership with the employees with LD themselves. In the absence of guid-ance and expertise in their workplace, employees with LD had to be "experts" in their own right when it came to LD and the ADA.

## People with LD and the ADA

A series of investigations were made to discover the realities of the workplace for people with LD in the ADA era. Price, Gerber, and Mulligan studied 25 adults with LD. . . . Five of the 25 respondents mentioned their learning disability while pursuing their job, but they never mentioned the ADA. The remaining 20 adults mentioned neither. None of the adults asked for pre-employment testing accommodations that were allowable under the ADA. Moreover, 19 respondents had no knowledge of the ADA, with many saying that they had never heard of it. Specifically, these adults did not understand how the ADA applied to them or how to use it for their own self-advocacy.

In a pilot study for a larger national study, Gerber, Price, Mulligan, and Williams found that very little was known about the ADA, and thus the ADA was underused. Some of the participants believed that the ADA was solely for people with physical disabilities. Of the 18 adults in the pilot, only 3 participants had learned about the ADA before leaving high school or in a post-secondary setting, with only one receiving any type of secondary transition assistance. . . . Furthermore, this study revealed the importance of a new element within the issue of underutilization—the issue of self-disclosure.

This set of findings foreshadowed what was seen in the national study of 80 adults with LD. . . . The majority of adults with LD in this larger study did not know of the existence of the ADA. If the adults had heard about the ADA, they knew very few details about it. Moreover, they did not see how it applied to them or to their disability.

Interesting enough, the findings of this study paralleled research done on 24 Canadian adults with LD. . . . Canadians have the Charter of Rights and Freedoms that protects individuals with disabilities (including LD) in all facets of society. Even though the Charter is not as focused as the ADA, it guarantees against discrimination in the workplace, including people with disabilities. Despite its existence, it was underused by adults with LD and just played a minor role in employment settings. Many participants in the study did not know how the Charter specifically applied to the workplace. In a comparative study of the American and Canadian data sets, the overall conclusion was that disability laws, whether American or Canadian, were not readily being used by adults with LD. This might be to the disadvantage of employees with LD not only at job entry but also in job advancement.

# Reasons for ADA Underutilization

## Transition-Oriented Materials

Ever since transition became an important initiative of the federal government in the 1980s, special educators have implemented curricula to prepare students with disabilities for their beyond-school years. Such has been the case for students with LD, although they have generally been grouped in a high-incidence, generic-like category. Curricula have been delivered to students with LD who were going from school to work as well as school to school to work. Granted, when the transition initiative was first proffered to the field, the ADA had not yet become law. It was during the decade of the 1990s that the ADA became part of the conversation regarding transition. Indeed, the ADA was enthusiastically received by the LD community because approximately 85% of people with LD go straight to work in competitive employment settings.

Perhaps one of the reasons for the underutilization of the ADA can be explained by a lack of relevant information on the ADA and LD currently available for the transition planning process. This hypothesis was addressed in a preliminary manner through an examination of widely known transition materials used in secondary schools, taught in personnel preparation courses, and developed for adults with LD. . . .

The 10 transition materials selected were subjectively chosen by the authors as representative of what is currently available in terms of transition ideology and methodology. . . .

[Despite] the best efforts to develop relevant materials for the transition process—some pertaining to students with LD and some not—little or no information is available on the ADA in these materials. Of equal importance, virtually no information is presented on how the ADA and transition specifically apply to individuals with LD. . . .

[The] professional transition literature has not kept up with the challenges of individuals with LD in this critical and frequently neglected area.

The reason for this glaring omission is not entirely certain at this time, but it begs the question: If students do not receive information about the ADA and how to use it effectively in their latter years of school, then when do they ever learn it? Moreover, if the vast majority of students with LD go straight to work, then when will they ever learn about the ADA?

## Self-Disclosure in the Workplace

Another issue interwoven with the connections of LD, transition planning, and adulthood is *self-disclosure*. Unlike the school-age special education laws (e.g., IDEA and Section 504), the ADA is predicated on self-disclosure. If people with LD do not self-disclose, then the protections laid out in the ADA are moot. Sadly, this seems to be the case for the vast majority of people with LD in employment settings, as noted in the preceding discussion. . . .

It should be noted that recent work by Gerber et al. has underscored self-disclosure as a significant and complex process in the lives of adults with LD. One component of this process, which is directly relevant to transition and ITPs, is the notion of personal choice. Currently, more than 120 adults with documented LD have reported to the authors that they make new decisions everyday about revealing—and not revealing—their disability. However, such critical decisions are often based on adult-oriented environments (e.g., family, employment, college classroom, [and] church). These choices mirror exactly the five consistent areas of transition planning anticipated by IDEA: postsecondary education, integrated employment, independent living, community participation, and recreation/leisure. Preliminary studies in this area have revealed that most adults with LD are much more comfortable discussing their LD at home with parents or immediate family members, where legislation is not an issue. However, these same individuals are often very reluctant to self-disclose at work—the exact location where the ADA could be a valuable asset for job performance. . . .

## Discussion

The underutilization of the ADA is an example of a missed opportunity for individuals with LD. The ADA can make a profound difference in competitive employment settings in job entry, in performance evaluation, and in job advancement. What is highlighted in the examination of the issue of the

ADA vis-à-vis LD is that there is a disconnection between the school-age and beyond-school years. If preparation for the beyond-school years is not sufficient or effective, it has lifelong consequences. In effect, insufficient preparation largely discounts the possibility of accessing the ADA throughout the adult years. Preparation for the adult years is multifaceted. Transition curricula and materials need to be specifically focused on understanding and using the ADA in the most authentic, research-based manner possible. As a result, materials need to be more in-depth, comprehensive, and LD-specific.

This article also suggests the need for greater examination of the ramifications of LD on transition preparation and effective use of the ADA. Clearly, many questions remain to be answered, including the following:

- How do we provide authentic transition training about the ADA for individuals with LD, their parents, teachers, and other related professionals?
- How do we integrate knowledge about the ADA and its consequences in the workplace for individuals with LD into local ITPs?
- How do we provide the most effective preservice and inservice training possible for secondary and postsecondary professionals (high school teachers and counselors, special needs college faculty, etc.) who, in turn, teach others about the transition, LD, and the ADA?

# EXPLORING THE ISSUE

## Has the Americans with Disabilities Act (ADA) Accomplished Its Goals?

## Challenge Questions

- Compare and contrast the positions of the YES and NO selections regarding whether the ADA has met its goals of providing equal access to individuals with disabilities.
- Which selection makes the best case for its argument? Why?
- Discuss the implications of the ADAA for school practices.
- Why are legal protections more extensive for children with disabilities while they are in school than when they graduate?
- Does society find it more acceptable to provide equal access to those with physical disabilities than to those whose disabilities are less visible? Why is the subway more accessible than a college classroom? What would the authors think?

## Is There Common Ground?

All the authors of the YES and NO selections agree that the ADA provides significant opportunities to help individuals with disabilities participate fully in society, school, and work. The benefits are substantial—for those who seek them.

## Additional Resources

Connor, D. J. (2012). Helping students with disabilities transition to college: 21 Tips for students with LD and/or ADD/ADHD. *TEACHING Exceptional Children, 44*(5), 16–25.

Cortiella, C. C. (2011). *The state of learning disabilities.* New York: National Center for Learning Disabilities. Retrieved from www.LD.org

Hockenberry, J. (2005, July 24). Yes, you can. *Parade Magazine,* 4–5. Retrieved July 24, 2005 from http://archive.parade.com/2005/0724/0724_disabilities.html

Kaloi, L. & Stanbury, K. (2009). *Section 504 in 2009: Broader eligibility, more accommodations.* Retrieved March 1, 2011 from www.LD.org

Holler, R. A. & Zirkel, P. A. (2008). Section 504 and public schools: A national survey concerning Section 504-only students. *NASSP Bulletin, 92*(1), 19–43.

Hong, B. S. S., Ivy, W. F., Gonzalez, H. R., & Ehrensberger, W. (2007). Preparing students for postsecondary education. *TEACHING Exceptional Children, 40*(1), 32–38.

Office of Civil Rights. (2012, January). *Protecting students with disabilities: Questions and answers on the ADA Amendments Act of 2008 for students with disabilities attending public elementary and secondary school.* Retrieved May 11, 2012 from www.ed.govADAAFAQ

Price, L. A., Gerber, P. J., & Mulligan, R. (2007). Adults with learning disabilities and the underutilization of the Americans with Disabilities Act. *Remedial and Special Education, 28*(6), 340–344.

Shah, N. (2011, July 26). *21 years after ADA, Census reveals some startling statistics.* Retrieved July 26, 2011 from www.edweek.org

Weatherly, J. J. (2012, January–March). Legal update: Further clarification from OCR on 504 "eligibility": A student can be found disabled but not in need of a 504 plan! *inCase, 5*, 9.

Zirkel, P. A. (2009). What does the law say? New Section 504 student eligibility standards. *TEACHING Exceptional Children, 41*(4), 68–71.

Zirkel, P. A. (2012, March/April). Section 504: An update. *Principal, 91*(4), 60–62.

# ISSUE 9

## Should RTI Interventions Be Delivered by Special Educators?

**YES: Douglas Fuchs, Lynn S. Fuchs, & Donald L. Compton**, from "Smart RTI: A Next-Generation Approach to Multilevel Prevention," *Exceptional Children* (vol. 78, no. 3, pp. 263–279, 2012)

**NO: Linda P. Blanton, Marleen C. Pugach, & Lani Florian**, from *Preparing General Education Teachers to Improve Outcomes for Students With Disabilities* (American Association of Colleges for Teacher Education and National Center for Learning Disabilities, April 2011), www.aacte.org

---

### Learning Outcomes

**At the conclusion of this issue, readers will be able to:**

- Compare and contrast the positions of the YES and NO selections addressing whether RTI interventions should be provided by special education teachers.
- Describe the strengths and the weaknesses of each side's arguments.
- Identify the elements of RTI and special education in your own school.
- Evaluate your school's programs against the criteria set forth by these authors.

---

### ISSUE SUMMARY

**YES:** Douglas Fuchs, Lynn S. Fuchs, and Donald L. Compton, professors at Vanderbilt University, and prolific scholars whose extensive research is in the area of student instruction and assessment, propose that the Smart RTI of the future taps the unique pedagogical training of special educators to implement Tier 3 interventions.

**NO:** Linda P. Blanton, Marleen C. Pugach, and Lani Florian, professors at Florida International University, the University of Wisconsin-Madison, and the University of Aberdeen, Scotland, respectively, blend the perspectives of two well-respected professional organizations to envision the future of RTI in the hands of general education teachers trained to teach all children who enter their classroom.

**W**ritten into IDEA 2004, Response to Intervention (RTI) was identified as an approach to help more children learn effectively in the general education classroom. The key elements of RTI include an integrated system that uses performance data to drive high-quality instruction; a problem-solving approach to student learning; and a progressive, multi-tiered system of interventions and assessments.

Echoing No Child Left Behind (NCLB), RTI emphasizes a connection between scientifically based instructional practices and continuously monitored student progress. Every student's performance is to be systematically and regularly measured. Careful attention to each child's rate of learning alerts educators to developing difficulties. If a student does not progress, then instruction must change.

There is no legal mandate for districts to implement RTI. Nevertheless, legislators were so committed to the goal of strengthening general education instruction that they authorized districts with disproportionate special education representation based on race and ethnicity to use up to 15 percent of their U.S. federal special education funds to develop and implement early intervening services.

Most districts have at least endeavored to incorporate RTI practices. As of 2010, over 61 percent of superintendents responding to a survey indicated they had implemented, or were in the process of implementing, an RTI model, compared to about 25 percent in 2007 (Samuels, *RTI: An approach on the march*, 2011, www.edweek.org).

Although some fretted because the U.S. federal government was not prescriptive about the structure and form of RTI, this gave educators the latitude—and the responsibility—to design programs tailored to their particular community of students (Kame'enui, *TEACHING Exceptional Children*, 2007). As a result, RTI programs, services, and criteria differ widely across districts as does the role played by special education professionals.

Intervention tiers correspond to instruction and assessment that are increasingly intense. To illustrate, three levels are described here. In Tier 1, children experience effective classroom instruction; teachers are appropriately prepared to use scientifically based teaching methods; all students are screened and assessed regularly; and educators scrutinize assessment data to identify students who are not progressing adequately. In Tier 2, small groups of students showing some difficulty receive additional focused, short-term instruction and assessments. Tier 3 is reserved for individual students who do not respond to Tier 2 and require longer, and more intensive, instruction and assessment. The tiers are expected to be fluid. As students respond to intervention, they return to a lower tier.

Although there is agreement that instruction in Tiers 1 and 2 is delivered by general education teachers, more variation exists about the most intense level of intervention in RTI. Some see Tier 3 as a further level of focused instruction within general education; others envision it delivered by special education faculty; still others view Tier 3 as the opportunity to evaluate whether a student has a disability and is eligible for special education (NASDSE, 2006).

This issue presents two different visions of ideal RTI practices, both proposed by university scholars who have all focused their research on the education of struggling students. Specifically, the YES and NO selections offer differing perspectives on the role special education professionals should play in Tier 3 RTI interventions. As you read, consider your knowledge of RTI tiers and practices in local schools.

In the YES selection, Douglas Fuchs, Lynne S. Fuchs, and Donald L. Compton propose Smart RTI, a method of combining school resources to maximize student success. This excerpt of the selection focuses on the best way to deliver what they refer to as tiers of prevention. Acknowledging the controversy in the field, the authors advocate that the third—and most intense—level of prevention should be delivered by special education professionals. They propose that Tier 3 might become special education. In Smart RTI, teachers would contribute their area of expertise. Classroom teachers would deliver solid core instruction, differentiated for learners. Special education teachers would return to their roots as data-based instruction experts for teaching the traditionally hardest-to-teach students.

In the NO selection, Linda Blanton, Maureen Pugach, and Lani Florian present a vision for the future that sees classroom teachers prepared to teach the entire range of diverse students they encounter, embracing a belief that all students are able to learn within the classroom. Student labels, levels, and characteristics are not relevant—there is more commonality among struggling learners than there is difference. The full policy brief lays out extensive recommendations for reconceptualizing teacher education; this excerpt includes multi-tier systems of support as one technique at the disposal of classroom teachers. Expanded preparation emphasizing universal design and the ability to collaborate with colleagues will enable classroom teachers to succeed with all students, including those with disabilities. In this re-envisioned comprehensive system, classroom teachers would anticipate and plan for a range of learning paces and strategies. Classroom teachers would have greater knowledge and skill about teaching struggling learners; special education teacher preparation would include expanded content area information. The lines between the two would become blurred.

Co-teaching is a technique, both authors predict, that will increase in use. However, the authors differ significantly in their view of co-taught classes, designed to combine the talents of general and special education professionals. Blanton, Pugach, and Florian project that co-teaching will be a strong methodology, with both general and special education teachers knowing more about each other's area of specialty. They believe teachers who use evidence-based practices can and do motivate all their students. In contrast, Fuchs, Fuchs, and Compton (2012) are troubled by co-teaching, which they see as delivering less focused attention than small-group Tier 2 interventions. These authors find benefit in specialized licensure areas, which allow teachers time to hone particular skills and knowledge; blurring categories would sacrifice time and opportunity for this specialization.

Since its inception, IDEA has required that schools provide any required service to children with disabilities, from consultation to individualized direct services. This long-established concept of continuum of services is acquiring a new meaning. Martin (www.rtinetwork.org, n.d.) suggests that RTI reaches beyond special education to create a modern continuum of services that spans services to children regardless of their designation or need.

The UCLA School Mental Health Project (SMHP) (http://smhp.psych.ucla.edu) researchers extend the continuum further. SMHP describes academically focused RTI efforts as "piecemeal" and "fragmentary" approaches to education reform. Commending the commitment to improving student success, SMHP emphasizes the importance of unified, comprehensive educational reform but advocates for attention to the broader range of circumstances that can affect student performance. Schools must first employ educational practices and programs that engage learners and their families, improving the fit between schools and students. When difficulties occur, instead of quickly moving to small-group instruction, SMHP recommends asking the student to discuss any barriers to learning. Perhaps there are economic, health, or family concerns that are taking priority in the student's mind and affecting school performance. In this case, appropriate personalized attention can be mobilized to address the root of the child's concerns. Short-term special assistance, perhaps expanding the continuum into the community, would re-engage the student's energy and improve academic performance.

Offering another perspective on student reaction, Schultz (*Nowhere to hide*, 2011) proposes that student stress could actually be worsened by additional pressured attention to academic performance. Focused, intense instruction only highlights difficulties already painfully evident to struggling students. Academic performance might be enhanced by helping students identify and build upon their strengths.

The RTI construct emphasizes the use of assessment to guide instruction. At a time when NCLB was emphasizing the use of scientifically based instruction, sparse research existed about RTI-type designs and practices. Studies are just now being published (Gersten, Compton, Connor, Dinino, Santoro, Linan-Thompson, & Tilly, *Assisting students struggling in reading: A practice guide*, 2009, What Works Clearinghouse, http://ies.ed.gov).

To fully experience the model, educators and researchers should gather and analyze data about the impact of RTI on students in their own schools and districts. Comparing findings across schools, districts, and states will deepen analysis and chart future actions. Perhaps the conclusion will be that one model of RTI practice best meets student needs. Conversely, since RTI programs to date have been locally adaptable to districts and schools, perhaps there will be room for many models of Tier 3 implementation.

# YES

**Douglas Fuchs, Lynn S. Fuchs, & Donald L. Compton**

# Smart RTI: A Next-Generation Approach to Multilevel Prevention

The 2004 reauthorization of the Individuals with Disabilities Education Improvement Act described and expressed a subtle preference for what was then a new and untested method of identifying students with learning disabilities. Specifically, the reauthorization encouraged use of a child's response to evidence-based instruction as a formal part of the disability identification process. This new method was called "responsiveness to intervention," or RTI. Since 2004, there has been much debate about whether and how to combine RTI with a multidisciplinary evaluation of a learner's strengths and weaknesses to determine disability status and special education eligibility.

RTI has also moved to the center of ongoing discussion about educational reform. For many, it represents a fundamental rethinking and reshaping of general education into a multilevel system oriented toward early intervention and prevention. Partly because its procedures were underspecified in the 2004 reauthorization of IDEA, RTI is currently implemented in numerous ways. It can include one tier or as many as six or seven tiers. Tiers designated by the same number may represent different services in different schools. In School A, for example, Tier 2 may involve peer tutoring in the mainstream classroom; in School B, it signifies adult-led, small-group tutoring in the auxiliary gym. Varying criteria define "responsiveness"; varying measures index student performance. Similar inconsistency extends to the role of special education. In Jenkins et al.'s survey of RTI-implementing teachers and administrators in 62 schools across 17 states, 12 separate approaches were described for serving students with individualized education programs (lEPs) in reading, reflecting disparate views about whether special education should exist within or outside RTI frameworks, and what services it should provide.

One constant among the many variants of RTI is that, as an early intervention and prevention system, it is costly in time and resources. It requires assessments and interventions that educators rarely conducted a decade ago. Moreover, because of its relative newness, there are serious inefficiencies in its application. This article offers research-backed guidance for designing more effective and efficient (next generation, if you will) multilevel prevention—an

Fuchs, Douglas; Fuchs, Lynn S.; Compton, Donald L. From *Exceptional Children*, vol. 78, no. 3, 2012, pp. 263–265, 268, 269–272, 273–277. Copyright © 2012 by Council for Exceptional Children. Reprinted by permission. www.cec.sped.org

approach we call, Smart RTI. We use the term to evoke such recent and popular innovations as *smart houses, smart cars,* and *smart phones.* . . . Each of these technologies reflects outside-the-box thinking that helps us become more effective and efficient. Put differently, although the inventors of these hi-tech homes, cars, and phones use "smart" to describe their products, the term also reflects their intent to make all of us—the users—smarter.

Our description of Smart RTI will not sizzle and dazzle as advertisements for smart phones do. We use plainer language to suggest a modest redesign of multilevel prevention systems to make users smarter and to help them make more efficient use of resources and promote school success among more of their students. . . . Our discussion focuses on K–12, not preschool; on academic performance, not school behavior. The academic focus should have relevance for students with high-incidence and low-incidence disabilities who are striving to meet academic goals. We address the *prevention-intervention* dimension of RTI, not its disability identification and eligibility dimension. Before discussing major components of Smart RTI, we clarify our terms.

## Levels Versus Tiers; Primary Versus Secondary Prevention

Some who write or speak about RTI intervention describe it in terms of "tiers." Others combine two or more tiers and refer to the aggregate as "levels." Most using this latter terminology describe a three-level prevention system. We, too, think of RTI this way with each of the levels distinguishable by the distinctiveness of the instruction delivered and by the skill set required of instructors. We use the descriptors *primary prevention, secondary prevention,* and *tertiary prevention* for our three levels. . . .

Primary prevention refers to the general instruction all students receive in mainstream classes. This includes (a) the core program, (b) classroom routines that are meant to provide opportunity for instructional differentiation, (c) accommodations that in principle permit virtually all students, access to the primary prevention program, and, (d) problem-solving strategies for addressing students' motivation and behavior. (Many view the core program as Tier 1 and instructional differentiation, accommodations, and problem solving as Tier 2.)

Screening in primary prevention identifies students at risk of not responding to the general instructional program. These students can then access more intensive secondary prevention in a timely manner. Screening in primary prevention is typically accomplished by administering a brief test to all students (i.e., a universal screen). A cut-point on the measure has been established through prior research, reflecting students' likelihood of successful or unsuccessful performance on important future outcomes such as teacher grades or high-stakes tests.

Secondary prevention differs from primary prevention in several ways. Probably the most important difference is that primary prevention programs are designed using instructional principles derived from research, but they typically are not validated empirically. This is partly because the commercial publishers of these programs usually lack the personnel or the desire to implement complex and costly experimental studies. Secondary prevention, by contrast often involves small-group instruction that relies on an empirically validated tutoring program. *Validation* denotes that experimental or quasi-experimental studies have demonstrated the efficacy of the instructional program. The tutoring program specifies instructional procedures, duration (typically 10 to 20 weeks of 20- to 45-min sessions), and frequency (three or four times per week). It is often led by an adult with special training. Schools can design their RTI prevention systems so students receive one or more tutoring programs in the same academic domain or in different domains.

Assessment during secondary prevention determines whether students have responded adequately to the tutoring. This assessment is usually based on progress monitoring during tutoring, on an assessment following tutoring, or on a combination of the two. Schools use these data to decide whether students should return to primary prevention without additional support or whether more intensive intervention is necessary. . . .

## Secondary Prevention: Necessary for Students Requiring Most Intensive Instruction?

Although the 2004 reauthorization of IDEA, and more recent "memoranda of understandings" from the federal government, require practitioners to conduct multidisciplinary evaluations of students suspected by parents or others of having special needs, students in most RTI systems almost always participate in less intensive levels of prevention before gaining access to more intensive levels. In a three-level system, for example, students must appear at risk for inadequate response to primary prevention before becoming eligible for secondary prevention services. Then, they must show lack of responsiveness to secondary prevention before becoming eligible for tertiary prevention. This typical lockstep process raises a basic question: Can practitioners identify students likely to be unresponsive to secondary prevention while they are still in primary prevention? That is, can practitioners identify the children who won't benefit from secondary prevention without placing them there? If so, such students may avoid an extended period of failure before gaining access to a more appropriate level of instructional intensity, and schools may avoid the cost of providing ineffective secondary prevention. . . .

. . . [A] multistage screening process in fall of first grade can be used to avoid both an RTI "wait-to-fail" model and the provision of secondary prevention to students who don't require it. In an RTI wait-to-fail model, children participate in 10 to 30 weeks of small-group tutoring, despite that their unresponsiveness to it can be determined before tutoring begins. A wait-to-fail approach delays the provision of more intensive intervention and increases RTI costs. *We recommend that schools practice Smart RTI by conducting multistage screening within primary prevention to avoid providing secondary prevention to students whose failure to respond to it can be predicted. These students should be fast tracked to tertiary prevention.*

# Tertiary Prevention, Special Education, and Three Assumptions

. . . [T]here is disagreement about whether special education should have a role in RTI. Some wish it would become a most intensive instructional level in RTI frameworks. Others say it should exist outside RTI or become an RTI component only after it has been redefined and "blurred" with general education. We are in the first of these two camps. Special educators should be charged with delivering specialized, expert, tertiary prevention to students who are not helped by prior levels of instruction. We base this belief on several assumptions we make about Smart RTI.

## Purpose of RTI

Our first assumption is that the purpose of Smart RTI is *not* to prevent special education placement—the implicit belief of many who argue against including special education in RTI frameworks. Rather, we believe educators should think about prevention as working with students to help them steer clear of school dropout, unemployment, incarceration, poor health, and other life-limiting sequelae of inadequate academic performance. . . . Dropout, incarceration, unemployment, and the like are the "big-picture" issues that will drive Smart RTI practitioners' prevention efforts. With such issues in mind, they will build frameworks that marshal the talents and efforts of all building-based professionals, including special educators.

## Comprehensive Framework

A second and related assumption is that if the purpose of Smart RTI is to prevent the numerous, undesirable consequences of school failure such as high school dropout and unemployment, it must reflect a comprehensive effort—as comprehensive (and complicated) as multilevel systems of effective health care. The overarching goal of full-spectrum health care . . . is to provide high-quality services at minimum cost. Where this occurs, it is achieved by reducing the need for intensive levels of prevention by offering effective primary care (e.g., regular screenings that may trigger early secondary prevention). The key distinction here is reducing, not eliminating, the need of intensive prevention. . . . [F]ull-spectrum RTI frameworks must be capable of helping both the "garden-variety" low achiever, who requires the intermittent attention of a co-teacher with expertise in modifying curricula and learning tasks, as well as the child with more serious and chronic learning and behavior problems, the severity of which requires 1 to 2 hours per day of one-to-one remediation from an expert instructor.

## Specialized Expertise

A third assumption: If practitioners adopt a comprehensive or full-spectrum framework of care, special and general educators (and others) must accept equally important, but uniquely different, responsibilities. This is because

Smart RTI is a highly articulated system: Many and varied activities must be implemented—activities that are interdependent and that call for different skills. We believe it is naïve to expect—and very bad policy to demand—that generalists will be cross-trained to teach skillfully to an academically diverse class of 28 children (primary prevention); to implement with fidelity a validated standard protocol to three to six students, some with behavior problems, while collecting and reviewing data on their progress (secondary prevention); and to use "experimental teaching" with the most difficult-to-teach children (tertiary prevention). In short, Smart RTI will be conducted by many specialists (including the classroom teacher) who are simultaneously applying different skills with different children at different levels of the prevention framework.

Among the multiple prevention levels, the one about which there is greatest uncertainty is tertiary prevention. Many teachers and researchers do not know how to conceptualize it, let alone conduct it. . . .

Smart RTI must include a level of tertiary prevention that is capable of serving most difficult-to-teach children and youth. Effective educators at this level will be instructional experts. They will be knowledgeable about curricula and instructional approaches across domains and will collect data on each of their students to understand whether and when their instruction is working. They will embrace the premise that, for many of their charges, effective treatments are derived across time through trial and error but guided by their knowledge and experience. They will be patient, persistent, and tolerant of ambiguity. Again, the need for such highly skilled clinician-researchers does not diminish the importance of equally talented teachers in primary and secondary prevention without whom RTI frameworks will simply collapse. In a comprehensive, full-spectrum system—irrespective of whether it's health care or educational care—specialization is pivotal at all levels.

Of course, it doesn't necessarily follow that special educators should be responsible for tertiary prevention. Nevertheless, there are at least two reasons for expressing this preference. First, for more than a century, special educators have worked with the most difficult-to-teach students, many of whom were previously rejected by general education. Second, during 25 years of funding by the Office of Special Education Programs in the U.S. Department of Education, special education researchers, often in collaboration with special education teachers, developed and validated a "technology" of assessment and instruction for the most instructionally needy students. This research, in turn, became the basis of a pedagogical approach known as "data-based instruction" or "experimental teaching," which has proved effective for many students with serious learning problems.

That said, there are precious few preservice or inservice programs currently preparing experimental teachers for our nation's schools. Special education has moved away from its unique history and tradition and distinctive practices. It is time for special educators to rediscover their roots and consider more ambitious roles for themselves in RTI frameworks. It is time, too, for policymakers, administrators, advocates, and academics to have high expectations of special educators—at least as high as the expectations they seem to have of general educators, despite the repeated failures of many to meet the needs of millions of students with disabilities as evidenced by data from the National Longitudinal Transition Study and other databases.

# Three Questions

. . . [R]eaders may be surprised to learn that *all* parts of our position are contested by various stakeholders. A need for a comprehensive framework, for example, is rejected by those who doubt the existence of "high-incidence disabilities"; who believe that, with the right general education (i.e., strong primary and secondary prevention), virtually all children, including those with learning disabilities, mild intellectual disabilities, and behavior disorders, will make satisfactory academic growth.

Similarly, some reject a need for specialized expertise. They champion generalists over specialists because of the purported absence of instructionally relevant differences between students with high-incidence disabilities and children without disabilities; also, because specialization, they say, divides educators from each other by necessitating different preservice majors and credentialing programs, and because it supposedly distances students from each other by contributing to the development of various instructional programs, categories of exceptionality, and learning environments. In short, some see specialization as working against collegiality among teachers and the inclusion of students in mainstream classrooms.

In light of these concerns, our perspective on RTI raises these three questions:

1. Is a third level of very intensive prevention necessary—or is primary and secondary prevention sufficient to prevent school failure?
2. If tertiary prevention is seen as necessary, how are practitioners currently implementing it?
3. What role(s), if any, should special educators play?

## Is Tertiary Prevention Necessary?

Among researchers who study RTI, there is growing recognition that a combination of strong primary and secondary prevention will fail to meet the needs of about 5% of the student population. These students require an additional tertiary level of intensive and expert instruction.

Findings . . . indicate that, although student learning improves with high-quality primary and secondary prevention, the level of intensity—by which we mean the frequency and duration of instruction, size and homogeneity of the instructional groups, and specialized expertise of the instructor—is not sufficient for a significant minority of students. . . . [T]o prevent school failure and associated poor-life outcomes, much more intensive intervention is required for about 5% of the school population. (This estimate does not include students with intellectual disabilities who typically are excluded from RTI studies.) *We conclude that Smart RTI requires a third level of instruction, which is distinguishable by its intensity from secondary prevention.*

## How Is Tertiary Prevention Typically Implemented?

Nobody has an authoritative answer to the question: How is tertiary prevention typically implemented? Our impression based on the work we do in schools and our understanding of others' research is when students do not benefit from secondary prevention, they often face one of two highly problematic scenarios. In the first, they remain indefinitely in secondary prevention, despite their long-running unresponsiveness. This averts tertiary prevention and special education, but does not address their instructional needs. (Relying on secondary prevention as a long-term solution for unresponsive students also violates IDEA for students with suspected disabilities and raises questions about due process and appropriate notification and participation of parents in decisions about the long-term provision of supplementary instruction.)

In a second scenario, the unresponsive students move from secondary prevention to special education, which in many school districts terminates their involvement in RTI frameworks. Rather than obtaining specialized expert instruction in special education, however, they frequently return to the general class with accommodations and co-teaching. . . .

We refer to this form of special education as *special education as accommodation* (or, perhaps *special education lite*). The apparent rationale for such an approach is that, despite the students' poor response to general education and to secondary prevention, access to the general education program (again) will meet their instructional needs. Sadly and ironically, this form of special education is often less intensive than secondary prevention. We have to wonder whether it signals that schools have given up on teaching their most instructionally needy students. Equally troubling is the possibility that these children and the specialized expert instruction they require—which may occur outside the classroom—are being sacrificed because of an inclusion policy that lacks necessary nuance. . . .

## What Might Special Education Look Like as Tertiary Prevention?

There is widespread recognition that special education and general education require reform. RTI provides opportunity for reforming both in coordinated fashion. We believe three changes are critical for strengthening connections between the two and making special education more effective for students with high- and low-incidence disabilities with academic goals. These changes are integral for practicing Smart RTI.

### Experimental Teaching

In a Smart RTI framework, special education (tertiary prevention) differs from secondary prevention because teachers set individual, year-end goals in instructional material that matches students' needs. The material may or may not be drawn from the students' grade-appropriate curriculum. Similarly, the instruction may address foundational, or precursor, skills necessary for eventual satisfactory performance in grade-appropriate material. In short, practitioners in a Smart RTI framework recognize that "off level," or out-of-level, curricula and instruction are sometimes required for creating meaningful access to the general education curriculum and content standards.

Because students in tertiary prevention, by definition, demonstrated insufficient response to "standard" instruction in primary and secondary prevention, special education instruction must be individualized; that is, no "off-the-shelf" instructional program or materials are likely to be helpful. The special educator may begin with a more intensive version of the standard protocol used in secondary prevention (e.g., longer instructional sessions, or smaller and more homogeneous groups), but she does not assume the protocol—more intensive or not—will be effective. Rather, she uses ongoing progress monitoring to evaluate instructional effects. The data are summarized in terms of weekly rates of improvement (i.e., slope) and, when slope indicates that goal attainment is unlikely, the teacher experiments by modifying treatment components and continues to evaluate student performance. In this way, the teacher uses her clinical experience and judgment to inductively design instructional programs—child by child. Research on the efficacy of this "data-based program modification," or experimental teaching, approach indicates that it accelerates academic performance among many special education students.

It seems that most school district's RTI systems omit experimental teaching, despite its demonstrated effectiveness with students with severe learning problems. Teachers and administrators often confuse it with informal, non-data-based problem solving. So, it is important to emphasize that in tertiary prevention informal problem solving (as well as implementing a standard tutoring protocol) is less intensive and will be less effective than experimental teaching.

### Meaningful Access

Experimental teaching requires a type of access to general education that differs from how "access" is typically understood. Conventional practice reflects the misunderstanding that access prohibits teaching below-grade-level content and requires students with disabilities to be in the classroom for all instruction. However, requiring students without prerequisite skills to participate in grade-level instruction violates notions of meaningful access in two ways: by subjecting children to inappropriate instruction and by depriving them of more appropriate instruction and the opportunity to learn. Access must be understood in terms of building foundational skills for eventual success in grade-appropriate material. In other words, concern about access should not prevent practitioners from providing out-of-level instruction to meet students' academic needs. A practice guide recently issued by the Institute of Education Sciences' What Works Clearinghouse, and written by a panel of academics and practitioners, supports this view. The panel reviewed the relevant literature and concluded, "Alignment with the core curriculum is not as critical as ensuring that instruction builds students' foundational proficiencies. Tier 2 and Tier 3 instruction must focus on foundational and often prerequisite skills that are determined by the students' rate of progress. In the opinion of the panel, acquiring these skills will be necessary for future achievement."

In Smart RTI, special educators must focus on instructional level material, even if this material does not represent grade-level content. Creating the opportunity for intensive intervention may also mean that children with severe learning problems miss portions of the general education program from which they are not likely to benefit. Special educators and their building-based colleagues need clarifying language from federal and state governments about what *alignment with the general education curriculum* means. Such information can help educators practice what they know about student learning. At the same time, care must be taken. No student should be excluded from components of the general education program from which he or she can and does benefit. A national dialogue is needed about meaningful access; a thoughtful conversation driven by concern for students with serious learning problems and not shaped by an ideological commitment to inflexible interpretations of access, which diminish opportunity for students to obtain the education they require and deserve.

### *Movement Across Prevention Levels*

Many students who are unresponsive to secondary prevention have uneven profiles of academic development. Consider a fifth grader who requires primary prevention instruction to learn about whole numbers, secondary prevention to learn about rational numbers, and tertiary prevention to boost reading skills. As the intensity of a student's instructional needs varies, so does the meaning of access. For the fifth grader, meaningful access for reading may require instruction from a second-grade text, whereas meaningful access for math means instruction in fifth-grade material. Similarly, a first grader with reading problems who is not helped by secondary prevention may enter tertiary prevention, respond well and, within 6 months, achieve a level of performance indicating a need for access to first-grade material.

Consideration of a student's instructional requirements across academic domains at a single point in time (e.g., the previously mentioned fifth grader), and within an academic domain at various points in time (e.g., the just-described first grader), illustrate the need for linkages between general and special education that facilitate flexible entering and exiting from tertiary prevention. Students with special needs require open IEPs (developed with parental participation) that permit strategic movement into and out of special education. . . .

Without such special education, schools will not make smart use of special education dollars to prevent the life-long difficulties associated with school failure. Schools will fail to rescue their most vulnerable students—those unresponsive to secondary prevention—requiring them instead to remain in secondary prevention or to exit the RTI system only to be warehoused in primary prevention under the guise of special education as accommodation. By contrast, if special education becomes tertiary prevention and is reformed as suggested, then school-based practitioners will mitigate the negative effects of disability and save their students with special needs not from special education, but from a litany of well-known failures that trail closely behind persistently poor academic performance.

# Coda

. . . We hope a majority of readers will see th[is] article . . . holistically as an effort to push the boundaries of accepted practice and to find more successful solutions to strengthen the academic performance of children with severe learning problems.

Trying to find more successful solutions should not imply a lack of respect for the many teachers and administrators who have worked very hard to make RTI work. But, as we and our colleagues have written elsewhere, there has been a rush to orthodoxy across the country with respect to RTI. That is, there has been a too frequent, unexamined acceptance of untested practices, which may not represent the smartest way of implementing multilevel prevention. Examples of this uncritical acceptance include the very quick and broad adoption of one-stage screening procedures; the lockstep dance among the instructional levels, requiring children with serious learning disabilities to participate in primary prevention before secondary prevention and both primary and secondary prevention before tertiary prevention; and the popular belief that special education should exist outside RTI frameworks or be admitted inside only after it has been changed into something indistinguishable from general education. There are alternate ways of thinking about each of these important issues.

We encourage practitioners and researchers to think dispassionately and critically (not negatively) about what they do; to rigorously and fearlessly test the effectiveness of their assessments and instruction; and to be innovative in exploring alternatives to how they are attempting to strengthen students' academic performance. We hope that this will be understood as the overarching, undergirding, integrating theme of the article.

Linda P. Blanton, Marleen
C. Pugach, & Lani Florian

 **NO**

# Preparing General Education Teachers to Improve Outcomes for Student With Disabilities

## Introduction

The education of students with disabilities has held a prominent place of concern in the United States since the first federal legislation to protect their educational rights was passed in 1975. This law and its implementing regulations specified that students with disabilities should be educated with their nondisabled peers in the least restrictive environment to the maximum extent appropriate. . . .

Since this time, the focus has been on preparing an adequate supply of special education teachers to meet this challenge. Less attention has been paid to the preparation of general education teachers, who also teach students with disabilities. While the adequate supply of special education teachers remains a challenge and warrants continued attention, 96% of students with disabilities spend at least part of their day in general education classes and general education teachers serve as the teacher of record on students' Individualized Education Programs (IEPs), which outline the supports and services students will receive annually to meet their goals. . . .

Today, the academic performance of too many students with disabilities does not meet expectations. For example, a student with a learning disability—when provided with effective instruction, accommodations, and supports—should be expected to graduate from high school with a regular diploma, ready for college and a career. Yet the graduation rate for students with learning disabilities—the largest group of students with disabilities identified under the law—is only 64%, and for students with orthopaedic impairments it is only 68%, each a full 10% below that of the general population. . . . Data from the 2005 National Longitudinal Transition Study show that although the participation rate of students with disabilities in postsecondary education has increased, it still lags behind that of other students, and the unemployment rate for adults with disabilities is higher than for other groups—14.5% for persons with disabilities compared to 9.0% for persons without a disability.

This policy brief asserts that the time has come to consider additional, innovative approaches to improving the outcomes for students with disabilities

Blanton et al., Linda P. From *Preparing General Education Teachers to Improve Outcomes for Students with Disabilities*, April 2011, pp. 7–12, 13–16, 17, 18, 20–21, 25, 26. Copyright © 2011 by American Association of Colleges for Teacher Education—AACTE. Reprinted by permission.

*by focusing on the preparation of general education teachers* because of the overwhelming evidence on school effectiveness that classroom teachers are the single most important factor influencing student achievement. Yet how general education teachers are prepared to work with students with disabilities has been largely overlooked. This brief urges investment in the preparation of general educators as key to improved outcomes for students with disabilities. . . .

# A Vision for the Future

## All Teachers Are Prepared to Act on the Belief That All Students, Including Students with Disabilities, Belong in General Education Classrooms

Today the demographic profile of students in our nation's schools is more complex than ever before. The idea of the regular classroom as offering the best opportunity for learning, and therefore the one to which all students are entitled, is supported by research that suggests that students who do not have access to this environment, and those who are excluded from it, are disadvantaged not only in their immediate educational opportunities but long into adult life. This disadvantage is particularly acute for students with disabilities, a group of over 6 million students defined by 13 categories in federal legislation who make up more than 13% of all school students ages 3–21.

Both the Individuals with Disabilities Education Act (IDEA) of 1997 and the Elementary and Secondary Education Act (ESEA) of 2001 emphasize the importance of a more inclusive approach to education. IDEA requires annual assessments for all students with disabilities and also reinforces that schools must provide greater access to the general classroom; however, most states did not include students with disabilities in annual assessments until ESEA required standardized annual assessments in mathematics and reading . . . for all students, including students with disabilities. Since that time, public scrutiny of and discussion about access to the general education curriculum for students with disabilities has intensified. However, research indicates that one of the greatest barriers to inclusive education is that too many teachers feel they have not been sufficiently prepared to address the diverse needs of students. As federal legislation such as IDEA and ESEA increasingly emphasize that students with disabilities are expected to be taught and learn the general education curriculum and achieve grade-level standards, *teacher education has an important role to play in ensuring that classroom teachers are better prepared for the challenges of teaching diverse groups of students* who, contrary to some misconceptions, can perform well in inclusive classrooms.

The notion that special education students are first and foremost general education students was forcefully advanced by the President's Commission on Excellence in Special Education in 2002. The Commission noted the need for an increase in efforts for early identification and prevention prior to referral to special education. . . . Preparing *every* student for the promise of college or a career requires that general education teachers view the full range of students they teach as *their* responsibility. Classroom teachers must be prepared to accept that all students differ—that responding to differences among learners is an essential aspect of teaching all children and something that they routinely do already for students who are not labeled. While students may need support from special educators and other specialists to fulfill this responsibility to students with disabilities and other diverse learners, general education teachers are not exempt from responsibility for all students' learning. Reforming the preparation of general education teachers to improve outcomes for students with disabilities requires addressing the following challenges.

# The Challenges

## "It's Not My Job"—Teacher Education Program Structures and Teacher Licensure

Although teachers routinely work with a wide range of students in their classrooms, their teaching license often limits them to work in an elementary or secondary school, as a bilingual specialist, a special education teacher, or a general education teacher. Even where teacher education programs offer candidates the option for multiple licenses, teachers tend to identify themselves as being one kind of teacher or another. This mentality is a key barrier to innovation in preparing teachers for working with diverse populations. . . .

Preparing teachers according to categories of learners such as bilingual, special education, or English language learners reinforces the idea that different groups of teachers are needed for different types of learners and that the normally wide range of students found in so many of today's general education classrooms in the United States cannot be met in the absence of such specialization. As a result, teachers may resist efforts to include students with disabilities—or students who are English language learners, or students who require bilingual education—in their classrooms on the grounds that they are not qualified or sufficiently prepared to teach them. . . . Equally important, categorizing students does not wholly define what teachers must do to provide a good education. As the persistent low achievement of students with disabilities indicates, it has proved limited in its power to overcome the fundamental barriers that are put into place when students are divided into groups based on personal attributes, such as autism or attention deficit disorder.

Finally, in this regard, serving students with disabilities is fundamentally about building strong classroom communities. When students are taught by teachers who recognize the unique learning needs of each and every individual, they learn that the effort required for learning may be different for each student—and it is effort that should be celebrated. Therefore, an important part of teacher professionalism includes an ethic of persistence and a belief in the learning capacity of every student in their, classroom. The passion for serving diverse learners is a professional commitment supported by a professional knowledge base that makes such practice possible.

## Unintended Consequences of Closing the Achievement Gaps Among School Groups

. . . [T]he increased pressure on schools to show improved results on achievement tests means that teachers may experience pressure to exclude students who are struggling. In such situations, students with disabilities are not the only vulnerable group. Students whose first language is not English are also achieving poorly on standardized measures of academic performance. In addition, the achievement gap between White and African American students and between White and Hispanic students in the nation remains wide.

The pressures teachers feel to "get the job done" in the current accountability climate—in which the stakes keep getting higher for teachers, and international comparisons shape perceptions of how well the nation's schools are preparing students to participate in the global economy—are also factors that affect achievement. One unintended consequence of the pressure to show increased student performance on academic achievement measures has been an increase in the exclusion of students who do not do well on these measures. In the United States, as in many other countries, standards-based reforms intended to improve national competitiveness and close the achievement gap between the highest performing students and those who do not perform as well have created some perverse incentives. Under these conditions, it is hardly surprising that dropout rates for students with disabilities far exceed those reported for all students and that high school graduation rates remain a problem. Learning to grapple with these conditions is an important part of both teacher education and teacher professional development.

Although one clear value of standardized achievement tests has been to lay bare the differences between groups of learners, they have not allowed teachers to be readily acknowledged for growth that remains below established goals. Neither have they been universally designed to create greater access to the test and allow students to more fully demonstrate what they know. Nor are they widely administered with appropriate accommodations that would yield more accurate assessment results. Modifications of the accountability system to explicitly include provisions to acknowledge teachers for student growth, even when it is below grade level, would help create a more positive environment for general education teachers to more readily support including students who have disabilities.

Today, teachers are being asked to do more than ever before with less than ever before as financial support for public education is dwindling across the country and they are voicing concerns about the challenge of getting the job done and getting it done well. The complexity of what it means to include all learners in today's classrooms is a challenge not only for general education teachers, but also for the teacher education programs that prepare them. Preparation programs must equip teachers with the essential skills to counteract the effects of the "silos" by which schools are organized and students are separated. Reinvigoration and innovation in preparing general education teachers are needed to conceptualize their role as competent to teach all students. . . .

## All Teachers A Are Prepared to Treat All Students, Including Students with Disabilities, as Capable Learners Who Are Entitled to High-Quality Instruction and Access to Challenging Content That Fully Prepares Them for Careers and Postsecondary Education

The goal of education in the United States, as in other countries, should be to include educating students with disabilities as part of a broader diversity agenda for education—an agenda that has been limited in this country by approaches that have been designed to address the specific needs of particular groups rather than focusing on systemic reform for the new realities of the school population. Federal funding focuses on the preparation of special education teachers, for example, addressing only one aspect of what students with disabilities need to achieve a good-quality education in inclusive schools. Students with disabilities also need highly skilled, well prepared general education teachers—with whom they spend most of their time—to view them as capable learners and as full members of the classroom community, rather than as the primary responsibility of special educators. . . .

General education teachers need to support all children's learning. They must provide a challenging academic curriculum that motivates and interests all students, and they also should be prepared to work creatively with specialists to achieve this goal. At the same time, special educators need to reconsider the role that they can play in 21st-century schools and have teaching the academic curriculum as the central focus of their preparation. Reinvigorated, innovative preparation programs for both general and special education teachers can help tackle the problems of underachievement for all students.

### Reinvigorating Teacher Education: What Do Distinctly Good Teachers Look Like?

Reinvigorating teacher education depends on a vision of what distinguishes teachers who are well equipped to meet the needs of all students, especially those who struggle in school. The qualities that characterize such teachers involve a complex interplay of the specific attitudes, knowledge, and skills that have been identified in the research on teacher education for inclusion. Beyond holding the fundamental belief that every child who comes through the classroom door is a child who belongs in that classroom, such teachers hold high expectations for all of their students and demonstrate a willingness to work with students with disabilities to ensure that they can reach those expectations.

In fact, there is evidence that students with disabilities can perform across the spectrum of proficiency. . . . While special education students are disproportionately low scorers, some general education students are also performing at the lowest levels, and some special education students are also performing at very high levels of proficiency. This evidence counters the common belief that students with disabilities cannot learn to high standards.

Distinctly good teachers also recognize that student diversity is the norm rather than the exception. For students who struggle, teachers must be skilled in providing instruction that is responsive not only to the academic standards expected, but also to the students themselves—their prior experiences, their cultural and community knowledge, their individual interests—and be able to use this kind of student knowledge as a bridge to new academic learning. They anticipate their students' high-priority instructional needs and accommodations allow students to express their knowledge in a variety of ways, use multiple technologies, implement peer tutoring programs, and engage in other evidence-based interventions. They recognize that many of the instructional methods they use can be effective with a wide range of students, and they consciously design instruction for a variety of learner needs from the outset of their planning. In other words, they expand their view of what is generally available to all students. This way of teaching is demanding because in order to embrace it, teachers must set aside the overarching assumption that students of similar age can and will learn similar content in a relatively straightforward manner. Viewing all students as capable learners who deserve and can learn challenging content, such teachers do not let the labels that may be used to describe particular groups of students divert them from this goal.

To teach in this way, teachers must be highly skilled practitioners who can embed specific evidence-based teaching practices within a broad view of the academic curriculum that both challenges and motivates all of their students. To meet the needs of their most challenging students, teachers continuously monitor student progress and routinely respond to their assessment of student learning by adjusting instruction accordingly.

The ability to do all of this arises from a complex combination of skills. In general teacher education, for example, current research on "high-leverage teaching practices" by Deborah Ball and her colleagues is pointing the way to preparing teachers for specific and robust teaching tasks that have implications for the success of students with disabilities, including practices that span classroom management, content planning, and instruction and assessment for learning. As schools respond to specific instructional expectations to make the general education curriculum accessible to a diverse school population, good teachers can also rely on approaches such as Multi-Tier System of Supports (commonly known as Response to Intervention), Positive Behavioral Intervention and Supports, and Universal Design for Learning, all of which draw on evidence-based instructional strategies that can be used by general and special education teachers alike to support students with disabilities. These school-wide approaches were designed to keep struggling students in the general education classroom all or most of the time, to provide interventions to individual students when needed, and to reduce the number of children who are mistakenly identified as having learning disabilities when their learning problems are actually a result of cultural difference or lack of adequate instruction.

In Multi-Tier System of Supports (MTSS), teachers monitor progress frequently to make appropriate changes in instruction and apply these ongoing assessments to important educational decisions. The results of monitoring student progress are used to make decisions about the need for further evidence-based instruction in general education, in special education, or both.

Positive Behavioral Intervention and Supports (PBIS) assists school personnel in adopting and organizing evidence-based behavioral interventions into an integrated continuum that enhances academic and social behavior outcomes for all students. In PBIS, classroom management and preventive school discipline are integrated with effective academic instruction to create a positive and safe school climate to maximize success for all students.

Universal Design for Learning (UDL) is a framework for designing curricula that provides cognitive as well as physical access to learning to enable all students to gain knowledge, skills, and motivation for learning. Using the power and flexibility of technology to make education more inclusive and effective for all learners, UDL includes multiple means of representing content, multiple means of expression, and multiple means of engagement, and it provides new ways for teachers to customize their teaching for students with a range of abilities, interests, and backgrounds. . . .

Another critical set of teaching skills has to do with general education teachers working collaboratively with their colleagues, as part of a team, to put into practice inclusive education that is challenging and motivating for students. When general education teachers take primary responsibility for the learning of their students, they should do so as part of a professional learning community alongside their special education colleagues. In this approach to professional development, staff across the entire school have been successful working together on assuring student progress. This learning community includes not only special education or bilingual education teachers but also parents and families who are viewed as expert sources of knowledge.

As a uniquely complex job, teaching demands a high level of collaboration, particularly when students need additional supports to improve outcomes on challenging content. In this vision of teaching, both general and special education teachers possess a shared base of professional knowledge for teaching that is anchored in the general education curriculum; from this shared base they can collaborate to ensure students' learning of this curriculum. Moreover, collaborative models of teaching, in which general educators and support personnel coordinate their work to support all students in diverse classrooms, have emerged as a promising set of practices in schools. These models can include coteaching, in which general and special education teachers share responsibility for instruction, as well as creating instructional teams in middle and high schools in which the special education teacher is a permanent member of the team of subject specialist teachers. . . .

# All Teacher Candidates Complete Their Initial Preparation with the Knowledge and Skills Necessary to Successfully Enter the Profession and Meet the Instructional Needs of Students with Disabilities

. . .

## Teachers Report Lacking Skills in Instructing Students with Disabilities

Numerous studies have reported that general education teachers do not feel prepared to teach the diversity of students in their classrooms effectively. In 2008, half of middle and high school teachers reported that the learning abilities of their students were so varied that they could not teach them effectively. At the same time, teachers increasingly realize how important it is to be able to address the needs of diverse learners. . . .

Teachers themselves, then, understand the need for more robust pre-service experiences to prepare them for their work in increasingly challenging classrooms. Learning to teach the changing student population well will take new approaches to clinical preparation to ensure that teachers have adequate opportunities to gain these essential practices. . . .

## New Roles for Special Educators

Achieving a new vision for general education teachers—one that enables them to build educational environments that result in significant learning gains for the full range of students they teach—also requires a reinvigoration of the preparation of special education teachers. What should the role of special education teachers be in an educational system that is focused on making sure that every child learns and is ready for college or a career?

As the practice of general education teachers is reframed to encompass a broad diversity perspective, a simultaneous reframing of the role of special education teachers should also occur, especially regarding their knowledge of the general education curriculum. In order for special educators to work effectively with their general education colleagues, their base in the general education curriculum should be strong and sound. Although the "highly qualified" requirements of IDEA and ESEA have been helpful in the expectation for special educators to acquire content knowledge at both the elementary and secondary levels, much more needs to be done to ensure a base in general education. Just as general education teachers need preparation programs that support them in taking responsibility for the learning of all students, special education teachers need core knowledge of the general education curriculum and how to make it accessible to students. Currently, 17 states require persons seeking special education licensure to first complete a general education license, a trend that holds promise for their preparation and that moves beyond preparation that has traditionally, at least for many programs, focused on instructional strategies in isolation from the general education curriculum.

The focus on collaborative teaching in recent years also requires consideration of how new roles for special education teachers will be shaped. Although the research on the effectiveness of such practices as coteaching, for example, is mixed, the use of these practices has increased in PK-12 schools. For aspiring teachers to succeed in collaborative teaching, they need opportunities to practice different approaches as part of their professional development. As various collaborative practices evolve, the expectations for what takes place in the general education classrooms will change, as will the relationship between general and special education.

# State and Federal Policy Invest in High-Quality Teacher Preparation for All Candidates, While Assuring That Every New Teacher Is Qualified with Demonstrated Skill to Educate Students with Disabilities

. . .

## Program-Level Redesign

The most promising developments are full-scale program redesign efforts in which teacher educators across general and special education collaborate on new designs for entire teacher education programs. These new program designs employ innovative curriculum configurations that address the preparation of general and special education teachers through a shared core curriculum in general education that ensures that new teachers are better prepared to work with students who have disabilities, as well as with other students who struggle in school. . . .

Such redesigned programs have approached reforming the preservice curriculum and dual certification in different ways. In *integrated programs*, prospective general and special education teachers study a redesigned, common core curriculum together to become general education teachers, and only those who want to become advanced specialists go on for additional studies to develop specialized expertise and an additional license in special education built on this common base of knowledge. In fully *merged programs*, all graduates obtain both a general and a special education license by completing a single, completely unified curriculum; there is no distinction between a special and general education teacher. Importantly, what these two program redesign models have in common is that teacher educators participate together to develop a preservice curriculum that addresses the practices all teachers should possess if they are going to be better prepared to work with students who have disabilities, and indeed, with all of their most challenging students.

These emerging program redesigns are significant because they reveal a growing willingness on the part of teacher educators in both general and special education to work together to improve the quality of teaching for students who have disabilities. They represent significant opportunities for rethinking how general education teachers are prepared to work with diverse groups of students and how teacher educators in special education can work collaboratively with colleagues in general education to support the development of teachers who feel qualified and well-prepared for the challenges of teaching in inclusive general education classrooms.

Many of these promising integrated and merged program redesign projects, however, are taking place without sufficient support, which limits what can be achieved in terms of systemic reform, even with the best of intentions and the best of curriculum innovations. To take full advantage of the opportunity that program redesign across general and special teacher education offers, it will have to be viewed as an opportunity for deep program transformation in the service of improved outcomes for all students. . . .

# All Providers of Teacher Education Must Embrace Preparation for Diverse Learners as a Core Component of Their Mission, Prioritizing It, Strengthening It, and funding It accordingly

. . .

## Strong Professional Teacher Education Programs

Recent activities to improve the preparation of teachers to work with students who have disabilities should be viewed in the broader perspective of the history of teacher education. Over time, as knowledge about curriculum, teaching, and learning has developed, the preparation of teachers has also evolved from a 19th-century model of apprenticeship to a largely university-based endeavor supplemented by a mix of school and university partnerships. Locating teacher education in the university is an important achievement in the professionalization of teaching, but it has also resulted in devaluation of the clinical work done in partnership with PK-12 schools that is so essential to teacher education. . . .

Today there are many alternative pathways preparing teachers through course work, distance education, and on-site mentoring. Alternative routes into teaching are heterogeneous in length, support, and program intensity, and they vary in quality. Federal policy allows candidates in alternative certification programs to serve as the teacher of record while completing their preparation, and many states utilize this practice. Given today's challenge of preparing teachers for a more diverse population of students than ever before, among them students with disabilities whose outcomes are not up to par, the logic of regularly allowing untrained teachers to take on the full responsibility for teaching in diverse classrooms simply does not stand up to scrutiny.

Alternative certification practices designed to address shortage problems may have the unintended effect of exacerbating rather than closing the gap in outcomes between different groups of pupils. What is important is that all teacher education programs, whether they are traditional or alternative, deliver curriculum that is motivating and evidence-based in a coherent programmatic fashion and develop new teachers with demonstrated skill in generating student learning gains for our most challenging students.

What will it take to achieve the vision of having teachers prepared to teach all of their students well, especially those who have disabilities and other diverse students? We know that it takes a good teacher to understand and respond to the complexity of educating every student. It takes a highly educated teacher to balance the demand for high performance on standardized tests with the more complex problem-solving skills that effective teaching requires. And it takes a strong teacher to raise questions in the face of institutional biases in schools that often put students at a disadvantage based on race, socioeconomic class, culture, gender, and/or disability status and to create a classroom where every student who comes through the door can thrive. Achieving the vision for preparing general education teachers to improve outcomes for students with disabilities is within our reach, but it will require changes in policy and practice.

# EXPLORING THE ISSUE

## Should RTI Interventions Be Delivered by Special Educators?

## Challenge Questions

- Compare and contrast the positions of the YES and NO selections regarding the role special education should play in RTI.
- Which selection makes the best case for its argument? Why?
- How is RTI being implemented in your neighborhood school? Who delivers services at the various tiers? How was that decision made?
- How would you use information from the YES and NO selections to affect your thinking as an RTI Leadership Team member? As a special education teacher?

## Is There Common Ground?

The YES and NO selections' authors see promise in the ability of RTI practices to improve the educational and life outcomes of today's diverse student body. None of the authors support abandoning RTI in favor of a return to past practices. All agree that RTI has brought about sea changes in schools and that now is the time to modify existing RTI models, maximizing educators' strengths.

## Additional Resources

Blanton, L. P., Pugach, M. C., & Florian, L. (2011, April). *Preparing general education teachers to improve outcomes for students with disabilities*. Washington, DC: American Association of Colleges for Teacher Education and National Center for Learning Disabilities. Retrieved April 25, 2012 from www.aacte.org

Fuchs, D., Fuchs, L. S., & Compton, D. L. (2012). Smart RTI: A next-generation approach to multi-tiered prevention. *Exceptional Children, 78*(3), 263–279.

Gersten, R., Compton, D., Connor, C. M., Dinino, J., Santoro, L., Linan-Thompson, S., & Tilly, W. D. (2009). *Assisting students struggling in reading: Response to Intervention and multi-tier intervention in the primary grades: A practice guide* (NCEE 2009–4045). Washington, DC: National Center for Educational Evaluation and Regional Assistance, Institute of Education Sciences, U.S. Department of Education. Retrieved from http://ies.ed.gov/ncee/wwc/publications/practiceguide

Kame'enui, E. J. (2007). A new paradigm: Responsiveness to intervention. *TEACHING Exceptional Children, 39*(5), 6–7.

Martin, J. L. (n.d.). *Understanding the modern menu of public education services for struggling learners: RTI programs, Section 504 and special education.* Retrieved January 29, 2012 from www.rtinetwork.org

National Association of State Directors of Special Education and Council of Administrators of Special Education. (2006, May). *Response to intervention: NASDSE and CASE white paper on Rtl.* Retrieved from www.nasdse .org/Portals/0/Documents/Download%20Publications/RtlAnAdministratorsPerspective1-06.pdf

Samuels, C. A. (2011, March). RTI: An approach on the march. Special Report: *Monitoring progress: Response to Intervention's Promise and Pitfalls,* XXX: Education Week, S2–S5.

Schultz, J. J. (2011). *Nowhere to hide: Why kids with ADHD and LD hate school and what we can do about it.* San Francisco, CA: Jossey-Bass.

UCLA Center for Mental Health in Schools. (2012, April). *RTI and classroom & schoolwide learning supports: Four units for continuing education.* Retrieved April 25, 2012 from http://smhp.psych.ucla.edu/pdfdocs/rtiii.pdf

# ISSUE 10

## Should Special Education and General Education Merge?

**YES: Mary T. Brownell, Paul T. Sindelar, Mary Theresa Kiely, & Louis C. Danielson**, from "Special Education Teacher Quality and Preparation: Exposing Foundations, Constructing a New Model," *Exceptional Children* (vol. 76, no. 3, pp. 357–377, 2010)

**NO: Margaret J. McLaughlin**, from "Evolving Interpretations of Educational Equity and Students with Disabilities," *Exceptional Children*, (vol. 76, no. 3, pp. 265–278, 2010)

---

### Learning Outcomes

**At the conclusion of this issue, readers will be able to:**

- Compare and contrast the positions of the YES and NO selections addressing whether special education and general education should merge.
- Identify the strengths and the weaknesses of each side's arguments.
- Discuss the implications of each option for the education of all children.
- Consider how each position would affect a person's desire and plans to become a special education teacher.

---

ISSUE SUMMARY

**YES:** Mary T. Brownell, Paul T. Sindelar, and Mary Theresa Kiely, policy scholars from the University of Florida, Gainesville, and Louis C. Danielson at the American Institutes for Research link political changes with special education teacher preparation. They conclude that the future of special education rests within content-rich RTI practices.

**NO:** Margaret J. McLaughlin, policy architect and analyst from the University of Maryland sees a disconnect between the singular academic outcomes of NCLB/ESEA and the individualized needs of students with disabilities. Merging is not wise when some students with disabilities are treated unjustly if held to unitary academic outcomes.

$\mathbf{G}$eneral education and special education have long been engaged in a dance. Sometimes the two have moved separately, sometimes in harmony; rarely in unison. Tension exists between their two fundamental education laws.

Current key legislation for general education, No Child Left Behind (NCLB), the latest reauthorization of the Elementary and Secondary Education Act (ESEA), focuses on academic standards and performance targets to be met by all students. The Individuals with Disabilities Education Improvement Act (IDEA) emphasizes ensuring Free Appropriate Public Education individually designed for all eligible students with disabilities.

During their last reviews, NCLB/ESEA and IDEA began to address related topics. The reauthorization of IDEA is on hold, pending that of NCLB/ESEA, which was scheduled for 2007. Many wonder if this delay signifies an impending merger of the two laws and educational systems.

Special education legislation initially focused on opening school doors for students with disabilities. At first, many received specially designed instruction in small self-contained groups. Over time, some children were enrolled in typical classes, but *pulled out* to receive intensive instruction from specialists; others remained in the general education classroom, but were *pulled over* for specially designed instruction. When remediation occurred, students often missed out on the curriculum and activities of the *regular* classroom. Inclusionary practices, ranging from co-teaching to full inclusion, attempted to link the two systems. Although they were bringing students closer together for learning, students with disabilities were often excluded from large-group assessments, simply because of the existence of their disability.

IDEA 97 required districts to include students with disabilities in large-scale assessment programs, ensuring access to the general curriculum, not just exposure. Some claimed that access did not "guarantee excellence of educational services and outcomes" (Eisenman & Ferretti, *Exceptional Children*, 2010).

NCLB addressed this concern by holding districts accountable for the academic performance of students with disabilities. Acknowledging the variety in students with disabilities, assessment participation includes alternate assessment methods, and, depending on the state, altered standards.

Striving for consistency with NCLB, IDEA 2004 required the highly qualified special education teacher to demonstrate competence in each core subject area taught. Those providing consultative services or support services must possess at least a bachelor's degree and full state certification in special education.

IDEA 2004 also included Response to Intervention (RTI), an approach encouraging general education teachers to use data to drive their use of evidence-based instructional practices. Students who struggled would be eligible for tiers of increasingly intensive services, many within the general education setting. Special education teachers play a role in RTI's intervention tiers, although that role differs across schools (Mellard, McKnight, & Woods, *Learning Disabilities Research & Practice*, 2009).

As each of the key laws references topics connected to the mission of the other, it is impossible not to wonder if U.S. federal legislators intend to merge special education and general education into one, unified system. The YES and NO selections consider whether such a merger is wise.

In the YES selection, Mary T. Brownell, Paul T. Sindelar, Mary Theresa Kiely and Louis C. Danielson note that success in special education has come to mean satisfactory progress in the general education curriculum. In today's accountability "pressure cooker," the authors claim the key to the future is dual licensure of all teachers. Special education and general education teachers must collaborate through RTI to ensure all students succeed academically.

By contrast, in the NO selection, Margaret McLaughlin urges legislators and educators to recognize there can be no equity if all students are expected to achieve the same academic outcomes. The NCLB/ESEA academic achievement targets may not result in the same benefit for everyone. McLaughlin believes educators must uphold their legal responsibility to provide appropriate individualized programs focused on what each learner needs to succeed in post-school life.

The Council for Exceptional Children (CEC), the largest international professional organization advocating for individuals with disabilities and/or gifts and talents, has developed a set of policy recommendations for ESEA reauthorization (www.cec.sped.org). Demonstrating how close the laws are, CEC's opening statements urge that ESEA be "carefully coordinated and balanced" with IDEA. Their first recommendation urges Congress to "emphasize the importance of special education pedagogy that centers on the evidence-based expertise of special educators to alter instructional variables to individualize instruction for individuals with exceptional learning needs." The third recommendation encourages Congress to support special education teachers who "also possess a solid base of understanding of the general content area curriculum sufficiently to collaborate with general education" with stronger knowledge for each subject they teach directly. Another recommendation urges that RTI be included in ESEA as well as IDEA.

Brownell, Sindelar, Kiely, and Danielson (2010) see the future in RTI for all children. General educators should have increased knowledge about disabilities, and special educators must utilize a solid content base as a foundation for specialized instruction. Tier 3 intervention should be virtually synonymous with special education. Avoiding this path will leave special education "marginalized" and adrift.

McLaughlin thinks an "appropriate" education is not the same for every student. All educators must acknowledge that individuals have unique goals and needs. Insisting that all must pursue the same outcomes "can seem counter to the principle of individualization" and actually be unjust. There must be specialized education—for some a specialized curriculum—that is substantially different from that appropriate for typical learners. Special educators must possess knowledge of disabilities and pedagogical tools beyond reasonable expectations for classroom teachers.

Several authors describe how special education can fit "seamlessly" into general education. Discussing how special educators can be redefined as interventionists, Simonsen, Shaw, Faggella-Luby, Sugai, Coyne, Rhein, Madaus, and Alfano (*Remedial and Special Education*, 2010) stated that special education "can be blended seamlessly" into a schoolwide RTI model, with special educators contributing to each tier. Weber (*Phi Delta Kappan*, 2008) asks whether special education "has to be special," since all children deserve services and support. If these were provided, students would "fit seamlessly into the mainstream of public education." Even McLaughlin (2010) notes that, for most students, special education services could blend "seamlessly" into general education.

In sharp contrast, Zigmond, Kloo, and Volonino (2009) ask, "If a differentiated education is provided in the same place as everyone else, on the same content as everyone else, with adapted instruction that is not unique to the student with disabilities, is the student receiving special education?" (p. 201).

In the same thematic issue that included the YES/NO selections, Fuchs, Fuchs, and Stecker (*Exceptional Children*, 2010) consider the "blurring of special education." They view merger discussions as evidence that special education has veered from its original mission to teach students with the most severe educational challenges. The authors call teachers, administrators, and policy makers to remember the charge to special education and think carefully about how to use their specific knowledge in tomorrow's schools—in both RTI and specially designed instruction.

Doubtless, this discussion will continue for some time. In each option, legislators and states will also consider funding. Although never fully funded to the extent promised by the legislature, IDEA does provide grant monies to states and districts. NCLB/ESEA also provides funds. Many feel that district special education funding is sacrosanct—it must continue even through difficult financial straits (Samuels, *Education Week*, 2011). IDEA 2004 allowed districts some latitude to use special education funds to support early intervention efforts in general education.

Blending the laws could create additional flexibility in how funds are used. It is possible that increased flexibility will provide richer experiences in the general education classroom for all students and perhaps even reduce the number of students found eligible for special education. On the other hand, this flexibility could be a temptation to dilute finances for students with disabilities.

The authors differ on what the future should be. In one vision, educators combine talents in service of common curriculum standards designed to lead to college or career readiness. In the other, teachers use their expertise differentially to address unique individual needs for adult life. Striking the right balance is challenging. Careful attention to reauthorization deliberations will ensure stakeholders have opportunities to provide input on these important elements.

# YES ◀ Mary T. Brownell, Paul T. Sindelar, Mary T. Kiely, and Louis C. Danielson

## Special Education Teacher Quality and Preparation: Exposing Foundations, Constructing a New Model

Special education teacher preparation has evolved over the past 150 years, since special education teachers were first prepared in residential settings. Shifting perspectives on disabilities, effective practice, and providing services to students with disabilities has led to changes in how special education is conceptualized and organized, and, consequently, how special education preparation programs are structured. Today, special education teacher preparation has lost focus, and there is enormous heterogeneity among programs. Redefining *special education teacher preparation* is difficult, especially when the need to do so occurs as serious questions are being raised about the effectiveness of teacher education generally, and when, for students with disabilities, *successful teaching* has been redefined to mean satisfactory progress in the general education curriculum. These changes occur against a backdrop of high-stakes assessments, rigorous academic standards, and individualized accountability—and persistent shortages of highly qualified special education teachers. . . .

## Major Trends in Preparing Special Education Teachers

The first teacher preparation programs in special education emerged in residential facilities and were directed by pioneering clinicians such as Seguin, Gallaudet, and Itard. With the advent of compulsory education and demands to improve the quality of public education, the preparation of special education teachers gradually moved away from these residential settings to teachers' colleges. By the 1960s and early 1970s, a series of public laws designed to increase the provision of high-quality educational services to students with disabilities produced an era of explosive growth in special education teacher education. These early programs were predominantly categorical in focus and, as such, were designed for the purpose of training individuals to teach students with specific disabilities. This categorical orientation dominated special education teacher education well into the 1970s, but by the early 1980s it gave way to a noncategorical approach. Proponents of this approach viewed the learning and behavioral needs of

Brownell et. al., Mary T. From *Exceptional Children*, vol. 76, no. 3, Spring 2010, pp. 357–359, 366–374. Copyright © 2010 by Council for Exceptional Children. Reprinted by permission. www.cec.sped.org

students with disabilities on a continuum of severity and questioned the relevance of disability categories to effective planning, instruction, and behavior management. In the 1990s, the push to educate students with disabilities in general education classrooms prompted further reconsideration of special education teachers' roles. Because collaboration figured more prominently in inclusive service delivery than it did when students with disabilities were educated in resource rooms or self-contained classrooms, it became an essential feature of special education teacher preparation. As more students with disabilities were included in general education classrooms, teacher educators designed and implemented programs in which classroom teachers and special education teachers were prepared together.

Today, special education teacher preparation is once again in transition. IDEA has mandated that students with disabilities have access to the general education curriculum. The No Child Left Behind Act of 2001 (NCLB) has mandated that schools are accountable for the performance of these students on assessments aligned with the general education curriculum. In addition to knowing how disability-related problems can derail learning and how research-based strategies can be implemented to intervene, special education teachers must be highly qualified in the core content areas they teach. Yet, conversations about special education teacher preparation have not focused on the knowledge and skills needed to execute content-area instruction for students with disabilities, but rather on traditional views of effective special education practice: knowledge of effective interventions, assessment, and collaboration. The current emphasis on access to the general education curriculum and the need for special education teachers who can facilitate access have raised questions about what "high-quality" special education teachers do and how they are prepared to do it. . . .

# Reconceptualizing Special Education Preparation: Thoughts for the Future
. . .
## Political Context

The political context for educating students with disabilities has shifted considerably over the past 3 decades. Initial focus on access to educational opportunity has given way to a focus on equitable outcomes. Now, an expectation exists that students with disabilities meet general education standards. This shift has occurred in part as a response to concerns about American children's poor performance on international assessments and the poor performance of students with disabilities on high-stakes assessments. Politicians and political pundits have leveled harsh criticism at teachers and schools that fail to produce desired results in spite of billions of tax dollars being invested in the enterprise. In the special education community, disappointing longitudinal data on the academic performance of students with disabilities, particularly in high-needs schools, have intensified the public outcry. Even parents of students with disabilities are demanding that schools and teachers be held accountable for the performance of their children. The overidentification of students with learning disabilities has compounded concerns about the degree to which students are being educated appropriately. Many scholars and policy makers believe that overidentification results in part from schools' failure to employ effective, evidence-based practices. The use of such practices minimizes the misidentification of students as learning disabled by ruling out the possibility of inadequate instruction. Concern over the failure of public schools to produce results has led to an accountability movement in schools that is unparalleled in any other educational era.

In this accountability pressure cooker, schools and teachers have become targets of reform. The availability of strong scientific evidence that effective practices can mitigate if not prevent learning problems and improve outcomes for all students has led to a strong push for teachers to use such practices in their classrooms. In fact, both NCLB and the Individuals with Disabilities Education Improvement Act (IDEA) speak to the need for schools to provide professional development that will enable teachers to use them. Moreover, that IDEA emphasizes the use of "research-based interventions" such as RTI as the preferred method for identifying students with learning disabilities is a reflection of the heightened role that evidence-based practice has taken in schools. RTI has emphasized the importance of teacher accountability for using evidence-based practices in reading and mathematics. In concept, RTI provides students increasingly explicit, intensive, and individually tailored instruction when achievement data suggests they are not making progress. Those who require the most intensive intervention are identified as learning disabled. Under this approach, general and special education teachers are required to employ evidence-based assessments and instructional strategies. At present, RTI has been applied mostly to reading during the primary grades, where a preponderance of research evidence for effective intervention and assessment exists. As states step up their capacity to implement RTI, its application to writing and mathematics should follow, as well as its application to content-area instruction in middle and secondary schools.

Research on teachers and teacher education has been used both to ratchet up expectations that students have access to highly qualified teachers, and to discredit formal teacher preparation. Large-scale analyses of student achievement data show that teachers are one of the strongest effects in the educational system. Value-added studies of teacher effects demonstrate that the most effective general education teachers can achieve student achievement gains that are as much as 50 percentile points greater than those secured by the weakest teachers. These findings, combined with evidence suggesting that teachers' subject matter knowledge has more impact on student achievement than teacher education courses have precipitated questions about the value of teacher education. Although these studies were conducted in the general education context, decisions about accountability based on policy makers' interpretations of them may apply to special education teachers as well.

As a result of accountability pressures and research findings pointing out students with disabilities' poor academic progress, IDEA and NCLB have mandated that students with disabilities be included in state assessments and meet annual yearly progress goals. IDEA also requires that students with disabilities have access to general education curriculum and receive individually designed instruction appropriate to their academic and behavioral needs. Both pieces of legislation also require that students with disabilities, particularly at middle and high school levels, have access to teachers who are highly qualified in both special education and the subjects they teach. At minimum, teachers can achieve highly qualified status by having a bachelor's degree and meeting state requirements for licensure in a content area and special education, which in some states simply means passing a state certification exam. Most special education professionals reject such a minimalist approach to preparing special education teachers, arguing that they will have no avenue for mastering the array of evidence-based practices they will need to teach students with disabilities.

## Research on Teaching and Learning: Implications for Teacher Quality

Rapid advancements in technology and the increasing sophistication and accumulation of research on learning, disability, and teaching have contributed to a knowledge base that holds promise for improving the education of students with disabilities. These advances also demonstrate the sophisticated knowledge and skills teachers must have to educate students with disabilities successfully. Technological innovations (such as digitized text combined with scaffolds to assist comprehension) have enabled teachers to provide students with disabilities access to complex concepts and to engage them in higher order thinking. Technological advances also have helped students with disabilities compensate when performing certain academic tasks. For example, speech-to-print software has become increasingly accurate in its ability to record the human voice and subsequently enable students with significant spelling and writing problems to generate text independently. Universal design for learning provides a framework for curriculum design in which these technological innovations may be situated. Such innovations enable general and special education teachers to provide curricular access while individualizing instruction, making the lofty goals of IDEA attainable. . . .

In addition to advances in technology, research on learning and disability has grown in volume and sophistication. Researchers in neuropsychology, psychology, educational psychology, and special education are beginning to amass evidence about the brain and how it functions, how brain functioning might influence the information-processing capacity of some students with disabilities, and how intervention can be structured to improve the brain's capacity for processing information. . . . Although such research is more developed in decoding and spelling, research in mathematics also has begun to connect cognitive deficits and intervention strategies. This intervention research harkens back to scholarship undertaken in the categorical era; it represents a second generation of diagnostic/prescriptive research, done now with more sophisticated assessments, more well-established instructional practices, and stronger ties to academic curriculum. Findings from this research suggest that special education teachers need an understanding of how disability presents itself in an academic area and what must be done to intervene in academic processing deficits.

Findings from recent research on the cognitive processes underlying typical academic development demonstrate that students must receive instruction that engages them in deep processing of selected concepts so that discipline-specific information becomes well integrated in memory. As students progress from novice to expert learners, they abandon simple cognitive strategies, such as paraphrasing, and adopt deeper processing strategies, such as analyzing text to determine its credibility. DI and cognitive strategy instruction, routines known to be effective for special education students, cannot be applied universally across disciplines without careful consideration of how knowledge within a specific discipline will be acquired. For example, competent performance in algebra depends on a conceptual understanding of decimals, fractions, and percents; it also depends on efficiency in solving computational problems involving these concepts. To assist students with disabilities, teachers understand mathematical concepts and relationships among them and how procedural knowledge can support conceptual knowledge. Otherwise, they cannot diagnose how student understanding and procedural knowledge is breaking down and respond with the more intensive, carefully articulated math instruction that students with disabilities need.

Learners require a well-integrated knowledge base in a particular content area to be considered experts; it is reasonable to assume that expert teachers would also have well-integrated knowledge that allows them to recognize problems in their discipline and retrieve knowledge to solve them. Research over the past decade examining the knowledge and classroom practice of effective teachers suggests that such teachers have domain expertise and are able to demonstrate that expertise during instruction. *Domain expertise* refers to skill in teaching a subject and includes knowledge of how the discipline is structured and how students build knowledge within it. By contrast, some researchers and policy makers have touted the importance of subject matter mastery over domain expertise. However, although the portion of variance that subject matter knowledge contributes to between classroom gains in student achievement is statistically significant, it also is trivial in magnitude. This fact as well as findings from recent research on teacher knowledge and expert teacher practice have led some educational researchers to suggest that the domain expertise teachers possess is tied closely to the task of teaching. Several recent studies in both special and general education demonstrate linkages between the specialized domain knowledge needed for teaching and teachers' classroom practice in mathematics and reading. Observational studies reveal how effective teachers engage in content-rich instruction that is carefully crafted, well orchestrated, and responsive to students' diverse needs. Through their instruction, these teachers reveal a sophisticated understanding of knowledge needed to teach in a particular content area.

The research on teaching and learning suggests that special education teachers must have well-integrated knowledge bases, including an understanding of (a) content and how to teach it, (b) specific problems that students with disabilities may experience in a particular content area, (c) the role of technology in circumventing learning issues or supporting access to more sophisticated learning, and (d) the role of specific interventions and assessments in providing more intensive, explicit instruction within a broader curricular context. Taken together, several earlier assumptions about teacher quality support a more contemporary view of special education teacher quality and preservice preparation. Teachers will need disability-specific knowledge as they did in the categorical era; however, now they must understand how certain processing deficits affect academic learning. They also must be knowledge-able of evidence-based intervention strategies that address disability-specific needs. Further, their knowledge must fit within the framework of the general education curriculum, requiring collaboration with general education. Unlike we imagined in previous eras, the diagnostic and intervention knowledge of special education teachers must be well integrated with content domain knowledge. . . .

## Using an RTI Framework to Rethink Special Education Teacher Preparation

The RTI movement holds potential to clarify and articulate special and general education teachers' instructional roles. During the integrated era, contributions that general education and special education teachers made to instruction were not well differentiated, in part because the boundaries between their roles had blurred. By contrast, RTI clarifies the roles that special and general education teachers play, and both roles require more sophisticated preparation. RTI . . . involves at least three tiers of instruction and intervention. At Tier 1, in addition to teaching the general curriculum, classroom teachers assume responsibility for monitoring student progress, developing and implementing instructional modifications when needed, and assessing the impact of those modifications on student performance. At Tier 2, classroom teachers retain primary responsibility for students who fail to thrive academically. However, at this point, they begin to work with a multidisciplinary team or other professionals (e.g., content-area specialists or special educators), to plan and evaluate more intensive intervention. Although students remain in the general education classroom, instruction is more intensive and monitoring more frequent and precise. Only when teams determine that students are not progressing satisfactorily in spite of Tier 2 accommodations and modifications are they referred for Tier 3 interven-tion. At Tier 3, students are provided intensive, explicit instruction to address their unremediated literacy and numeracy needs. Tier 3 instruction involves ongoing assessments and interventions based on those assessments. Many scholars recommend that, at Tier 3, instruction should be the purview of special education and special education teachers; we concur, as specially designed, individualized instruction is a defining feature of a free and appro-priate education for students with disabilities.

RTI's ultimate success hinges not just on general and special education's ability to assign responsibility for who provides instruction at each tier but also on how instruction will be conceptualized at each tier. Although detailed explanations of tiered instruction lie beyond the scope of this article, we provide examples of how tiered literacy instruction might be enacted in elementary and secondary contexts. These illustrations are intended to serve as a foundation for discussing general and special education teachers' roles in an RTI framework and articulating how special education teachers can be prepared for those roles.

In the early elementary grades, research on how assessment and intervention can be used in the prevention of reading disabilities has demonstrated that increasingly explicit and intensive intervention in essential language and reading skills reduces the number of students requiring remedial reading services and mitigates the impact of learning disability. In the case of early reading instruction, then, Tier 1 would involve whole-class reading instruction that incorporates research-based practices focused on the essential components of reading (i.e., phonemic awareness, phonics, vocabulary knowledge, fluency, and comprehension). Tiers 2 and 3 instruction would target specific language deficits in reading and increasingly intensive ways of remediating them, with Tier 3 involving the most intensive instruction and frequent progress monitoring. Such intensive and responsive instruction requires deep knowledge of language, literacy, and potential processing deficits, and extensive experience with struggling learners.

Describing how tiered instruction operates in the later grades, however, is more challenging. In an article critiquing the feasibility and consequences of applying an RTI framework to content-area instruction, Mastropieri and Scruggs (2005) suggested that educators have not conceptualized what tiered instruction looks like in different content areas and caution that the field is a long way from doing so. Further, they suggest that poorly articulated frameworks for operationalizing tiered instruction do not help schools improve teaching quality. They argue that secondary instruction is fast-paced, lecture-based, and focused on abstract learning, and that it emphasizes memorizing content for high-stakes assessments. As a result, most secondary instruction in general education classrooms is not accessible to students with learning difficulties. Thus, little room is left for differentiating instruction or identifying areas of learning that could be remediated intensively within the general education curricular framework.

Although few would disagree with concerns about secondary instruction and its suitability for RTI, many educators—including school-based professionals already implementing RTI—would argue that the time is right for implementation. These educators posit that students' abilities to handle the literacy, language, and mathematics demands posed in content-area instruction are essential for genuine access to the general education curriculum. They assert that schools should move forward now with RTI, using the demands of content-area instruction and struggles that students with high-incidence disabilities experience as a way of describing how RTI works at the secondary level.

As students progress in school, the literacy and language skills they need to profit from content-area instruction change. The language and literacy skills students need to understand narrative texts differ from the skills required for reading and writing in different academic disciplines. For example, comprehension strategy instruction, an approach supported by the National Reading Panel, typically involves teaching students generic strategies, such as making graphic representations of text and summarizing text. Although both are important generic strategies that enable students to comprehend many genres of academic writing, they are insufficient for fully comprehending academic text. Each academic discipline has its own particular way of communicating ideas. In the area of science, to comprehend the natural world, students must be able to observe, measure, predict, and explain phenomena and relationships among them. Thus, comprehending and writing scientific texts require that students be able to activate prior knowledge, connect it with new knowledge, make predictions, question understandings of ideas being presented, raise questions about data, and summarize what they have learned from texts or experiments. By contrast, readers of historical text are less concerned with explaining phenomena and more focused on trying to determine the historical lens of the author and how an author's biases might influence the position he or she took when writing about a historical event or person. Students with high-incidence disabilities may experience difficulties acquiring the cognitive strategies as well as basic literacy and language skills needed to comprehend texts, and they are likely to struggle with adjusting their strategies to meet the demands of different disciplinary texts. . . .

Although the intricacies of RTI implementation are not well understood at this time, it is clear that successful RTI implementation demands greater teaching expertise and better preparation for the roles teachers will play at each tier. At Tiers 1 and 2, in addition to providing high-quality instruction in the general education curriculum, general education teachers must have knowledge of evidence-based remedial practices and be amenable to implementing them. Further, general education teachers need a solid grasp of CBM procedures. At Tier 2, special education teachers require solid understanding of the general education curriculum, and all teachers require collaborative skills to engage successfully in the multidisciplinary planning needed for cohesive instruction at this tier. Thus, integrating special and general teacher preparation is once again a top priority, as it was during the integrated era. However, preparation now must help general and special education teachers integrate evidence-based practices into content instruction.

Success at Tier 3 demands specialized expertise. Special education teachers must demonstrate, at minimum, a sophisticated knowledge base that extends beyond that of general education teachers, and this expertise must add value to the general education that students with disabilities receive. Research on expert learners and teachers and research on interventions for students with high-incidence disabilities can serve as a basis for identifying this expertise. Findings from this research strongly suggest that special education teachers will need domain knowledge in areas targeted for Tier 3 instruction as well as knowledge of interventions, technological adaptations, and assessments for high-risk learners. As students with disabilities are likely to need intensive assistance in reading, writing, and mathematics, special education teachers should have sufficient preparation in these content areas to enable them to teach students in elementary, middle, and high school. They also need to develop an instructional repertoire that integrates domain knowledge with knowledge of intensive interventions and assessments. Moreover, preparation should focus on either the elementary or the secondary level, as content literacy demands change depending on the grade level taught.

To develop such extensive expertise, special education teachers will require preparation in both general and special education. Research evidence has demonstrated that general education teachers with special education preparation are better prepared to meet the literacy and mathematics needs of students with disabilities than teachers who lack it. Feng and Sass also showed that special education teachers with special education preparation produced higher achievement scores for students in reading but not math. We believe that, after entering the field, special education teachers should undertake advanced preparation in special education focused on either elementary or secondary level. This advanced preparation would target knowledge and skills needed to (a) provide direct services to students receiving Tier 3 instruction, and (b) collaborate with general education colleagues to provide Tier 2 instruction. Such expertise is important for two reasons. First, according to Feng and Sass's preliminary analyses, preparation in special education has a value-added effect on the achievement of students with disabilities. Also, expertise in how to assess, support, and remediate literacy and numeracy skills is essential for providing access to the general education curriculum. If special education teachers do not help students access the general education curriculum, then they fail to add value to their students' education.

## Strategies for Improving Special Education Teacher Quality

To improve special education teacher quality and preparation, policy makers and educators must address long-standing concerns about shortages of special education teachers and the inadequate preparation of general education teachers. Special education teacher shortages continue to be severe, hovering around 10% since the passage of EHA. Licensure strategies have often been designed to remedy quantity issues with little attention paid to the impact on teacher quality. Noncategorical certification and, more recently, the emergence of fast-track, alternative routes to licensure reflect special education's emphasis on addressing shortages (as opposed to improving quality). Although concerns about remedying shortages are well justified, the problem with these licensure strategies is that they fail to articulate and support the concept of unique expertise. Moreover, many general education teachers are unprepared to cope with the diverse needs of students who fail to thrive in response to good classroom instruction. Studies of general education teachers demonstrate that they have difficulty differentiating instruction for students with disabilities and other at-risk learners, especially at the secondary level.

Attempts to improve teacher quality must meet these two powerful issues head on. There must be reform of general education preparation if Tier 1 and 2 instruction is to be responsive and provide a foundation that special education teachers can build on. Moreover, well-designed, effective Tier 2 and 3 instruction will be impossible unless special education teachers, particularly at the secondary level, have the expertise in content, language, literacy, and numeracy to engage in such instruction. To ensure that students with disabilities have access to high-quality teaching in both general and special education, policies and practices needed for supporting the RTI movement need to be integrated with those related to licensure, teacher education, and teacher salaries. The RTI movement must be supported by policy makers through legislation, policies, and public funding for implementation and teacher education. The strong push for RTI to be included in the reauthorization of NCLB is an example of how policy could be used to broaden support in general education. Many schools across the country are implementing RTI, and this trend is likely to hasten with passage of comprehensive federal legislation.

Public schools, acting alone, will be unsuccessful in responding to these pressures if general and special education teachers are not prepared for their designated roles. Colleges of education must embrace conceptions of preparing teachers that will ready them for their roles in RTI. Key changes in state teaching standards and licensure policies provide levers for changing the nature of preparation for both general and special education teachers. In light of emerging evidence on the importance of special education preparation for both classroom and special education teachers, states must require dual certification for all beginning teachers, advanced preparation in literacy and numeracy for all special education teachers, and content-area literacy for those working in secondary schools. At a minimum, however, states must implement standards and licensure systems that make clear the knowledge and skills general education teachers will need for teaching students with disabilities and the knowledge and skills special education teachers will need for providing both access to the general education curriculum and more intensive instruction at Tiers 2 and 3. Moreover, what special education teachers need to know to provide Tier 2 and 3 instruction in elementary schools should be differentiated from what they will need for secondary schools. . . .

## Conclusion

The changes we propose for improving the quality and preparation of special education teachers are lofty and dramatic—and difficult to attain. However, the risks of failing to improve the quality of instruction are unacceptable. The ability of many students with disabilities to access the general education curriculum and make adequate annual yearly progress depends on the skill and motivation of their teachers. Students with disabilities continue to lag well behind their peers. Requiring special education teachers to become highly qualified in the subjects they teach prior to entering the classroom offers less promise as a solution to this problem than recruiting highly qualified general education teachers into special education. Good general education teachers know content and how to teach it, and they are skilled collaborators. They have a framework for understanding and integrating the specialized knowledge they acquire in preparing for RTI and so will be better positioned to meet the needs of students with disabilities. Of course, encouraging general education teachers to become special educators necessitates fundamental reform in school practice, incentives for teachers, and teacher education. Because RTI requires fundamental change in school practice, the time is right for undertaking this ambitious agenda.

The viability of special education as a profession rests on our capacity to be recognized as a legitimate contributor to RTI implementation. Special education teachers must be responsible for providing Tier 3 instruction, as well as collaboratively planning Tier 2 instruction with their general education colleagues. If special education teachers are not perceived as adding value to the education of students with disabilities in an RTI model, they may be marginalized in schools, and special education would risk losing its identity as a profession. . . . We can no longer afford to be unclear about who high-quality special education teachers are and how they should be prepared. . . .

Margaret J. McLaughlin

 **NO**

# Evolving Interpretations of Educational Equity and Students with Disabilities

The education of students with disabilities in today's schools is being shaped by two very powerful laws: the 2004 Individuals with Disabilities Education Improvement Act (IDEA) and the 2001 Title I of the Elementary and Secondary Education Act (ESEA) also known as the No Child Left Behind Act (NCLB). These laws are changing our conceptions about the meaning of special education and are the source of confusion and frustration among general and special educators as they attempt to implement the various provisions. Much of the frustration arises from the tension between the core policy goals and assumptions that underlie Title I and IDEA. . . .

## The Tension

There is increasing recognition of a fundamental tension between the prevailing K–12 educational policy of universal standards, assessments, and accountability as defined through Title I and the entitlement to a Free Appropriate Public Education (FAPE) within IDEA. The possibility of such a conflict between the standards-driven reform model and special education policies was acknowledged more than a decade ago by a National Research Council (NRC) committee that concluded that the two policies were not incompatible; however, there were definite areas of misalignment. . . . The challenges that educators are confronting in aligning Title I and IDEA arise from differing interpretations of what constitutes educational equity. . . .

## Educational Equity and K–12 Education

What constitutes an equitable education has been subject to much debate and discussion among educational policy makers over the years. . . . A recurrent theme in the debates is distinguishing between the ideals of educational equity and educational equality. As Green notes, equity is not the same as equality, "Inequity always implies injustice. . . . Persons may be treated unequally but also justly." (p. 324). Thus, equitable treatment in education may conflict with

McLaughlin, Margaret J. From *Exceptional Children*, vol. 76, no. 3, Spring 2010, pp. 265–272, 273–276 (refs. omitted). Copyright © 2010 by Council for Exceptional Children. Reprinted by permission. www.cec.sped.org

what constitutes equality depending on the particular interpretations as well as how we choose to measure it. At the core of the conflict between Title I and IDEA is the belief that students with disabilities may be treated unjustly in being held to universal standards. . . .

## The Evolution of the Equity Concept

As noted earlier, the meaning of what constitutes educational equity shifted throughout the 19th and 20th centuries and has been confounded with interpretations of educational equality. However, the increase in publicly funded education in the United States in response to industrialization and increased immigration made visible issues related to equity. Coleman (1968) noted that, with the exception of the very poor children who did not go to school, children with disabilities, and Native American and African American children who did not have schools, educators' earliest interpretations of equity had three foci: (a) providing a free education up to the point that a child entered the workforce; (b) providing a common curriculum for all children regardless of background; and (c) providing that children of diverse backgrounds attend the same school within a specific locality.

Equity assumed society had an obligation to remove the economic barriers to education, that is, provide a free education in a geographically accessible area and provide exposure to a common or core curriculum. To be denied these things was to be treated inequitably. The need for the state to provide an opportunity for all students to have equal access to a public education grew out of an increasing recognition that education was linked to larger economic goals such as the need to create potential employees and reduce economic dependency. In this interpretation of equity, the state must only provide or make available specific educational opportunities; whether or not a child chooses to access education or benefits from this education is left up to the student and the family.

A number of events in the early part of the 20th century shaped the interpretations of the role of the state in providing publicly funded education, such as curricular reforms. Most of these, however, changed the opportunities that were provided but did not alter the fundamental notion that public education only needed to provide equal access to achieve equity. The 1954 *Brown v. Board of Education* decision altered this interpretation when it repudiated the notion that simply providing exposure to the same curriculum, regardless of location, constituted equity. Although the findings in the *Brown* decision were supported by the wide disparities in resources (i.e., funding, facilities, and teachers) existing in the segregated, all Black schools, the *Brown* decision began to link conceptions of equitable treatment to the effects or results of the education a child received. That is, giving the same to every child was not sufficient to determine equality without considering how the child benefited from the opportunity. Yet, following the *Brown* decision, equitable treatment as articulated in U.S. educational policy was measured in terms of reducing resource disparities between White and African American students. This focus on inputs remained grounded in the notion that states must provide equal opportunities but not equal benefit. Further, an important factor was the idea that measuring equitable treatment should be at the group and not at the individual student level primarily because measurement at the individual level would be infeasible and unproductive.

In 1966, the Equality of Educational Opportunity Study (EEOS), also known as the "Coleman Study," was commissioned by the U.S. Department of Health, Education, and Welfare to assess the availability of equal educational opportunities to children of different race, color, religion, and national origin. This study was conducted in response to provisions of the Civil Rights Act of 1964 and focused on inequities across schools in terms of facilities, staff, class size, and so forth and their connection to variation in student background and achievement. The assumption underlying this report was that two students attending schools with the same resources should have the same opportunities. The report also introduced the concept of equal access and used this phrase repeatedly and almost synonymously to mean equality in funds, facilities, teachers, and curriculum.

The findings of the Coleman Study documented the disparities among schools in terms of critical educational resources, but it is probably best known for its conclusion that a child's economic status accounted for more of the variation in achievement than did school resources. Subsequent to the publication of this report, Jencks and his colleagues reanalyzed the Coleman data and reached similar conclusions. However, whereas both studies documented that substantial inequalities in both educational resources and outcomes existed among children of different races and backgrounds, the reports differed in terms of what constituted evidence of equity. Jencks's (1972) concept of equity focused on providing individual students with, "as much schooling as he (sic) wants. [Noting that] equal opportunity in this sense guarantees unequal results" (p. 109). Equity was interpreted as equal claims to public resources while acknowledging the possibility of different or unequal outcomes. The Coleman study focused on establishing equal access for different groups of students (e.g., minority and poor students) to the same schools, same curriculum, and same expenditures. . . .

The shift toward a focus on measuring the outcomes of education was driven by the belief that larger societal and cultural forces may have limited opportunities for students from certain backgrounds. Thus, an African American student or a student living in poverty might not aspire to certain educational outcomes; therefore, it was the role of the state to promote the same outcomes. This notion of equity was embraced by liberal and progressive educators and became a driving theme in federal education policy. In this interpretation, equity is measured in terms of equality of outcomes as opposed to inputs and evolved into what Berne and Stiefel (1984) later defined as horizontal and vertical equity. Horizontal equity is interpreted as schools having equal or equivalent inputs such as funding or teacher-student ratios; whereas vertical equity assumes that different or unequal inputs may be required to attain equal outcomes—in short, that unequal students require unequal treatment. This version of equity requires a way to define and measure the desired universal educational outcomes of the standards-based model of education.

Spurred by events such as the release of the 1983 *A Nation at Risk . . .*, there were calls for greater curricular rigor and of state-imposed standards for what students must achieve. The passage of the Goals 2000: Educate America Act and the 1994 reauthorization of ESEA, Improving America's Schools Act, increasingly defined a state's responsibility in ensuring educational equity. That is, if states wished to access the federal funding associated with these programs, they were to be responsible for providing all school-age children access to the same rigorous content and be held accountable for ensuring that children reached, at a minimum, state-defined levels of proficiency in that content. Equity was to be measured in terms of student achievement on state assessments and the gap in performance between specific subgroups of students. The 2001 ESEA reauthorization built on the earlier versions of this law by adding provisions for assessing annually the performance of students in three key content areas and by specifying mandatory consequences for schools, districts, and states that fail to meet specific performance benchmarks. Notably, both the 1994 and 2001 ESEA reauthorizations revised the formula for distributing federal funds to states and schools. The formula began to shift resources toward the neediest schools consistent with the notion of vertical equity.

# Educational Equity and IDEA

The quest for educational equity for children with disabilities paralleled to some extent the broader K–12 policies. Equal access to a free, public education for all children with disabilities—a major policy goal for much of the latter half of the 20th century—was achieved at the national level with the passage of the Education of All Handicapped Children Act of 1975 (EAHCA). Providing equal access followed the reasoning in the *Brown* decision that when a state provides an opportunity for an education in its public schools, such an opportunity is a right that must be made available to all on equal terms. . . . However, EAHCA was also deeply grounded in the policy goals of the emerging disability rights movement.

## Disability Rights Goals

As conceptualized by Silverstein (2000), there are four major goals that guide all federal laws and other policies pertaining to children and adults with disabilities. These are (a) equality of opportunity, which encompasses individualization, integration, or inclusion; (b) full participation (i.e., self-determination); (c) economic self-sufficiency; and (d) independent living. These goals are expressed through various provisions within IDEA as well as Section 504 of the Rehabilitation Act of 1973 and the Americans with Disabilities Act (ADA).

Individualization is central to the concept of equality of opportunity in all disability policies and arises from the heterogeneous nature of disabilities as well as the impact of disabling conditions on functioning. The goal requires that each person with a disability be considered in terms of his or her strengths and needs. The latter includes considerations for accommodations, supports, and services. Adherence to the goal requires that educational programs and policies be flexible enough to respond to individual differences and not be based solely on categories, labels, preconceptions, or biases. As interpreted in IDEA, the concept of individualization is found in the core entitlement to a FAPE, which is operationalized through the individualized education program (IEP).

Another core element of equality of opportunity is the full integration or inclusion of persons with disabilities into all those activities and policies designed for persons without disabilities. Based on the principle of normalization, inclusion means making available to each person with a disability the opportunity to experience all of the conditions of everyday living in the same way and place as individuals without disabilities. Within IDEA, the goal of inclusion is expressed primarily through the least restrictive environment (LRE) provision. However, this principle also extends to ensuring that individuals with disabilities are considered in federal and state educational policies. . . .

Thus, a student with a disability who is being treated equitably is being considered as an individual, is given full access to those aspects of life available to persons without disabilities, has opportunities to make decisions about both mundane and important life events, and has opportunities to become independent and self-sustaining. As interpreted in IDEA, these goals are reflected in the provisions that govern the IEP process and content. The procedural requirements associated with the IEP ensure that each child is treated justly. There are also substantive requirements associated with the IEP that require that there be educational benefit to the child.

## Educational Benefit

The notion of educational benefit is central to interpreting what constitutes an "appropriate" education for an individual student. The prevailing legal standard for determining an appropriate education comes from the very first U.S. Supreme Court case to consider IDEA and its provisions. The decision in this case established the precedent that the federal statute was not intended to maximize the potential of a student served under the law. Instead, the Court determined that the statute was intended to provide access to education that would allow the student to "benefit" from educational programs and services. . . .

Subsequent to the *Rowley* decision, lower federal court cases further established that the educational benefit due to students with disabilities must be "more than trivial."

Under current interpretation, a student with a disability served under IDEA has claims on public resources as required to meet what an IEP team determines will provide a level of educational benefit, determined on an individual basis. This is a somewhat Jencksian concept of equity in that a child may get as much as he or she needs to receive educational benefits determined by a team of professionals and the child and/or his parents. The concept of equity as determined by attainment of equal outcomes was not articulated in the 1975 EAHCA until the 1997 reauthorization of IDEA when the first adjustments to K–12 policy began to appear. The 1997 amendments required that states and local districts include students with disabilities in assessments with accommodations where appropriate, to report the performance of these students with the same frequency and in the same detail that they use to report the performance levels of students without disabilities and to develop alternate means of assessment for those students who are unable to participate in standard assessments. The 1997 amendments also required that IEP teams consider how a child's disability affects his or her involvement and progress in the general education curriculum and develop IEP goals that promote the child's progress in that curriculum.

## The NCLB Influence

Of course, major changes occurred with the passage of the 2001 amendments to Title I of ESEA. The Act made a clear statement regarding the state's responsibility in providing an equitable education to all students, including those with disabilities. Students with disabilities are expected to participate in all aspects of the Title I provisions. . . . The regulations define how students with disabilities are to be assessed and how schools are to be accountable for their performance. Most notably, the accountability provisions require schools (and districts and states) to be held accountable for the performance of the *subgroup* of students with disabilities and for closing the achievement gap between this subgroup and all others. Two specific regulations deserve mention. In December 2003, the U.S. Department of Education (ED) issued regulations for the inclusion of students with "the most significant cognitive disabilities" in Title I assessments. These regulations grant states the flexibility to measure the achievement of the selected students against alternate achievement standards, but in terms of accountability, the proficient or advanced scores of not more than 1% of the student population tested may be counted. An alternate achievement standard is defined as "an expectation of performance that differs in complexity from a grade-level achievement standard." It is important to note that only the achievement standards and not the content standards are permitted to be altered. Thus, students' performance expectations are based on the same academic content as their peers without disabilities.

In April 2007, the ED issued another set of regulations permitting states to adopt "modified" achievement standards. These regulations make clear that modified academic achievement standards are intended for a small group of children, in addition to the "1% of students" whose disability precludes them from achieving grade-level proficiency and whose progress is such that they will not reach grade-level achievement standards in the same time frame as other students. The expectations for whether a student has mastered those standards, however, may be less difficult than grade-level academic achievement standards. Not more than 2% of proficient scores of students who are held to modified standards may be included in adequate yearly progress (AYP) calculations at any level. . . . Modified academic achievement standards must be based on a state's grade-level academic content standard and the student's IEP must include goals that are based on the academic content standards for the grade in which the student is enrolled. The 2004 IDEA amendments acknowledged these regulatory requirements and made several explicit references to ESEA in terms of requirements for such things as assessment, highly qualified special educators, and so forth. These changes signal the intent of Congress to better align if not merge the two major policies.

## Standards-Based IEPs

As a result of the Title I regulations as well as the general move toward standards-based education, a new practice is emerging with respect to IEP development. Referred to as standards-based IEPs the practice directly links IEP goals to a state's grade-level content standards and assessments. Each child receives an individually designed plan of services and supports that are geared to moving the student toward attaining state-determined standards. The tensions between IDEA and Title I become quite evident in the implementation of standards-based IEPs. There is an assumption that all students with disabilities need or will benefit from the same educational outcomes (albeit some will be measured against different standards) and that the IEP team is to determine what resources the student may need to reach these common outcomes. From the perspective of IDEA, these IEPs can seem counter to the principle of individualization and subvert the procedural rights for determining what constitutes a FAPE for a student.

# Considerations for Reconciling IDEA and Title I of the Elementary and Secondary Education Act

Including the group of children covered under IDEA within the basic policies of Title I of ESEA is consistent with the notion of equity that asserts that public education has a larger role in ensuring equity beyond providing whatever an individual student wants, or in the case of a student with a disability, what an IEP team decides he or she needs. This is tricky and contested territory because one needs to respond to the question "Needs to do what?" . . . The issue of whether all children may benefit from or need the same curriculum has long been debated as part of our nation's efforts to increase the achievement of children. Concerns about what happens to those who cannot or choose not to meet standards are not exclusive to students served under IDEA. However, for students served under IDEA the question of whether or not they are being treated unjustly when held to such standards becomes more potent given their entitlement to a FAPE.

The Purpose section of IDEA 2004 states that the goals of educating children with disabilities are: ensuring that all children with disabilities have available to them a free appropriate public education that emphasizes special education and related services designed to meet their unique needs and prepares them for further education, employment, and independent living. These goals are not dissimilar from those of all children; rather, it seems that the tension is as Green (1983) argues, that "We cannot [provide] an education that is uniquely suited . . . for each individual and at the same time give to each an education that is as good as that provided for everyone else" (p. 319). Yet, that is implicitly the intent of an appropriate education and also fuels the tension between standards and the determination of an appropriate education. However, at the same time that IDEA has accepted unequal, that is, individual treatment and unequal educational outcomes, there has been intense scrutiny and far less tolerance of inequalities in post-school employment and other functional outcomes. . . .

## Employment, Further Education, and Independent Living

. . . The National Longitudinal Transition Study–2 (NLTS2) provides the most current national data on the postschool outcomes of students with disabilities who received special education services. The first wave of data was collected in 2003 from the first cohort of students within the sample to leave high school. Among this group, 31% of the sample had enrolled in some type of postsecondary institution, compared to 41% of students in the general population. . . .

About 40% of the youth were employed at the time of the first follow-up, which was substantially below the 63% employment rate among students with-out disabilities in the same age group. About 40% of the sample was working full time and about 40% of this group of former students was earning more than $7.00/hour, but only a third of all those employed were receiving any benefits with their employment. In terms of independent living, about three fourths of the youth were living with their parents 2 years after high school, which is similar to the general population. However, these outcomes varied by type of disability as well as by whether the student had received a high school diploma. Notably, students with more significant intellectual disabilities expe-rienced lower rates of employment and independence. . . .

Clearly, receiving a high school diploma is an important outcome for students with disabilities, but also important is the rigor of graduation requirements. The National Center on Educational Outcomes (NCEO) con-ducted a survey of the 50 states and the District of Columbia in 2002 to 2003 to examine graduation requirements for students with and without disabili-ties. Results . . . indicated that 28 states had increased their requirements for all students, whereas two states increased requirements only for students without disabilities. However, in all but three of the 28 states, students with disabilities were allowed to obtain a standard diploma without completing all requirements. . . . At that time six states offered IEP/special education diplomas, 19 states granted certificates of attendance, 10 states granted cer-tificates of achievement, and three states offered occupational diplomas. In addition, 32 states permitted IEP teams to make adjustments to graduation requirements. The unequal expectations for graduation may likely reflect an attempt to treat some students with disabilities differently in an effort to provide them an equitable opportunity to receive a diploma. Although such treatment may be fair, it may promote greater inequities if it results in loss of opportunity to gain knowledge and skills that are relevant and necessary for postschool success.

. . .

# Concluding Thoughts About Educational Equity and Students with Disabilities

Obviously, there are some fundamental differences underlying the policy ideals expressed in NCLB and IDEA 2004. These are reflected to some degree in the policy goals. Although I would argue that the goals are less divergent than the means for reaching those goals. The stress of trying to implement standards-based IEPs, provide instruction in grade-level subject matter content while addressing the unique needs of an individual student with a disability can quickly obscure the ultimate goals of education for all students. Further, measuring progress in terms of aggregate versus individual measures of achievement creates a sense of unfairness. Yet, the data on employment and achievement inform us that, in the aggregate, students with disabilities are not receiving the same outcomes. The data also raise legitimate questions about the level of benefit the subgroup of students with disabilities are receiving from public education. But, do the data suggest inequities in the educational system? By that I mean, are students receiving equitable treatment in terms of access to curriculum, qualified teachers, and other inputs critical to the attainment of academic and educational outcomes important to their postschool success? . . .

The NLTS2 documented differences in course taking among students with disabilities. On average, more than half (59%) of the courses that secondary students with disabilities took were academic. However, the data also indicate that students with disabilities were less likely to be enrolled in higher level math and science courses. Not surprising, course taking differed by disability category, with more students identified as having mental retardation and other cognitive disabilities enrolled in vocational and special classes and more students identified as having specific learning disabilities enrolled in grade-level academic courses. In addition, a recent analysis of math achievement among secondary students with and without disabilities found that students with IEPs who attended schools that provided a range of math courses had significantly lower achievement than those in schools that provided only a more rigorous math curriculum. Are differences in access legitimate, meaning do they reflect the unique needs of a student even if they lead to unequal outcomes? As noted by Gelber (2007), prior discrimination or inequities can and do shape current inequalities in educational achievement. We can only speculate the extent to which preconceived and historic notions about students with disabilities as well as conceptions about their needs are reflected in their current educational outcomes. We also cannot know with certainty whether greater access to rigorous courses and higher expectations would make a difference to both in school and postschool outcomes. However, experience with the IEP has suggested that there are low expectations and lack of accountability suggesting that differences in access and outcomes between students with and without IEPs may result from a system that permits inequities as part of the individualization mandate and yet is vulnerable to preconceived and historic notions about students with disabilities. Without standards that guide the process, how are we to know if a student is being treated equitably?

The concepts of standards and individualization reflect different beliefs about equity. As noted by Brighouse and Swift (2008), it is not unusual for different values to conflict in political discourse, nor is it unusual to conclude that one value is more important than the other. However, they argue that in some instances, one has to make a judgment of whether Policy Y, which we believe to be so critical (e.g., IEPs with individually referenced outcomes), has a moral priority over Policy X (e.g., IEPs that are based on common standards). That is, does Y always trump X or only in some instances? For example, under what conditions might a parent of a child with a disability argue for individualized outcomes? Would a parent argue for lower standards for graduation if their child's diploma was not at risk? Would some educational outcomes matter more to some groups of students with disabilities? One cannot argue for individualizing outcomes only when it is convenient or beneficial. However, we must be explicit about if or when a comparative or relational concept of equity is called for and when certain inequities are tolerable.

In the case of students with disabilities, equity can be measured in terms of the procedural integrity of the IEP. These standards are consistent across individuals. Educational benefit, however, is relational. It must be determined in relation to something and this something must be consistent across some or all students with disabilities. The implications are that requiring each student with a disability to meet the same standards may, in fact, be inequitable. For instance, requiring all students with IEPs to pass the same exam in algebra in order to receive a high school diploma may not be just, particularly if this proficiency is unnecessary for independent living or certain jobs. However, who gets to decide? Is it truly equitable to allow the IEP team to determine that a specific child will not be provided access to algebra because they believe it will not be important to that student's future or because they believe the child will not be able to benefit? At what point can we accept as legitimate unequal outcomes among students with disabilities, and are the procedural requirements and safeguards of the law sufficient and reasonable for ensuring equitable treatment? I would argue that they are not and that we need to include in our measure of equity consideration of attainment of important educational outcomes. To go forward with a true alignment of the Title I and IDEA we must reconsider the structure, if not the purpose, of the IEP, which ultimately will affect what constitutes an appropriate education.

## A New Way Forward

I believe that the concept of the IEP needs to reflect differential educational outcomes, based not on a case-by-case basis but on some rational grouping of students with disabilities. Although I believe that core procedural requirements can be maintained, the specific implementation of these may need to differ based on educational expectations measured in terms of attainment of certain levels of academic and, for some students, functional competence. Such a model was recently proposed by Gándara and Rumberger (2008) for linguistic minority students. They proposed defining four groups of students based on their educational goals: (a) English language proficiency, (b) English language proficiency and academic proficiency, (c) biliteracy, and (d) biliteracy and academic proficiency. Under their model, each group would have a defined set of educational outcomes based on the goal, and there would be different needs and resource implications for students as defined by the goals of their instruction.

A similar model could be applied to students with IEPs. I believe that IEPs could be differentiated for three groups of children and youth: those held to regular, modified, and alternate achievement standards. The first group, and certainly the largest of the groups, need IEPs that focus on accommodations and special education and related services that are tailored to their needs and directly related to enabling the students to fully *access instruction in grade-level subject matter content and to progress toward predetermined NCLB achievement goals.* Educational goals for these students should not differ from those of any other student, nor should the assessments used to determine educational needs or progress. After determining eligibility for services and that the student will be held to regular achievement standards, the IEP team can focus on meeting that student's needs, both in the academic as well as the social or behavioral areas as they impact access to the grade-level curriculum. The IEPs for these students should be simplified to reflect only the accommodations, services, and supports needed to progress toward proficiency on state standards. Progress should be monitored as it would be for students without IEPs. This approach to IEP development removes the risks of lowered expectations and denial of opportunity.

The IEPs for students held to modified achievement standards would also be based on grade-level content standards and would also focus on access to grade-level subject matter instruction and services to access and progress in that curriculum. However, the expected outcomes, benchmarks, and measures must reflect the modified achievement standards as established by the state. The IEPs for these children should reflect the more intensive and specialized services and supports required to enable them to meet the modified standards and progress toward proficiency on the regular state achievement standards. These students should not be permanently assigned to some sort of "modified" track, thus it is critical that progress measures be benchmarked to both the modified and regular achievement standards. It is difficult to know at this point what modified standards will look like as states are in the early stages of developing them along with the alternate assessments by which they will be measured. It is also unclear which students will be included in this group. Nonetheless, the role and function of IEP teams will be critical in identifying these students, designing educational interventions, and carefully monitoring progress.

The third and smallest group of students are those identified as having significant cognitive disabilities as defined by NCLB regulations. Alternate assessments based on alternate achievement standards must show a clear link to the content standards for the grade in which the student is enrolled, but the grade-level content may be reduced in complexity or modified, in some instances substantially, in order to meet the need of a student to develop skills. These alterations to curriculum will be reflected in the highly differentiated and individualized performance of the students in both academic and functional domains. Educational benefit must be measured in terms of differentiated outcomes, which will likely be individualized and should consider performance on alternate assessments and progress toward economic self-sufficiency and independent living. The IEPs of these students will contain goals and objectives that reflect the differentiated outcomes. Further, the claims on special education resources may be substantial and continue through age 21.

The differentiation in IEPs should in no way prohibit full and equal access to general education classrooms as determined on an individual basis. Decisions about least restrictive environment should be made after full consideration of the educational needs. However, regardless of where a student receives special education and related services, the regular, modified, or alternate achievement standards must establish the desired outcomes or benefits of education.

Just changing the IEP goals is really insufficient to address a fundamental shift in considering equity. A more radical suggestion is to consider what happens once a student with an IEP meets the regular education achievement standard. Should students who are at least proficient on the established achievement standards continue to have claims on special education resources? Under the notion of vertical equity, once a student has achieved the state-determined outcomes, the claims to unequal educational resources should cease. That is, these students would not be entitled to more than students who are similarly situated in terms of educational performance. As Green (1983) notes, "Some inequalities are fair and some are not" (p. 338). Just as it is inequitable to deny an individual student with an IEP access to the educational benefits as defined through state standards, it is also inequitable to provide resources to students beyond those required to achieve this "benefit." . . .

Changes to how one thinks about equity and students with disabilities affect much more than IEP decision making. The purpose of special education in the schools will also be altered. For the majority of students currently served under IDEA 2004, special education resources will support student progress toward regular state achievement standards and resources will be seamlessly blended into general education. For a lesser number of students with IEPs, special education will be more intensive and with more personalized goals. Resources and services will be more distinguishable from general education. The overall effect should be a more rational model of special education delivery that is more consistently applied across schools and districts.

This new policy model intentionally does not speak to the merits of the current standards, neither the subject matter content that is assessed nor how we are measuring students. These are political decisions and technical issues that affect all students and should be debated within that context. Nonetheless, interpretations of equity as seen in the national standards have reached the point where a significant reexamination of IDEA 2004 is required. It is in the best interests of the children and youth with disabilities in America's public schools for policy makers to come to terms with the conflicting beliefs and understandings of equity that underlie current policies and engage in serious debate of their relative merits. This will be necessary to truly align K–12 and special education in policy and practice.

# EXPLORING THE ISSUE

## Should Special Education and General Education Merge?

## Challenge Questions

- Compare and contrast the positions of the YES and NO selections regarding whether special education and general education should merge.
- Which side makes the best case for its argument? Why?
- What professional benefits do you see from having all teachers dually licensed in general education and special education?
- If IDEA and NCLB/ESEA are combined, how will parents' rights be affected?
- Compare and contrast reactions of parents, general education teachers, and special education teachers to each option.

## Is There Common Ground?

This issue's authors agree on three key points. First, the current educational system prizes academic outcomes for each child. Second, special education is in transition, responding to changes in general education. Third, the two reauthorizations provide a rare opportunity to influence the future of both general education and special education.

## Additional Resources

Brownell, M. T., Sindelar, P. T., Kiely, M. T. & Danielson, L. C. (2010). Special education teacher quality and preparation: Exposing foundations, constructing a new model. *Exceptional Children, 76*(3), 357–377.

*CEC's ESEA Policy Recommendations.* (2010). Council for Exceptional Children. Retrieved June 5, 2010 from www.cec.sped.org

Eisenman, L. T. & Ferretti, R. P. (2010). Introduction to the special issue: Changing conceptions of special education. *Exceptional Children, 76*(3), 262–263.

Fuchs, D., Fuchs, L. S., & Stecker, P. M. (2010). The "blurring" of special education in a new continuum of general education placements and services. *Exceptional Children, 76*(3), 301–323.

McLaughlin, M. J. (2010). Evolving interpretations of educational equity and students with disabilities. *Exceptional Children, 76*(3), 265–278.

Mellard, D. F., McKnight, M., & Woods, K. (2009). Response to Intervention screening and progress-monitoring practices in 41 local schools. *Learning Disabilities Research & Practice, 24*(4), 186–195.

Samuels, C. A. (2011). Finding efficiencies in special education programs. *Education Week, 30*(16), 32–34.

Simonsen, B., Shaw, S. F., Faggella-Luby, M., Sugai, G., Coyne, M. D., Rhein, B., Madaus, J. W., & Alfano, M. (2010). A schoolwide model for service delivery: Redefining special educators as interventionists. *Remedial and Special Education, 31*(1), 17–23.

Weber, M. C. (2008). Special education law: Challenges old and new. *Phi Delta Kappan, 90*(10), 728–732.

Zigmond, N., Kloo, A., & Volonino, V. (2009). What, where, and how? Special education in the climate of full inclusion. *Exceptionality, 17*, 189–204.

# ISSUE 11

## Does NCLB Leave Some Students Behind?

**YES: Jennifer Booher-Jennings**, from "Rationing Education in an Era of Accountability," *Phi Delta Kappan* (vol. 87, no. 10, pp. 756–761, 2006)

**NO: U.S. Department of Education**, from "Working Together for Students with Disabilities: Individuals with Disabilities Education Act (IDEA) and No Child Left Behind Act (NCLB) (2005), http://ed.gov, January 31, 2006

---

### Learning Outcomes

**At the conclusion of this issue, readers will be able to:**

- Compare and contrast the positions of the YES and NO selections addressing whether NCLB leaves some children behind.
- Describe the strengths and the weaknesses of each side's arguments.
- Determine whether, as a result of NCLB, students with disabilities have been left behind or included more than ever.
- Discuss elements of NCLB/ESEA that you think should be revised, as well as those you would like to keep.

---

**ISSUE SUMMARY**

**YES:** Jennifer Booher-Jennings, a doctoral candidate at Columbia University when she wrote this issue, finds the accountability pressures of No Child Left Behind lead some administrators to advise teachers to focus only on those children who will improve their school's scores; other students don't count much.

**NO:** The U.S. Department of Education FAQ Sheet on IDEA and No Child Left Behind (NCLB) advises readers that the link between these two statutes is sound, emphasizing how they work together to ensure that every student's performance and needs receive appropriate attention.

**P**rior to 1997, the very fact that students had a disability often meant they—and their performance—were excluded from any large-scale testing programs. This was the case whether the student had a mild learning disability, or a complex combination of sensory, physical, and cognitive challenges. The existence of the disability was sufficient to preclude participation. Some thought this was the right thing to do; it spared students the frustration of testing on the general curriculum, which everyone knew they could not master. Since their scores did not count, the students did not count. Schools were not accountable for the performance of students with disabilities.

Beginning with IDEA 97, districts were required to include students with disabilities in all large-scale testing programs. NCLB increased the stakes. Districts must now report, and be held accountable for, the academic performance of students with disabilities.

To comply with NCLB and IDEA, IEP teams decide how students can best demonstrate what they know and can do in large-scale testing. Although parents may contest the manner of testing, students cannot be exempted from the process. The following participation options exist:

- Regular assessment (that is administered to all students in that grade)
- Regular assessment with accommodations
- Alternate assessment based on grade-level achievement standards
- Alternate assessment based on alternate achievement standards
- Assessment based on modified achievement standards

NCLB required states to determine academic standards and assessment programs as well as their own method of alternate testing. Modified and alternate standards, as well as all alternate assessments, must be based on state academic standards. Some states use one set of standards for all students.

Under NCLB, every school is accountable for the adequate yearly progress (AYP) of all students toward the goal of academic proficiency by 2013–2014. Every child is expected to reach that target. These goals remain in place until/ unless reauthorization changes NCLB. States have been permitted to count as proficient a limited number of students taking an alternate assessment based on modified or alternate achievement standards.

If schools do not make AYP, their leadership must take actions to improve. Parents must be notified of the status and have the option of transferring to higher performing schools. Supplemental educational services must be available. In the extreme, schools are subject to "corrective actions" under the guidance/supervision of external experts.

This issue considers whether, despite the claim to reach everyone, NCLB efforts have left students with disabilities behind. As you read the YES and NO selections, ask yourself how the schools in your neighborhood have addressed the mandates and consequences of NCLB, particularly the progress of subgroups.

In the YES selection, Jennifer Booher-Jennings learned that teachers in one Texas school were being encouraged to focus on "the kids who count" because their improvement could increase school scores. Since students with disabilities didn't "count," or because they were "hopelessly" unlikely to do well, they were not deemed worthy of teacher energy.

In the NO selection, the U.S. Department of Education, responding to frequently asked questions, maintained that NCLB and IDEA act in concert to ensure that every child with a disability reaches high standards. The FAQ notes that most children with disabilities are in general education placements and are already participating in high numbers. The information gleaned from frequent assessments should "shine a light on student needs and draw attention to how schools can better serve (them)."

Some schools appeared to be successful, but certain groups within their walls did markedly less well than others. To hold schools accountable for the achievement of all students, NCLB specified particular subgroups, including students from low-income families; students from major racial and ethnic groups; those with limited English proficiency; and those with disabilities. Unless each subgroup makes AYP, a school is deemed not making total AYP.

The pressure to avoid being deemed a failing school has led some to adopt strategies to "game the system." Two of these are adjusting subgroup size and setting lower standards.

Under NCLB, states set their own minimum subgroup size. Subgroups falling below the minimum size are considered as having met AYP, regardless of student performance.

Subgroups, and their sizes, elicit much discussion. Scores from a very small number of students may not be statistically valid. With small subgroups, privacy can be compromised when scores become public. These situations are particularly relevant in small and/or rural schools (McLaughlin, Embler, Hernandez, & Caron, *Rural Special Education Quarterly*, 2005).

Some states have been accused of adjusting subgroup sizes to obscure the results of particular groups. An interim report addressing *Inclusion of students with disabilities in school accountability systems* found subgroup sizes ranged from 5 to 100 (Harr-Robins, Song, Hurlburt, Pruce, Danielson, Garet, & Taylor, 2012, http://ies.ed.gov/ncee/pubs/20124056). An earlier study (Simpson, Gong, & Marion, www.nciea.org, 2005) noted that larger minimum subgroup sizes mask the performance of students with disabilities. Schools might meet their targets without being accountable for these students. Interestingly, the Commission on No Child Left Behind (2006) found that disability subgroup scores were "very often not the sole reason a school is identified as not making AYP."

Another way to reach full proficiency is to lower the bar students must cross. The authors of *The proficiency illusion* (Cronin, Dahlin, Adkins, & Kingsbury, 2007) lament how greatly standards vary from state to state. They allege that some reported increases in proficiency actually reflect declines in test difficulty.

Checker Finn, a strong proponent of NCLB at its inception, thinks lawmakers made a "noble yet misleading promise" that all children would reach proficiency (Troublemaker, 2008). He writes that states dealt with this mandated promise by reducing standards so that more would pass. Finn now thinks NCLB should have held states accountable for reaching uniform academic expectations (Finn, 2009).

Senator Lamar Alexander (R-TN) and former Secretary of Education under the first President Bush reflects the positive side of NCLB when he notes that schools are now reporting school progress and being held accountable for the results. Using appropriate assessments to measure clear academic standards was an effective way to track progress. Referring to universal proficiency as a laudable, ambitious goal, Alexander described a one-size-fits-all approach inadequate and unrealistic in a society as diverse as ours. States, not the U.S. federal government, should drive this reform (Alexander, 2012).

Ten years after its passage, there is general agreement that NCLB has effected some positive changes, but is in need of significant revision. Commentaries of the law's background, successes, and shortcomings are abundant. Two extensive documents were recently published by the *National Journal* (Johnson, 2012, www.newnationaljournal.com) and West's *Education Law Reporter* (Umpstead & Kirby, 2012).

One positive change has been the success in having schools be accountable for all students. Performance data have revealed specific successes and areas needing attention. Because all kids count, all scores count. The National Journal Study (Johnson, 2012) found that the mandated subgroups drew attention to students whose performance might otherwise have been obscured.

Attention to student achievement did result in modest gains, but for unusual reasons. Umpstead and Kirby (2012) determined that the performance gap between students was narrowed, one of NCLB's goals. The reasons they uncovered are not admirable. Some of Umpstead and Kirby's commentators noted that, under pressure of making AYP targets, teachers did focus on "bubble kids," those most likely to influence the score of the class. Lower scoring students received attention, especially if they were part of a subgroup. Unfortunately, higher scoring students received little attention. The result was a narrowed gap: but not equal attention to all students.

The Obama administration's *Blueprint for Reform* (www2.ed.gov/policy/elsec/leg/blueprint/blueprint.pdf, 2010) identifies specific readjustments for ESEA reauthorization. Within the *Blueprint*'s elements, the goal of having every student academically proficient by 2014 would be replaced by having every student ready for college and/or career by 2020. Absolute scores on one-time assessments would be replaced by growth assessments and multiple measures. Punishments for struggling schools would be replaced by emphasis on a district's lowest performing schools.

Reviewing the *Blueprint* through the lens of its impact on students with disabilities, Boundy and Karger (*Responding to "A Blueprint for Reform" through the lens of students with disabilities*, 2011, www.cleweb.org) maintain that IDEA and NCLB formed a strong bond to include students with disabilities meaningfully in school reform. Noting that the *Blueprint* "is basically silent" on students with disabilities, they hope this does not signal a lowering of standards or a diminution of services.

The bipartisan support that heralded the passage of NCLB has all but evaporated and reauthorization is unlikely until 2013 at the earliest. With the 2014 proficiency date looming, and more districts unlikely to make the NCLB target, President Obama and Secretary Arne Duncan announced an opportunity for states to find relief through flexibility requests, referred to as waivers. State waiver proposals must include plans to move to college- and career-ready standards, develop rigorous accounting systems to monitor student achievement; deliver interventions to the lowest performing schools; and improve educator evaluation systems to incorporate student progress as one element—many elements of *The Blueprint*.

Advocates for students with disabilities remain vigilant and vocal. In a letter to Secretary Duncan, the advocacy group Consortium for Citizens with Disabilities (www.c-c-d.org, 2011) urges that waiver applications include meaningful information about the state plan that will address students with disabilities.

Both NCLB and IDEA are long overdue for reauthorization. Decisions will have a significant impact on students with disabilities. Educators can influence these policies. Highlighting the contributions of advocacy groups, Whitby and Wienke (*Intervention in School and Clinic*, 2012) urge educators to contribute their experiences, noting that every story can make an important difference. Don't let your own work be left behind!

# YES

**Jennifer Booher-Jennings**

# Rationing Education in an Era of Accountability

**M**eet Mrs. Dewey, 46 years old and a veteran fourth-grade teacher at Marshall Elementary School. Mrs. Dewey entered the teaching profession in the wake of *A Nation at Risk* and has weathered the storm ever since. For the last 20 years, she has survived the continuous succession of faddish programs that have characterized American education reform. Year after year, administrators have asked Marshall teachers to alter their practice to conform to the latest theory. Mrs. Dewey's colleagues, frustrated by the implementation of such silver-bullet approaches, have often flouted the administrative directives and chosen instead to serve as the sole arbiters of their classroom practice.

But it is the newest of the new solutions that worries Mrs. Dewey most. The language of accountability is swift and uncompromising: hold educators responsible for results. Identify those teachers who, as President Bush says, "won't teach." Fair enough, Mrs. Dewey thinks. The consummate professional, Mrs. Dewey always looks for the silver lining.

Like other reforms, accountability requires teachers to embrace a new strategy. Data-driven decision making, a consultant told the faculty at a professional development session, is the philosophy Marshall teachers must adopt. The theory is simple. Give students regular benchmark assessments, use the data to identify individual students' weaknesses, [and] provide targeted instruction and support that addresses those areas. Mrs. Dewey remembers nodding approvingly. After all, this approach—gathering textured information on each student to guide instructional activities—was one she had been using for 22 years.

The consultant moved on. "Using the data, you can identify and focus on the kids who are close to passing. The bubble kids. And focus on the kids that count—the ones that show up at Marshall after October won't count toward the school's test scores this year. Because you don't have enough special education students to disaggregate scores for that group, don't worry about them either." To make this concept tangible for teachers, the consultant passed out markers in three colors: green, yellow, and red. Mrs. Dewey heard someone mutter, "What is this? The traffic light theory of education?"

"Take out your classes' latest benchmark scores," the consultant told them, "and divide your students into three groups. Color the 'safe cases,' or kids who

From *Phi Delta Kappan,* June 2006, pp. 756–761. Copyright © 2006 by Phi Delta Kappan. Reprinted by permission of Phi Delta Kappan and Jennifer Booher-Jennings.

will definitely pass, green. Now, here's the most important part: identify the kids who are 'suitable cases for treatment.' Those are the ones who can pass with a little extra help. Color them yellow. Then, color the kids who have no chance of passing this year and the kids that don't count—the 'hopeless cases'—red. You should focus your attention on the yellow kids, the bubble kids. They'll give you the biggest return on your investment."

As the bell tolls a final warning to the boisterous 9-year-olds bringing up the rear of her class line, Mrs. Dewey stares blankly into the hallway. Never did she believe that the advice offered by that consultant would become Marshall's educational mantra. Focus on the bubble kids. Tutor only these students. Pay more attention to them in class. Why? It's data-driven. Yet this is what her colleagues have been doing, and Marshall's scores are up. The community is proud, and the principal has been anointed one of the most promising educational leaders in the state. At every faculty meeting, the principal presents a "league table," ranking teachers by the percentage of their students passing the latest benchmark test. And the teachers talk, as they always do. The table makes perfect fodder for faculty room gossip: "Did you see who was at the bottom of the table this month?"

Mrs. Dewey has made compromises, both large and small, throughout her career. Every educator who's in it for the long haul must. But this institutionalized policy of educational triage weighs heavily and hurts more. Should she focus only on Brittney, Julian, Shennell, Tiffany, George, and Marlena—the so-called bubble kids—to the exclusion of the other 17 students in her class? Should Mrs. Dewey refuse to tutor Anthony, a persistent and eager little boy with no chance of passing the state test this year, so that she can spend time with students who have a better shot at passing? What should she tell Celine, a precocious student, whose mother wants Mrs. Dewey to review her entry for an essay contest? Celine will certainly pass the state test, so can Mrs. Dewey afford the time? What about the five students who moved into the school in the middle of the year? Since they don't count toward Marshall's scores, should Mrs. Dewey worry about their performance at all?

In her angrier moments, Mrs. Dewey pledges to ignore Marshall's approach and to teach as she always has, the best way she knows how. Yet, if she does, Mrs. Dewey risks being denounced as a traitor to the school's effort to increase scores—in short, a bad teacher. Given 22 years of sacrifices for her profession, it is this reality that stings the most.

Mulling over her choices, Mrs. Dewey shuts her classroom door and begins her class.

# Unintended Consequences of Accountability Systems: Educational Triage

Test-based accountability systems aim to direct the behavior of educators toward the improvement of student achievement. The No Child Left Behind (NCLB) Act codified accountability as our national educational blueprint, requiring schools to increase test scores incrementally so that all students are proficient in reading and math by 2014. Yet, despite the stated intent of NCLB to improve outcomes for all students, particularly those who have been historically neglected, educators and others may adopt a series of "gaming" practices in order to artificially inflate schools' passing rates. Such practices include giving students a special education classification to exclude them from high-stakes tests, retaining students in grade to delay test-taking, diverting attention away from subjects not evaluated on high-stakes tests, teaching to the test, and cheating.

In what follows, I discuss two of the dilemmas presented by a less well-known gaming practice: educational triage. The insights offered here derive from an ethnographic study of an urban elementary school in Texas, to which I have assigned the pseudonym "Beck Elementary." Educational triage has become an increasingly widespread response to accountability systems and has been documented in Texas, California, Chicago, Philadelphia, New York, and even England. By educational triage, I mean the process through which teachers divide students into safe cases, cases suitable for treatment, and hopeless cases and ration resources to focus on those students most likely to improve a school's test scores. The idea of triage, a practice usually restricted to the direst of circumstances, like the battlefield or the emergency room, poignantly captures the dynamics of many schools' responses to NCLB. In the name of improving schools' scores, some students must inevitably be sacrificed. And the stakes are high—for schools, which face serious sanctions for failing to meet adequate yearly progress targets; for students, who increasingly face retention if they do not pass state tests; and for teachers, who are judged by the number of students they "save."

**Dilemma 1.** *Data can be used to improve student achievement, but they can also be used to target some students at the expense of others.* Data-driven decision making has become something of a sacrosanct term in education policy circles. Who could be against it? The public face of data-driven decision making—identifying the needs of each individual child and introducing interventions to remediate any learning difficulties—is sensible and beyond question.

But the Achilles' heel of education policy has always been implementation. When I listened closely to the conversations that educators at Beck Elementary School had about "being data-driven," the slippage between evaluating the individual needs of every student and deciding which students to target to maximize school performance quickly became evident. As I moved closer and closer to the classroom, the administrators' ideal version dissipated and gave way to a triage-based understanding of data-driven decision making. Teachers were most attuned to the chasm between administrators' theoretical proclamations and how the same administrators expected them to operate: teachers understood that the bottom line in this numbers game was the percentage of students who passed. Because of the unrelenting pressure to increase test scores, one mode of using data became dominant at Beck: the diversion of resources (e.g., additional time in class; enrichment sessions with the literacy teacher; and after-school, Saturday, and summer tutoring) to students on the threshold of passing the test, the "bubble kids."

All my questions about which students received extra help were met with the deferent maxim, "It's data-driven." When I asked one teacher how the school allocated additional services to students—for example, the reading specialist or after-school and Saturday tutoring—she provided the following response:

> It's all data-driven. . . . We do projections—how many of them do you think will pass, how many of them do you think will need more instruction, how many teachers do we have to work with, what time limit do we have? Based on that, who are we going to work with? It comes down to that. . . . We really worked with the bubble kids . . . that's the most realistic and time-efficient thing we can think of.

In this conception of data-driven practice, the choice to privilege one group of students over another is viewed as neutral and objective. The decision to distribute resources to those most advantageous to the school's pass rates is not understood as a moral or ethical decision. Instead, it is seen as a sterile management imperative. Protected by its scientific underpinnings, the data-driven focus on the bubble kids is difficult for teachers to attack. In sum, at Beck Elementary, the invocation of the phrase "data-driven" obscures, neutralizes, and legitimates a system of resource distribution that is designed to increase passing rates rather than to meet the needs of individual students.

The blunt vocabulary of triage infiltrated every corner of Beck. The tenor of the phrases used to describe students—"the ones who could make it" and "hopeless cases"—speaks not only to the perceived urgency to improve test scores but also to the destructive labeling of those children who find themselves below the bubble. Driven by the pressure to increase the passing rate, teachers turned their attention away from these students. As one teacher related in an interview:

> I guess there's supposed to be remediation for anything below 55%, but you have to figure out who to focus on in class, and I definitely focus more attention on the bubble kids. If you look at her score [pointing to a student's score on her class test-score summary sheet], she's got a 25%. What's the point in trying to get her to grade level? It would take two years to get her to pass the test, so there's really no hope for her. . . . I feel like we might as well focus on the ones that there's hope for.

To say that hope is absent for a 10-year-old child is a particularly telling comment on how dramatically the accountability system has altered the realm of imagined possibility in the classroom. Now, with an unforgiving bottom line for which to strive, teachers can retain hope only for those perceived as potential passers. To assert that students below the bubble are just too low-performing to help establishes that the only worthwhile improvement in this brave new world is one that converts a nonpasser to a passer.

The problem is that those students who arrive at school as the most disadvantaged are often the lowest scoring. And since the focus on the bubble kids at Beck Elementary begins not in the third grade—the first year that students take state tests—but the moment students enter kindergarten, they are branded as "hopeless cases" from the very first days of their schooling.

An important shift occurs in a system focused on the percentage of students above a particular threshold. When a low-performing student enters a teacher's classroom, he or she is seen as a liability rather than as an opportunity to promote individual student growth. As Michael Apple trenchantly wrote, the emphasis changes "from student needs to student performance, and from what the school does for the student to what the student does for the school."

Certainly one can imagine uses of data that could turn attention to the individual needs of each and every student. However, the current monolithic discourse on data-driven decision making begs for a discussion of unintended consequences. Data can be used to target some students at the expense of others, and it is happening today.

When we blindly defer to "the data," we abdicate responsibility for tough decisions, all the while claiming neutrality. But data are not actors and cannot do anything by themselves. Data do not make decisions; people make decisions that can be informed by data. Decisions about resource allocation are ethical decisions with which educators and communities must grapple and for which they must ultimately take responsibility.

What we need above all is a sustained discussion among educators and the broader polity about the very real tradeoffs involved in schools' responses to accountability systems. If schools adopt the practices of educational triage in response to NCLB, the consequence may be suboptimal outcomes for students "below the bubble," as well as for their peers who are mid-level and high-achieving students. And all of these unintended consequences can happen while official pass rates increase.

**Dilemma 2.**   *It is unfair to hold schools accountable for new students or for subgroups that are too small to yield statistically reliable estimates of a school's effectiveness; however, the consequence of excluding some students may be to deny them access to scarce educational resources.* Educational triage does not end with the diversion of resources to the "bubble kids." Because of the fine print in NCLB, all students are not equally valuable to a school's test scores. Subgroups are not disaggregated if the number of test-takers does not meet a minimum size requirement, and students are not counted at all in a school's scores if they are not enrolled in a school for a full academic year. For example, in Texas, the scores of students who arrive at the school after the end of October do not count toward schools' scores. Such a definition is logical, for it attempts to isolate the impact of schools on students. Including students who have not attended the school for a reasonable period of time might bias estimates of the school's quality and unfairly penalize schools serving more mobile students.

However, if resources flow only toward those students who affect a school's outcomes, students who do not "count" may be denied access to scarce educational resources. I found that another pithy term, "the accountables"— those students who count toward a school's scores—was incorporated into the lexicon of Beck educators. Teachers engaged in a second kind of educational triage by focusing resources on the "accountables," to the virtual exclusion of students who "did not count." In accountability's ultimate contradiction, the protean word "accountable" retained only a semblance of its intended meaning—taking responsibility for each and every student.

How many students are affected by the mobility provisions of NCLB? Take the Houston Independent School District as an illustrative example. Serving 211,157 students, this district is the largest in Texas and the seventh largest in the nation. The average Houston school excludes 8% of its students from its "accountables." Almost one-third of Houston schools (31%) exclude more than 10% of their students from scores used for accountability. By any measure, this is not an insignificant number of students. Moreover, because mobility is not uniformly distributed across the population, some demographic groups have much higher numbers of mobile—and thus unaccountable—students. In Houston, an average of 16% of special education students and 11% of African American students are not counted in schools' scores because they have not been enrolled in a school for a full academic year. Ironically, the very students NCLB was designed to target are often those least likely to be counted.

A second way that students may "not count" stems from states' definitions of the subgroup size required for disaggregation. If states define subgroup size expediently, the scores of various subgroups will continue to be buried in schoolwide averages. Again, Texas is a good example of artful definition of subgroup size. Under the Texas state accountability system, subgroups must include at least 30 students and account for at least 10% of all students—or include 50 or more students—to be evaluated. Under Texas' NCLB implementation plan, subgroups must include at least 50 students and make up at least 10% of all students—or include 200 or more students—to be evaluated. Under the state system, 82% of Houston schools with African American test-takers disaggregate scores for African American students, while for the purposes of NCLB, only 66% do.

Though Texas does not include a special education subgroup in its state system, the impact of using the 50 and 10% or greater than 200 definition rather than the lower threshold is significant. Shifting the definition upward reduces the percentage of Houston schools that disaggregate scores for special education from 55% to 24%. Other states have similarly gamed the subgroup-size provision of the law. In 2005, the U.S. Department of Education allowed Florida to change its minimum subgroup size to 30 students who also make up 15% of test-takers. Because special education students rarely account for more than 15% of a school's population, very few schools in Florida will be required to disaggregate scores for these students.

There is an irreconcilable tension between accurately measuring school effects and forestalling the potential negative consequences of excluding some students from accountability calculations. If accuracy of measurement is privileged, some students will necessarily be excluded from accountability calculations. In order to best estimate school effects, a school should not be responsible for students who attend it for a short period of time. Similarly, small subgroups may yield statistically unreliable estimates of the school's efficacy with a particular group of students. Moreover, mainstream state tests may be inappropriate measures for some English-language learners or special education students. In other words, there are valid reasons, from a measurement perspective, for excluding students from schools' scores. On the other hand, the consequence of excluding these students may be to deny them access to scarce educational resources.

## Better Choices?

So Mrs. Dewey can choose to teach all of her students, regardless of their potential contribution to her school's bottom line, or she can participate in educational triage. If she refuses to focus her time and attention on those students most likely to raise the school's scores, she risks not only the school's survival but her professional reputation as a good teacher and, potentially, her job.

Mrs. Dewey should not be asked to make such choices, and it is unconscionable to question her ethics when she does what she has little choice but to do. Systems of public policy cannot be designed solely for those with the moral certitude to qualify them for sainthood.

Educators will respond to systemic incentives, and NCLB's current incentives structurally induce behaviors that are inimical to broader notions of equity and fairness. In many cases, these perverse incentives turn educators' attention away from NCLB's intended beneficiaries. Until these issues are addressed, we can expect to see educational triage practices flourish across the country.

# Working Together for Students with Disabilities: Individuals with Disabilities Education Act (IDEA) and No Child Left Behind Act (NCLB)

## Frequently Asked Questions

### 1. Are *NCLB* and *IDEA* in conflict with each other?

No. Both laws have the same goal of improving academic achievement through high expectations and high-quality education programs. *NCLB* works to achieve that goal by focusing on school accountability, teacher quality, parental involvement through access to information and choices about their children's education, and the use of evidence-based instruction. *IDEA* complements those efforts by focusing specifically on how best to help students with disabilities meet academic goals.

*NCLB* aims to improve the achievement of all students and recognizes that schools must ensure that all groups receive the support they need to achieve to high standards. That is why *NCLB* requires that schools look at the performance of specific subgroups of students, including students with disabilities, and holds schools accountable for their achievement. By including students with disabilities in the overall accountability system, the law makes their achievement everybody's business, not just the business of special education teachers. Shining the light on the needs of students with disabilities draws attention to the responsibility of states, districts, and schools to target resources to improve the achievement of students with disabilities and to monitor closely the quality of services provided under *IDEA*.

### 2. If *NCLB* focuses on school performance while IDEA focuses on individual students, how can a student's individual rights not be compromised under *NCLB*?

The requirements of *NCLB* do not infringe on the rights of students with disabilities under *IDEA*.

*IDEA* requires that schools provide special education and related services to meet the individual needs of each student with a disability. To provide these services, a team of educators and parents develop a plan (referred to as an

From http://www.ed.gov/admins/lead/speced/toolkit/index.html, December 2005. Published by the U.S. Department of Education.

"Individualized Education Program," or IEP) for each student with a disability that maps out what achievement is expected and what services are needed to help the student meet these expectations. With the appropriate supports and services, students with disabilities can and should be held to high standards.

NCLB is designed to ensure that schools are held accountable for educational results so that each and every student can achieve to high standards. Setting the bar high helps all students, including students with disabilities, reach those standards. The expectation of *NCLB* is that students with disabilities can achieve to high standards as other students, given the appropriate supports and services.

### 3. Was *NCLB* the first federal law to require states to include students with disabilities in the state's assessment system?

*NCLB* is the first law to hold schools accountable for ensuring that all students participate in the state assessment system, but it is built on earlier law. The 1997 amendments to the *IDEA* required that students with disabilities participate in state and district assessments and that their results be reported publicly in the same way and with the same frequency as those of other students. The federal law that preceded *NCLB*, the *Improving America's Schools Act of 1994*, required schools to include the assessment results of students with disabilities in accountability decisions for Title I schools. *NCLB* and the 2004 *IDEA* amendments strengthened a commitment to this requirement, and now all states are paying attention to testing students with disabilities and are using those results to hold schools accountable for the performance of these students.

Data indicate that participation and achievement levels are rising each year. Data from the National Council on Educational Outcomes (NCEO) show that in 2003, most states had 95 percent to 100 percent participation in state math and reading assessments by students with disabilities in elementary school, middle school, and high school. By including students with disabilities in the assessment and accountability systems, we raise our expectations for them while giving schools the data they need to help all of their students to be successful. *NCLB* is helping special education programs and each child's IEP team know what academic goals children need to achieve so that they are given the appropriate supports and services. *NCLB* tells us what we're working toward, while *IDEA* brings to bear multiple resources and services to help students attain the learning standards.

### 4. My school did not make Adequate Yearly Progress (AYP) because students with disabilities did not score well on the state test. Is that fair?

Only by holding schools accountable for *all* students will the spotlight of attention and necessary resources be directed to those children most in need of assistance and most often left behind academically.

Schools need to be accountable for all students. To achieve that goal, AYP is intentionally designed to identify those areas where schools need to improve the achievement of their students. What we are learning is that some schools perform well on average, but they may miss their AYP goals as a result of the student achievement of one or a few groups of students. The requirement for states, districts, and schools to disaggregate their data (i.e., separate their assessment data by the results of the different subgroups of students) is one of the fundamental principles of NCLB. This ensures that all schools and districts are held accountable for the performance of subgroups of students, not just the school as a whole.

The Department recognizes the challenges educators face in helping all children achieve to high standards. But allowing overall school performance to mask the lower performance of particular groups of students who need additional academic assistance would be *unfair* to those struggling groups of students.

### 5. Why should students with disabilities be tested and included in accountability systems?

Students with disabilities deserve the same high-quality education as their peers. Ever since Congress enacted the 1997 amendments to the IDEA, the nation has been working to improve the participation of students with disabilities in state assessments and provide students with disabilities access to the general education curriculum. Many states have been committed to this goal for an even longer period of time. The purpose of requiring participation in assessments is to improve achievement for students with disabilities. As Secretary Spellings has said on more than one occasion, "What gets measured gets done." Too often in the past, students with disabilities were excluded from assessments and accountability systems, and the consequence was that they did not receive the academic attention and resources they deserved.

Students with disabilities, including those with the most significant cognitive disabilities, benefit instructionally from such participation. One state explains the instructional benefits of including students with the most significant cognitive disabilities in its assessment system in the following way: "Some students with disabilities have never been taught academic skills and concepts, for example, reading, mathematics, science, and social studies, even at very basic levels. Yet all students are capable of learning at a level that engages and challenges them. Teachers who have incorporated learning standards into their instruction cite unanticipated gains in students' performance and understanding. Furthermore, some individualized social, communication, motor, and self-help skills can be practiced during activities based on the learning standards."

To ensure that adequate resources are dedicated to helping these students succeed, appropriate measurement of their achievement needs to be part of school and district accountability systems. Furthermore, when students with disabilities are part of the accountability system, educators' expectations for these students are more likely to increase. In such a system, educators realize that students with disabilities count and that they can learn to high standards, just like students without disabilities.

### 6. Is it fair to make students with disabilities take a test that they cannot pass?

For too long in this country, students with disabilities have been held to lower standards than their peers and unjustly routed through school systems that expected less of them than of other students. Several states have found that once students with disabilities are included in the assessment system and expected to achieve like other students, performance improves. In 2005, for example, 60 percent of fourth-graders with disabilities in Kansas were proficient in reading. This represented an increase over 2003, when 51 percent of students with disabilities were proficient.

Students with disabilities can achieve at high levels. That is why *NCLB* requires states and school districts to hold all students to the same challenging academic standards and have all students participate in annual state assessments. We test students to see what they are learning, identify academic needs, and address those needs. The purpose is not to frustrate children. Rather, it is to shine a light on student needs and draw attention to how schools can better serve their students.

If students are excluded from assessments, they are excluded from school improvement plans based on those assessment results. If all students are to benefit from education reforms, all students must be included. Only by measuring how well the system is doing will we clearly identify and then fill the gaps in instructional opportunities that leave some students behind.

We do, however, need to improve tests for students with disabilities. We need tests that measure what students know and can do without the interference of their disability. The Department is currently looking at ways to make tests more accessible and valid for a wider range of students so that all students can participate and receive meaningful scores. For more information about this work, please refer to item 13 of this document and to the proposed regulation that was released in December 2005. . . .

### 7. Why can't a student's Individualized Education Program (IEP), instead of the state assessment, be used to measure progress?

There are several reasons why IEPs are not appropriate for school accountability purposes. In general, IEP goals are individualized for each student and may cover a range of needs beyond reading/language arts and mathematics, such as behavior and social skills. They are not necessarily aligned with state standards, and they are not designed to ensure consistent judgments about schools—a fundamental requirement for AYP determinations. The IEP is used to provide parents with information about a student's progress and for making individualized decisions about the special education and related services a student needs to succeed. Assessments used for school accountability purposes must be aligned to state standards and have related achievement standards.

### 8. Students in special education get extra privileges in taking the state tests. Some of them get more time and get tested by themselves or in small groups. Isn't this unfair?

These "privileges" are called "accommodations." Accommodations are changes in testing materials or procedures, such as repeating directions or allowing extended time, that, by design, do not invalidate the student's test score. In other words, accommodations help students access the material but do not give students with disabilities an unfair advantage. These accommodations instead help level the playing field so that a test measures what the student knows and can do and not the effect of the child's disability. It is not unfair to allow valid accommodations during a test because these accommodations allow a test to measure the student's knowledge and skills rather than the student's disability.

The state is responsible for analyzing accommodations to determine which are acceptable on the basis of the test design. It is important for the state to make sure that students use only those accommodations that result in a valid score. For example, if the assessment is supposed to measure how well a student decodes text, reading the test aloud to the student would result in an invalid score.

9. **Isn't it unrealistic to expect *all* students with disabilities to meet grade-level standards? Students are in special education for a reason.**

Students receive special education services for a reason. They are in special education because a team of professionals has evaluated the child using a variety of assessment tools and strategies to gather relevant functional, developmental, and academic information about the child, including information provided by the parent, and determined that the child has a disability and needs special education services. Their achievement on grade-level standards is only part of the picture. It does not determine whether or not they need services. Assessments and other evaluation materials include those tailored to assess specific areas of education need. The child must be assessed in all areas related to the suspected disability including, if appropriate, health, vision, hearing, social and emotional status, general intelligence, academic performance, communicative status, and motor abilities. The impression that students are receiving special education services because they cannot pass a state test is a misunderstanding of what it means to be eligible for *IDEA* services.

Being in special education does not mean that a student cannot learn and reach grade-level standards. In fact, the majority of students with disabilities should be able to meet those standards. Special education provides the additional help and support that these students need to learn. This means designing instruction to meet their specific needs and providing supports, such as physical therapy, counseling services, or interpreting services, to help students learn alongside their peers and reach the same high standards as all other students.

10. **What about students with significant cognitive disabilities? Is it realistic to expect them to meet the same level of achievement as all other students?**

The expectation of *NCLB* is that the majority of students with disabilities can and should participate in and achieve proficiency on state assessments. We understand, however, that there is a small percentage of students with disabilities who may not reach grade-level standards, even with the best instruction. These are students with the most significant cognitive disabilities (about 10 percent of all special education students). The Title I regulations allow these students to take an alternate assessment based on alternate achievement standards that is less difficult and more tailored to their needs. Their proficient scores can be counted in the same way as any other student's proficient score on a state assessment. The Department has developed certain safeguards around this policy to help prevent students from being placed in an assessment and curricula that are inappropriately restricted in scope, thus limiting their educational opportunities (see item 11).

11. **It seems like the Department has said the following: "Only 1 percent of students with disabilities can take an alternate assessment based on alternate achievement standards." Is this true?**

The Department has not made such a statement. In fact, it reflects several common misunderstandings about federal education policy. Current Title I regulations permit a student's proficient score on assessments based on alternate achievement standards to count the same as any other student's proficient score on a state assessment, subject to a 1.0 percent cap at the district and state levels. If more than 1.0 percent of proficient scores come from such assessments, then the state must establish procedures to count those scores as nonproficient for the purposes of school accountability.

*MYTH. The Department expects that only 1 percent of students with disabilities should take a test based on alternate achievement standards (1 percent cap).*

*FACT.* The 1.0 percent cap reflects the following: 1 percent of *all* students represents about 10 percent of students with disabilities. While all children can learn challenging content, evaluating that learning through the use of alternate achievement standards is appropriate only for a small, limited percentage of students who are within one or more of the existing disability categories under the *IDEA* (e.g., autism, multiple disabilities, traumatic brain injury), and whose cognitive disability prevents them from attaining grade-level achievement standards, even with the very best instruction. The 1 percent cap (or approximately 10 percent of students with disabilities) is based on current incidence rates of students with the most significant cognitive disabilities, allowing for reasonable local variation in prevalence.

*MYTH. IEP teams are limited in the number of students with disabilities that they may determine need an alternate assessment based on alternate achievement standards.*

*FACT.* The cap is a limit on the number of proficient scores that may be included in AYP decisions at the district and state levels. The cap is not a limit on the number of students who may take such an alternate assessment based on alternate achievement standards.

*FACT.* IEP teams must make informed and appropriate decisions for each individual student, based on each student's unique needs. If more than 1 percent of all students in a district need to take an assessment based on alternate achievement standards, then all such students may take them. To protect students from inappropriate, low standards, however, districts and states are limited in the use of proficient scores based on alternate achievement standards in making AYP decisions.

*FACT.* Alternate assessments based on alternate achievement standards must only be given to students with the most significant cognitive disabilities. States must develop guidelines to help IEP teams determine which assessment is most appropriate for a student with a disability to take. If those guidelines are appropriately developed and implemented, IEP teams should be making the right decisions for their students.

### 12. Don't such "caps" interfere with IEP decisions?

No. The policies on including students with disabilities in assessment and accountability systems do not affect the IEP team's role in making specific individual decisions about how to best address the needs of children with disabilities. The policies do not restrict the number of students who can participate in an alternate assessment. Instead, the policy restricts, solely for purposes of calculating AYP for school accountability, the number of scores that can be counted as proficient or advanced based on alternate achievement standards on alternate assessments.

### 13. How will the Department's recent proposed regulations change the policy on assessing and including students with disabilities in school accountability?

Since the regulation permitting a state to develop alternate achievement standards for students with the most significant cognitive disabilities was issued, information and experience in states, as well as important recent research, indicate that there may be an additional number of students who, because of their disability, have significant difficulty achieving grade-level proficiency, even with the best instruction, within the same time frame as other students.

The best available research and data indicate that this group of students comprises about 2 percent of the school-age population (or approximately 20 percent of students with disabilities). The progress of these students with disabilities in response to high-quality instruction, including special education and related services designed to address the students' individual needs, is such that the students are not likely to achieve grade-level proficiency within the school year covered by the students' IEPs.

The Department is publishing proposed regulations to address how these students may be included in a state's assessment and accountability systems. The proposed regulations would permit a state to (1) develop modified achievement standards, that is, standards that are aligned with the state's academic content standards for the grade in which a student is enrolled, but may reflect reduced breadth or depth of grade-level content; (2) develop assessments to measure the achievement of students based on such modified achievement standards; and (3) include the proficient and advanced scores based on modified achievement standards in determining AYP for school accountability purposes only, subject to a cap of 2.0 percent at the district and state levels.

The goal of the proposed regulations is to recognize, based on research, the specific needs of an additional group of students with disabilities while ensuring that states continue to hold schools accountable for helping these students with disabilities meet challenging standards that enable the students to approach, and even meet, grade-level standards. The proposed regulations would require certain safeguards, such as requiring that modified achievement standards provide access for students with disabilities to grade-level curricula and do not preclude a student from earning a regular high school diploma. They would also require a state to develop clear and appropriate guidelines for IEP teams to apply in determining which students should be assessed based on modified achievement standards and to ensure that parents are informed that their child's achievement will be measured on those standards. The proposed regulations would also permit a state, in determining AYP for the students with disabilities subgroup, to include, for a period of up to two years, the scores of students who were previously identified as having a disability but who are no longer receiving special education services.

The proposed regulation affects both *IDEA* and *NCLB* by ensuring that the requirements for participation in state assessment systems are the same. With this proposed change, students with disabilities must participate in an assessment that results in a valid score.

### 14. How will *IDEA* and *NCLB* work together for students with disabilities in the future?

*IDEA* and *NCLB* reinforce and strengthen the goal of accountability for all children. Both laws require states to include students with disabilities in state assessments and to report publicly the achievement of students with disabilities. In addition, state performance goals under the *IDEA* must be aligned with the state's definition of AYP. Such consistency across these two laws will facilitate greater collaboration between special education and general education teachers and realize the goal of considering children with disabilities as general education students first. One of the ways that *IDEA* supports this effort is through new provisions added by the 2004 reauthorization of the *IDEA* that allow local education agencies (LEAs) to use federal special education funds to provide early intervention services for students who are at risk of later identification and placement in special education. (There is nothing precluding state funds from also being used for this purpose.) This provides an opportunity for educators to work together to implement scientifically based instructional practices like curriculum-based measurement to identify and address academic problems early.

# EXPLORING THE ISSUE

## Does NCLB Leave Some Students Behind?

## Challenge Questions

- Compare and contrast the positions of the YES and NO selections regarding whether NCLB leaves some children behind.
- Which selection makes the best case for its argument? Why?
- Do the teachers in your local school believe they are encouraged to teach all children—or do some matter more than others? How is this message conveyed? What do teachers think about this practice?
- Discuss the ways in which, under NCLB, students with disabilities have been left behind as well as the ways they have been included more than ever.
- Has your state filed for a waiver from NCLB's provisions? Will students with disabilities fare better under the waiver or become uncounted?

## Is There Common Ground?

Both the authors of the YES and NO selections want students to succeed. They both state that schools need to be accountable for the performance of all children and believe that teachers play a critical role in improving that performance.

## Additional Resources

*A Blueprint for Reform*: The reauthorization of the Elementary and Secondary Education Act. (2010). U.S. Department of Education. Retrieved April 10, 2010 from www2.ed.gov/policy/elsec/leg/blueprint/blueprint.pdf

Alexander, L. (2012, January 11). Assessing No Child Left Behind: NCLB lessons: It is time for Washington to get out of the way. *Education Week, 40*, 29.

Booher-Jennings, J. (2006). Rationing education in an era of accountability. *Phi Delta Kappan, 87*(10), 756–761.

Commission on No Child Left Behind. (2006). *Commission staff report: Children with disabilities and LEP students: Their impact on the AYP determinations of schools*. The Aspen Institute. Retrieved June 1, 2006 from www.nclbcommission.org

Commission on No Child Left Behind. (2008). *Beyond NCLB: Fulfilling the promise to our nation's children*. Retrieved May 1, 2008 from http://nclbcommision.org

Consortium for Citizens with Disabilities. (2011, December 22). *Letter to Secretary Duncan regarding ESEA flexibility requests*. Retrieved May 1, 2012 from www.c-c-d.org

Cronin, J., Dahlin, M., Adkins, D., & Kingsbury, G. G. (2007). *The proficiency illusion*. The Fordham Institute. Retrieved March 1, 2010 from www.edexcellence.net

Finn, C. E., Jr. (2009). The end of the education debate. *National Affairs*. Retrieved April 5, 2010 from www.nationalaffairs.com

Harr-Robins, J., Song, M., Hurlburt, S., Pruce, C., Danielson, L., Garet, M., & Taylor, J. (2012). *The inclusion of students with disabilities in school accountability systems*. (NCEE 2012-4056). Washington, DC: National Center for Education Evaluation and Regional Assistance, Institute of Education Sciences, U.S. Department of Education.

Johnson, F. (2012, January 12). *Education report card: With help from education experts, National Journal grades the landmark No Child Left Behind*. Retrieved January 29, 2012 from www.newnationaljournal.com

McLaughlin, M. J., Embler, S., Hernandez, G., & Caron, E. (2005). No Child Left Behind Act and students with disabilities in rural and public schools. *Rural Special Education Quarterly, 24*(1), 32–39.

*No Child Left Behind Act and the Individuals with Disabilities Education Act: A Progress report*. (2008). National Council on Disability. Retrieved May 1, 2008 from www.ncd.gov

Simpson, M. A., Gong, B., & Marion, S. (2005). *Effect of minimum cell sizes and confidence interval sizes for special education subgroups on school-level AYP determinations*. National Center for the Improvement of Educational Assessment. Retrieved April 11, 2006 from www.nciea.org

Umpstead, R. R. & Kirby, E. (2012, March 29). Commentary: Reauthorization revisited: Framing the recommendations for the Elementary and Secondary Education Act's reauthorization in light of No Child Left Behind's implementation challenges. *West's Education Law Reporter*. Retrieved May 9, 2012 from Campus Research.

Whitby, P. J. S. & Wienke, W. (2012). A special educator's call to action for advocacy in national education policy. *Intervention in School and Clinic, 47*(3), 191–194.

# ISSUE 12

## Should Students with Cognitive Disabilities Be Expected to Demonstrate Academic Proficiency?

YES: **Kevin S. McGrew & Jeffrey Evans**, from *Expectations for Students with Cognitive Disabilities: Is the Cup Half Empty or Half Full? Can the Cup Flow Over?* (Synthesis Report 55) (University of Minnesota, National Center on Educational Outcomes, 2004)

NO: **James M. Kauffman**, from *Education Deform: Bright People Sometimes Say Stupid Things about Education* (Scarecrow Press, 2002)

---

### Learning Outcomes

**At the conclusion of this issue, readers will be able to:**

- Compare and contrast the positions of the YES and NO selections addressing whether students with cognitive disabilities should be expected to demonstrate academic proficiency.
- Describe the strengths and the weaknesses of each side's arguments.
- Identify how students with significant disabilities participate in No Child Left Behind (NCLB)-required testing.
- List the benefits and disadvantages of holding higher academic expectations for students with significant disabilities—from the perspective of teachers and parents.

---

#### ISSUE SUMMARY

YES: Kevin S. McGrew, director of the Institute for Applied Psychometrics (IAP) and educational researcher, and Jeffrey Evans, consultant and educational researcher for IAP, are wary that stereotypes of individuals with cognitive disabilities are used to form limited (and limiting) expectations and self-fulfilling prophecies.

NO: James M. Kauffman, professor Emeritus of Education at the University of Virginia, Charlottesville, and special education philosopher-researcher, believes that educators and parents must acknowledge that some students with cognitive disabilities cannot reach high academic standards and are best served by programs that develop other skills.

$T$he Elementary and Secondary Education Act (ESEA), sometimes called Title I, was signed by President Lyndon B. Johnson in 1965. Its funding supported state efforts to improve educational performance of children from low-income families. In ESEA's 2001 reauthorization, the U.S. federal government demanded a return on its investment. Titled the No Child Left Behind Act of 2001 (NCLB), this reauthorization changed the vocabulary and practice of educators in every publicly funded school in America.

Four principles formed the foundation of NCLB:

- Schools must be accountable for student performance and teacher qualifications.
- States and districts must set growth targets and have the latitude to achieve them.
- Parents must have more information about their schools and broader educational options if their schools do not reach growth targets.
- Schools must use research-based instructional strategies.

The principle most on the minds of educators has been accountability. NCLB mandated that all children be proficient in math and reading/language arts by 2013–2014. States determined their own educational standards, as well as specific benchmark goals, staged to reach the proficiency target. Results of regular testing in reading, math, and science document if a school is making adequate yearly progress (AYP) toward the target.

From the beginning, there have been questions about the intersection of NCLB and IDEA. NCLB focuses on the same goal for every student. IDEA's emphasis is on designing individualized programming, with goals tailored to each child's needs. Referencing questions about possible conflicts between NCLB and IDEA, then Secretary Margaret Spellings said:

> Special education is no longer a peripheral issue. IDEA and NCLB have put the needs of students with disabilities front and center. We've torn down the final barrier between special and general education. And now everyone in the system has a stake in ensuring students with disabilities achieve high standards. (2005)

To comply with IDEA and NCLB, IEP teams decide the way in which students can best demonstrate what they know and can do in large-scale testing.

Although students cannot be exempted from the process, parents may contest the manner of testing. The following participation options are available:

- Regular assessment (that is administered to all students in that grade)
- Regular assessment with accommodations
- Alternate assessment based on grade-level achievement standards
- Alternate assessment based on alternate achievement standards
- Assessment based on modified achievement standards

Modified and alternate standards, as well as all alternate assessments, must be based on state academic standards. NCLB requires states to determine their own method of alternate testing. Some use portfolios; others select out-of-level testing, administering a test from a lower grade. Some states require one set of standards for all learners.

Clearly, it is sensible to help every individual develop into a competent, independent adult. Educators generally agree that the historical blanket exclusion of all students with disabilities was not wise and failed to provide an accurate view of the accomplishments of the total student body. Now some ask if it is wise to expect all students to reach the same goal.

The YES and NO selections are somewhat longer than is typical for Taking Sides. Their length reflects the complexity of the controversy about whether students with cognitive disabilities should be expected to reach academic proficiency. Before you read these selections, decide how you would answer the question posed by this issue. After reading, decide whether the selections changed your response.

In the YES selection, Kevin S. McGrew and Jeffrey Evans caution that there are dangers in relying on disability labels or IQ scores to anticipate what a student might achieve. They discuss the powerful impact expectations can have on accomplishments and worry that stereotypes will limit possibilities for students with cognitive disabilities.

In the NO selection, James Kauffman maintains that some students, particularly those with cognitive disabilities, simply will not be able to reach high academic standards. He sees this as a reality that should be accepted and urges people to focus on what these individuals can do, creating programs to develop their strengths.

The Center on Educational Policy (CEP) (www.cep-dc.org, 2010) has conducted a series of studies to determine the impact of NCLB. The fourth segment investigated whether progress has been made in raising achievement for students with disabilities. Findings were mixed. Progress was evident in reading and math at the fourth-grade level. Nevertheless, CEP found a far smaller percentage of children with disabilities reached proficiency than did typical children.

People sometimes live up to our expectations for them—or down to other expectations. The power of positive thinking drives many to unimagined levels of success. McGrew and Evans remind us not to let IQ scores constrain the opportunities offered to children with cognitive disabilities.

Listen to the voices of teachers who have used alternate assessments to engage their students in academic standards. "My attitude (about her abilities) was denying her the opportunity to succeed." "Now I look at the possibilities instead of the limitations." "He is doing things I didn't realize he could do." These optimistic comments represent the findings of Moore-Lamminen and Olsen (n.d., Alliance for Systems Change), documenting the positive experiences of teachers who have stretched their students to excel.

Measuring and reporting the performance of students using alternate assessments based on alternate standards are challenging (Ahearn, *NASDSE inForum*, 2009). Even though both are based on state curricula, alternate standards may differ substantially from those used for standard assessments. CEP noted that "fuzzy data" make it difficult to assess the performance of those who used alternate assessments; tests varied widely across states as did scoring and reporting practices.

Following a successful pilot experience, states are now permitted to use growth models rather than one-time status model assessments. These track changes in the achievement of individual students. States can be acknowledged for the progress of each learner.

U.S. federal regulations stipulate that growth must be measured on academic standards, not IEP goals; that students using alternate assessments must be included as much as possible; and that schools need to justify the nonparticipation of any child. The Council for Exceptional Children (CEC) (www.cec.sped.org), an international professional association, has consistently advocated for a longitudinal growth model to document and validate the progress of students who may not reach grade-level standards.

Tracking student growth is a complex task. In 2010, the Institute for Educational Sciences announced grants to 20 states for the design and implementation of statewide longitudinal databases. The stated intent is the creation of systems to track student growth over time, matching students to teachers.

Federal NCLB waiver applications require plans for refined evaluation systems that use student progress as one aspect of teacher evaluations. Although this is relatively straightforward in academic situations with one teacher, there is little clarity in special education or co-teaching situations.

Basing teacher evaluations on student growth is complex, especially for students with significant learning challenges. The teachers quoted above talking about student performance on alternate tests might welcome the opportunity to be evaluated based on the growth of their students from one year to another. Apportioning student growth to members of teaching teams, no matter their field, will be challenging. Linda Darling-Hammond (*Education Week*, 2012) is concerned that teachers will avoid special education students for fear of being judged by their slower gains compared to classmates.

# YES

Kevin S. McGrew and
Jeffrey Evans

# Expectations for Students with Cognitive Disabilities: Is the Cup Half Empty or Half Full? Can the Cup Flow Over?

## Introduction

Over the past 30 years the United States has slowly and steadily clarified the meaning of access to a free and appropriate public education for students with disabilities. . . . Unfortunately, there is still limited consensus among educators regarding appropriate achievement expectations for students with disabilities, particularly those with cognitive disabilities.

A concern about low expectations and the need for high expectations was reflected in the IDEA's 1977 Preamble: "Over 20 years of research has demonstrated that the education of children with disabilities can be made more effective by . . . having high expectations for such children and ensuring their access to the general education curriculum to the maximum extent possible. . . ." IDEA 1997 clarified that all students with disabilities are to have access to instruction focused on the same skills and knowledge as all other students, and that their achievement is to be measured with the same district and statewide assessment programs as used for all students (and, adding an alternate assessment for those students unable to participate in the general assessment).

The *No Child Left Behind (NCLB) Act of 2001* further clarified that schools are to be held accountable for the adequate yearly progress (AYP) of all groups of students. NCLB specifically requires the disaggregation of assessment data for specified subgroups, including students with disabilities. The intended purpose of NCLB is "to ensure that all children have a fair, equal, and significant opportunity to obtain a high-quality education and reach, at a minimum, proficiency on challenging state academic achievement standards and state academic assessments." In other words, the expected educational outcomes for students with disabilities . . . are the same high expectations held for all students.

McGrew, K. S., Evans, J. *Expectations for Students with Cognitive Disabilities: Is the Cup Half Empty or Half Full? Can the Cup Flow Over?* (NCEO Synthesis Report 55, December 2004). Published by University of Minnesota, National Center for Educational Outcomes. http://education.umn.edu/NCEO/OnlinePubs/Synthesis55.html

Although data show that some students with disabilities are reaching the state-determined level of proficiency, many students with disabilities are still far from performing at this level. . . .

Many educators have grown increasingly concerned about the performance of students with cognitive disabilities who are appropriately working toward grade-level achievement standards, but whose current performance is far from a proficient level on grade-level achievement standards as measured by current statewide assessments. Considerable controversy surrounds the issue of what can and should be expected for these students. Some people argue that the vast majority of students with disabilities, when given appropriate access to high-quality curriculum and instruction, can meet or exceed the levels of proficiency currently specified. Many special education advocates believe that subscribing to the same high expectations and accountability for student progress will ultimately lead to improved instruction and learning for all students. Others argue that a student's disability will ultimately prevent the student from attaining grade-level achievement standards, even when provided appropriate instruction and accommodations. This latter group believes that it is unjust to punish schools when these students fail to perform at the proficient level.

The discrepant "expectations" arguments reflect very different perspectives regarding the nature of cognitive disabilities. These two perspectives have existed for many years. To make informed decisions about the best instruction and assessments for students with cognitive disabilities, several questions need to be answered. For instance, how many students with cognitive disabilities can be expected to achieve the same level of proficiency as other students? To what extent can we predict who these students are? Can we discern whether a student's failure to meet proficiency is due to the student's disabling condition or lack of appropriate instruction? Finally, what effects do teacher expectations have on student achievement?

This report was prepared to begin to address these issues. It includes an analysis of nationally representative cognitive and achievement data to illustrate the dangers in making blanket assumptions about appropriate achievement expectations for individuals based on their cognitive ability or diagnostic label. . . .

# Overview

Few would argue that the concept of intelligence (IQ), and tests that measure the construct, has played a long and significant role in education, and special education in particular. The use of practical IQ tests is typically traced to the beginning of the century when Alfred Binet developed a battery of tasks to help identify children with learning difficulties. Binet's goal was to develop a means by which to identify struggling students who would then receive remediation via "mental orthopedics." Clearly, Binet did not believe that his measure of intelligence quantified an innate or "fixed" ability. Binet was an optimist who believed that the ability "glasses" of children with lower ability were half full, and that their vessels could be filled further.

In stark contrast to Binet's optimistic position was that of English psychologist Sir Cyril Burt, [whose] . . . work was based on the then popular view that intelligence was a genetically based fixed entity. Burt's ideas influenced the design of educational systems that segregated children in different educational tracks based on ability. According to Burt, "capacity must obviously limit content. It is impossible for a pint jug to hold more than a pint of milk; and it is equally impossible for a child's educational attainments to rise higher than his educable capacity permits." Clearly Binet and Burt viewed the proverbial half-filled glass differently.

A final view, based on the 1994 feel-good movie *Forrest Gump,* can be considered the "cup overflowing" perspective. Briefly, this movie portrayed the fictitious life history of Forrest Gump, an individual who was classified in the mental retardation range early in school. The exchange between the school principal and Forrest's mother clearly illustrated an educational approach grounded in the Burt philosophy:

*School principal:* "Your boy's . . . different, Miz Gump. His IQ's 75."

*Ms. Gump:* "Well, we're all different, Mr. Hancock. He might be a bit on the slow side. He's not going to a special school to retread tires!"

Ms. Gump's response, and the subsequent string of life achievements of her son Forrest (e.g., star football player in college, world-class ping-pong player, Vietnam war hero, CEO of successful shrimp company) reflects the "cup flowing over" perspective on IQ test scores. That is, Forrest's achievements were beyond his measured IQ (which was below the average sized "jug" according to Burt).

When faced with students whose classroom performances or achievement test scores surpass their measured . . . IQ scores by significant amounts, laypersons and professionals (e.g., educators and psychologists) frequently demonstrate an implicit subscription to a Burt philosophy that a person can achieve only up to his or her level of intelligence when they characterize Gump-like students as "overachievers." Ms. Gump's implicit intelligence conception, which was subsequently manifested in Forrest's accomplishments, would suggest that there is more to school learning than the size of a child's "IQ cup or jug"—other variables contribute to achievement.

Half-full or half-empty? Filled to-the-brim or the cup flowing over? Which intelligence-learning metaphor is correct? Burt versus Binet/Gump? Who should be believed during the current standards-driven educational reform fueled by the mantra that "no child shall be left behind" (NCLB), and that all children should reach grade-level standards. More importantly, which philosophy should guide educational expectations for students whose primary special education classification is tied closely to IQ scores below the normal range (i.e., students with mental retardation or cognitive disabilities)? Should educational expectations for students with cognitive disabilities be grounded in a Burt philosophy (i.e., expect academic performance and achievement no higher than the student's estimated cognitive ability), or should expectations be based on the more optimistic Gump philosophy (i.e., it is possible for students with cognitive disabilities to achieve higher than their IQ test score and at grade level)? . . .

## Diversity within Disability Distributions

Probably no environment elicits individual differences sooner in life than formal education. In classrooms teachers strive to arrange conditions to elicit optimal performance among a diverse class of unique learners. However, due to the only true "law" in psychology (the law of individual differences), optimal learning conditions and techniques are not universal across learners.

This holds true for all learners—those with and without disabilities. It is important that students with disabilities not be saddled with group-based stereotyped low academic expectations. Just as the diversity of learning rates for students without disabilities is acknowledged, so it should be for students with disabilities. . . .

The federally funded *Special Education Elementary Longitudinal Study* (SEELS), the first ever nationally representative longitudinal investigation of elementary students with disabilities (ages 6 to 12), recently provided empirical support for the diversity of achievement levels of students with disabilities. According to the SEELS project director . . . the data indicate that "you can find kids with disabilities who are scoring right near the top—above the 80th percentile—and you'll find some in the middle . . . and then a lot more kids in the lowest quartile. So it's heavily weighted toward the low end but there's quite a bit of diversity." Although students with disabilities, as a group, tend to achieve in the lower half of the distribution of achievement, "individuals with disabilities can be found across the full range of academic performance." . . .

## IQ and Disability: The Misunderstood Common Denominator

Despite their diversity of characteristics, the majority (58%) of students receiving special education services under IDEA share a common experience—most have been classified as having a learning disability or cognitive impairment (mental retardation) with the aid of an intelligence test. Despite many disputes over competing theoretical conceptualizations of intelligence and the utility of intelligence test scores, even the most ardent critics recognize that IQ tests "predict certain forms of achievement—especially school achievement—rather effectively."

Despite a defensible rationale for their early development and continued deployment in the schools, many people have developed . . . the inaccurate belief, often reinforced by court decisions, that measured intelligence is a genetically determined, largely fixed, global, and enduring trait that explains most of a student's success (or failure) in school learning. Such a Sir Cyril Burt conceptualization of intelligence can doom a student to low expectations if his or her IQ score is significantly below the norm. This fixed entity view of intelligence, summarized in the belief in the predictive power of the single global IQ score, represents the mental jug or cup being "half-empty" or "filled-to-the-brim" philosophy. According to this view, to expect more academic achievement than a person's estimated or measured IQ score is simply not possible.

A recent *Education Week* (2004) national survey (*Count me in: Special Education in an Era of Standards*) of 800 special and general education teachers suggests that most educators implicitly subscribe to the Burt IQ-potential philosophy. Eighty-four percent of surveyed teachers did not believe that students in special education should be expected to meet the same set of academic standards as students without disabilities. In addition, approximately 80% of the teachers felt that students with disabilities should not be included in the same state tests as students in general education, especially if the results are used for accountability purposes.

The surprising extent to which educators appear to hold alternative (and typically lower) standards and expectations for students with disabilities, although appropriate for many of these students, is troubling given the empirical reality of the predictive power of IQ test scores—scores that are often at the root of lowered expectations. Sir Cyril Burt's IQ-fixed potential legacy appears to be alive and well in America's schools (albeit not typically adopted maliciously or explicitly articulated).

Fortunately, decades of research on intelligence tests have repeatedly converged on a near unanimous consensus on the predictive accuracy of IQ test scores[;] it is time to "leave the Burt IQ-potential philosophy behind."

## Reality of the IQ–Achievement Relationship: Statistics Made Simple

In an era of standards-driven educational reform, educators and policymakers must recognize the truth about IQ test scores and the resulting disability categories that are based on a continuum of IQ test scores. . . . The reality is simple. Given the best available theoretically and psychometrically sound, nationally standardized, individually administered intelligence test batteries, three statements hold true. Each of these can be explained in depth. . . . For greater conciseness here, the statements that hold true are:

- IQ test scores, under optimal test conditions, account for 40% to 50% of current expected achievement.
- Thus, 50% to 60% of student achievement is related to variables "beyond intelligence."
- For any given IQ test score, half of the students will obtain achievement scores at or below their IQ score. Conversely, and frequently not recognized, is that for any given IQ test score, half of the students will obtain achievement scores at or *above* their IQ score.

. . . Using the general IQ and Total Achievement (average across reading, math, and written language) scores for "real" norm subjects from the standardization of the *Woodcock-Johnson Battery Third Edition* (WJ III, . . . there is a strong linear relation between IQ and achievement, as evidenced by a strong correlation of .75. . . .

[However,] . . . even IQ tests that demonstrate some of the strongest correlations with achievement . . . cannot be used to provide perfect estimates of predicted achievement for *individual* students. . . . [For] subjects with IQs from 70–80, expected achievement scores range from a low of approximately 40 to a high of approximately 110. . . . [Half] of the individuals with IQs between 70–80 achieve at or below IQ-predicted achievement, and the other half . . . score at or *above* IQ-predicted achievement.

[These] data . . . suggest that the proper metaphor for the IQ-achievement prediction relationship is that the "cup can flow over." The carte blanche assumption that all students with disabilities should have an alternative set of educational standards and an assessment system is inconsistent with empirical data. . . .

The current reality is that despite being one of the flagship developments in all of psychology, intelligence tests are fallible predictors of academic achievement. IQ test scores (and associated IQ-based disability category labels) are adequate, but not nearly sufficient metrics, by which to make reasonably precise predictions about any particular *individual* student's future expected achievement progress. It simply cannot be done beyond a reasonable doubt.

The fallibility of IQ tests, coupled with the enduring presence of the ghost of Sir Cyril Burt's deterministic IQ-achievement educational philosophy, in the context of today's high-stakes educational accountability environment, raises the specter of many children with disabilities being denied the right to appropriate and demanding expectations. Stereotyping students with disabilities (often on the basis of disability label or test scores) as a group that should be excluded from general education standards and assessments is not supported by the best evidence from current science in the field of psychological and educational measurement. The potential soft bigotry of setting a priori IQ or disability label–based low academic expectations (for students with disabilities) needs to be recognized, understood, and minimized, if all children are not to be left behind.

# Expectancy Effects: A Brief History and Literature Review

Since the 1970s, the notions of the "self-fulfilling prophecy" (SFP), the "Pygmalion Effect," . . . and more recently, "expectancy effects" (EE) have become commonplace in the educational psychology literature. In general, these terms refer to similar phenomena. . . .

Merton is recognized as the first to coin the term "self-fulfilling prophecy" which has now evolved into the more general phenomena of "expectancy effects." According to Merton, SFP occurs when an inaccurate definition of a situation elicits new behaviors which, in turn, make the originally inaccurate conception a reality. SFP is a compelling theory, largely because of its potential implications and elegant simplicity.

> The concept is simple enough: If we prophesy (expect) that something will happen, we behave (usually unconsciously) in a manner that will make it happen. We will, in other words, do what we can to realize our prophecy.

In most EE research, it is usually a person in a position of authority (e.g., an employer, medical professional, parent, teacher, . . .) who holds expectations about an individual (or group) under their supervision. According to the EE research, expectations expressed by an authority figure via verbal and non-verbal communication often influence the self-image and the behavior of the supervised person in such a way that the expectations held come to pass.

## Origins of Expectancy Effects

. . . SFP is also often referred to as the "Pygmalion Effect" which was drawn from the title of the original book (Rosenthal & Jacobson, *Pygmalion in the Classroom*) that reported the phenomenon. SFP first appeared in early psychological research studies where it was demonstrated that experimenters could unwittingly influence the behavior of animal and human subjects during an experiment. In 1968, Rosenthal and Jacobson substituted teachers for experimenters in order to investigate the effects of teachers' expectancies on the intelligence test scores of their pupils. The Rosenthal and Jacobson study was designed to measure "whether those children for whom the teachers held especially favorable expectations would show greater intellectual growth than the remaining or control-group children" when evaluated . . . months later. Cotton provided a succinct summary of the original Pygmalion study:

> The Rosenthal/Jacobson study concluded that students' intellectual development is largely a response to what teachers expect and how those expectations are communicated. The original Pygmalion study involved giving teachers false information about the learning potential of certain students in grades one through six in a San Francisco elementary school. Teachers were told that these students had been tested and found to be on the brink of a period of rapid intellectual growth; in reality, the students had been selected at random. At the end of the experimental period, some of the targeted students—and particularly those in grades one and two—exhibited performance on IQ tests which was superior to the scores of other students of similar ability and superior to what would have been expected of the target students with no intervention.

The Rosenthal and Jacobson report suggested that teacher expectations could increase or decrease . . . IQ . . . test scores. Understandably, this report created a media sensation. The possibility that teachers could effect change (either positive or negative) in a student's IQ scores held considerable popular interest and appeal. . . .

# Expectancy Effects and Intelligence

It would be an understatement to describe the EE research focused on the relations between teacher's expectations and intelligence as contentious. Post hoc re-analysis of the . . . Rosenthal and Jacobson investigation raised many questions about the study's methodology. Numerous attempts to replicate the Pygmalion effect . . . have proven unsuccessful. . . . In many of the subsequent follow-up studies the control groups often gained more IQ points than the experimental groups. . . .

Many . . . researchers have continued to examine the teacher–student expectancy effect. A clear connection between [EE] and IQ has not been established. However, *expectancy effects and academic achievement do appear to correlate positively.*

# Expectancy Effects: How Large?

A frequently quoted estimate of the magnitude of Expectancy Effects (EE) in education is that 5% to 10% of student achievement performance might be ascribed to the influence of differential teacher expectations. More recently, average expectancy effect sizes from 0.1 to 0.3 have been reported. On first inspection, effect sizes of 0.1 to 0.3 appear to be of little practical import. This is wrong. According to Jussim et al., when discussing students who are the "targets" of EE, "a naturally occurring effect of 'only' .2 means, that on average, of all targets of high expectations, 10% show substantial improvement; and of all targets of low expectations, 10% show substantial decreases in performance." . . .

To reassure the reader of the importance of what appear to be significant, yet small correlations or effect sizes, one only needs to be reminded that many significant public and social policy decisions have been made on the strength of relations between variables that are of the same magnitude or lower than those reported for EE. . . . [A] special American Psychological Association . . . *Psychological Assessment Work Group* . . . provided the following examples:

- The reduction of the risk of dying from a heart attack by taking aspirin is based on $r = 0.02$
- The impact of chemotherapy on breast cancer survival; $r = .03$
- The value of antihistamines for reducing sneezes and a runny nose; $r = .11$
- The impact of Viagra on improved sexual functioning; $r = .38$

Furthermore, much like the long-term insidious effect of long-term exposure to subclinical levels of lead, asbestos, secondhand smoke, and other toxins, some research studies have suggested that even small EE can result in larger cumulative effects over time. Small EE could exert a substantial influence on student achievement, particularly for more vulnerable and "at risk" students.

# Expectancy Effects and Student Characteristics

In the field of special education, EE was first investigated . . . with regard to the potential negative consequences of being labeled "mentally retarded." In general, this "stigma" research suggested that being labeled mentally retarded often led to changes in the behavior of adults who encouraged "learned helplessness." These studies reported that the attribution for success or failure for a mentally retarded person was more frequently assigned to the person's inherent low ability, while failure attribution for others was more frequently assigned to the person's effort.

Researchers have found that, in general, EE in classrooms are often related to a number of different student characteristics. "Teachers overestimate the achievement of high achievers, underestimate that of low achievers, and predict least accurately the responses of low achievers." Although low-achieving students have been found to receive more learning support, they also are communicated lower expectations via less pressure to achieve than high-achieving students. Additional student characteristics associated with teacher expectations include race, ethnicity, SES, physical appearance or attractiveness, . . . use of standard English . . . , prior negative comments or evaluations about a student by other teachers, readiness/maturity, and grouping/tracking effects. Similar to the early MR-stigma research, some teachers have been found to associate success to inherent ability in the case of high-achieving students and luck or chance for perceived low achievers. . . .

# Expectancy Effects: Educator Behaviors

Although the claim that teacher expectancies can raise student intelligence has been effectively rebuked, most . . . critics have expressed the belief, supported by research, that expectancy effects do influence teacher-to-student performance and behavior. . . .

Expectancies can be expressed both verbally and non-verbally. Although most teachers report that they can fully control their behavioral affect and deceive students whenever necessary, at times the two primary modes of communication can send mixed signals. . . .

Even brief exposure to a teacher's face or body movements (e.g., differences in voice inflection) can provide a student with enough information to communicate expectancies. Teacher behaviors associated with the communication of low achievement expectancies to low achievement students have included:

- The provision of fewer opportunities to learn new material.
- Less "wait" time provided to answer questions.
- Providing answers or calling on someone else.
- Inappropriate feedback (more frequent and severe criticism for failure; insincere praise), limited reinforcement (e.g., giving reinforcement that is not contingent on performance), or rewarding more incorrect answers or inappropriate behavior.

- Providing less attention and more interaction in private settings.
- Providing differential treatment in grading (less frequently giving "the benefit of the doubt") and personal interactions (e.g., teachers less friendly or responsive; making less eye contact; giving fewer smiles).
- Providing briefer and less informative feedback.
- Providing less stimulating, and lower-level cognitive questions.
- Providing less effective (but time-consuming) instructional methods.

# Expectancy Effects: Why Do They Occur?

Although the original research on [EE] was based primarily on studies where educators were provided false information regarding student potential, "most researchers have concluded that teacher expectations are not generally formed on the basis of 'false conceptions.'" Rather, they are based on the best information available about the students. Furthermore, even if the initial expectations a teacher forms for a student are realistic and appropriate, student learning and self-concept development can be limited as a result of *sustained expectation effects.* The adverse impact of sustained expectations can occur when teachers continue to engage in behaviors that result in the maintenance of previously formed low expectations (e.g., by giving low-expectation students only drill work). . . .

## Attribution Theory

Certain beliefs about intelligence and learning may lead to lowered expectations for low-achieving students and students with cognitive disabilities . . . [Contemporary] social cognitive psychology research has suggested that *attribution theory* is a "useful framework for exploring teachers' response to children's academic outcomes, such as success or failure, in the general education classroom."

Briefly, attribution theory research has demonstrated that individuals (e.g., teachers) tend to attribute success or failure for an individual (e.g., students) to one of two different human characteristics—*ability* or *effort.* Graham and Weiner's studies found that the initial response of many classroom teachers to a negative student outcome is either anger or pity. Furthermore, the elicitation of anger or pity was differentially linked to the degree to which teachers perceived the student as responsible for his or her failure. Typically, when faced with student failure, a teacher pity response was elicited for students of low abilities while anger was the more frequent response to high-ability students (due to a perceived lack of effort or motivation). Furthermore, these researchers found that the anticipation of future failure for students was directly related to the perceived stability of the cause of the student failure. "Failure due to causes that are viewed as stable, such as low ability, will result in a high expectation that failure will recur, whereas failure due to unstable causes, such as effort or task difficulty, will result in a lower expectation of repeated failure. . . ."

Clark found . . . [that when] students use attribution information to make inferences about their own ability and effort, these inferences are manifest in the students' self-esteem, expectations for their own future successes and failures, and their classroom performance." . . .

# Group Stereotyping

Expectancy effects may also reflect the differential treatment of an individual based on group membership stereotypes. Group-based self-fulfilling prophecies differ from individual-based self-fulfilling prophecies and are relevant to the educational practices of grouping, tracking, and institutionalized segregated instruction (e.g., separate special education classrooms). . . .

Researchers have reported the communication of differential expectations as a function of placement in different ability or tracked groups in classrooms. According to Cotton's research synthesis, "students in low groups and tracks have been found to get less exciting instruction, less emphasis upon meaning and conceptualization, and more rote drill and practice activities than those in high-reading groups and tracks." . . . In general, . . . tracking or ability grouping "may lead to the type of rigid teacher expectations that are most likely to evoke self-fulfilling prophecies and perceptual biases. Teachers often prepare more for and are more supportive toward students in high-ability groups."

Stereotype-based low expectations for "different" students . . . can beset anyone who belongs to a group with a specific reputation. When the stereotype or reputation is pejorative, . . . the effects can be significantly disruptive to individual development. Stereotypes have two salient characteristics: (1) they polarize perceptions and sharpen differences, and (2) they are rigidly held, readily fixated and resistant to change. Thus, the development of stereotypically based differential student academic expectations (based on group membership or label) can serve to fixate and exaggerate existing differences. . . .

Probably one of the more potentially insidious forms of stereotype-based expectation formation is that which results from the attachment of diagnostic labels (e.g., learning disabled, mentally retarded, emotionally disturbed, . . .) to students. Although all forms of social stereotypes (e.g., gender, social class, race, ethnicity, . . .) can produce harmful effects, diagnostic educational or medical disability labels almost always have the authoritative stamp of approval by a credible expert (e.g., psychologist, doctor). This major source of lowered teacher expectations has been repeatedly demonstrated in the special education research literature. Based on the previously summarized *Education Week* national survey of teachers, lowered expectations for all students with disabilities continue to be a latent force in many of America's classrooms, and may be exacerbated by the current wave of high-stakes educational accountability.

## Beware of Silent, Shifting Standards

Research during the past decade has revealed that group-based stereotypes can be conceptualized as functioning as "standards against which individual members of stereotype groups are judged." Briefly, *stereotyping effects* occur when individual group members are evaluated in a direction consistent with group-based expectations or stereotypes. "For example, a man is judged a better leader than a woman; a physician is judged more intelligent than a hairdresser . . . these types of effects certainly indicate that stereotypes have been used to judge individuals and that the outcome is *assimilation*." The self-fulfilling prophesies previously described are examples of the commonly recognized assimilative stereotype effect.

Research on the "shifting standards model" suggests that assimilative effects alone fail to capture the complexity and extent to which stereotype-based expectations operate in group settings: "Less well recognized is the fact that stereotyping can also be manifested in other ways, most notably in counter-stereotypical or contrast effects."

*Within-category* standards are typically used when a person evaluates or judges an individual . . . of a stereotyped group . . . on stereotyped dimensions. For example, given the stereotype that students with mental retardation are "slower learners" than students of normal intelligence, one is likely to judge the learning capability of a particular student with mental retardation relative to (lower) standards for students with mental retardation and, the learning ability of a particular non-retarded student relative to (higher) standards of competence for non-retarded students. . . . "Good" does not mean the same thing for the student with mental retardation and the student of normal intelligence. . . .

Probably the most pernicious masked effect of the shifting standards model is that "evidentiary standards are lower for members of the group stereotyped as deficient on an attribute." When an individual . . . is a member of a group that is stereotyped as deficient on a trait or attribute (i.e., intelligence), evidentiary standards or expectations are often shifted in the direction of leniency, less challenge, and minimal competencies. [This] shift, . . . in turn, often produces behavior in the evaluator in the opposite direction of the stereotype. This shifting of standards "activates low (patronizing) minimizing standards that are more readily surpassed, producing a subjective sense of positivity—a 'wow' effect. That this positivity is not borne out in outcomes that matter for the target (getting a job or the key fielding position) suggests that the favorable treatment is more apparent and ephemeral than real." The essence of this phenomena is captured in the words of Alexa Pochowski, the assistant commissioner for learning services in the Kansas education department, . . . quoted in *Education Week* as saying:

> For too long, we held these students to lower standards . . . I hate to say
> it: I think we almost felt sorry for them."

. . . In summary, for students with cognitive disabilities, expectancy effects can be viewed as a form of **standards-based stereotyping.** This stereotyping can either produce direct . . . or indirect "hidden" stereotyping effects, both of which can exert negative influences on academic performance. The silent, subjective shifting (towards lower) evidentiary academic standards (for students with disabilities) represents a subtle, yet potentially potent force operating against the goal of "leaving no child behind."

# Education Expectations: Caveats and Concerns

Teachers, like all humans, develop personal beliefs, opinions, and stereotypes. During most teacher preparation programs, educators are taught to become aware of potential expectancy effects and how to control their overt day-to-day teaching behavior to be more equitable, and to refrain from dispensing differential praise and criticism.

Given the popularity of the expectancy effects and self-fulfilling prophesies in the educational and psychological research and popular press, one could be led to believe that these negative influences are pandemic in school classrooms. This is not the case. Although some researchers have concluded that differential treatment of students is widespread, most researchers have concluded that the majority of educators (particularly experienced teachers and teachers who are very familiar with their students) form expectations based on the initial available information and "tweak" or adjust their expectations and instruction based on changes in student performance.

It is inappropriate to infer that the majority of educators are biased simply because they may hold differential expectations for some students. Often, differential treatment of students represents the appropriate implementation of individualized adaptive instruction responsive to the individual differences in a classroom. . . .

It is important to note that educators who may hold inappropriately low expectations for some students "are rarely acting out of malice; indeed, they are often not even aware that their low expectations have developed based on specious reasoning."

Nevertheless, the literature raises numerous issues that are directly relevant to today's educational context for students with disabilities in which both IDEA and NCLB are requiring improved performance. Particularly for those students with cognitive disabilities, the information on expectancy effects should cause us much concern. Is it possible that expectancy effects have been holding students back in the past? Are we under the influence of silently shifting standards—especially for students with cognitive disabilities? These and other questions are ones that states, districts, schools, administrators, and teachers need to ask themselves and others—as our nation strives to improve the performance of all of its students, including . . . those with cognitive disabilities.

James M. Kauffman  **NO**

# Education Deform: Bright People Sometimes Say Stupid Things about Education

## Test Bashing Is Part of the "Progressive" Rhetoric That Thwarts Progress

Standardized testing has become the Great Satan of education in the minds of some, a "monster" that must be put out of schools. For example, Alfie Kohn condemns standardized testing—not just certain tests or the misuse of tests, but standardized tests as tools. . . . His suggestions for fighting standardized tests include not only civil disobedience by educators but printing bumper stickers with slogans such as "Standardized Testing Is Dumbing Down Our Schools." Like most slogans in education, this one, too, in my opinion, is vapid. Standardized testing can, indeed, be stupid or be used stupidly, but I doubt very seriously that it is the ogre responsible for dumbing down our schools. And rejecting standardized tests can only deprive parents, teachers, school officials, and governing bodies of an important tool in monitoring students' performance. . . .

Now it is undoubtedly true that some standardized tests are poorly made or misused, as are many teacher-made tests and other forms of "alternative assessment" such as portfolios. In fact, *any* form of assessment of which I'm aware can be (and has been) crudely made and badly used. So, why the seething hostility toward "standardized" testing? The answer is not simple, but I think much of the outrage over standardized tests is prompted by fears of comparisons of various individuals and groups who take the tests. Furthermore, educational theory has become, to some, a matter of religious conviction in which evidence doesn't matter. Too many educators—and, as well, too many people who are not educators—embrace "progressive" theory that relies on pet phrases and terminology for its defense of educational "quality" that tests are said not to be able to measure. These "reformers," who actually hold educational theories originated nearly a century ago, call for "real learning" that standardized tests are assumed not to be able to assess. . . .

Kohn and others who take a position against standardized tests also often raise the specter of uniformity across schools and states, which they

Kauffman, James M. From *Education Deform: Bright People Sometimes Say Stupid Things About Education* (Scarecrow Press, 2002), pp.184–192, 247–252, 254–260. Copyright © 2002 by Rowman & Littlefield Education. Reprinted by permission.

see as being overly rigid. Even such politically conservative opinion writers as George F. Will suggest that America probably should not have a standard examination for high school graduation or a national curriculum. Perhaps it is inevitable that people of nearly all political persuasions will figure out some day that math and reading and much of what we need to know about science and geography and the United States government is not really different in different places. People might figure out that uniformity of expectations and curricula and testing might actually be beneficial in a society in which children move often to different localities or states. But it may take decades for people to arrive at these conclusions.

All the more reason, in my opinion, that standardized testing has a valuable role to play in measuring students' progress. . . . [One] argument against standardized testing is that comparisons of schools and states—perhaps of individuals as well—are insidious. No one is to be "left behind." . . . [Any] measure of progress—but most obviously a standardized measure—produces a distribution that by nature finds some to have performed better than others; for any measure that is not simply "yes/no" or "pass/fail" or in some other way a truncated range, there is a bottom fourth (first quartile) as well as a top fourth (or any other percentage of the sample one wishes to examine). So alternative assessment procedures that obscure if not obviate comparisons seem, to some, a godsend. Such alternative measures can help maintain the fiction that all students are excellent or give the misimpression that nobody is actually behind. The "progressive" idea seems to be that an "authentic" assessment will show that everyone and everything is cool—nobody can fail.

For some purposes there is no good substitute for the test that is standardized and can be failed—normed on a large sample of test takers by which we want to judge the achievement of individuals and groups. It is easier to shoot the messenger that brings unwelcome tidings than to confront the differences among individuals and groups that tests may reveal. . . . And it is easy to overlook the advantages of standardized tests while describing the tests themselves as monsters to be driven from our schools.

Some scholars have pointed out that the current popularity of standardized testing is really based on public concern about standards or accountability. The standards of performance that a state or school adopts are nearly always linked to a standardized test, and for this reason some writers refer to "test-linked standards." We do, I think, want to know how a student's performance compares to others' and to be able to compare average student performances across schools and states. It is only through such comparisons that we can address some problems, including the problem of how well we're doing and the problem of equity. Nevertheless, some people seem to be in favor of accountability—but without knowing how students are doing on any standardized test. To them, standardized tests seem to be a way of holding people responsible for teaching a standard curriculum, which they find anathema.

Mary Anne Raywid has voiced a familiar complaint: "One problem with the vast majority of tests, of course, is that they are curriculum-based." Well, it seems to me that we do want curriculum and testing to be aligned. That is, we want to teach what students are going to be tested on and to test what we teach.

In fact, curriculum-based assessment is what some of us are after. It makes no sense to test students on things they haven't been taught, and it makes good sense to base assessment on the curriculum. The curriculum could determine what is tested; the tests could determine what is taught. But, either way, it only makes sense for the two to be in sync. In fact, one is not likely to be developed without the other: Testing and curriculum *should* influence each other. To me, it makes little difference which comes first, as long as what is taught is really important stuff for students to learn. I suppose the question actually becomes what we think is important for students to know. Another way of putting it is to ask whether we think there is a common core of knowledge that most students should learn. I think there is this common content that most students should be expected to master, and I see no reason not to check up on how well we're doing it—to test it with a standardized instrument.

Others, particularly E. D. Hirsch, Jr., have described eloquently how having a core body of knowledge or core curriculum increases equity among groups of students differing in ethnicity or social privilege—or, at least, opportunities for achieving such equity. Standardized tests were invented, at least in part, to be fairer to students without social privileges—to focus on a student's performance rather than his or her genetic or social heritage that brought privilege in spite of what a student could do. Standardized tests *can* be used to increase equity if they measure important knowledge and if all schools and individuals are provided the resources needed to allow them to attain a reasonable standard. Standardized tests *can* be used to improve the clarity of schools' objectives and focus on instruction. Standardized tests *can* be used to allocate resources more efficiently, and they *can* be used as a common metric—a common, readily understood language of measurement—for communicating educational outcomes.

Please notice that I have *not* suggested that *all* students should learn exactly the same thing or be taught exactly the same way. I suggested that *most* students would benefit from a standard, core curriculum. . . . Some students are not going to be successful in the regular, general curriculum that may be right for the majority of students. I think it's essential that we provide alternatives for those students who cannot reasonably be expected to learn the core curriculum and be tested on it. . . . But, of course, here's the problem: Who should decide, and on what basis, that an alternative to the core curriculum is a better choice for a given student? Here are some givens, in my opinion: First, the decision should not be based on the student's ethnicity, gender, or social privilege. Second, the decision should be based on the student's estimated ability to learn the core curriculum. Third, there are no perfect decision makers. Any decision making scheme we can devise will produce some false positives (students thought to be able to learn the core curriculum but who cannot) and false negatives (students who are thought to be unable to learn the core curriculum but who can). The goals should be to make as few errors of judgment as possible in either direction and to correct errors as soon as they can be detected by changing the student's curriculum. But don't miss this given: Assuming that any core curriculum should be studied and mastered by *all* students simply guarantees a very large number of false positives. For a substantial number of kids and a significant percentage of the student population, it's not in the cards. The majority of the students I'm referring to have disabilities of one kind or another, although some of those with disabilities can and should learn the standard—general, core—curriculum.

Standardized tests, like every other human invention and some natural phenomena, will be abused. That is a given. We are well advised to recognize abuses without proscribing the use of the instruments that are abused, to use instruments responsibly. Obscuring or hiding differences on good standardized measures merely locks in place the social inequities that anti-testing forces say they oppose. We cannot address inequities that we will not admit are real and important. . . . [I] think we have yet to invent a better or more reliable way than standardized testing of finding out fairly what someone knows. The fact that some test questions are bad and that some people use scores unwisely should not be used as an excuse for bashing the very notion of standardized testing.

Every educational policy has a downside as far as I know, standardized testing and test-linked standards included. It is possible to narrow a curriculum unreasonably in efforts to prepare students for tests, and this is true for standardized tests or any other kind of assessment. It is possible to define good teaching simply as that which maximizes test performance—standardized tests or any other type of assessment. It is possible to use standardized test performance to devalue those who do not score well on them, but the same is true for any type of assessment—kids can be devalued because their performance is judged to be inferior, not up to expectations, not acceptable. And standardized tests or any other type of assessment can preclude certain opportunities for students who fail to meet expectations. Any kind of assessment of performance—standardized test or any alternative—can create anxiety in the person being assessed. Alternatives to standardized tests, such as "portfolio assessment" in which a student's work is judged in some way, have their downsides, too. They are cumbersome, extremely time-consuming, and present problems of reliability, validity, and comparisons across individuals and groups.

If our schools are being "dumbed down," I doubt that it's because of standardized tests. Much more likely, I think, is that the dumbing down is a result of fumbled thinking about issues in education, including mindless rhetoric that misleads people's thinking about the tools we use to assess educational progress. And make no mistake about this, either: *Standardized testing cannot take the place of the type of frequent teacher monitoring or assessment that is an essential part of good teaching.* Imagining that standardized testing provides sufficient early warning for failing students is similar to imagining that reporting tornado damage provides sufficient early warning of severe weather. Standardized tests can assess instructional success or failure long after the fact, and for that they're important, but they can't be relied upon to guide the instruction of individuals. . . .

Some who write about education policy see the advantages of good standardized testing but suggest "criterion-referenced" tests that set "benchmarks" of performance. Sometimes, these individuals even suggest that an advantage of such criterion-referencing is that the test does not rely on norms, that students' performance is simply compared to the criterion, not to other students' performance. This is quite a misleading interpretation of "criterion" or "benchmark." A reasonable person would, I think, have to ask something like this: How'd we come up with this criterion or benchmark?

A criterion or benchmark can be pulled out of the air or be based simply on someone's opinion of what a student should know at a particular age. But "pull-them-out-of-the-air" criteria are ultimately seen as arrogant and unworkable. Eventually, people come to their senses and inquire about what most students know at a given age. The criterion is then set based on a comparison to what most students can do. Otherwise, it is unreasonably high or unreasonably low.

People I think should know better than to refer to criterion-referenced tests as not comparative or non-normative. They're right in only a very restricted way—a student is judged to perform acceptably or not based only on comparison to the criterion or benchmark of performance. However, a reasonable person has to ask where the criterion comes from, and this inevitably takes us back to a normative sample or normative comparison. Witness the difficulties various states or school districts have in deciding on a "cut point" or benchmark on a standards of learning test. If the criterion is something that too few students can reach, then it's abandoned as unreasonable (and for good reason). If the criterion is something just about every student reaches without difficulty, then it's abandoned as too low (and with good reason). A criterion-referenced test does force the issue of manufacturing failure (just how much is enough, desirable, or too much?). But here's something I think you can go to the bank on: If a criterion is set that results in what is deemed a reasonable rate of failure and a few years down the road we find that nearly every child is passing it, we will see efforts to raise the bar because the benchmark is now judged too low.

Criterion-referencing might be a good idea. That is, it might be a good idea to set a standard that we think merits promotion to the next grade or graduation or the need for remediation. But nobody should be fooled into thinking that the criterion isn't based on some comparison to a normative group. And nobody should be fooled into thinking that every last student will reach whatever criterion is set. Some students will fail to reach the benchmark unless it is set at zero, and some will find reaching the benchmark ridiculously easy. That's one of the reasons we need special education. . . .

# Failure of Some Students with Disabilities to Reach a Standard Is Predictable

Why is the failure of some exceptional students to profit from standard educational programs utterly predictable? The answer seems obvious to me. It is because they differ significantly from the modal or typical student in instructionally relevant ways. Standard programs are designed for modal (most frequently occurring) students, not those at the extremes of a distribution. These standard educational programs simply cannot, and can't be expected to, accommodate extreme differences in instructionally relevant characteristics, like abilities to read, perceive, organize, store, retrieve, and apply information to the solution of particular problems. Some students with disabilities are going to fail to meet standard educational goals regardless of the instructional strategies a teacher uses.

Some students with disabilities can meet state testing standards, but not with the standard instructional program or in the standard amount of time or by the typical chronological age. And some students who are gifted will be bored out of their minds by having to repeat and by being expected to *appear* to learn things they learned long ago.

Pixie Holbrook described the futility and cruelty of requiring all students with disabilities to take state-mandated examinations that are appropriate for the majority of students. She describes the agony for herself and one of her pupils, Sarah, a fourth-grader with a learning disability. Sarah is a good and diligent student, but because of her learning disability she hasn't the skills required for the test.

> She knows she doesn't know. And she knows that I know she doesn't know. This is so very humiliating.
>     Her eyes are wet now, but she's silent and stoic. I check in, and she re-assures me she's fine. She appears to be on the verge of weeping, but she will not be deterred. I cannot help her in any way; I can only sit nearby and return a false smile. I can offer a break, nothing more. Later, I calculated the reading level of this selection. Sarah reads like a second-grader, and the poem is at the high end of the fifth-grade scale. Her eyes are not just scanning the paragraphs. I know she has stopped reading and is just glancing and gazing. It's meaningless, and it hurts. Yet she attempts to answer every question.
>     It is now 2 ½ hours, and my anger is growing. This is immoral and has become intolerable. And it's only the first day.

. . . Teachers and school administrators have, it seems to me, a moral obligation to recognize the fact that many special education students should not be required to take state competency exams.

Moreover, teachers have to be allowed, even encouraged, to recognize the limits of their instructional competence. Teachers should decline to teach students for whom their training is inadequate and decline to teach a curriculum that isn't right for their students. . . .

. . . [For] the life of me I can't figure out how someone . . . can . . . argue that teachers in elementary and secondary schools should just try to teach all students, regardless of students' characteristics. And, so some argue, if a teacher has a student that he or she can't seem to teach and manage or one who seriously interferes with teaching the rest of the class, then that teacher should just suck it up and learn to deal with it, never work to get the student taught in a special class or school. Maybe that teacher could ask for help, so the full-inclusion or merge-general-and-special-education argument goes, but not give up responsibility for the student and turn education of that student over to someone else.

I try to make this add up with any other profession's attitudes toward its clients, and I can't. What would we think of a dentist who said, "Well, no, I don't know what to do here, but I'm not going to refer you to someone else, because I am responsible for treating *all* of my patients? So I'll ask another dentist what to do and then do my best to follow the advice I get." Would we not want to wring the neck, if not sue, a mechanic or plumber or builder or lawyer who was in over his or her head—didn't have the skills demanded of the case and knew it—yet wouldn't give the job over to someone with the necessary skills?

Knowing the limits of one's knowledge and skill and being given the responsibility for refusing clients whose problems don't match one's training and skills are rather basic professional and moral responsibilities, it seems to me. Those who do not want teachers to decline to teach a child for whom they are not prepared believe one of two erroneous things, I think: (a) teachers shouldn't be professionals in any true sense or (b) students don't actually differ much in what's required to teach them. Teaching is teaching, they seem to believe, and if you can teach one student you can teach any student. I find that kind of denial maddening.

## Students Who Fail at Certain Things Aren't Total Failures

Some people fail at few things, others at many. We have a tendency to write people off as failures if they fail at anything we think is important, regardless of the values or abilities of the person whose performance we judge to be failing. Much as we are too quick to judge someone who makes a vapid statement a stupid person, we overgeneralize. Surely, there are people whom failure seems to dog, and I believe there are people who could be described as *being* failures or as having failed generally at life. But those cases are, I think, rare. And, although some people may act like test scores are everything, we know that they're not—and we need to act like they're not.

Some people fail at something because of a disability, and their disability is then used against them in an unfair manner. True, we can't eliminate failure, and we can't and shouldn't "protect" people from confronting their own and other people's failures. But keeping failure at a particular thing or things in perspective is also important. Dan Hallahan and I, as well as many of our colleagues in special education, have noted that although people with disabilities can't do certain things (and, thus, could be said to fail in some respect) it is essential that we focus on what they *can* do, which for most people with disabilities is most of the things we consider normal or expected.

Failure at something doesn't make a person bad, nor does success make them a good person. Sometimes I think people misunderstand this and suppose that those who are gifted are better people and those who are disabled are not as good as others. Achievement or success at something doesn't make someone a better person, but it does enhance a person's opportunities. The more you know and are able to do, the more opportunities you have to learn and succeed. We do want to give students the greatest opportunity we can, and that means teaching them things that will open up new opportunities. I tried to make this clear in a previously published essay.

> Clearly, we do not want a human's worth to be measured simply by what he or she can do. That criterion would, for example, result in very little worth being attached to infants and young children. Yet, what someone can do is not a trivial matter. A just and humane society does not value people *for* what they can do, but it does unequivocally value peoples' ability to do certain things. If we do not value what people can do, then we have no reason to teach anyone anything. We value what people can do because of what accomplishment does for them, the additional opportunities it brings them—not because it makes them better people but because it makes them people who are better off.

Certainly, assuming that the test score is all that matters is perverse. It's the kind of perversion and stupidity we would be much better off without. We want kids to be happy and go to school excited about learning. Those objectives aren't incompatible with test scores unless we act as if, and teach kids that, test scores are all that matter. Still, avoiding test scores is just a way of evading reality.

One more thing here: It's important to note that failure once doesn't mean failure always. Most people can and do learn lots of things. Sometimes they have to try again, sometimes many times, before they learn a particular thing. Sometimes things just start to "click," and away they go. Sometimes people just seem to hit a "wall" and don't progress beyond it. Anyone who's practiced a musical instrument or sport knows the phenomenon most people call a learning "plateau," a point at which progress seems to stop. But persistence usually pays off, in that progress resumes with repeated practice—sometimes people experience a "breakthrough" in their progress, but not unless they're persistent. Yes, people differ in aptitudes for particular things and in skill in picking them up, but we have to be really careful not to assume that because a person is progressing only slowly (or rapidly) they'll always continue at that rate. . . .

✦

# Exceptional Students Need Options for Curriculum, Instruction, and Placement

Because public education must serve all children's educational needs, the largest part of general education must be designed for the modal (most frequently occurring) characteristics of students and teachers. Public education is by definition a service designed for the masses. Any product or service intended for the public at large has to be designed around the typical characteristics of consumers. Economies of scale alone require this. The size, shape, and abilities of the typical citizen fall within a fairly narrow band of variability around the mean, and simple economics demand that things be designed with this in mind.

Surely, what some call "universal design" is important, and good design will accommodate a large range of individual characteristics. But, like "all," "universal" has its limits, often unspoken, sometimes not even recognized. If "universal" design can accommodate a larger segment of the population, that is all well and good. But remember that it is neither economically feasible nor necessary to eliminate all stair steps because some people can't use them or to design and equip every car so that a person with quadriplegia can drive it. Neither is it feasible or desirable to design a reading program for most children that will be appropriate for students with severe mental retardation.

Education has to be designed for what the average teacher and the average student can be expected to do, not what the exceptionally able or those with disabilities can accomplish. I'm not suggesting that the performance of the average teacher or student can't be improved, simply that expectations in the general education program can't outstrip what the average teacher can do with appropriate training or what the typical student can do with good instruction.

Because public education must address all children's educational needs, it must include explicit structures ensuring the accommodation of exceptional students. By definition, exceptional students require an extraordinary response from educators—something different from the ordinary, even if the ordinary is good. The standard educational program can serve most students very well, but it can't serve exceptional students without additional, explicit components—special structures that go beyond the normal or routine in such matters as goals, lines of authority, roles and responsibilities of personnel, budgets and purchases, allocation of time and space, modification of curriculum, evaluation of performance, and assignment of students to classes. Failure to create these explicit structures to accommodate students at the extremes of the performance distribution inevitably results in their neglect. They are forgotten. They don't just fail a little. They fail a lot, and their noses are rubbed in their failures.

The requirement of alternative educational goals and programs must be explicit for exceptional students. It's as simple as this, I think: When the interests of students with disabilities or those who are gifted are not explicitly mandated, they get lost in the shuffle. The implicit or explicit assumption that standard educational goals and programs will accommodate the needs of exceptional students is not just logically untenable. It also places the onus of proof that the program is inappropriate wholly on the student when questions arise about his or her performance. However, if there is an explicit requirement of alternative goals and programs for exceptional students, then the burden of proof is at least partly on the school to show that those alternatives are available to students for whom the typical program is unsatisfactory and in which an exceptional student cannot be expected to make satisfactory progress.

Alternative goals and programs must be expressed as alternative curricula and educational methods for exceptional students. It is not enough to have a separate place—a special class or school. Some exceptional learners need to learn something other than the standard curriculum, not just learn the standard curriculum in a different way or in a different place. And they may need instructional or behavior management procedures that are not needed by most students.

People not familiar with instruction may miss the distinctions of method that are important for exceptional students. For example, students with disabilities may require more trials, more examples, a different pace, smaller steps in a sequence, more reinforcement (praise, encouragement, or other rewarding consequences), more careful monitoring, more structure (e.g., higher predictability, more explicit instructions, more immediate consequences) than is desirable for typical students. There may be other distinctions that I have not listed here, but at least all of these are involved in more precise teaching. In short, the instruction of students with disabilities may need to be considerably more precise than the instruction that produces good results for typical students.

In many types of performance, it is the precision with which something is done that makes the difference, not the basic operation. This is true in driving, flying, playing music, shooting guns, and so on. Just consider the differences in level of performance of the same basic operations in the following comparisons: the typical drive to work versus driving in a high-speed race; flying from city *A* to city *B* versus flying with a stunt team; playing in a municipal band versus playing in one of the world's virtuoso combos; shooting targets in the backyard versus sharp-shooting for a SWAT team. Highly expert, precision performance requires extensive training. You don't give all soldiers the competence of the Special Forces by giving them a beret. You don't make every teacher a special educator by telling them good teaching of exceptional children is just good teaching because, after all, kids are more alike than they are different and good teachers use the same basic operations regardless who their students are.

# EXPLORING THE ISSUE

## Should Students with Cognitive Disabilities Be Expected to Demonstrate Academic Proficiency?

## Challenge Questions

- Compare and contrast the positions of the YES and NO selections regarding whether students with cognitive disabilities should be expected to demonstrate academic proficiency.
- Which selection makes the best case for its argument? Why?
- How did your perspective on this question change while reading the selections? Why?
- If teachers are to be evaluated partly by the progress of their students with disabilities, what procedures would be fair to both teachers and students?

## Is There Common Ground?

The authors of the YES and NO selections have all given considerable thought to the dynamics of assessment. They agree that both standardized testing and less formal assessment can be useful, if used appropriately. They would warn educators to avoid the temptation of stereotypes and caution that isolated test scores should not limit possibilities. And they would all support having high expectations for all individuals.

## Additional Resources

*A Blueprint for Reform:* The reauthorization of the Elementary and Secondary Education Act. (2010). U.S. Department of Education. Retrieved April 10, 2010 from www2.ed.gov/policy/elsec/leg/blueprint/blueprint.pdf

Ahearn, E. (2009). *inForum: Growth models and students with disabilities: Report of state interviews.* National Association of State Directors of Special Education. Retrieved June 8, 2010 from www.nasdse.org

Darling-Hammond, L. (2012, March 14). Value-added teacher evaluation: The harm behind the hype. *Education Week, 32,* 24.

Gewertz, C. (2010, April 15). Advocates push new definition of career readiness. *Education Week,* 9.

Kauffman, J. M. (2002). *Education deform: Bright people sometimes say stupid things about education.* Lanham, MD: Scarecrow Press.

Markheim, M. (2010). What if a college education just isn't for everyone? *USA Today,* Retrieved March 18, 2010 from www.usatoday.com

McGrew, K. S. & Evans, J. (2004). *Expectations for students with cognitive disabilities: Is the cup half empty or half full? Can the cup flow over?* (Synthesis Report 55). Minneapolis, MN: University of Minnesota, National Center on Educational Outcomes.

Moore-Lamminen, L. & Olsen, K. (n.d.). *Alternate assessment: Teacher and state experiences.* Alliance for Systems Change/Mid-South Regional Resource Center. Retrieved June 22, 2006 from http://osepideasthatwork.org/toolkit/index.asp

Spellings, M. (2005, December 14). *To raise achievement of students with disabilities, greater flexibility available for states, schools.* Retrieved December 30, 2005 from www.ed.gov

U.S. Department of Education. (2005). *Working together for students with disabilities: Individuals with Disabilities Education Act (IDEA) and No Child left Behind Act (NCLB): Frequently asked questions.* Retrieved January 31, 2006 from http://ed.gov

# ISSUE 13

## Is Full Inclusion the Least Restrictive Environment?

**YES: Rosalind Vargo and Joe Vargo**, from "Voice of Inclusion: From My Friend, Ro Vargo," in R. A. Villa & J. S. Thousand, eds., *Creating an Inclusive School* (Association for Supervision and Curriculum Development, 2005, 2nd ed., pp. 27–40)

**NO: Amy D. Marcus**, from "Eli's Choice," *The Wall Street Journal* (2005, December 31), http://online.wsj.com/article/SB113598974559935259-search.html?KEYWORDS=marcus&COLLECTION=wsjie/6month}, December 31, 2005

---

### Learning Outcomes

At the conclusion of this issue, readers will be able to:

- Compare and contrast the positions of the YES and NO selections about full inclusion and the least restrictive environment.
- Describe the strengths and the weaknesses of each side's arguments.
- Compare and contrast the points of view of the two students who are the focus of the YES and NO selections.
- Identify actions team members and parents should take when considering educational placements.

---

### ISSUE SUMMARY

**YES:** Rosalind Vargo and Joe Vargo, parents of Ro, use their voices to tell a powerful story of their daughter's success in fully inclusive educational programs, from kindergarten through college.

**NO:** Amy D. Marcus, staff reporter at *The Wall Street Journal*, conveys the voices of Eli's parents and teachers as they react to his message to leave a fully inclusive program in favor of a separate special education class.

IDEA requires all schools to ensure that students with disabilities are educated in the least restrictive environment (LRE): "removal from the regular education environment occurs only if the nature or severity of the disability is such that education in regular classes with the use of supplementary aids and services cannot be achieved satisfactorily." Although never used in IDEA, the term *inclusion* is frequently linked to LRE discussions.

Ask a group of people to define *inclusion* and they will usually come up with a statement like, "all children being educated in the same school." Ask again, "Do you mean *all* children?" The reply is likely to be a bit less certain, "Well, maybe not *all*." Probe a bit further and someone might admit (with a bit of trepidation) that inclusion should mean all students except . . . The words that follow may vary, but usually there are doubts about including students with severe cognitive challenges—those who have intellectual disabilities, or disabilities in multiple areas, and require complex and comprehensive support in order to communicate, move, and/or learn. Inclusion, for many people, really does not include *all* children.

Proponents of full inclusion have a very different answer. They say—and mean—*all* children being educated in the same school. Full inclusion advocates maintain that all children, regardless of level of need, have a moral and legal right to attend their home school; be enrolled in general education classes; and receive all necessary supports within those classes. In a full inclusion environment, students don't need to fit into the school; the school adapts to all students. Children are not sent out (or away) because what they need is not available or difficult to deliver; needed services and supports are brought to the child.

Those who oppose full inclusion cite the difficulties of adapting instruction; meeting student needs; and acquiring material, training, and professional supports. Accustomed to traditional academic goals for some students and pressing vocational, life-skills based goals for others, they ask how the demands of both can be met.

The challenge of full inclusion is perhaps greatest at high schools, with their focus on distinct academic disciplines and college aspirations. Communication between teachers is complicated by the increased number of individuals who interact with each student and the large numbers of students taught by each educator. The conversation has become even more intense with the advent of high stakes testing, causing some to wonder if the needs of every child can be met within a typical classroom.

This issue focuses on whether full inclusion is the least restrictive environment for all students. There are legal, philosophical, educational, and interpersonal dimensions to this topic. All will be addressed, but the YES and NO selections present the compelling voices and experiences of two sets of parents who have had much in common. They each had a child—now grown—with a significant disability. Both chose fully inclusive educational programs for their children. By their accounts, both children flourished. Then their experiences diverged.

In the YES selection, Rosalind Vargo and Joe Vargo, parents of a young woman who communicates through sign language and uses a wheelchair, describe Ro's inclusive schooling experiences, from kindergarten through university studies. They share vivid illustrations of how Ro was recognized for her capabilities rather than judged by her appearance.

In the NO selection, Amy Dockser Marcus communicates the reactions of Eli's parents, who were also strongly committed to inclusion. They were surprised when their son, who has Down syndrome, reached high school and actively rejected inclusion to be with his friends with disabilities. Although Eli's parents decided to abide by his preference, they each have different questions about the wisdom of their son's choice.

The field of disability studies focuses on the role of individuals with disabilities in society. Some of the field's most powerful language speaks to disability discrimination—people segregated and oppressed because of their difference. The line between *normal* and *different* is context-specific. Too often, individuals are divided into those who succeed and those who don't. The problem gets situated in the individual, rather than the setting. The key may be to consider the range of human experience and capability. Disability studies prefer that educators adjust the curriculum to embrace the range of learners, rather than focus on *fixing* individuals. To ensure that educational plans are made in the most informed fashion, Baglieri, Valle, Connor, and Gallagher (*Remedial and Special Education*, 2011) propose that we include Eli and Ro in decision making. Each of us knows what works for us and would like to be part of important decisions.

Sandra Houghton (*Education Week*, 2011), a woman with cerebral palsy, shares her feelings of isolation. Even within a warm and caring family, she believes her experiences were restricted, compared to her siblings. Houghton thinks the key skills are "soft" (social) skills that help an individual navigate diverse situations. She has built upon her experiences, creating the Self-Advocacy Leadership Series (SALS). Through this unique program, which emphasizes communication and interpersonal interactions, Houghton and others strengthen the self-advocacy skills of students with developmental disabilities. Knowing and communicating their own wants and needs help the individuals feel more successful.

Drawing on student voices, Chadsey and Han (*TEACHING Exceptional Children*, 2005) address the peer connections essential to successful inclusion. The students think "segregation is unfair" and urge educators to provide opportunities where friendships can flourish naturally, as they would between any students.

Segregation is not always physical. Consider the experiences of a deaf student, whose primary language is American sign language (ASL). Interactions with children and adults are limited unless there are opportunities to use a common language. Contemplate the experience of a student educated primarily by a 1:1 paraprofessional. Individualized attention may be helpful, but prevent connections with peers.

Another group of students found friendships—and inclusion—less important than their educational environment (Moore & Keefe, *Issues in Teacher Education*, 2004). These high school students, asked about their educational experiences, favored separate programs. Although disliking the accompanying stigma, they felt special education classes offered a more responsive environment that attended to their learning requirements.

Inclusion literature abounds with stories that melt hearts and open eyes. Horowitz and Klein (*Educational Leadership*, 2003) describe their efforts to include a child with Down syndrome into their religious school kindergarten. They discovered that, through working to include Michael, they learned to see the potential in every child and the interconnectedness of us all.

Most writers acknowledge that successful complete inclusion is far from easy to achieve. In two instructive articles, Villa and Thousand (*Educational Leadership*, 2003) and McLeskey and Waldron (*Phi Delta Kappan*, 2002) provide numerous examples of lessons learned through schools' efforts to become inclusive. Their practical suggestions emphasize that successful inclusive programs require collaborative, sustained partnerships between administrators, teachers, and parents.

Teachers, too, are concerned about the full inclusion learning environment. Kavale and Mostert (*Exceptionality*, 2003) reviewed several studies that explored the "empirical evidence" of full inclusion. Teachers embraced the democratic, just goals of full inclusion, but were concerned about its responsibilities. Their enthusiasm often moderated as they struggled to meet daily challenges.

Preparation for teaching in a fully inclusive setting is critical to consider and, unfortunately sometimes overlooked. Reflecting on a San Diego decision to phase out separate classes in favor of an inclusive model, Carless (www.voiceofsandiego.org, 2011) noted that teachers were offered an optional single day of training and preparation—not nearly enough. Teacher reactions to the new model were varied; their ability to go to the training was inconsistent, as were the outcomes.

Many inclusive settings involve co-teaching, a methodology that partners general education and special education teachers in the same classroom. The intention is to draw on the content knowledge of the general education teacher and the pedagogical knowledge of the special educator. The best of these models differs significantly from the one described above.

Ideally, the teacher pair is involved in choosing both the assignment and their teaching partner. Building a solid relationship is a key; teachers need to share responsibilities equitably and feel open to do so (Sileo, *TEACHING Exceptional Children*, 2011). Regular planning time is essential, as is the willingness to discuss operational details and resolve conflicts at an early stage. Good inclusive programming takes time and money as well as administrative support and encouragement. Friend and Cook (*Interactions*, Pearson, 2010) provide an essential treatment of the ways teachers can successfully collaborate to meet student needs.

Zigmond (*The Journal of Special Education*, 2003) maintains the diverse perspectives about placement may arise from the questions we ask. Instead of asking whether full inclusion is desirable for all, perhaps Americans should return to the individual focus that has been the hallmark of special education to ask: For whom is full inclusion the best course? What instructional goals are best served by full inclusion? And which by focused specialized settings?

All teachers seek to prepare students to be successful adults. In partnership with parents, Americans endeavor to support and guide the young people along this journey. Americans cannot help but respond to the compelling narratives of these parents. Eli and Ro come alive in their words.

For these families, the road was not always easy and branched into two different paths. Doubtless, in years ahead, everyone concerned will wonder about "the road not taken" (Frost, 1920). This reflective question is one each of the Americans will face, for their students and themselves. The overriding responsibility of Americans is to understand the gravity of these choices.

# YES

Rosalind Vargo and
Joe Vargo

## Voice of Inclusion: From My Friend, Ro Vargo

It was Tuesday, a beautiful autumn morning at Syracuse University. Ro had just finished her class "Topics in American Music—20th Century" in Bowne Hall and was walking back to the car (with my assistance) to go home. Joe, Ro's dad, was waiting in the car. He and I looked at each other and at Ro and wondered how we had gotten here. After all, it seemed like only yesterday. . . .

### Kindergarten

Among our vivid memories is kindergarten and Ro's first invitation to a birth-day party. Kristen's mother phoned to ask if she should make any special arrangements for Ro to attend. Fighting back tears, we responded, "No, but thanks for asking." Kristen's mom said her daughter was so looking forward to Ro coming. Then we said it: "We love Ro because she's our daughter. But do you know why other kids like her?"

The mom replied, "Well, I can speak only for my daughter, Kristen. She says she likes Ro's smile and that Ro is someone you can really talk to . . . and that she wears really neat clothes." Kristen's mom continued, "I think kids like Ro because she isn't a threat to them; they can just be them-selves around her."

### 2nd Grade

In 2nd grade, we invited several kids to Ro's birthday party. Because we would be picking them up at school, we needed to know who would be coming. The night before the party, we called Eric's mom and politely asked, "Is Eric coming to Ro's party tomorrow?"

She said, "I'm sorry I didn't call you, but Eric said he just told Ro in school yesterday that he was coming. Was that all right?" It was more than all right! To Eric, the fact that Ro couldn't talk didn't mean that she couldn't understand him. . . .

Vargo, Rosalind and Vargo, Joe. From *Creating an Inclusive School,* 2nd ed. (ASCD, 2005), pp. 27–40. Copyright © 2005 by Association for Supervision & Curriculum Development. Reprinted by permission.

# 4th Grade

In 4th grade, a time when pressure to have the "right" clothes and hairstyles had already begun, Ro was voted "Best Friend" by her 25 "typical" 4th-grade classmates. Somehow, Ro's inclusion in the school life was making a tremendous difference in many kids as well. Her "giftedness" was recognized and celebrated.

We recall another night when a puzzling phone call came for Ro. Sharing the same nickname as my daughter, I thought the call was for me and I replied, "Speaking."

The young girl at the other end of the line clarified, "No, I'd like the Ro who goes to Ed Smith School."

I said, "Hold on," and exclaimed to Joe, "Someone wants to talk with Ro on the phone!" We got Ro from the dinner table and put the phone to her ear. Immediately recognizing the voice of her friend Ghadeer, Ro started laughing. She then nodded her head to indicate "yes" and followed with a head shake indicating "no." Curiosity got the best of me and I took the phone, reporting to Ghadeer, "Ro's listening and nodding her head."

Ghadeer said, "Great, I'm asking her advice about a birthday present for a friend. Now, did she nod 'yes' for the jewelry or 'yes' for the board game?"

# Ro's 11th Birthday

We remember with pleasure Ro's 11th birthday party. Before the party, the mother of one of Ro's friends called to ask if the present she had picked out for Ro was OK. Apparently, her daughter hadn't been with her when she went shopping. She had just wrapped it and given it to her daughter to take to school that morning. She wasn't sure if the gift was the "in" thing and feared that her daughter would die of embarrassment if it weren't.

She had bought a jump rope for Ro—a deluxe model. Without hesitation, I said that it was a wonderful idea and a gift that Ro would love using with her sisters.

With a sigh of relief, the mom responded, "Well, I am glad. I was hoping that Ro was not handicapped or anything. Is she?"

For the life of me, I wanted to say "No" and save this mom obvious embarrassment. So I said, "Well, a little bit." After many of her apologies and my reassurances, we got off the phone as friends. She had made my day, my week, my life! The thought that an 11-year-old girl had received a birthday party invitation, wanted to go, and asked her mom to buy a present, *never thinking it important to mention that her friend had a disability*, still makes me cry with wonder and happiness. . . .

When Ro unwrapped the jump rope, all the girls were elated, shrieking, "I hope I get one of those for my birthday," and "Oh, cool." The girls immediately dragged Ro down the stairs and outside to the driveway, where they tied one end of the jump rope to her wrist. With the strength of her twirling partner, Ro was able to rotate the rope for her friends. It was Ro's best adaptive occupational therapy activity in months.

# A Gift for Ghadeer

Probably the most profound testimony to inclusive education occurred in January 1993. Ghadeer, Ro's friend who had called to ask for advice on gift selection, suffered a cerebral hemorrhage, or severe stroke. At the age of 12, she was comatose for almost four weeks. . . . [After] weeks of having family, teachers, and friends read at her bedside, Ghadeer miraculously, although not completely, recovered. Her voice and articulation were so severely impaired that she could not communicate orally. To the amazement of the child's doctors and nurses, her disability did not stop her from communicating; she began to use sign language. An interpreter was quickly found who asked Ghadeer, "Where did you learn sign language?"

Ghadeer replied in sign, "From my friend, Ro Vargo!"

After four months of intensive rehabilitative therapy, Ghadeer returned to school, but now as a "special education" student requiring speech and language services plus physical and occupational therapy. Her family proudly reports that Ghadeer turned away the "special" bus and rode the regular school bus on her first day back to school. Furthermore, she advocated for herself to get a laptop computer to assist her with her schoolwork. Inclusive education enabled Ghadeer to get to know someone like Ro and to learn about augmentative communication systems and her rights, particularly her right to be part of her school, class, and friendship circle. She had learned that a person can still belong even if something unexpected—like a disability—happens.

# What's Hard About Being Ro's Friend?

Ghadeer was one of many of Ro's friends who became quite capable of articulating for themselves what Ro meant to them and the kinds of things that they learned at school with her. That relationship became clear when Ro and a group of her friends responded to questions from parents and teachers in a session titled "Building Friendships in an Inclusive Classroom" at a national education conference that they attended.

Tiffany said, "I think Ro should be in class with all of us because how else is Ro going to learn the really important stuff? Besides, we can learn a lot from her."

Teachers asked Ro's friends some unusual questions, such as "Have you ever discussed her disability with her?"

Stacey replied, "No, I know she is different, but I never thought it important to ask. Like, for instance, I never thought to go up to a black kid in my class and say, 'You're black. How come you're different?'"

A "popular" question among teachers and parents—judging by their nods—was "What is the hardest thing about being Ro's friend?" As Ro's parents, we held our breath, waiting for responses such as "She drools," "She walks funny," or "She's a messy eater."

But again Stacey spoke up, saying, "The hardest thing about being Ro's friend is that she always has a parent or an adult with her." Ouch! That hurt. But Stacey's observation taught us, Ro's parents, an important lesson that will surely have a positive effect on our daughter's future.

# Transition to Middle School

The transition from elementary to middle school was tough socially for Ro, as it can be for any adolescent. For Ro, the first months were spent in isolation, but her isolation was not one of physical proximity. Ro attended a regular 6th grade program and had to gain acceptance from her new middle school peers. Initially, she was ignored or stared at; a few classmates even teased her. When Ro was assigned to a work group, no group members complained out loud, but Ro noticed non-verbal signs of rejection. In those first months, we began to doubt our decision to include Ro in middle school. We recalled the comment a teacher from the previous year had made: "Middle school kids don't like themselves. How can you expect them to like your kid?"

Mauricha, a classmate, became Ro's closest new friend. It was Mauricha who broke the social barrier. Asked how the two became friends, Mauricha said, "I saw her. She saw me. We've just been friends ever since." One night when I was taking Mauricha home, she looked at me and touched my arm. "You know, Mrs. Vargo," Mauricha said, "lots of teachers think I'm friends with Ro cuz it gets me more attention. That isn't true. The truth is, I need her more than she needs me."

Ro's father and I would have to summarize Ro's middle school experience as fairly typical. When reflecting on our other daughters' experiences in middle school, we realized that there were many of the same issues: isolation at times, hot and cold friendships, recognition of and a growing interest in boys, physical changes, teasing, challenging class work, and parents who didn't know anything! Oh, yes. Ro went to her first dance and danced with Jermaine. . . .

# Arrival at High School

. . . Ro and six other students with disabilities entered Henninger High School. Early on, Ro communicated, "I like . . . zoology . . ., and the kids and I have learned a lot. I have had some classes I didn't like. It is hard for me when classes have no small groups and no homework for me. Sometimes there is too much information. The worst is when neither the kids nor the teachers talk to me." . . .

Inclusive education in high school was offering Ro a whole new world of opportunities and choices. She joined the Key Club. . . . She accrued service hours through her volunteer job at a . . . fully inclusive day care. Ro was acting as a role model for many young students with disabilities, as well as for the whole class and her fellow workers.

During her early high school years, Ro communicated many things to us in various ways. . . . Her "voice" gave us a clearer vision of where and what Ro wanted to do with her life. . . .

On the afternoon of her first volunteer job, Ro had to fill out an application. Her teaching assistant completed it with Ro's input. However, 10 minutes later, Ro totally dissolved into a full-blown temper tantrum.

The panicked teaching assistant questioned Ro, "Does it have anything to do with the application?"

Ro nodded, "Yes."

"Was it #1, #2, #3 . . . ." until the question, "What has been your biggest challenge?"

Without consulting Ro, the teaching assistant had written "Rett syndrome." That was the one! Ro wanted it removed. Yes, the line about Rett syndrome.

Another time that Ro clearly expressed her thoughts was when she was nominated by her teachers for Student of the Month. She had to complete an information sheet for the committee who would select the winner. After much deliberation, Ro opted not to include any of her work with local university students and their numerous papers on her life experiences or any of her work with other girls with Rett syndrome. Basically, her nomination went in with just her name, age, and favorite teacher. Ro was making it clear that she didn't think that Rett syndrome was something important to share about herself. It wasn't really who she was, or what she did, or even what she wanted to have. . . .

The voice of Ro's peers was also becoming clearer and louder. While on the zoology trip to New York City, Ro and her dad struggled for three days to keep up with the fast pace of a very busy itinerary. Ro's classmates seemed oblivious to her tiring easily and to the locomotion problems that caused her to lag behind. It appeared that they hardly noticed her at all that weekend—at least that was Joe's observation. Ro still enjoyed the trip, and it was a wonderful bonding experience for her and dad.

Months later, we came to understand the ramifications and the benefits of Ro's participation in that trip. Students in the class began to vocalize, without our knowledge, concerns about Ro's support person in school. They complained to their teacher at first about how they thought the teaching assistant was disrespectful to Ro. When the teacher heard their complaints, she notified the principal. When there was no action, kids went to their parents and parents came to us. When the school administration failed to act, Ro's peers did!

The vision for inclusive education was a reality. We had hoped that the kids who sat in class with Ro would not seek to harm her now or in the days to come. We had hoped that they would protect her and take care of her, seek the social and legislative reforms to support the inclusive lifestyle that she had grown accustomed to, and gladly be her neighbors and her friends because they had shared the same space, the same hopes, and the same dreams. Ro and her peers in an inclusive high school setting were already living out the dream, and there was no going back for any of us.

After Ro's third year in high school, . . . Ro was clearly envious of the planning and choices that her sister Josie was engaging in. College visits, college applications, and senior pictures were taking place. We were unclear about what Ro's choices could be, and she communicated that the situation was not fair.

One night I read about an inclusive college setting in Kentucky. The ONCAMPUS program had been initiated as a collaborative effort between the Inclusive Elementary and Special Education Program of Syracuse University (SU) and the Syracuse City School District. . . . ONCAMPUS brought six high school students . . . with moderate to severe disabilities to the SU campus where they would participate with other SU students in . . . learning experiences.

Ro. . . . actively communicated her absolute delight with her peers that she was going to attend SU next year. She decided which courses to take, what clubs to belong to, and where she would eat lunch.

However, getting a handicapped parking permit proved to be no easy task. After much discussion and hassle, Ro was secured her permit. When I picked it up, the receptionist asked, "Oh, is this for Ro Vargo who went to Henninger High School?"

"Yes," I replied.

"Tell her I said 'Hi.'"

"You know Ro?" I asked.

"Yeah, I graduated with her from Henninger last year."

Inclusive education . . . another voice heard and in all the right places . . . another confirmation.

## Syracuse University Students

Jacqueline[,] . . . is a sophomore at SU in the School of Social Work. She began to spend time with Ro on campus through her job as a residential habilitation counselor. She shared with Ro the names of all the good professors and the courses she should pass up! . . . Jackie was a member of SU's jazz and pep band, as well as the dance band. She would clue Ro in on any musical performances on campus. . . .

Justine had seen Ro on campus. . . . She was a senior in the Maxwell School of Communication at the time. As part of her final grade, Justine had to produce a short documentary. She approached Ro and asked if she would be willing to be part of a presentation highlighting the ONCAMPUS program. Ro agreed. A relationship developed that spanned a whole year. Justine introduced Ro to Gregg, another senior, who would be the codirector. They met frequently to talk and shoot videotape.

The final project culminated in a video titled *Ro.* Justine and Gregg's perspective was clearly evident in their work. It was respectful, serious, and funny, and Ro's hopes and dreams of being on a university campus were unfolded in the video. The images were searing and thought-provoking as Ro traversed the campus. Justine and Gregg's voice on this tape will last forever, and so will Ro's voice.

Ro's inclusion in high school and college settings has certainly caused my daughter some pain as she acknowledged her limitations and struggled to belong. Yet inclusion also prompted Ro's self-actualization, self-determination, and self-acceptance and her growing belief that there is nothing that she cannot do. Placing herself in a "regular" environment was a risk that Ro was willing to take.

Inclusive education has always been an emotional and physical risk for all of us, especially Ro. But it has clearly been worth it! . . . Today, Ro uses adult services, and we're starting all over again: justifying, rationalizing, sharing vision, relaying data, and information.

When parents of children with disabilities become lonely and fatigued, their voices can become silent. There are limited routes of appeal and no federal mandates to support Ro's inclusive lifestyle. Frankly, we are exhausted and frustrated. Nothing prepared us for this new fight to belong in a community outside of school. This adult, segregated mentality has taken its toll. We have been diligent advocates, articulate spokespersons. We've awakened—not only in Ro but also in many other students—the idea that inclusive education can mean college.

The impact of Ro's inclusive education is made clear by the relationships she forged along the way. Ghadeer called Ro to attend Ghadeer's high school graduation party. . . . Ro received a Christmas card from Mauricha, the middle school friend who broke the social barrier for Ro. The note began, "Hi, Ro. I know you probably don't remember me, but I have never forgotten you." Mauricha explained that she was working as a home health aide and taking a sign language course at night.

Kristen, Ro's teaching assistant, married Gavin. Ro was invited to the wedding, and she reminisced with the bridal party about the last time that they had all been in a limo together! . . . In a newspaper article highlighting the . . . high school graduations in the area, Kristen told a reporter that . . . "Ro was the sister I never had."

## The Future?

Our "severely impaired" child has already accomplished more than we had ever thought possible, and she continues to grow. . . . We believe in those young adults who sat in class with Ro. They will not seek to harm her but will be her community—the ones who will protect and care for her. They will advocate social and legislative reform to support the inclusive lifestyle to which Ro and they have grown accustomed. They will gladly be her neighbors, caretakers, job coaches, and friends because they shared the same classes, space, hopes, and dreams.

Amy D. Marcus

 **NO**

# Eli's Choice

For years, Eli Lewis was the only student in his class with Down syndrome.

The genetic condition, which causes a range of cognitive and physical impairments, made it harder for him to do his schoolwork. But his parents felt strongly that he could succeed. They hired a reading tutor. An aide worked with his teachers to modify tests and lessons so that he could be in the same classroom as everyone else. He participated in his middle school's award-winning chorus and was treated as a valued member.

But when all the other kids in his class were making plans to go to the local high school this fall, Eli, 14 years old, said he didn't want to go. He wanted to be in a small class with other students like him. "I don't want to get lost in a big crowd," Eli says.

Eli's declaration surprised his parents. Then his mother recalled the many times she stopped by the school to check on her son, only to find him eating by himself. Once, when she came to pick him up from a dinner that chorus members attended, she says she found Eli sitting with his aide, while the other students sat at a different table.

"The kids liked him, they knew him, they spoke to him," says his mother, Mary Ann Dawedeit. "They just didn't think of him as a peer." Eli, she says, was tired of "being the only kid who was different."

Federal law mandated in the 1970s that children with disabilities be offered a "free and appropriate public education" in the "least restrictive environment," rather than being separated only in special schools or institutions. Over the years, advocacy and additional laws resulted in efforts to get children with disabilities placed in regular classrooms, with proper support, whenever possible. The process, called "inclusion" or "mainstreaming," has largely been an academic success.

Studies have shown benefits for all children, not only those with disabilities, who study together. Many researchers argue this is one reason why people with Down syndrome have made such remarkable progress in recent decades. People with Down syndrome who learn in regular classrooms do much better academically, research has found. They also have significantly higher rates of employment after they graduate and earn more money than peers who studied mainly in self-contained classes.

And yet, Eli Lewis's experience poses a difficult dilemma, one that is only now starting to be recognized and addressed. With help, he had succeeded academically in a regular classroom. . . . [R]esearchers at the Center for Social Development and Education at the University of Massachusetts in Boston say that although people with intellectual disabilities made enormous gains academically due to inclusion, their social integration at school "remains stagnant."

In a survey of 5,600 seventh- and eighth-grade students from 70 schools across the country, more than half of the youths said they were willing to interact with students with intellectual disabilities at school. But only one-third said they would be willing to invite such students to their house or go to the movies with them, according to the survey done by the University of Massachusetts center and the Washington-based opinion firm, ORC Macro. "Student attitudes continue to remain the most formidable barrier to inclusion," the researchers concluded.

At first, Ms. Dawedeit and her husband, Howard Lewis, thought Eli might change his mind. The couple—who have two other sons who don't have Down syndrome—felt there were many advantages to Eli staying in a regular classroom, including greater independence and more interaction with the general student body. But eventually, Mr. Lewis says he began to recognize that having Eli in a regular classroom might not be "as important to Eli as it is to me."

Ms. Dawedeit remained reluctant. She talked with a friend who had a son with Down syndrome, who was also learning in a regular classroom. "I felt like I had let her down," Ms. Dawedeit says. "I had preached a mantra for so long to so many."

In May, at the science exposition at Eli's middle school, her feelings changed. The eighth-graders took over the school hallway and parents were invited to visit. Some students demonstrated elaborate experiments they had been working on. Eli worked with his aide to do research online about the chemical properties of silver. He learned where to find it on the periodic table. For the exposition, he printed out some of the documents he had found.

When his mother came to see his project, Eli again raised the subject of where he was going to high school. For Ms. Dawedeit, the contrast was sharp. Here was Eli, successfully participating in a science exposition with peers who didn't have disabilities—but still talking about wanting to be with other people with Down syndrome.

She says she realized she needed to try to accommodate her son's desire for a social group. "I really had to step back from my personal beliefs," she says.

In the fall, Eli enrolled in the ninth grade at Bethesda's Walter Johnson High School, a sprawling building of over 2,000 students. He is in a special program with 20 other students who have disabilities, including one who gets around in a wheelchair and has difficulty talking. Six of the students in the class have Down syndrome. Eli already knew some of the kids from various extracurricular activities, such as drama class and Special Olympics, where he participated in soccer, basketball, swimming, and bowling.

Getting out of the mainstream has meant trade-offs. His school is about 10 miles from Eli's house, farther than the local high school that his older brother attends. (The local high school doesn't have a separate special-education program.) A special-education bus now comes each day to pick up Eli, along with other students with disabilities.

"This was one of our big compromises," says his mother. In middle school, Eli walked to a bus stop and rode a regular school bus. "Other kids knew him," says Ms. Dawedeit. "Now he's a special-ed kid on a bus."

One evening in November, after a dinner of chicken burritos and salad, Eli helped his brothers, ages 12 and 17, clear the dishes. Then his parents watched him, as he started making his way through his homework—a worksheet to practice using nouns and verbs. Since Eli was born, they had fought to have him included in regular classrooms. Now it sometimes felt as if Eli might end up outside the world they had tried so hard to keep him in.

All along, they shared a similar goal: for their son to be able to live independently. But Mr. Lewis, a lawyer, began to worry that the academic gap between Eli and other classmates was getting wider in the regular classroom as he grew older, and might be too difficult to bridge in high school. "I'm not married to inclusion at the expense of Eli's getting the skills he needs," he says.

Ms. Dawedeit, a manager at a retail store, was less certain. She knew how much Eli, like all kids his age, wanted to belong. But without spending significant amounts of time in regular classrooms, how would he ever learn the skills he needed to reach the goal of living on his own? "The truth is he has to go out and get a job," she says. "If he's educated with his regular peers, then maybe a regular peer will hire him."

Eli finished his English worksheet, and got up to take a break. He came over and gave his father a hug. "Are you meeting any new kids at school, Eli?" his dad asked. "Not just yet, Dad," Eli answered. "Why are you hanging out only with the kids in your class?" his father queried. "Because I know them," Eli answered, and went into the kitchen to get some cookies.

At his new school, the Parent Teacher Student Association has put the issue of how to promote the inclusion of students with disabilities in extra curricular activities on the agenda for its January meeting. A student group that pairs students with disabilities with a buddy without disabilities has already scheduled several activities for the coming months, including ice skating and bowling.

Still, for most of his school day, Eli is now in a separate classroom from the general school population. Last month, ninth-graders in the general-education classes were reading the novel, "To Kill a Mockingbird." In the special-education classroom, the teacher was going over worksheets that had been adapted from the book, with some related questions.

Eli was signed up for a regular physical-education class, but asked his parents if he could switch to one with only special-education students. His mother was reluctant to change because it was one of his only chances to meet kids in the general-student population. She offered a compromise: He could switch to the special-education gym class with his friends if next semester he took weight-training as part of the regular class. Eli agreed.

Janan Slough, the assistant principal who oversees the special-education department at Eli's school, says the school has difficulty finding certified special-education teachers because of a national shortage.

The school tries to foster as many opportunities as possible for those with disabilities to be in general classrooms, she says. Still, she adds, "I feel caught" between juggling the need for socializing with the need to teach basic, crucial tasks, such as handling money. On one field trip, the special-education kids went to a grocery store; they were supposed to buy something their family might use at home, pay for it, and make sure they got correct change.

Most of the kids with disabilities need to focus on independent-living and job skills, rather than college preparation. "I'm charged with thinking about where they are going to be at 21," she says. "I don't want parents to come back and say, 'It's nice they were socially included and had parallel instruction, but you didn't prepare them for the world of work.'"

For now, Eli has only one class—ceramics—that he attends with the general school population. On a recent morning, Eli sat next to a boy assigned to help him. The students were designing tiles, and from time to time his peer assistant would look at what he was doing, or go with him to get more clay. For much of the class, the boy bantered with one of his friends, who had pulled up a chair next to him and was regaling him with a story. From time to time, Eli made a joke and the boys all laughed together.

But when they walked Eli back to the special-education classroom, there was no suggestion that they meet up again that day. When Eli was asked if he enjoyed spending time with his assigned partner, he shrugged and said, "It's OK."

Eli has a lot of ideas about what he wants to do after high school. In middle school, he took a media class and worked in the school's TV studio. Along with the other kids in the class, he was given a homework assignment to make a public-service announcement. Eli made one about the Special Olympics. "I want to be a director," he said, when asked about his plans after high school.

"Eli has serious career aspirations for himself that may not have anything to do with what the rest of the world sees for him after high school," said his mother, one afternoon last month, while waiting for him at a drama class he takes outside of school. The class, made up of students with and without disabilities, was planning a variety show, and Eli was excited about performing. Every night, he went to his room to work on a dance routine he had created to accompany a song from the soundtrack of the movie, "Holes."

His girlfriend, whom he met in elementary school and also has Down syndrome, had invited him to be her date to the upcoming Winter Ball at her private school. Next month, Eli will turn 15 and is planning a big party. The only kids he plans to invite also have disabilities, his mother says.

While she's glad he has found a social circle, she still wonders about what he's missing by going to special-education classes instead of staying in regular classes. "I go back and forth on it all the time," she says. For instance, his school has a state-of-the-art TV studio with editing facilities and a control room, where a class is given. Eli's parents wanted him to be in that class, but it's not possible right now because he needs to attend the special-education math class, which is held during the same period.

On a recent morning at school, Eli weaved around the teenagers lining the hallway. Some sprawled on the floor, catching up on homework. Others joked with each other by their lockers, or rushed to get to their next class.

Eli didn't talk to any of the students. He walked with purpose, heading to the special-education room.

When he got there, his face brightened when he saw one of his friends. "This is my best friend," he said, throwing his arm around the other boy, who also has Down syndrome. He pressed his face close to his friend's until their cheeks almost touched. Eli smiled. "What table are you sitting at lunch today?" he said as they walked together down the hall. "Come on, make sure you sit with me."

# EXPLORING THE ISSUE

## Is Full Inclusion the Least Restrictive Environment?

## Challenge Questions

- Compare and contrast the positions of the YES and NO selections regarding whether full inclusion is the least restrictive environment.
- Which selection makes the best case for its argument? Why?
- What successes and challenges did Ro and Eli experience? Why did their paths diverge? Would you accede to their preferences or advocate for a different path?
- Discuss the implications of each option for the education of all children.
- How would you use information from the YES and NO selections to affect your actions at a team meeting?

## Is There Common Ground?

Ro's and Eli's parents regain common ground when they speak of the future. The Vargos believe Ro's typical peers "will be her community—the ones who will protect and care for her. They will advocate social and legislative reform to support the inclusive lifestyle." Eli's mother hopes, "The truth is he has to go out and get a job. If he's educated with his regular peers, then maybe a regular peer will hire him."

## Additional Resources

Baglieri, S., Valle, J. W., Connor, D. J., & Gallagher, D. J. (2011). Disability studies in education: The need for a plurality of perspectives on disability. *Remedial and Special Education, 32*(4), 267–278.

Carless, W. (2011, October 5). *Becoming a special education teacher almost overnight.* Retrieved October 30, 2011 from voiceofsandiego.org

Chadsey, J. & Han, K. G. (2005). Friendship facilitation strategies: What do students in middle school tell us? *TEACHING Exceptional Children, 38*(2), 52–57.

Friend, M. & Cook, L. (2010). *Interactions; Collaborative skills for school professionals* (6th edition). Upper Saddle River, NJ: Pearson.

Frost, R. (1920). The road not taken. In *Mountain interval.* New York: Henry Holt and Company.

Horowitz, E. & Klein, M. (2003). What Michael taught us. *Educational Leadership, 61*(3), 84.

Houghton, S. (2011, March 11). Social skills are critical for those with disabilities. *Education Week.* Retrieved March 22, 2012 from www.edweek.org

Kavale, K. A. & Mostert, M. P. (2003). River of ideology, islands of evidence. *Exceptionality, 11*(4), 191–208.

Mcleskey, J. & Waldron, N. L. (2002) School Change and Inclusive Schools: Lessons Learned from Practice. Phi Delta Kappan, Vol. 84. No. 1

Marcus, A. D. (2005, December 31). Eli's choice. *The Wall Street Journal.* Retrieved December 31, 2005 from http://online.wsj.com/article/SB113598974559935259-search.html?KEYWORDS=marcus&COLLECTION=wsjie/6month]

Moore, V. M. & Keefe, E. B. (2004). "Don't get your briefs in a bunch": What high school students with disabilities have to say about where they receive their services. *Issues in Teacher Education, 13*(1), 7–17.

Sileo, J. M. (2011). Co-teaching: Getting to know your partner. *TEACHING Exceptional Children, 43*(5), 32–38.

Vargo, R. & Vargo, J. (2005). From my friend, Ro Vargo. In R. A. Villa & J. S. Thousand, (Eds). *Creating an Inclusive School* (2nd edition, pp. 27–40). Alexandria, VA: Association for Supervision and Curriculum Development.

Villa, R. A. & Thousand, J. S. (2003). Making inclusive education work. *Educational Leadership, 61*(2), 19–23.

Zigmond, N. (2003). Where should students with disabilities receive special education services? Is one place better than another? *The Journal of Special Education, 37*(3), 193–199.

# ISSUE 14

## Should Colleges Be More Accommodating to Students with Disabilities?

**YES: Hazel Denhart**, from "Deconstructing Barriers: Perceptions of Students Labeled with Learning Disabilities in Higher Education," *Journal of Learning Disabilities* (vol. 41, no. 6, pp. 483–497, 2008)

**NO: Melana Z. Vickers**, from *Accommodating College Students with Learning Disabilities: ADD, ADHD, and Dyslexia* (The John W. Pope Center, 2010), www.popecenter.org, March 1, 2010

---

### Learning Outcomes

**At the conclusion of this issue, readers will be able to:**

- Compare and contrast the positions of the YES and NO selections addressing whether institutions of higher education should be more accommodating to students with disabilities.
- Describe the strengths and the weaknesses of each side's arguments.
- Identify how services at the college level differ from those in elementary/secondary schools.
- Discuss the implications of each position for transition service plans for high school students with disabilities.

---

#### ISSUE SUMMARY

**YES:** Hazel Denhart, who lectures at Portland State University, uses a disability theory perspective to analyze how students with learning disabilities perceive their experiences in higher education. Her interviewees identify social barriers that make college a less-than-welcome experience and recommend steps to reduce institutional intolerance.

**NO:** Melana Zyla Vickers, an editorial writer for *USA Today*, uses information from interviews with on-campus experts, professors, and students, to raise serious questions about the legitimacy of accommodations and disability services. Many of her interviewees think disabilities leading to accommodations can be purchased, to the detriment of everyone's experience.

**H**ave you used a curb-cut to ease the passage of your bike or a stroller? Or pushed the automatic door opener button when your arms were full? Do you know the now-ubiquitous food processor was designed for a cook with disabling arthritis?

All the above are accommodations, originally designed to make the world more accessible for people with disabilities. Without the accommodations listed, someone using a wheelchair might not be able to cross streets or open doors. U.S. federal laws (Section 504, ADAA) require that reasonable accommodations be provided so that people with disabilities have fair and equal access to life's activities.

Most people would agree that Braille signs and ramps in buildings are reasonable accommodations, making school accessible for those with sensory or motoric disabilities. These accommodations are visible to us all, as are their associated disabilities.

The use of scribes to transfer a student's words into print, or extended time for exams, is not always so readily accepted. These can be accommodations as well—for people with disabilities affecting writing, processing material quickly, or sustaining attention. These accommodations are sometimes more difficult to understand, as is existence of their related *invisible* disabilities. Some wonder whether they cross the line, making things a little too easy.

In elementary and secondary schools, accommodations are adjustments to setting, timing, presentation mode, and/or response mode that allow students with disabilities to demonstrate what they know and can do. They are not intended to change the nature of a task, make it easier, or ensure that a student passes.

Accommodations achieved controversial status with the advent of high-stakes testing and accountability. Consider a student with a reading disability who receives a low score on a high-stakes math test; it is important to know whether the student's score reflects math knowledge or struggles reading the items. U.S. federal laws require that schools provide appropriate accommodations so that students with disabilities can participate fully in education and assessment.

Elementary and secondary educators have become accustomed to regulatory rigor when selecting accommodations, especially for high-stakes assessments. Analyzing 12 years of research on accommodation policies, Lazarus, Thurlow, Lail, and Christensen (*The Journal of Special Education*, 2009) found states have formalized regulations and guidelines, particularly regarding large-scale test situations. There is general consensus that appropriate accommodations ensure an assessment measure its intended content knowledge, rather than the effects of a disability.

According to the National Longitudinal Transition Study-2 (NLTS2, 2009), 45 percent of students with disabilities pursue higher education. Some of these students might have been covered by 504 plans; others by IEPs. Both documents could include accommodations.

Several circumstances might contribute to the rise in numbers of students with disabilities seeking higher levels of education. Early identification, services, and successful use of accommodations throughout PreK–12 might have increased student skills and competencies. IDEA and NCLB require that students with disabilities participate in the general curriculum and large-scale assessments may have broadened the students' knowledge base. The increase might be a consequence of IDEA 2004's emphasis on transition planning that can embrace postsecondary goals. Finally, the rise might also reflect the growing availability of college disability support centers (Sparks & Lovett, *Journal of Learning Disabilities*, 2009).

This issue explores whether students with disabilities encounter an unwelcome learning environment when they make the move to higher education. While people with various disabilities attend college, the YES and NO selections focus primarily on students with learning disabilities, although the NO selection includes people with attention deficit hyperactivity disorder (ADHD). As you read these selections, consider the differing perspectives of those interviewed: students are seeking access to higher education; faculty and administrators are striving to understand what they are asked to do.

The YES selection is written by Hazel Denhart, herself a person with a learning disability. For her doctoral dissertation, Denhart interviewed students who were identified in college as having a learning disability. She sought to relate and summarize their perceptions and experiences. The voices of her participants speak of their significant struggles. Despite considerable efforts, they feel they are often regarded as poor students. Once found eligible for accommodations, many did not want to use them, sensing disdain from their peers and professors.

In the NO selection, columnist Melana Zyla Vickers offers a sharply contrasting view. Based on statistical reports and interviews with higher education administrators and professors, Vickers concludes that postsecondary schools have already made far too many concessions. She questions the legitimacy of the growing number of disability diagnoses, and the accommodations that accompany them, referencing claims that both can be purchased. Hinting that faculty are reluctant to share their accommodations' reservations, Vickers raises concerns about a possible student backlash at this special treatment.

IDEA includes disability categories, which all states enhance with specific regulations. In elementary and secondary schools, accommodations are seen as leveling the playing field, so individuals with disabilities have equal access to education. Multidisciplinary teams, including the student, convey information about accommodations and their direct relationship to a disability. IDEA entitlements to special education expire when a student turns 22 or receives a high school diploma.

Postsecondary education is governed by the Americans with Disabilities Amendment Act and Section 504. No specific disability categories are listed in either. To be eligible for reasonable accommodations, individuals must have (or be regarded to have) a major physical or mental impairment that substantially limits one or more major life activities. Individuals must self-disclose their disability and accommodation status.

Denhart conveys the voices of college students diagnosed with learning disabilities who feel they are silenced, and limited by intolerance at the college level. Reluctant to use accommodations because of the stigma they encounter, some of the students develop advocacy skills through the support of specialists. The perceptions Denhart shares are underscored by Egan and Guiliano (*North American Journal of Psychology*, 2009), who found students with disabilities to be in a no-win situation. The undergraduates they interviewed expressed negative views of those who did well using accommodations. Without the accommodations, the students may not have equal access.

Complicating the situation, Denhart's participants were not identified as needing disability-related accommodations during their PreK–12 education. Not having been part of IDEA's transition process, they would be coming fresh to the complexities of discussing a disability and identifying accommodations.

Given the breadth of IDEA's influence on PreK–12 education since 1975, it is important to consider the individuals mentioned by both authors in this issue. Several indicate they received no accommodations before they entered higher education, implying they had never been found eligible under Section 504 and/or IDEA. In contrast, the NLTS2 found that only 24 percent of students who received disability-related accommodations in high school did so in postsecondary settings. Consider why these different situations might have occurred.

Vickers raises a key point when she notes that evaluations at the college level are inconsistent, as are procedures for determining eligibility and assigning accommodations. In many colleges, a single individual determines a student's status. Faculty receive notices of accommodations and have limited avenues to learn about disabilities and their impact on learning. Describing postsecondary identification as a "heterogeneous mess," Sparks and Lovett (2009) find "the sheer number of criteria . . . is dizzying and the range of criteria is depressing" (p. 507).

Both Denhart and Vickers refer to accusations that some people fake disabilities to gain an advantage in college. Indeed, high school faculty are often asked to evaluate students for the presence of a learning disability or ADHD to support requests for accommodations that would hopefully increase SAT scores. Newton (*Psychology Today*, 2010) related incidents of people who wanted to fake ADHD to gain access to stimulant drugs with the aim of increasing their performance. Newton discusses a research study that asked individuals to try to feign ADHD. After preparation time with background information about ADHD and the struggles it presents, individuals were asked to perform tasks that were difficult for those who really did have ADHD. Results indicated that neither test performance nor self-reports could differentiate between those faking ADHD and those who actually experienced the disorder.

The Association on Higher Education and Disability (AHEAD), a rich source of information, offers best practice advice in disability documentation at the postsecondary level (www.ahead.org). AHEAD notes that accurate information is necessary to establish protection from discrimination/harassment as well as to select accommodations, and recommends groups of stakeholders establish policies and practices that are consistent, individualized, and informative. Using existing information, knowledgeable examiners, and clear communication, colleges can design a disability support system that is consistent and not masked in mystery.

Discussing disability theory and disability studies, Baglieri, Valle, Connor, and Gallagher (*Remedial and Special Education,* 2011) agree that it might be difficult to discern those who experience the characteristics of a disability, especially those which are as invisible as dyslexia or ADHD. Rather than situating the problem within an individual, the authors emphasize the range of human behavior and learning. Instead of labeling individuals as different and problematic, the authors recommend more flexibility for all students through universal design for learning (UDL) (www.udlcenter.org). UDL principles include multiple means of representing information, expressing knowledge, and class engagement. Incorporating UDL principles in college courses would require some redesign and readjustment, but might markedly reduce the need to consider changes for a single individual.

The current emphasis on preparing students to be college- and/or career-ready signals that the time is right to address this situation for the benefit of all.

# YES

Hazel Denhart

# Deconstructing Barriers: Perceptions of Students Labeled with Learning Disabilities in Higher Education

Since the 1960s, intensive scientific inquiry into learning disabilities (LD) has yielded an immense body of excellent knowledge about its manifestation. . . . Medical researchers have identified physical differences in the brains of dyslexics altering visual perception, phonemic processing, semantic understanding, working memory, and muscle coordination. Brain researchers can see precisely where phonemic difficulties unfold when dyslexics wrestle the written word for meaning, and geneticists are tracking multiple entry points for the flow of dyslexia through the human genome. Meanwhile, social scientists from the relatively new field of disability studies are discovering how diversity in brain structure and brain function can be misunderstood as disability. From this perspective, LD is seen as socially created by values restricting how one's brain is permitted to function.

However, despite our vast knowledge of LD those who live with it still struggle for success. While their enrollments are up in postsecondary institutions the dropout rate of those labeled with LD remains high locking many into higher unemployment rates, more placement in lower prestige jobs, lower income from employment, and higher rates of poverty.

Since the early 1990s an expanding stream of qualitative research has invited the voice of those labeled with LD to illuminate the barriers facing them in higher education. That voice speaks to being silenced, misunderstood, and misrepresented by others.

The issue of being silenced is apparent in policy and practice where the voice of those labeled with LD has gone missing. Even to the present moment it continues to be nonlabeled researchers, policy makers, and practitioners debating the issues and setting agendas regarding services and accommodations for those who are labeled. . . . Few studies in LD research seek the voice of those labeled as to the impact of scientifically based interventions imposed on them or other possible solutions yet to be recognized by researchers who do not experience the phenomenon. It is puzzling that the voice of those labeled

Denhart, Hazel. From *Journal of Learning Disabilities,* vol. 41 no. 6, November/December 2008, pp. 483–488, 490–493, 494–495 (refs. omitted). Copyright © 2008 by Hammill Institute on Disabilities and Sage in association with American Rehabilitation Counseling Association (ARCA). Reprinted by permission via Rightslink.

LD is missing considering scientific research has provided them with adequate accommodations for equal participation, because federal civil rights law guarantees their inclusion in social and civic life. . . .

## Theoretical Framework

This [doctoral] study was conducted through the lens of *disability theory* based in the emerging, interdisciplinary field of disability studies. The following interpretation of disability theory offers the reader a simple, common reference for understanding this particular study and is not given as theoretical currency or to canonize any particular elements of this dense body of literature.

Three foundational ideas form a rudimentary core of disability theory viewing disability as (a) socially constructed, (b) part of normal human variation, and (c) requiring voice to deconstruct it.

First, disability theory asserts that disability cannot be understood outside of the context where it arises because it is a *product of social interaction*. Indeed in the United States even the mere perception of disability is enough to disable as evidenced in the Americans with Disabilities Act (ADA) of 1990 giving federal protection to those not actually disabled according to societal norms but who are only regarded as such. Thus, one can be free of impairment and still be disabled.

Higgins, Raskind, Goldberg, and Herman (2002) illustrated the social construction of disability in *master status* where the label of disability spreads from a single-task incompetence across one's totality obliterating other quite sound abilities. For example, in societies where reading ability is considered a measure of intelligence, master status makes it inconceivable for a person who cannot read or write well to be regarded as an intellectual. Here, the dyslexic who cannot encode or decode print might have no difficulty comprehending an audio text or dictating into a recording device but this person will still be considered disabled or intellectually inferior because literacy through the eyes is privileged over literacy through the ears.

An example of *institutionally* held master status was found on an advertisement for a "therapeutic support group" at one university in the Pacific Northwest. A flyer posted across campus by the psychological services office depicted a large heading "A.D.H.D." with a subheading asking, "Do these describe you?" followed by a list of 18 negative attributes including "social misfit," "underachiever," and "undisciplined." Only one positive attribute, "creative," appeared near the bottom of the list. Here, the university's chief medical authority on attention-deficit/hyperactivity disorder (ADHD) publicly announced that students with an ADHD label necessarily belong to a stereotype invalidating their overall competence and capacity. . . .

Second, disability studies scholars argue impairments are a natural and productive part of *normal human variation* known to all at some point in the life span.

Finally, disability scholars posit that *voice* is necessary to deconstruct disability and to authentically understand it in research. Indeed the field of disability studies is characterized by action research comprised of scholars openly claiming their personal labels of disability, with the exception of scholars labeled with LD who largely remain missing from any research field.

## Research on Students Labeled with LD in Higher Education

Three themes appear consistently in qualitative inquiry of students labeled with LD in higher education: (a) being misunderstood, (b) needing to work harder than nonlabeled others, and (c) seeking out strategies for success in education.

The theme of feeling misunderstood appears from the earliest ethnographies to more recent emancipatory research conducted as political action, and within autobiographical work. The voice of those labeled with LD speak of being regarded as intellectually inferior, incompetent, lacking effort, or attempting to cheat or use unfair advantages when requesting accommodations. The phenomenon of being misunderstood occurs both *intrapersonally* as well as interpersonally leading to devaluation and marginalization.

Intrapersonal (self) misunderstanding appears commonly in the use of the term "stupid" (or synonyms of this) by informants as a descriptor of themselves. Shessel and Reiff (1999) identified internalized master status in their use of the term *imposter phenomenon* to describe informants feeling they must have presented false impressions of themselves or somehow "cheated" the system by having been admitted to college as persons with LD traits. These informants feared being exposed as "frauds.". . .

Interpersonal misunderstanding with others is also common in the qualitative and autobiographical literature (as well as in some quantitative) where informants speak of being mistaken as intellectually inferior. Higgins et al. (2002) traced some issues of depression to informants' unhappy early school experiences of being bullied, teased, ridiculed, and hounded to a degree far exceeding the severity of their challenges. These qualitative findings might serve to illuminate those in clinical studies indicating high rates of loneliness, despair, depression, anxiety, and low self-esteem among LD subjects.

Feelings of being misunderstood have a direct impact on requesting accommodations. Studies found students labeled with LD feared they would be perceived as cheating if they tried to use accommodations. Hill's (1994) informants reported faculty members believed accommodations provided an unfair advantage. Hill's informants "were told certain modifications could not be made (e.g., extended time allowance on exams) because of the perceived 'advantage' it might give the student with a disability when compared to the non-disabled student . . ." (p. 11). In a study by Sarver (2000), one informant recalled "[some professors] have a really negative attitude towards me, even though they don't even know me" (p. 86). Elaqua, Rapaport, and Kruses's (1996) informants felt professors believed they "were trying to take advantage of the situation and attempted to 'pull a fast one' on them" (p. 6).

Abundant in the literature are tales of experiencing discrimination and even harassment after revealing LD to get accommodations. An engineering student in Barga's (1996) study was labeled a "dangerous engineer" (para. 18) by faculty after revealing her LD label to secure accommodations for an exam. Barga stated, "A meeting was held to have her removed from his class. Another meeting was held to have her removed from the department" (para. 18). Informants also speak of being advised to choose programs of study based on their disability rather than on their ability. Greenbaum, Graham, and Scales (1996) found fear of discrimination was a critical barrier for success among those labeled with LD. Not surprisingly, voice-based literature indicates a strong desire among informants for faculty and staff to undergo training about the nature of LD and how it is misunderstood.

The second major theme in the perceptions of students labeled with LD in higher education comes from the heavy workload they experience well beyond the scope of nonlabeled peers. Abundant in the literature are reports of students labeled with LD working themselves into a state of exhaustion even to the point of experiencing headaches and becoming physically ill from the workload. Ironically, these individuals are often judged as lazy or not trying hard enough as indicated in Lock and Layton's (2001) findings where some professors believed students use learning disabilities as an excuse to get out of work. Fearing stigma and misunderstanding, college students labeled with LD often avoid using their legally mandated accommodations that could ease their workload, fearing they would be misunderstood as cheating. . . .

Finally, the third theme from the perspective of students labeled with LD in the qualitative and autobiographical literature focuses on seeking empowerment strategies for practical as well as emotional needs.

Practical strategies include securing accommodations when possible such as audio texts, note takers, having exams read, demonstrating course mastery through alternative means, having extended time on exams, and receiving assistance from an LD specialist.

However, to receive these accommodations students must first be labeled with LD. From the perspective of students labeled with LD in higher education are emergent findings indicating the assessment experience can be oppressive. Most colleges implement a standard assessment process developed by the Association for Higher Education and Disability (AHEAD) for diagnosing LD in their college students. The AHEAD guidelines are based almost entirely on the original Individuals with Disabilities Education Act (IDEA) guidelines developed for children in public schools. The AHEAD guidelines call for intelligence testing as well as a battery of cognitive and psychological inventories and a complete diagnostic interview where clinicians gather from students detailed intricacies about their medical, developmental, social, and family history as well as probing into their psychological state and current social life. It is unquestionably an invasive experience. The interview is not limited to learning issues and can cover nearly any aspect of the student's being. . . . The testing for labeling is also expensive (equivalent to 6–8 weeks' pay for fulltime work at the minimum wage). Whereas some colleges subsidize the testing, others do not and not all colleges will accept the diagnosis granted free in K-12. Also, because current policy directs testing be repeated every 3 years, a K-12 diagnosis will expire and need to be redone before graduation with a bachelors degree.

Little is known from the perspective of college students labeled with LD as to the effectiveness and appropriateness of prescribed accommodations or what might work better. Studies indicate problems with accommodations such as recorded texts being inaudible or arriving too late—even long after the course concluded. While accommodations such as audio texts on tape will lighten the workload it cannot fully reduce it to the level of students with average reading skills. Taped texts use speech at a rate of 150 words per minute whereas the average reader reads at a rate of 300. Thus, reviewing audio texts take twice as long. Further, recorded texts cannot yet be highlighted or flagged as easily as printed texts. Trying to review a passage before an exam could require sorting through hours of audio recordings to find the correct passage, complicated when readers fail to note page numbers. However, technology is advancing quickly to remedy the highlighting issue. . . .

## Purpose of the Study

The purpose of this phenomenological study was to identify commonly held structures of consciousness among a subset of college students labeled with LD as to their educational barriers and the ways they overcome them. . . .

## Methodology

Where the anthropologist seeks to understand what a culture *looks* like from the position of an expert observer using an approach of "otherness," of "difference," of "not of us", the phenomenologist by contrast seeks to understand how it *feels* to be in a culture using an approach of "we," of "identification" between the informants and the reader. As a researcher labeled with LD, I was in the position of both expert and insider translating experience from the LD perspective to that of the scholarly, professional one.

### Role of the Researcher

My capacity to learn remained largely invisible throughout the first quarter-century of my life when I lived in relative illiteracy with little promise of an adequate education. As a dyslexic with a visual perceptual disability I was misunderstood by those around me as being "slow," yet today I hold a doctorate in educational policy. Where my intellect was invisible to the educational institutions I encountered in my youth and young adulthood, it is now recognized and even given accolades. As a researcher I wanted to know what changed. It seemed unlikely that the neurophysiology of my brain changed that much. I am still dyslexic and struggle for the meaning of each printed word I encounter with my eyes. It seemed more likely that the dramatic change necessary for me to become literate and then to become a scholar occurred in the social environment around me. I embarked on this study seeking to understand the nature of the barriers I and others like me face and to identify the shared strategies we use to overcome them. This was a risky enterprise because education for me was oppressive, silencing, and marginalizing. This experience threatened to bias my study. The first step in addressing bias was to admit it will exist to some degree and that I cannot free myself of the strong emotion I feel at having my intellect—the most precious attribute of a human being—dismissed for the first two and a half decades of my history. It penetrates my life, saturating my every thought and move. The second step I took was to be as open as possible about my biases by telling my story to everyone concerned with this study; my doctoral committee, my informants, the gatekeepers associated with the study, and interested others watching it unfold. I sought criticism from everyone as to where I might be overlaying my story on the data. . . . Additionally, I guarded against personal experience by seeking informants who had very different histories from my own. I came from a working-class family, achieved literacy late, did not graduate from high school with my peers, attended community college for 5 years and then a public university (with minimal admission requirements) for another 9 years before earning a bachelor's degree. I had no LD specialist and no accommodations for the first 12 years of higher education. In contrast, my informants came from middle and upper-middle class families, some attended private grade schools and high schools, 10 of 11 graduated from high school on time, and all but one were attending an exclusive, private university with stringent admission requirements. . . . In other words, I intentionally looked for informants who had the opportunity for the best possible educational experience and the most resources to attain it. However, seeking to balance my experience with my informants' comes at the price of not being able to generalize these findings to the wider LD population. Still, the findings could offer something else; as an insider I established considerable trust with my informants and reached a level of candor and depth in the interviews unlikely to be attained by outsiders.

## Participants

After receiving human subjects approval from my university, I approached informants through the offices of disability services at two colleges located in the Pacific Northwest; one an exclusive, private college (PC) with stringent admission requirements and the other a public, community college (CC) with no admission requirements. Criteria for participation required informants to be native speakers of English, have a diagnosis of LD determined by the [AHEAD] guidelines, and have no other physical or emotional impairments that could complicate the LD experience. . . .

## Characteristics of Participants

Three male and eight female participants represented European American ancestry from the American middle and upper-middle class. All 10 of the PC students attended regular K-12 classes completing their schooling on time with their nonlabeled peers. Only one received accommodations (extra time on tests) in high school. These informants are not representative of the *identified* LD population in K-12, which might concern some readers. However, given that medical research indicates as much as 20% of the human population carries the genes for dyslexia and only about 5.5% are identified by the schools, one could argue that those moving through K-12 who could be identified with LD but who go unrecognized are actually more representative of the LD population than those who are identified. Some readers might also be concerned that if these informants were not identified with LD in K-12 they might be "faking" LD to seek advantage at a highly competitive school, an issue candidly discussed among professionals in the field. However, the informants in this study were labeled with LD by licensed clinical psychologists using the AHEAD guidelines for assessing LD in college students. This testing is rigorous and extensive taking about 8 hours to complete in the presence of a skilled clinician whose training is focused on screening out those who genuinely do not have the characteristics of LD. Also, considering the LD label leads to powerful and irrevocable stigma, it seems less likely that one would try to gain intellectual advantage by using a label that undermines one's intelligence. . . .

# Findings

. . .

## RQ I: What Are the Similarities in the Described Experiences of a Subset of College Students Labeled with LD?

The shared experiences of informants included (a) working harder than nonlabeled others, (b) having the workload unrecognized, (c) generating products incommensurate with the workload, (d) viewing the college LD specialist as crucial to success, and (e) experiencing rapport with others labeled with LD.

Nine of 11 informants spoke of working significantly longer hours than their nonlabeled peers on the same assignments. JJ commented, "People spent 2 or 3 hours on this paper. I spent 20 hours, easily." Porter observed, "I would turn in papers to my professors, papers I had spent, like, days on. And people around me were spending, like, hours."

Four informants indicated the workload went unrecognized. JJ said, "I think usually that I turn things in late and . . . they [professors] think I'm not good, that I'm just putzin' around." Rocky Top said, "I don't think my professors know how much, how hard I work."

Eight informants noted the excessive workload did not produce a commensurate product and feared the mediocre quality would reflect laziness. Bering noted, "I think that they might even think that I'm lazy, and that I don't spend time." Porter commented, "I have put so much into this and you can't even tell."

Eight of the 10 PC students spoke of the crucial role of the LD specialist in their success. This appears in part from her ability to see their perspective and recognize their workload. . . . Mac noted the professor's attitude toward him "totally turned around" when the LD specialist intervened and explained the situation to the professor who then allowed Mac to demonstrate his course mastery privately. The professor thus came to understand Mac as a dedicated student. Some regarded the LD specialist as a transformative figure. . . .

Finally, five of 11 informants experienced an *LD rapport* where communication flowed easily and without disability among them. Lea detailed a conversation style in the LD community at the PC, "We're all speaking in fragments at the exact same time, on top of one another . . . We are speaking this weird piece language, and everyone gets it." Porter said, "We're in the same zone, you know?" Beth said, "People who don't have learning disability can't understand what I'm doing."

## RQ II: How Does This Subset of Students View Themselves Based on Their Experiences?

All these informants emphasized they had a healthy cognitive difference rather than a disability and 9 of 11 informants used the term learning difference at some point in the interviews to reference themselves. Only the CC informant used the term *learning disabled* to describe herself saying, "I say I have a learning disability which basically means that I learn differently than other people."

Ten of [11] informants spoke of being misunderstood by faculty. For example, Lea noted those labeled with LD were seen as "weird," "wacky," "not quite on the ball," and "not getting it together like they could if they really pushed the pedal to the metal." . . . When Sarah sought testing for dyslexia, one professor commented to her, "I think people just do it nowadays to get medicine for it." Beth's professor told her "Well, I don't know if you need to be taking this class if you have a learning disability." . . . Isaac and JJ viewed themselves as ideal students (hardworking, committed to scholarship, etc.) but argued the college could not accept them as such because the labels "LD" and "ideal" were incompatible. . . .

## RQ III: What Has Been the Experience of This Subset of College Students . . . in the Process of Assessment and Accommodations?

. . . Five themes emerged . . . (a) positive and negative testing experiences, (b) surprise at the LD label, (c) validation of intelligence, (d) not receiving adequate information from the testing process, and (e) reluctance to use accommodations.

Three informants had positive experiences with the testing stemming from the novelty of first time testing and anticipating discovering what was "wrong." Positive experiences came with flattering remarks from the test administrator. For example, Sarah commented, "I was giving these really good stories and she [clinician] was just blown away by them." However, those who enjoyed testing indicated they would not want to repeat the process.

Five of 11 informants reported strong negative reactions to assessment testing. Negative experiences included emotional and physical pain (apparently related to cognitive exhaustion but this is not clear). Comments included, "It was so painful," "I felt awful and then I went home and cried," "It was horrible," and, "Oh, I hate them [assessment tests]. With a passion."

Some informants were surprised to be labeled with LD. Three had previously attributed their academic difficulties to being lazy or stupid before testing. Lea commented, "Well, I've learned about it that I'm not stupid."

All 11 participants felt pride at having their intellects clinically validated and often reminded themselves of their IQ scores or percentile ranking in times of alienation.

Eight participants reported not receiving enough information (or were not able to recall enough information) from the assessment to clearly understand how the LD impacted their daily living. For example, Sarah said, "I know that I have dyslexia, but I don't really understand what that means." . . .

Finally, 9 of the 10 informants who were granted accommodations expressed reluctance to ask for them. JJ said, "I feel like I can never ask for an extension because I feel like I don't . . . don't deserve it or something." Isaac commented, "I kind of feel like you're slacking, like you're failing in some way, which, [pause] for me, is one of the hardest things to get over . . . I'm not giving up, I'm not giving in . . . I'm just getting the help I deserve." . . . Kai was reluctant to ask for accommodations for fear "that they'll see me as different and not the same as the other students. Inferior almost."

In addition to their reluctance to ask for accommodations, five informants devalued the work accomplished with them. Lea said, "I feel like the less people utilize accommodations, the more valued their work is." . . .

## RQ IV: What Does This Subset of College Students . . . See as Barriers to Their Access of Higher Education?

[O]ther barriers facing these informants included difficulties with (a) organizing concepts for reading and writing, (b) oral and written comprehension, (c) verbal communication, and (d) having a different way of thinking than nonlabeled peers.

Six informants spoke of difficulties with organizing concepts. Mac said, "I have trouble funneling all my concepts into sentences" adding, "I can get it out, but it takes forever. I write paragraph-long sentences. I cannot put periods in there." Rocky Top explained when it comes to organizing concepts, "I literally can't do it . . . I've never been explained how I can improve this." . . . Narrowing large texts and selecting key information to write papers was another source of organizing difficulties. JJ said, "The point is, is everything's important to me, so making an outline that's only supposed to be like two pages . . . I have no idea. It's all important . . ." . . .

Four informants also spoke of verbal communication challenges (potentially related to organizing concepts). For example, Mac said, "I don't talk much at all. And I definitely don't talk under pressure, in class . . . I just like, freeze up." Sarah said, "I had these great things to say, but they just never came out right."

Finally, six informants indicated they experienced a *different way of thinking* than nonlabeled peers. . . . Porter explained, "My brain is just like a pomegranate and they want it to be like an orange." Mac's different way of thinking drove him to contextualize new knowledge. Mac said, "I need to see the process, but they wanted you to just look at the equation and just associate the number, instead of seeing why."

## RQ V: What Do This Subset of College Students . . . View as Their Accommodation Needs?

Participants indicated they needed: (a) self-understanding (including their different way of thinking), (b) traditional accommodations, (c) writing assistance, (d) organization strategies, and (e) visual strategies.

Ten of 11 informants felt self-understanding was a key strategy to overcome barriers. This understanding often came through the LD community group. For example, Lea said,

> Meeting other people and seeing myself in them and seeing, "oh, my god," that's the thing we share in common and it's not a flaw in me or something that I need to work out. It's like a way of being in the world. And when I see [it] in other people, it's like I like it in them.

Lea added, "It's not about how we fix ourselves with that group, it's like, how do we get this system to give us what we need. What do we need?". . .

Seven informants spoke of overcoming barriers with traditional accommodations, such as extra time on exams/papers, audio books, note takers, and tutors, whereas three benefited from medication for ADD/ADHD. Mac said, "Without the medication, like, I can get to the library and [pause] who knows what happens, it's like rolling the dice."

Five informants sought writing assistance. Rocky Top commented, "I work hard, I get tutors, I get note takers, I have an editor that does all of my papers for me." . . .

Five informants overcame barriers by using systems for organization. . . . Rocky Top commented that although she cannot learn to organize concepts she is otherwise an "organizational freak" commenting, "I make lists of everything and they are everywhere." Beth remarked, "I have to write everything down, and get everything organized, things have to be in little organized compartments."

Finally, five informants used visual strategies to overcome barriers such as multicolor highlighting, drawing outlines, and using visual imagery (metaphor) for organizing, learning, and remembering. Porter used the metaphor of a rug to narrow information for a paper saying, "When you write a paper you're not writing about the rug. You're writing about one, like, the cream in the rug. And pulling that out for people.". . .

## Implications for Practice and Future Research

The issue of students labeled with LD being reluctant to ask for accommodations for fear of triggering discrimination is a serious matter. Adequate studies now demonstrate those labeled with LD in higher education do fear discrimination. But the degree to which it is present is not yet known. Larger scale quantitative studies need to be conducted to confirm if the discrimination is real and to what degree it might be experienced. These should be followed by qualitative studies exploring the nature and context of the discrimination and how those who experience it believe it should be addressed.

Universities might enhance educational success of their students labeled with LD through university-wide diversity training to raise awareness of LD, emphasize the importance of accommodations, and illuminate potential discrimination. Such training should be grounded in a basic disability theory where the social cause of the disability is identified, where normal human variation is recognized, and where the voice of those labeled with LD informs the training. Socially constructed disability can also be addressed in the development of democratic LD communities (not to be confused with therapy groups) on campuses where those labeled with LD can gather as citizens, identify problems, develop strategies, and speak on their own behalf. The role of the LD specialist could also be instrumental in both community building and diversity training. . . .

The issue of assessment testing also has implications. [F]uture studies need to investigate the psychological, emotional, and economic impact this testing might have on the population of those required to undergo it. It is not yet clear to what degree this testing has unrecognized, unintended consequences for those experiencing it especially in light of their needing to repeat it every 3 years. [F]uture studies need to investigate how well those undergoing testing are given beneficial information from it and to what degree they are invited to collaborate in determining accommodations. Finally, action research studies should inquire as to the feasibility of engaging disability theory to inform new policies and revise existing ones. Such studies could also inquire as to the possibility of replacing some aspects of diagnostic assessment and special accommodations with universal access. For example, if audio texts were available to any student paying the copyright fee and duplication costs then there would be no need for expensive diagnosis, labeling, and the resulting stigma. . . .

## Conclusion

The finest accommodations based on the most sophisticated science will have no value if intolerance denies their use. I believe the most important change that can be made for students labeled with LD in education today is to grant them the agency to speak of the disabling force of discrimination. Those labeled with LD need the opportunity to gather of their own accord, share experience, discover an identity, and find a collective voice with which to turn outward and claim their place as equal citizens in the democracy. As it is for the birth of any newly recognized community this move will be a slow and arduous one. The journey to self-representation will be more complex than simply gathering into community and taking the floor for those whose intellect has gone unrecognized and whose true identity brings suspicion and stigma.

We must awaken to one another, to the essence of the phenomenon we share, and shatter the silence together. . . .

Melana Z. Vickers  **NO**

# Accommodating College Students with Learning Disabilities: ADD, ADHD, and Dyslexia

**S**can an undergraduate lecture hall at any U.S. college or university, and odds are that two out of every 100 students there will have Attention Deficit Disorder (ADD), Attention Deficit Hyperactivity Disorder (ADHD), or another learning disability such as dyslexia. These students are entitled to ask for special academic treatment under federal disability law. Such "accommodation" can include extra time to take exams, alternative exam formats such as oral or take-home, and classroom assistance such as the help of a note taker.

In the last decade, the proportion of undergraduates designated as learning disabled (LD) or as having ADD/ADHD has almost doubled, to reach more than 2 percent of the total U.S. undergraduate population, or 394,500 students. These figures do not include those disabled by mental retardation, autism, brain injuries, and other severe conditions, which are not considered in this paper. At colleges and universities that attract more affluent students, the numbers of LD and ADD/ADHD are even higher as a percentage of undergraduates. Most of the LD and ADD/ADHD (hereafter shortened to ADD) students are white males.

It would be natural for legally mandated special treatment of the LD and ADD students to rise along with their numbers. But the special treatment appears to be rising even more rapidly than the number of students. [At] the University of North Carolina at Chapel Hill, the number of LD and ADD students seeking eligibility for accommodations has almost doubled since 2002 and has grown eightfold since the 1980s. What's more, the rate of growth is still accelerating.

The diagnosis and accommodation of cognitive disabilities have helped some students a great deal. Students who in the past were unable to perform well now have the opportunity to achieve their true potential. Yet the accommodation of LD and ADD college students is becoming controversial, because neither all the diagnoses, nor all the accommodations, are perceived as legitimate. Some professors have spoken out against accommodating students whose condition doesn't warrant the special treatment, and many others have complained privately about the power and secrecy of the disabilities offices that decide whether students are to be accommodated.

The American Association of University Professors (AAUP) has published calls for reform. Organizations that administer national, standardized entrance exams such as the College Board have been criticized in the media and by scholars for their accommodation policies. And as the news reports of well-to-do students obtaining unwarranted LD or ADD diagnoses for the sole purpose of obtaining academic accommodations multiply, other students are likely to speak out against the practice.

The issue will gain new attention . . . when the U.S. District Court for the Western Division of Kentucky will reconsider a case called *Jenkins v. National Board of Medical Examiners*. The case involves a medical student (Jenkins) with a reading disability who has received accommodations on exams in his past schooling and now seeks accommodations, including extra time, on his medical school exams. A lower court denied the accommodations, but a federal appeals court . . . ordered the court to reconsider its decision and to re-evaluate whether the student is disabled under new, looser definitions of learning disability signed into law in . . . 2008 as amendments to the Americans with Disabilities Act.

If the lower court reverses itself, accommodations in colleges nationwide are likely to expand. There is, however, an "out." Postsecondary institutions may seek exemptions under the new amendments to the Americans with Disabilities Act. Besides redefining disability more loosely, the amendments state that postsecondary institutions may be exempted from the new language if they can show that it would cause them to fundamentally alter the nature of the academic services involved. Such an exemption could keep schools from having to accommodate students under the new standards. Even so, some professors see the current accommodations as an infringement on their freedom to set academic standards for their students. . . .

This paper will review the controversy over ADD and LD accommodations and suggest how schools might better address this growing problem. Until now, the issue has had a low profile, both because of federal laws that keep the details of a student's accommodation private and because faculty members have avoided discussing a problem affecting disabled students for fear of being viewed as politically incorrect. Indeed, few faculty members were willing to be interviewed on the record for this paper. . . .

# Background

No other disability has seen as dramatic a rise in numbers of diagnoses in recent decades as have LD and ADD. In 2006, fully 5.6 percent of all Americans aged 3–21 and enrolled in public education (preschool through high school) were diagnosed with LD or ADD, up from 3.6 percent of that population in 1981. By contrast, the proportion of Americans aged 3–21 with hearing, visual, orthopedic, and other impairments has stayed steady over the same period, at about 0.1 percent apiece. Speech and language impairments rose slightly from 2.9 percent to 3 percent, and mental retardation has been cut in half from 2 percent to 1 percent of this population. Autism has grown to 0.5 percent of this school-age population, up from 0.1 percent in 1995–96, the frst year it was measured.

The National Institutes of Health (NIH) define ADD/ADHD as a disorder whose symptoms include difficulty in staying focused and paying attention, difficulty in controlling behavior, and hyperactivity. NIH defines learning disabilities, including dyslexia, as disorders that affect the ability to understand or use spoken or written language, do mathematical calculations, coordinate movements, or direct attention. School-aged children are diagnosed with these disorders by licensed psychologists or doctors who use as their guide the *Diagnostic and Statistical Manual of Mental Disorders* of the American Psychiatric Association. . . .

Since there is no single test to determine whether a child has such a disorder, there can be—and there is—great variance in the diagnoses from specialist to specialist and from demographic group to demographic group.

The LD and ADD diagnoses are not randomly distributed, either in the school-age population or in the postsecondary population. An undergraduate student with ADD or LD is exponentially more likely to be white, male, and from a family with high income and college-educated parents, than female, nonwhite, or with parents with lower income or level of education. There are no recorded Asian undergraduates disabled by ADD, and only 0.7 percent of Asian students have a learning disability, according to government data. Only 1.6 percent of disabled Latinos are disabled by ADD, 5.8 percent by learning disabilities, or 7.4 percent in total. In contrast, white undergraduates with ADD represent 7.7 percent of the white disabled population, and 5.8 percent of the LD population. For black, disabled undergraduates, the numbers are 3.8 percent ADD, and 1.2 percent LD.

The diagnosis numbers suggest several possibilities. For one, white male undergraduates from upper-income, high-education families may be disproportionately afflicted by ADD and LD. Alternatively, they may be overdiagnosed. Other possibilities are that nonwhites and lower-income, lower-educated undergraduates are underdiagnosed or that they are not predisposed to ADD and LD. Whatever the case, the unevenness of the distribution of the diagnosis—and thus of accommodations that can be acquired with the diagnosis—adds contentiousness in an area of mental health that has seen a high degree of controversy in recent years. . . .

Regional distinctions in the proportions of ADD and LD diagnoses are evident as well. The disabled undergraduate population in New England colleges and universities is 22.8 percent LD or ADD. By contrast, in the Plains region, it is 15.1 percent. The variations aren't huge, but they raise questions about the reliability of the diagnoses. . . .

Perhaps the biggest changes driving the diagnoses were the Americans with Disabilities Act of 1990 (ADA), the Individuals with Disabilities Education Improvement Act of 1997 (IDEA), and its reauthorization and revision in 2004. Along with the Rehabilitation Act of 1973, these federal laws mandate that disabled students from age 3 to 21 (but to a lesser degree college-age) must be provided with services, monitoring, assessment, and other aspects of treatment in publicly funded education. By mandating services and treatment, the laws have driven up the number of school mental health professionals and raised the level of awareness of teachers. Many actively seek to identify and assist students who they suspect should have their learning abilities assessed.

The rise in LD and ADD diagnoses has stirred controversy. One reason is evidence that some diagnoses are illegitimate. Various news organizations including *ABC News* and *USA Today* have reported that for a price it's possible to secure an illegitimate ADD diagnosis in order to obtain academic advantage. Scholarly journals have also studied the topic of what one termed the "undesirable incentives to seek diagnosis"—in order to obtain extra time for taking exams, for instance. A psychologist in California advertises his diagnostic services online at testaccommodations.com, with his principal message being that an ADD or LD diagnosis can provide extra time for testing for the SAT as well as professional programs such as medical school or law school. . . .

The director of disability services at UNC-Chapel Hill, Jim Kessler, says that "oh yes, you can" buy an LD diagnosis, and that one can therefore buy accommodations as well. He adds, however, that it would require "a lot of work" for an otherwise nonqualifying student to buy the diagnosis and the accommodation, and that those who do it are "going to be such a small, small group of people." He says that this concern is tiny in the greater scheme of issues facing the disabled and that professors or other observers who are concerned about such illegitimate accommodations "need to get a life."

## How to Obtain Accommodations

To obtain accommodations, students must apply to college disabilities offices. To use typical language from a disabilities office website, an LD or ADD student may request accommodations to "overcome limitations that keep him or her from meeting the demands of college or university life."

Such accommodations can include providing note takers or scribes who write what the student dictates, converting textbooks or course packs into accessible mediums such as audio recordings, giving extended time on tests, alternative forms of tests (i.e., using scribes, tape recorders, computers, or oral administration of the test) or alternative locations for tests (such as a quiet room for one person), a lessened load of courses while having full-time status, and course substitutions.

In order to qualify for such accommodations, the student must provide the college's disabilities services office with evidence of the disability and how it limits the student. The University of North Carolina-Chapel Hill requires a "description of *current substantial limitations* as they relate to meeting the various demands of University life" and a documented discussion (typically from a medical professional and a school professional) of academic achievement in the last two to three years and how it has been affected by the disability.

College disabilities websites typically make clear that the threshold for special treatment in college is higher than it was in elementary and high school, and that accommodations aren't automatic for students who had received them in K-12. The UNC-Chapel Hill site notes that the medical documentation must address the student's current level of functioning. Having had IEPs (Individualized Education Plans, mandated by law for disabled students in grade school), 504 Plans (mandated by the Rehabilitation Act of 1973), and Summary of Performance plans (which discuss the student's readiness for postsecondary education, and are described in the IDEA Act of 2004), provides historical evidence of accommodations but these are generally not considered sufficient to make a student eligible for services. . . .

The student identifies himself or herself to the disabilities office voluntarily, then follows up with the documentation. A single administrator or a committee then decides if the student can qualify for disability services. If so, a disabilities expert meets with the student to determine what services, including accommodations, are warranted. The office then sends the student's relevant professor(s) a note on the need for the accommodation on such-and-such a date or over such-and-such a period. The paperwork does not describe the disability, only the requirement for accommodation.

Of all disabled students on a campus (orthopedically disabled, vision-impaired, hearing-impaired, depressed, etc.) statistics show that the LD and ADD students are the most likely to receive disability-related services. Nationally, 51.1 percent of LD and ADD students receive services (most likely accommodations) on campus, compared with 19 percent of mobility-impaired students, and 22 percent of visually or hearing-impaired students.

These data suggest several things. First, the ADD and LD population is more inclined than any other disabled group to request special services and also to receive them. The reason may be that the adjustments made for, say, physically or visually impaired populations—ramps, Braille signs, and the like—exist as permanent structures whose presence doesn't need to be requested by a disabled group; they're part of the campus universal design. By contrast, the academic accommodations have to be requested student-by-student. . . .

## The Rules for Higher Education

Because of the different federal laws under which colleges and K-12 schools operate, some students who were eligible for accommodations/special treatment and services in K-12, and even when taking their SAT exam, find that they are not eligible for accommodations or services in college. Postsecondary institutions are not governed by the Individuals with Disabilities Education Improvement Act of 2004, which mandates services and intervention for students with special needs and disabilities in K-12 education.

Rather, higher education is governed by Section 504 of the Rehabilitation Act of 1973 and also the Americans with Disabilities Act. These are civil rights statutes, as opposed to education statutes, requiring that all postsecondary institutions make reasonable and necessary modifications to rules, policies, and practices to prevent discrimination and ensure access and opportunity for students with disabilities. "Equal access and opportunity" means the same access and opportunity available to the general population. Disability is defined under the ADA as "a physical or mental impairment that substantially limits one or more of the major life activities of such individual" who is disabled.

The requirement for "equal access and opportunity" is more uncertain and difficult to put into practice with respect to academic services than with, say, getting a physically disabled student to the second story of a building or to view a film. Until the ADA was amended in 2008, the threshold for providing accommodation for LD or ADD was that the student must prove not only that the disability exists but also that the disability prevents functioning in a given academic setting (say, a lecture, lab, or exam) at a level equal to that of the general population.

Some campuses appear more willing to grant accommodations than others. UNC-Chapel Hill turned down only one applicant for disability services, including accommodations, last year. By contrast, the University of North Alabama turns down half its applicants for disability services. . . . If more data were available on accommodations at various colleges, their differing rates of refusal would be easier to measure.

The difference from one college to the next also has to do with the different application processes. As noted, UNC-Chapel Hill has a committee that reviews the initial applications for services, but the decision whether to grant an accommodation is made by an individual disabilities expert. Other North Carolina colleges use individual administrators, not committees, to review disabilities cases.

Leaving the decision to a single administrator is the prevailing practice across the country. Yet that is where some of the trouble begins. A 2007 report by a coalition of LD and ADD advocacy groups and mental health professionals found that the disability experts in these offices do not always apply a consistent or legally rigorous standard in judging eligibility for accommodations. The report from the National Joint Committee on Learning Disabilities says that:

> at the postsecondary level, there is a lack of uniformity in determining whether an individual is eligible as a person with a disability and in identifying needed supplemental services and accommodations for access. There are no consistent or agreed upon principles related to interpretation of data and information to determine student eligibility, access to services, and appropriate accommodations.

This report, *The Documentation Disconnect for Students with Learning Disabilities: Improving Access to Postsecondary Disability Services*, also notes that "[s]econdary and postsecondary institutions differ in their programs and expectations . . . [and] educational decisions are made by postsecondary personnel with varying qualifications.". . .

Among the kinds of documentation sought is evidence that the applicant's level of intelligence and level of academic achievement are several standard deviations apart. This "discrepancy model" type of documentation demonstrates that the applicant's ability to achieve the level of academic performance typically associated with his or her level of intelligence would be impaired if the applicant's disability were not accommodated. . . .

On the majority of campuses where individuals, not committees, decide whether to grant accommodations, there remains concern about their fairness and legitimacy. Transparent, committee-based processes would ensure greater uniformity in decision making. A committee process would also provide a sturdier base from which to defend a decision to refuse a request for accommodation, if the refusal were appealed.

# Faculty Views of Accommodation

For the most part, professors accept and cooperate with the accommodations system, this author's interviews suggest. Indeed, UNC-Chapel Hill disabilities administrators could think of only a handful of cases in the last two decades where professors disputed an accommodations request. The coordinator of UNC-Chapel Hill's Academic Success Program for Students with LD and ADHD, Theresa Maitland, explains that "[i]t's very rare to meet someone who isn't cooperative because in today's world these disabilities touch everyone. Often these professors have children or a grandchild who has these conditions, or they may have them themselves."

The experience of UNC-Chapel Hill history professor Richard Kohn is consistent with that assessment: In his 18 years at UNC, Kohn has found the staff of the disabilities services offices "reasonable in their recommendations, requirements, and behavior." He says that the offices "have extraordinary power, or at least used to: they can and probably occasionally do compel faculty to abide by their ruling." But he adds that "the bother to us faculty is truly minor."

But whether professors' cooperation comes about because all professors agree with an institution's LD and ADD accommodations policy or because some choose not to oppose it publicly for fear of the consequences of their opposition is far less clear.

A 2008 survey of 192 professors at a large Midwestern university on the subject of accommodations for LD students shows that some professors are ambivalent about whether testing and other accommodations of LD students are fair to students without accommodations. . . . Moreover, . . . professors were somewhat unwilling to provide major accommodations to students, including extra credit assignments, fewer assignments, reduced reading, or a different grading curve. [P]rofessors were somewhat willing to provide test accommodations. . . .

This author's interviews found similar results, albeit from a smaller sample. Few professors interviewed by this author were willing to have their names associated with criticism of the accommodations system, or even to be quoted anonymously on the subject. The criticism itself was forthcoming, however. Faculty members said that they thought that criticism of current accommodation practices was widely shared but unlikely to surface publicly. In the prevailing inclusive and egalitarian context of most colleges, their colleagues would want to avoid being associated with a position that may be construed as being anti-disabled. Several professors also noted that disabilities services offices are very powerful and that when the professors had had occasion to choose between trying to oppose their decisions or backing down, they had chosen simply to back down.

The role faculty members play in the accommodations process is one of implementation, not of judging the validity of the request. Their role is to agree to give the student the extra exam time or other accommodation, produce an exam several days early and submit it to the disabilities office, or prepare written lecture notes for the student, and the like.

To illustrate with a typical example involving exams, a student whose request for an accommodation has been granted by the disabilities office takes a paper form to his or her professor and requests extra time on an exam or a noise-free exam room, or, in the case of UNC-Chapel Hill, has a letter from the disabilities office e-mailed directly to the professor. The professor signs the paperwork, and then must plan accordingly. The professor must prepare a copy of the exam several days early to be sent to the disabilities office. Then, the student may start the exam, say, two hours earlier than the rest of the class, isolated from the other students so as not to share the exam's contents to those who are starting at the scheduled exam time. Or, if the accommodation relates to distractability, the student may start at the scheduled exam time but in a noise-free room. Other requests might include giving a disabled student advance notice of a pop quiz, providing extra time for submitting assignments, or submitting written lecture notes for the student.

It's easy to see how such requests might raise concerns among professors about cheating. UNC-Chapel Hill's Kessler recounts that one student's accommodation, which allowed the student to take an exam home to complete, led to questions about whether the student would cheat. Also, professors noted in interviews that when accommodated students don't begin the exam at the same time as the remaining students, or are not sequestered for the full duration of the other students' exam, they fear that the student could compromise its contents.

Other concerns were more minor, including the fact that sometimes professors must respond to students who bring in their accommodations forms a day or two before the accommodation is needed, requiring a scramble to produce an exam at the required deadline. It was also noted that students overall, in recent years, appear to have a sense of entitlement—albeit expressed politely—that students in the past did not. . . .

A final aspect of accommodations that raises concerns among professors is the accommodation's secrecy, or the accommodated student's right to privacy. For a start, under the federal Family Educational Rights and Privacy Act of 1974, the student's type of disability is kept secret from the professor and is not noted on the accommodations paperwork. Theoretically, a professor could request that the disabilities office supply more information about the student's disability—for example, by sharing the educational and medical documentation supporting the student's request for accommodations. The professor could do this on the grounds that he or she has a "legitimate educational interest" in understanding the disability's effects, according to an interpretation of the law provided by the U.S. Department of Education after some confusion was reported. But the department adds that a university or college would be free to deny such requests by having a policy against them.

Some professors chafe at this secrecy, objecting to changing their academic standards for one student in response to an assertion that is backed by secret evidence known only to the disabilities office, and not by verifiable fact. (Other professors said they have no interest in knowing about the student's condition, because they have no qualifications for assessing it.)

The wider problem with the secrecy surrounding the student's disability, however, is that professors must in turn keep the accommodation secret as well. Richard L. Stroup, an economics professor at North Carolina State University in Raleigh, says that professors are told by the disabilities office not to discuss accommodations with anyone. He and other professors interpret that to mean that if someone asks for an assessment of the student—in the form of a graduate school or job recommendation, for instance—the professor is obligated to withhold the information that the student had, say, twice as much time on exams as other students did. Stroup questions the propriety of drawing a professor into that sort of evasion. He also says that the accommodations process may not ultimately be beneficial to disabled students, because they acquire a false sense that they will be accommodated in the workplace, for instance by being given extra time to complete a task that is time-sensitive.

To be sure, a more open process for granting accommodations won't address all professors' concerns. But a review of accommodations policies could lead to explicit policy changes that would address the sense some professors have that they being required to mislead third parties on the student's behalf. In addition, a committee system for granting accommodations in which professors could participate would tamp down the latent criticism that the accommodations process can be unfair. Such reforms wouldn't address all the controversy surrounding accommodations, however. Legal issues, questions about legitimacy of the diagnoses, as well as students' questions about fairness, would remain. . . .

## ADA Amendments

A second legal development is likely to have a great infuence as well. In the fall of 2008, Congress amended the Americans with Disabilities Act, lowering the standard for assessing whether a person is "substantially limited in performing a major life activity" (to use ADA language), and therefore disabled. Congress's amendment, signed into law by President George W. Bush, states that its purpose is "to reject the standards enunciated by the Supreme Court in *Toyota Motor Manufacturing, Kentucky, Inc. v. Williams* . . . (2002)." Specifcally, Congress rejected the finding that

> the terms "substantially" and "major" in the definition of disability under the ADA "need to be interpreted strictly to create a **demanding** standard for qualifying as disabled," and that to be substantially limited in performing a major life activity under the ADA "an individual must have an impairment that prevents or severely restricts the individual from doing activities that are of central importance to most people's daily lives."

In practice, this change has significantly lowered the threshold for accommodation. . . .

As if that language in the amendment weren't enough to keep lawyers at postsecondary institutions busy, the amendment also states that "reasonable modifications in policies, practices, or procedures shall be required" to comply with its language—with a key exception. That exception occurs when "an entity can demonstrate that making such modifications in policies, practices, or procedures, including academic requirements in postsecondary education, would fundamentally alter the nature of the goods, services, facilities, privileges, advantages, or accommodations involved."

In other words, colleges and universities may be exempt from the new, looser definition of disability if they can show that applying it would alter the nature of their academic program and standards. Certainly, some professors might argue that the looser definition would indeed affect their academic freedom to assess their students fairly and according to their existing standards. . . .

Unless the institutions successfully use the loophole provided by the amended ADA, this legal trend may facilitate more eligibility for accommodations in college and university and bring with it associated costs in terms of personnel needed to administer the requests, faculty time in providing the additional required materials, and legal work required to comply with the new standards. At a time when both education budgets and budgets for disabilities programs are being cut by state governments, it's difficult to see how the changes to accommodations policy mandated by new federal law can be implemented with any ease.

## Fairness Questions

Disabilities services experts on campus recognize that there is a risk that the accommodations they offer may be perceived by non-disabled students as unfair, particularly if the accommodations are granted too freely or subjectively, or if the requests come from students who are improperly qualified for them. The website of the disabilities services office at the University of Mississippi has gone so far as to post an article saying that over-accommodation of students who aren't entitled to them "may contribute to prejudices, lower academic standards, and fuel backlash by students and faculty that cannot be easily dispelled.". . .

[T]his author was unable to find students who were willing to talk about the fairness issue for this study. It would seem unlikely that the reason for the silence is full agreement with the policies. The director of disability services at UNC-Chapel Hill, Jim Kessler, said he hadn't heard of any overt student backlash against accommodations and attributed that to the fact that the accommodations such as extra time for exams are arranged privately, without other students knowing about them. He did note, though, that disabled students who do not participate in exams with the rest of the class face the risk of being asked by fellow students about their perennial absence during tests. . . .

One can see how controversy could arise over the demographic imbalance in ADD and LD diagnoses—as indicated earlier, the preponderance of these diagnoses are for white males from high-income families. Some minority and economically disadvantaged students may be entitled to disabilities diagnoses but don't receive them, either because their high schools didn't offer them the services that would have led to their diagnosis or because their parents couldn't afford private diagnoses or weren't aware of the issue to begin with. Thus, they might perceive the demographic imbalance as unfair. It's also worth recalling here that experts ranging from the UNC-Chapel Hill disability services director to administrators at the College Board say that students can and do buy diagnoses and accommodations. . . .

## Recommendations and Conclusion

Learning disabilities and ADD are an important issue in campus life, if only because of the growing number of students diagnosed with these disabilities. The accommodation of these students through extra time on exams and other such provisions is increasing. Yet it is not widely discussed in public, for a variety of reasons including fear of being seen as anti-disabled.

But the issue is evoking controversy. As newspaper reports, scholarly publications, legal battles, and a handful of writings by professors imply, not everyone is in agreement about the degree to which LD and ADD students are accommodated, or should be accommodated, in higher education.

The controversy won't end anytime soon—indeed, there's a high probability it will grow if a less stringent disabilities law and upcoming legal decisions trigger more LD and ADD accommodations on campuses. Meanwhile, well-meaning administrators will be caught between a desire to serve the genuine needs of their disabled students and the need to avoid unfairness by granting accommodations to students who don't really deserve them.

At the very least or as an initial step, administrators should . . . open up their accommodations processes for closer scrutiny. They should include faculty members on panels that consider initial applications for accommodations— not just for appeals—so that legitimate concerns about academic quality and fairness can be addressed. Schools should have strict standards for determining eligibility and produce data on the numbers of accommodations granted, refused, and appealed per year.

Reporting on the numbers of requests for accommodation that are granted will reveal inconsistencies in ADA enforcement across campuses. It will also force openness on the subject while preserving the individual privacy of disabled students. It's surprising that the federal government doesn't require such reporting already.

A radical alternative would be to open up the accommodations to every student, where practicable. The idea has been floated among some testing and disabilities experts recently. It would follow the principle—attractive among disabilities experts—of universal design. For example, postsecondary institutions could let all students decide whether to have extra time (time-and-a-half, or double-time, say) on an exam, but make their extra time publicly known by flagging it on their grade reports. Thus, disabled students would have equal opportunity to do well on exams and would be able to avail themselves of accommodations without having to go through the ordeal of applying for them and being accepted or rejected. And other students who want the extra time could have it just by asking. This might help their performance, leveling the academic playing field for all, rather than only for those with a diagnosis, and undercutting any argument that the extra time is unfair. Flagging the grade reports would be a measure of extra time only, rather than a measure of disability, and thus would not be discriminatory.

To be sure, some professors may see time-and-a-half or double-time as unreasonable or impractical. In some fields, such as emergency medicine, it would indeed be unreasonable, because speedy completion of a task is of central importance. but that would not be the case in all areas of study. As accommodations rise, this "universal design" solution may be the greatest leveler of the playing field.

Accommodations of LD and ADD students are here to stay as long as there is an Americans with Disabilities Act and Section 504 of the Rehabilitation Act—and as long as there are students who suffer from impediments to learning. Unfortunately, the potential for abuse of LD and ADD diagnoses, as well as the accommodations process, is here to stay as well. Wise administrators would do well to report more fully on their accommodations process and make it more transparent and rigorous. Only that way can any latent perception of unfairness or compromised standards, whether from faculty or students, be done away with. Such openness would be to the benefit of the campus as a whole and disabled students in particular.

# EXPLORING THE ISSUE

## Should Colleges Be More Accommodating to Students with Disabilities?

## Challenge Questions

- Compare and contrast the positions of the YES and NO selections regarding whether colleges should be more accommodating to students with disabilities.
- Which selection makes the best case for its argument? Why?
- What policies and practices does your college's disability support center utilize? Do counselors think students with disabilities encounter bias and prejudice?
- Acknowledging the difference in laws, what consistent practices can higher education adopt from PreK–12 systems and IDEA?
- How can the information on both sides of this Issue affect the practices of those who teach high school students with disabilities?
- What aspects of universal design are apparent in the classes you teach and the ones you attend? How do they impact teaching and learning for everyone? Which others could be adopted?

## Is There Common Ground?

Denhart and Vickers relate painful struggles and significant confusion about higher education experiences of individuals with invisible disabilities and their faculty. The fields of disability theory/studies (Denhart's philosophical and methodological foundation) and universal design (Vickers' "radical alternative") provide a meeting place for ideas.

## Additional Resources

Baglieri, S., Valle, J. W., Connor, D. J., & Gallagher, D. J. (2011). Disability studies in education: The need for a plurality of perspectives on disability. *Remedial and Special Education, 32*(4), 267–278.

Denhart, H. (2008). Deconstructing barriers: Perceptions of students labeled with learning disabilities in higher education. *Journal of Learning Disabilities, 41*(6), 483–497.

Egan, P. M. & Giuliano, T. A. (2009). Unaccommodating attitudes: Perceptions of students as a function of academic accommodation use and test performance. *North American Journal of Psychology, 11*(3), 487.

Lazarus, S. S., Thurlow, M. L., Lail, K. E., & Christensen, L. (2009). A longitudinal analysis of state accommodations policies: Twelve years of change, 1993-2005. *The Journal of Special Education, 43*(2), 67–80.

Newman, L., Wagner, M., Cameto, R., & Knokey, A. -M. (2009). *The post-high school outcomes of youth with disabilities up to 4 years after high school. A report from the National Longitudinal Transition Study-2 (NLTS2)* (NCSER 2009-3017). Menlo Park, CA: SRI International. Retrieved June 12, 2010 from http://ies.ed.gov/ncser/pdf/20093017.pdf

Newton, P. (2010, July 3). *How easy is it to fake ADHD?* Retrieved August 23, 2011 from www.psychologytoday.com/

Sparks, R. L. & Lovett, B. J. (2009). College students with learning disability diagnoses: Who are they and how do they perform? *Journal of Learning Disabilities, 42*(6), 494–510.

Vickers, M. Z. (2010). *Accommodating college students with learning disabilities: ADD, ADHD, and dyslexia.* Raleigh, NC: The John W. Pope Center. Retrieved March 1, 2010 from www.popecenter.org

# Internet References . . .

## Council for Exceptional Children

The Council for Exceptional Children (CEC) is the largest international professional organization addressing issues surrounding education of students with
disabilities, as well as those who are gifted and talented. CEC's site introduces
you to current events in the field, recent legislative developments, and an array
of specialized divisions focused on particular aspects of special education.

**www.cec.sped.org**

## Technical Assistance Alliance for Parents

The ALLIANCE is a federally funded technical assistance network for parents.
Seven projects support and coordinate over 100 parent training and information centers and community parent resource centers in each state. The website
provides links to each center and helps parents to participate effectively in the
educational lives of their children with disabilities, from infancy through young
adulthood.

**www.taalliance.org**

## Children and Adults with Attention-Deficit/
## Hyperactivity Disorder

Children and Adults with Attention-Deficit/Hyperactivity Disorder (CHADD),
founded in 1987 by families seeking information about this disorder, is now a
national organization linked to a variety of activities. The CHADD website contains extensive information on ADHD and ADD and is helpful to anyone who
wants to learn more about these conditions.

**www.chadd.org**

## Autism Society of America

The mission of the Autism Society of America is to promote lifelong access and
opportunity for all individuals within the autism spectrum, and their families, to
be fully participating, included members of their community. Education, advocacy at state and federal levels, active public awareness, and the promotion of
research form the cornerstones of ASA's efforts.

**www.autism-society.org**

## National Institute of Mental Health

A branch of the National Institutes of Health, the National Institute of Mental
Health (NIMH) is focused on generating and disseminating information regarding mental health conditions.

**www.nimh.nih.gov**

## National Association for Gifted Children

The National Association for Gifted Children is a professional association dedicated to increasing public awareness about gifted learners, their needs, and
appropriate services.

**www.nagc.org**

# Exceptionalities

*E*arlier units focused on global issues regarding the education of children who learn differently than their peers. In addition to the arenas of law, policy, and practice, controversies exist about the reality of particular exceptionalities and the efficacy of unique methodologies. The fervent desire of parents and educators to help children nurtures the development of approaches, which promise success. The challenge of evaluating new ways of thinking will be with us as long as there are children who need extra support to realize their potential. We will face that challenge best when we work collaboratively.

- Do Gifted and Talented Students Need Special Schools?
- Is Mental Health Screening an Unwarranted Intrusion?
- Should the Government Prohibit the Use of Restraint and Seclusion in Schools?
- Is ADHD a Real Disorder?
- Are Evidence-Based Practices Sufficient for Educating Students with Autism?
- Does Working with Parents Have to Be Contentious?

# ISSUE 15

## Do Gifted and Talented Students Need Special Schools?

**YES: John Cloud**, from "Are We Failing Our Geniuses?" *Time Magazine* (vol. 170, no. 9, pp. 41–47, 2007, August 27)

**NO: Susan Winebrenner and Dina Brulles**, from *The Cluster Grouping Handbook* (Free Spirit Publishing, 2008)

---

### Learning Outcomes

**At the conclusion of this issue, readers will be able to:**

- Compare and contrast the positions of the YES and NO selections addressing whether gifted and talented students need specialized schools.
- Describe the strengths and the weaknesses of each side's arguments.
- Identify ways to analyze program options for gifted and talented students.
- Evaluate the options available in your district and state.

---

### ISSUE SUMMARY

**YES:** John Cloud, a staff writer for *Time Magazine* since 1997, profiles a number of extraordinarily gifted young people challenged for the first time in a specialized school that pushes them to reach their potential in a way that public schools could not.

**NO:** Susan Winebrenner and Dina Brulles work with educators to design and deliver cluster-based programs that address the needs of the gifted within their neighborhood school and provide options for a range of students to reach their potential.

T his *Taking Sides* book focuses on individuals who have disabilities and may require 504 plans or special education services. These students struggle with learning, requiring supplemental supports and services to make the progress that comes easily to others.

Another group of exceptional learners also requires attention. These students are at the other end of the spectrum of school success—gifted and/or talented far beyond most of their agemates.

No Child Left Behind defines the gifted and talented as: "students, children, or youth who give evidence of high achievement capability in areas such as intellectual, creative, artistic, or leadership capacity, or in specific academic fields, and who need services and activities not ordinarily provided by the school in order to fully develop those capabilities" (Title IX, Part A, Section 9101(22), p. 544).

There is no U.S. federal requirement to identify, or develop programs for students who have unique gifts and/or talents. Despite their need for programming "not ordinarily provided by the school," these students are not covered by special education law because they do not have disabilities that have a negative impact on their ability to make effective progress in school.

The National Association for Gifted Children (NAGC, 2011) monitors and reports on the status of gifted/talented education. NAGC's *2010–2011 State of the nation in gifted education executive summary* (www.nagc.org) noted that although 26 (of the responding 36) states mandate gifted education, most programming decisions are delegated to individual districts. The consequence is "a crazy quilt collection of services."

Extraordinarily gifted/talented minds have long fascinated psychologists, teachers, and parents. NAGC publishes a comprehensive reference evaluating existing research and indicating pressing needs in a range of topics, from policy to identification to instructional strategies (Plucker & Callahan, *Critical issues and practices in gifted education* 2007).

We each know our own children are brilliant, but who, exactly, is gifted? There is no universal definition. In one key chapter, Miller (P&C, 2008) reviews several ways giftedness is conceptualized. Proponents of Terman look for an IQ score more than two standard deviations above the average of 100. Gardner finds giftedness in one or more of eight independent multiple intelligences, ranging from linguistic to musical to intrapersonal. Renzulli differentiates between the schoolhouse-gifted and those who create/produce original products that impact society. Ruf (*Losing our minds*, 2005) identifies five levels of giftedness, emphasizing the critical need for specialized programming. Without this, students become frustrated with the boredom of everyday work and can appear to have behavior problems.

Educational options range as widely as the conceptualizations of giftedness. A sampling includes early school admission; curriculum acceleration in small classes; acceleration through grade skipping; enrichment activities based on the standard curriculum; home schooling; mentoring (by professionals or older students); correspondence courses; summer institutes; and advanced coursework.

This issue invites you to consider the best way to meet the learning needs of children who are gifted/talented. The authors describe two very different worlds.

In the YES selection, John Cloud explains his belief that the United States is failing our geniuses; stifling them in a bureaucratic system that lacks the knowledge or creativity to support challenging programs. Cloud presents compelling profiles of young learners who have outgrown their neighborhood schools and will wither and fade unless their talents are nurtured and guided. Cloud's students find room to grow at The Davidson Academy, a unique private school focusing exclusively on extraordinarily gifted students.

The Davidson Academy website (www.davidsonacademy.unr.edu) describes the school as designed for the "profoundly gifted," those whose SAT scores are in the top one-tenth of the top 1 percent. Closely linked with the University of Nevada, Reno, Davidson devises "Personalized Learning Plans," designed to guide student experiences at their own level and pace. Socialization with "intellectual peers" is a school goal as is engaging parents in the process of educating their exceptional children.

In the NO selection, Susan Winebrenner and Dina Brulles discuss the Schoolwide Cluster Grouping Model (SCGM): "an inclusion model in which students with exceptional learning needs are integrated into mixed-ability classrooms and teachers are expected to provide appropriate differentiation opportunities for any students who need them." By careful clustering, and attention to teacher professional development, SCGM stimulates the full range of students to flourish without having to leave home.

The model presented by Winebrenner and Brulles provides the benefits of ability grouping without the isolation of tracking. Educators maintain high levels of professional skill, which benefits all learners. Carol Ann Tomlinson, who writes extensively about differentiated instruction, underscores the need to support teachers through the hard work of continuous differentiation.

Efficacy research is not conclusive, partially due to the inability to use control groups, but Schroth (P&C, 2008) finds one absolute: any service is better than none. As described, cluster models benefit a range of students, and more students are identified as high-achievers. They are "financially friendly." On the other hand, students in public special schools with a disciplinary focus outperform gifted peers in all other learning environments. The logistics of residential schools, however, are frequently impractical.

Two other aspects of gifted education demand consideration: underrepresentation of minorities and of those who are twice-exceptional. Both must be addressed.

The underrepresentation of ethnically diverse students in gifted programs is a long-acknowledged fact (Gentry, Hu, & Thomas, P&C, 2008). This is especially the case with African American boys and Latino children. Although Asians are frequently described as "overrepresented" in gifted education, a finer breakdown reveals that this is not uniformly so of all Asian groups. Ford (*Journal for the Education of the Gifted*, 2003) is concerned that the effects of poverty can mask the strengths of a gifted child. She advises a move away from traditional normed IQ tests to alternative measures that take into consideration the complex contexts of student lives.

Context is also critical for twice-exceptional children—those who are gifted and have a disability. An illuminating study by the National Education

Association (www.nea.org/specialed, 2006) described three basic categories of twice-exceptional children. First are those who have been formally identified as gifted, but not as having a disability: their giftedness masks the disability (think of a very bright child with a learning disability). Second are those formally identified as having a disability, but not as gifted: the disability masks the giftedness (consider someone's first impression of Helen Keller). Too often, once a disability has been identified in a twice-exceptional child, attention shifts to the Individuals with Disabilities Education Act (IDEA) and difficulties, with little attention paid to the child's exceptional strengths (Kennedy, Banks, with Grandin, *Bright not broken*, 2011). The third group of children may not have been formally identified under either category: the characteristics combine to present the appearance of an average student.

Concern for gifted education has another dimension given NCLB's target of universal proficiency by 2013–2014. Especially in working class schools, Carnevale (*Education Week*, 2007) warns that gifted students are left behind as the majority struggle to get to "average."

Each of these concerns becomes more compelling when funds are in short supply, locally and federally. Local funding information is gathered biannually by the NAGC. According to the *NAGC Annual Report* (www.nagc.org), "of the 36 reporting states, 10 provided $0 in state funds to support gifted education in 2010–2011; another 4 states spent less than $1 million. . . . Since the last *State of the States* report, 14 states have reduced funding for gifted education."

The sole source of U.S. federal monies has traditionally been a grant competition funded by the Jacob K. Javits Gifted and Talented Student Education Act. According to the Javits Awards website (www.ed.gov/programs/javits/awards. html), "In 2007, the Javits appropriation was cut substantially. As a result, a new competition . . . will not be held. Future competitions are contingent upon future appropriations." In 2008, seven grants (out of 57 proposals) were funded. For the following three years, the wording reads: 2010: No New Awards; 2011: No Funding Available; 2012: No Funding Available.

Cloud challenges Americans to explain why society's commitment to the gifted should not be at least as large as its commitment to athletes, or to those with disabilities. If Americans are committed to leaving no child behind, they must consider their gifted children. Ignoring preparation for their future can lead to lost opportunities for all Americans.

# YES

John Cloud

# Are We Failing Our Geniuses?

## In U.S. Schools, the Highest Achievers Are Too Often Challenged the Least. Why That's Hurting America—and How to Fix It

Any sensible culture would know what to do with Annalisee Brasil. The 14-year-old not only has the looks of a South American model but is also one of the brightest kids of her generation. When Annalisee was 3, her mother Angi Brasil noticed that she was stringing together word cards composed not simply into short phrases but into complete, grammatically correct sentences. After the girl turned 6, her mother took her for an IQ test. Annalisee found the exercises so easy that she played jokes on the testers—in one case she not only put blocks in the correct order but did it backward too. Angi doesn't want her daughter's IQ published, but it is comfortably above 145, placing the girl in the top 0.1% of the population. Annalisee is also a gifted singer: last year, although just 13, she won a regional high school competition conducted by the National Association of Teachers of Singing.

Annalisee should be the star pupil at a school in her hometown of Longview, Texas. While it would be too much to ask for a smart kid to be popular too, Annalisee is witty and pretty, and it's easy to imagine she would get along well at school. But until last year, Annalisee's parents—Angi, a 53-year-old university assistant, and Marcelo, 63, who recently retired from his job at a Caterpillar dealership—couldn't find a school willing to take their daughter unless she enrolled with her age-mates. None of the schools in Longview—and even as far away as the Dallas area—were willing to let Annalisee skip more than two grades. She needed to skip at least three—she was doing sixth-grade work at age 7. Many school systems are wary of grade skipping even though research shows that it usually works well both academically and socially for gifted students—and that holding them back can lead to isolation and underachievement. So Angi home schooled Annalisee.

But Angi felt something was missing in her daughter's life. Annalisee, whose three siblings are grown, didn't have a rich social network of other kids. By 13, she had moved beyond her mother's ability to meaningfully teach her. The family talked about sending her to college, but everyone was hesitant. Annalisee needed to mature socially. By the time I met her in February, she had been having trouble getting along with others. "People are, I must admit it, a lot of times intimidated by me," she told me; modesty isn't among her many talents. She described herself as "perfectionistic" and said other students sometimes had "jealousy issues" regarding her.

The system failed Annalisee, but could any system be designed to accommodate her rare gifts? Actually, it would have been fairly simple (and virtually cost-free) to let her skip grades, but the lack of awareness about the benefits of grade skipping is emblematic of a larger problem: our education system has little idea how to cultivate its most promising students. Since well before the Bush Administration began using the impossibly sunny term "no child left behind," those who write education policy in the U.S. have worried most about kids at the bottom, stragglers of impoverished means or IQs. But surprisingly, gifted students drop out at the same rates as nongifted kids—about 5% of both populations leave school early. Later in life, according to the scholarly *Handbook of Gifted Education,* up to one-fifth of dropouts test in the gifted range. Earlier this year, Patrick Gonzales of the U.S. Department of Education presented a paper showing that the highest-achieving students in six other countries, including Japan, Hungary and Singapore, scored significantly higher in math than their bright U.S. counterparts, who scored about the same as the Estonians. Which all suggests we may be squandering a national resource: our best young minds.

In 2004–05, the most recent academic year for which the National Opinion Research Center (NORC) has data, U.S. universities awarded 43,354 doctorates— more than ever during the 50 years NORC has gathered the data. But the rate of increase in the number of U.S. doctorates has fallen dramatically since 1970, when it hit nearly 15% for the year; for more than a decade, the number of doctorates has grown less than 3.5% a year. The staggering late-1960s growth in Ph.D.s followed a period of increased attention on gifted kids after Sputnik. Now we're coasting.

To some extent, complacency is built into the system. American schools spend more than $8 billion a year educating the mentally retarded. Spending on the gifted isn't even tabulated in some states, but by the most generous calculation, we spend no more than $800 million on gifted programs. But it can't make sense to spend 10 times as much to try to bring low-achieving students to mere proficiency as we do to nurture those with the greatest potential.

We take for granted that those with IQs at least three standard deviations below the mean (those who score 55 or lower on IQ tests) require "special" education. But students with IQs that are at least three standard deviations above the mean (145 or higher) often have just as much trouble interacting with average kids and learning at an average pace. Shouldn't we do something special for them as well? True, these are IQs at the extremes. Of the 62 million school-age kids in the U.S., only about 62,000 have IQs above 145. (A similar number have IQs below 55.) That's a small number, but they appear in every demographic, in every community. What to do with them? Squandered potential is always unfortunate, but presumably it is these powerful young minds that, if nourished, could one day cure leukemia or stop global warming or become the next James Joyce—or at least J.K. Rowling.

In a no-child-left-behind conception of public education, lifting everyone up to a minimum level is more important than allowing students to excel to their limit. It has become more important for schools to identify deficiencies than to cultivate gifts. Odd though it seems for a law written and enacted during a Republican Administration, the social impulse behind No Child Left Behind is radically egalitarian. It has forced schools to deeply subsidize the education of the least gifted, and gifted programs have suffered. The year after the President signed the law in 2002, Illinois cut $16 million from gifted education; Michigan cut funding from $5 million to $500,000. Federal spending declined from $11.3 million in 2002 to $7.6 million this year.

What's needed is a new model for gifted education, an urgent sense that prodigious intellectual talents are a threatened resource. That's the idea behind the Davidson Academy of Nevada, in Reno, which was founded by a wealthy couple, Janice and Robert Davidson, but chartered by the state legislature as a public, tuition-free school. The academy will begin its second year Aug. 27, and while it will have just 45 students, they are 45 of the nation's smartest children. They are kids from age 11 to 16 who are taking classes at least three years beyond their grade level (and in some cases much more; two of the school's prodigies have virtually exhausted the undergraduate math curriculum at the University of Nevada, Reno, whose campus hosts the academy). Among Davidson's students are a former state chess champion, a girl who was a semifinalist in the Discovery Channel Young Scientist Challenge at age 11 (the competition is open to kids as old as 14) and a boy who placed fourth in both the Nevada spelling and geography bees even though he was a 12-year-old competing against kids as old as 15. And last year the school enrolled another talented kid from a town 1,700 miles (some 2,700 km) away: Annalisee Brasil, whose mother moved with her to Reno so Annalisee could attend the school (her father was working in Longview at the time).

The academy is being watched closely in education circles. The Davidsons are well-connected philanthropists who made their fortune in the education-software business—Jan and a friend conceived the hit Math Blaster program in the early 1980s. She and her husband sold Davidson & Associates for roughly $1.1 billion in 1996. They have given millions of dollars to universities and tens of thousands to Republican politicians like George W. Bush and Senator John Ensign of Nevada. Gifted kids often draw only flickering interest from government officials, but Secretary of Education Margaret Spellings attended the Davidson Academy's opening.

At the academy, the battered concept of IQ—complicated in recent years by the idea of multiple intelligences, including artistic and emotional acuity—is accepted there without the encumbrances of politics. The school is a rejection of the thoroughly American notion that if most just try hard enough, we could all be talented. Many school administrators oppose ability grouping on the theory that it can perpetuate social inequalities, but at the Davidson Academy, even the 45 élite students are grouped by ability into easier and harder English, math, and science classes. The school poses blunt questions about American education: Has the drive to ensure equity over excellence gone too far? If so, is the answer to segregate the brightest kids?

# How We See Them

As a culture, we feel deeply ambiguous about genius. We venerate Einstein, but there is no more detested creature than the know-it-all. In one 1996 study from *Gifted Education Press Quarterly*, 3,514 high school students were asked whether they would rather be the best-looking, smartest, or most athletic kids. A solid 54% wanted to be smartest (37% wanted to be most athletic, and 9% wanted to be best looking). But only 0.3% said the reason to be smartest was to gain popularity. We like athletic prodigies like Tiger Woods or young Academy Award winners like Anna Paquin. But the mercurial, aloof, annoying nerd has been a trope of our culture, from Bartleby the Scrivener to the dorky PC guy in the Apple ads. Intellectual precocity fascinates but repels.

Educators have long debated what to do with highly gifted children. As early as 1926, Columbia education professor Leta Hollingworth noted that kids who score between 125 and 155 on IQ tests have the "socially optimal" level of intelligence; those with IQs over 160 are often socially isolated because they are so different from peers—more mini-adults than kids. Reading Hollingworth, I was reminded of Annalisee, who at 13 spoke in clear, well-modulated paragraphs, as though she were a TV commentator or college professor. For an adult, the effect is quite pleasant, but I imagine other kids find Annalisee's precision a bit strange.

In Hollingworth's day, when we were a little less sensitive to snobbery, it wasn't as difficult for high-ability kids to skip grades. But since at least the mid-1980s, schools have often forced gifted students to stay in age-assigned grades—even though a 160-IQ kid trying to learn at the pace of average, 100-IQ kids is akin to an average girl trying to learn at the pace of a retarded girl with an IQ of 40. Advocates for gifted kids consider one of the most pernicious results to be "cooperative learning" arrangements in which high-ability students are paired with struggling kids on projects. Education professor Miraca Gross of the University of New South Wales in Sydney has called the current system a "lockstep curriculum . . . in what is euphemistically termed the 'inclusion' classroom." The gifted students, she notes, don't feel included.

We tend to assume that the highly gifted will eventually find their way—they're smart, right? The misapprehension that genius simply emerges unbidden is related to our mixed feelings about intelligence: we know Alex Rodriguez had to practice to become a great baseball player, and we don't think of special schools for gymnasts or tennis prodigies as élitist—a charge already leveled against the Davidson Academy. But giftedness on the playing field and giftedness in, say, a lab aren't so different. As Columbia education professor Abraham Tannenbaum has written, "Giftedness requires social context that enables it." Like a muscle, raw intelligence can't build if it's not exercised.

People often wonder how to tell if their child is gifted. Truly gifted kids are almost always autodidacts. Take Max Oswald-Selis. He moved to Reno from Sydney with his mother Gael Oswald so that he could attend Davidson. Max is 12. The first time I saw him at the academy, he was reading an article about the Supreme Court. He likes to fence. He loves Latin because "it's a very regimented language. . . . There's probably at least 28 different endings for any given verb, because there's first-, second- and third-person singular and plural for each tense. . . ." He went on like this for some time. Max didn't get along especially well with classmates in Sydney and later Kent, England, where his mother first moved him in search of an appropriate school—and where she says he was beaten on the playground.

Max is Gael's only child, so when he taught himself to read at 3—she says she hadn't even taught him the alphabet—she wasn't sure it was so unusual. Then around age 4, he read aloud from a medical book in the doctor's office, and the doctor recommended intelligence testing. At 4, Max had the verbal skills of a 13-year-old. He skipped kindergarten, but he was still bored, and his mother despaired. No system is going to be able to keep up, she thought.

Gael, a math teacher, began to research giftedness and found that high-IQ kids can become isolated adults. "They end up often as depressed adults . . . who don't have friends or who find it difficult to function," she says. Actually, research shows that gifted kids given appropriately challenging environments—even when that means being placed in classes of much older students—usually turn out fine. At the University of New South Wales, Gross conducted a longitudinal study of 60 Australians who scored at least 160 on IQ tests beginning in the late '80s. Today most of the 33 students who were not allowed to skip grades have jaded views of education, and at least three are dropouts. "These young people find it very difficult to sustain friendships because, having been to a large extent socially isolated at school, they have had much less practice . . . in developing and maintaining social relationships," Gross has written. "A number have had counseling. Two have been treated for severe depression." By contrast, the 17 kids who were able to skip at least three grades have mostly received Ph.D.s, and all have good friends.

At the Davidson Academy, all the kids are skipping ahead quickly—in some cases they completed more than two years of material last year. There's no sixth grade or ninth grade or any grade at the academy, just three tracks ("core," "college prep," and "college prep with research"). The curriculums are individualized and fluid—some students take college-prep English but core-level math. I sat in on the Algebra II class one day, but it wasn't so much a traditional class as a study session guided by the teacher, Darren Ripley. Kids worked from different parts of the textbook. (One 11-year-old was already halfway through; most Americans who take Algebra II do so at 15 or 16.) Occasionally Ripley would show a small group how to solve a problem on the whiteboard, but there was no lecture.

## The Founders

Ultimately the academy's most important gift to its students is social, not academic. One of the main reasons Jan and Bob Davidson founded the school was to provide a nurturing social setting for the highly gifted. Through another project of theirs, the Davidson Institute for Talent Development, each year the Davidsons assist 1,200 highly gifted students around the U.S. who need help persuading their schools to let them skip a grade or who want to meet other kids like them. Often the kids are wasting away in average classes, something that drives Bob Davidson crazy: "I mean, that's criminal to send a kid [who already reads well] to kindergarten. . . . Somebody should go to jail for that! That is emotional torture!"

Davidson, 64, carries an air of peremptory self-assurance. He unself-consciously enjoys his place in the plutocracy. During a tour of the Lake Tahoe manse he and Jan, 63, call Glen Eagle, he showed me his red Ferrari, his private theater, and the two 32-ft. totem poles just inside the entry. They are made from cedar at least 750 years old and feature carvings of the Davidsons and their three kids, who are now grown. Bob sees his work for the gifted as akin to the patronage that sustained the artists and inventors of the Renaissance. His view of giftedness is expressed through simple analogies: Educators often "want people to have equal results. But that's not likely in our world. You know, I would love to be equal to Michael Jordan in my basketball talents, but somehow I never will be."

But such an uncomplicated view of intelligence—one that esteems IQ scores and raw mental power—has had at least one awkward consequence for the Davidson Academy: it doesn't mirror America. Twenty-six of the 45 students are boys; only two are black. (A total of 16 are minorities.) The school is unlikely ever to represent girls and African Americans proportionately because of a reality about IQ tests: more boys score at the high end of the IQ scale (and, it should be said, more score at the low end; girls' IQ variance is smaller). And for reasons that no one understands, African Americans' IQ scores have tended to cluster about a standard deviation below the average—evidence for some that the tests themselves are biased.

Not everyone at the academy embraces a strict IQ-based definition of giftedness. Its curriculum director, Robert Schultz, emphasizes the importance of interpersonal skills, passion, and tenacity in long-term success. Still, the Davidsons point out, correctly, that they are serving an underserved population, kids whose high IQs can make them outcasts. The academy provides a home for them and also functions to check their self-regard since they finally compete day to day with kids who are just as bright. Because everyone at Davidson performs so well, says Claire Evans, 12, "other kids can't say, 'Well, I'm better than you because I did this good.' I did that good too!" (Of course, being labeled prodigies in stories like this one probably inflates them, but researchers have found that outside labeling has less effect on your self-concept than where you fit in with peers you see every day.) Going to Davidson has been an adjustment for kids used to "being on the top of the pile," in the words of Colleen Harsin, 36, the academy's director. Harsin has heard Davidsonians arrive at difficult realizations: "I'm not as smart as I thought I was." "Somebody's better at math than I am. That's never happened."

## A New Isolation?

No matter their IQs, these are still kids on the rocky promontory of adolescence. Hormones crackle; tempers rise. The boys shove; the girls gossip; a kid hits another kid during volleyball. "They are O.K. with the team sports, but this is a group that really loves the individual sports—the rock climbing was a big hit," says Kathy Dohr, the gym teacher. You do get the sense sometimes that the Davidson students are alone together. An older boy who says he was beaten up at other schools told me, "I can't say I have many friends here, but I'm not hated. . . . The school does tend to be pretty much sort of cliquish."

The academy has been good for Annalisee Brasil, even though dividing into two households has been expensive and stressful for the Brasils. She has made friends at the academy and at the university, where this summer she completed a precalculus course so that she can take college calculus in the fall. She has also developed an interest in biochemistry. Socially, Annalisee is finally learning to get along with others in a close-knit setting. "It's been interesting having to deal with that and getting used to, you know, the judgments of other kids," she told me in February. "We get into arguments a lot, because we're all really smart people with opinions, and it doesn't always turn out that great. Sometimes I take things a little too personally. You know, I'm the typical sensitive artist, unfortunately."

The Davidson kids feel less isolated, but have the Davidsons simply created another kind of isolation for their students? When I asked curriculum director Schultz this question, he replied in an e-mail that schools can nurture traits like "civic virtue and community development." And he warned of the alternative: "Essentially these individuals are left to their own devices [in regular schools] and really struggle to find a space for themselves. . . . Some successfully traverse society's pitfalls (for instance, Albert Einstein); others are less successful (for instance, Theodore Kaczynski). In either case, unless performance was noted as deficient (in Einstein's case, he was believed to be a mute) via school personnel, schools did nothing to provide services. This continues today."

But there is something to be said for being left to one's own devices and learning to cope in difficult surroundings. Einstein is a good example: it's a myth that Einstein failed math, but he hated his Munich school, the Luitpold Gymnasium. Like many other gifted kids, he chafed at authority. "The teachers at the elementary school seemed to me like drill sergeants, and the teachers at the gymnasium are like lieutenants," he later said. Einstein was encouraged to leave the school, and he did so at 15. He didn't need a coddling academy to do O.K. later on.

That's not to say the best approach is a cold Dickensian bed. But Einstein's experience does suggest a middle course between moving to Reno for an élite new school and striking out alone at age 15. Currently, gifted programs too often admit marginal, hardworking kids and then mostly assign field trips and extra essays, not truly accelerated course work pegged to a student's abilities. Ideally, school systems should strive to keep their most talented students through a combination of grade skipping and other approaches (dual enrollment in community colleges, telescoping classwork without grade skipping) that ensure they won't drop out or feel driven away to Nevada. The best way to treat the Annalisee Brasils of the world is to let them grow up in their own communities—by allowing them to skip ahead at their own pace. We shouldn't be so wary of those who can move a lot faster than the rest of us.

# Susan Winebrenner and Dina Brulles

**NO**

# *The Cluster Grouping Handbook*

**W**ithin the current politics of education, the focus of most educators is on the learning needs of students who score below grade-level standards. There is a general assumption that students who can score well on standardized tests must be learning. When we speak of children being "left behind," we are usually referring to those students who are scoring below desired levels. The need for students performing below grade level to be supported so they can meet and even exceed standards is not in dispute. Equally indisputable are the consequences faced by students, teachers, parents, administrators, and schools when students do not reach these standards. But in our efforts to reach and teach struggling students in order to bring all students to grade-level performance standards, are some students being overlooked or underserved? What attention is focused on learners who readily master the content and are ready to move forward even though many of their classmates are not? Or on those exceptional students who walk in the classroom on the first day of school already able to pass state grade-level tests with exemplary scores? If learning can be described as forward progress from the entry point at the beginning of a school year, then the students who are most likely to be "left behind" when it comes to individual academic growth may be the students with exceptionally high ability—those we call gifted learners.

The field of gifted education is currently experiencing its lowest level of political support since the early 1960s. The launching of *Sputnik I* by the Soviet Union had created intense interest in nurturing America's most capable students so they could help the United States compete with the Soviets in the space race. Now, decades later, attention to No Child Left Behind (NCLB) has significantly reduced political interest in challenging gifted students in our school. Budget cuts have led to the reduction or elimination of gifted-education positions in many school districts. This affects not only gifted students but also high-performing students not necessarily categorized as gifted. Fewer students in the United States are majoring in science and mathematics than in past years. At the present time, more than 90 percent of the scientists in the world are being educated in Asia.

The United States' position as a world leader may be at greater risk from the challenges to its educational system than from any other factor. Egalitarian issues and budget concerns have led to the elimination of ability grouping in favor of heterogeneous grouping practices. The absence of ability grouping

Winebrenner, Susan and Brulles, Dina. From *The Cluster Grouping Handbook: How to Challenge Gifted Students and Improve Achievement for All* (Free Spirit Publishing, 2008), pp. 1–8 (excerpts). Copyright © 2008. Reprinted by permission of Free Spirit Publishing, Inc., Minneapolis, MN. All rights reserved. www.freespirit.com

practices has led to the loss of attention to the differentiated learning needs of gifted and high-achieving students. As a consequence, many highly able students are leaving their established public schools in favor of charter schools and homeschooling, taking away from their school districts valuable talent along with considerable tax dollars.

Without visible and continuous support for gifted students, forces now present in the field of gifted education are being impacted. Some state legislatures have abandoned the practice of earmarking funds specifically for gifted education, which leaves the decision of funding gifted services to the discretion of each school or district. Fewer jobs are available for educators who want to specialize in teaching gifted students. Little state or national attention is directed toward the fact that gifted students may be consistently denied regular opportunities to experience at least one year's academic growth for each year they are in school. Most importantly, many parents are being told that their gifted children will experience differentiation in the regular classroom, while the reality is that very little of classroom teachers' efforts at differentiation are being addressed to gifted learners. It takes specialized training for classroom teachers to know how to challenge gifted students. Effective differentiation for the gifted will generally not take place until teachers have noticeable numbers of those students in their classes and until they have received training in how to effectively motivate and challenge them.

## Why Meet the Learning Needs of High-Ability Students?

On a day-to-day basis, the highest-ability students usually receive the least amount of the teacher's time. Based on their high test scores and grades, these students are expected to make it on their own or with a minimal amount of guidance.

Looking at students on a bell curve provides a striking illustration of the inequity of this situation, and of what can be lost as a result. While the bell curve has the potential to create unease among some educators, we use it for one purpose only: to demonstrate that the learning needs of students at both ends of the learning continuum are identical.

. . . To teach a class of students, effective teachers usually plan the content, pacing, and quantity of instruction based on what is known about typical students of the age and grade for that class. In a mixed-ability classroom, these are the students in the middle of a heterogeneous group—those students of average abilities on the bell curve. In this same classroom, there will be a number of students who come to the grade level missing many of the basic understandings that typically would have been acquired in earlier grades. These are the students to the left on the bell curve. A third group of students will also be part of this classroom: those who are ahead of their grade-level peers in what they know and can do. These are the students to the right on the bell curve.

When teachers discover struggling students in their class—those below or left of average on the bell curve—they make instant adjustments to their methods of teaching. They may change the pace by moving a bit slower. They may lessen the amount of work for some students. They may change the methods they use to accommodate the learning styles of struggling students. They may change the way in which they interact with the students and try to pair them up with partners who can work well with them. They may adjust the content to reinforce prerequisite concepts that were not learned in earlier grades.

Teachers make these necessary adjustments because the students' learning needs *differ from the average*. Now imagine folding that bell curve in half, left to right. You will clearly see that gifted students are *as far removed from average* on the right side of the curve as are struggling students on the left side. While there are myriad reasons for supporting gifted children's educational growth, this fact alone provides a clear justification for exactly the same intervention to accommodate their needs—an adjustment of pacing, content, workload, and approach to teaching and learning. Gifted students need a faster pace, a smaller amount of practice with grade-level standards, an understanding of their independent work style, a teacher who is comfortable acting as a guide and coach, and opportunities to work with partners who are similar in learning ability, style, and preferences. They need this not because they are gifted, but because they are *not average*.

Gifted students are no more "special" than any others. However, grade-level standards describe what typical students should be able to learn at a certain age. When we accept the fact that gifted children are able to learn at levels that exceed their chronological age expectations, we immediately understand why grade-level standards must be adjusted for them. We do this because, like those students who struggle to meet the standards, gifted students are equally divergent from the "norm."

# Meeting the Needs of All Students: The Schoolwide Cluster Grouping Model (SCGM)

We present a unique approach to help schools meet the needs of all students, including those who are gifted. It is called the Schoolwide Cluster Grouping Model (SCGM). The practice of cluster grouping students is gaining popularity in many states since the method can provide full-time academic services to gifted students without major budget implications and it has the potential to raise achievement for all students in the grade levels that are clustered. With the SCGM, gifted students are grouped into classrooms based on their abilities, while all other students are placed according to their achievement levels. Cluster grouping with the SCGM is different from other cluster grouping methods because the classroom compositions are carefully structured with two main goals: (1) to ensure a balance of abilities throughout the grade level *without returning to the practice of tracking* and (2) to reduce the learning range found in every classroom.

. . . These two goals can be accomplished by dividing the students at a given grade level into five groups. Group 1 represents the identified gifted students who will be in the gifted cluster. Group 2 represents high-achieving students who are not gifted but are very capable learners. These students will be clustered and placed in the classes that do not have the gifted-cluster group. (Clustering gifted students and high-achieving students not identified as gifted in separate classrooms is a key component of the SCGM, which has been shown to expand academic growth for both groups.) Group 3 represents students with average academic performance. Group 4 represents students whose performance is below average, and Group 5 represents students who produce work that falls considerably below grade-level expectations, or those with significant learning challenges. Students who are identified as "twice-exceptional"—those who are gifted and also have a learning challenge—are placed in Group 1, as are identified gifted students who are not fluent in English. . . . Typical gifted-cluster classrooms will include students from Groups 1, 3, and 4; the other classrooms at the grade level will include students from Groups 2, 3, 4, and 5. Ideally, no classroom will include both gifted students *and* students who perform far below average, so the achievement range in all classrooms will be narrower than that of a randomly heterogeneous classroom.

How does this type of clustering differ from tracking? The two main differences are that, in the SCGM, all classes are heterogeneous and all students are provided a varied curriculum. Opportunities for moving faster or going deeper into the curriculum are consistently offered to the entire class, which means there are times when some students in the gifted-cluster group (Group 1) will be experiencing differentiation and times when they won't. There are also times when students not identified as gifted can benefit from available differentiated learning opportunities.

This is different from a tracking system, in which all students are grouped by ability for much of the school day and are rarely exposed to learning experiences that extend their expected achievement ranges. In a tracking system, students are assigned a set curriculum based on their ability level, and they generally do not veer from that curriculum. With schoolwide cluster grouping, every class in the grade level has students with a range of learning abilities and levels. In order to reach that range, the teachers naturally have to modify or extend the grade-level standards.

In the SCGM . . ., all classes have high-performing students. While one or two classes have a cluster of gifted students, all other classes have a cluster of high-achieving students who, while not identified as gifted, can easily serve as positive academic role models. In a cluster model, learning opportunities are open to all students in the class, and teachers use their students' entry points, or readiness, to determine levels and pace of curriculum. Teachers are trained in differentiation and curriculum compacting, students receive ongoing assessment, and the results of schoolwide cluster grouping are continually evaluated.

## What the Research Says About Cluster Grouping

Research documenting the benefits of keeping gifted students together in their areas of greatest strength for at least part of the school day supports the philosophy behind schoolwide cluster grouping. Moreover, the research suggests that all students, including those categorized as average and below-average students, thrive when gifted students are placed in their own cluster groups within heterogeneous classes.

The SCGM is an inclusion model in which students with exceptional learning needs are integrated into mixed-ability classrooms and teachers are expected to provide appropriate differentiation opportunities for any students who need them. An inclusion model has already been in use for many years as a method for providing special education services to students who have been identified as having exceptional educational needs. However, it is only when a class has a noticeable group of gifted students—a cluster—that teachers will be most likely to accommodate *their* exceptional educational needs. When there are only one or two gifted students in a class, teachers often tend to assume the students are learning as long as they are getting high grades and, as a result, minimize or overlook their need for expanded learning opportunities. Teachers are also likely to count on these students to help other students with their learning, a practice that robs the gifted students of opportunities to move forward in academic areas.

Clustering requires that teachers differentiate instruction. Differentiation occurs when teachers modify the curriculum and their instructional methods in response to the needs, strengths, learning styles, and interests of individual students so that *all* students have an opportunity to learn at their full potential. To be successful, the gifted-cluster teacher must have ongoing training in how to teach high-ability students in the cluster model. The SCGM creates a setting for providing appropriate instruction that is feasible for teachers and for enhancing the likelihood that differentiation will take place.

# The SCGM: Who Benefits, and How?

The SCGM offers a win-win educational approach that benefits all stakeholders in the school community—students, teachers, administrators, and parents. Grouping gifted children in a regular classroom can provide academic, social, and emotional advantages to the students and make teaching gifted students more manageable for teachers. Gifted students feel more comfortable when there are other students like them in the class. They are more likely to choose challenging tasks when they can do that work in the company of other students. Teachers attuned to differentiating instruction are more likely to provide appropriate learning opportunities for gifted students and for other students as well. The school is able to provide a full-time, cost-effective program for gifted students since their learning needs are being met every day. Parents who are satisfied that their children are experiencing consistent challenge at school are more ready to work cooperatively with the school and the teachers and less likely to remove their children from public education.

## Impact of the SCGM on Gifted Students

Gifted students who are clustered demonstrate high achievement because they experience more consistent challenge in their learning activities. Their scores on achievement tests show forward progress—rather than lost ground, as has been the case in some schools where gifted students are not placed in clusters or are not consistently challenged in other ways.

When gifted students are purposefully clustered in otherwise heterogeneous classes, rather than split up so that each class has one or two gifted students, their learning needs are much more likely to be noticed by the teacher. They also enjoy more attention to their social and emotional needs because of the specialized training the teacher receives.

Cluster grouping also makes it more likely that gifted kids will work to their full potential and take advantage of available differentiated learning opportunities because they will have other students to work with on these advanced learning tasks. Having serious competition from other students like themselves, they begin to develop more realistic perceptions of their abilities and to better understand and accept their learning differences. With so many opportunities to work and learn together, gifted students become more comfortable working at extended levels of complexity and depth in a given subject or topic. Their willingness to take risks in learning experiences increases when they spend time with others who share the same interests, have similar abilities, and can also benefit from the available differentiation opportunities.

## Impact of the SCGM on English Language Learners

Cluster grouping offers exciting opportunities for schools to meet the needs of gifted English language learners (ELL students). When gifted students are served only in a pull-out model, gifted students who are not proficient in English are frequently kept out of services because of their inability to work at the same pace and level as the gifted students already proficient in English. With cluster grouping, extended learning opportunities are available in the regular classroom. When ELL students with high learning potential are present in classes where consistent challenge is available, they make faster progress in attaining English fluency and academic achievement.

A significant increase in achievement in students of different ethnic groups can also be expected from using cluster grouping. These findings result from classes in which teachers can be more focused and effective in their teaching. Another reason for the achievement gains is that gifted-education training required for cluster teachers helps the teachers set high expectations for *all* students—expectations to which students respond positively.

## Impact of the SCGM on All Students

It has already been noted that students at all ability levels benefit from this model because teachers have more training in how to differentiate the curriculum and the pacing for all types of students, ensuring that learning success can be within the reach of all. A further benefit results from the fact that gifted and high-achieving students are motivated, work more independently and are allowed to spend more learning time on activities that interest and challenge them, opening up more time for teachers to spend with those who need additional assistance.

As teachers become more adept at recognizing giftedness in their students, the number of students they nominate for gifted testing increases yearly in schools that use the SCGM. This is especially noticeable in classes that do *not* have the gifted cluster, demonstrating the benefit of clustering high-achieving children who are *not* identified as gifted in separate classrooms. These classroom structures provide opportunities for the high-achieving students to thrive and emerge as new academic leaders.

## Impact of the SCGM on Teachers

Student achievement is positively correlated with effective teaching. The SCGM allows teachers to be more effective because they are teaching a class with a smaller range of learning levels. The system provides opportunities for teachers to more readily respond to the needs of all their students, to challenge gifted students clustered together in mixed-ability classes, and to engage in practices that lead to improved academic achievement for students not identified as gifted, working at or above grade level. As a result, over time with the SCGM, more students in a school are identified as high achievers and fewer as low achievers.

For a school that already has a pull-out program for gifted students, the cluster model makes scheduling out-of-class activities easier. The resource (pull-out) teacher has to work with only one classroom teacher's schedule per grade level instead of the schedules of all the teachers at a particular grade level. The gifted-cluster teacher, whose gifted students venture to another classroom for pull-out services, understands that while they are gone, students who remain should be experiencing activities that reinforce standards the gifted students have already mastered. Therefore, when the students return from the pull-out program, they do not have any "missed" classroom work to "make up," and the teacher does not have the added layer of planning and record keeping that typically comes with makeup work.

When the SCGM is implemented with the goal that all teachers will eventually receive the related staff development, over time it is possible to ensure that all teachers who wish to teach a classroom with a gifted cluster will have the opportunity. At the same time, students in all classrooms benefit from the teachers' facility with differentiating the curriculum to meet students' varied learning needs.

## Impact of the SCGM on Administrators

Schools that use the SCGM find that they can still offer valuable services for their gifted students even in the presence of reduced budgets or lack of political support. This helps administrators assure parents of gifted students that their children's learning needs will be served. Cluster grouping actually provides full-time placement and service for gifted students in the schools *without* the cost of creating and maintaining a separate gifted-education program. Gifted students are retained in the public school system and, moreover, gifted education becomes part of the school culture.

When schools take the time to implement the SCGM strategically, carefully planning the groups for cluster classrooms, training as many teachers as possible to implement gifted-education strategies, educating parents about how their children's school experience will be affected, and conducting ongoing student assessments and program evaluations, the result can be a cohesive and budget-friendly schoolwide approach to gifted education that brings the school community together as it raises student achievement levels.

## Impact of the SCGM on Parents

Providing a cluster grouping model announces to the community that the school is committed to recognizing and serving its gifted students and enhancing achievement opportunities for all students. As parents of gifted students come to understand how clustering impacts their children's learning opportunities, they see that the schools are providing full-time gifted services, that teachers are responding to their children's needs, and that their gifted children spend time learning with other students of similar ability. Parents of students *not* identified as gifted are also likely to appreciate the opportunities the clustering arrangements and differentiation strategies afford their children. When these parents become familiar with the research that shows how the SCGM facilitates the emergence of new leaders in classes that do not have a gifted cluster, they may realize that, for the first time, their children have more opportunities to demonstrate academic leadership roles. Many students have had this very positive experience as a result of schoolwide cluster grouping.

# EXPLORING THE ISSUE

## Do Gifted and Talented Students Need Special Schools?

## Challenge Questions

- Compare and contrast the positions of the YES and NO selections regarding whether gifted and talented students need special schools.
- Which selection makes the best case for its argument? Why?
- Compare the student experiences mentioned with deliberations regarding the inclusion of students with disabilities.
- How does your state/district conceptualize giftedness? What types of programs are available?
- Discuss the implications of each option for the education of all children.
- If your child were identified as gifted/talented, how would you determine the best educational option?

## Is There Common Ground?

Authors of the YES and NO selections agree that gifted and talented children need specialized educational programming. They provide strong support and examples for the models they propose. They also mention significant stumbling blocks to the implementation of these models.

## Additional Resources

Carnevale, A. P. (2007, September 26). No child gets ahead. *Education Week*, 40.

Cloud, J. (2007, August 27). Failing our geniuses. *Time Magazine, 170*(9), 41–47.

Ford, D. Y. (2003). Two other wrongs don't make a right: Sacrificing the needs of diverse students does not solve gifted education's unresolved problems. *Journal for the Education of the Gifted, 26*(4), 283–291.

Gentry, M., Hu, S., & Thomas, A. J. (2008). Ethnically diverse students. In J. A. Plucker & C. M. Callahan (Eds). *Critical issues and practices in gifted education* (pp. 195–212). Waco, TX: Prufrock Press, Inc.

Kennedy, D. M., Banks, R. S., with Grandin, T. (2011). *Bright not broken: Gifted kids, ADHD and autism*. San Francisco, CA: Jossey-Bass.

Miller, E. M. M. (2008). Conceptions of giftedness. In J. A. Plucker & C. M. Callahan (Eds.). *Critical issues and practices in gifted* education (pp. 107–117). Waco, TX: Prufrock Press, Inc.

National Association for Gifted Children. (2011). *2010–2011 State of the nation in gifted education: A lack of commitment to talent development. Executive Summary*. Retrieved April 6, 2012 from www.nagc.org

National Education Association. (2006). *The twice-exceptional dilemma.* Retrieved January 8, 2008 from www.nea.org/specialed

Plucker J. A. & Callahan C. M., eds. (2007) Critical Issues and Practices in Gifted Education: What the Research Says. Waco, Tex: Prufrock Press.

Ruf, D. L. (2005). *Losing our minds: Gifted children left behind*. Scottsdale, AZ: Great Potential Press.

Schroth, S. T. (2008). Levels of service. In J. A. Plucker & C. M. Callahan (Eds.). *Critical issues and practices in gifted education* (pp. 321–334). Waco, TX: Prufrock Press, Inc.

Winebrenner, S. & Brulles, D. (2008). *The cluster grouping handbook* (Introduction, pp. 1–10). Minneapolis, MN: Free Spirit Publishing.

# ISSUE 16

# Is Mental Health Screening an Unwarranted Intrusion?

YES: Nathaniel S. Lehrman, from "The Dangers of Mental Health Screening," *Journal of American Physicians and Surgeons* (vol. 11, no. 3, pp. 80–82, 2006)

NO: Mark. D. Weist, Marcia Rubin, Elizabeth Moore, Steven Adelsheim, & Gordon Wrobel, from "Mental Health Screening in Schools," *Journal of School Health* (vol. 77, pp. 53–58, 2007)

---

## Learning Outcomes

**At the conclusion of this issue, readers will be able to:**

- Compare and contrast the positions of the YES and NO selections addressing whether mental health screening is an unwarranted intrusion.
- Describe the strengths and the weaknesses of each side's arguments.
- Cite resources that can inform mental-health screening decisions for local schools.
- Identify methods to ensure that parents are active partners in any screening.

---

ISSUE SUMMARY

YES: Nathaniel Lehrman, clinical director (retired) of the Kingsboro Psychiatric Center, New York, warns that new mental health screening requirements, heralded as a way to increase the health of the nation, will intrude on basic freedoms, lead to inappropriate labels, and increase revenue for pharmaceutical companies.

NO: Mark Weist, Marcia Rubin, Elizabeth Moore, Steven Adelshiem, and Gordon Wrobel, consultants and researchers in mental health, view this screening as a way to identify those who need early intervention in order to prevent the development of debilitating mental illnesses.

**S**chools such as Virginia Tech, Northern Illinois, Columbine, and others, and countless now-silent adolescents, remind Americans how fragile their existence can be. They make them wonder about the students they teach. Many friends, teachers, and parents have worried whether they missed a clue that could have saved a life.

Noting that between 5 percent and 7 percent of all adults and children have a serious mental illness, President Bush's New Freedom Commission on Mental Health (NFC) observed "(m)ental health ranks first among illnesses that cause disability in the United States, Canada, and Western Europe. This serious public health challenge is under-recognized as a public health burden. In addition, one of the most distressing and preventable consequences of undiagnosed, untreated, or under-treated mental illnesses is suicide" (www.mentalhealthcommission.gov, 2003).

The NFC Final Report lists six goals for an improved quality of mental health in the United States. *Goal 4: Early Mental Health Screening, Assessment, and Referral to Services Are Common Practice* includes a recommendation to screen for mental health disorders. This goal would be achieved through regular screenings of children and youth. The intent is to identify those in need, and deliver intervention to prevent the development of a mental illness. Seemingly benign, the call for regular screening has stimulated much debate.

This issue explores the controversial topic of whether mental health screening is an intrusion or a prudent early warning strategy. As you read the YES and NO selections, consider how to determine the best way to balance cherished individual rights and freedoms with the desire to be proactive and avert a tragedy. Consider, also, who should decide where the line should be drawn.

In the YES selection, psychiatrist Nathaniel Lehrman describes mental health screening as an unwarranted intrusion into individual and family privacy. Acknowledging the good intentions of the NFC, Lehrman is concerned that inadequate screening tools will stigmatize people with unfounded diagnoses. Only the pharmaceutical companies will benefit.

In the NO selection, Mark Wiest and colleagues, who practice and conduct research in psychiatry, support systematic mental health screening. They emphasize the effectiveness of early intervention, especially through school mental health services. Mark D. Weist, Marcia Rubin, Elizabeth Moore, Steven Adelsheim, and Gordon Wrobel maintain that, delivered in a timely fashion, mental health interventions can reduce the stigma of mental illness.

The Executive Summary of the New Freedom Commission's final report, *Achieving the Promise*, begins with this statement: "We envision a future when everyone with a mental illness will recover, a future when mental illnesses can be prevented or cured, a future when mental illnesses are detected early, and a future when everyone with a mental illness at any state of life has access to effective treatment and supports—essentials for living, working, learning, and participating fully in the community." As the outcome of its work, the NFC anticipated transforming the current complex fragmented system of mental health into a more integrated system of care for all.

Representative Ron Paul (R-TX), who has sought the Republican presidential nomination, is one of several legislators who introduced a bill (H.R. 2387) prohibiting the use of U.S. federal funds for any universal mental health screening. To support this measure limiting government intrusion into private lives, the bill's authors cited efforts to formalize a diagnosis of "extreme intolerance" as well as the suggestion of one federally funded program that children who share their parents' traditional values may instigate school violence. Like Lehrman, these legislators see such claims as leading to stigmatizing labels, which result in the pressure for pharmaceutical treatment.

Responding to an earlier version of H.R. 2387, and in support of screening, the National Alliance on Mental Illness (www.nami.org) appealed to Congress to reject the misinformation provided by anti-screening advocates. To NAMI, the tone of anti-screening legislation engenders fear, enhances stigma, and keeps people away from needed help. NAMI holds that screening merely identifies those who need more intensive evaluation. This, and any medical treatment, can happen only with full parental involvement and consent.

Meet four young women, whose riveting stories illustrate this controversy: Aliah, Rosie, Chelsea, and Courtney. Lehrman depicts Aliah's and Chelsea's experiences as examples of the intrusive consequences of screening; Weist et al. would cite Rosie and Courtney as solid reasons to screen.

Lehrman tells Aliah's story: on the basis of an in-school screening, and against the wishes of her parents, Aliah was hospitalized, isolated from her parents, and subjected to heavy medication. Compare Aliah to Rosie D, the lead named plaintiff in a class action suit against the State of Massachusetts. The suit charged that nine children were hospitalized, or at-risk for hospitalization, because Massachusetts did not provide Medicaid-mandated screenings, and necessary home-based mental health services. The court ruled in Rosie's favor, reinforcing the need for these services in hopes that no other children would get "lost in the system" (Kenny, 2007, www.massmedicaid.org).

Lehrman also shares the experiences of Chelsea Rhoades, said to have mental health problems as a result of a brief in-school screening. Angered that they had not been notified of this intrusion into their lives, Chelsea's parents filed a lawsuit against her school (www.rutherford.org). Contrast this to Courtney, whose experience with in-school screening, and resultant mental health services, led her to say, "I'm not sure where I would be today if I didn't get screened. I'm not even sure I would be here at all" (Friedman, *The New England Journal of Medicine*, 2006).

One key element of this debate focuses on the type of parental permission requested. Methods of participation in any activity can be mandatory or voluntary; granting permission can be either active or passive. A mandatory activity is just that; everyone must participate. Statewide assessment systems are mandatory activities. Active voluntary permission requires a parent/guardian to sign a paper supporting their child's participation. Because permission slips can get lost—in transmission or on the kitchen table—passive/opt-out permission is sometimes employed. In this method an informational permission note indicates that the student will participate in the stated activity unless the parent/guardian sends an objection to the school. *Achieving the Promise* is clear that screening is to be voluntary and that "parents should be included in the process of making choices and decisions for minor children" (*Executive Summary*). Some suggest a more active permission process would result in fewer children being screened (Effrem, www.education.org/2005/021405.htm, 2005).

The website of the American Association of Suicidology (www.suicidology .org) displays the following quote: "There are some things you do not want to learn by experience. One of them is recognizing suicide risk in one of your clients."

Barbara Schildkraut (*Unmasking psychological symptoms*, 2011) counsels therapists to look beyond behavior. Medical conditions such as Lyme disease, sleep disorders, or HIV might affect behavior, thinking, and emotions in ways that simulate mental health disorders. Identifying an accurate reason for an apparent mental health difficulty can lead to finding the right remedy.

Actress Glenn Close, whose sister and nephew have been diagnosed with mental health disorders, spearheads a campaign to reduce the stigma of mental illness. Addressing the negative perceptions about mental illness, bringchange2mind.org asks: "Imagine if you got blamed for having cancer."Acknowledging each family's need for support, and society's need for information, Close's organization (http://bringchange2mind.org) contains accessible resources and public education materials.

Few would deny the benefits of providing help to those in need, especially to avoid a tragic event. It is harder to find agreement on how to identify those in need of services.

# YES

**Nathaniel S. Lehrman**

# The Dangers of Mental Health Screening

## The New Freedom Commission on Mental Health

According to the President's New Freedom Commission on Mental Health (NFC), all American parents will receive notice from their youngsters' schools of the new screening program during the 2005–2006 school year. It will test for mental illness in the 52 million students and 6 million adults working in schools, and expects to find at least 6 million in need of treatment. The force of government will then urge or compel them to receive that treatment.

But children aren't the only targets. The commission's final report looks forward to having both children and adults screened for mental illnesses during their routine physical examinations.

The sale of psychiatric medications—antipsychotics and antidepressants—rose from $500 million to $20 billion between 1987 and 2004, a 40-fold increase. A pharmaceutical stock analyst recently predicted that continuing to widen our definitions of illness will result in increased sales of medications. This amounts to corporate-sponsored creation of illness, to enhance revenue. With the new screening program, the government-sponsored "discovery" of illness will augment the already existing corporate "promotion of undiscovered illness"—which means even more medication sales. And by allowing experts to define peaceful, law-abiding citizens as ill and in need of treatment (which increasingly is becoming involuntary), the program comes to resemble the witchhunts of 16th-century Europe.

## Screening and Its Victims

This is how the program works. In December 2004, as part of the TeenScreen program created to implement the NFC blueprint, Chelsea Rhoades and her Indiana public high school classmates were given a 10-minute, yes-or-no computer test, which had no room for alternate answers or explanations. A few students were not given the test because their parents had opted them out, an option the Rhoades family had not known about in advance.

Lehrman, Nathaniel S. From *Journal of American Physicians and Surgeons*, 11(3) Fall 2006, pp. 80–82 (refs. omitted). Copyright © 2006 by Association of American Physicians and Surgeons. Reprinted by permission. www.jpands.org/

Shortly after Chelsea took the test, a local mental health center employee told her that she was suffering from obsessive-compulsive disorder because she liked to help clean the house, and from social anxiety disorder because she didn't party much. The worker then suggested that if her condition worsened, her mother should bring her to the center for treatment. Chelsea says all her friends were also told they had something mentally wrong with them. The only youngsters not supposed to be suffering from some mental disorder were those with opt-out slips.

Furious at this intrusion into their privacy and parental rights, the Rhoadeses sounded the alarm. With the help of the Rutherford Institute, they have filed a lawsuit against the school district for failing to inform them about the test or to obtain permission for Chelsea to take it.

Even more frightening was the experience of 13-year-old, black Aliah Gleason, an average, but rather obstreperous seventh-grade student in an Austin, Texas, suburb. After her class was screened for mental illness, her parents were told that she needed further evaluation because she scored high on a suicide rating. She was referred to a university consulting psychiatrist, and thence to an emergency clinic. Six weeks later, a child protection worker appeared at her school, interviewed her, summoned her father to the school, and ordered him to take the girl at once to Austin State (psychiatric) Hospital. When he refused, she took Aliah into emergency custody and had a police officer drive her to the hospital.

During Aliah's five terrible months in the hospital, her parents were forbidden to see or speak to her. While there, she was placed in restraints more than 26 times and given at least 12 different psychiatric medications, many of them simultaneously. After that, she spent four more months in a residential facility, where she received even more psychotropic medications.

Despite her caretakers' uncertainty about her clinical diagnosis (and whether she even had a psychiatric illness), her parents had to go to court to have her released. The professionals they chose for her then tapered her off all medication and successfully addressed problems—both hers and the family's. She is now doing well in school, participating in extracurricular activities, and according to her psychologist, Dr. John Breeding of Austin, recovering her high spirits.

At a Colorado homeless shelter, 50 percent of the 350 young people given the TeenScreen were found to be suicidal risks, and 71 percent screened positive for psychiatric disorders. Although such youngsters are certainly suffering from residential and social instability, and probably from not eating or sleeping properly, the TeenScreen diagnoses lead to medications instead of appropriate interventions.

The particular purpose of children's mental health screening is supposedly to prevent suicide. But the Columbia University TeenScreen program acknowledged that 84 percent of the teens who tested positive were found to be not really at risk. And, as Sharav points out, an evaluation by the authoritative U.S. Preventive Services Task Force (USPSTF) concluded that screening for suicide failed to demonstrate any benefit at reducing suicide. The report noted that the screening instruments have not been validated. Moreover, there is insufficient evidence that treatment of those identified as high risk reduces either suicide attempts or mortality.

## What Is Mental Illness?

What is the mental illness for which we are now screening? Years ago, the term "mental illness" referred only to the insane: people with bizarre ideas who were unable to function socially. Such disabled individuals were social annoyances who might also be dangerous to themselves, others, or both. Other maladaptive psychological patterns such as nervousness or sadness have also been called mental illness, but these produce distress rather than disability. Over the past several decades, however, the term has been expanded to include increasingly more of the thousand natural ills to which the flesh is heir. A recent report from Harvard and the National Institute of Mental Health, for example, says that 46 percent of Americans will at some point in their lives develop a mental disorder.

Many of those thousand natural ills are included among the 400-odd disorders listed in the latest edition of the American Psychiatric Association's (APA) *Diagnostic and Statistical Manual of Mental Disorders,* the DSM. Calling it the psychiatric bible, Herb Kutchins, professor of social welfare at California State University, Sacramento, and Stuart A. Kirk, professor of social welfare at the University of California at Los Angeles (UCLA) point out that since there are no biological tests, markers, or known causes for most mental illnesses, psychiatric diagnosis is based almost entirely on symptomatology—depression, anxiety, disorganization, obsessive thinking, compulsive behavior, and other subjective symptoms.

Depression, for example, has as many causes as there are people suffering from it: job difficulties, failure to attain expectations, and problems in relationships are but a few. Basing psychiatric diagnosis entirely on symptoms can be compared to making fever a definitive diagnosis; symptoms are not disorders in themselves, but products of other psychological and/or physiological phenomena. The cure of depression—a term rarely used today although a common occurrence yesterday—requires that an individual's particular problems be addressed. Psychiatry's dependence on symptom-based diagnostics is a major reason for the specialty's mounting pessimism.

One reason for higher estimates of the prevalence of mental disorders is that the APA keeps adding new disorders and more behaviors to the manual, as Kutchins and Kirk point out. The increase in the number of these disorders, along with the greatly increased use of new medications to treat them, parallels the increase in individuals disabled by these disorders. Rates for psychiatric disability in America have risen from 3.38 per thousand in 1954; to 13.75 in 1987, when the atypical anti psychotics and SSRI antidepressants were introduced; to 19.69 in 2003. The number of patient care episodes—the amount of care given, as measured by the number of people treated each year for mental illness at psychiatric hospitals, residential facilities for the mentally ill, and ambulatory care facilities—rose similarly: from 1,028 per 100,000 population in 1955; to 3,295 in 1987; and to 3,806 in 2000. Since the start of the "medication era," the number of mentally disabled people has risen nearly sixfold.

# How the History of ADHD Predicts the Effects of Screening

Kutchins and Kirk point out that children are considered to exhibit signs of attention deficit hyperactivity disorder (ADHD) when they are deceitful, break rules, can't sit still or wait in lines, have trouble with math, don't pay attention to details, don't listen, don't like to do homework, lose their school assignments or pencils, or speak out of turn. This common childhood behavior is defined as a disorder by the psychiatry department of the New York University (NYU) School of Medicine. ADHD is now diagnosed in 6 to 9 percent of school-age children and 4 percent of adults. Its "symptoms"—acting impulsively; easy distractibility; interrupting others; constant fidgeting or moving; and difficulty in paying attention, waiting one's turn, planning ahead, following instructions, or meeting deadlines—can be found in any of us. With diagnosis and treatment, the department contends, ADHD symptoms can be substantially decreased.

The process through which ADHD became accepted is important, but little recognized. In 1980, the list of symptoms then called ADD (attention deficit disorder) was first accepted into the DSM. Seven years later, hyperactivity was added, thus making ADHD. Within a year, 500,000 youngsters were assigned this diagnosis.

A few years later, ADHD was classified as a disability, and a cash incentive program was initiated for low-income families with children diagnosed with ADHD. A family could get $450 a month for each child so labeled, and the cost of treatment and medication for low-income children would be covered by Medicaid. Then in 1991, schools began receiving educational grants of $400 annually for each ADHD child. The same year, the U.S. Department of Education classified the disorder as a handicap, which required special services to be provided to each disabled child.

By 1996, close to $15 billion was spent annually on the diagnosis, treatment, and study of this supposed neuropsychiatric disorder. Recently, public health officials in the United States, Canada, and the United Kingdom have issued warnings about previously known, but undisclosed risks associated with the stimulant medications used to treat ADHD.

What has happened with ADHD presages what can be expected from government-sponsored mental health screening. One example is the case of the first-grade son of Patricia Weathers. After a school psychologist diagnosed the "disorder," she was pressured into medicating him.

"The medication eventually made him psychotic," she said. But when she stopped giving it to him, the school reported her to state child protection officials for "child abuse." Weathers cofounded AbleChild . . . and filed a lawsuit against school officials.

"We have 1,000 stories like this," she states. Meanwhile, her son is now 15 and "doing fine."

Rep. Ron Paul, M.D., (R-TX) a congressman who has been a physician for more than 30 years, has criticized government agencies for charging parents with child abuse if they refuse to drug their children. Some parents have even had their children taken from them for refusing to give them medications.

Mrs. Weathers's experience is far from unique. According to Dr. Andrew Mosholder of the FDA's Office of Drug Safety, about 2.5 million children in this country between ages 4 and 17 currently take ADHD drugs, 9.3 percent of 12-year-old boys, and 3.7 percent of 11-year-old girls. And although these medications have been used for years, the harm they can cause to the heart and circulatory system, and the psychiatric difficulties they can produce, is only now being publicly discussed.

No matter how we define mental illness in children or adults, it cannot be diagnosed by simple screening. Nobody can, by merely looking at someone else, or even on the basis of a questionnaire, differentiate the transient emotional disturbances we all have from those that last longer.

The ephemeral nature of suicidal ideation and depressive feelings among teens is specifically mentioned by the Columbia TeenScreen report. Screenings won't prevent suicide because those who are contemplating it usually won't tell. Indeed, the screening process itself can produce significant anxiety among those in whom mental illness is being "diagnosed." Such efforts to find their troubles by frightening people, and thus aggravating those troubles, are misdirected. Only when gross insanity exists can mental illness be recognized on inspection, and then we need neither experts nor screening.

Troubled people can indeed benefit from good mental health care. But good treatment requires that a physician actually examine a patient and address that individual's unique problems, with the patient's knowledge and consent. This requires time, and busy practitioners are often under severe time constraints. Thus, they are pressured to quickly prescribe medications to relieve symptoms that are often transient even if untreated.

In my opinion, relying on medication as the definitive treatment of psychiatric complaints, rather than addressing their real causes in patients' lives, is responsible for the gross overuse of psychiatric medications, especially among children, but also among seniors:

- Twenty-nine million prescriptions were written last year in the United States for Ritalin and similar medications to treat ADHD, 23 million of them for children.
- From 60 to 70 percent of children in foster care in Massachusetts are now being given psychiatric medications.
- About 40 to 50 percent of students arrive at some colleges with psychiatric prescriptions.
- Approximately 41 percent of prescriptions for one group of 765,000 people over 65 were for psychotropics.
- As many as 75 percent of elderly, long-term-care nursing home residents in another study were being given psychotropics.

The screening program will aggravate this already unfortunate situation.

## Conclusions

Good intentions notwithstanding, the mental health screening program created by the president's NFC probably will harm thousands of Americans by giving them stigmatizing diagnoses that can follow them for the rest of their lives. The program's government-sponsored promotion of long-term medications will compound the harm, as the experience with ADHD has shown.

As Sharav points out, screening for mental illness serves no medical or societal purpose. Screening will, however, do much to increase the benefits to the drug manufacturers and to the mental health provider industry. Good psychiatric care is voluntary, and based on trust between patient and physician. The involuntary government-sponsored mental health screening program, as demonstrated by the cases of Aliah Gleason and Chelsea Rhoades, represents psychiatric malpractice.

Their cases also demonstrate how the program undermines basic American freedoms, as parents are coerced to medicate their children, sometimes with severe adverse effects.

We need to start to undo psychiatry's 50 years of overdependence on psychopharmacology, rather than expanding it through mental health screening.

# Mark D. Weist et al.

 **NO**

# Mental Health
# Screening in Schools

## Background

A significant gap between the mental health needs of children and adolescents and the available services has been well documented. For example, between 12% and 27% of youth might have acting-out behavioral problems, depression, and anxiety; yet, as few as one sixth to one third of these youth receive any mental health treatment. In this context, school mental health (SMH) programs have grown progressively. This growth reflects increasing recognition of the need to address the mental health needs of children and youth and the many advantages of SMH programs. These include reducing barriers to student learning, unmatched access to youth, and ability to engage youth in an array of strategies that can simultaneously address their educational, emotional, behavioral, and developmental needs. In fact, for youth who do receive mental health services, most receive them in schools. In addition, SMH programs can reduce stigma, enhance the generalization and maintenance of interventions, increase opportunities for preventive services, and promote efficiency and productivity of staff and programs. Program evaluation data and early research suggest that *when done well*, SMH services are associated with satisfaction by a number of different stakeholder groups including students and contribute to achieving outcomes valued by families and schools.

Strong federal support for SMH programs and services is found in the US Surgeon General's reports on mental health and child and adolescent mental health; large federal initiatives such as the Safe Schools/Healthy Students Program and the Child and Adolescent Service System Program. *Achieving the Promise: Transforming Mental Health Care in America,* the report issued by the President's New Freedom Commission on Mental Health in 2003, emphasized the large gap between needs and effective services and the lack of a national priority on child and adolescent mental health. The 6 goals and 19 recommendations of the report strongly support SMH, including recommendation 4.2 to "improve and expand school mental health programs" and a related recommendation 4.3 to "screen for co-occurring mental and substance use disorders and link with integrated treatment strategies."

Weist et al, Mark D. From *Journal of School Health*, 77(2) February 2007, pp. 53–57 (refs. omitted). Copyright © 2007 by American School Health Association. Reprinted by permission of Wiley-Blackwell via Rightslink.

*Achieving the Promise* calls for an approach that connects policy, training, practice, and research on mental health services and that improves behavioral, emotional, and academic functioning of youth. This approach is reflected in a pyramid of programs and services. The foundation aims to improve school environments and broadly promotes health as well as academic success. The second tier encompasses targeted prevention programs and early identification practices that help recognize and refer students with unmet mental health needs. Providing access to effective treatment services for serious and/or chronic disorders occupies the top of the pyramid. This model is congruent with a public health approach to disease prevention and detection. It incorporates a continuum of educational messages that promote health and prevention and incorporates early identification practices that ensure cost-effective treatment for disabling health conditions. This pyramid model for health and mental health promotion has been embraced by the World Health Organization and other groups but unfortunately does not reflect the way programs and services are delivered to children and youth in the United States.

Although historically, school-based mental health services were provided primarily to students qualified for special education services, more recently, schools have expanded mental health and social services for all students as part of their coordinated school health program. Today, there are a number of different models for offering these services in schools, with an array of service components ranging from alcohol and other drug use treatment, case management, individual and group counseling, and referrals to community mental health systems and providers. Despite this, there remain numerous barriers including

- insufficient funding
- inadequate training and supervision of staff
- difficulty coordinating a full continuum of prevention and intervention services
- maintenance of quality and empirical support of services
- limited evaluation of outcomes of services to improve programs and contribute to policy improvement.

Providing treatment services within school buildings is often challenging for additional reasons, including

- environmental characteristics (poor office spaces, crowded classrooms)
- frequent changes in personnel (high teacher and administrator turnover)
- distinctive knowledge bases and cultures (education and mental health)
- difficulties in fully engaging families
- academic demands stemming from the No Child Left Behind educational reforms.

These issues are increasingly documented in the published literature, especially in relation to research-based interventions.

# Mental Health Screening in Schools

Youth with internalizing disorders such as depression, anxiety, or suicide ideation are not as easily identified as those with acting-out or externalizing disorders. Individuals with internalizing conditions comprise a significant population; the 2003 Youth Risk Behavior Survey, a nationally representative sample of more than 15,000 high school students throughout the United States, found that in the 12-month period preceding the survey 16.9% had seriously considered attempting suicide, 16.5% had made a plan for attempting suicide, 8.5% had attempted suicide one or more times, and 2.9% had made an attempt requiring medical attention. In addition, studies have shown that students contemplating suicide or even those who had previous attempts were not known or detected by school personnel. Furthermore, 90% of teens who commit suicide have a mental health issue at the time of their death but are usually not receiving treatment.

For these reasons, formal screening programs that detect depression and suicide ideation are recommended. The New Freedom Commission on Mental Health recommended screening in multiple settings as a critical component of a public health approach to prevention and early intervention for mental health issues in youth. The Commission went so far as to name the Columbia University TeenScreen program as a model program for identifying at-risk youth and linking them to critical intervention services. TeenScreen is currently implemented in 460 sites in 42 states and involves systematic and supported assessment of youth mental health needs in schools along with technical assistance and guidance on addressing identified needs. Other effective programs such as Dominic and the Signs of Suicide program are also widely available. These recommendations have led to increasing discussion among mental health providers of the need to advance mental health screening in schools. A few states, such as Ohio, Illinois, and New Mexico, have moved to expand screening in multiple settings as part of their efforts to transform their child's mental health system.

However, screening in schools is not without controversy. Some perceive screening as government intrusion, and others describe it as a violation of the family's right to privacy. These concerns appear to be based on the erroneous belief that screening programs in schools require all students to be screened against their wishes or against those of the parents. In fact, "mandatory universal screening" for behavioral health issues does not exist anywhere and has never been recommended by any federal agency or community screening program. All existing mental health screening programs are voluntary and require active informed consent of the family and the assent of the student. It is likely that another factor contributing to the misunderstanding surrounding screening is stigma. The President's Commission acknowledged the pervasive nature of stigma and the need to actively address it.

While there are no currently agreed-upon national standards for mental health screening in schools, a number of federal agencies, professional organizations, and advocacy groups have issued helpful resources. Both the Substance Abuse and Mental Health Services Administration and the National

Alliance for the Mentally Ill recently released documents confirming the importance of screening as part of a public health approach to early identification and intervention for behavioral health problems and offering guidelines for the appropriate use of screening. Well-established screening programs such as TeenScreen generally have experientially based recommendations for implementation and strongly recommend active parental consent for any screening in schools. Another helpful resource on screening and assessing mental health and substance use disorders was issued by the Office of Juvenile Justice and Delinquency Prevention of the US Department of Justice, which includes a set of criteria for selecting screening methods. The American Medical Association's Guidelines for Adolescent Preventive Services includes recommendations for screening behavioral and emotional conditions, such as substance abuse, eating disorders, depression, suicide risk, and school or learning problems. All these guidelines and criteria for mental health screening can provide a foundation for developing standards for the school setting.

## Other Issues

In trying to decide whether to implement a screening program, there are other factors that districts will need to consider. For example, strategic planning should attempt to gauge the needs of individual schools in relation to the school/community's abilities to respond to those needs. This will require a self-assessment process. In addition, prior to advancing the agenda related to mental health screening in schools, the community should consider:

1. Availability of trained staff and other resources to conduct screening.
2. Availability of mental health providers with training in evaluating and treating those children and youth identified by screening.
3. Need for technical assistance in system development for ensuring parental consent and student assent for participation in screening.
4. Selection of age-appropriate screening measures.
5. Logistics including when to do the screening, finding the right confidential space for screening, and provision of alternative activities for youth who do not have parental permission for screening.
6. Resolution of liability concerns.

## First Steps

Once a district has addressed the issues outlined above and decided to move toward implementing a formal screening program, five additional elements will need to be considered: inclusive planning, collaborative relationships, logistics, training and supervision, and integration.

### Inclusive Planning
Planning should involve all significant stakeholders including families, education professionals, primary care providers, mental health professionals, and other representatives from the community. Once configured, the planning body might begin with a policy review to ensure that sufficient safeguards are in place to protect privacy and confidentiality. Districts can also benefit from

ongoing technical expertise from community agencies that respond to related mental health issues such as substance abuse, child welfare, law enforcement, or other specialty systems.

### Collaborative Relationships

To promote collaboration, the sharing of resources, and to address liability concerns, memoranda of agreement should be established between schools and collaborating community agencies to ensure adequate clarification of responsibility. Ideally, local initiatives and agreements between child serving systems should be approved of and supported by state systems, such as state departments of education, mental health, juvenile justice, and child welfare.

### Logistics

The time to conduct screening must be determined. Some have recommended transitional years such as sixth and seventh and ninth and 10th grades as critical times when clinical symptoms often linked to increased suicide risk sometimes develop. However, screening efforts at these ages should ideally be part of broader efforts within communities to promote wellness, mental health, and learning success for youth from preschool through young adulthood. Locally collected data such as emergency room data can assist in identifying age groups at particular risk. In the absence of locally available data, state and national data such as the Youth Risk Behavior Survey . . . can be helpful. However, if the planning group determines that there are inadequate resources to provide adequate follow-up to the screen, the screening process should be delayed until adequate resources are marshaled and confidence of adequate follow-up is increased.

### Training, Supervision, and Support

Staff that participate in screening will require adequate training and supervision. Personnel will be needed who can coordinate the work; select age-appropriate and culturally sensitive measurement tools; manage associated technology for administering, scoring, and interpreting the data; and establish and sustain relationships with school and community providers.

Regardless of whether a school implements a systematic screening program, all schools should enhance their capacity to identify youth who present signs of emotional/behavioral disturbance. These disturbances represent barriers to learning and are indicative of the development of serious mental health concerns. Schools should connect these youth to appropriate resources and services. Professional development will be required to raise awareness and increase knowledge of child and adolescent mental health needs, the factors that promote healthy youth development and those that contribute to mental health problems, specific signs of distress, and strategies to assist distressed youth in obtaining help. All staff should have a clear understanding of referral procedures and know how to determine when a youth is in crisis and needs an immediate intervention.

### Integration

Mental health screening should be one aspect of a full continuum of effective mental health programs and services in schools. Such programs can only exist when there is a full partnership between families, schools, and child serving systems, particularly the mental health system. There must be strong emphases on quality assessment and improvement, empirically supported practice, and evaluating outcomes of services. Findings from outcome evaluations should be used to continuously improve services and should connect to advocacy and policy agendas.

## Conclusion

The President's New Freedom Commission on Mental Health provides specific recommendations to improve and expand school mental health programs and to screen for co-occurring mental and substance use disorders and link with integrated treatment strategies. The New Freedom Initiative and its 19 specific recommendations represent a call to action for communities and states to move beyond fragmented and ineffective approaches to illness care for a small percentage of those in need toward a true public mental health promotion system that ensures quality and effectiveness along a full continuum of services. Consideration of the issues outlined in this article should help schools and communities determine whether they are ready to include screening in schools as part of their SMH program.

When implemented with appropriate family, school, and community involvement, mental health screening in schools has the potential to be a cornerstone of a transformed mental health system that identifies youth in need, links them to effective services, and contributes to positive health and educational outcomes valued by families, schools, and communities.

# EXPLORING THE ISSUE

## Is Mental Health Screening an Unwarranted Intrusion?

## Challenge Questions

- Compare and contrast the positions of the YES and NO selections regarding whether mental health screening is an unwarranted intrusion.
- Which selection makes the best case for its argument? Why?
- What services/plans does your local school have for addressing mental health needs? Do they screen? Why/why not? Do you agree with their reasoning?
- How would you use information from the YES and NO selections to affect your actions as an educator?

## Is There Common Ground?

The authors agree that mental health needs are burgeoning. They also agree that the consequences of failing to appropriately address mental health problems can be dire.

## Additional Resources

Effrem, K. R. (2005). *Myths and facts regarding mental health screening programs and psychiatric drug treatment for children*. Retrieved February 10, 2008 from www.education.org/

Friedman, R. A. (2006). Uncovering an epidemic: Screening for mental illness in teens. *The New England Journal of Medicine, 355*(26). Retrieved March 23, 2008 from www.nejm.org

Kenny, H. A. (2007). *Implementing the Rosie D remedy: The opportunities and challenges of restructuring a system of care for children's mental health in Massachusetts*. Boston, MA: Massachusetts Medicaid Policy Institute. Retrieved March 1, 2008 from www.massmedicaid.org

Lehrman, N. S. (2006). The dangers of mental health screening. *Journal of American Physicians and Surgeons, 11*(3), 80–82.

NAMI (2005, January). *Mental Health Screening: Fact vs. fiction*. Retrieved January 4, 2008 from www.nami.org

President's New Freedom Commission on Mental Health. (2003). *Achieving the promise: Transforming mental health care in America. Final report*. Department of Health and Human Services. Retrieved January 7, 2008 from www .mentalhealthcommission.gov

Schildkrout, B. (2011). *Unmasking psychological symptoms: How therapists can learn to recognize the psychological presentation of medical disorders.* Hoboken, NJ: Wiley.

Weist, R., Rubin, M., Moore, E., Adelsheim, S., & Wrobel, G. (2007). Mental health screening in schools. *Journal of School Health, 77,* 53–58.

# ISSUE 17

## Should the Government Prohibit the Use of Restraint and Seclusion in Schools?

**YES: National Disability Rights Network,** from *School Is Not Supposed to Hurt: The U.S. Department of Education Must Do More to Protect School Children from Restraint and Seclusion* (2012), www.ndrn.org, March 20, 2012

**NO: Sasha Pudelski,** from *Keeping Schools Safe: How Seclusion and Restraint Protects Students and School Personnel* (2012), www.aasa.org, March 20, 2012

---

### Learning Outcomes

**At the conclusion of this issue, readers will be able to:**

- Compare and contrast the positions of the YES and NO selections addressing whether schools should be banned from using restraint and seclusion with students.
- Describe the strengths and the weaknesses of each side's arguments.
- Discuss pending/existing legislation and its impact on students and educators.
- Consider implications of each position for addressing extreme student behavior.

---

**ISSUE SUMMARY**

**YES:** The National Disability Rights Network (NDRN) has authored three major reports highlighting concerns about the use of restraint and seclusion in schools. In the face of continuing legislative gridlock, the latest report urges the U.S. federal Department of Education to issue clear guidance limiting restraint and seclusion to situations posing an imminent danger.

**NO:** Sasha Pudelski, government affairs manager for the American Association of School Administrators (AASA), presents her organization's position that restraint and seclusion need to be available tools in schools. Banning their use with any and all students could actually increase the potential for injury.

"**V**ictim Information: Female, 4, born with cerebral palsy and diagnosed as autistic. West Virginia Public School. Case details: Child suffered bruising and post traumatic stress disorder after teachers restrained her in a wooden chair with leather straps—described as resembling a miniature electric chair—for being uncooperative." This is one illustration provided during the testimony of Gregory Kurtz of the Government Accounting Office (GAO) in front of the House of Representatives in May 2009 (www.gao.gov). The hearing was titled *Examining the Abuse and Deadly Use of Restraints and Seclusion in Schools*. GAO, the audit, evaluation, and investigative arm of Congress, had been charged with reviewing current laws regarding restraint and seclusion in schools and examining cases where students "had died or suffered abuse" as a result of these techniques. GAO did not seek to assess any possible beneficial outcomes of the use of restraint and seclusion.

GAO's study revealed little legal or regulatory structure. No U.S. federal laws addressed the use of restraint and seclusion practices in public and private schools. State laws varied. Individuals with Disabilities Education Act (IDEA) does not preclude identifying seclusion and restraints as methods in individualized education plans (IEPs).

Other voices were heard at the hearing. One witness spoke to the essential need for restraint and/or seclusion in times of emergency and/or danger where no other techniques have worked. Another noted that adoption of positive schoolwide behavioral supports reduced the use of restraint and seclusion.

Subsequent to the House hearing, legislators in both houses of Congress proposed bills addressing the use of restraint/seclusion, required training for staff, and mandatory notice to parents. Although containing many of the same elements, the bills differed in emphasis. The 2009 bills passed in the House, but not the Senate. The 2011 proposals of the Keeping All Students Safe Act are referred to as H.R. 1831 and S2020. The Senate bill prohibits discussing restraint/seclusion in an IEP; a violation of this injunction would be considered a denial of free and appropriate education. These bills are moving slowly, with support from fewer legislators than before.

Jessica Butler (*How safe is the schoolhouse?* www.autcom.org, 2012) tracks how states have reacted to the U.S. federal congressional debates. As of her April 2012 update, 30 states had legislation governing the use of restraint/seclusion; 12 of these either adopted or strengthened their laws incorporating elements of U.S. federal proposals. Twelve additional states had nonbinding guidance for districts. Some states addressed only students with disabilities; others addressed all students. Definitions of restraint and seclusion were not consistent. Commenting on the wide differences, Butler concluded, "Where a child lives still determines the protection he/she gets."

Although there is no universal description of these tools in schools, definitions and standards have been established for psychiatric institutions and residential settings by the Center for Medicare and Medicaid Services. For the purpose of this text, these will be used as cited on the Restraints and Seclusion Rules Chart, on the website of The National Council for Community Behavioral Healthcare (www.thenationalcouncil.org, 2012). Restraint is defined as "Any manual method or physical or mechanical device, material or equipment attached or adjacent to a patient's body that he or she cannot easily remove that restricts freedom of movement or normal access of one's body." Chemicals or medication can also be used as restraint. The Council defines seclusion as "The involuntary confinement of a person in a room or an area where the person is physically prevented from leaving." Seclusion does not include time-out spaces, which differ because the student is free to leave the space.

Other professional and advocacy organizations have contributed their perspectives on restraint and seclusion. Much of this input has informed the proposed legislation. The Council of Parent Attorneys and Advocates (COPAA) issued a declaration of principles (2008, www.copaa.net) claiming repeated use of restraints/seclusion demonstrates "the failure of educational programming." COPAA advocates the use of positive behavioral interventions, focusing on de-escalation and positive behavioral supports. In cases of imminent danger, where less restrictive measures have not succeeded, restraint/seclusion could be employed for the minimum amount of time necessary. COPAA found some techniques so dangerous that they should be banned; these include prone restraints, and aversive techniques such as pain, shock, or seclusion in a room from which the child cannot escape.

The Council for Children with Behavioral Disorders (CCBD) issued Position Statements on the use of restraint and on the use of seclusion (2009, www.ccbd.net), both of which are extensive in their exploration of the topic. Like COPAA, CCBD recommends de-escalation techniques; limits appropriate use of restraint/seclusion to situations of imminent danger, and lists some techniques so unsafe that they should never be used. The CCBD Position Statements also recommend that legislation address both typical learners and those with disabilities; guidelines are not strong enough to protect everyone involved.

CCBD and COPAA both emphasize the need for staff to be trained in a range of techniques, from positive supports to de-escalation and restraint/seclusion. Proposed legislation incorporates this emphasis. Opposition to training has been expressed by The Alliance to Prevent Restraint, Aversive Interventions and Seclusion (APRAIS, http://tash.org), which seeks to eliminate the use of restraint and seclusion. Training would only increase their use—and the consequent potential for harm to individuals.

The Office of Civil Rights (*Revealing new truths about our nation's schools*, 2012, www2.ed.gov) presented information about a student's likelihood to experience restraint and/or seclusion. Males make up approximately 50 percent of the school population, but 70 percent of those experiencing restraint and or seclusion. Although students with disabilities are 12 percent of the school population; they were almost 70 percent of those physically restrained in schools. There is a racial divide as well: African American students comprise 21 percent of those with disabilities, but 44 percent of students with disabilities who experience mechanical restraint.

This issue explores the complicated and emotional topic of whether the government should prohibit the use of restraints and seclusion in schools. The selections address current practices and concerns, emphasizing the role of government.

In the YES selection, the National Disability Rights Network (NDRN, www.ndrn.org) restates and expands upon its concerns about the use of restraint and seclusion, using riveting case illustrations. The first version of this report spurred the GAO actions, which led to legislative proposals. In the continuing absence of any U.S. federal standard of practice, NDRN urged the Department of Education (ED) to issue mandatory guidance to ensure that restraint and seclusion are used only when necessary to protect individuals from imminent physical danger. NDRN encourages ED to hold stakeholder summits and fund demonstration projects, which will develop practices to ultimately end the use of these techniques and the suffering of children who endure them.

In the NO selection, Sasha Pudelski presents the view of the American Association of School Administrators (AASA), also using vivid examples. Acknowledging that there are problems in some schools, Pudelski maintains that restraint and seclusion are used very rarely and help students stay in the least restrictive environment. Informed, careful use of restraints and seclusions—for typical students as well as those with disabilities—prevents injury and protects against dangerous situations. The role of the U.S. federal government should be limited to funding training so that educators are well informed about an array of intervention techniques.

There is little question that educators should intervene to protect students from harm. There are many questions about the appropriate timing of that intervention as well as the possible physical consequences to adults and students alike.

Student misbehavior ranges from small infractions to more intense challenges and dangerous acts. Allday (2011, *Intervention in School and Clinic*) observed that minor misbehaviors can trigger frustration and overreaction from a teacher, especially one new to the field. A hasty word or act can snowball into a confrontation that leads to excluding a child from class. This action actually rewards both the undesirable behavior and the exclusion, rather than improves the situation. The teacher is relieved of the challenging student; the student escapes an unpleasant situation. Instead of reacting, Allday recommends that teachers endeavor to prevent misbehavior through the use of rules and routines, and subtle actions such as teacher proximity and rule reminders.

Repeated misbehavior and teacher frustration sometimes lead unprepared teachers to use restraint and seclusion even after these tools have been found to be ineffective in changing unwanted—even dangerous—behavior (Smith, Katsiyannis, & Ryan, *Behavioral Disorders*, 2011). Identifying the reason for the behavior is a more productive course of action.

IDEA requires the use of a functional behavioral assessment (FBA) when a student has experienced 10 days of suspension, brings drugs or a weapon to school, or is determined to be a danger to self or others. Although this is a time-consuming process, conducting an FBA at an earlier stage can help everyone determine a productive course of action before behavior escalates (Menzies &

Lane, *Preventing School Failure*, 2011). Recording and analyzing occurrences of the target behavior as well as its antecedents and consequences yield powerful information. If the educator can discern patterns in the behavior, a less drastic solution might emerge.

In late May 2012, the U.S. Department of Education issued a long-awaited *Restraint and seclusion: Resource document* (www.ed.gov/policy/restraintseclusion). Containing 15 nonbinding principles to be used in forming local policy, the *Resource document* addresses all children, not just those with disabilities. Prevention of restraint and isolation should be the priority; use should be limited to dangerous situations and never as a punishment or convenience.

# School Is Not Supposed to Hurt: The U.S. Department of Education Must Do More to Protect School Children from Restraint and Seclusion

## I. Executive Summary

Many schools are regularly using restraint and seclusion to control student behavior. Students are suffering, especially very young students. Congress has failed to act. Some states enacted laws and regulations to protect school children, but the progress is slow and the laws are often inconsistent and incomplete.

[The Department of Education (ED)] is in the unique position to issue strong national guidance to state education agencies and local school districts about when the use of restraint and seclusion might violate anti-discrimination and education laws, similar to the guidance that the Office of Civil Rights has already issued on bullying and harassment. The guidance at a minimum must also limit the use of physical restraint or seclusion to circumstances when necessary to protect a child or others from imminent physical danger and not weaken existing protections in the states.

ED is also in the unique position to pull together a national summit of researchers, educators, mental health professionals, and others to discuss whether restraint and seclusion has any therapeutic value . . . to develop evidence-based best practices to prevent and reduce the use of restraint and seclusion. ED should collaborate with the Substance Abuse and Mental Health Services Administration (SAMHSA) in this effort because SAMHSA has successfully supported efforts over the last decade to reduce the use of restraint and seclusion in mental health facilities. ED should fund demonstration projects to test what works.

ED can prevent future injuries and deaths by investigating restraint and seclusion (even where there is no individual complaint) and requiring school districts to take appropriate corrective action.

Finally, ED can define the scope of the problem and how to address it by immediately [analyzing] data it has collected for the 2009–2010 school year

National Disability Rights Network (NDRN). From *School Is Not Supposed to Hurt: The U.S. Department of Education Must Do More to Protect School Children from Restraint and Seclusion*, March 2012. Copyright © 2012 by National Disability Rights Network. Reprinted by permission. www.ndrn.org

about the use of restraint and seclusion. . . . [It] should . . . determine which school districts and schools have unusually high numbers of restraint and seclusion incidents, analyze what might be causing this and then fund demonstration and research projects to reduce—and eventually eliminate—restraint and seclusion in those schools.

# II. School Children Are Continuing to Suffer

NDRN issued reports about the use of restraint and seclusion in 2009 and 2010. Since then many others, including the Government Accountability Office, have reported on deaths and injuries resulting from the use of restraint and seclusion in schools. Despite the alarms that have been raised, students are continuing to be hurt in our nation's schools. Below are only a few of the examples that protection and advocacy agencies have collected since NDRN issued its January 2010 report.

## Arizona—Misuse of Postural Support Chairs as Restraints

Rifkin, a manufacturer of postural support chairs, has explicitly warned that postural support chairs are not supposed to be used to restrain children and youth to control their behavior. Nevertheless, schools continue to use postural support chairs "off-label." For example, in 2011, a public school teacher strapped a 7-year old child into a postural support chair and moved him into another room because he was disrupting the class. The child tried to twist out of the chair, ending up with his face against the back of the chair and getting scratched by nails in the chair when the teacher tried to untangle him. The school did not take any corrective action. It could have prohibited staff from using postural support chairs to restrain children. Use of postural support chairs for behavioral reasons violates the IDEA because it is not an evidence-based practice and violates the ADA and § 504 because only students with disabilities are being restrained in postural support chairs.

## Colorado—Duct Taping Child to Wheelchair

The teacher in a public middle school duct-taped a 12-year-old student's only ambulatory arm to his wheelchair, claiming that she was trying to keep him from choking himself, but his grandmother claimed that the reflex in his arm was the only way for him to communicate. The Legal Center for People with Disabilities and Older People did an investigation and recommended that the school do more training on the state law regarding restraint and seclusion because restraints, such as the duct tape, was a mechanical restraint prohibited under state law.

## Connecticut—Scream Rooms

According to a complaint filed with the Office of Civil Rights of the U.S. Department of Education, elementary school students with disabilities at Farm Hill School in Middletown, Connecticut, were being held against their will in what administrators called "time out rooms," but which parents called "scream rooms."

The complaint stated that these are small, cement-walled rooms and that students in regular education report hearing their classmates screaming and banging on the door and school staff have reported having to clean up blood and urine from these rooms. Students with disabilities are apparently being secluded, restrained and injured at school repeatedly. The school has acknowledged publicly that it is treating students with disabilities differently from their non-disabled classmates. The school's superintendent stated that "unless you have an IEP, this is not part of your plan." The superintendent later stated that he had directed all staff to cease using the rooms for students who do not have Individualized Education Programs (IEPs) and that the room had been moved to the second floor of the school so general education classes would not be disrupted by the screaming. . . .

## Idaho—Repeatedly Secluded, Restrained and Sprayed

A middle school child with Asperger's Syndrome was repeatedly placed in seclusion for non-compliant behaviors—"shutting down" and being generally non-responsive. The child sustained rug burns on his back from being dragged across the floor to the room by his hands and/or feet; he also indicated he was sometimes sprayed by the teacher with a water bottle containing a chemical cleaning solution for the white board. The child's mother filed complaints with Child Protection Services, the school district and the police, who investigated the allegations. The child was removed from the teacher's classroom; no other disciplinary action was disclosed by the school, citing "personnel matters." An advocate from the DisAbility Rights Idaho intervened. Independent behavior consultants were brought in to conduct assessments and draft an appropriate behavior plan, with positive behavior services provided by trained staff. . . .

### Iowa—Tied to a Lunch Table

The Individualized Education Program of a 15-year-old student with autism, cerebral palsy, intellectual disabilities and epilepsy stated that he must have two aides with him at all time, but the school failed to consistently provide the aides. When there was only one aide, the school used a gait belt and other means to restrain the child to the lunch table and a recliner "for his own safety." Disability Rights Iowa assisted his parents in filing a complaint with the Iowa Dept. of Education. The complaint alleged that the restraint violated state law, the IEP and behavior plan were inappropriate and the school had failed to provide the student with a free and appropriate public education (FAPE). The state ruled in favor of the child on denial of FAPE, inappropriate restraint and ordered compensatory education for the child and also training for the school district on restraint and seclusion and health programs. . . .

### Kansas—Secluded as Punishment

The mother of a 13-year-old child with disabilities contacted the Disability Rights Center of Kansas with allegations of extensive improper seclusion. Her son has been diagnosed with intellectual disabilities, speech delays significantly limiting his ability to communicate, and epilepsy. He has no mental health diagnosis, but he has been placed at a school for students with behavior issues. The child has a behavior plan which prohibits him from touching anybody without permission. Impermissible touching includes a hug, high five, or fist bump. If he does not follow the plan, he is sent immediately without warning to the in-school suspension room (ISS) room in the principal's office. The school also has a separate seclusion room in each classroom which is also called an ISS room. All rooms have no windows and only a door. The mother has learned that during the past several weeks her son has spent 8-1/2 days in a seclusion room. The child has been sent to the room for as long as the entire day and sometimes into the following day. The door is always closed. The mother understands that the school does not record the removals on exclusion report forms, and they are noted only on his daily point sheets which she must sign and return to the school. Her son has been suspended over 10 times and has never had a manifestation hearing. . . .

## New Hampshire—Secluded When Anxious

A child with a disability had a history of bolting out of the room whenever her anxiety increased. Her classroom teachers came up with an informal plan (permitting her to have some 1:1 time with a preferred staff member when she became anxious) but never conducted a functional behavioral assessment. Unfortunately, the school did not implement this plan consistently and the student continued to refuse to do work and bolt out of the classroom when she became anxious. In response, school personnel repeatedly put her into an 8' × 10' seclusion room for about 20–30 minutes at a time. Rather than helping the student calm down, secluding her made her even more anxious. After the Disabilities Rights Center . . . investigated, the school agreed to stop using the room for this particular student and developed protocols requiring functional behavioral assessment before seclusion is even contemplated, monitoring during seclusion, and documentation of antecedents and consequences of seclusion. . . .

# III. Congress Has Not Passed Legislation

In January 2009, NDRN issued "School Is Not Supposed To Hurt," the report included policy recommendations for federal, state, and local policymakers that included banning prone restraint and seclusion and was the catalyst for then Chairman George Miller of the House Education and Labor Committee to request a report from the Government Accountability Office that further documented the abuse, at times deadly, that students have experienced as a result of the use of restraint and seclusion in the nation's schools.

A hearing was held on May 19,2009, at which then Chairman Miller stated that the report issued by NDRN was the inciting force behind the development of the legislation to prevent the harmful use of restraint and seclusion in schools. On December 9, 2009, George Miller (D-CA) and Cathy McMorris Rodgers (R-WA) introduced the Preventing Harmful Restraint and Seclusion in Schools Act (H.R. 4247). On the same day, Senator Christopher Dodd (D-CT) also introduced legislation with the same title. The bills would have established minimum federal standards on the use of restraint and seclusion in schools, and limited the use of these practices to situations where students present an imminent risk of harm to themselves or others. The legislation was renamed the Keeping All Students Safe Act, and the House of Representative's Committee on Education and Labor passed the legislation in February 2010, and the full House of Representatives passed it by a vote of 262 yeas to 153 nays on March 3, 2010. Right before Congress recessed for the 2010 elections, Senators Christopher Dodd and Richard Burr (R-NC) introduced a new version of the legislation in the Senate (S. 3895). This legislation had many similarities to the version that passed the House of Representatives, but also had some very important differences. Ultimately, time ran out for the Senate to mark-up and bring a bill to the floor to debate in the 111th Congress.

On April 6, 2011, Ranking Member George Miller reintroduced the Keeping All Students Safe Act with Representative Gregg Harper (R-MS) as the lead co-sponsor (H.R. 1381). H.R. 1381 is the same bill that passed the House of Representatives in the 111th Congress, and as of February 22, 2012 has 31 co-sponsors. On December 16, 2011, Senator Tom Harkin (D-IA) introduced a new Senate version of the Keeping All Students Safe Act (S. 2020) with many significant changes; most notable is a prohibition on the use of seclusion.

Even though the stories of abuse and neglect through the use of restraint and seclusion continue to occur on almost a daily basis and some legislators have tirelessly worked to protect school children from restraint and seclusion, others have stopped passage of a federal law based on the misperception that this can be addressed at the state or local level. This ignores the fact that without strong federal leadership on this topic, changes at the state and local level are inconsistent and slow in occurring.

## IV. States Are Slow to Put Adequate Protections in Place

The activity on the federal level made states more aware of the dangers of restraint and seclusion and spurred some states to improve their legal protections. In 2009, when NDRN published its first report on restraint and seclusion in schools, the Government Accountability Office reported that state laws and regulations about restraint and seclusion in schools varied widely. According to the Government Accountability Office, 19 states had no laws or regulations. Seven states placed some restrictions on the use of restraints, but did not regulate seclusion. Only 17 states required that selected staff receive training before being permitted to restrain children. Only 19 states required parents to be notified after restraint had been used.

Unfortunately, almost three years later, there are only 29 states with protections against restraint and seclusion of school children. Another 7 states have laws that do not create any meaningful protection for children. There are 13 states with voluntary guidelines that are not legally binding. And, 6 states have no protection whatsoever: Arizona, Idaho, Mississippi, North Dakota, New Jersey, and South Dakota, although at least 3 of them have tried to take some action.

Thus, with the legislation in Congress blocked by a few members and inadequate and inconsistent state legislation, the only entity that can provide national leadership in protecting school children from the harmful use of restraint and seclusion is the ED, which is in a perfect position to fund demonstration projects, issue strong guidance, and follow through on the recommendations outlined at the end of this report.

# V. ED's Failure to Protect School Children from Restraint and Seclusion

ED has made some promising statements and taken some promising steps to reduce the use of restraint and seclusion in schools. However, ED has also sent out mixed signals and has not clearly stated what is and what is not permissible under either the Individuals with Disabilities Education Act (IDEA) or Section 504 of the Rehabilitation Act of 1973 (Section 504) or antidiscrimination laws. ED has also failed to issue strong guidance that at a minimum must also limit the use of physical restraint or seclusion to circumstances when necessary to protect a child or others from imminent physical danger.

## A. Office of the Secretary

In 2009, after legislation was introduced in the House of Representatives to severely curtail the use of restraint and seclusion in schools, . . . Secretary Arne Duncan issued letters to Representatives George Miller and Cathy McMorris Rodgers supporting their proposed legislation. In his letter, the Secretary noted several "principles" that Congress should consider as it developed legislation:

- Any behavioral intervention must be consistent with the child's right to be treated with dignity and to be free from abuse regardless of the child's educational needs or behavioral challenges;
- Physical restraint and seclusion should never be used as punishment or discipline;
- Physical restraint and seclusion should never be used that restricts a child's breathing;
- Limit the use of physical restraint and seclusion in schools . . . except when it is necessary to protect a child or others from imminent danger;
- Every instance of physical restraint and seclusion should be appropriately monitored to ensure the safety of the child, other children, teachers, and other personnel;
- Parents should be notified promptly following the use of restraint or seclusion on their child, and any such use should be documented in writing;
- Teachers and other personnel should be trained regularly on the appropriate use of restraint and seclusion and the use of effective alternatives, such as positive behavioral intervention and supports.

Unfortunately, . . . ED has not consistently applied these principles in its policy announcements on restraint and seclusion.

On July 31, 2009, the Secretary issued a letter to the Chief State School Officers, requiring them to provide copies of the restraint and seclusion guidelines in their states. ED published the information obtained from the states in response to the letter at http://www2.ed.gov/policy/seclusion/seclusion-state-summary.html.

In the letter, the Secretary urged the States to revise their policies and again made some very promising statements concerning limiting the use of restraint and seclusion in schools. . . .

The Secretary also emphasized the important role that Positive Behavior Intervention Strategies (PBIS) can provide in limiting the use of restraint and seclusion in schools:

> PBIS provides a framework for decision making that guides the implemen-
> tation of evidence-based academic and behavioral practices throughout
> the entire school, frequently resulting in significant reductions in office
> disciplinary referrals, suspensions, and expulsions. While the successful
> implementation of PBIS typically results in improved social and academic
> outcomes, it will not eliminate all behavior incidents in a school. However,
> PBIS is an important preventative approach that can increase the capacity
> of the school staff to support children with the most complex behavioral
> needs, thus reducing the instances that require intensive interventions.

Unfortunately, in a letter issued . . . on January 26, 2010, the Secretary undercut much of what he had said in his prior letters. The letter starts out promising. The Secretary noted that . . . he was "very concerned that we do all we can to help ensure that schools are places of safety for all our children and that the use of seclusion and restraint is very limited." The Secretary also stated that "no child should be subjected to the abusive or potentially deadly use of seclusion or restraint in a school."

However, the Secretary went on to state that although the "IDEA emphasizes and encourages the use of positive behavioral interventions and supports, [it] does not prohibit the use of other measures, such as seclusion, *non-emergency* restraint, or *aversive* behavioral intervention when appropriate" (emphasis added). By stating that restraint or seclusion may be used in non-emergency situations contradicts the Secretary's prior statements that these measures should be used in only limited circumstances. Further, by stating that aversives may be used, the Secretary undercuts his statements that students should be treated with dignity and be free from abuse.

Additionally, with respect to Section 504, the Secretary stated that it "does not expressly authorize us to ban . . ."—"electric shock, other *painful* and aver-sive procedures, seclusion, and *unnecessary* restraint, and food deprivation" (emphasis added). In spite of the Secretary's comment, it is hard to imagine that the infliction of pain and the use of unnecessary restraint is consistent with the basic protections to be free from discrimination under Section 504.

## B.  Office of Civil Rights

ED's Office for Civil Rights (OCR) has also taken some promising steps to address the use of restraint and seclusion in schools. OCR added restraint and seclusion to its data collection of 7,000 school districts for the 2009–10 school year. It also maintained restraint and seclusion in its data collection for all school districts in the country for the 2011–2012 school year. However, OCR has taken an exceedingly long time to publish the data from the 2009–10 school year. . . . ED . . . should promptly analyze it to determine which school districts and schools have unusually high numbers of restraint and seclusion incidents, analyze what might be causing this and then fund demonstration and research projects to reduce—and eventually eliminate—restraint and seclusion in those schools.

OCR has also issued several decisions over the years regarding the use of restraint or seclusion of which NDRN is aware, yet only a handful have found any violation of Section 504. When looking at claims that the use of restraint or seclusion [is] a violation of Section 504, OCR should adopt the seven principles set out in Secretary Duncan's letters to Representatives George Miller and Cathy McMorris Rodgers.

In addition, it would be very useful to all stakeholders—students, parents, school personnel and advocates—if OCR provided some clarity about when the use of restraint and seclusion would violate the IDEA, the Americans with Disabilities Act (ADA), Section 504 and other anti-discrimination laws with respect to the following:

### i. Safe Environments

In addition, OCR can borrow from principles enunciated in cases involving Peanut and Tree Nut Allergies (PTAs). For example, OCR has said, "As the vast majority of District students without disabilities do not face a significant possibility of experiencing serious and life-threatening reactions to their environment while they attend District schools, Section 504 and Title II of the ADA require that the District provide the Student with an environment in which he also does not face such a significant possibility." But, such is the case if PTAs are not accommodated.

In the same way, what parent sends a child to school expecting the child will be subjected to dangerous, abusive or traumatic practices, as documented in this report. These practices have nothing to do with whether there is anything in an IEP. Similar to its PTA cases, OCR must look at the nature of the intervention and at some point it becomes discriminatory, regardless of whether it is in the IEP.

### ii. Harassment

ED and other federal departments have rightly devoted significant resources to bring attention to bullying and to develop strategies to combat it. . . . ED composed *Anti-Bullying Policies: Examples of Provisions in State Laws,* a guidance document outlining common key components of state anti-bullying laws. Following [a] Summit, ED's Policy and Program Studies Service contracted researchers to compile the analysis on state laws and policies. The White House held a bullying conference in March 2011. Then, in September 2011, ED held a second summit to discuss continued strategies for combatting bullying.

As Secretary Arne Duncan said at the White House Summit:

> Students should not be threatened physically, isolated socially, or hurt emotionally based on their skin color, their ethnicity, any physical

or mental disabilities, their sex, their sexual orientation, their gender identity, religion or any other reason. Through our collective efforts, we're going to be able to reduce this harassment and make schools a better place for students to learn . . . I start with a simple premise that no school can be a great school until it is a safe school . . . You cannot do your best or concentrate academically if you are scared.

His comments about the harm caused to school children by bullies apply equally to the harm caused by school staff when they restrain or seclude a child. In both cases, students may be threatened physically, isolated socially and hurt emotionally. In both cases, students cannot be expected to learn if they do not feel safe at school.

In fact, ED's definition of bullying accurately describes instances in which school staff use restraint and seclusion for the purpose of coercion, discipline, convenience or retaliation, rather than to ensure immediate physical safety of the student or others (emergency situations):

Although definitions of bullying vary, most agree that bullying involves:

- **Imbalance of Power:** people who bully use their power to control or harm and the people being bullied may have a hard time defending themselves
- **Intent to Cause Harm:** actions done by accident are not bullying; the person bullying has a goal to cause harm
- **Repetition:** incidents of bullying happen to the same person over and over by the same person or group.

Under this definition, the only potential difference between bullying and restraint and seclusion used for non-emergency purposes is the actors. Typically, bullying involves student-on-student abuse while restraint and seclusion in non-emergency situations involve staff-on-student abuse.

As ED states on its StopBullying website:

Everyone can help prevent and stop bullying. Adults have the responsibility to protect and be a role model for kids, teens, and young adults.

School staff cannot be a role model to stop bullying if staff is simultaneously using violence in the forms of restraint and seclusion in non-emergency situations. Students who witness such violence are traumatized themselves and may believe that violence is an appropriate way to act.

Many of the strategies for stopping bullying are the same strategies for stopping restraint and seclusion. We urge ED to start viewing these acts as being on the same continuum of school safety and take appropriate actions to stop them.

### iii. Disparate Treatment
Another strategy that OCR should use when analyzing restraint and seclusion cases is disparate treatment—whether between students with disabilities and students that do not have disabilities or racial and ethnic minorities with

disabilities compared with students that do not have disabilities. Statistically significant discrepancies create a prima facie case of discrimination which the school will have to rebut, including by addressing what efforts they are taking to reduce the need for restraint and seclusion system wide when disparate treatment is found.

### iv. Informed Consent

Finally, OCR should uniformly adopt the standard enunciated in a decision from the California Regional Office to analyze whether the parents were properly informed of and consented to the use of restraint or seclusion, even if their use is in an IEP or behavior plan. In that case OCR noted that a district "that chooses to educate students in a highly restrictive placement, including seclusion under adverse conditions for extended periods of time, must meet the highest standard of procedural adherence in order to receive deference and comply with Section 504." OCR concluded that the County program did not meet this standard.

## C. Office of Special Education and Rehabilitative Services [OSERS]

. . . Like OCR, OSERS should issue revised policies that reflect the seven principles outlined by Secretary Arne Duncan.

### i. Free and Appropriate Public Education (FAPE)

The IDEA has other core principles which OSERS should adopt to limit the use of restraint and seclusion in schools. First, the definition of FAPE includes the requirement that services must meet state standards. Therefore, although the IDEA provides the basic floor of opportunity, any state law, regulation or policy that creates greater protections is also binding within that state. Therefore, all laws, regulations or policies in a state that provide greater protections on restraint or seclusion are binding on the covered educational programs in that state.

Additionally, OSERS policy should recognize the basic educational principle that behavior is a form of communication. Given school districts' obligations to ensure that students receive FAPE, when a student's behavior rises to the point where it is so severe that school staff decide to restrain or seclude the student, the school must take steps to identify the issues giving rise to the behavior and undertake steps to ensure that this behavior does not recur. When less informal measures are not successful in reducing this behavior, these steps must include a Functional Behavioral Assessment (FBA) and meetings with the individualized education program team to address the student's program.

### ii. "Off-Use" of Equipment

OSERS should also flatly prohibit the "off-use" of equipment. A chair is a chair for sitting, not for being tied into. A Rifton chair and wheelchairs are designed for specific types of disabilities and are not intended to be used for restraint other than for the specific purposes for which they are designed.

### iii. Evidence-Based Practices

The IDEA requires that services be research based to the extent practicable. There is no research to support the use of either restraint or seclusion for therapeutic purposes. Therefore, OSERS should state that they are not permitted for these purposes. Moreover, given the dangers associated with the use of restraint and seclusion, restraint and seclusion should not be permitted as forms of discipline for student misconduct.

### iv. Least Restrictive Environment

OSERS should also build into its policy the obligations based on the least restrictive environment requirement—that the IDEA requires that removal "from the regular educational environment occurs only when the nature or severity of the disability is such that education in regular classes with the use of supplementary aids and services cannot be achieved satisfactorily." Seclusion is most definitely a removal from the "regular educational environment" and, arguably so is a restraint. Therefore, school districts must be required to provide necessary supplementary aids and services to prevent both seclusion and restraint. Supplementary aids and services may include supports for the student, such as an individual aid, and program modifications or supports for the school personnel. Such support should include training in how to meet the needs of the student in such a way as to obviate the need for either seclusion or restraint.

### v. Monitoring

Finally, to avoid the danger of harm, no seclusion should ever be used where the student is not constantly monitored. Instances of students' soiling themselves or being traumatized or otherwise harmed by the use of seclusion or restraint as documented in this report are not acceptable and should not be tolerated.

## Specific Recommendations for Guidance

ED should provide strong guidance to state departments of education, school districts, school personnel, students and families about when restraint and seclusion violate federal antidiscrimination and education laws. The guidance at a minimum must also limit the use of physical restraint or seclusion to circumstances when necessary to protect a child or others from imminent physical danger, and not weaken existing protections in the states. In analyzing whether a restraint or seclusion would violate the federal anti-discrimination and education laws, the decision should not be governed by whether or not their use is in an IEP. The nature of the restraint or seclusion, the effects on the student, and steps taken to obviate the need for restraint or seclusion need to be independently analyzed. In addition, States can have additional restrictions on the use of either restraint or seclusion. . . .

Sasha Pudelski

# Keeping Schools Safe: How Seclusion and Restraint Protects Students and School Personnel

## Introduction

AASA has long opposed the prohibition of seclusion and restraint in public schools. We believe the use of seclusion and restraint has enabled many students with serious emotional or behavioral conditions to be educated not only within our public schools, but also in the least restrictive and safest environments possible.

Some of the approximately 4.7 million school personnel working in our public schools are not perfect. The unfortunate reality is that they make a variety of mistakes, sometimes intentionally, that can hurt children. However, AASA does not support federal policies built around the few wrongful individuals who choose to disobey school policies, state regulations, or state and federal criminal laws. Because circumstances where seclusion and restraint are used inappropriately are the vast exception to the rule, we advocate for policies that support the 99 percent of school personnel that use seclusion and restraint safely, responsibly and only when circumstances truly demand their application.

In early 2012, AASA conducted a randomized survey of school administrators across the U.S. on how often seclusion and restraint was used in their school districts and whether school personnel were injured as a result of working with students who needed to be secluded or restrained. The results of our survey are as follows:

- 10 percent of respondents used seclusion and restraint more than 5% of the time in a single school year.
- 97 percent of respondents said that staff who perform seclusion and restraint are either trained or certified in how to perform safe and appropriate seclusion and restraint.
- 95 percent of school personnel who perform seclusion and restraint are trained in prevention and conflict de-escalation or positive behavioral interventions and supports.

- 25 percent of school districts reported that at least 20 times in the last school year, an administrator, teacher, paraprofessional, aide or other school professional trained in proper seclusion and restraint techniques has been physically threatened or attacked by a student.
- 30 percent of school districts responded that within the last five years, there have been at least five hospitalizations of school staff due to unanticipated behavioral outbursts by students.

In light of these survey results, AASA solicited stories and examples from school districts nationwide that would be affected by federal legislation that would prohibit, limit or undermine their ability to use seclusion and or restraint techniques.

## Seclusion and Restraint Allows Students to Remain in Public School Settings

In response to a request from the Kansas State Board of Education for guidelines on the use of seclusion and restraint, a parent and special-education teacher anonymously submitted this letter in 2011.

TO: Kansas Legislators & State Board of Ed.,

I am writing this letter in response to concerns regarding the use of seclusion and restraints in public school. My daughter, "Jane," has attended school in the Auburn-Washburn (USD 437) district since kindergarten. She is currently in the 7th grade. Jane has multiple behavioral, cognitive and sensory issues that have made school a tremendous struggle for her since the start. She was evaluated for services immediately upon entering the school system, as it became apparent right from the start that she could not manage herself nor learn appropriately in the general education setting. We had muddled through preschool, and as I am a special educator, I thought we could at least get through kindergarten without special services.

Through her school years, Jane has continued to struggle to manage her behavior, regardless of the strategies and supports utilized by the district and myself. And please understand, we have been down every road: therapy, medication, behavioral, consultation through the school, use of an alternative school, 1:1 paraprofessionals, her own special education teacher half-time. The district has been so incredibly supportive and accepting of my daughter and myself that I am overwhelmed by their desire to help her succeed.

With that, it should be noted that without the appropriate use of seclusion and restraint procedures, I am 100% certain that my daughter would not have been able to stay in public school. Her "meltdowns" over the years have been intense! They include every behavior you can imagine and she has succeeded in hurting several adults and damaging property on numerous occasions. This has been an incredibly difficult journey for our family. **Without the use of seclusion and restraints, Jane would have been placed out of home in a residential school setting, which honestly, would have been intolerable for me. However, there is no chance a public school could have managed her behavior without appropriate techniques.**

I have always been kept apprised of techniques being suggested, IEP meetings were held, daily and weekly correspondence sent to me so that I have always been aware when seclusion or restraint was needed. Jane's teachers have always treated her with respect and dignity and Jane has always understood why these procedures were necessary and she could verbalize what happened.

It would be disastrous for some students if seclusion and restraints were not options in public school. While I would be appalled to see any child hurt or their self-esteem damaged, those instances of abuse of seclusion and restraint should be dealt with on an individual basis. **We should not punish schools and students where things are going well.**

---

Another example submitted by a medium-sized school district in Georgia about a student named "Dave" illustrates how seclusion and restraint techniques actually keep students in school.

---

"Dave" is a fourth grade student who is significantly cognitively disabled and autistic. He began to demonstrate aggressive behavior during fall 2010. Dave will bite, slap, hit, and punch himself and others. A teacher and a paraprofessional have been injured and required medical treatment. The only way that we have found to keep injury from occurring and to keep Dave in school is to restrain him when de-escalation strategies and positive supports are not effective. **Dave's parents are aware of his outbursts and have witnessed the school staff restrain their child. They also use restraint at home for the same reason. The school system and the parents have sought other outside opinions and evaluation, but no one has been able to provide a strategy or treatment that is completely effective in preventing the occasional need for restraint.** Dave's parents and school district personnel have worked with the two Board-Certified Behavior Analysts (BCBAs) who are in the school weekly to provide coaching in applied behavior analysis, but there is still no way to help Dave control his outbursts. Through the use of restraints, Dave has been able to remain in a public school setting and not be institutionalized.

---

Although the district implemented a Positive Behavioral Interventions and Support (PBIS) system-wide for four years and had personnel from general education and special education trained in de-escalation strategies and appropriate restraint, the use of physical restraint was still necessary.

Because school districts can utilize practices like seclusion and restraint when necessary, students like "Jane" and "Dave" are learning in America's public schools today. If school districts were unable to occasionally use these techniques with students with severe behavioral or emotional disorders, then these students would have to be institutionalized or sent to private facilities where they may not have the same rights and services available to them.

For these students, federal legislation that prohibits these practices from being written into an individualized education plan (IEP) or behavioral intervention plan means that school personnel are unable to work with parents to create a plan for coping with the student when their behavior becomes unmanageable. Legislation that prohibits parents and school personnel from communicating about the student's needs and corresponding school interventions runs counter to the entire purpose of the Individuals with Disabilities in Education Act (IDEA). If IEP teams comprised of both parents and school personnel agree the use of seclusion and restraint will enable a student to remain in the least restrictive environment possible and to educationally benefit from the teaching and services the student needs, then these techniques should be allowed to be written into the student's IEP. The IDEA statute was never meant to restrict parents from receiving a unique, effective education plan for their child. Prohibiting seclusion and restraint in the IEP or behavioral plans where past behavior clearly indicates a need will only lead to further conflicts and misunderstandings between parents and school staff. Consequently, IEP teams cannot reach agreements with parents on individualized protocols for emergency situations that may require physical restraint, which could lead to harm for other students and school personnel.

## Prohibiting Seclusion and Restraint for General Education Students Is Dangerous, Especially When the Standard for Intervention Is So High

School personnel around the country understand that seclusion and restraint should only be used in rare circumstances where other interventions have failed to address student behavior. While the students highlighted in the aforementioned examples have serious, diagnosed behavioral conditions, there are times when restraint or seclusion must be used on general education students with no prior history of behavioral misconduct or emotional disabilities. For example, Tammie Morin, Director of Special Services of the Middleton School District in Idaho, wrote that sometimes her staff needs to use seclusion and restraint during a student fight.

> "Two students who are upset enough to engage in physical aggression do not typically de-escalate through the use of the words 'calm down and come with me.' As educators, we are responsible for the safety of all students; therefore, we must intervene and disengage the students from this aggressive behavior. This may result in restraining the students and escorting the students to a conference room or other location away

from others to allow the student to calm down and talk with an administrator or counselor."

Federal legislation under consideration by the Senate would prohibit the use of seclusion and restraint on a general education and special-education student unless the student was at risk of inflicting "serious bodily injury" on himself or another student. Accordingly, if a fight breaks out, school personnel are not allowed to intervene unless the students are at risk of inflicting "serious bodily injury" on each other or themselves.

The "serious bodily injury" standard is a major flaw in the current federal legislation that has been proposed in the Senate. In the *Keeping All Students Safe Act* (S.2020), restraints can be used in emergency situations by trained personnel, but only when the student is at risk of imposing "serious bodily injury" on himself or others. Applying the "serious bodily injury" standard is problematic because seclusion and restraint techniques are most often used to *prevent* the risk of injury, not to determine the extent of the injury in the aftermath of the incident. Imagine the difficulty of trying to determine during a fight whether a student is at risk of inflicting "serious bodily injury" to himself or to another individual or whether the student is only at risk of inflicting "bodily injury," particularly if school personnel are fearful for themselves or the student.

Moreover, the standard for "serious bodily injury" is very high and could lead to considerable litigation by parents who second guess school personnel decisions to intervene. Although not defined in the text, S.2020 cites the IDEA's definition of **"seriously bodily injury,"** which states that it is a sub-**stantial risk of death; extreme physical pain; protracted and obvious dis-figurement; or protracted loss or impairment of the function of a bodily member, organ, or mental faculty."** Bodily injury is defined as "a cut, abrasion, bruise, burn, or disfigurement; physical pain; illness; impairment of the function of a bodily member, organ, or mental faculty; or any other injury to the body, no matter how temporary." Consequently, in the vast majority of cases, the standard simply cannot be met, and will likely lead to litigation that the school district acted inappropriately when school personnel restrained a child. Morin articulates this concern in the following statement:

> If the legal ramifications for unwarranted intervention compel school personnel to refuse or delay intervening when a student or group of students are at risk of endangering themselves or others, how can schools ensure the safety of all students they serve? **How would you feel if a student in a classroom became violent and the school staff could do nothing but evacuate the room? What if, as an evacuated student was leaving the room, he/she was stabbed with a pencil? How do you explain to the injured student's parent that you were unable to stop the behavior? Or, how do you explain to a teacher who physically placed himself/herself between the behavioral student and that of the others, (which is what we would expect our teach-ers to do) that it is expected that they might be physically injured on the job?** Training staff in de-escalation and PBIS is vital and neces-sary as we teach students replacement/appropriate behaviors. However,

sometimes the behavior of a student leaves you no other choice than to restrain them and/or seclude them for safety reasons.

What does this mean for school districts? School staff would be in the unenviable position of either risking a violation of S.2020 and subjecting themselves or the school to litigation over whether they improperly restrained a student, or risking a civil rights action from their failure to intervene. Under general principles of common law, parents are liable for the torts of their minor children and would be at risk for being sued by other parents for the injuries that are the result of their child's outburst. For example, if a student assaults another student and there are medical costs or other damages involved, the parents of the assaulting student may be subject to a civil action for those expenses.

# Teachers and Other School Personnel Would Be Injured More Frequently If Seclusion and Restraint Were Prohibited

In AASA's survey of school districts regarding the rate of injury of school personnel, we were surprised to find that a quarter of school districts reported that at least 20 times in the last school year, an administrator, teacher, paraprofessional, aide or other school professional trained in proper seclusion and restraint techniques was physically threatened or attacked by a student when trying to calm the student during a behavioral outburst.

The following three stories illustrate the serious health risks to teachers and school personnel when they delay using seclusion and restraint in favor of alternative de-escalation measures. These examples demonstrate how school personnel trained in de-escalation techniques and proper seclusion and restraint can be harmed when these techniques fail to calm down students. If school personnel are afraid to use these techniques because they could risk litigation for their school district, or if school personnel are prohibited from using these techniques entirely, the rate of injury for school personnel and for the students with whom they are trying to work would increase dramatically.

## A Special Education Teacher at a Junior High School in the State of Missouri Shared This Story in the AASA Survey

"I teach students with Behavior Disorder, Emotional Disorders, and Students with Autism. I am professionally trained in de-escalation techniques and an instructor for our district. During this school year one of my students became upset because he could not have an item from my desk. The student became very agitated and began yelling at me. I moved away from the student and calmly verbalized other choices for him. The student began to throw items from my desk which prompted me to have another adult in the room remove the other students for their personal safety. I continued to speak to the student about calming down and again giving him the choices he could make. The student continued to approach me while yelling. I kept backing away from the student in an effort to not have a physical event. The student eventually backed me against a counter top and began to swing at me and kick at me. Using my training, I blocked several hits and kicks. **During one swing at me, the student grabbed my index finger and twisted it. This caused a spiral fracture. My finger was placed in a cast for six weeks. Five months later, I am still unable to have full range of motion in that finger."**

## A Special Education Director at a New Mexico Elementary School Disclosed This Story

A trained staff member was compelled to use physical restraint after two hours of de-escalation techniques did not calm the first grade student. The student displayed extremely high levels of aggressive behavior toward himself, the staff, and his mother who had been contacted to come to the school site and try to help de-escalate the situation. The student threw furniture, kicked, bit and threw objects at the staff and at his mother. The team attempted several techniques to calm the student, including: verbal de-escalation, nonverbal de-escalation (increasing the student's personal space to reduce his feelings of being threatened or controlled) and positive limit setting (including being offered choices of preferred activities, etc.) **The school social worker was severely bitten during the course of the attempted two-hour de-escalation.** Ultimately, the student was physically restrained for almost three minutes, according to CPI techniques and the restraint ended when he showed physical and behavioral signs of having calmed down. The parent supported the decision to use restraint.

---

**A school district in Florida shared these two examples regarding the effects of delaying manual physical restraint.** Both examples are about the same student. School personnel who restrained the child were trained in de-escalation techniques as well as the way to properly restrain a child.

An 8th grade male student stands about 6 foot 2 inches tall, and weighs about 185 pounds. In order to ensure all appropriate strategies and interventions were first implemented, a teacher delayed using manual physical restraint. *After punching another student repeatedly, the student kicked the teacher hard enough to cause nerve damage. The teacher was transported for emergency medical care by ambulance and continues to have difficulty.*

In another incident, the student physically attacked another student with force in the face, causing injury. The room was cleared to ensure student safety. During verbal de-escalation intervention, the student attacked an administrator by *thrusting his finger into the administrator's eye, causing severe bleeding and injury that required emergency medical attention at a hospital and ongoing treatment.*

---

# Conclusion

Despite the efforts of some organizations to convince the public otherwise, AASA is confident that school personnel are not trying to hurt children when they restrain and seclude them.

> "When a public education staff member opts for student seclusion or restraint, it is at the end of many proactive attempts of de-escalation. I know this, because in addition to being a certified school psychologist and special education director, I am a fair, reasonable, calm, and compassionate person who would rather not spend my days restraining a child. None-the-less, I *have* restrained students in the past and bear the literal scars of student violence."

— James Stevens, East Wenatchee, Washington

AASA refuses to accept the idea that public school employees are overusing seclusion and restraint and/or using it inappropriately. Rather, we believe that teachers, administrators and other school personnel did not enter this profession with the intention of harming children. These individuals chose to work in schools to support the most successful and undemanding students as well as the most vulnerable and difficult-to-teach students.

AASA believes the issue of how schools use seclusion and restraint is a local and state policy decision and we are pleased that states are taking it upon themselves to pass laws, regulations or guidance that best meet the needs of the districts they represent. Between 2010 and 2012, seven states adopted executive orders, statutes or regulations governing the use of seclusion and restraint in schools. The total number of states with statutes or regulations related to the use of seclusion and/or restraint is 36. Thirteen states have created guidance issued by the State Board of Education or documents authored by the State Department of Education or Department of Special Education related to the use of seclusion and restraint and how school districts should design policies on the use of these techniques. Only six states lack any formal guidance, regulation or statute on the use of seclusion and restraint.

If there is a role for the federal government when it comes to seclusion and restraint, it is to ensure school districts have the funding they need to train as many staff and school personnel as necessary in positive behavioral interventions and support systems, crisis prevention interventions and de-escalation techniques. These techniques have shown to be an effective way of reducing, but not eliminating, the need for seclusion or restraint.

**In conclusion, AASA does not think the use of seclusion and restraint should be commonplace, or used as a means for punishing bad behavior. Rather, AASA believes seclusion and restraint are necessary tools in the toolbox of school personnel to defend themselves and their students from incidents that could be dangerous for everyone who attends or works in a school.**

# EXPLORING THE ISSUE

## Should the Government Prohibit the Use of Restraint and Seclusion in Schools?

## Challenge Questions

- Compare and contrast the positions of the YES and NO selections regarding whether restraint and seclusion should be available tools to educators.
- Which selection makes the best case for its argument? Why?
- What policies are in place in your district? How have people reacted to the new U.S. federal guidelines? Are these sufficient?
- If restraint and seclusion were allowed to be used in emergencies, how would each author define an emergency? How does your own definition of emergency compare with that of the authors—with others in your group?
- How would you use information from the YES and NO selections to affect your actions when facing a student whose behavior is escalating?

## Is There Common Ground?

Both selections contain deeply disturbing descriptions of student/staff behaviors and interactions, some of which have resulted in injury and death. The full NDRN report contains almost eight pages of documented incidents. Both organizations, NDRN and AASA, want schools to be safe places for students and educators. Both agree that emergencies might call for the use of restraint and/or seclusion.

## Additional Resources

Allday, R. A. (2011). Responsive management: Practical strategies for avoiding overreaction to minor misbehavior. *Intervention in School and Clinic, 46*(5), 292–298.

Butler, J. (2012). *How safe is the schoolhouse? An analysis of state seclusion and restraint laws and policies*. Retrieved April 16, 2012 from www.autcom.org

Council for Children with Behavioral Disabilities. (2009). *Position statement on the use of physical restraints in school settings*. Retrieved July 24, 2009 from www.ccbd.net/advocacy/papers

Council of Parent Attorneys and Advocates. (2008). *COPAA declaration of principles opposing the use of restraints, seclusion, and other aversive interventions upon children with disabilities.* Retrieved July 24, 2009 from www.copaa.net/news/Declaration.html

*Department of Education, Office of Civil Rights, Civil Rights Data Collection, Revealing New Truths about Our Nation's Schools.* (March 2012). Retrieved April 18, 2012 from www2.ed.gov

Government Accounting Office. (2009, May 19). *Seclusions and restraints: Selected cases of death and abuse at public and private schools and treatment centers* (GAO-09-719T). Washington, DC: Author. Retrieved June 15, 2009 from www.gao.gov/productsGAO-09-719T

Menzies, H. M. & Lane, K. L. (2011) Using self-regulation strategies and functional assessment-based interventions to provide academic and behavioral support to students at risk within three-tiered models of prevention. *Preventing School Failure, 55*(4), 181–191.

National Disability Rights Network. (2012). *School is not supposed to hurt: The U.S. Department of Education must do more to protect school children from restraint and seclusion.* Retrieved March 20, 2012 from www.ndrn.org

Pudelski, S. (2012). *Keeping schools safe: How seclusion and restraint protects students and school personnel.* Retrieved March 20, 2012 from www.aasa.org

Smith, C. R., Katsiyannis, A., & Ryan, J. B. (2011). Challenges of serving students with emotional and behavioral disorders: Legal and policy considerations. *Behavioral Disorders, 36*(3), 185–194.

TASH. (n.d.). *Restraint and seclusion (APRAIS).* Retrieved April 18, 2012 from http://tash.org

The National Council for Community Behavioral Healthcare. (2012). *Policy resources: Restraints and seclusion—Rules chart.* Retrieved April 19, 2012 from http://thenationalcouncil.org

# ISSUE 18

# Is ADHD a Real Disorder?

YES: **Evelyn B. Kelly,** from *Encyclopedia of Attention Deficit Hyperactivity Disorders* (Greenwood Press, 2009)

NO: **Todd E. Elder,** from "The Importance of Relative Standards in ADHD Diagnoses: Evidence Based on Exact Birth Dates," *Journal of Health Economics* (vol. 29, pp. 641–656, 2010)

---

## Learning Outcomes

**At the conclusion of this issue, readers will be able to:**

- Compare and contrast the positions of the YES and NO selections addressing whether ADHD is a real disorder.
- Describe the strengths and the weaknesses of each side's arguments.
- Discuss the implications of ADHD identification for young children.
- Identify questions to ask your school's kindergarten teachers about the link between student age and behavior.

---

### ISSUE SUMMARY

**YES:** Evelyn B. Kelly, a science writer, journalist and adjunct professor at the College of Education, St. Leo University, presents an encyclopedia of characteristics, causes, and interventions for the several conditions, which are all very real attention deficit hyperactivity disorders.

**NO:** Todd E. Elder, a faculty member in the Economics Department of Michigan State University, presents evidence from a longitudinal study indicating that the likelihood of a child's diagnosis with ADHD is more dependent on his age relative to kindergarten peers than it is to any discrete, absolute behavior characteristics.

$\mathbf{A}$DHD—four letters that evoke images of a person who moves incessantly, has difficulty concentrating, and is distracted by what happens around him or her. A frequently discussed disorder, ADHD is likely the topic of at least one magazine article in your pediatrician's office or at the grocery or drugstore check-out counter.

Three types of ADHD are identified: predominantly inattentive, predominantly hyperactive-impulsive, and combined. Here are the official diagnostic criteria:

A. Either (1) or (2):

(1) Six (or more) of the following symptoms of inattention have persisted for at least 6 months to a degree that is maladaptive and inconsistent with developmental level:

- often fails to give close attention to details or makes careless mistakes
- often has difficulty sustaining attention in tasks or play
- often does not seem to listen when spoken to directly
- often does not follow through on instructions and fails to finish chores or duties (not due to oppositional behavior or failure to understand)
- often has difficulty organizing tasks and activities
- often avoids, dislikes, or is reluctant to engage in tasks that require sustained mental effort
- often loses things necessary for tasks or activities
- often forgetful

(2) Six (or more) of the following symptoms of hyperactivity-impulsivity have persisted for at least 6 months to a degree that is maladaptive and inconsistent with developmental level:

- often fidgets with hands or feet or squirms in seat
- often leaves seat unacceptably
- often runs about or climbs excessively when inappropriate (in adolescents or adults, may feel restless)
- often has difficulty playing quietly
- often talks excessively
- often blurts out answers before questions completed
- often has difficulty awaiting turn
- often interrupts or intrudes on others.

B. Some symptoms present before age 7
C. Present in two or more settings
D. Clear evidence of clinically significant impairment
E. Symptoms are not due to another disorder

(Adapted from DSM-IV-TR, 2000)

A developmental condition, ADHD is often considered by parents and teachers when a child seems to have difficulty focusing or behaving at home, school, or both. Mention of ADHD is routinely accompanied by the name of a frequently used prescription medication.

According to a Centers for Disease Control survey of parents in 2007, 9.5 percent of school-aged children (ages 4–17) had been given an ADHD diagnosis by a health-care provider, up from 7.8 percent in 2003 (*Morbidity and Mortality Weekly*, 2010, www.cdc.gov). The Center for Disease Control and Prevention (CDC) found the highest rates of ADHD were among multiracial children and those covered by Medicaid.

In March 2012, the American Academy of Pediatrics released new guidelines for diagnosing ADHD (http://pediatrics.aapublications.org). These extended practice recommendations from the current age of 6 to children as young as 4 years of age. Behavioral therapy was recommended as primary intervention, and medication as a possible treatment.

The scientific community has not identified a specific cause or universally effective interventions; few believe ADHD can be cured. Standard treatments include medication, behavioral supports, and counseling. A combination of these is usually found to achieve the most significant and long-lasting change.

Information about ADHD and its treatments is abundant. The National Institute of Mental Health offers the online booklet *Attention deficit hyperactivity disorder* (www.nimh.nih.gov, 2006), accompanied by extensive references. National Institute of Mental Health (NIMH) describes ADHD as a neurobiological condition with genetic linkages. Environmental toxins can also be contributors.

The U.S. Department of Education, Office of Special Education and Rehabilitative Services, regularly updates two companion documents on ADHD. One addresses identification and treatment; the other contains an extensive array of strategies and practices for instruction and behavior management (www2.ed.gov).

ADHD is acknowledged by IDEA and referenced under Other Health Impairment, although some mistakenly refer to it as a learning disability. Organizations, websites, clinics, and medications attest to its impact. Despite this proliferation of information, the existence of ADHD is not universally accepted.

The YES and NO selections explore whether ADHD is a real disorder or a term used to disguise other life conditions. As you read these selections, ask yourself how often you have wondered if you or someone you know has ADHD. Consider how each author would respond to your concerns.

In the YES selection, Evelyn B. Kelly discusses the serious nature of ADHD and the wide-ranging consequences it can have on schooling and life, emphasizing the history of ADHD-like behaviors, their diagnosis, and their appearance in adults. The source document, the *Encyclopedia of Attention Deficit Disorders*, is a comprehensive volume containing over 150 entries. Kelly cautions readers not to view every active moment as convincing evidence of ADHD, but not to ignore behavior that could signal this condition. While supporting the existence of ADHD, Kelly often acknowledges that there are "no concrete medical tests" for ADHD, making diagnosis "subjective." The *Encyclopedia's* section on the diagnosis of ADHD describes a complex set of procedures to rule out other conditions. The *Encyclopedia* closes with an appendix of close to 50 "conditions that may be confused with ADHD." These range from emotional disturbances to hearing problems to food allergies.

In the NO selection, Todd E. Elder considers diagnoses of ADHD in light of the age of children and kindergarten entry cutoff dates of their districts. Elder found August-born children in districts with September cutoff dates were more likely to be identified as having ADHD than would children with the same birthday in districts with December kindergarten entry dates. Teachers appeared to judge student behavior in comparison to that of others in the class, rather than to the age of the child. The younger child might be showing age-appropriate behavior, not a medical condition. Nevertheless, medication was frequently prescribed, leading to possible side effects and unnecessary medical costs.

Studying three groups of children over time, Rabiner, Murray, Rosen, Hardy, Skinner, and Underwood (*Journal of Developmental and Behavioral Pediatrics*, 2010) found instability in teacher ratings of student attention. Many children rated as inattentive in one year were not rated that way the next school year. Rabiner et al. suggest that maturity, improved nutrition, or changed classroom situations may affect students' attention in school. They recommend annual evaluations to confirm whether the condition really exists.

Careful assessment of ADHD-like behavior is urged by Smith, Barkley, and Shapiro (*Assessment of childhood disorders*, 2007), who describe three levels of diagnostic procedures. Checklists and brief interviews are minimally sufficient. An extensive "ADHD Checkup" combines assessment (including consideration of the effects of motivation, time of day, and fatigue) and some intervention. The third, and best, type considers the Checkup with the way the child responds to a series of interventions. Barkley feels medication helps, but sometimes reduces the motivation to try more complex approaches.

Posing the question "Are Americans More Prone to ADHD?" the Room for Debate section of the *New York Times* (www.nytimes.com/roomfordebate.2011) drew responses from prominent authors. Ned Hallowell believes that the adventuresome spirit of America's beginning established ADHD characteristics of impulsiveness and quick action as part of American "national DNA." Peter Breggin's view is that every diagnosis of "so-called ADHD" is "harmful," leading to labeling and drugging of our children rather than solving their real-life problems. Noting the disproportionate representation of minorities in special education, Donna Ford looks at ADHD prevalence as greatly exaggerated because of a cultural mismatch between African American boys and their white female teachers; Ford recommends that culture and gender considerations be part of the diagnostic procedure.

Another *New York Times* discussion (Hu, 2011, May 27, www.nytimes.com) explored whether some children were "Too young for kindergarten," reporting community responses over changing Connecticut's kindergarten entry cutoff date. The proposal would restrict September entry to those who turned 5 by October 1 rather than the following January 1 (which would occur in the middle of the school year). The decision was motivated by concerns that younger children were simply not ready to tackle the increasing academic demands in kindergarten. Hu relates several perspectives on the consequences of such a change. Wealthy parents whose children missed the deadline would likely pay for a private preschool program and gain school experience. In contrast, children of families who could not afford costly private programs would spend another year away from school. Responses to Hu's article showed a range of reactions: one recommended that kindergarten return to its traditional non-academic character; another postulated that the cutoff change would decrease ADHD diagnosis for younger children who were not developmentally ready to handle the academic demands. Still another favored a return to the practice of two entry-dates per year, ensuring that children entered school with others closer to their age.

Hara Marano discusses ADHD within her book, *A nation of wimps* (2008), claiming that today's competitive environment has led parents to see every childhood event as important to future status and financial well-being. Dedicated to ensuring the success of their children, Marano describes "invasive" parents who structure every moment, "cheating" their children from the opportunity to engage in "simple" play. ADHD develops as a reaction to forced academic pressure and deprivation of unstructured playtime. Marano recommends increasing unstructured play time; she believes children will use this opportunity to develop focus, resilience, and creativity.

Writing in the *Wall Street Journal* (2008, April 17), Schellenbarger explores "the silver lining" of ADHD. Interviewing the founders of Jet Blue and Kinko's, she sees signs that their ADHD masked remarkable creativity and ingenuity. Although negative messages from school could be overwhelming, their outcome was much different because supportive parents reinforced what their child did right.

# YES

Evelyn B. Kelly

# Encyclopedia of Attention Deficit Hyperactivity Disorders

## Introduction

Frazzled and befuddled, the mother of 5-year-old John brought him to the specialist's office. His teacher said he was the terror of the kindergarten, and his parents were concerned about his nonstop destructive behavior at home. In the doctor's office he jumped from chair to chair, climbed under a table, and flailed his arms like an animated rag doll. He picked up the tape and stapler from the receptionist's desk and then began to flip the light switch off and on, to everyone's annoyance. He ambled over to a group of children and butted into a game they were playing. They complained about his bossiness and moved away from him. The doctor immediately suspected John had attention-deficit hyperactivity disorder (ADHD). Is it really ADHD or is it something else?

The words "attention-deficit hyperactivity disorder" or ADHD are on the lips of many teachers, parents, and physicians. Generally, the child displays a persistent pattern of inattention and/or hyperactivity and impulsivity, which developed in the early years. When other symptoms such as forgetfulness, poor impulse control, and distractibility begin to interfere with the child's performance in the classroom or at home, parents become concerned. Unfortunately, the condition may persist into adulthood.

In 1998, the American Medical Association stated that ADHD is one of the best researched disorders in medicine. It is also one of the most controversial. Yet, with all the interest and research, no one knows what causes ADHD or how to cure it.

ADHD is considered to be a developmental disorder largely neurological in origin. The term "developmental" means that certain traits such as impulse control are slower to develop in these children than in the general population. That degree of lag appears to relate to the degree of severity of the disease. The compound terms "neurobehavioral" or "neurodevelopmental" disorders are frequently used to describe the disorder. The Greek root *neuro* means "nerve." ADHD is not thought to be a disorder relating to the brain and nervous system. However, the origin, causes, and treatments are subjects of debate and controversy.

ADHD is not just a fad that has been created in the latter half of the 20th century. It is documented in history. In 493 B.C. Hippocrates, the great physician on the Greek island of Cos, described a condition in patients who had quick sensory experience and their souls moved quickly on to the next impression. Believing that an imbalance of the four humors—water, fire, earth, and air—causes all diseases, Hippocrates attributed this condition to an over-balance of fire over water. He recommended a diet of barley rather than wheat bread and fish rather than meat; he also recommended adding water drinks and natural and diverse physical activities. Even Shakespeare referred to a seri-ous malady of attention in King Henry VIII.

In 1845 a German, Dr. Heinrich Hoffman, wrote an illustrated book of children's poetry that described a boy named Fidgety Phillip, who obviously had all the symptoms of ADHD and who met a tragic end when he pulled all the food on the table over on top of him. Dr. Hoffman attributed the problem to bad behavior and certainly never considered it could be inherited from parents.

ADHD was first observed clinically in 1902. Sir George F. Still described a group of impulsive children who had behavioral problems. He added the idea that the problems of these children could be traced to a genetic disorder and not poor parenting. Still called the condition a "morbid defect of moral control." Others studied the condition and found the condition to be one that had identifiable symptoms.

Twentieth century scientists began to look for the causes of ADHD. In 1918, a terrible influenza epidemic left many survivors with neurological dysfunctions; some survivors exhibited behaviors that corresponded to ADHD. Dr. Bradley made a chance discovery in 1937; he found that a group of children with behav-ioral problems in Providence, Rhode Island, improved after receiving stimulant medication. In 1957, the stimulant methylphenidate (Ritalin) became available and in various forms and is still one of the most prescribed medications. . . .

Although it does affect 3–5 percent of school-age children, no simple test exists for ADHD. According to the American Psychiatric Association (2004), the condition is more common in boys with a ratio of two to one. Girls may hide the condition by sitting back and refusing to participate and consequently go undiagnosed. An estimated 60 percent of children diagnosed with ADHD retain the disorder as adults.

In a classroom not paying attention, losing things, making careless mistakes, and forgetting to turn in homework are normal to some degree, and taken individually may not indicate anything problematic. However, the child with ADHD may have a constellation of symptoms that interfere with school, home, and friends. Many of these children will carry the disorder into adult-hood, when it will also cause tremendous problems. . . .

# Diagnosis of ADHD

Diagnosis of ADHD is not an all-or-nothing concept. If one has food poisoning or measles, the diagnostician can point to an absolute cause based on symptoms and behavior. However, there are no concrete medical tests to diagnose ADHD, which therefore makes the diagnosis of ADHD subjective.

Although the diagnosis is not like other medical conditions, several strategies for determining ADHD are in play. These strategies lie in careful observation and analysis of the behaviors of the individual from many sources. Because many conditions can mimic ADHD, a thorough physical examination is essential. ADHD may be diagnosed by excluding many other possible conditions.

There are four important reasons for the proper diagnosis of ADHD:

1. Diagnosis gives information regarding treatment planning and the long-term course.
2. Diagnosis is necessary to obtain special services.
3. It is necessary for medical and legal reasons.
4. Diagnosis guidelines are important for consensus on who is included and how many are treated in research projects.

To the physician or psychologist, diagnosing ADHD is much more like trying to determine if the person has clinical depression. Everyone feels sad from time to time, but clinical depression will significantly impair the function of the person over a sustained period of time. Thus, the ADD/ADHD diagnosis is not for people who have occasional symptoms but for those whose function over a period of time is affected.

Making the problem even more perplexing is that some people will demonstrate proficiency at times. For example, a high school student is the star of the football team; he can remember and execute complex plays to perfection and concentrate to catch the ball with efficiency. He is bright, with an IQ in the superior range, but is in constant trouble with his teachers for not doing work, not paying attention in class, and making inappropriate comments in class. His teachers might ask, "If you can pay such attention on the football field, why can't you pay attention in class?" It may not just be the field where the person may concentrate; some may be involved in playing video games, drawing, building with Legos, or completing mechanical tasks. Yet, these same people may have trouble preparing for a major exam.

To diagnose ADHD, several types of professionals are involved: pediatricians, clinical psychologists, educational psychologists, teachers and school staff, and neurologists. Guidelines in the United States are provided in a manual known as the *Diagnostic and Statistical Manual*, 4th ed., revised, usually referred to as DSM-IV-R, which gives direction for diagnosis of recognized mental illnesses. To begin the diagnosis of ADHD, DSM-IV-R lists six essential steps:

1. The parent interview. This should include discussing problems, developmental history, and family history. Parents are encouraged to recount specific situations and instances and try not to make general statements about behavior, such as "he is bad" or "he just won't pay attention."
2. Interviewing the child about home, school, and social functioning.
3. Teachers and parent complete behavior-rating scales describing home and school functioning.

4. Obtaining data from the school. The data should include grades, achievement test scores, current placement, and other pertinent information.
5. The psychological testing for IQ and screening for a learning disability. This step may have been completed previously but is pertinent here for completing the picture of ADHD.
6. Physical and/or neurological exams.

DSM-IV states that these steps are only suggested and are not universally followed. The diagnosing professional should always consider other possibilities and rule them out before making a diagnosis of ADHD. . . .

[N]ot all may have specific training in the disorder. It is important to look for a professional who does have special interest and training for the disorder.

Knowing the differences in the qualifications and services may help the family choose the health care provider who can best meet their needs. Child psychiatrists are doctors who specialize in diagnosing and treating childhood mental and behavioral disorders. Pediatricians and psychiatrists can provide therapy and prescribe medications. Child psychologists can diagnose and help the family in many ways with the disorder, but they are not medical doctors and must rely on the child's physician to do medical exams and prescribe medication. Neurologists are medical doctors who work with disorders of the brain and nervous system; they can diagnose ADHD and prescribe medicine. However, unlike psychiatrists and psychologists, neurologists usually do not provide therapy for the emotional aspects of the disorder.

## What Are the Subtypes of ADHD?

Although DSM-III used the term Attention Deficit Disorder (ADD), DSM-IV uses only the term Attention Deficit/Hyperactivity Disorder (ADHD) but classifies it into three different subtypes: ADHD predominantly hyperactive, ADHD inattentive, and a combined type.

Dr. Thomas Brown of Yale University has championed the recognition of children who have ADHD without hyperactivity. He believes these children are underdiagnosed because they are not the restless, intrusive, driven as if by a motor, Dennis-the-Menace stereotype. He notes these children are more like the stereotypes of "space cadet" or "couch potato" rather than the "whirling dervish" that one depicts as being the person with ADHD. Brown believes that even publications about ADHD offer little guidance about this disorder without hyperactivity.

Adults tend to overlook three specific groups of people with ADHD:

- Bright students. Adults think these people who underachieve are lazy and choosing not to do their work. However, individuals with ADD are found at all IQ levels.
- Females. Girls with ADD do not tend to stand out in the crowd and usually do not draw attention to themselves with dramatic disruptive behavior.

- Students under stress. When a student is daydreaming, the adult may explain away such behavior with family circumstances, such as divorce, unemployment, poverty, or multiple moves. What may be forgotten is that ADD is common in families under psychosocial distress. . . .

The **Centers for Disease Control and Prevention (CDC)** believes that only trained health care professionals should make a diagnosis of ADHD. This position is held because the symptoms may be part of other physical conditions, such as hyperthyroidism. Some normal individuals may exhibit some of these conditions from time to time. It is the pervasiveness of the symptoms that keep the person from functioning in school, work, and social relationships that form the strength of the factors in diagnosis. . . .

The diagnosis and evaluation of ADHD actually currently has no reliable objective tests. Because several of the symptoms overlap with other conditions, even a skilled clinician can have difficulty in determining differences. An astute clinician must perform a thorough medical and psychiatric evaluation. Useful tests include urine drug screening, serum thyroid-stimulating hormone, complete blood count, chemistry panel, and a history of central neurologic illness, infection, or trauma. Many common medications may contribute to psychiatric symptoms. One of the main factors in diagnosis is the presence of chronic ADHD symptoms since childhood, without a major depressive episode. Several other scales have been developed for diagnosis. . . .

## Adult ADHD

The idea of adult ADHD is fairly new and somewhat controversial. Papers dealing with an adult equivalent of childhood hyperactivity/minimal brain dysfunction were found in the late 1960s and 1970s, but they did not get widespread acceptance of the adult equivalents in the fields of psychiatry and clinical psychology. In 1994 Edward Hallowell and John Ratey wrote *Driven to Distraction,* which became a best seller and brought adult ADHD to the public's attention. Scientists, such as S. Goldstein (1997), K. Nadeau (1995), and Paul Wender (1995), conducted serious and rigorous scientific research on adults with ADHD. During the 1990s, more and more scientists began to consider the disorder as a real condition worthy of diagnosis and treatment. . . .

Several other popular books, as well as the media, also called attention to ADHD in adults. Internet chat rooms, Web pages, and bulletin boards were dedicated to this topic, and support groups such as ADDA and CHADD began to include adults with ADHD in their discussions. Adults with the disorder began to ask questions that challenged the old idea of the 1960s that they would outgrow the condition. The adult form of ADHD was found to share many of the attributes of childhood ADHD and was found to respond to similar medications and treatments. The acceptance of ADHD in adults continues at the present time and is likely to increase in the decades ahead.

Many adults realize they have ADHD when they seek diagnosis for a son or daughter. Up to 65 percent of children diagnosed with ADHD will continue to manifest symptoms of the disorder in adulthood. . . .

Adults are diagnosed under the same criteria as young people, including the fact that the symptoms began prior to age 7. Adults with ADHD may face challenges in self-control, self-motivation, executive functions, and inattention. They usually exhibit fewer of the impulsive and hyperactive tendencies that children have. However, they exhibit secondary symptoms such as disorganization, lack of follow-through, thrill-seeking, and impatience. These attributes may cause numerous problems in the work world.

Joseph Biederman, professor of psychiatry, Harvard Medical School, in a 2004 AMA briefing, observed that adults with ADHD had significant problems in the quality of their lives. According to Biederman, eight million adult Americans are estimated to struggle with inattention, impulsivity, and hyperactivity. He referred to his study of a large-scale survey that estimates yearly loss of household earning potential due to ADHD in the United States to be $77 billion. In the study he matched patients by educational levels. ADHD patients with high school education earn significantly less than their non-ADHD counterparts. On the average those with ADHD had household incomes $10,000 lower for high school graduates and $4,334 lower for college graduates. About 50 percent of those with ADHD reported they have lost or changed jobs because of the disorder. . . .

Although the existence and burden of ADHD have previously been questioned, ample data now support the validity of ADHD as diagnosis. Many successful people proclaim their struggle with ADHD as children and adults. . . .

Todd E. Elder

 **NO**

# The Importance of Relative Standards in ADHD Diagnoses: Evidence Based on Exact Birth Dates

## Introduction

Attention-deficit/hyperactivity disorder (ADHD) is the most commonly diagnosed behavioral disorder among children. . . . Fueled largely by increasing recognition of ADHD as a legitimate disorder within the medical community, prescriptions of psychostimulants to children diagnosed with ADHD rose by more than 700 percent in the U.S. between 1991 and 2005. In 2006, the Centers for Disease Control and Prevention estimated that 4.5 million children under age 18 were diagnosed with ADHD, with roughly 2.5 million of these children regularly using prescription medication to treat their symptoms.

Despite the rapid growth in ADHD diagnoses, treatment, and related expenditures, researchers and practitioners disagree about the disorder's underlying incidence—published estimates vary from less than 2 percent to nearly 17 percent. This lack of consensus has contributed to intense public debate about whether ADHD is over- or under-diagnosed in American children. The dramatic increase in the use of prescription stimulants intended to treat ADHD has also spawned widespread concern that millions of children regularly use potentially harmful medications to treat a disorder with inherently subjective symptoms.

In this paper, we investigate the role that subjective comparisons across children play in ADHD diagnoses by assessing whether children who are young relative to their classmates in school are disproportionately diagnosed with and eventually treated for ADHD. We also analyze the relationship between a child's age relative to his classmates and both teacher- and parent-reported assessments of ADHD symptoms. . . .

We analyze data from the Early Childhood Longitudinal Study-Kindergarten cohort (ECLS-K), which is uniquely suited to studying ADHD because it includes parent and teacher reports of ADHD symptoms, diagnoses, and stimulant-based treatments. We study the relationship between a child's age-for-grade and these measures of ADHD by focusing on discontinuities in

Elder, Todd E. From *Journal of Health Economics*, September 2010, pp. 641–642, 643–644, 649–650, 653–654. Copyright © 2010 by Elsevier Health Sciences. Reprinted by permission via Rightslink.

school starting age between children born just before and just after statewide kindergarten eligibility cutoff dates, which determine whether a child is eligible to enroll in kindergarten in a given school year. For example, a child born in October may begin kindergarten the year he turns five if he lives in a state with a cutoff of December 1, but the same child would have to delay kindergarten enrollment until the following year if he lived in a state with a cutoff of September 1.

Our analyses produce three substantive findings. First, ADHD diagnoses among children born just prior to their state's kindergarten eligibility cutoff are more than 60 percent more prevalent than among those born immediately afterward. This discontinuity implies that the ADHD diagnosis rate among the youngest children in a classroom is 5.4 percentage points higher than it would have been if those children had instead waited an additional year to begin kindergarten. . . . Children born just before a cutoff are more than twice as likely to regularly use methylphenidate as those born immediately afterward. If these patterns are driven entirely by inappropriate diagnoses and treatment among the youngest children in a grade, our estimates imply that roughly 20 percent of the 2.5 million children who use stimulants intended to treat ADHD have been misdiagnosed. Such inappropriate treatment is particularly worrisome because of the unknown impacts of long-term stimulant usage on children's health. . . .

Finally, a child's school starting age strongly affects teachers' perceptions of whether the child exhibits ADHD-related symptoms but only weakly influences similarly measured parental perceptions. . . . These patterns suggest that teachers' opinions of children are the key mechanisms driving the relationship between school starting age and ADHD diagnoses. Current National Institute of Mental Health (NIMH) guidelines for diagnosis explicitly instruct health professionals to consider whether a child exhibits attention deficits and hyperactivity relative to his or her peers, but these relative assessments are presumably intended to compare children of the same ages, rather than children of different ages within the same grade. Our results are consistent with teachers using within-grade comparisons across students to assess whether a child has ADHD symptoms, but these "symptoms" may merely reflect emotional or intellectual immaturity among the youngest children in a classroom. . . .

# Data and Descriptive Findings

The ECLS-K is a National Center for Education Statistics (NCES) longitudinal survey that initially included 18,644 kindergarteners from over 1000 kindergarten programs in the fall of the 1998–1999 school year. Individuals were resampled in the spring of 1999, the fall and spring of the 1999–2000 school year (when most of the students were in first grade), and again in the spring of 2002, 2004, and 2007 (when most were in third, fifth, and eighth grade, respectively). NCES also interviewed parents and teachers in each survey wave.

We match each child in the ECLS-K to the state-mandated kindergarten eligibility cutoff that applied in the child's state of residence in 1998. . . . Excluding children living in states without statewide cutoffs results in a sample of 11,784 children. . . .

# Binary Indicators of ADHD Diagnoses and Medication Usage

In all waves of the ECLS-K, restricted-use data files include parental reports of whether a child has been diagnosed with a learning problem such as ADHD, autism, dyslexia, developmental delays, or learning disabilities. We create a binary indicator equal to one if a child was ever diagnosed with ADHD as of the spring 2007 survey and zero otherwise. Additionally, in the spring of 2004 and 2007, parents who reported in any survey that their child had been diagnosed with ADHD or related disorders were asked a follow-up question about the usage of prescription medication intended to treat them. . . .

Parents who answered affirmatively were then asked an open-ended question about which medication their child was currently taking. . . . We create two indicator variables based on these questions; the first equals one if a child uses any prescription medication in either 2004 or 2007 and zero otherwise, and the second equals one if the child specifically uses methylphenidate and zero otherwise.

Fig. 1 presents graphical evidence of the relationship between ADHD diagnoses and a child's month of birth. The darkly shaded bars in Panel A show average ADHD diagnosis rates by birth month in the 15 states with September 1 cutoff dates. The results are striking: diagnosis rates rise steadily with birth month from January to August but then fall sharply between August and September. 10.0 percent of children born in August are diagnosed with ADHD, more than twice the 4.5 percent diagnosis rate among those born in September. These rates are statistically distinguishable at conventional significance levels ($t = 3.10$). The lightly shaded bars in the figure show the corresponding fractions of children who regularly use prescription stimulants to control ADHD symptoms. The monthly averages track diagnosis rates closely, and children born in August are more than twice as likely to use stimulants as those born in September (8.3 percent versus 3.5 percent; $t = 2.47$). These sizeable differences in diagnosis and medication rates between the youngest (born in August) and oldest (born in September) children in a grade suggest that the youngest children may be over-diagnosed (and over-medicated), the oldest children are under-diagnosed, or both.

Panel B of the figure presents analogous findings for states with December 1 or 2 kindergarten entrance cutoffs. In these states, the biggest month-to-month change now appears between November and December. The ADHD diagnosis rate among children born in November is 6.8 percent, more than triple the 1.9 percent rate among those born in December. The corresponding rates of stimulant usage are 5.0 and 1.5 percent, respectively. Only 4.1 percent of children born in August in these states are diagnosed with ADHD, compared to 10.0 percent of August-born children living in the September 1 cutoff states. This 5.9 percentage-point difference is surprising because both samples of August-born children start school at approximately the same age; the average school starting age among August-born children is 5.17 in the September 1 cutoff states and 5.09 in the December 1 and 2 cutoff states. The discrepancy in diagnoses may partly be driven by more

*Figure 1*

**Rates of ADHD Diagnosis and Behavioral Medication Usage by Birth Month, ECLS-K. (A) States with September 1 Kindergarten Entrance Cutoffs: (B) States with December 1 or 2 Kindergarten Entrance Cutoffs**

A: States with September 1 Kindergarten Entrance Cutoffs

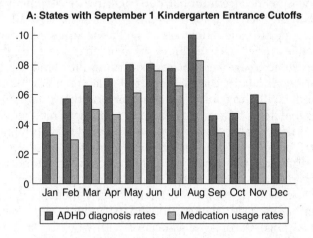

B: States with December 1 or 2 Kindergarten Entrance Cutoffs

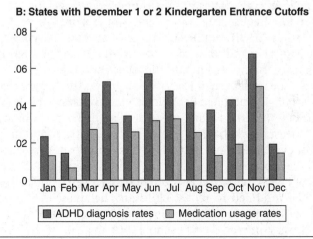

aggressive diagnostic practices in the September 1 cutoff states, which have 2.3 percentage-point higher overall diagnosis rates than do the December 1 and 2 cutoff states. . . . This pattern suggests that what matters for ADHD diagnoses and treatment is not merely that these children are young when they enter kindergarten, but that they are young *relative* to their classmates. Put differently, many August-born children diagnosed with ADHD and living in states with September 1 cutoffs may have never been diagnosed had they simply lived in a state with a December cutoff.

## ADHD-Related Symptoms Based on Teacher and Parent Reports

Teachers in the first, second, and fourth waves of the ECLS-K rate individual students on scales from 1 ("never") to 4 ("very often") on 24 different dimensions intended to measure social, emotional, and cognitive development. NCES does not release data on each of these 24 items individually, instead aggregating them to five composite scales known as Social Rating Scales (SRS). The first, the "approaches to learning" scale, includes six items that rate a child's attentiveness, task persistence, eagerness to learn, learning independence, flexibility, and organization. Similarly, the "self-control" scale includes four items that measure a child's ability to control his behavior, and the "interpersonal skills" scale includes five items that measure a child's ability to interact with others. For all three of these scales, higher scores are associated with higher levels of development. The fourth scale, "externalizing problem behaviors," includes five items that rate the frequency with which a child acts impulsively, interrupts ongoing activities, fights with other children, gets angry, and argues. Finally, the "internalizing problem behaviors" scale includes four items that rate the presence of anxiety, sadness, loneliness, and low self-esteem. In these latter two scales, higher scores are associated with worse social development. All five of the composite scales are measured as averages of the underlying items and therefore have a range of possible values from 1 to 4.

A diagnosis of ADHD requires evidence of at least six symptoms of inattention or at least six symptoms of hyperactivity, with these symptoms persisting for six or more months before the age of seven (as noted above, these symptoms much be present in at least two settings). The "approaches to learning" and "externalizing problem behaviors" scales overlap with DSM-IV-TR criteria most closely, with the former measuring several aspects of attentiveness and the latter measuring behaviors related to hyperactivity and impulsiveness, and we present evidence below that all five SRS composites are correlated with actual ADHD diagnoses.

Parents of ECLS-K children also provide SRS assessments, although some of the scales are modified to reflect children's behavior in the home rather than at school. The "approaches to learning" and "self-control" scales are identical to those completed by teachers, but instead of an "interpersonal skills" scale, parents complete a "social interaction" scale intended to measure similar concepts. Parents also complete "impulsive/overactive" and "sad/lonely" scales which are similar to the "externalizing problem behaviors" and "internalizing problem behaviors" scales, respectively; for example, three of the four items on the "sad/lonely" and "internalizing problem behaviors" scales are identical. . . .

## The Role of Teachers in ADHD Diagnoses

. . . [S]chool starting age has much stronger effects on teachers' perceptions of child behavior than on similarly measured parental perceptions. What drives this discrepancy? The answer may stem from teachers and parents using different reference groups in assessing a child's behavior and development. Teachers presumably form their opinions of a child's behavior by comparing the child to others in the same classroom. Like teachers, parents likely form their assessments based on comparisons across children, but they might compare their child's behavior to that of others of roughly the same age, not others in the same grade. This difference in reference groups may be particularly pronounced at the beginning of the kindergarten year. . . . Parents may be unable to accurately gauge the developmental level of their child's classmates so soon after the beginning of formal schooling, making those classmates an uninformative reference group.

Although the use of different reference groups by teachers and parents is one plausible reason for the relatively large discontinuity in teacher-reported predicted ADHD, other explanations could produce similar results. For example, teachers may simply be better equipped than parents to objectively assess a child's development, possibly because parents are susceptible to social desirability bias in evaluating their children. . . .

Another alternative explanation for the large discontinuity in teacher-reported predicted ADHD may stem from teachers' use of *absolute* standards, rather than relative standards, in evaluating a child's development. The SRS questions ask how often a child exhibits a particular behavior without explicitly asking for relative comparisons, so teachers might have absolute standards in mind when assigning ratings. Moreover, the discontinuities in SRS composites at eligibility cutoffs are consistent with the use of absolute standards if young children truly are less emotionally and cognitively developed than their older classmates. . . .

# Summary and Discussion

Diagnoses of attention-deficit/hyperactivity disorder (ADHD) among children have increased dramatically in recent decades, along with prescriptions of stimulants intended to treat the symptoms of ADHD. These rapid increases have been the source of much controversy about the definition and treatment of ADHD, and even about whether ADHD is a "real" condition. Substantial variation in diagnosis rates across states, races, and ethnicities has amplified these concerns, leading researchers to suspect that diagnoses and treatments are not solely based on underlying neurological conditions.

We have presented evidence that ADHD diagnosis rates vary systematically with the age at which a child begins kindergarten, with an additional year of school starting age reducing the likelihood of diagnosis by 5.4 percentage points. . . . Similarly, beginning kindergarten one year later reduces the likelihood that a child uses behavior-modifying stimulants in eighth grade by 4.4 percentage points and reduces the likelihood of using methylphenidate in particular by 3.8 percentage points.

The ECLS-K data used in this study are unique in that they include measures of ADHD diagnoses as well as teacher and parent reports of ADHD-related symptoms. These teacher and parent assessments shed light on the mechanisms underlying the negative effects of school starting age on diagnoses.

Specifically, teachers' evaluations of a child's development are closely related to the child's location in the classroom age distribution. In contrast, parental assessments are only weakly related to a child's age-for-grade, perhaps because parents' frames of reference include children of similar ages, rather than children in the same *grade*. Our estimates suggest that teachers play a vital role in decisions to refer children to medical professionals for evaluation and possible diagnosis. This role is reinforced by current NIMH diagnostic guidelines that require evidence of ADHD symptoms in at least two settings, such as at home and in the classroom.

The most troubling aspect of the close association between school starting age and ADHD is that it suggests that many children diagnosed with ADHD may not have any underlying biological markers of the disorder. In particular, children who are young for their grade may be diagnosed inappropriately if teachers and parents mistake their immaturity for ADHD. . . . If medical professionals diagnose these relatively old children if and only if it is medically appropriate to do so, and if the true incidence of ADHD does not vary by birth date, then 20 percent of the 4.5 million children currently identified as having ADHD have been misdiagnosed. For many of these 900,000 children, transient deficiencies in maturity led to comparatively long-lasting use of stimulants intended to treat ADHD symptoms. . . .

Inappropriate diagnoses may impose substantial costs, in the form of adverse health impacts and the direct financial costs of stimulant therapy. Although no large-scale studies have assessed the long-term physical effects of the medications used to treat ADHD, the existing evidence suggests that chronic stimulant use may have numerous harmful effects. First, randomized clinical trials have consistently found that ADHD medications affect the cardiovascular system, raising users' pulse rates and . . .

In addition to possibly harming cardiovascular health, ADHD medications dramatically reduce children's growth rates. The NIMH's Multimodal Treatment Study of ADHD found that in a 24-month randomized trial, children continuously treated with stimulants grew 1.92 cm (0.76 inches) less in height and gained 3.80 kg (8.36 pounds) less in weight than those treated with placebo, on average. Moreover, children who ended treatment after 14 months continued to grow more slowly over the next 10 months than those continuously given placebo, suggesting that these growth deficits may be irreversible. These unexpected findings suggest that chronic stimulant usage may harm children in a number of ways, only some of which are well understood. These potential risks may be justified by therapeutic effects for children who have the biological markers of ADHD, but those who are diagnosed merely because of transient immaturity may not experience any offsetting benefits.

Inappropriate ADHD diagnoses also impose substantial financial costs on the families of affected children, insurance providers, and taxpayers. [It is] estimated that stimulant treatments for ADHD cost $1.6–2.5 billion annually in the U.S., and [also] that $400–450 million of these costs are paid by Medicaid. If 20 percent of diagnosed and treated cases are medically inappropriate, roughly $320–500 million is spent annually on ADHD treatments for inappropriately diagnosed children, at a cost to Medicaid of $80–90 million.

These estimates merit consideration in assessing whether Medicaid should continue to cover stimulant-based treatments for ADHD.

Finally, we note that the use of within-grade standards as a basis for ADHD diagnoses may harm the oldest children in a classroom, rather than the youngest. ADHD symptoms in relatively old children may be difficult to recognize in comparison to the hyperactivity and inattentiveness exhibited by their "normal" younger classmates. As a result, legitimate cases of ADHD in older children may go undiagnosed, possibly leading to long-term adverse effects on academic success and social adjustment. Whether relatively young children are over-diagnosed, relatively old children are under-diagnosed, or both, current efforts to define and diagnose ADHD evidently fall short of an objective standard.

# EXPLORING THE ISSUE

## Is ADHD a Real Disorder?

## Challenge Questions

- Compare and contrast the positions of the YES and NO selections regarding whether ADHD is a real disorder.
- Which selection makes the best case for its argument? Why?
- What is your school's policy on kindergarten entry dates? How was their decision reached? Are there ever any exceptions to the policy?
- What does your local pediatrician think of ADHD and how to best diagnose its existence?

## Is There Common Ground?

Both Kelly and Elder acknowledge the dimensions of the construct of ADHD. It is an undeniable force in today's world and can have serious repercussions and costs.

## Additional Resources

American Academy of Pediatrics. (2012). *ADHD: Clinical practice guidelines for the diagnosis, evaluation, and treatment of attention-deficit/hyperactivity disorder in children and adolescents*. Retrieved May 5, 2012 from http://pediatrics .aappublications.org/content/early/2011/10/14/peds.2011-2654

*Attention deficit hyperactivity disorder handbook*. (2006). Washington, DC: National Institute of Mental Health. Retrieved May 22, 2008 from www.nimh.nih.gov/

*Centers for Disease Control and Intervention Morbidity and Mortality Weekly*. (2010, November 12). *Increasing prevalence of parent-reported attention deficit/hyperactivity disorder among children—United States, 2003 and 2007, 59*(44). Retrieved May 6, 2012 from www.cdc.gov/

Elder, T. E. (2010). The importance of relative standards in ADHD diagnoses: Evidence based on exact birth dates. *Journal of Health Economics, 29*, 641–656.

Hu, W. (2011). Too Young for Kindergarten? Tide Turning Against 4-year-olds. New York Times, May 27th.

Kelly, E. B. (2009). *Encyclopedia of attention deficit hyperactivity disorders*. Santa Barbara, CA: Greenwood Press (pp. ix–xi, 9–12, 85–87, 91–92).

Marano, H. E. (2008). *A nation of wimps: The high cost of invasive parenting*. Chapter 5: Cheating Childhood. New York: Broadway Books.

Rabiner, D. L., Murray, D. W., Rosen, L., Hardy, K., Skinner, A., & Underwood, M. (2010). Instability in teacher ratings of children's inattentive symptoms: Implications for the assessment of ADHD. *Journal of Developmental & Behavioral Pediatrics*.

Schellenbarger, S. (2008, April 17). The creative energy behind ADHD. *Wall Street Journal*.

Smith, B. H., Barkley, R. A., & Shapiro, C. J. (2007). Attention-deficit/hyperactivity disorder. In E. J. Mash & R. A. Barkley (Eds). *Assessment of childhood disorders* (4th edition, pp. 53–131). New York: The Guilford Press.

U.S. Department of Education, Office of Special Education and Rehabilitative Services, Office of Special Education Programs. (2008a). *Identifying and treating Attention Deficit Hyperactivity Disorder: A resource for school and home.* Washington, DC: Author. Retrieved from www2.ed.gov

U.S. Department of Education, Office of Special Education and Rehabilitative Services, Office of Special Education Programs. (2008b). *Teaching children with Attention Deficit Hyperactivity Disorder: Instructional strategies and practices.* Washington, DC: Author. Retrieved from www2.ed.gov

# ISSUE 19

## Are Evidence-Based Practices Sufficient for Educating Students with Autism?

YES: Samuel L. Odom, Lana Collet-Klingenberg, Sally J. Rogers, & Deborah D. Hatton, from "Evidence-Based Practices in Interventions for Children and Youth with Autism Spectrum Disorders," *Preventing School Failure* (vol. 54, no. 4, pp. 275–282, 2010)

NO: Ken Siri & Tony Lyons, eds., from *Cutting-Edge Therapies for Autism, 2010–2011* (Skyhorse Publishing, 2010)

---

### Learning Outcomes

**At the conclusion of this issue, readers will be able to:**

- Compare and contrast the positions of the YES and NO selections addressing whether EBPs are sufficient for educating students with autism.
- Describe the strengths and the weaknesses of each side's arguments.
- List the steps necessary to identify an EBP.
- Identify procedures to take in determining treatments/ interventions for children with autism.

---

**ISSUE SUMMARY**

YES: Samuel L. Odom, Lana Collet-Klingenberg, Sally J. Rogers, and Deborah D. Hatton, researchers affiliated with the National Professional Development Center, describe a procedure for determining whether focused intervention practices have sufficient evidence to be deemed evidence-based practices (EBPs). Identifying 24 practices that meet the research criteria, the authors also provide guidance and advice about implementation.

NO: Ken Siri and Tony Lyons are fathers of children on the autism spectrum. Dr. Mark Frielich is a developmental pediatrician who practices in New York. They view children with autism as individuals whose bodies have fallen victim to a perfect storm of problems.

They introduce an edited book of "cutting-edge therapies," designed to inform readers of possible treatments, many of which have not been vetted by research.

In 1943, Leo Kanner described a puzzling type of young child who preferred "aloneness" to the company of others. Seemingly uninterested in people, these children did not respond readily to the smiles and speech of adults. They did not react with anticipation when a caretaker reached out to pick them up. Kanner identified a combination of social isolation, significant delays in language development, and a tendency to engage in repetitive behavior and resist change; he called this group of behaviors *infantile autism*. The personal story of "Autism's first child," whose father approached Kanner with almost 40 pages of developmental notes, describes theories of the time and life outcomes for this influential man (Donovan & Zucker, 2010, www.theatlantic.com).

Early in the recognition of autism, Bruno Bettleheim and other psychoanalytically oriented psychologists believed that the condition stemmed from cold, unloving "refrigerator mothers" who failed to provide warm, responsive parenting. This theory was disproven by other researchers who found no evidence of difference between parents of children with autism and those with typical children. Parents of children with autism often had other children who developed without difficulty.

Autism occurs with varying levels of severity. Children with high functioning autism (termed Aspergers syndrome) display defining characteristics to a moderate degree. More significant challenges are experienced by children diagnosed with autism, Rett's syndrome, and/or PDD/NOS (pervasive developmental disability/not otherwise specified). Collectively, these are referred to as autism spectrum disorders (ASDs). The website for the Autism Society of America (www.autism-society.org) contains abundant information and resources about ASDs.

For the first 30 years of its recognition, autism occurred two to five times per 10,000 births. Prevalence figures have sky-rocketed. The Centers for Disease Control report 1 in every 88 children was classified as having an ASD in 2008, an increase of 78 percent since 2002 (*Morbidity and Mortality Weekly Report,* March 2012).

Considerable dispute exists about the cause/s of autism, and the reason/s behind the sudden rise in its occurrence. Many speculated that vaccines cause autism. Most (but not all) believe this issue has been resolved in the negative, especially since thimerisol, the mercury-containing vaccine preservative, has been removed from most childhood vaccines. Brown, author of *Babies 411* (2008), provides a concise review of this controversy (www.immunize.org/catg.d/p2068.pdf) from the perspective of a pediatrician who advocates vaccinating children.

There is little disagreement about parental reaction to a diagnosis of autism: "Our boy, our beautiful boy, was floating away from us, and there was nothing we could do" (Isaacson, *The horse boy,* 2009). There is little disagreement about a parent's drive to take positive action: "I was on a race against time to set him on a developmental path that would lead to independent living. The urgency to help him was almost primal" (Lytel, Washingtonpost.com, 2008).

Reaching agreement on what constitutes effective intervention is another matter entirely. A recent Amazon search for books on autism yielded a total of 7,178 results. Some claim to describe medical facts about autism. Many speak movingly about children "cured" of autism by a particular method, medical treatment, or diet. Over 50 were pre-orders for books not-yet-released

In the midst of what has been called an autism epidemic, No Child Left Behind (NCLB) and IDEA tasked educators to use practices proven to be effective. A number of similar terms are defined clearly by Kretlow and Blatz (*TEACHING Exceptional Children*, 2011). *Research-based practices,* the broadest category, describe methods that have been studied in some way, but not with experimental rigor. *Scientifically based research* connotes a methodology including replicated cause-and-effect studies, reviewed by scholarly peers and published in journals. *Evidence-based practices* denote those that have been vetted through quantitative research revealing a cause-and-effect relationship; the latter is most desirably demonstrated through participation of a control/comparison group or replicated single-subject research.

Parents, reeling from the diagnosis of their child, feel compelled to make a rapid choice rather than lose crucial learning time. Powerful narratives of how an unusual therapy led to a cure may influence them. Educators want to respond to parents, yet are bound by U.S. federal regulations requiring them to use proven techniques. This issue asks whether EBPs are sufficient for educating children with autism.

Affiliated with a number of professional research facilities, Samuel Odom, Lana Collet-Klingenberg, Sally Rogers, and Deborah Hatton, in the YES selection, also collaborate in the federally funded National Professional Development Center (NPDC), which provides guidance to educators seeking to follow the U.S. federal mandate to use EBPs. They identify 24 practices with sufficient research to qualify as EBPs; practices tested through well-designed experimental research studies involving students with autism. The authors acknowledge that some promising techniques might not yet have been fully researched. Odom et al., and the NPDC website (http://autismpdc.fpg.unc.edu), explain how teachers can develop their own evidence base, by gathering data and evaluating the success of interventions. Their selection discusses only educational interventions.

In the NO selection, Ken Siri and Tom Lyons, each a father of a child with autism, describe ASD as a medical condition with many different variants, the outcome of a "perfect storm" of challenges to a child's developing immune system. Beginning with a clear disclaimer that that they are not giving medical advice, Siri and Lyons present an array of treatments for parent consideration, noting their plans for annual updates. The authors state that most of the treatments, ranging from allergy desensitization to art therapy to craniosacral to gastrointestinal disease to equine therapy, have not undergone rigorous trials. Each of the 66 chapters is written by a professional well-versed in the particular therapy. In the book's Introduction, Dr. Mark Freilich (2010) advises parents to create a team, the cornerstone of which is a primary pediatric care provider who is open to both alternative and traditional approaches. The authors identify with parents fighting to get their child as healthy as possible. Although some educational approaches are included in *Cutting Edge*, the majority are medical in nature.

One of the most widely used treatments is applied behavioral analysis (ABA). An intensive therapy based on the work of Lovaas and colleagues, ABA methods require many daily hours of 1:1 work, reinforcing children for increasingly complex behaviors. This approach begins with an emphasis on eye contact and basic attention and moves on to academic and social interactions. Supporters assert ABA has *cured* their child. Detractors maintain that learned behavior does not generalize to new settings and that existing research studies are flawed. The What Works Clearinghouse (WWC, http://ies.ed.gov) found ABA to have "potentially positive effects on cognitive development . . . and no discernable effects for communication/language competencies, social-emotional development/behavior, and functional skills." These conclusions were reached after reviewing the two studies that met WWC criteria for evidence standards.

Claiming that her son is her science, actress Jenny McCarthy adopted a combination of behavioral therapy, diet, and supplements that "became the key to saving Evan from autism" (*Mother warriors*, 2008). Doctors don't have an answer but she, and the mothers she quotes, know what evidence they have seen and who they believe.

Paul Offit (*Autism's false prophets*, 2008), empathizes with the helpless feelings of parents and acknowledges that the "glacial pace of research," combined with a child's slow progress, can lead to frustration and a demand for a solution. Despite inspiring anecdotal claims, Offit cautions that proponents of alternative therapies such as stringent diets, chelation, and anti-yeast medications offer false hope, wasting time and money. He shares the words of parents who feel betrayed by misleading promises of recovery.

Writing to parents, Rader (*EP*, 2008) reminds readers that the phrase, "there is presently no cure for this condition," is simply not acceptable to people seeking to help their child. Many currently accepted methods began as nontraditional therapies before they were validated by extensive research. Every intervention began with one person's observations of change.

Endeavoring to determine the treatments parents are using and which are seen as effective, the Interactive Autism Network (IAN, www.iancommunity.org) links families to the research base of the Kennedy Krieger Institute. To date, almost 400 different therapies have been identified by parents. Preliminary results reveal that the average child with autism receives five separate interventions; approximately 5 percent receive none; one respondent described a child who received 56 distinct interventions.

IAN recommends several procedures that help parents determine the effectiveness of any intervention, including the following. Know your child's baseline performance before the intervention; this is critical for comparison. Be aware that everyone has good and bad weeks. Start one treatment at a time to best observe the impact. Be observant of other elements that could affect change, including hope for success or a new environment.

Not everyone wants a cure for autism. The Autistic Self-Advocacy Network (ASAN) (www.autisticadvocacy.org) promotes the idea of neurological diversity, advocating "a world in which Autistic people enjoy the same access, rights and opportunities as all other citizens." Read this first stanza of "A poem" by Dora Raymaker (2012) (at ASAN): "When the numbers roll in, I see where I fall: 1 in 1,000; 1 in 150; 1 in 88 children America has committed to prevent from being born."

Gary Mesibov and Victoria Shea (*Autism,* 2011), speaking from their experience with Project TEACH, address benefits and problems with evidence-based practices. Formalized methods and procedures can clarify language and ease communication. The same formality may restrict the types of interventions explored and preclude the rigorous evaluation of multipart interventions. Counseling that "generally effective approaches sometimes fail and unlikely approaches sometimes succeed," Mesibov and Shea seek to balance inquiry with observation and the complex lives of people with autism.

# YES

Samuel L. Odom et al.

# Evidence-Based Practices in Interventions for Children and Youth with Autism Spectrum Disorders

**B**asing educational practice on scientific evidence of its effectiveness has become a necessary feature of programs for infants, children, and youth with autism spectrum disorders (ASD). This policy is based in part on the precedents set in the fields of medicine and health care (Sackett, Rosenberg, Gray, Haynes, & Richardson, 2002), and educational policy in the United States that requires teachers and school systems to implement scientifically proven practices (U.S. Department of Education, 2008). Yet, a perusal of the professional literature may lead a reader to conclude that most practices are evidence-based because their developers or purveyors describe them as such. It is the brand put on many programs and practices. To date, however, there is not a universally agreed-on standard or set of standards by which to identify a practice as evidence-based, although the field is moving in that direction.

Teachers and other practitioners working with children and youth with ASD and their families are required by agencies and insurance companies to implement evidence-based practices, but there may be little guidance regarding where to locate those practices and what criteria to use to verify that a practice is evidence based. The aims of the present article were (a) to provide a definition of evidence-based practices (EBP) used with infants, children, and youth with ASD and their families; (b) to describe a process for identifying EBPs; (c) to identify the practices that meet the offered definition and thus have sufficient empirical support to qualify as evidence-based; and (d) to describe how teachers and practitioners might use such information to select practices to address specific goals and objectives for individual children.

## A Short History of EBP in ASD

In the 1970s, members of the health care community in England began a concerted effort to employ the findings from medical and health care sciences in their practices with patients (Cutspec, 2003). The movement was based on the realization that medical doctors and health care providers were not using the most current and strongly evaluated procedures or treatments with their patients. This resulted in the formation of an organization called the Cochrane Collaboration, which summarizes scientific evidence for specific health care treatments or practices. This systematic approach to gathering evidence of effectiveness was subsequently created for social intervention through formation of the Campbell Collaboration, whose mission is to summarize evidence that will support policy and practice decision making. In the United States, the Institute for Education Science funded the What Works Clearninghouse (WWC) to summarize evidence about educational practices or interventions that have evidence of efficacy. The WWC has made progress on identifying practices in general education but little information has been provided about practices for children and youth with ASD. One reason for this omission is that WWC has, to date, chosen not to include single-case research studies as an acceptable form of empirical evidence.

Within the field of practice for individuals with ASD, national professional organizations, such as the American Academy of Pediatrics (Johnson, Myers, & Council on Children with Disabilities, 2007), have established guidelines for practices around early screening and diagnosis for ASD. In 2000, the National Academy of Sciences convened a committee to review research on educational practices for children with ASD and their families, which subsequently generated general recommendations for practice (Committee on Educational Interventions for Children with Autism, 2001). Some states such as New York have followed systematic processes for identifying intervention and educational practices for children with ASD. Also, there have been national initiatives to review the research literature and identify the quality of research that has examined individual practices (National Autism Center, 2008). In 2007, the Office of Special Education Programs in the U.S. Department of Education funded the National Professional Development Center on Autism Spectrum Disorders (NPDC) to promote the use of evidence-based practices in programs for infants, children, and youth with ASD and their families, and an initial activity of this center has been to identify EBPs. In the present article, we describe the process established and followed by the NPDC and use this process as the basis for our discussion of EBPs.

# Evidence-Based Practice: The Devil in the Details

An initial devilish, but critically important detail is in the definition of practice. We propose an important distinction, existing in the ASD literature, between comprehensive treatment models (CTMs) and focused intervention practices (Odom, Boyd, Hall, & Hume, 2010). CTMs are conceptually organized packages of practices and components designed to address a broad array of skills and abilities for children with ASD and their families. The models should be described well enough to be replicated by others and have a process for assessing implementation to verify replication. CTMs from the Denver Model (Rogers et al., 2006), LEAP (Hoyson, Jamieson, & Strain, 1984), Lovaas Institute, the May Institute, and the Princeton Child Development Institute are examples of well-documented CTMs. We refer the reader to Odom et al. (2010) for more information about these models. However, in our work with the NPDC, we concentrated only on focused intervention practices.

Focused interventions, in contrast with CTMs, are individual instructional practices or strategies that teachers and other practitioners use to teach specific educational targets—skills and concepts—to children with ASD. The practices may take place in classrooms, clinics, homes, or communities and, ideally, are based on explicit teacher behaviors that can be described and measured. Most also involve multiple steps. Prompting, reinforcement, Picture Exchange Communication System, and visual supports are examples of focused intervention practices. Intervention practices that have been tested in high quality research designs and found efficacious are considered EBPs. This is the important devilish detail that is often overlooked in service programs. Many practices are considered to be EBPs only because the practice is based on theory, research on typical child development, or research findings that do not come from intervention studies (e.g., neuroscience, attachment, Erickson, Skinner, Bronfenbrenner). However, a focused intervention practice is empirically based and supported when the practice has been specifically tested in an experimental and research study, with learners who resemble the target students in critical ways (e.g., age, diagnosis, intellectual level, language level).

# A Process for Identifying Evidence-Based Practices for Children with ASD

Providing a definition for EBP and establishing criteria for the amount of evidence needed to qualify as an EPB are two necessary initial steps for identifying practices from the research literature.

## Evidentiary Criteria

Several professional organizations have established criteria for determining a social intervention as being efficacious or evidence-based (Chambless & Hollon, 1998; Kratochwill & Stoiber, 2002; Odom et al., 2004). The criteria converge around several common indicators for the level of evidence provided by experimental or quasiexperimental group designs or single case designs. For our work in the NPDC, we drew from the criteria discussed by Nathan and Gorman (2007), Rogers and Vismara (2007), Odom et al. (2004), and Homer et al. (2005).

For us to accept evidence about a practice from a particular study, the study had to (a) have been conducted with participants having ASD who were between birth and 22 years, (b) have outcomes for those participants as dependent measures, (c) clearly demonstrate that the use of the practice was followed by gains in the targeted teaching skills, and (d) have adequate experimental control so that one could rule out most threats to internal validity (Gersten, Fuchs, Compton, Coyne, Greenwood, & Innocenti, 2005; Horner et al., 2005). When a research study met these criteria, it could qualify as evidence for a specific practice. For a specific practice to meet our criteria for an EPB, the practice had to have evidence from (a) at least two experimental or

*Table 1*

### Criteria for Evidence-Based Practice

| Practice | Criteria |
| --- | --- |
| Experimental or quasiexperimental group design evidence | At least two peer-reviewed studies that meet acceptable methodological criteria and are conducted by different research groups |
| Single-case design evidence | At least five peer-reviewed studies that meet acceptable methodological criteria and are conducted by at least three different research groups. |
| Complementary evidence | At least one experimental or quasi-experimental design and at least three single case design peer-viewed studies meeting acceptable methodological criteria and conducted by three different research groups. |

quasiexperimental group design studies carried out by independent researchers, (b) at least five single case design studies from at least three independent investigators, or (c) a combination of at least one experimental and one quasi-experimental study and three single case design studies from independent investigators (see Table 1).

## Searching the Research Literature

Initially, researchers from the NPDC conducted broad literature searches using search engines in the following databases: Academic Search, ERIC, LEXIS/NEXIS Academic, PsycINFO, PubMed/Medline, and SocIndex. Search terms included keywords such as *autism, ASD, autism spectrum,* and PDD-NOS; as well as terms related to specific domains including *academics/cognition, behavior, communication, play, social skills,* and *transition.* In each domain, the NPDC researchers identified additional keywords. For example, in the domain of behavior, search terms also included words such as *adaptive, functional, idiosyncratic, perseverative, repetitive,* and *stereotypical.*

When potential research articles were identified, NPDC staff first screened potential studies by reading the abstracts and then obtained original articles for those studies that appeared to meet inclusion criteria. They scrutinized the *Methods* sections of articles to assess whether the article met the methodological criteria and, if so, it would be grouped with other articles about the same intervention practice. For all groups of intervention studies, a second senior researcher with training in research methodology conducted a second review of the articles to make sure they met criteria.

To categorize practices, researchers used the terminology for a well-known practice as it appears in the literature (e.g., discrete trial training, Picture Exchange Communication System). In other instances, practices with various names were found to have similar, if not identical, procedural features. In this instance, a generic name, or summary descriptor, was developed and the evidence for these closely related practices was pooled. For example, naturalistic intervention is a summary descriptor we created to label interventions identified by researchers as applying behavioral principles inside an interaction style that involved following rather than directing. These interventions were known in the field by a variety of different names: milieu teaching (e.g., enhanced milieu, prelinguistic milieu), activity-based interventions, and incidental teaching, but they were similar in delivery style, and thus the development of the summary descriptor. The studies supporting one of these was considered to support the class of practices named by the summary descriptor.

# Evidence-Based Practices for Infants, Children, and Youth with ASD

From the review of the literature, researchers with the NPDC have thus far identified 24 EBPs (see Table 2). The practices are generally organized in alphabetical order. Two sets of practices are grouped within a larger descriptor. The first subgroup is *behavioral teaching strategies,* which are fundamental intervention techniques (e.g., prompting, reinforcement) based on the principles of applied behavior analysis. These strategies appear as parts of other focused interventions (e.g., prompting and reinforcement is a part of Discrete Trial Training), but they also have sufficient evidence to be listed independently. Second, we grouped a set of strategies used primarily to reduce or eliminate interfering behaviors (e.g., tantrums, disruptive behavior, aggression, self-injury, repetitive behavior) under a general classification of positive behavior support (PBS).

*Table 2*

### Identified Evidence-Based Practices with Descriptors

| Evidence-based practice | Descriptor |
| --- | --- |
| Behavioral strategies | |
| Prompting | Behaviorally based antecedent teaching strategy |
| Reinforcement | Behaviorally based consequence teaching strategy |
| Task analysis and chaining | Behaviorally based antecedent teaching strategy that breaks down steps and links them for prompting |
| Time delay | Behaviorally based antecedent teaching strategy that promotes errorless learning |
| Computer-aided instruction | The use of computers for varied instruction |
| Discrete trial training (DTT) | One-to-one instructional strategy that teaches skills in a planned, controlled, and systematic manner |
| Naturalistic interventions | A variety of strategies that closely resemble typical interactions and occur in natural settings, routines and activities |
| Parent-implemented interventions | Strategies that recognize and use parents as the most effective teachers of their children |
| Peer-mediated instruction/ intervention (PMII) | Strategies designed to increase social engagement by teaching peers to initiate and maintain interactions |

*Table 2 (Continued)*

### Identified Evidence-Based Practices with Descriptors

| Evidence-based practice | Descriptor |
| --- | --- |
| Picture exchange communication system (PECS)™ | A system for communicating that uses the physical handing over of pictures or symbols to initiate communicative functions |
| Pivotal response training (PRT) | An approach that teaches the learner to seek out and respond to naturally occurring learning opportunities |
| Positive behavioral support strategies | |
| Functional behavior assessment (FBA) | A systematic approach for determining the underlying function or purpose of behavior |
| Stimulus control/Environmental modification | The modification or manipulation of environmental aspects known to impact a learner's behavior |
| Response interruption/redirection | The physical prevention or blocking of interfering behavior with redirection to more appropriate behavior |
| Functional communication training (FCT) | A systematic practice of replacing inappropriate or ineffective behavior with more appropriate or effective behaviors that serve the same function |
| Extinction | Behaviorally based strategy that withdraws or terminates the reinforcer of an interfering behavior to reduce or eliminate the behavior |
| Differential reinforcement (DRA/I/O/L) | Behaviorally based strategies that focus reinforcement on alternative, incompatible, other, or lower rates of the interfering behavior in order to replace it with more appropriate behavior |
| Self-management | A method in which learners are taught to monitor, record data, report on, and reinforce their own behavior |
| Social narratives | Written narratives that describe specific social situations in some detail and are aimed at helping the individual to adjust to the situation or adapt their behavior |
| Social skills training groups | Small group instruction with a shared goal or outcome of learned social skills in which participants can learn, practice, and receive feedback |
| Structured work systems | Visually and physically structured sequences that provide opportunities for learners to practice previously taught skills, concepts, or activities |
| Video modeling | Utilizes assistive technology as the core component of instruction and allows for pre-rehearsal of the target behavior or skill via observation |
| Visual supports | Tools that enable a learner to independently track events and activities |
| VOCA/ Speech Generating Devices (SGD) | Electronic, portable devices used to teach learners communication skills and as a means of communication |

The general PBS approach comprises individual focused interventions, organized around the results of functional behavioral assessment and ordered in level of intensity (Horner, Carr, Strain, Todd, & Reed, 2002). In this grouping, we included Differential Reinforcement of Other Behavior as a special application of the use of reinforcement to the reduction of interfering behavior.

Table 3 shows the EBP by domain matrix, which indicates what EBP practices have evidence of efficacy for teaching skills in specific educational domains. For example, for naturalistic intervention, Table 3 indicates that this

*Table 3*

## Evidence-Based Practices × Learner Outcome Matrix Key

| | Academic | Behavior | Communication | Play | Social | Transitions |
|---|---|---|---|---|---|---|
| **Evidence-based practice** | | | | | | |
| *Behavioral intervention strategies* | | | | | | |
| Prompting | X | | | | | |
| Reinforcement | X | X | X | X | | |
| Task analysis and chaining | X | | X | X | X | X |
| Time delay | X | | *X* | X | X | |
| Computer-aided instruction | X | | X | | X | |
| Discrete trial training (DTT) | | X | X | | | |
| Naturalistic interventions | | X | X | | X | |
| Parent-implemented interventions | | X | X | | | |
| Peer-mediated instruction/ | | | X | | X | X |
| intervention (PMII) | | X | | | X | X |
| Picture exchange communication system (PECS) | | X | X | | X | |
| Pivotal response training (PRT) | | X | X | X | X | |
| *Positive behavioral support strategies* | | | | | | |
| Functional behavior assessment (FBA) | | X | X | | | |
| Stimulus control/Environmental modification | X | X | | X | | |
| Response interruption/redirection | X | X | X | | | |
| Functional communication training (FCT) | | X | X | | | |
| Extinction | | X | X | | | |
| Differential reinforcement (DRA/I/O/L) | | X | X | | | |
| Self-management | X | X | X | | X | X |
| Social narratives | | X | X | | X | |
| Social skills training groups | | | X | | X | |
| Structured work systems | X | | | | | X |
| Video modeling | | X | X | X | X | |
| Visual supports | X | | X | X | X | X |
| VOCA/ Speech Generating Devices (SGD) | | | X | X | | |

*Note.* X indicates that the studies making up the evidence base for specific practice.

practice has shown efficacy for teaching communication and social skills. We did not find studies documenting efficacy for teaching play. This does not mean that naturalistic interventions may not be a useful practice for teaching play skills. In fact, we suspect that this would be an effective approach for promoting play (e.g. see Kasari, Freeman, & Paparella, 2006). It means that we did not find sufficient published studies in which this practice was used to teach play skills that fit the aforementioned criteria stated. Specific advice on how to interpret and apply information on identified EBPs in practice follows.

## How to Use EBPs

Definitions of EBP often include the qualifier that the selection and use of practices established by the best available evidence must be blended with professional expertise (Buysse & Wesley, 2006; Sackett, Rosenberg, Gray, Haynes, & Richardson, 2002). One feature of professional expertise is the knowledge that EBPs must be used strategically if they are to be valuable. Their strategic use includes basing the selection of practices for individual children on carefully identified learning objectives for learners with ASD and careful implementation of the practice as it was designed.

## Basing Selection of EPB on Learning Objectives

The first necessary step in building a program for learners with ASD is through assessment of learners' skills, assessment of the requirements of their school, home, or community environment, and use of the information to establish learning objectives (i.e., as in a learner's IEP goals). We anticipated that practitioners, family members, and perhaps the learner with ASD would be involved in this process. Once a learning objective is established, practitioners can consult the practice (outcome matrix in Table 3 to identify EBPs that are applicable to the general skill area of the objective and select a practice to use to teach the objective).

However, in some cases, there may not be an EBP that has been used successfully in teaching a particular content to a learner with ASD. The teacher may be aware of a promising practice that could be applicable, but researchers have not yet conducted or published studies that document the efficacy of that specific practice. When this occurs, the practitioner may draw on his or her teaching or clinical experience to select a practice having some evidence of efficacy for other outcomes and in the practitioners' judgment has a high likelihood of teaching the learner the identified objective. In this situation, the data that the educator collects while teaching determines efficacy of that practice for teaching the target objective to the target child and helps the educator make further instructional decisions.

## Implementation

The efficacy of an EBP assumes implementation in the manner and level of intensity used in the efficacy studies. However, the research literature seldom describes the implementation of the practice in enough detail for a practitioner to immediately use the practice (although some EBP researchers have translated their research into practitioner friendly resources; e.g., Lovaas, 2002). The NPDC staff has examined thoroughly the publications of each of the EBPs listed in Table 2 to construct step-by-step guidelines and corresponding implementation checklists to guide teachers and other practitioners in their use of practices. When possible, the original developers of the identified EBPs reviewed these materials to make sure they accurately reflected the practice. As a final step, educators in the field reviewed these guidelines and implementation checklists to ensure that they were clear, understandable, and applicable in a school setting. These step-by-step guidelines and implementation checklists are being assembled into Web-based modules, developed by the NPDC in collaboration with the staff at the Ohio Center for Autism and Low Incidence Disabilities and the Autism Intervention Module Web site. In addition to the implementation guidelines, the modules also contain information on the evidence base for each practice, procedural details of the EBP, descriptions of how to collect data for this practice, case examples, picture examples, video examples, and additional resources (e.g., data sheets, where to find materials).

## Administrative Support for Implementation

When federal law, state policy, or litigation dictates that practitioners need to use EBP for learners with ASD, administrators may expect practitioners to implement EBPs and change their educational practices immediately. However, sometimes practitioners are already using EBPs, and all that is needed is documentation of their use. In this situation, the NPDC products that may be helpful in documenting the use of EBPs include data collection procedures, evidence-based summaries, steps for implementation, and implementation checklists. In other situations, practitioners may be using an identified EBP in part but not completely. The NPDC products involving procedural guidelines and implementation checklists can aide the professional in assuring that the EBP is being implemented in the correct way, as demonstrated in the studies making up the evidence-base. For example, when asked if they use PECS, many practitioners reply, "yes." However, when queried further they admit that they use the acronym PECS for the use of pictures with learners; not that they use the complete picture exchange system for communication instruction. The NPDC products support and promote the EBP practices in their entirety, helping practitioners to be confident of the ways in which they are implementing the EBPs that they use.

For many practitioners, however, the adoption of EBPs may require learning to implement new practices in their programs. Rarely can a supervisor hand a procedural manual to a practitioner, say "Do this," and see an immediate and accurate implementation of a practice. Even single-training workshops may produce limited sustainable change in practices (Fixsen, Naoom, Blase, Friedman, & Wallace, 2005). The educational literature has long documented the variables that affect practitioner adoption of "innovation" (i.e., EBPs). These variables include training, administrative support (e.g., from the principal or supervisor), time for planning, and clear delineation of roles (Fullan, 1991;

Leiber et al., 2009). The emerging science around implementation documents the need for an ecological systems perspective for moving EBPs into daily educational practice for learners with ASD (Fixsen et al., 2005).

## Conclusion

To translate research about focused interventions for learners with ASD from the research lab into the classroom begins with a systematic process for identifying and describing evidence based practices. In the present article, we described one approach to this task. We established criteria and identified 24 practices that met the criteria established for EPB. We also used the research methods from the studies to develop step-by-step guidelines, implementation checklists and web-based modules for educators and other practitioners. These 24 are not a final set of EPBs. The research literature in ASD is active, with new research studies about focused interventions being published monthly. One should expect this set of practices to grow along with the literature. Additional lines of research are providing empirical evidence for methods for implementing EBPs into daily practice in educational settings for learners with ASD. The work of the NPDC is one source of information that is supporting this effort.

## References

Buysse, V., & Wesley, P. W. (2006). Evidence-based practice: How did it emerge and what does it really mean for the early childhood field? In V. Buysse & P. W. Wesley (Eds.), *Evidence-based practice in the early childhood field* (pp. 1–34). Washington, DC: Zero to Three Press.

Chambless, D. L., & Hollon, S. D. (1998). Defining empirically supported therapies. *Journal of Consulting and Clinical Psychology, 66,* 7–18.

Committee on Educational Interventions for Children With Autism. (2001). *Educating children with autism. Washington,* DC: National Academy Press.

Cutspec, P. A. (2003). *Evidence-based medicine: The first evidence-based approach to best practice.* Asheville, NC: Center for Evidence-Based Practices, Research and Training Center on Early Childhood Development, Orlena Puckett Institute.

Fixsen, D. L., Naoom, S. F., Blase, K. A., Friedman, R. M., & Wallace, F. (2005). *Implementation research: A synthesis of the literature.* Tampa, FL: University of South Florida, Louis de la Parte Florida Mental Health Institute, The National Implementation Network (FMHI Publication #231).

Fullan, M. G. (1991). The *new meaning of educational change.* New York: Teachers College Press.

Gersten, R., Fuchs, L. S., Compton, D., Coyne, M., Greenwood, C. & Innocenti, M. S. (2005). Quality indicators for group experimental and quasi-experimental research in special education. *Exceptional Children, 71,* 149–164.

Horner, R. H., Carr, E. G., Halle, J., McGee, G., Odom, S., Wolery, M. (2005). The use of single-subject research to identify evidence-based practice in special education. *Exceptional Children, 71,* 165–179.

Horner, R. H., Carr, E. G., Stain, P. S., Todd, A. W., & Reed, H. K. (2002). Problem behavior interventions for young children with autism: A research synthesis. *Journal of Autism and Developmental Disorders, 32*, 423–446.

Hoyson, M., Jamieson, B., & Strain, P. S. (1984). Individualized group instruction of normally developing and autistic-like children: The LEAP Curriculum Model. *Journal of the Division for Early Childhood, 8*, 157–172.

Johnson, C. P., Myers, S. M., & Council on Children with Disabilities. (2007). Identification and evaluation of children with Autism Spectrum Disorders. *Pediatrics, 120*, 1185–1215.

Kasari C., Freeman S., & Paparella T. (2006). Joint attention and symbolic play in young children with autism: a randomized controlled intervention study. *Journal of Child Psychology and Psychiatry. 47*, 611–20.

Kratochwill, T. R., & Stoiber, K. C. (2002). Evidence-based interventions in school psychology: Conceptual foundations of the Procedural and Coding Manual of Division 16 and the Society for the Study of School Psychology. *School Psychology Quarterly, 17*, 341–389.

Lieber, J., Butera, G., Hanson, M., Palmer, S., Horn, E., Czaja, C., et al. (2009). Factors that influence the implementation of a new preschool curriculum: Implications for professional development. *Early Education and Development, 20*, 456–482.

Lovaas, I. O. (2002). *Teaching individuals with developmental delays.* Austin, TX: PRO-ED.

Nathan, P. E., & Gorman, J. M. (2007). *A guide to treatments that work* (3rd ed.). New York: Oxford University Press.

National Autism Center. (2008). *National Standards Project.* Randolf, MA: Author. Retrieved December 4, 2008, from www.nationalautismcenter.org/about/national.php

Odom, S. L., Brantlinger, E., Gersten, R., Horner, R. D., Thompson, B., Harris, K. (2004). *Quality indicators for research in special education and guidelines for evidence-based practices: Executive summary.* Arlington, VA: Council for Exceptional Children Division for Research.

Odom, S. L. (2009). The tie that binds: Evidence-based practice, implementation science, and outcomes for children. *Topics in Early Childhood Special Education, 23*, 53–61.

Odom, S. L., Boyd, B., Hall, L. J., & Hume, K. (2010). Evaluation of comprehensive treatment models for individuals with autism spectrum disorders. *Journal of Autism and Developmental Disabilities, 40*, 425–437.

Rogers, S. J., Hayden, D., Hepburn, S., Charlifue-Smith, R., Hall, T, & Hayes, A. (2006). Teaching young nonverbal children with autism useful speech: A pilot study of the Denver model and PROMPT interventions. *Journal of Autism and Developmental Disorders, 36*, 1007–1024.

Rogers, S. J., & Vismara, L. A. (2008). Evidence-based comprehensive treatments for early autism. *Journal of Clinical Child and Adolescent Psychology, 37*, 8–38.

Sackett, D. L., Rosenberg, W. M., Gray, J. A., Haynes, R. B., & Richardson, W. S. (1996). Evidence based medicine: What it is and what it isn't. *British Medical Journal, 312*, 71–72.

U.S. Department of Education. (2008). *No Child Left Behind.* Washington, DC: Author. Retrieved December 12, 2008, from http://www.ed.gov/nclb/landing.jhtml.

# Cutting-Edge Therapies for Autism 2010–2011

**EDITOR'S NOTE:** Ken and I both have children on the autism spectrum. We don't have any financial connection to any organization, doctor or therapist included in this book. We conceived of the book as a way to learn more ourselves in order to help our children. We are happy to be able to present what we have learned regarding the resources and treatments currently available and those which are emerging. Our team of contributors is impressive. It includes leading doctors, therapists, teachers, scientists, educators, social workers and parents.      **—Tony Lyons**

The central purpose of this book is to provide people interested in autism therapies—including parents, grandparents, teachers, therapists, doctors and researchers—with articles about the cutting-edge work being done in the field. This field changes rapidly and we plan to update the book annually. *Cutting-Edge Therapies for Autism* is for people who want to learn as much as they possibly can about the therapies available, and about how to do everything in their power to help the growing number of children who are suffering.

Autism is the country's fastest-growing medical emergency, affecting more children than cancer, diabetes, Down syndrome and AIDS combined. Approximately 1 million people in the United States currently suffer from some form of autism.

Autism is difficult to define. No two kids have the same exact set of symptoms or respond to the same combination of therapies. Each child's treatment plan needs to be unique, taking into consideration the specific symptoms the child exhibits, the results of tests administered, and the observations of the child's doctors, therapists, teachers and, just as importantly, parents.

There is no general consensus on what causes autism—either classic Kanner's autism or the regressive kind. Some people think it's entirely genetic, while others think it's caused by Pitocin, fluoride in tap water or tooth paste, GAMT (guanidinoacetate methyltransferase) deficiency, chemicals in foods or household products, parental age, stress, treatments for asthma given to pregnant women, vaccines and/or the preservative thimerosal in some vaccines,

# CASE STUDY #1: LINA

My daughter Lina was a bright, happy, talkative, social little girl. She had some ongoing problems with eczema but, other than that, was very healthy. Just before she turned three, she was given a regimen of antibiotics for bronchitis. Shortly thereafter, she received her measles mumps and rubella (MMR) booster shot. About two weeks later, she started to drool uncontrollably. It looked like her lips and jaw muscles had gone totally numb. The pediatrician took some tests and found that she had been exposed to the Epstein Barr Virus, but couldn't tell us anything more. The drooling episode lasted a couple of weeks, during which time her speech became garbled and she began to stutter. It took an incredible effort for her to push words out of her mouth. She was like a toy running low on batteries, losing steam, losing control. As things inside of her began to disconnect, she was becoming disconnected from the world around her. A friend came over with her daughter for a play date and, after a few minutes with Lina, she asked, with real fear in her eyes: "What's going on with Lina? She seems like a different person." Lina seemed to improve after that, but then gradually deteriorated. She was first diagnosed with Sensory Processing Disorder, then Pervasive Development Disorder (PDD), and then, finally, autism. For some kids autism means screaming, biting, throwing things out the window, breaking everything in sight, even head banging. Life with them and for them can be harsh. When I look at Lina I see a peaceful, loving, gentle girl struggling to get out of a body that isn't functioning correctly. She's the victim—not me, not her mother, not her teachers, not society. The other day after slamming doors, screaming uncontrollably, and throwing things, she was able to calm down and walked over to me. I was sitting in my home office and, exhausted, she put her cheek on my arm, pulled my fingers to her back and said: "Can I please have a tickle, scratch, scratch." Lina clearly has attention deficit hyperactivity disorder (ADHD), she's obsessive compulsive (OCD), she has sensory processing disorder (SPD), is often manic, has gut and sleep issues, and her language is a constant struggle. But her mother, Helena, and I are fighting these symptoms and Lina is fighting them and we'll keep fighting them together and, God willing, we'll continue to see progress.

viruses in the stomach or perhaps a specific retrovirus known as XMRV (which is under investigation by the CDC), gastrointestinal (GI) tract problems, immune problems, impaired intestinal functioning, environmental toxins, vitamin D deficiency, seizures, mobile phone radiation, encephalitis, hypoglycemia, antibiotics, and the list goes on and on. In compiling this book we have noticed a consensus beginning to emerge that the symptoms of autism result from a perfect storm of factors that come together to create a kind of system overload, a tipping point, in a genetically predisposed child's developing immune system. Recent studies point toward this overload causing problems

## CASE STUDY #2: ALEX

My son Alex was born in June of 1998 and developed normally, meeting or exceeding all his milestones until just after the age of 3. He attended daycare early (from age 4 months old) and was a popular and happy kid. While at daycare, Alex was able to pick up some Spanish in addition to his native English and could count to 10 in English, Spanish and Japanese by his second birthday. Medically, Alex was healthy as an infant and toddler, although he did have frequent sinus and ear infections that were treated with inhaled albuterol. He had all his vaccinations on time, the last of which followed his third birthday. By late summer folks at daycare began to comment that Alex was uncharacteristically spending more time on his own, sometimes staring out the window. A visit to his pediatrician produced an all too common "Don't worry, it's just a stage." Then Alex began to lose some speech, though he was still able to say, "Turn that off, that's scary," in response to TV coverage of 9/11. By Christmas 2001, Alex had lost a significant amount of speech, frequently stimmed by clapping his hands loudly (you never heard such a clap) and clearly had ADHD. At a holiday party that season, a person who owned a daycare center told me she thought Alex was autistic. This began our yearlong journey into the autism abyss. By the end of 2002 Alex was non-verbal and a fully diagnosed member of the autism epidemic.

at the cellular level, impairing the ability of nerve cells to transmit information properly through the synapses of the brain. Furthermore, the dramatic increase in the incidence of autism spectrum disorders points toward environmental factors playing a significant role. Further supporting this is the fact that scientists have found that by introducing environmental toxins or antibiotics they can create autistic symptoms in rats.

So what happened to Lina and Alex? We believe that they were genetically predisposed to contract autism, but required a big push and that the push came from a virus and a high fever, followed by antibiotics and a barrage of vaccines, all of which occurred at a fragile developmental stage. The antibiotics disregulated the immune system and the vaccines, thrown in as an additional stressor at the worst possible time, were the final straw. We also believe that the disregulated, hyper-active immune system created an autoimmune response whereby the immune system couldn't tell the difference between healthy tissue and the antigens that it normally fights and then probably attacked the healthy tissue of both the stomach lining and the brain. We believe that this combination of factors created a gut malfunction, a kind of climate change in the stomach that made it difficult for our kids to digest certain proteins that are necessary for healthy blood-cell development and healthy nerve cell activation. The proteins in the blood cells are necessary for the healthy development of the cognitive centers of the brain and in the nerve cells they help the neurotransmitters fire up correctly, send proper messages (like pain, hot and cold, sound etc.) and connect the right and left lobes of the brain. We think that the human body can normally withstand severe complications and stressors but, for the young, predisposed child, this chain of events is just too much. While we're not scientists, like everyone reading this book, we're doing our very best to try to solve the puzzle.

As far as treatments for autism, most doctors still tell parents with absolute certainty that it is an incurable lifelong condition and that treatments simply don't work. Kim Stagliano, author of the upcoming book *All I Can Handle, I'm No Mother Teresa* about life with three autistic daughters writes:

> An autism diagnosis can erase a person's ability to get solid medical care. If you brought your 6-year-old to a hospital in the throes of a seizure, the neurologists would run tests and look for the cause. When I brought my 6-year-old in, I was told, "She has autism. She has different circuitry." And then when I requested tests, I was told, "We're just not that aggressive with autism." My child has a brain and a gut and immune system just like any other child. Why does her autism negate that?

In looking at a more than 50 percent increase in the incidence of autism between 2002 to 2006, Dr. Thomas Insel director of the National Institute of Mental Health (NIMH) and chair of the Interagency Autism Coordinating Committee (IACC) the nation's top autism research coordinator, had this to say in an interview with David Kirby for the *Huffington Post:*

> This tells you that you really have to take this very seriously. From everything they are looking at, this is not something that can be explained away by methodology, by diagnosis.

He goes on to say that we should not be looking at autism as a single thing, with one cause, one treatment, one explanation. There may, in fact, be 10 or 20 or more distinct variations.

> I think this is a collection of many, many different disorders. . . . It's quite believable to me that there are many children who develop autism in the context of having severe gut pathology, or having autoimmune problems, or having lots of other problems. And some of these kids really do recover. And this is quite different from the autism that was originally described in the 1940s and 1950s—where it looks like you have it and you are going to have it for the rest of your life.

If autism is caused by the comorbidity of the underlying medical conditions, and if there are really endless variations of autism, then why on earth wouldn't we treat these conditions, mandate that insurance companies pay for these treatments, and get on to the business of trying to heal the underlying conditions. Dr. Insel agrees and says: "We've got to be able to break apart this spectrum disorder into its component parts and identify who's going to respond to which interventions." He advocates for genetic mapping as a way to pinpoint the underlying medical conditions so that we can figure out whether an individual had been "exposed to organophosphates, or perhaps to some infection, or some autoimmune process" that interferes with the way the brain develops. Others are beginning to express similar sentiment. Dr. Christopher Walsh, Ballard Professor of Neurology and Chief of the Division of Genetics at Children's Hospital in Boston says: "I would like every kid on the spectrum to have not 'autism' but a more specific disorder. By isolating the genes involved and understanding their functions, researchers can begin to develop particular treatments aimed at particular disorders." Dr. James Gusella, Ballard Professor of Neurogenetics and director of the Center for Human Genetic Research at Massachusetts General Hospital (MGH) says: "Autism is a problem that no one person or discipline can figure out alone."

Throughout the book, we use the word "treatment" in the broadest possible sense. Nevertheless, the therapies included by no means constitute an exhaustive list. Most of the practitioners included can tell you about cases where their therapy helped decrease the symptoms of a specific child, helped the child relate better, speak better, helped minimize gut problems, or helped control behavioral problems. And they have parents to support their claims. On the other hand, most of these therapies have not undergone rigorous trials, the kind of trials that cost substantial amounts of money and often take years to complete and evaluate. As a result, there are some people who contest the claims of the practitioners or parents. In any case, by including a specific treatment, we are not endorsing that treatment or telling you that it will work for your child or patient. Nor are the 84 doctors, teachers, therapists, parents, and other experts who have contributed to this book endorsing any treatment other than the one that they are writing about. Furthermore, practically none of these therapies are endorsed by any state or the federal government or covered by health insurance.

We certainly believe that the government should mandate insurance coverage for extensive genetic, blood and spinal fluid testing before any definitive diagnosis can be given. We have heard of cases where children showed the symptoms of autism or other disorders such as cerebral palsy, multiple sclerosis, or schizophrenia, but in fact had easily treatable disorders and were fully rehabilitated. We believe these kids, like any other kids, deserve the best medical care available, including full coverage for any treatment that is recommended by a specialist in any specific underlying medical condition. Some states have already started heading in this direction. For now, the only FDA approved drugs are Abilify and Risperdal and the only therapy approved by most states is applied behavior analysis (ABA), based on the teachings of B. F. Skinner. Recently, however, practitioners and researchers have begun advocating for approaches that combine the various therapies and scientists are trying to develop ways to measure how particular therapies improve brain connections in a specific individual.

Autism costs families an incredible amount of money. Estimates range from $60,000 to $100,000 per year and that assumes that you can either find an adequate public school in your district or, more likely, a private school that your city will agree to pay for. If you can't get the school paid for, then the cost could be as high as $200,000 per year. Whoever pays, autism is a growing problem and states and the federal government need to address it. Right now, autism costs the United States an estimated 35 billion dollars per year, but that could well be the trickle that turns into a flood. We believe that by funding more research and by agreeing either to pay for a broader range of therapies or to require insurance companies to do that, states and the federal government will save money in the long run.

Dr. Insel admits that when he was in training as a psychiatrist he "never saw a child with autism." He says that he wanted to see kids with autism, but he simply couldn't find any. Now, Insel says, "I wouldn't have to go any further than the block where I live to see kids with autism." This is an epidemic. We've come from a time when 1 in 10,000 babies born in the United States exhibited symptoms of autism to a time when the statistics are roughly 1 in 100. Think about that for a moment, 1% of kids born in this country become autistic. And those statistics, which come from the Centers for Disease Control (CDC), are based on data collected four years ago, so that the current rate is estimated to be 1 in 91.

If you were to take the 57% increase in the incidence of autism between 2002 and 2006, as calculated by the CDC (which the CDC itself says cannot be explained away by a shift in diagnostic criteria) and extrapolate forward, then at least half of all children born in the United States will be autistic by 2046. And these statistics fail to differentiate between classic autism, which is characterized by a child sitting in a corner rocking back and forth with little interest in social interaction, and regressive autism, where a normally developing child suddenly loses speech, interest in social interaction with peers and develops various biomedical symptoms. Ten years ago no one talked or wrote about regressive autism and now this is the fastest growing segment of the autistic population. What if this is just a different disorder? What if it's a disorder that has gone from 1 in 200 million to 1 in 200 in a 10 year period? Then, certainly, we're looking at a medical disaster of unprecedented proportions that is here, now and warrants a response at least as dramatic as the CDCs response to swine flu or the AIDS epidemic. We could well be at the tipping point of a crisis that will soon consume our future.

We are not doctors or scientists or government officials, but dads who love our kids and want to do the very best we can for them. We don't know for sure what caused our kids' autism and maybe we never will. If it was an immune system overload, we think that in most cases the cure is going to come not from a one-off drug, but from a counterassault, an all-out systemic approach, from DIR, from ABA, from dietary interventions, from GI tract treatments, from nutritional supplements, from anti-virals, from physical therapy, from sensory integration therapy, from brain therapy, from whatever fits the individual child. The current unwillingness of insurance companies, states and the federal government to pay for therapies is typical short-term thinking. Costs will only escalate, as untreated children become adults who need to be cared for by the state. A long-term approach will ultimately save money and will undoubtedly lead to at least some children being cured. This is war and if we want these children back, if we want to stop the progress of this disorder, we are going to have to fight. There will be people, lots of people, who will keep pointing out that there is no known cure, that they believe the struggle is hopeless. They will tell you that the best thing to do is to try to protect your own sanity and save your money. Our mission is to give our children, everyone's autistic children, their lives back to the fullest extent possible. We want to be involved in finding a remedy or a series of therapies that act together to bring these kids back to themselves and to their families and to the world.

Lina and Alex may never be typical kids. But perhaps they can be in a position to make informed decisions about their own lives, to communicate with people, to experience friendship and love and passion and hope. And who knows, perhaps if we help cure them, they will be the ones who develop a cure for cancer! Whatever the outcome, until there is a cure, we will do our very best to look for promising therapies for the symptoms of autism and continue to publish *Cutting Edge Therapies for Autism* in March of every year.

# Navigating the Autism Superhighway: How to Determine if a Therapy Is Right for Your Child and Family, by Dr. Mark Freilich

If you are intently reading or just skimming through the chapters of this book, the assumption is that your child or a child you know was recently or at some time in the past diagnosed with an autism spectrum disorder.

At this point you have hopefully, to one degree or another, started to come to terms with the diagnosis and what it means for your child, for you, and for your family. You are now ready to enter the Autism Superhighway, inch by inch, or at full speed.

In either case, it is now time to gather your team of co-navigators who will assist you in putting together a GPS system with the appropriate approaches, methods, and interventions. These should all be based on your child's unique and individual profile. This profile is essential in guiding the course of treatment.

For any child with autism, determining a course of treatment using only information you have read in a book or researched on the Internet is ill-advised. One needs a qualified team of specialists to properly evaluate, diagnose, prescribe, and monitor your child's strengths and areas of need.

This book is intended to provide an overview of a variety of approaches, methods, and interventions that alone or in combination may help place a child on the road to recovery from autism. It needs to be said that at this time there is no cure for autism. There are many children, however, who have received timely and comprehensive interventions and no longer meet the diagnostic criteria for an autism spectrum diagnosis. No matter the severity of manifestations, significant benefit can be gained by the child, the family, or both, with early and intensive interventions. However, if any clinician, specialist, or intervention approach promises a cure, be very leery and scrutinize carefully the validity of these claims.

Your primary pediatric care provider should be knowledgeable about the various medical, developmental, and behavioral issues that children with autism spectrum disorders may encounter. They should be aware of the available treatment options and the specialists in your area to whom you need to be referred. They need to be open minded to ALL treatments, whether they are based on a Western medicine approach or an alternative/complementary medical philosophy. Most importantly, there needs to be close collaboration and communication between your family, your specialists/therapists, and your child's primary care pediatric physician.

Unfortunately a common etiology for autism has not been discovered. Each child may broadly share common general manifestations but the triggers and causes for these manifestations may vary greatly from one child to another. It appears that the way parents and professionals view autism today is in transition. Although many continue to view it as strictly a psychiatric or a neurologic disorder, newer viewpoints are being embraced. Autism is increasingly being viewed as a disorder with multifactorial etiologies defined by its behavioral manifestations. These include impairments in communication and social interactions, repetitive behaviors, and sensory processing and regulatory issues. Therefore, autism needs to be considered a "spectrum" disorder that not only is impacted by issues in the brain and nervous system but one that is impacted by dysfunction in the immune, gastrointestinal, and metabolic systems. Since the etiology as well as the manifestations of autism are influenced by a variety of multiple factors, a cookie-cutter or a one-size-fits-all approach to treatment and intervention programming is steering you onto the wrong road. Creating an individual profile is therefore essential to navigating the Autism Superhighway. This profile must include an assessment of the child's present developmental level. It needs to analyze the child's individual medical, genetic, behavioral, sensory processing, and regulatory profile. Consideration of parenting skills, cultural beliefs, and expectations [needs] to be factored in.

The child's profile should and will change over time. The key to successful outcomes is establishing a cohesive team approach, with ongoing monitoring of progress to ensure treatments remain relevant and goals are always current and realistic.

One cannot promise that the Autism Superhighway your child and your family will be travelling on will offer a smooth or detour-free trip. There will be bumps, curves, and forks in the road. Remember, this is a long journey, not a short road trip. There will be many moments when you think "are we there yet?" but there will also be many scenic road stops and enjoyable attractions. Be sure to take the time to enjoy the major highlights along the way.

---

# WARNING

The editors and contributors are not giving medical advice. They are just describing the various therapies that are available. Tony Lyons, Ken Siri, Skyhorse Publishing, and the contributors cannot take the medical or legal responsibility of having the information contained within *Cutting-Edge Therapies for Autism* considered as a prescription for any person. Every child is different and parents need to consult with doctors, therapists and others to determine what is best for their child. Failure to do so can have disastrous consequences.

# EXPLORING THE ISSUE ⟳

## Are Evidence-Based Practices Sufficient for Educating Students with Autism?

## Challenge Questions

- Compare and contrast the positions of the YES and NO selections regarding whether evidence-based practices are sufficient to educate children with autism.
- Which selection makes the best case for its argument? Why?
- What interventions are used in the schools you know? By the parents you know? How do these compare to those discussed in the selections?
- How do educators of your school determine whether a practice is evidence-based? How do their practices compare to those discussed in the selections?
- If there are multiple variations of autism, what is the best path to identifying the treatments that work with each type?

## Is There Common Ground?

This issue's authors agree on several points. Autism is a complex disorder, which is manifested in many different ways. To date, no single treatment has been identified as successful with every child with autism. Research in this field is active; new lines of inquiry appear daily. Children with autism require early intervention; it is essential to begin effective therapy as early as possible.

## Additional Resources

Brown, A. (2008). *Clear answers & smart advice about your baby's shots*. Retrieved January 5, 2010 from www.immunize.org

Donovan, J. & Zucker, C. (2010, October). *Autism's first child*. Retrieved July 10, 2011 from www.theatlantic.com

Freilich, M. (2010). Introduction: Navigating the autism superhighway: How to determine if a therapy is right for your child and family. In Ken Siri & Tony Lyons (Eds). *Cutting-edge therapies for autism, 2010–2011*. New York: Skyhorse Publishing.

Isaacson, R. (2009). *The horse boy: A father's quest to heal his son*. New York: Little, Brown & Co.

Kretlow, A. G. & Blatz, S. L. (2011). The ABCs of evidence-based practice for teachers. *TEACHING Exceptional Children, 43*(5), 8–19.

Lytel, J. (2008, November 18). My son was autistic. Is he still? *Washington Post*. Retrieved November 28, 2008 from www.washingtonpost.com/wp-dyn/cotent/article/2998/11/14

McCarthy, J. (2008). *Mother warriors: A nation of parents healing autism against all odds*. New York: Dutton.

Odom, S. L., Collet-Klingenberg, L., Rogers, S. J., & Hatton, D. D. (2010). Evidence-based practices in interventions for children and youth with autism spectrum disorders. *Preventing School Failure, 54*(4), 275–282.

Offit, P. A. (2008). *Autism's false prophets: Bad science, risky medicine, and the search for a cure*. New York: Columbia University Press (pp. xix–xxi, 1–3, 6, 13, 17, 119–126).

Rader, R. (2008). Now if we just had some evidence. *EP Magazine, 38*(11), 8.

Raymaker, Dora. (2012). *A poem*. Retrieved May 21, 2012 from http://autisticadvocacy.org/

Siri, K. & Lyons, T. (2010). Preface. In Ken Siri & Tony Lyons (Eds). *Cutting-edge therapies for autism, 2010–2011*. New York: Skyhorse Publishing.

U.S. Department of Health and Human Services, Centers for Disease Control and Prevention. (2012, March). Prevalence of autism spectrum disorders—Autism and Developmental Disabilities Monitoring Network, 14 sites, United States, 2008. *Morbidity and Mortality Weekly Report* (81), 3. Retrieved April 9, 2012 from www.cdc.gov/mmwr/

# ISSUE 20

# Does Working with Parents Have to Be Contentious?

**YES: Jenna Goudreau**, from "Parenting Through Special Education," *Forbes* (2009, August 5), www.forbes.com/2009/08/05/special-education-needs-autism-forbes-woman-time-working-mother_print.html, August 6, 2009

**NO: Jennifer Krumins**, from "Choose Your Advocates Wisely: Getting the Best for Your Child," *EP Magazine* (vol. 39, no. 8/9, pp. 34–36, 2009)

---

## Learning Outcomes

**At the conclusion of this issue, readers will be able to:**

- Compare and contrast the positions of the YES and NO selections addressing whether working with parents needs to be contentious.
- Identify possible grounds for contentious interaction between parents and educators.
- Identify educator practices, which can affect the quality of their working relationship with the parents of their students.
- Compare the perspectives of parents and teachers in tense situations.

---

### ISSUE SUMMARY

**YES:** Jenna Goudreau, journalist in two prominent publications, relates the compelling stories of several parents who have had to fight with school systems and battle legal complexities to get the free appropriate public education they feel is right for their children with disabilities.

**NO:** Jennifer Krumins, a special education teacher and mother of a child with autism, advises parents to ease tension, stress, and pressure by finding an advocate who can serve as an "interpreter" in a complex educational system and teach them how to secure the necessary supports with a positive approach.

$\mathbf{T}$ he meeting will convene in five minutes. In attendance are 10 educators and Mr. and Mrs. Jones. The group will be discussing a recent evaluation of their child, Jessie, to consider eligibility for special education. This is the middle of a very long process. Everyone looks ready for a serious conversation.

Let's take a few steps back to see what led to this meeting. Jessie is a sociable child who enjoys sports, videogames, and family time. School is another matter. Unlike others in the class, Jessie began kindergarten with no preschool experience. Although most classmates had mastered the basics of numbers, letters, and school routines, it was all new to Jessie, who has never caught up with classmates.

Jessie's third-grade teachers decided it was time to formally explore the reasons behind these continuing learning difficulties. Mr. and Mrs. Jones reluctantly agreed to an evaluation to determine if Jessie qualified for special education. They were not happy with the possibility that Jessie could be identified as having a disability, but everyone agreed Jessie might need more than a classroom teacher could provide.

Along with the form asking written permission for a battery of unfamiliar tests came a dense brochure explaining parental rights within the special education process. Mr. and Mrs. Jones learned that no evaluation could be conducted without their written consent. They would meet with school staff to discuss the evaluation results, after they had received a copy of all reports. If this team established that Jessie had a disability requiring specially designed instruction, it would formulate an IEP specifying recommended services and projecting goals to be reached in one year. The brochure repeated what Jessie's teachers had said: no special education services could be provided (or changed) without written parental approval on that IEP.

There was also a lengthy section on due process: what could happen if the parents and the schools disagreed, now or in the future. If they disagreed with the school's evaluation, Mr. and Mrs. Jones might be eligible for a second opinion at school expense. If they disagreed with the school's proposals, they could ask for a resolution meeting to discuss their concerns. In their state, Mr. and Mrs. Jones could also ask for mediation, where a neutral third person would attempt to find common ground between the school and parents. If that did not succeed, the brochure outlined increasing levels of appeal, where other neutral parties would decide whether the school's IEP met the letter of the law. Parents could even go to state or U.S. federal courts. This would be costly, but prevailing parents might be compensated for their legal fees. On the other hand, if the complaint is found to be frivolous, parents might be required to compensate the district.

Mr. and Mrs. Jones knew parents with good experiences in the special education process, but had spoken to others who were frustrated and unhappy. Right now, at the beginning of this meeting, they were anxious and uncertain. So many people were sitting on *the other side* of the table. They felt concerned and alone. The reports they received had been full of complex terms and unfamiliar information about Jessie. They worried they would not understand;

would not ask the right questions; would not make the right decisions. They had known Jessie's teachers for a long time, but could they trust them now?

In any endeavor, people of good hearts and minds may have different views, equally supported by reason. Optimally, the parties reason together and come to a conclusion beneficial to all, especially when a child is involved. Unfortunately, other motives and concerns can intervene to prevent this meeting of the minds. Disagreements do not need to become battles, but sometimes they do. This issue explores contrasting perspectives on the interactions between parents and educators as they collaborate for a child with a disability.

In the YES selection, Jenna Goudreau, professional journalist, relates the experiences of several parents who have fought their way through "the maze of education laws" to ensure their child with disabilities was well served. Each presents a story of unending frustration, battling school personnel about the type, location, and amount of services needed.

In the NO selection, Jennifer Krumins, a teacher, author, and parent of a child with autism, acknowledges the isolation felt by parents who are entrusting their vulnerable child to a suddenly legalistic bureaucracy. Krumins counsels that a knowledgeable, objective advocate can be a guide through this unfamiliar territory. She encourages parents to choose an advocate who focuses on solutions and options rather than blame and arguments.

Returning to the meeting with Mr. and Mrs. Jones, think of the possibilities. Like many, their experience may be positive. They might feel part of a mutually respectful collaborative team that crafts a strong plan for Jessie (Fish, *Preventing School Failure*, 2008). Then again, Mr. and Mrs. Jones might feel unheard and lose the trust they had in teachers to do the best for Jessie (Angell, Stoner, & Sheldon, *Remedial and Special Education*, 2009).

Friction can arise when teams discuss appropriate services. Berlin (*Phi Delta Kappan*, 2009) explains that the Supreme Court has ruled that schools are required to provide the "floor of educational opportunity," not maximize the potential of each child. In words sure to strike an emotional cord, Berlin notes that some courts refer to appropriate services as a Chevrolet, not a Lexus, even though every parent wants the very best for their child. Goudreau rails against the money spent on lawyers and evaluations, and educators who might choose "the option that costs the least money."

The cost of special education is frequently criticized, particularly when budgets are tight and cuts must be made. In a review of the special education "spending spiral" in Massachusetts, Mohl and Sullivan (www.massinc.org, 2009) complained that state efforts to "tighten the rules" for eligibility and "narrow the standards for services" had not put "the brakes" on spending. Increased special education costs were bemoaned, without comparative analysis of general education spending. This viewpoint could motivate anyone to fight hard to secure scarce resources for their child. It also demoralizes educators trying to work in partnership with parents.

Regardless of finances, educators and parents alike should advocate for appropriate educational programs. Parents can focus solely on their own child. Krumins says a wise advocate can discover the range of available supports and strategies and help parents understand that schools have a responsibility to all children.

After interviewing an array of parents involved in special education, Trainor (*Remedial and Special Education*, 2010) identified four advocacy styles. "Intuitive advocates" rely on personal knowledge of their children, whereas "disability experts" add information gathered from specialists and independent research. "Strategists" use more sophisticated awareness of the Individuals with Disabilities Education Act (IDEA), including the powerful role parents should play. "Change agents" move beyond the school, using their knowledge to help other parents. Different styles lead to different results. Trainor found parents were more successful at achieving their ends as they moved beyond the intuitive style.

Other circumstances can affect parental participation. Trainor recommends that educators be sensitive to the impact of cultural and linguistic differences. Parents who feel marginalized may need support to believe they are equal partners in this process. Studying Chinese families, Lo (*Preventing School Failure*, 2008) learned they thought educators who left meetings early were rude, especially when the parents had taken time off from work, resulting in a loss of income. Lo also discovered the words of interpreters frequently did not match those of the speaker, adding to confusion and misunderstanding.

Special education is based on laws written to ensure an appropriate education for children with disabilities. Teachers and administrators are professionally bound to uphold these laws and implement strong programs. Districts are also charged with informing parents of their legal rights to approve and appeal the processes of special education. Unfortunately, brochures designed to meet this goal often sound more like legal contracts than guides for parents trying to plan an education for their child with a disability.

Facilitated IEPs represent an emerging practice utilized when parent/school interaction has been contentious, or less than productive (Mueller, *TEACHING Exceptional Children*, 2009). This process is designed to avoid more litigious routes, which are costly in time, money, and relationships. A neutral, expert facilitator maintains focus and order, whereas parents and educators attend to the content of the meeting. The facilitator helps identify key concerns, respond respectfully, and stay on topic.

Pressures to identify the right educational option are intense. In any special education meeting, well-meaning people might disagree about what is best. Educators must listen actively, speak clearly, and engage parents as partners. Parents must feel comfortable enough to respect educators, and knowledgeable enough to voice their concerns. Disagreements do not need to become battles. In stressful times, can we reach this goal?

# YES

# Parenting Through Special Education

It's a typical summer morning for Maureen Blasko, an associate director at Ernst & Young's Washington, D.C., office. While she helps her 8-year-old twins get ready for the day, her husband makes their lunches and shuffles them out the door—one is off to golf camp; the other to figure skating.

Katie, her eldest, is 15. From birth, she's suffered a host of medical issues and now attends a special education school for her epilepsy, learning disabilities and ADD. Blasko still gets her dressed, ties her shoes and reminds her to brush her teeth and hair after she finishes breakfast. She will stay and see that Katie gets safely on the summer school bus (at 7:30 a.m., it's late again), but her mind is already jumping ahead to her packed work schedule. When the bus rumbles in, it's one kiss on Katie's cheek and she's off to the office.

Working moms are expert jugglers. While many are putting in long hours to grow their careers, they are also striving to get their kids in the best schools or classrooms, and watching over homework and after-school activities. Having children with special needs complicates things exponentially. And it's not just a small few dealing with disabilities. According to the U.S. Department of Education, 13.6% of students have disabilities and 6.5 million children are enrolled in special education.

There are federal laws in place to help parents and their special needs kids, but the education system can be difficult to navigate. Parents have to be constant advocates, adding a whole other layer to the familiar working mother balancing act.

## The Basics

The Individuals with Disabilities Education Act (IDEA) is a federal requirement, enacted in 1975 and still evolving, that ensures children with disabilities receive a "free appropriate public education" from ages 3 to 22. Each state must provide the minimum requirements, though some provide more, and all interpret the law differently and on a child-by-child basis.

Every child confirmed to have one of 13 disabilities—ranging from autism or learning disabilities like dyslexia to physical or sensory impairments—is administered an Individualized Education Plan (IEP) catered to his or her specific needs. An IEP team that includes the child's parent, a general educa-

From *Forbes,* August 5, 2009. Copyright © 2009 by Forbes Media. Reprinted by permission of Forbes Media LLC.

tion teacher, a special education teacher, a school representative and others with special knowledge of the child or disability creates the plan and meets annually (or more, if needed) to discuss the student's progress.

## What the Laws Lack

Taking care of her now 23-year-old son, who has several physical and learning disabilities, consumed much of Carol Berman's time—so much so that the former market researcher at a large brokerage firm had to give up her job. His disabilities, and the attendant physical therapy, fights with health insurance companies and "the maze of education laws" had to take precedent. It was a financial blow to her family on top of everything else.

"The basic tenet of the law, that each child is entitled to a 'free appropriate education in the least restrictive environment' becomes tricky," she says. "To a parent, 'appropriate' means 'best,' which is not necessarily the case for the school districts."

She hit several roadblocks. The general policy of inclusion, when special needs children and mainstream kids share a classroom, made it difficult for her son to keep up with the advancing curriculum. She also felt that the advisers who recommended services did so based more on funding and statistics than to the specific strengths and weaknesses of her son.

Ellen Notbohm, author of the best-selling *Ten Things Every Child with Autism Wishes You Knew,* agrees that there are "100,000 interpretations of the law." She tells parents that constant communication with the school is their best bet and suggests they "look for a school that will see the child as a whole child and not as a baggie of broken parts." But the power—and ultimate responsibility—lies with the parent.

## A Second Job

Marilyn Haese, mother of two sons, ages 19 and 17, both diagnosed with dyslexia and AD/HD, runs her own PR agency, Haese & Wood, in Century City, Calif. She is the first to admit a working mom with special needs kids must devote a Herculean amount of time to their education. It becomes a second job.

Every school year she has had to reintroduce her children's ever-changing needs to the school—classroom teachers, yes, but also the librarian, gym teacher and even the principal. Their report cards had measurements that changed and became harder to decipher as the boys aged. But her biggest obstacle has been her battles against her children's IEP teams.

Haese discovered that she had to champion what *she* knew was in the best interests of her boys. When her older son was in elementary school, for example, he was moved from a mainstream school to a special ed school. Concerned about the social and educational ramifications of extracting him from a "normal" setting, she moved him back to public school—after much ado and against adviser recommendations. He's now in college and she believes the transfer made all the difference. She now tells other parents to be proactive, address problems early and to be the voice your child doesn't have.

Early on Chantai Snellgrove of Vero Beach, Fla., realized she was naive to blindly trust the school system and has been battling it ever since. "It's very frustrating," she says. "If you don't know the right questions, you won't get very far." As the mother of a 12-year-old daughter with language and learning disabilities, she's had to immerse herself in the research, keep meticulous records and negotiate fervently with an "intimidating" team of professionals to ensure her daughter gets what she needs.

Advocating for her child was so complicated and time consuming that, once Snellgrove learned the ropes, she found a new career—helping others embarking on the same path. Last year, she founded the online magazine, *Parenting Special Needs,* a resource she says she wished she had from the start.

Ernst & Young's Blasko admits that she has also applied her business acumen to IEP meetings. "Everything is a negotiation, just like work," she says. She got into a boardroom-style broil recently. When Katie, her 15-year-old, was placed in three job skills training classes and had no time in her schedule for science, Blasko refused. Katie will be taking biology in the fall.

## What's Next

Rich Robinson, executive director of the Federation for Children with Special Needs, a services and support organization for parents, says he keeps an eye on the controversial issues surrounding special education. Full federal funding, he says, is the "politically hot debate."

[In 2009, p]rograms falling under the Individuals with Disabilities Education Act (IDEA) are set to receive $12.2 billion as part of the American Recovery and Reinvestment Act (ARRA). Half was given out in April and the other $6.1 billion will be released in September. The funds, in part, will go toward retraining displaced teachers to specialize in special education.

In other words, it appears that the federal government is looking at special education to help stimulate the economy. To many of these working mothers, shifting funds sounds like a sigh of relief.

# Age-Old Problem, Perpetually Absent Solution: Fitting Special Education to Students' Needs

### Jay Mathews

Miguel Landeros is a lanky, well-spoken 12-year-old about to begin seventh grade in Stafford County. He is severely learning disabled, with reading, writing and math skill levels at least two years below his peers, and needs special teaching, according to a licensed clinical psychologist at the Kennedy Krieger

Institute in Baltimore and other specialists. Last February, Stafford officials refused to accept that evaluation and left him in regular classes. He performed poorly, failing all core subjects. Recently, they promised to give him more specialized services, but not the ones the experts who examined him say he needs.

I admit that education writers in general, and I in particular, write very little about learning disabilities and the many failures of federally mandated public school programs to help students who have them. I often say the cases are so complicated I have difficulty translating them into everyday language, and even then readers struggle to understand.

But that is not the whole truth. I also avoid special education stories because they all seem the same, one tale after another of frustrated parents and ill-equipped educators trying but failing to find common ground, calling in lawyers while the children sit in class, bored and confused.

That is not a good reason for ignoring what is probably the most aggravating part of our public school system, at least for the millions of parents who have to deal with it. Many prefer to fight these battles in private. But occasionally, someone like Kelli Castellino, Miguel's mother, shames me by emailing a thick file of her correspondence and asking me to tell the story. I will give it a try, without much hope anything will come of it.

Castellino says Miguel attended first through fifth grades at two Howard County elementary schools, Bryant Woods and Phelps Luck. He struggled to learn to read, she says, but the schools did not test him for learning disabilities until she made a formal request in fifth grade. She was told he did not qualify for an Individualized Education Plan, which under one federal law would require special teaching to address his disabilities. He received the lesser option, called a 504 plan, which under another federal law guarantees him special accommodations in a regular classroom setting, such as more time to complete tests.

Castellino, like other parents of children with learning disabilities, had fallen into a jabberwocky world of legal, educational and psychological jargon that makes money for lawyers but leaves parents with headaches and empty bank accounts. Different evaluators might have different views of a child's needs. The laws are vague, although a recent U.S. Supreme Court decision gave parents more sway in such cases. School district evaluators—good people placed in impossible situations—might choose the option that costs the least money in hopes that will be enough. They know their budgets may not support much else.

When Castellino moved to Stafford last year and enrolled Miguel at Shirley C. Heim Middle School, she told school administrators that she thought Howard County had overlooked severe problems (a Howard spokeswoman said "not every child with a disability qualifies for an IEP") and asked that Miguel be tested again. School officials told her that because the Howard tests had been so recent, they wanted to wait and see.

In November, Castellino had Kennedy Krieger evaluate Miguel. That report identified these disabilities, with numbers referring to entries in the Diagnostic and Statistical Manual of Mental Disorders: "Reading Disorder (315.00); Mathematics Disorder (315.1) and Disorder of Written Expression, 315.2 (Specific Learning Disability); Attention Deficit Hyperactivity

Disorder-Combined Type, by history, (Other Health Impaired)." Still, the school kept Miguel in regular classes the rest of the school year. Stafford agreed recently to offer him special services, but in a class with mentally disabled or emotionally disturbed children, not the placement his private evaluators recommended.

Castellino, an office manager, says her insurance has covered the nearly $10,000 spent on neuropsychological, speech and language, occupational therapy, hearing, vision and assistive technology tests by seven different evaluators, including the $2,000 Kennedy Krieger bill. But she anticipates tapping her own funds for future legal and private school expenses. "I am selling my car and will be riding my bike to work, selling anything I can in my house to come up with the money to place my child where he should be," she says.

I asked Stafford for a response. A spokeswoman said the school system provides "an outstanding education for all of our special-needs students," but she would not comment on any individual student "even if the parent signs a waiver of privacy rights."

Why do you suppose that is? Castellino is following the usual course, making plans to seek a court order for a better placement in a private school. The school district has lawyers, too. They do not want their spokeswoman to say anything that might weaken their case.

Here we go again. Is there an alternative, some innovative way to help kids like Miguel? Special education vouchers? Charter schools for the learning disabled? The old way is rutted, bumpy and slow. It is not taking us very far. We need something new.

Jennifer Krumins

# Choose Your Advocates Wisely: Getting the Best for Your Child

**I**magine . . . after months of waiting and anticipation, the moment has finally arrived! Your beautiful baby enters the world and life is the fullest it has ever been! As the nurse gently places your newborn in your arms she slips a book into your hands. "This is your child's manual," she explains. "Be sure to read it as soon as possible. Oh, and pay close attention to the section regarding special needs."

A crazy scenario, I know, but at times I wish that I had been given that manual! Navigating the parenting role is tricky at the best of times but, finding your way with a child that has special needs is even more demanding and difficult. This is a path that may not have been traveled by family and friends. Loneliness, disappointment, frustration, and a sense of failure can make the journey miserable. The challenges can become overwhelming once your child reaches school age. It is at that time that you enter a whole world of professionals that will have your precious child for six hours out of the day! It is a world that is a culture unto itself with its own language and its own set of rules. You may feel like an outsider. You may feel that you need help. You may need someone to act as an interpreter in this new land.

You begin the investigation . . . look on the Internet and the Yellow Pages . . . can someone out there help me do the best for my child in school? Before you choose the person who will be your guide and advocate for your child, you must do some homework, for the sake of your child and for your own sanity. There are many people who call themselves advocates, but it is up to you—the parent—to make an informed decision as to whether the person is truly qualified to advocate for a student with special needs and whether this person is a "good fit" with you, your child, and your goals. Take the time to do your research. The decision you make can literally affect your own and your child's life in ways that you never dreamed possible. The person that you choose will impact your relationship with school personnel, your spouse, your child, and the members of your family. The advocate will have a direct effect on your marriage, your personal relationships and your family. You are inviting someone to enter into your world. Be very careful to whom you give this precious gift.

From *Exceptional Parent (EP) Magazine,* vol. 39, no. 8/9, pp. 34–36, August/September 2009.

## What Role Can an Advocate Play?

- Assist parents in finding supports and resources that are available
- Model effective relationship building and problem solving skills
- Listen to all parties in a genuine and non-judgmental manner
- Clarify issues
- Suggest options and possible solutions
- Document meetings or help parents to understand documents such as psychological assessments
- Locate and provide information
- Speak on the parent/child's behalf when they cannot speak for themselves
- Help the family with written correspondence, documentation or phone calls
- Attend meetings
- Follow up on decisions made and actions taken

The following are a few points to ponder before deciding whom you will choose:

## Advocates Should Have the Qualifications to Be Able to Speak with Integrity and Knowledge about Exceptionalities in Learning

A high level of qualification brings a level of respect to the table. Humans are far more likely to listen to someone who has "walked in their shoes" and has experience in education and special needs. It is probably safe to say that very few people are willing to modify their own expertise and professional methods based on the ideas and opinions of someone who has little or no experience and credentials in the field. As an educator, sitting in meetings with someone who has no special education qualifications and having them point out your deficiencies is a waste of time and money. Any parent who has experienced being lectured on the best methods of raising children by a person who has no children may know how frustrating this can be. Teachers are more likely to be open to the opinions and suggestions of someone who is at least qualified to make such statements. It makes sense that if you want to cultivate the best education for your child, you would expect an advocate that had the special education credentials and experience that would enhance your role as parent. Maintaining professional development by attending conferences, keeping up to date on current policy documents and procedures are important qualifications to have. Special education is a constantly evolving science and an advocate must be up to date. A solid knowledge of local resources, services providers, and community programs facilitates problem solving. It is equally important that the advocate you choose have the interpersonal skills necessary to work collaboratively with others to create solutions. As a parent, expect the person that you hire to be qualified to help you to work with the school.

## Advocates Should Know Your Child

People who are chosen to represent your child need to read assessments, report cards, interact and spend time with the child in order to really know who they are working for. Then the role of advocacy is authentic and not a matter of fighting for a cause or for an ego boost. When an advocate knows the parent and the child well, he or she can help to uncover the common ground between school and home. The advocate should be able to explain how your child's disability may impact their learning and then work with you to help prioritize your child's needs. A wise advocate is someone who will look for solutions and not blame. Advocates should see the child in the context of his classroom. A child's program on paper can never tell the whole story. There is no way that a teacher can put into words all of the supports, plans, visuals, tools and strategies that are employed to make the child successful. The child's world tells far more than any documentation could ever describe. It important to note that entering a classroom is opening a "sacred trust." Just as you would not let someone that you do not trust into your home, teachers must be wary to whom they open their classrooms. If someone is entering the room to "observe" and then report back to the parent all of the things that they think are being done incorrectly and to "build a case" against the school, the relationship has then been destroyed. Would you want someone coming into your home to "observe and critique" you as you carry out the daily functions of parenthood?

## Advocates Should Be Objective and Solution Minded

While interviewing an advocate, listen carefully for language that promotes solutions rather than vengeance. The advocate's personal experience with a school district, board, or previous personal history has no place in the discussion. This is about YOUR child. The advocate may utilize background knowledge of the people and resources to facilitate a workable plan for your child. In order to secure a positive proactive response from the people that are in relationship with your child, the advocate is best to be respectful, courteous, considerate, and open minded. Of course, this is true of every member of a team.

Can the advocate help your child access the best education possible without putting undue stress on the resources and personnel involved? Sometimes in the hopes of helping a parent, promises are made that are overly taxing on a personal or financial level . . . the school must educate all students, not just yours. Parents may disagree and say that it is really their child that they care about. While that is very true, schools cannot operate on this premise. Educational institutions have a duty to look after the collective while at the same time ensuring that each individual receives what is needed. It is not fair to assume that school staff should take from one child in order to provide for another. Imagine someone suggesting that a parent take away resources from one of their children in order to give to another. There are solutions that can work for everyone. We need to be searching for them as a team.

## Advocates Should Be Facilitators, not Dictators

Listen and observe an advocate carefully. Are they talking as if they are going into battle? Using words like "them" and "us?" Watch for an ego that is using your child to feed itself! Egos look out for egos, not children. Red flags should wave wildly when an advocate sees only negatives in a child's education, or when promises of specific outcomes for your child are made. An advocate that speaks with an "I'll show them" attitude is not going to effectively negotiate a plan that makes everyone want to do their part. Problems are not solved that way. Children do not win in these scenarios.

Humans need to be acknowledged for the effort that they invest; we need to feel supported and respected. We are more open to solutions when we are not feeling defensive. No person, neither educator nor parent, should leave a discussion feeling that they have been ignored, rejected or discounted if they were genuinely promoting a child's needs and not their own. When the disagreement lowers itself to the level of acting like children who are demanding that everyone play by their rules, the child with special needs is no longer the center of the discussion. An advocate is worth their weight in gold when they can objectively look at a situation without an emotional charge and create solutions that work for the child.

Each member of a team has a perspective on how to best help a child: a principal, community agency member, speech pathologist, teacher and a parent have ideas that stem from their training and experience. A skilled advocate is able to listen to each member's ideas and see solutions that draw on the strengths of each person at the table.

Ultimatums, threats, and accusations drive a wedge between parents and teachers that is extremely damaging to the child because the message that the parent is giving is that they trust this person more than the teacher.

## The End of the Road

As a parent, it can be intensely frustrating when you feel that a system is failing your child. At times, the anger and resentment can be too much to bear. It is easy to fall into the trap of vengeance and revenge. Going to the press or calling a lawyer should never be done without serious thought of the repercussions. These actions should never be born from an emotional reaction. The cost will be high. Before taking any action, the question that should be front and center is: "How will this benefit the child? How could this hurt the child?" It is all too easy to get caught up in the feeling of retribution. When we feel helpless it is almost intoxicating to gain a sense of power. We need to be honest with ourselves about what is driving our course of action. Before taking such steps, consider that your child may have many years in school ahead of him. Your child's siblings may have many years in the educational system. The damage caused by legal action and/or public humiliation cannot help but affect your relationships with the very people that you will rely on to give your children the best, I am speaking of the deep-seated hurt, mistrust and fear that sinks into the soul of anyone that has been affected by litigation and bad press. Public humiliation and bad press may make a school system give in to your demands but it does nothing to draw out the best of any human being or relationship.

This is not to say that legal action is not necessary at times but, it is a LAST resort. Advocates may or may not be affiliated with an attorney but they are not lawyers and they should not be giving legal advice.

## Final Thoughts

Hiring an advocate does not take away the parent's role in decision-making. Advocates make sense of the documents, technical language and educational jargon. They may explain options or the requirements of special programs, attend meetings and ask clarifying questions but, as the child's parents, you make the decision. Your child needs YOU to be in charge: your role is long term!

Educators need to listen, really listen to what it is that parents are asking for. We may have to sort through layers of hurt, anger, resentment and fear to see the authentic concern for their child. I believe that most times we can meet the requests of the parent at some level. Look for common ground.

The relationship between parent and school can be difficult because a child's life is at stake and emotions run high but, with hard work, respectful dialogue and child-centered problem solving, it is possible to work as a team to make the most of a child's education. It is up to the adults to make it work for the sake of the children.

# EXPLORING THE ISSUE ⮂

## Does Working with Parents Have to Be Contentious?

## Challenge Questions

- Compare and contrast the positions of the YES and NO selections regarding whether working with parents needs to be contentious.
- Which selection makes the best case for its argument? Why?
- Did you feel frustration about the surprising, bureaucratic attitude of Jessie's teachers and administrators who seemed so nice before this lengthy process began? What happened to create his attitude? In retrospect was it justified?
- Did you feel frustration about the surprising, emotional concerns of Jessie's parents who seemed so nice before this lengthy process began? What happened to create these feelings? In retrospect were they justified?
- What did parents and teachers do to keep communication open and consider alternative points of view? How did each handle disagreement?
- How would you use information from the YES and No selections to affect your actions at a team meeting?

## Is There Common Ground?

Each of this issue's selections mentions a desire to collaborate to meet the needs of a child with a possible disability. Goudreau and Krumins note the tension involved in this process as well as the necessity to resolve the tension so that people can concentrate on developing and implementing a free and appropriate public education.

## Additional Resources

Angell, M. E., Stoner, J. B., & Shelden, D. L. (2009). Trust in educational professionals: Perspectives of mothers of children with disabilities. *Remedial and Special Education, 301*(3), 160–176.

Berlin, L. F. (2009). Public school law: What does it mean in the trenches? *Phi Delta Kappan, 90*(10), 733–736.

Fish, W. W. (2008). The IEP meeting: perceptions of parents of students who receive special education services. *Preventing School Failure, 63*(1), 8–14.

Goudreau, J. (2009, August 5). Parenting through special education. *Forbes*. Retrieved August 6, 2009 from www.forbes.com/2009/08/05/special-education-needs-autism-forbes-woman-time-working-mother_print.html

Krumins, J. (2009). Choosing your advocates wisely: Getting the best for your child. *EP Magazine, 39*(8/9), 34–36.

Lo, L. (2008). Chinese families' level of participation and experiences in IEP meetings. *Preventing School Failure, 63*(1), 21–27.

Mathews, J. (2009, August 17). Age-old problem, perpetually absent solution: Fitting special education to students' needs. *The Washington Post*. Retrieved August 17, 2009 from www.washingtonpost.com

Mohl, B. & Sullivan, J. (2009, Spring). *Spending spiral*. Retrieved November 25, 2009 from www.massinc.org/index.php?id+732&pub_id=2452

Mueller, T. G. (2009). IEP facilitation: A promising approach to resolving conflicts between families and schools. *TEACHING Exceptional Children, 41*(3), 60–67.

Trainor, A. A. (2010). Diverse approaches to parent advocacy during special education home-school interactions. *Remedial and Special Education, 31*(1), 34–47.

# Contributors to This Volume

## EDITOR

**MARYANN BYRNES** is an educational consultant who collaborates with schools and districts on issues of policy, the implementation of IDEA, program evaluation, and professional development. Dr. Byrnes has a broad portfolio of experience in education; she began as a classroom teacher in Chicago and soon moved into the field of special education, teaching at elementary and secondary levels. MaryAnn served as a special education administrator for 18 years and as an associate professor at the University of Massachusetts, Boston. She is past president of the Massachusetts Federation of the Council for Exceptional Children and past president of the Massachusetts Association of Administrators of Special Education (ASE). Dr. Byrnes earned her BA from the University of Chicago, her MA in learning disabilities at Northwestern University, and her EdD in learning theory at Rutgers University.

## AUTHORS

**HOWARD S. ADELMAN** is a professor of psychology and codirector of the School Mental Health Project and the National Center for Mental Health in Schools at UCLA. He began his professional career as a remedial classroom teacher in 1960 and received his PhD in psychology from UCLA in 1966. He directed the Fernald School and Laboratory at UCLA from 1973 to 1986 and has codirected the School Mental Health Project since 1986.

**STEVEN ADELSHEIM** is the director of New Mexico School Mental Health Programs.

**LINDA P. BLANTON** is a professor, Department of Educational and Psychological Studies, Florida International University, Miami, Florida, USA.

**JENNIFER BOOHER-JENNINGS** is a doctoral candidate in the Department of Sociology at Columbia University in New York City. Her research focuses on accountability, school organization, and school choice.

**MARY T. BROWNELL** is a professor of special education at the University of Florida as well as the Irving and Rose Fien Endowed Professor and director of the National Comprehensive Center to Improve Policy and Practice in Special Education Professional Development. Her research efforts focus on improving the reading instruction of both general and special education teachers and improving the induction of beginning special education teachers into the classroom.

**DINA BRULLES** is a school administrator and the gifted-education director for Arizona's Paradise Valley Unified School District. Recognized for her expertise in creating and supervising schoolwide cluster grouping, she also assists districts throughout the United States in developing gifted-education programs, including those districts serving culturally and linguistically diverse gifted students.

**JOHN CLOUD** is a staff writer for *Time Magazine*, where he has worked since 1997.

**DONALD L. COMPTON** is chair and a professor of special education at Vanderbilt University. He has written extensively about cognitive and social/environmental factors that affect children's ability to learn and to read.

**LOUIS C. DANIELSON** is currently a statistician in the Division of Innovation and Development at the Bureau of Education for the Handicapped.

**HAZEL DENHART** is experienced in service learning development and implementation that started in 1994 when she worked on the design of Portland State University's Service Learning Program where she taught until 2008. This program was recently named to the U.S. President's Higher Education Community Service Honor Roll with Distinction, one of the highest federal recognitions a college or university can receive for its commitment to volunteering, service-learning, and civic engagement.

**TODD E. ELDER** is an associate professor of economics at Michigan State University.

**JEFFREY EVANS** does research with the Institute for Applied Psychometrics (IAP) and the Woodcock–Johnson development team. He has published in the area of reading achievement. Jeff is currently working on educational test development and writing projects with IAP. He also serves on the volunteer board of directors of United Cerebral Palsy (UCP) of Central Minnesota. Jeff holds a master's in communications disorders from St. Cloud State University.

SUSAN C. FAIRCLOTH is an assistant professor at Pennsylvania State University. Dr. Faircloth's publications and research interests center on leadership, special education, higher education, cultural diversity, and the education of American Indians and Alaska Natives.

EDWARD FERGUS is an NYU professor who teaches courses on Latinos in urban education. Fergus has helped various organizations develop standards for evaluating the effectiveness of after-school programs.

LANI FLORIAN is a professor of social and educational inclusion at the University of Aberdeen in Scotland. Previously she was a senior lecturer in inclusive and special education in the Faculty of Education, University of Cambridge and a fellow of St. Edmund's College, Cambridge.

WILLIAM C. FRICK is an assistant professor at the University of Oklahoma.

DOUGLAS FUCHS is a professor of special education at Peabody College of Vanderbilt University. He also serves as the codirector of the National Research Center on Learning Disabilities, funded by the Office of Special Education Programs in the U.S. Department of Education.

LYNN S. FUCHS is the Nicholas Hobbs Professor of special education and human development at Vanderbilt University, where she also codirects the Kennedy Center Reading Clinic. She has conducted research on assessment methods for enhancing instructional planning and on instructional methods for improving reading and math outcomes for students with learning disabilities.

PAUL J. GERBER is the Ruth Harris Professor of Dyslexia Studies in the Department of Special Education and Disability Policy in the School of Education at Virginia Commonwealth University in Richmond, Virginia. He has researched and written extensively about post-school and lifespan issues for adults with learning disabilities.

JENNA GOUDREAU is an editorial assistant at *Forbes* magazine.

DEBORAH D. HATTON has recent research focused on Fragile X syndrome, comorbid Fragile X and autism, and visual impairment/blindness. In addition to the phenotypic characteristics of children with these disabilities, Hatton's work also examines the neural underpinnings of the disorders, and intervention research that can help families, educators, and professionals promote optimal development and learning in children with disabilities.

THOMAS HEHIR is a professor at Harvard Graduate School of Education. He has also served as director of the U.S. Department of Education's Office of Special Education Programs from 1993 to 1999.

JOHN HOCKENBERRY is an award-winning television commentator, a radio host, and a foreign correspondent who became a paraplegic in an auto accident when he was 19. He lives in Brooklyn, New York, with his wife, Alison, and their two sets of twins—Zoe and Olivia, and Zachary and Regan.

JAMES M. KAUFFMAN is the Charles S. Robb Professor of education at the University of Virginia in Charlottesville, Virginia, where he also serves as director of the doctoral program in special education. His primary areas of interest in special education are emotional and behavioral disorders and learning disabilities. He is coeditor of *Behavioral Disorders*, the journal of the Council for Children with Behavioral Disorders, and he is coprincipal investigator of the Center of Minority Research in Special Education (COMRISE). Among his many publications are *Characteristics of Emotional and Behavioral Disorders of Children and*

*Youth*, 7th ed. (Prentice Hall PTR, 2000) and *The Least Restrictive Environment: Its Origins and Interpretations in Special Education*, coauthored with Jean B. Crockett (Lawrence Erlbaum, 1999). He received his MEd in teaching in the elementary school from Washburn University in 1966 and his EdD in special education from the University of Kansas in 1969.

**EVELYN B. KELLY** has been an independent writer, speaker, and educator. Her books include *Encyclopedia of Attention Deficit Hyperactivity Disorders* (Greenwood, 2009) and *Gene Therapy* (Greenwood, 2007).

**MARY THERESA KIELY,** as an assistant scholar in special education at the University of Florida, has helped to develop teacher instrumentation and data analysis for a study on the impact of collaborative professional development on literacy instruction. Her research interests include teacher learning, reading, writing, language arts, and teaching and learning for students with high-incidence disabilities. She has delivered more than 25 conference presentations and authored five peer-reviewed publications.

**LANA COLLET-KLINGENBERG** earned her PhD in special education from the Department of Rehabilitation Psychology and Special Education at the University of Wisconsin-Madison in 1996. She has focused on communication and social skills and on the transition from school to adult life for persons with disabilities. Since 1998, she has been involved in pre-service teacher education at UW-Whitewater and UW-Madison, as well as having worked on a number of federal and state grant initiatives focusing on nonverbal communication of persons with significant disabilities, improving transition services, and creating authentic schools that address special education needs.

**JENNIFER KRUMINS** has been a teacher in Ontario, Canada, for 20 years. She earned her special education specialist and undertook extensive training from Queen's University in Kingston, Ontario, and the Geneva Centre for Autism in Toronto, Ontario.

**NATHANIEL S. LEHRMAN** is clinical director (retired) at the Kingsboro Psychiatric Center in Brooklyn, New York.

**TONY LYONS** is the president and publisher of Skyhorse Publishing. He is the author of *The Little Red Book of Dad's Wisdom* and *Cutting-Edge Therapies for Autism*.

**AMY D. MARCUS** is a Boston-based staff reporter for the New York bureau of *The Wall Street Journal*. Born in Boston, Massachusetts, Marcus earned a bachelor's degree from Harvard University.

**JOSE L. MARTIN** is a partner with the school law firm of Richards Lindsay & Martín, L.L.P. in Austin, Texas. His practice focuses exclusively on disabilities issues and litigation affecting the schools, including special education consulting and litigation under the Individuals with Disabilities Education Act (IDEA).

**KEVIN S. McGREW** is the director of the Institute on Applied Psychometrics (IAP) and is currently a visiting professor in the Department of Educational Psychology at the University of Minnesota. Dr. McGrew has extensive experience in both clinical (1:1) and large-scale assessment, and in data management and analysis. Dr. McGrew has published over 60 journal articles, books, or book chapters covering many areas of special education.

**MARGARET J. McLAUGHLIN** has been involved in special education all of her professional career, beginning as a teacher of students with serious emotional and behavior disorders. Currently she is the associate director of the Institute for the Study of Exceptional Children, a research institute within the College of Education at the University of Maryland.

**ELIZABETH MOORE** is a research coordinator at the Center for School Mental Health Analysis and Action, University of Maryland School of Medicine.

**ROBERT MULLIGAN** is the director of special education and counseling in the Point Pleasant Beach Public Schools (New Jersey).

**NATIONAL DISABILITY RIGHTS NETWORK (NDRN)** is the nonprofit membership organization for the federally mandated Protection and Advocacy (P&A) Systems and Client Assistance Programs (CAP). Collectively, the P&A/CAP network is the largest provider of legally based advocacy services to people with disabilities in the United States.

**SAMUEL L. ODOM** is an assistant professor of education and Otting Professor of special education in the School of Education, Indiana University, Bloomington.

**LYNDA A. PRICE** is an associate professor of special education at Temple University. She received her MA from the University of Minnesota in 1979 and her PhD in 1995. Her professional interests include qualitative research methods and design in special education.

**SASHA PUDELSKI** is government affairs manager for the American Association of School Administrators where she monitors and evaluates the legislative and regulatory actions concerning education by the U.S. federal government.

**MARLEEN C. PUGACH** is a professor of teacher education in the Department of Curriculum and Instruction at the University of Wisconsin-Milwaukee.

**SALLY J. ROGERS** is a professor in the Department of Psychiatry and Behavioral Sciences at the UC Davis MIND Institute. She specializes in conducting research into autism and other developmental disorders and treating patients with developmental disabilities, especially young children with autism and their families. Dr. Rogers studies early social, cognitive, and emotional development, development of motor skills, communication, imitation, and language in children with severe disabilities, development of social relationships in people with disabilities, and treatment efficacy in autism at the UC Davis MIND Institute.

**MITT ROMNEY** is the son of the former Michigan Governor George Romney. He founded the investment firm Bain Capital. He ran for Massachusetts Senate in 1994 but was defeated by incumbent Edward Kennedy. Romney took over the Salt Lake Organizing Committee and helmed the successful 2002 Olympic Games. He was elected governor of Massachusetts in 2003 and made a run for the Republican presidential nomination in 2008 and 2012.

**RICHARD ROTHSTEIN** is a research associate of the Economic Policy Institute and senior fellow of the Chief Justice Earl Warren Institute on Law and Social Policy at the University of California (Berkeley) School of Law.

**MARCIA RUBIN** is the director of Research and Sponsored Programs at the American School Health Association.

**GWYN W. SENOKOSSOFF** is an instructor at the College of Education, University of South Florida, St. Petersburg.

**SCOTT M. SHANNON** is a pediatric psychiatrist who is board-certified in general psychiatry, child/adolescent psychiatry, and holistic medicine. He currently has a private practice in holistic child psychiatry and serves as medical director of four residential treatment centers for children in Northern Colorado.

**PAUL T. SINDELAR** is a professor of special education and the co-director of the Special Education Department at the University of Florida. Research interests are instructional methods for students with educational disabilities.

**KEN SIRI** is the author of *Cutting edge therapies for autism* and *1001 tips for the parents of autistic boys*. He is the single parent of a child with autism. Ken is active in the autism community in New York City, where he and his son reside.

**AUTISM SPEAKS** is a leading autism science and advocacy organization dedicated to funding research into the causes, prevention, treatments, and a cure for autism; increasing awareness of autism spectrum disorders; and advocating for the needs of individuals with autism and their families.

**KIM STODDARD** is an associate professor in the College of Education at the University of South Florida, St. Petersburg. Her research interests include the development of school–university partnerships, the implementation of inclusive practices, teacher education, and implementation of thematic units.

**LINDA TAYLOR** is codirector of the School Mental Health Project and the National Center for Mental Health in Schools at UCLA. Throughout her career, she has been concerned with a wide range of psychosocial and educational problems experienced by children and adolescents. Her early experiences included community agency work.

**H. RUTHERFORD TURNBULL III** is the cofounder and codirector of the Beach Center on Disability at the University of Kansas. He is a professor of special education and former courtesy professor of law there, and his research interests include special education law and policy, disability policy generally, and, most recently, the effects of U.S. federal policy on treatment issues raised by the Schiavo cases.

**U.S. DEPARTMENT OF EDUCATION (USDE)** promotes educational excellence for all Americans. Created in 1980 by combining offices from several U.S. federal agencies, the USDE remains true to its original directive to ensure equal access to education and to promote educational excellence throughout the nation.

**ROSALIND VARGO AND JOE VARGO**, mother and father of Ro Vargo, respectively, use their voices to tell a powerful story of their daughter's success in fully inclusive educational programs, from kindergarten through college.

**MELANA Z. VICKERS** is a widely published journalist who writes editorials on education and public policy for *USA Today*. She also is a regular contributor to *The Weekly Standard* and *National Review Online* and has appeared on the PBS show *Newshour*, CNN, Fox, and other news channels.

**MARK D. WEIST** is a professor and director of the Division of Child and Adolescent Psychiatry in the Center for School Mental Health Analysis and Action, University of Maryland School of Medicine.

**J.P. WIESKE** is the director of state affairs for the Council for Affordable Health Insurance (CAHI).

**SUSAN WINEBRENNER** is a full-time consultant who works with school districts to help them translate current educational research into classroom practice. She received her BS in education and her master's degree in curriculum and instruction from the University of Wisconsin.

**GORDON WROBEL** has worked as a psychologist for Minneapolis Public Schools and the state of Minnesota.